The Infraordinary

Inhaltsverzeichnis
Contents

Buchrezensionen
Book Reviews

Faculty News

Editorial

Gewöhnliche Räume, alltägliche Situationen
Begegnungen zwischen Architektur und Soziologie

Ordinary Places, Everyday Situations
Encounters between Architecture and Sociology

Julian Müller, Matthias Castorph

Die zwanzigste Ausgabe von GAM begibt sich auf die Suche nach dem Alltäglichen in der Architektur. Den Titel, den wir diesem Vorhaben voranstellen, borgen wir uns von dem französischen Schriftsteller Georges Perec, in dessen Werk der Kunstbegriff *infra-ordinaire* auftaucht. Das Infraordinäre kann als das Gegenteil des Extraordinären verstanden werden. Es ist aber eben nicht einfach nur das Ordinäre, in einem despektierlichen Sinne, sondern vielmehr das Nicht-Extraordinäre, also das Nicht-Außergewöhnliche. Perec ging es darum, in seinen literarischen Werken all das einzufangen, was zumeist übersehen wird, all das, „was jeden Tag geschieht und jeden Tag wiederkehrt, das Banale, das Alltägliche, das Selbstverständliche, das Allgemeine, das Gewöhnliche, das Infragewöhnliche (*l'infra-ordinaire*), das Hintergrundgeräusch, das Übliche".[1] Es sind vor allem Alltagsbeobachtungen an gewöhnlichen Orten, an Pariser Straßen, Plätzen oder in Mietshäusern, die im Mittelpunkt der Perec'schen Literatur stehen. Immer wieder insistiert er darauf, all diese gewöhnlichen Orte nicht für selbstverständlich zu nehmen. „Das, was wirklich befragt werden muss, ist der Ziegelstein, der Beton, das Glas, unsere Tischmanieren, unsere Gerätschaften, unsere Zeiteinteilung, unsere Rhythmen."[2] Perec erweist sich für die Architektur somit als ebenso produktiver Stichwortgeber wie für die Soziologie. Diese beiden Fächer sollen in der vorliegenden GAM-Ausgabe auch ins Gespräch gebracht werden; geschieht doch das meiste, was wir tun, in gebauten Räumen, die von ihrem alltäglichen Gebrauch nie zu trennen sind. Sie werden bewohnt,

1 Perec, Georges: „Annäherungen an was?" [1973], in: Ders.: *Warum gibt es keine Zigaretten beim Gemüsehändler?*, Zürich/Berlin 2014, 5–8, hier 6.
2 Ebd. 7.

The twentieth issue of GAM sets out in search of the everyday in architecture. We have borrowed its title from the French writer Georges Perec, in whose oeuvre the coinage "infra-ordinaire" is found. The infraordinary can be understood as the opposite of the extraordinary. It is, however, precisely not just the ordinary in a disrespectful sense but rather the non-extraordinary. In his literary works Perec sought to record everything that is usually overlooked, "what happens every day and recurs every day: the banal, the quotidian, the obvious, the common, the ordinary, the infra-ordinary, the background noise, the habitual."[1] Perec's literature is primarily about everyday observations of ordinary places, in the streets, on the squares, or in apartment buildings in Paris. Again and again, he insists on not taking these ordinary places for granted: "What we need to question is bricks, concrete, glass, our table manners, our utensils, our tools, the way we spend our time, our rhythms."[2] Perec proves to be just as much a productive source of inspiration for architecture as for sociology. These two fields are to be brought into a dialogue in the present issue of GAM, since most of what we do takes place in built spaces that can never be separated from their everyday use. They are lived in, redesigned, converted, improved, and sometimes even desecrated. That is not always beautiful but should be taken seriously.

Everyday uses of extraordinary architecture as well as extraordinary practices with everyday architecture that have come to our attention, hybrid forms of things worth seeing and things not worth seeing, or simply

1 Georges Perec, "Approaches to What?" (1973), in Perec, *Species of Spaces and Other Pieces*, ed. and trans. John Sturrock (London, 1997), 205–207, esp. 206.
2 Ibid.

umgestaltet, umgenutzt, aufgewertet und bisweilen auch entweiht. Das sieht nicht immer schön aus, sollte aber doch ernstgenommen werden.

In den Blick geraten alltägliche Gebrauchsweisen außergewöhnlicher Architektur ebenso wie außergewöhnliche Praktiken in alltäglicher Architektur, Mischformen des Sehenswürdigen und Nicht-Sehenswürdigen oder einfach nur banale Orte, die jedoch eine konzentrierte Beobachtung verdienen. Dabei geht es uns weder um eine Ästhetisierung des Alltäglichen noch um eine Emphase des Banalen. Wir wollen es vermeiden, den Alltag in irgendeiner Form zu intellektualisieren, zu ästhetisieren oder zu ironisieren und bemühen uns stattdessen um Sachlichkeit und Nüchternheit. Zu diesem Zweck werden in GAM 20 Methoden und Techniken erprobt, die es erlauben, sich mit dem Alltäglichen aus größtmöglicher Nähe und doch mit der gebotenen Distanz zu beschäftigen. Die teilnehmende Beobachtung ist dabei ein ebenso geeignetes Verfahren wie die Verfremdung, die Imitation, die Archivierung, die Serialisierung oder der Vergleich. Lernen konnten wir dabei von der Ethnologie, dem Dokumentarfilm, der Alltagssoziologie, dem realistischen Roman, der frühen Stadtforschung oder auch der Architekturethnographie.

Die Hinwendung zu alltäglicher Architektur ist immer auch eine Hinwendung zum Bestand. Und doch betreibt dieses Heft keine Apologetik des Bestehenden. Ganz im Gegenteil: Die Beschäftigung mit dem Alltag zwingt dazu, sowohl die Beharrungskräfte als auch das kreative Potential der Praxis – und zwar der architektonischen wie der sozialen Praxis – anzuerkennen. Bisweilen ist die Architektur klüger, innovativer, moralischer, politischer und subversiver als ihre alltägliche Nutzung – Gleiches gilt aber auch umgekehrt. Gerade hier können Architektur und Soziologie viel voneinander lernen. Gleichwohl sollte nicht der Eindruck entstehen, der Alltag sei nur harmlos und friedlich. Es gibt auch eine Bösartigkeit des Banalen, weswegen uns die Auseinandersetzung mit dem Alltag immer auch in die Lage versetzen sollte, entsprechend Kritik zu formulieren. Was wir im Folgenden präsentieren, kann freilich keine umfassende Bestimmung oder Inventarisierung des Alltags sein. Nicht nur konzentrieren sich die Beiträge auf unterschiedliche Fälle unterschiedlicher geographischer und kultureller Regionen, sie führen auch je unterschiedliche Zugänge und Methoden aus unterschiedlichen Disziplinen vor. Die Kamera kann dabei ein ebenso wichtiges Forschungsinstrument sein wie das Interview, der Gang ins Archiv oder die eigene Feldforschung vor Ort. Die Disparatheit der Fälle und die Komplementarität der Zugänge sehen wir dabei nicht als Schwäche, sondern als Stärke dieses Vorhabens an.

Michael Heinrich verdanken wir etwa eine Fotoserie von Gebäuden in der Serranía Celtibérica, einem nur wenig besiedelten Gebiet im Nordosten Spaniens. Es handelt sich dabei um einfache Schutzhütten, Taubenhäuser und Ställe. Den Fotografien geht es keineswegs um ein Lob

banal places that nevertheless deserve concentrated observation. It is neither about aestheticizing the everyday nor emphasizing the banal. We want to avoid intellectualizing, aestheticizing, and ironizing the everyday in any form and instead strive for objectivity and sobriety. To that end, GAM 20 explores methods and techniques that permit the greatest proximity to the everyday and yet are concerned about the distance offered. Participant observation is a method just as suitable for this as alienation, imitation, archiving, serializing, or comparison. We have learned from ethnology, the documentary film, the sociology of the everyday, the realistic novel, early urban research, and even architectural ethnography.

The turn to everyday architecture is always a turn to the existing building fabric as well. And yet this issue is no apology for the existing. Quite the contrary, working with the everyday forces one to recognize both the forces of persistence and the creative potential of practice—and specifical architectural and social practice. Sometimes, architecture is more intelligent, more innovative, more political, and more subversive than its everyday use—but the reverse is also true. This is where architecture and sociology can learn from each other. Nevertheless, this should not create the impression that the everyday is merely harmless and peaceful. There is also an evilness of the banal, which is why we must always be in a position to formulate criticism as well whenever we engage with the everyday. What we present in what follows cannot, of course, be a complete definition or inventory of the everyday. Not only do the essays concentrate on different cases in different geographic and cultural regions, but they also demonstrate different approaches and methods from different disciplines. The camera can be an instrument of research of equal importance as the interview, the visit to an archive, or one's own field research. But we see the disparateness of their cases and the complementarity of their approaches not as a weakness but as a strength of this project.

We are indebted to Michael Heinrich for a series of photographs of buildings in the Serranía Celtibérica, a sparsely settled region in northeast Spain. They are of simple shelters, dovecotes, and stables. These photographs are by no means praising the simple or aestheticizing lost places but instead capturing the proportions, materialities, and details of buildings that cease to appear simple only after extended observation.

The history of the term "infra-ordinaire" and its position in the work of Georges Perec are the focus of the essay by Johanna-Charlotte Horst. She argues that Perec's fascination with ordinary places is by no means merely a characteristic of an idiosyncratic literary project but must rather be understood from his turn to the ordinary and everyday as a result of his own lack of biographical orientation and as an attempt to interpret his lifelong work of memory and mourning. After reading this essay at the latest, the theme of this issue should lose any appearance

des Einfachen oder um die Ästhetisierung von Lost Places, sondern darum, die Proportionen, Materialitäten und Details von Gebäuden einzufangen, die erst nach längerer Betrachtung den Anschein des Einfachen verlieren.

Der Entstehungsgeschichte des Begriffs *infra-ordinaire* und seiner Stellung im Werk Georges Perecs geht der Beitrag von Johanna-Charlotte Horst nach. Perecs Faszination für gewöhnliche Plätze sei keineswegs nur Kennzeichen eines eigenwilligen literarischen Projekts, vielmehr müsse dessen Hinwendung zum Gewöhnlichen und Alltäglichen aus seiner eigenen biographischen Orientierungslosigkeit heraus verstanden und als Versuch einer lebenslangen Erinnerungs- und Trauerarbeit gedeutet werden. Spätestens nach der Lektüre dieses Beitrags sollte der Themenzuschnitt dieses Heftes jeden Anschein des Frivolen verloren haben. Es muss eben ganz schön viel in Ordnung sein, damit einem das Alltägliche banal erscheinen kann.

Dass nicht nur das Schreiben, sondern auch das Bauen eine therapeutische Funktion haben kann, macht Ajna Babahmetović deutlich. Sie gewährt uns Einblicke in ihre Feldforschung zu Diaspora-Architektur in Kozarac, einer Ortschaft im Nordwesten Bosnien-Herzegowinas. Die von ihr untersuchten Einfamilienhäuser der im Ausland lebenden GastarbeiterInnen deutet sie als Versuche, der eigenen Entwurzelung zu begegnen. Das Haus in der Heimat wird für viele GastarbeiterInnen somit zu einer *extension of man*, die lebenslange Arbeit an diesem Haus zu einem Akt architektonischer Psycho- und Physiotherapie: „Körper bauten Häuser, und die Häuser machten im Gegenzug die Körper ganz."

Der Schriftsteller Thomas Meinecke wiederum öffnet uns die Türe zu einem der berühmtesten und meistfotografierten Gebäude der Architekturgeschichte: Le Corbusiers Unité d'Habitation in Marseille. Im Interview mit ihm erfahren wir etwas über den Alltag in diesem Haus, in dem er seit einiger Zeit lebt. Er berichtet von Bengalo-Rauchschwaden um das Haus bei Heimspielen von Olympique Marseille, von Hausversammlungen, Hundewiesen und tobenden Kindern auf dem Dach und zeichnet ein anderes Bild dieses ikonischen Bauwerks, als wir es aus Architekturbüchern kennen.

Auch Alberto Calderoni und Luigimanuele Amabile stellen den Wohnalltag in den Mittelpunkt, erzählen allerdings von den Hinterhöfen der zumeist von anonymen Architekten gebauten neapolitanischen Palazzi, in denen sie „intuitive, offenkundig nicht aus Berechnung entstandene urbane Räume" jenseits von unmittelbarer Nützlichkeit erkennen. Die begleitenden Fotografien fangen die zahlreichen Spuren der alltäglichen Benutzung – wir sehen Topfpflanzen und Wäscheleinen – dieser unkalkulierten Räume ein.

Wer nur einen flüchtigen Blick in den Beitrag von Ena Kukić wirft, könnte darin einen Hauch Retrotopie vermuten; schließlich widmet sie sich einem Denkmal des jugoslawischen Alltags, dem massenhaft produzierten K67 Kiosk, der als Zeitungsstand ebenso wie als Skilift-

of the frivolous. A great deal has to be in order for the everyday to seem banal.

Ajna Babahmetović makes it clear that not only writing but also building can have a therapeutic function. She offers us insights into her field research on diaspora architecture in Kozarac, a town in the northwest of Bosnia and Herzegovina. The single-family home of migrant workers living abroad that she studied are thus an *extension of man*, and lifelong work on such a house becomes an act of architectural psycho- and physiotherapy: "Bodies built houses, and the houses, in return, rendered the body whole."

The writer Thomas Meinecke, in turn, opens doors for us to one of the most famous and most photographed buildings in the history of architecture: Le Corbusier's Unité d'Habitation in Marseille. In the interview with him, we learn something about daily life in this building in which he has been living for some time. He tells of clouds of smoke around the building from flares during the home games of Olympique Marseille, of resident meetings, dog parks, and children romping on the roof and sketches a different picture of this iconic building than the one we know from books on architecture.

Alberto Calderoni and Luigimanuele Amabile also look at everyday housing, though they tell of the backyards of Neapolitan palazzi, whose architects are usually anonymous, which they see as "intuitive and apparently uncalculated urban spaces" beyond immediate utility. The accompanying photographs capture numerous traces of daily use: we see flowerpots and clotheslines from these spaces characterized by lack of calculation.

Anyone who casts even a fleeting glimpse on the essay by Ena Kukić may suspect a hint of retrotopia; it is, after all, dedicated to a monument of everyday life in Yugoslavia, the mass-produced K67 Kiosk, which was used as a newspaper stand, a ski-lift hut or a florist's. Kukić is by no means interested in a nostalgic look at an object from the past. Although she traces the history of the K67 Kiosk, she is primarily interested in its astounding persistence and the forms of its use today.

If one wishes to approach the everyday through research as Denise Scott Brown does, it is wise to follow the heuristic method of deferring judgment: "Judgment is withheld in the interest of understanding and receptivity." The text in which this important instruction is found is titled "Learning from Pop" and dates from 1971. We are pleased to have been allowed to reprint this still-relevant text in GAM and to publish it in German translation for the first time.

Next, Andrea Canclini focuses on the developments of simple single-family homes in Italy that were built after World War II. As modest as they may appear, the history of their origin is noteworthy, in which a social-reformist Catholicism of the postwar years converged with the Italian image of an American suburban lifestyle.

In recent years, the documentation of one's own life has become a universal cultural technique. It pays all

häuschen oder Blumenladen eingesetzt wurde. Kukić geht es aber keineswegs um einen nostalgischen Blick auf ein Objekt der Vergangenheit. Zwar zeichnet sie die Geschichte des K67 Kiosks nach, interessiert sich aber in erster Linie für dessen erstaunliche Persistenz und für heutige Formen des Gebrauchs.

Will man sich mit Denise Scott Brown dem Alltäglichen forschend nähern, so empfiehlt es sich, der heuristischen Methode des aufgeschobenen Urteils zu folgen: „Man hält sich mit dem Urteilen zurück, um etwas besser aufnehmen und verstehen zu können". Der Text, in dem diese wichtige Anweisung zu finden ist, trägt den Titel „Learning from Pop" und stammt aus dem Jahr 1971. Wir sind froh, diesen noch immer aktuellen Text in GAM abdrucken und erstmals in deutscher Übersetzung veröffentlichen zu dürfen.

Andrea Canclini richtet im Anschluss den Fokus auf einfache italienische Einfamilienhaussiedlungen, die nach dem Zweiten Weltkrieg errichtet wurden. So unscheinbar diese in ihrer Anmutung sind, so erstaunlich ist deren Entstehungsgeschichte, in der ein sozialreformerischer Katholizismus der Nachkriegsjahre auf die italienische Imagination eines amerikanisch-suburbanen Lifestyles traf.

Die Dokumentation des eigenen Alltags ist in den letzten Jahren längst zu einer allgemein gebräuchlichen Kulturtechnik geraten. Umso mehr lohnt es sich, die Fotografien von Helmut Tezak aufmerksam zu betrachten. Nur auf den ersten Blick ähneln sie jenen Formen ubiquitärer Street Photography. Bei genauerem Hinsehen stechen jedoch die Akribie, die Beharrlichkeit und Repetitivität ins Auge, die dieses bereits Jahrzehnte andauernde Projekt einer fotografischen Auseinandersetzung mit dem Alltag in der Stadt Graz auszeichnen.

Beatrice Azzolas Beitrag nimmt uns mit auf einen Roadtrip über italienische Autobahnen und macht Halt an den vielen berühmten italienischen Autogrill-Raststationen. Dabei rekonstruiert sie deren Entstehungs- und Faszinationsgeschichte, legt aber auch jene vergangene Zukunft frei, die mit dieser markanten Autobahn-Architektur verbunden war. Die zunehmende Veralltäglichung dieser einst fantastischen Bauten stellt uns heute vor die Herausforderung des Umgangs mit dieser Architektur, aber gleichzeitig auch mit deren längst verschwundenen utopischen Energien.

Der Zusammenhang zwischen Automobil und Architektur spielt auch im Beitrag von Svenja Hollstein eine zentrale Rolle. Mobilität wird hier jedoch auf eine ganz eigene Weise gedeutet, geht es doch nicht um das Auto als Fortbewegungsmittel, sondern um das Auto als beweglichen Einrichtungsgegenstand. In Auseinandersetzung mit Josef Franks Überlegungen zur Möblierung von Innenräumen fragt Hollstein nach möglichen Übertragungen auf die Straßenraumgestaltung von Graz.

Im Jahr 1966 erschien das Buch *Liquor License. An Ethnography of Bar Behavior*. Es handelte sich um die Doktorarbeit der Soziologin Sherri Cavan, die mehrere

the more to look carefully at the photographs of Helmut Tezak. Only at first glance do they resemble the forms of ubiquitous street photography. On closer inspection, however, one is struck by the meticulousness, persistence, and repetitiveness that distinguish this decades-long project of grappling with everyday life in the city of Graz through photography.

Beatrice Azzola's essay takes us on a road trip via Italian highways, stopping at many of Italy's famous Autogrill rest stops. She reconstructs the fascinating history of their origins but also reveals the "past future" that was associated with this striking roadside architecture. The increasing familiarity of these once imaginative buildings presents us with a challenge today when addressing not only this architecture but also its long-since vanished utopian energies.

The connection between the automobile and architecture also plays a central role in the essay by Svenja Hollstein. But mobility is interpreted here in a unique way, as it is not about the car as a means of transportation but as a mobile piece of furniture. Reflecting on Josef Frank's thoughts about furnishing interiors, Hollstein asks how they can be applied to designing the streets of Graz.

Liquor License: An Ethnography of Bar Behavior was published in 1966. It was the dissertation of the sociologist Sherri Cavan, who spent several years conducting participant observation in bars in California to study the behavior of people in such places. In the excerpt reprinted here, and translated into German for the first time, Cavan looks more closely at the particularities of the bar as a concrete place, analyzes seating arrangements, reconstructs movements in the bar, and measures the distances between guests.

This issue ends with a series of photographs by Luc Merx that is part of an extensive study of plaster workshops in Cairo. Over time, several of them have set up in the cemeteries of the city and in the process became places where the ordinary and the extraordinary overlap. The photographs manage to document the process of gradual appropriation and also profanation by practical use but without making a moral judgment.

The image on the cover of this issue of GAM is titled "Teilansicht mit Besenschrank mit geöffneter Tür" (Partial view of broom closet with door open) and is a photograph of a domestic closet taken by Friedrich Weimer and commissioned by the state-owned furniture company Dresden-Hellerau for the autumn trade fair in Leipzig in 1988. Today, we can read it as an image of an everyday life that changed radically just a year later. Not a lot of sociological foreknowledge is required to recognize in this photograph the expectations of gender roles and the structures of domestic power inherent in this space and time. One is also struck by the private orderings of the everyday beneath the surface—*infra-orders*, as it were—that can be found in various forms in our apartments, suitcases, drawers, and of course also laptops and smartphones. This shot is part of a collection of just over 15,000 photographs of

Jahre teilnehmend beobachtend in kalifornischen Bars verbrachte, um das Verhalten von Menschen in derartigen Räumen zu studieren. In dem hier abgedruckten und erstmals ins Deutsche übersetzten Textausschnitt geht Cavan genauer auf die Eigentümlichkeiten der Bar als konkretem Raum ein, analysiert Sitzordnungen, rekonstruiert die Bewegungen in der Bar und misst die Abstände zwischen verschiedenen Gästen.

Das Heft endet mit einer Bilderstrecke von Luc Merx, die Teil einer umfangreichen Studie über Stuckwerkstätten in Kairo ist. Einige von ihnen haben sich im Laufe der Zeit in den Nekropolen der Stadt niedergelassen und wurden dadurch zu Orten, an denen sich Alltägliches und Außeralltägliches überlagern. Den Fotografien gelingt es, den Prozess der allmählichen Aneignung und auch Profanierung durch praktische Nutzung zu dokumentieren, jedoch ohne ein moralisches Urteil zu fällen.

Das Coverbild dieser GAM-Ausgabe trägt den Titel „Teilansicht mit Besenschrank mit geöffneter Tür" und ist die Aufnahme eines Haushaltsschrankes im Auftrag des VEB Möbelkombinats Dresden-Hellerau, fotografiert von Friedrich Weimer für die Leipziger Herbstmesse 1988. Wir können es heute als Abbild eines Alltags lesen, der sich schon ein Jahr später radikal geändert hat. Es ist nicht viel soziologische Vorbildung nötig, um an dieser Aufnahme dem Raum und der Zeit inhärente Rollenerwartungen und häusliche Machtstrukturen zu erkennen. Auch stechen die unterhalb der Oberfläche liegenden privaten Alltagsordnungen – gewissermaßen *Infra-Ordnungen* – ins Auge, die sich in unterschiedlichen Ausprägungen in unseren Wohnungen, Koffern, Schubladen, aber natürlich auch auf Laptops und Smartphones finden lassen. Die Aufnahme ist Teil einer Sammlung von knapp 15.000 Fotografien von Inneneinrichtungen für Möbelkataloge der DDR – ein Archiv des Alltags, dessen Entstehung sich weder künstlerischen noch wissenschaftlichen Impulsen verdankt. Wer sich die Mühe macht, diese unzähligen Fotografien durchzusehen, wird nicht nur staunen, mit welcher Genauigkeit hier alltägliche Räume nachgebaut und fotografiert wurden, sondern wird auch Bewegungsstudien von Alltagsmöbeln entdecken. Im Hinblick auf unsere Forschungsfragen handelt es sich um beeindruckendes Material: was die damit verbundene Ernsthaftigkeit und Präzision betrifft, haben wir uns dieses Projekt für die Gestaltung dieser GAM-Ausgabe zum Vorbild genommen.

interior designs for furniture catalogues of the German Democratic Republic, which were not taken for artistic or scholarly reasons. Anyone who makes the effort to go through these countless photographs will not only be astonished by the precision with which everyday spaces were reconstructed and photographed but will also discover motion studies of everyday furniture. It is impressive material for our research questions; we have taken the seriousness and precision associated with this project as a model for conceiving this issue of GAM.

Translation: Steven Lindberg

Friedrich Weimer: Sofa, 1988

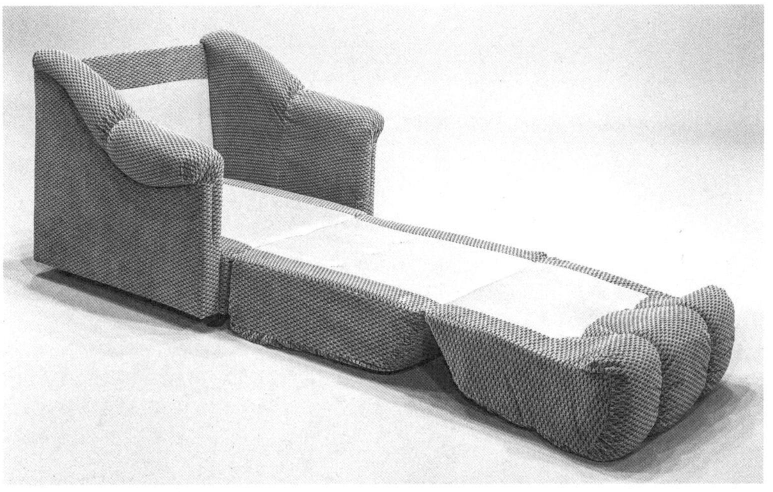

Friedrich Weimer: Sessel, 1989

Friedrich Weimer: Eckschrank, 1956

Casa 001-100

Einfache Bauten
Simple Structures

Michael Heinrich

In der Serranía Celtibérica, einem fast menschenleeren Gebiet im Nordosten Spaniens, gibt es viele einfache Gebäude, die ohne große Umbauten viele Jahrzehnte überdauert haben. Sie sind oftmals schlicht aus Lehmziegeln und im Inneren aus gestampfter Erde gebaut, sind unverputzt und haben meist nur eine Türe und ein Fenster. Die Gebäude dienen als Unterkünfte für LandarbeiterInnen, Taubenhäuser, Ställe oder Schutzhütten für wandernde SchäferInnen. Die folgende Bilderserie nimmt diese einsamen Bauten in den Blick, um sie vor dem Vergessen zu bewahren. Dabei geht es ihr nicht um Ruinenromantik, sondern um dokumentarische Genauigkeit: Im Fokus stehen Proportionen, Materialität und Details sowie die harmonische Interaktion der Gebäude mit ihrer Umgebung. Es wurden auch einige zeitgenössische Bauten in die Serie aufgenommen, um einen Vergleich zu ermöglichen. Die Aufnahmen entstanden im Spätsommer 2023 in den Regierungsbezirken Burgos und Soria und bilden den Anfang einer umfangreichen, für die nächsten Jahre geplanten fotografischen Dokumentationsserie.

In the Serranía Celtibérica region of northeastern Spain, which is nearly devoid of people, there are many simple buildings that have survived for decades without any major renovations. Often they are built of clay bricks in a straightforward style, and of tamped earth in the interior; they are unplastered and usually have just a single door and window. The structures serve as accommodations for farmhands, as dovecotes, as stables, or as shelters for migrant shepherds. The photo series following this introduction takes a look at these solitary buildings, aiming to protect them from falling into oblivion. The focus here is not on the romantic nature of ruins, but on documentary precision: on proportions, materiality, and details like the harmonious interaction of the buildings with their surroundings. Several contemporary buildings were also included in the series for the purpose of comparison. The photographs were taken in the late summer of 2023 in the administrative districts of Burgos and Soria and mark the beginning of an extensive photographic documentation series planned for the coming years.

Translation: Dawn Michelle d'Atri

MARCO

ANAMA

FOX

„Infra-ordinaire“

Zur literarischen Infrastruktur des Alltäglichen bei Georges Perec
On the Literary Infrastructure of the Everyday in Georges Perec

Johanna-Charlotte Horst

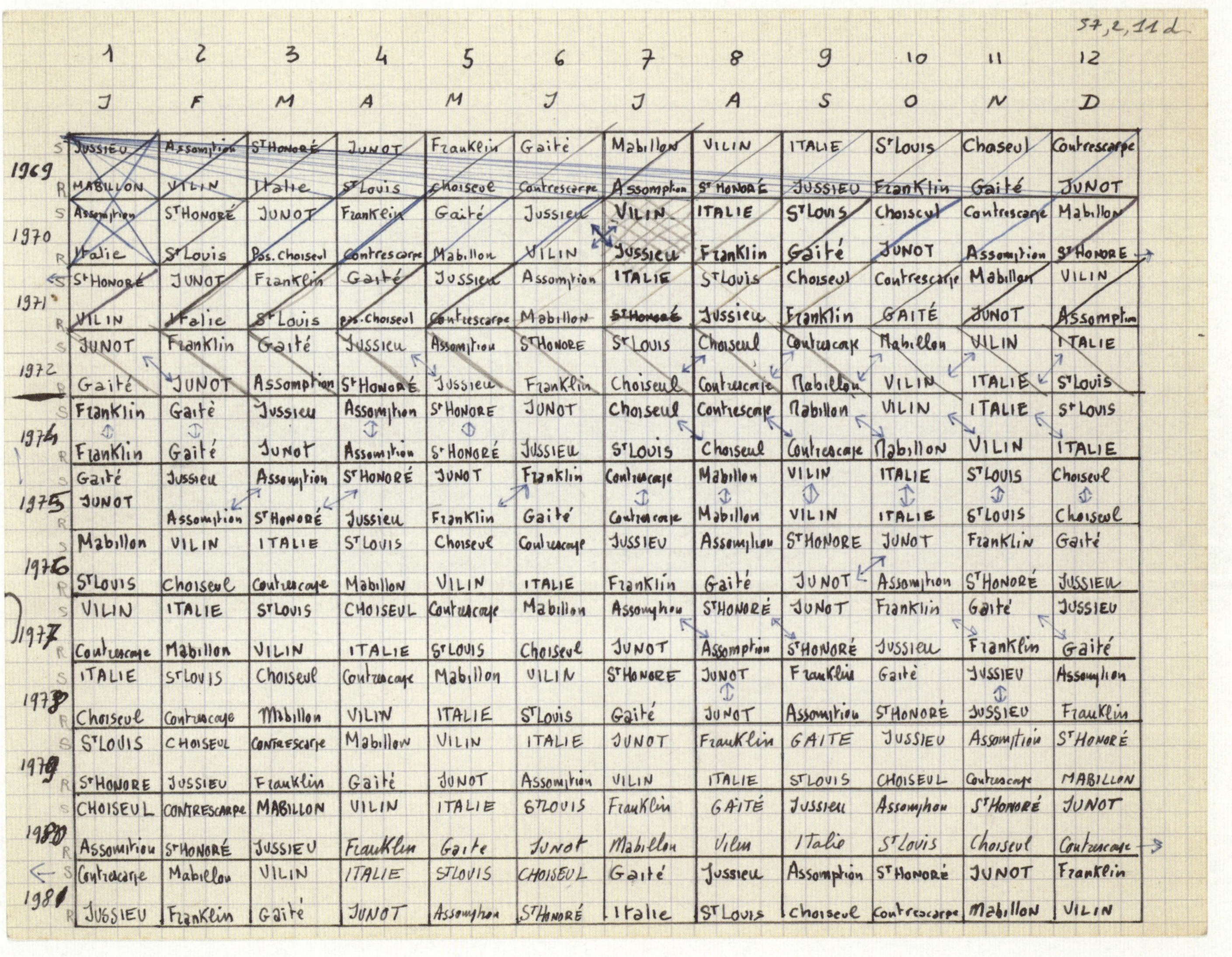

57,2,11 d

		1 J	2 F	3 M	4 A	5 M	6 J	7 J	8 A	9 S	10 O	11 N	12 D
1969	S	Jussieu	Assomption	St Honoré	Junot	Franklin	Gaité	Mabillon	Vilin	Italie	St Louis	Chaseul	Contrescarpe
	R	Mabillon	Vilin	Italie	St Louis	Choiseul	Contrescarpe	Assomption	St Honoré	Jussieu	Franklin	Gaité	Junot
1970	S	Assomption	St Honoré	Junot	Franklin	Gaité	Jussieu	Vilin	Italie	St Louis	Choiseul	Contrescarpe	Mabillon
	R	Italie	St Louis	Pas. Choiseul	Contrescarpe	Mabillon	Vilin	Jussieu	Franklin	Gaité	Junot	Assomption	St Honoré
1971	S	St Honoré	Junot	Franklin	Gaité	Jussieu	Assomption	Italie	St Louis	Choiseul	Contrescarpe	Mabillon	Vilin
	R	Vilin	Italie	St Louis	pas. Choiseul	Contrescarpe	Mabillon	~~St Honoré~~	Jussieu	Franklin	Gaité	Junot	Assomption
1972	S	Junot	Franklin	Gaité	Jussieu	Assomption	St Honoré	St Louis	Choiseul	Contrescarpe	Mabillon	Vilin	Italie
	R	Gaité	Junot	Assomption	St Honoré	Jussieu	Franklin	Choiseul	Contrescarpe	Mabillon	Vilin	Italie	St Louis
1974	S	Franklin	Gaité	Jussieu	Assomption	St Honoré	Junot	Choiseul	Contrescarpe	Mabillon	Vilin	Italie	St Louis
	R	Franklin	Gaité	Junot	Assomption	St Honoré	Jussieu	St Louis	Choiseul	Contrescarpe	Mabillon	Vilin	Italie
1975	S	Gaité Junot	Jussieu	Assomption	St Honoré	Junot	Franklin	Contrescarpe	Mabillon	Vilin	Italie	St Louis	Choiseul
	R		Assomption	St Honoré	Jussieu	Franklin	Gaité	Contrescarpe	Mabillon	Vilin	Italie	St Louis	Choiseul
1976	S	Mabillon	Vilin	Italie	St Louis	Choiseul	Contrescarpe	Jussieu	Assomption	St Honoré	Junot	Franklin	Gaité
	R	St Louis	Choiseul	Contrescarpe	Mabillon	Vilin	Italie	Franklin	Gaité	Junot	Assomption	St Honoré	Jussieu
1977	S	Vilin	Italie	St Louis	Choiseul	Contrescarpe	Mabillon	Assomption	St Honoré	Junot	Franklin	Gaité	Jussieu
	R	Contrescarpe	Mabillon	Vilin	Italie	St Louis	Choiseul	Junot	Assomption	St Honoré	Jussieu	Franklin	Gaité
1978	S	Italie	St Louis	Choiseul	Contrescarpe	Mabillon	Vilin	St Honoré	Junot	Franklin	Gaité	Jussieu	Assomption
	R	Choiseul	Contrescarpe	Mabillon	Vilin	Italie	St Louis	Gaité	Junot	Assomption	St Honoré	Jussieu	Franklin
1979	S	St Louis	Choiseul	Contrescarpe	Mabillon	Vilin	Italie	Junot	Franklin	Gaité	Jussieu	Assomption	St Honoré
	R	St Honoré	Jussieu	Franklin	Gaité	Junot	Assomption	Vilin	Italie	St Louis	Choiseul	Contrescarpe	Mabillon
1980	S	Choiseul	Contrescarpe	Mabillon	Vilin	Italie	St Louis	Franklin	Gaité	Jussieu	Assomption	St Honoré	Junot
	R	Assomption	St Honoré	Jussieu	Franklin	Gaite	Junot	Mabillon	Vilin	Italie	St Louis	Choiseul	Contrescarpe
1981	S	Contrescarpe	Mabillon	Vilin	Italie	St Louis	Choiseul	Gaité	Jussieu	Assomption	St Honoré	Junot	Franklin
	R	Jussieu	Franklin	Gaité	Junot	Assomption	St Honoré	Italie	St Louis	Choiseul	Contrescarpe	Mabillon	Vilin

Zeitplan für Georges Perecs *Lieux* © Bibliothèque nationale de France

Georges Perec wird 1981 auf eine Architektur-Konferenz zur Repräsentation des Raums eingeladen. Praktische ArchitektInnen sollen bei dieser Gelegenheit mit RaumsemiotikerInnen ins Gespräch kommen.[1] In den 1970er-Jahren publizierte Perec eine Vielzahl von Texten, in denen es um verschiedene Arten von Räumen geht. Zu ihnen zählen minutiöse Beschreibungen Pariser Plätze, etwa des Place Saint-Sulpice. Den Modus seiner Beschreibungen sowie das Beschriebene selbst bezeichnet Perec als ‚infra-ordinaire'. Auf der Konferenz soll er diese Praxis anhand eines von den Veranstaltern vorgegebenen Ortes vorführen. Der Wunsch bleibt jedoch unerfüllt. Sein Scheitern erklärt der Schriftsteller damit, dass er nur solche Räume ‚dekodieren' könne, die mit seinem Leben in Verbindung stän-den. Wenn dies nicht der Fall sei, bleibe der Ort für ihn stumm.Schließlich gibt Perec vor den ArchitektInnen zu, dass seine Beschreibungspraxis nicht primär auf das Studium von Räumen abziele, sondern in erster Linie Teil eines umfangreichen Erinnerungsprojektes sei.

Orientierung

Im Schreiben, so Perec, arbeite er stets gegen eine räumliche und zeitliche Orientierungslosigkeit an.[2] Diese lässt sich auf die traumatische Kindheit des jüdischen Autors zurückführen. Sein Vater starb an der Front im Zweiten Weltkrieg, die Mutter wurde entweder auf dem Weg in das oder in dem KZ Auschwitz-Birkenau umgebracht. In dem autobiografischen Roman *W ou le souvenir d'enfance* (*W oder die Kindheitserinnerungen*) stellt Perec traurig fest, er habe keine Erinnerungen an seine Eltern. An die Stelle von Kindheitserinnerungen sei die Geschichtsschreibung getreten, die die Lücken der eigenen Geschichte mit den historischen Schlagwörtern „KZ" und „Krieg" immer

1 Vgl. Perec, Georges: „À propos de la description", in: Dominique Bertelli und Mireille Ribière (Hg.): *Entretiens et conférences. 1965–1978*, Bd. 2, Nantes 2003, 227–243, hier 227. (Sofern nicht anders vermerkt, stammen die Übersetzungen von der Autorin.)

2 Nicht zuletzt aus diesem Grund geht es in Perecs Texten immer auch um Räume: In *Espécès d'espaces* (*Träumen von Räumen*), einer Sammlung literarischer Raumstudien, misst der Autor unterschiedliche Raumformate von der Buchseite bis zur Erde aus. In den Romanen *Les choses* (*Die Dinge*), *Un homme qui dort* (*Ein Mann, der schläft*) und *La vie mode d'emploi* (*Das Leben Gebrauchsanleitung*) geht es darum, wie man sich in Räumen bewegt, wie man sie bewohnt, aber auch, wie man aus ihnen herauskommt. Den Text selbst begreift Perec ebenso als einen Raum. Bevor er mit dem Schreiben beginnt, entwirft er fast immer einen Bauplan seiner Texte. Bei *La vie mode d'emploi* fällt der Romanentwurf gar mit der Skizze eines Hauses zusammen. Dabei ist jedem Zimmer ein Kapitel zugeordnet, jedem Zimmer bzw. jedem Kapitel wiederum bestimmte Wörter. Vgl. hierzu auch Dettke, Julia: *Raumtexte. Georges Perec und die Räumlichkeit der Literatur*, Paderborn 2021.

Georges Perec was invited to an architecture conference on the representation of space in 1981. It was intended as an opportunity for practicing architects to converse with semioticians of space.[1] In the 1970s, Perec had published a number of texts on different types of spaces. They included minutely detailed descriptions of squares in Paris, such as the place Saint-Sulpice. Perec called both the mode of his descriptions and the described things themselves "infra-ordinaire" (infra-ordinary). At the conference he was supposed to demonstrate this practice using the example of a place chosen by the organizers. This wish remained unfulfilled, however. The writer explained his failure by saying that he could "decode" only spaces that were connected with his life. When that was not the case, the place remained mute to him. In the end, Perec admitted to the architects that his practice of describing was not primarily focused on studying but rather part of an extensive memory project.

Orientation

When writing, said Perec, he was always working against a lack of spatial and temporal orientation.[2] This could be explained by the Jewish author's traumatic childhood. His father died on the front in World War II; his mother was murdered either en route to or in the Auschwitz-Birkenau concentration camp. In his autobiographical novel *W ou le souvenir d'enfance* (*W, or The Memory of Childhood*), Perec sadly observed that he had no memories of his parents. His childhood memories had therefore been replaced by history writing that had always filled the gaps in his own story with historical catchwords such as "concentration camp" and "war."[3] Only starting at the age of seven, that is, from 1943, did he have single fragments of

1 See Georges Perec, "À propos de la description" (1981), in Perec, *Entretiens et conférences, 1965–1978*, ed. Dominique Bertelli and Mireille Ribière, 2 vols. (Nantes, 2003), 2:227–43, esp. 227. (Unless otherwise indicated, all translations from German and French are my own.—*Trans.*)

2 Not least for this reason, Perec's texts are always about spaces: In *Espécès d'espaces* (*Species of Spaces*), a collection of literary studies of space, the author measures different spatial formats, ranging from the book page to Earth. The novels *Les choses* (*Things: A Story of the Sixties*), *Un homme qui dort* (*A Man Asleep*), and *La vie mode d'emploi* (*Life, A User's Manual*) are about how one moves in the spaces in which one lives but also about how one gets out of them. Perec thus understood the text itself as a space. Before he begins writing, he almost always drafts a construction plan for his texts. In the case of *La vie mode d'emploi*, the design for the novel even coincides with the sketch of a house. A chapter is assigned to each room, and in turn certain words to each room or each chapter. On this, see also Julia Dettke, *Raumtexte: Georges Perec und die Räumlichkeit der Literatur* (Paderborn, 2021).

3 On this and on its relationship to Perec's practice of memory and mnemonics, see Judith Kasper, *Sprachen des Vergessens: Proust, Perec und Barthes zwischen Verlust und Eingedenken* (Munich, 2003), 140–181.

schon gefüllt habe.[3] Erst ab dem Alter von sieben Jahren, also ab 1943, verfüge er über einzelne Erinnerungsfragmente. In dieser Zeit wird Perec in einem südfranzösischen Internat versteckt. Er weiß nicht, wo er ist, wie lange er bleiben und wann wieder Besuch von der Familie kommen wird. Die wenigen Erinnerungen an diese Zeit sind so fragmentarisch, dass sie zusammenhanglos nebeneinanderstehen. Es fehlt ein strukturierter Erinnerungsraum, in dem das Vergangene abgelegt und später wieder aufgesucht und reaktiviert werden kann. Dem Autor bleibt also nichts anderes übrig, als die vereinzelten „morceaux de vie" („Lebensfetzen")[4] in eine mehr oder weniger zufällige Reihenfolge zu bringen: „Nulle chronologie sinon celle que j'ai, au fil du temps, arbitrairement reconstituée [...]." („Keine Chronologie außer der, die ich im Laufe der Zeit willkürlich rekonstruiert habe [...].")[5]

Diese Orientierungslosigkeit, „son absence de repères" („das völlige Fehlen von Anhaltspunkten")[6], fungiert nicht nur als Metapher für das Fehlen von Erinnerungen, sie schlägt sich auch als körperliche Verlorenheit im Raum nieder. So berichtet Perec in *W ou le souvenir d'enfance* von einer Links-Rechts-Schwäche, „une incapacité à peu près chronique et toujours aussi vive à distinguer [...] la droite de la gauche" („eine fast chronische und noch immer gleich starke Unfähigkeit [...] links von rechts zu unterscheiden")[7]. Auch im Schreiben manifestiert sich Perecs fundamentale Desorientierung. Seine Handschrift sei bis ins Erwachsenenalter mehr Kritzelei als Schrift gewesen. Die lose auf dem Blatt zerstreuten Buchstaben, „incapables de se souder entre elles pour former un mot" („die unfähig sind, zusammenzuwachsen, um ein Wort zu bilden"),[8] spiegeln die Zerstreutheit der Erinnerungen wider. Die Fähigkeit, Buchstaben zu verbinden, konstelliert sich hier als Voraussetzung eines sinnvollen Erinnerungstextes. Denn der Schreibprozess, „le cheminement de mon histoire" („die Entwicklung meiner Geschichte"), fällt mit dem Erinnerungsprozess, „l'histoire de mon cheminement" („die Geschichte meiner Entwicklung"), zusammen.[9]

Perec berichtet davon, dass er nicht nur links und rechts, sondern alle möglichen Gegensätze durcheinanderbrachte. Geholfen hätten Merksprüche oder andere Eselsbrücken. So habe er sich über die Assonanz von ‚konkav' und dem französischen Wort für Höhle, ‚cave', eingeprägt, was konkav und konvex bedeutet. Daher stamme auch die

3 Vgl. hierzu und zum Verhältnis von Perecs Erinnerungspraxis und der Mnemotechnik Kasper, Judith: *Sprachen des Vergessens. Proust, Perec und Barthes zwischen Verlust und Eingedenken*, München 2003, 140–181.

4 Perec, Georges: *W ou le souvenir d'enfance*, Paris 1975, 98. (Perec, Georges: *W oder die Kindheitserinnerung*, Übers. Eugen Helmlé, Berlin/Zürich 2012, 76.)

5 Ebd., 98f. (Ebd.)

6 Ebd., 98. (Ebd.)

7 Ebd., 185. (Ebd., 144.)

8 Ebd., 97. (Ebd., 76.)

9 Ebd., 18. (Ebd., 13.)

memories. At the time Perec was hidden away in a boarding school in southern France. He did not know where he was, whether he could remain a long time, or when he would be visited by his family again. The few memories he had of that time were so fragmented that they stood side by side, unconnected. He lacked a structured space of memories where the past could be stored away and then later searched for again and reactivated. There was nothing for the author to do other than put the isolated "morceaux de vie" ("scraps of life")[4] into a more or less random sequence: "Nulle chronologie sinon celle que j'ai, au fil du temps, arbitrairement reconstituée [...]." ("No sequence in time, except as I have reconstructed it arbitrarily over the years [...].")[5]

This disorientation, the "absence de repères" ("absence of landmarks")[6], did not just function as a metaphor for his lack of memories but also took the form of being physical lost in space. In *W ou le souvenir d'enfance*, Perec reported of a left-right deficiency: "une incapacité à peu près chronique et toujours aussi vive à distinguer [...] la droite de la gauche" ("more or less chronic and still undiminished inability to tell [...] left from right").[7] Perec's fundamental disorientation was also manifested in writing. Even into adulthood his handwriting was more like scribbling than writing. The letters loosely scattered on the page were "incapables de se souder entre elles pour former un mot" ("unable to forge themselves into a word")[8], reflecting his scattered memories. For the process or writing, "le cheminement de mon histoire" ("the passage of my history"), coincided with the process of remembering, "l'histoire de mon cheminement" ("the story of my passage").[9]

Perec then reported that he confused not only left and right but all sorts of antitheses. Mnemonics and other tricks had helped. For example, he used the assonance of "concave" and the French word "cave" to remember what "concave" and "convex" mean. That was also the source of his fondness "pour les procédés mnémotechnique" ("for mnemonics")[10]. The word *mnémotechnique* is more common in French than its equivalent is in German. It is nevertheless etymologically related to the ancient rhetoric to which Perec came into contact through his teacher Roland Barthes. In his text "L'ancienne rhétorique," Barthes focused on to Aristotle, Cicero, and Quintilian. All three of them refer primarily to speaking in court, to either accuse or defend a person. According to Barthes, rhetoricians understand both the production and the finished structure of a speech as a spatial constellation.

4 Georges Perec, *W ou le souvenir d'enfance*, Paris 1975, 98; (Georges Perec. *W, or The Memory of Childhood*, trans. David Bellos (Boston, 1988), 68.)

5 Ibid., 98–99. (Ibid., 68–69.)

6 Ibid., 98. (Ibid., 68.)

7 Ibid., 185. (Ibid., 135.)

8 Ibid., 97. (Ibid., 68.)

9 Ibid., 18. (Ibid., 6.)

10 Ibid., 185; (Ibid., 136.)

Vorliebe „pour les procédés mnémotechnique" („für mnemotechnische Verfahren")[10]. Die Rede von der Mnemotechnik ist im Französischen zwar umgangssprachlicher als im Deutschen. Dennoch geht sie etymologisch auf die antike Rhetorik zu, mit der Perec durch seinen Lehrer Roland Barthes in Kontakt kam. In seiner Schrift „L'ancienne rhétorique" konzentriert dieser sich auf Aristoteles, Cicero und Quintilian. Alle drei denken in erster Linie über das Redenhalten vor Gericht nach, durch das eine Person entweder angeklagt oder verteidigt werden soll. Die Rhetoriker begreifen Barthes zufolge sowohl die Produktion als auch den fertigen Aufbau einer Rede als räumliche Konstellation. Entsprechend weisen sie die Lehre von der guten Rede als Topik, d.h. als Lehre von der richtigen Verortung aus. Die Inventio figuriert hier als eine Art Parcours, in dessen Verlauf die passenden Versatzstücke und Strukturierungen zu finden sind. Dieses Vorgehen konzipieren die antiken Rhetoriker nicht als kreativen Prozess, sondern als die Anwendung einer Methode, die jeder lernen kann. Um das richtige Argument zu finden, müsse man, so lässt sich exemplarisch in Ciceros *Topica* nachlesen, lediglich an der richtigen Stelle, „locis" („Stellen"), suchen, dort, wo das Gesuchte eingeschlossen liege: „in quibus argumenta inclusa sunt" („in denen die Argumente eingeschlossen liegen").[11] In diesem Sinn bezeichnet Barthes die topische Struktur, in der das schlagende Argument bereit liegt, als „accoucheuse de *latent*" („Geburtshelferin des *Latenten*")[12].

Perec insistiert nicht nur immer wieder auf dem Mangel an Erinnerungen, sondern auch an Inspiration. In beiderlei Hinsicht sucht er nach Vorformatierungen, die ihn zum Schreiben zwingen. Um dieses in Gang zu bringen, erprobt Perec verschiedene Praktiken. Unter anderem tritt er 1967 dem Künstlerkollektiv ‚Ouvroir de littérature potentielle', kurz: Oulipo, bei. Diese ‚Werkstatt für potentielle Literatur' wurde 1960 von dem Mathematiker François Le Lionnais und dem Schriftsteller Raymond Queneau gegründet. Das oulipotische Programm setzt auf selbstauferlegte formale Beschränkungen, die das sprachlich Mögliche erweitern sollen. In Perecs Fall zielt der Einsatz sogenannter ‚contraintes' vor allem darauf ab, Blockaden außer Kraft zu setzen. In diesem Sinn begreift er auch das topische Raster als eine „contrainte"-artige Vorstrukturierung.

10 Ebd., 185. (Ebd., 145.)

11 Cicero, Marcus Tullius: *Topica. Die Kunst, richtig zu argumentieren. Lateinisch und deutsch*, hg. v. Karl Bayer, übers. v. Karl Bayer, München 1993, 2,7ff.

12 Barthes, Roland: „L'ancienne rhétorique. Aide-mémoire", in: Ders.: *L'aventure sémiologique*, Paris 1985, 85–165, hier 139. (Barthes, Roland: „Die alte Rhetorik", in: Ders.: *Das semiologische Abenteuer*, Übers. Dieter Hornig, Frankfurt am Main 1988, 15–101, hier 69.)

Consequently, they identify the art of speaking well as a topic, that is, a theory of finding the right place. The *inventio* figures here as a kind of parcourse over the course of which suitable set pieces and structures can be found. The ancient rhetoricians conceived this approach not as a creative process but as the application of a method that anyone can learn. To find the right argument, as one can read in Cicero's *Topica*, it is merely necessary to search for the right place—*locis* means "places"—where the thing to be found is included: "locis in quibus argumenta inclusa sunt" ("topics under which arguments are included").[11] Barthes accordingly defines the topical structure in which the convincing argument already lies waiting as an "accoucheuse de *latent*" ("midwife of the *latent*")[12].

Perec insisted again and again that he lacked not only memories but also inspiration. In both cases, he sought preformatting to force him to write. Perec tried various practices to achieve this. Among others, in 1967 he joined the artist's collective *Ouvroir de littérature potentielle*, or *Oulipo* for short. This "workshop of potential literature" had been founded in 1960 by the mathematician François Le Lionnais and the writer Raymond Queneau. The Oulipian program consists of self-imposed restrictions intended to expand what is possible in language. Perec used so-called *contraintes* (constraints) above all to overcome blocks. He thus understood the topical model as a kind of *contrainte*-like prestructuring.

Perec explained to his editor, Maurice Nadeau, that he needed "une grille" (a grid)[13] through which the discourse could develop, a little like the lists of (common)places that rhetoricians compile. In the same letter Perec reported on a monumental memory project to be called *Lieux*. In *Lieux* Perec was to take up ancient rhetoric again. It reads: "[M]a seule tradition, ma seule mémoire, mon seul lieu est rhétorique [...]." (My only tradition, my only memory, my only place is rhetorical).[14] Perec repurposed one of rhetoric's central list of questions as a mnemonic in his autobiographical essay "Je suis né." They are questions related to a person. With the help of these *loci a persona* (person-related topics), Perec tried to put his life story

11 Cicero, "Topics," in *On Invention, The Best Kind of Orator, Topics*, trans. H. M. Hubbell (Cambridge, MA, 1949), 377–459, esp. 387 (2.7).

12 Roland Barthes, "L'ancienne rhétorique: Aide-mémoire," in Barthes, *L'aventure sémiologique* (Paris, 1985), 85–165, esp. 139; Roland Barthes, "The Old Rhetoric: An Aide-Mémoire," in *The Semiotic Challenge*, trans. Richard Howard (Berkeley, CA, 1994), 11–94, esp. 67.

13 Georges Perec, "Lettre à Maurice Nadeau" (1969), in Perec, *Je suis né*, ed. Maurice Olender (Paris, 1990), 51–66, esp. 56.

14 Georges Perec, *Lieux*, ed. Jean-Luc Joly (Paris, 2022), 188. On this, see also Philippe Lejeune, *La mémoire et l'oblique: Georges Perec autobiographe* (Paris, 1991), 141; Annelies Schulte Nordholt, *Georges Perec et ses lieux de mémoire: Le projet de Lieux* (Leiden, 2022), 12; Derek Schilling, *Mémoires du quotidien: Les lieux de Perec* (Villeneuve d'Ascq, 2006), 131–132.

Seinem Verleger Nadeau erklärt Perec, er brauche „une grille" („[ein] Gitter")[13], durch das sich der Diskurs entwickeln könne, ein wenig wie jene Verzeichnisse von (Gemein-) Plätzen, die die Rhetoriker aufstellten. In dem gleichen Brief berichtet Perec von einem monumental angelegten Erinnerungsprojekt, das *Lieux* heißen soll. In *Lieux* wird Perec die antike Rhetorik wieder aufnehmen. Dort heißt es: „[M]a seule tradition, ma seule mémoire, mon seul lieu est rhétorique […]." („Meine einzige Tradition, mein einziges Gedächtnis, mein einziger (Erinnerungs-)Ort ist rhetorisch […].")[14] Einen der zentralen rhetorischen Fragenkataloge zweckentfremdet Perec als Mnemotechnik in dem autobiografischen Essay „Je suis né". Es handelt sich dabei um Fragen, die sich auf eine Person beziehen. Mithilfe dieser „loci a persona" (‚personenbezogene Fragenkataloge') versucht Perec, seine Lebensgeschichte zu Papier zu bringen: „Tapons dans la topique: Quoi? Qui? Quand? Où? Comment? Pourquoi?" („Verlegen wir uns auf die Gemeinplätze: Was? Wer? Wann? Wo? Wie? Warum?")[15] Doch trotz der topischen Vorstrukturierung tauchen keine Erinnerungen aus dem Gedächtnis auf. Was eigentlich ein Text voller Erinnerungen werden sollte, gerät somit zu einem Text, der nichts anderes als die Struktur des Erinnerns selbst zu lesen gibt. Das topische Raster verschwindet dabei nicht als Hilfsstütze, sondern bleibt als Textstruktur sichtbar, trägt gewissermaßen die Statik des Textes.

In *W ou le souvenir d'enfance* greift Perec nicht auf die antike Rhetorik zurück, sondern bedient sich einer einfacheren Strukturierungsweise: Zwischen autobiografische Kapitel schaltet er eine Abenteuergeschichte, die in einem KZ-artigen Sportlager endet. Auch hier geht der Erinnerungstext nicht aus *Re*konstruktionen, sondern aus Konstruktionen hervor. Den katastrophalen Bruch, den der Holocaust für Perecs Kindheit bedeutet, überbaut der Autor dabei, so soll im Folgenden gezeigt werden, mit stabilen Texträumen. Sein Schreiben ist somit vor allem eine räumliche Arbeit, die den Aufbau eines Textes wie den Bau eines Gebäudes konzipiert.

Perecs autobiografisches Schreiben ist aber nicht nur im übertragenen Sinn als räumliches zu beschreiben.

13 Perec, Georges: „Lettre à Maurice Nadeau", in: Perec, Georges: „Lettre à Maurice Nadeau", in: Ders.: *Je suis né*, hg. v. Maurice Olender, Paris 1990, 51–66, hier 56.: *Je suis né*, Paris 1990, 51–66, hier 56. (Perec, Georges: „Brief an Maurice Nadeu", in: Ders.: *Geboren 1936*, hg. v. Maurice Olender, Übers. Eugen Helmlé, Berlin/Zürich 2015, 41–53, hier 45.)

14 Perec, Georges: *Lieux*, hg. v. Jean-Luc Joly, Paris 2022, 188. Vgl. zu *Lieux* auch Lejeune, Philippe: *La mémoire et l'oblique. Georges Perec autobiographe*, Paris 1991; 141, Schulte Nordholt, Annelies: *Georges Perec et ses lieux de mémoire: Le projet de Lieux*, Paderborn 2022, 12; Schilling, Derek: *Mémoires du quotidien: les lieux de Perec*, Villeneuve d'Ascq 2006, 131f.

15 Perec: „Je suis né", in: Ders.: *Je suis né* (wie Anm. 13), 9–14, hier 12. (Perec: „Ich bin geboren" in: Ders.: *Geboren 1936*, wie Anm. 13, 7–11, hier 9.)

to paper: "Tapons dans la topique: Quoi? Qui? Quand? Où? Comment? Pourquoi?" ("Let's keep on at the theme: What? Who? When? Where? How? Why?")[15] But despite the topical prestructuring, no memories emerge. What was supposed to be a text full of memories thus becomes a text that offers nothing to read other than the structure of remembering. The topical grid does not disappear as an aide-mémoire but remains visible as a structure of the text, supporting the statics of the text, in a sense.

In *W ou le souvenir d'enfance*, Perec does not resort to ancient rhetoric but rather uses a simpler structure: Between autobiographical chapters, he inserts an adventure story that ends in a concentration-camp-like sports camp. Here too the text on memory results not from *re*constructions but from constructions. As I will show in what follows, the author builds stable textual spaces over the catastrophic rift that the Holocaust represented in Perec's childhood. His writing is therefore above all a spatial work that conceives of constructing a text like a building.

Perec's autobiographical writing should not be thought of as spatial only in a metaphorical sense. It is also literally working in a space. In the writing project *Lieux*, Perec tried to describe twelve squares and streets in Paris twice a year over twelve years, once on location and once from memory. The selected streets and squares are important to the author's biography for different reasons. For example, he lived on rue Vilin with his parents; he lived on the Île Saint Louis with a former lover. Perec created an extensive plan for the temporal sequence of *Lieux*.[16] It was intended to ensure that the square to be described on location would not coincide with the one to be remembered in any month.[17] He sealed the finished descriptions in envelopes that were to be opened when the work was completed, that is, after twelve years. But it did not come to that because Perec abandoned the project early in 1975.

Visiting venues of past phases of life can be described as a strategy of mnemonics from antiquity. Its origins can be traced back to the Greek poet Simonides. In a fateful incident, he was the only person to survive the collapse of a building in which a banquet was taking place. The guests were also so crushed in the accident that they were unrecognizable. Simonides managed to identify them at the site by remembering the seating arrangement. This led to the conclusion that people remember things better when they arrange or place them in a mental space. In Perec's case, returning to the places of his past had no effect on the capacity to remember. He still had no

15 Georges Perec, "Je suis né" (1988), in Perec, *Je suis né* (see note 13), 9–14, esp. 12; Georges Perec, *Species of Spaces and Other Pieces*, ed. and trans. John Sturrock (London, 1997), 95–99, esp. 96.

16 See Jean-Luc Joly, "Introduction," in Perec, *Lieux* (see note 13), 27–45.

17 On the concept of *Lieux*, see Perec, "Lettre à Maurice Nadeau" (see note 13), 58–59; Lejeune, *La mémoire et l'oblique* (see note 14).

Es ist auch buchstäblich eine Arbeit im Raum. In dem Schreibprojekt *Lieux* nimmt Perec sich vor, über zwölf Jahre hinweg zwölf Plätze bzw. Straßen in Paris zweimal im Jahr zu beschreiben, einmal vor Ort, einmal aus der Erinnerung. Die ausgewählten Straßen und Plätze sind aus unterschiedlichen Gründen bedeutend für die Biografie des Autors. In der Rue Vilin lebte er zum Beispiel als Kind mit seinen Eltern, auf der Île Saint Louis wohnt eine ehemalige Geliebte. Für den zeitlichen Ablauf von *Lieux* erstellt Perec einen umfangreichen Arbeitsplan.[16] Dieser soll dafür Sorge tragen, dass in keinem Monat der vor Ort zu beschreibende Platz mit dem zu erinnernden zusammenfällt.[17] Die fertigen Beschreibungen werden in Briefumschlägen versiegelt und sollen nach Abschluss der Arbeit, also erst nach zwölf Jahren, wieder geöffnet werden. Soweit kam es aber nicht, da Perec das Projekt 1975 vorzeitig aufgibt.

Das Aufsuchen von Schauplätzen vergangener Lebensphasen lässt sich als eine Strategie antiker Mnemotechnik beschreiben. Deren Entstehung wird auf den griechischen Dichter Simonides zurückgeführt. Durch einen schicksalshaften Umstand überlebte er als einziger den Einsturz eines Hauses, in dem gerade ein Festmahl stattfand. Die Gäste waren nach dem Unfall derartig zerquetscht, dass man sie nicht mehr wiedererkannte. Simonides gelang es, sie vor Ort zu identifizieren, indem er sich an die Platzordnung erinnerte. Hieraus ist der Schluss gezogen worden, dass man sich besser an Dinge erinnert, wenn man sie in einem Gedankenraum anordnet bzw. ablegt. In Perecs Fall hat die Rückkehr an Orte der Vergangenheit keinen Effekt in Bezug auf seine Erinnerungsfähigkeit. Er bleibt ohne Erinnerungen und kann vor Ort nur beschreiben, was er sieht. Die Vor-Ort-Beschreibungen für *Lieux* sind die frühesten ‚infra-ordinaire'-Texte und damit die Vorbereitung und der Ausgangspunkt für die Rede vom ‚infra-ordinaire'.

‚Infra-ordinaire'

In den Vor-Ort-Beschreibungen protokolliert Perec das alltägliche Geschehen wie ein Ethnograf eine ihm fremde Umgebung: „[J]e décris", so Perec, „‚ce que je vois' de la manière la plus neutre possible, j'énumère les magasins, quelques détails d'architecture, quelques micro-événements" („[Ich] beschreibe [...] das, was ich sehe' so neutral wie möglich, ich zähle die Läden auf, einige Einzelheiten der Architektur, einige Mikro-Ereignisse").[18] Dazu wird eine verfremdende Perspektive eingenommen, die sich nicht auf die kleinen, anekdotischen Begebenheiten konzentriert, sondern auf außeralltägliche Weise aufmerksam für das Alltägliche ist. Auf den polemischen Kommentar, er würde in seinen Texten Tiefenbedeutung allein über

16 Vgl. hierzu Joly, Jean-Luc: „Introduction", in: Perec: *Lieux* (wie Anm. 14), 27–45.

17 Vgl. zum Konzept von *Lieux* Perec: „Lettre à Maurice Nadeau" (Anm. 13), 58f.

18 Perec: „Lettre à Maurice Nadeau" (Anm. 13), 58. (Perec: „Brief an Maurice Nadeau", (Anm. 13), 47.)

memories and on location could only describe what he saw. The in-situ descriptions for *Lieux* were the earliest "infra-ordinaire" texts and hence the preparation and point of departure for talking about "infra-ordinaire."

"Infra-ordinaire"

In the in-situ descriptions, Perec records everyday activities like an ethnographer does a foreign environment: "[J]e décris," writes Perec, "'ce que je vois' de la manière la plus neutre possible, j'énumère les magasins, quelques détails d'architecture, quelques micro-événements" (I describe "that which I see" as neutrally as possible; I list the stores, several details of the architecture, a few micro-events).[18] He also adopts an estranging perspective that is not concentrated on small, anecdotal events but is rather attentive to the ordinary in a way that is extraordinary. Perec responded to the polemical comment that in his texts he arrives at deeper meaning solely by accumulating the meaningless by saying that he found the meaningless especially fascinating.[19] He tried to describe those levels of life that escape conceptual access. For him, the "infra-ordinaire" is not about knowledge but about the process of approaching as a practice of seeing and writing.

Perec first spoke about the "infra-ordinaire" in the brief text "Approches de quoi?" ("Approaches to What?"). This manifesto-like program on the everyday was published in 1973 in the fifth issue of the journal *Cause commune*. Perec had been working on *Lieux* for four years at that point. In 1973, however, he took a break from this project, and the "infra-ordinaire" practice appears to liberate itself as proto-sociological method from autobiographical writing. That is perhaps also the motivation for coining a special word, the "infra-ordinaire," for this writing form. It is first mentioned in a list: "le banal, le quotidien, l'évident, le commun, l'ordinaire, l'infra-ordinaire, le bruit de fond, l'habituel" ("the banal, the quotidian, the obvious, the common, the ordinary, the infra-ordinary, the background noise, the habitual").[20] The "infra-ordinaire" is programmatically an element of a constellation as is clear from the double title of the corresponding issue of *Cause commune*: infra $\frac{\textit{quotidien}}{\textit{ordinaire}}$. Perec chose the "lower" variant over the "quotidian." For what one finds in a daily newspaper—*quotidien* in French—is always only the extraordinary spectacle. It distorts the view of the everyday: "Les journaux parlent de tout, sauf du journalier." ("The daily papers talk of everything except the daily.")[21] Whereas the second part of the compound word "infra-ordinaire" can be

18 Perec, "Lettre à Maurice Nadeau" (see note 13), 58.

19 See Georges Perec, "Pour Georges Perec, le banal est explosif" (1979), in Perec, *Entretiens et conférences, 1979–1981* (see note 1), 2:80–83, esp. 82.

20 Georges Perec, "Approches de quoi?" (1973), in Perec, *L'infra-ordinaire*, ed. Maurice Olender (Paris, 1989), 9–13, esp. 11; Georges Perec, "Approaches to What?" (1973), in Perec, *Species of Spaces* (see note 15), 205–207, esp. 206.

21 Ibid., 10; (Ibid., 201.)

die Anhäufung von Unbedeutendem erreichen, antwortet Perec, das Unbedeutende fasziniere ihn besonders.[19] Er versuche diejenige Ebene des Lebens zu beschreiben, die sich einem begrifflichen Zugriff entziehe. Es geht beim ‚infra-ordinaire' also nicht um Erkenntnis, sondern um den Prozess der Annäherung als einer Praxis des Sehens und Schreibens.

Perec spricht zum ersten Mal vom ‚infra-ordinaire' in dem kurzen Text „Approches de quoi?" („Annäherungen an was?"). Dieses manifestartige Programm zum Alltag erscheint 1973 in der 5. Ausgabe der Zeitschrift *Cause commune*. Zu diesem Zeitpunkt arbeitet Perec bereits seit vier Jahren an *Lieux*. 1973 pausiert er mit diesem Projekt, und die Praxis des Vor-Ort-Beschreibens löst sich mit dem ‚infra-ordinaire' als proto-soziologische Methode vom autobiografischen Schreiben. Aus diesem Grund entsteht möglicherweise auch der Impuls, ein eigenes Wort, nämlich das ‚infra-ordinaire', für diese Schreibform zu etablieren. Bei seiner ersten Nennung taucht es in einer Liste auf: „le banal, le quotidien, l'évident, le commun, l'ordinaire, l'infra-ordinaire, le bruit de fond, l'habituel" („das Banale, das Alltägliche, das Selbstverständliche, das Allgemeine, das Gewöhnliche, das Infra-Gewöhnliche, das Hintergrundgeräusch, das Übliche").[20] Dass das ‚infra-ordinaire' programmatisch Element einer Konstellation ist, zeigt sich auch in dem Doppeltitel der entsprechenden Ausgabe von *Cause commune*: infra $\frac{\textit{quotidien}}{\textit{ordinaire}}$. Perec entscheidet sich für die ‚untere' Variante und gegen das ‚quotidien'. Denn was in der Tageszeitung, auf Französisch ‚quotidien', zu finden sei, sei immer nur das außergewöhnliche Spektakel. Es verstelle den Blick auf das Alltägliche: „Les journaux parlent de tout, sauf du journalier." („Die Zeitungen schreiben über alles, außer über das Tagtägliche.")[21] Während sich der zweite Teil des Kompositums ‚infra-ordinaire' über den Gegensatz zum ‚quotidien' erklärt, lässt sich ‚infra' auf die französische Übersetzung des marxistischen Begriffs ‚Basis' als ‚infrastructure' zurückführen. Die sprichwörtliche Dialektik von Basis und Überbau ist in den 1970er Jahren zu einer bloßen Phrase verkommen. Sie ist schnell zur Hand und wird für alle möglichen Argumente benutzt. Nicht zuletzt um zu retten, was mit der Basis ursprünglich gemeint war, wird das neue Wort ‚infra-ordinaire' erfunden.

Auf diese marxistische Genealogie verweist Perec in „Approches de quoi?", wenn er konstatiert, dass die „malaises sociaux" („[d]as soziale Unbehagen")[22] nicht nur zu Zeiten der öffentlichen Aufmerksamkeit während der

19 Vgl. Perec, Georges: „Pour Georges Perec, le banal est explosif", in: Bertelli, Dominique/Ribière, Mireille (Hg.): *Entretiens et conférences 1979–1981*, Bd. 2, Nantes 2003 [1979], 80–83, hier 82.

20 Perec, Georges: „Approches de quoi?", in: Ders.: *L'infra-ordinaire*, Paris 1989 [1973], 9–13, hier 11. (Perec, Georges: „Annäherungen an was?", in: *Warum gibt es keine Zigaretten beim Gemüsehändler*, Übers. Eugen Helmlé, 5–8, hier 6.)

21 Ebd., 10. (Ebd.)

22 Ebd. (Ebd., 5.)

explained as being the antithesis of "quotidien," the "infra" can be traced back to the French translation of the Marxist term *Basis* (base) as "infrastructure." The proverbial dialectic of base and superstructure had become a mere phrase in the 1970s. It was handy and used for all possible arguments. Not least in order to save what was originally meant by "base," the new word "infra-ordinaire" was coined.

In "Approches de quoi?" Perec refers to this Marxist genealogy when he remarked that "malaises sociaux" ("social problems")[22] do not exist only when the public is paying attention to workers' strikes but also represent the permanent foundation of daily life beyond the spectacular. Karl Marx and Friedrich Engels noted something similar in *Die deutsche Ideologie* (*The German Ideology*). They refer to the means and conditions of production as the "wirklichen Lebensprozess" ("actual life-process") as the "irdische Basis der Geschichte" ("earthly basis for history").[23] Making history includes "vor Allem Essen und Trinken, Wohnung, Kleidung und noch einiges Andere" ("before everything else eating and drinking, a habitation, clothing and many other things.")[24] From these early discussions of the relationship between base and superstructure, one can conclude that the "Produktion des materiellen Lebens" ("production of material life")[25] as base determines the form of society. In order to understand this, according to Marx and Engels, we must analyze the conditions of everyday events rather than the ideas of the rulers.[26]

In this spirit, Lefebvre saw his studies of everyday life as preparing the way to liberating society from false ideas. They were to make people conscious of alienation and make de-alienation possible. Even if Perec did not agree with this analytical vanishing point, he shared with Lefebvre a preliminary objective: The first step is changing perception. Anyone who goes through everyday life blind can neither recognize nor change its structures. With the "infra-ordinaire," Perec was proposing a perspective whose radical neutrality can capture the everyday in its meaninglessness because, unlike Lefebvre's approach, it is not indebted to any preprogrammed political objective. Perec replaces de-alienation with estrangement that makes

22 Ibid.; (Ibid.)

23 Karl Marx and Friedrich Engels, "Die deutsche Ideologie: Kritik der neuesten deutschen Philosophie in ihren Repräsentanten Feuerbach, B. Bauer und Stirner, und des deutschen Sozialismus in seinen verschiedenen Propheten," in Marx and Engels, *Werke* ed. Institut für Marxismus-Leninismus, vol. 3, (Berlin, 1969), 9–533, esp. 28; Marx and Engels, *The German Ideology, Parts I and III*, ed. R. Pascal (New York, 1947), 14 and 16.

24 Ibid.; (Ibid., 16.)

25 Ibid.; (Ibid.)

26 Stuart Hall discusses that the superstructure has relative autonomy and the interrelationship of base and superstructure is accordingly complex. See Stuart Hall, "Rethinking the 'Base and Superstructure' Metaphor" (1977), in Hall, *Essential Essays*, ed. David Morley, 2 vols. (Durham, NC, 2018), 143–171.

Arbeiterstreiks beständen, sondern jenseits des Spektakulären den permanenten Untergrund des Alltags bildeten. Karl Marx und Friedrich Engels stellen in *Die deutsche Ideologie* Ähnliches fest. Sie bezeichnen die Produktionsmittel und -bedingungen als „wirklichen Lebensprozess", als „irdische Basis der Geschichte"[23]. Zum Geschichte-Machen gehöre „vor Allem Essen und Trinken, Wohnung, Kleidung und noch einiges Andere"[24]. Aus diesen frühen Überlegungen zum Verhältnis von Basis und Überbau lässt sich schlussfolgern, dass die „Produktion des materiellen Lebens"[25] als Basis die gesellschaftliche Form bestimmt. Um diese zu verstehen, so Marx und Engels, müssten die Bedingungen der alltäglichen Abläufe und nicht die Ideen der Herrschenden analysiert werden.[26]

In diesem Sinn sieht Lefebvre die gesellschaftliche Befreiung von falschen Ideen durch seine Studien zum Alltagsleben vorbereitet. Sie sollen die Entfremdung bewusst und die Ent-Entfremdung möglich machen. Auch wenn Perec diesem analytischen Fluchtpunkt nicht zustimmt, teilt er mit Lefebvre ein ‚Etappenziel': In einem ersten Schritt geht es um die Veränderung der Wahrnehmung. Wer blind durch den Alltag gehe, der könne dessen Strukturen weder erkennen noch verändern. Mit dem ‚infra-ordinaire' schlägt Perec eine Perspektive vor, deren radikale Neutralität das Alltägliche in seiner Bedeutungslosigkeit einfangen kann, weil sie im Gegensatz zu Lefebvres Ansatz keinem vorprogrammierten politischen Ziel verpflichtet ist. An die Stelle der Ent-Entfremdung rückt Perec die Verfremdung, die das Übersehene sichtbar macht. Man solle so lange beobachten, bis vertraute Orte nicht mehr wieder zu erkennen seien, bis „le lieu tout entier devienne étranger, que l'on ne sache même plus que ça s'appelle une ville, une rue, des immeubles, des trottoirs …" („der ganze Ort fremd wird, bis man nicht mehr weiß, daß das eine Stadt ist, eine Straße, Wohnhäuser, Bürgersteige heißt …")[27].

Mit gleicher Stoßkraft fordert Paul Virilio in einem Text zum ‚infra-ordinaire', der ebenfalls in der fünften Ausgabe von *Cause commune* erscheint, zur Unterbrechung von Sehgewohnheiten auf. Man solle zur Seite schauen,

23 Marx, Karl/Engels, Friedrich: „Die deutsche Ideologie. Kritik der neuesten deutschen Philosophie in ihren Repräsentanten Feuerbach, B. Bauer und Stirner, und des deutschen Sozialismus in seinen verschiedenen Propheten", in: Institut für Marxismus-Leninismus (Hg.): *MEW*, Bd. 3, Berlin 1969 [1932], 9–533, hier 28.

24 Ebd.

25 Ebd.

26 Stuart Hall diskutiert, dass der Überbau relative Autonomie besitzt und das Wechselverhältnis von Basis und Überbau entsprechend ein komplexes ist. Vgl. Hall, Stuart: „Rethinking the ‚Base and Superstructure' Metaphor", in: Ders.: *Essential Essays*, hg. v. David Morley, Bd. 1, New York 2018 [1977], 143–171.

27 Perec, Georges: *Espèces d'espaces*, Paris 2000 [1974], 105. (Perec, Georges: *Träume von Räumen*, Übers. Eugen Helmlé, Bremen 1990, 68.)

the overlooked visible. The goal is to observe for so long that familiar places can no longer be recognized, until "le lieu tout entier devienne étranger, que l'on ne sache même plus que ça s'appelle une ville, une rue, des immeubles, des trottoirs …" ("the whole place becomes strange, and you no longer even know that this is what is called a town, a street, buildings, pavements …").[27]

With the same urgency, Paul Virilio calls for breaking habits of seeing in a text on the "infra-ordinaire" that was also published in the fifth issue of *Cause commune*. People should look to the side, let the gaze drift, and observe the edges of sidewalks and thresholds of doors.[28] In the words of Michel de Certeau, the "infra-ordinaire" could be called an art of practice.[29] It pursues a tactic of estrangement that undermines the usual ways of dealing with everyday spaces.[30] Perec too understood his "infra-ordinaire" texts in this way, as exercises in observing whose proto-ethnological approach makes the most familiar thing foreign. The topology of the deceptive surface and true underground that still concerned Lefebvre loses its validity. Perec's "infra-ordinaire" texts depend on minute-detailed descriptions of the superficially visible that record the infrastructure of public squares used daily such as the frequency of bus service.

Lieux

In an interview on memory work, Perec explained that the "infra-ordinaire" and the autobiographic essays start out from a need to "faire le tour de quelque chose pour le situer" ("to define something in order to situate it")[31]. Both in the case of the childhood in the past and in the case of everyday life in the present, writing revolves around something that cannot be grasped and located. Whereas Perec's practice in autobiography struggles for the few fragments of memory there are, the "infra-ordinaire" gathers what is ordinarily overlooked as unimportant. This commonality is structured in the two-track structure of in-situ descriptions and memory texts in *Lieux*. Autobiographical and "infra-ordinaire" texts condition or stabilize one another in the process. The writing strategy of opposed poles is ultimately reflected in the narrative

27 Perec, *Espèces d'espaces* (Paris, 2000), 105; Georges Perec, *Species of Spaces* (see note 15), 46–56, esp. 53.

28 See Paul Virilio, "La défaite des faits," in "Le pourissement des sociétés," special issue, *Cause commune*, no. 1 (1975): 257–60, esp. 260.

29 See Michel de Certeau, *L'invention du quotidien*, vol. 1, *Arts de faire*, ed. Luce Giard, 2nd ed. (Paris, 1990); Michel de Certeau, *The Practice of Everyday Life*, trans. Steven F. Rendall (Berkeley, CA, 1984).

30 De Certeau cites Perec early on as a tactical expert on the everyday. See ibid., 226 n. 27.

31 Georges Perec, "Le travail de la mémoire (entretien avec Franck Venaille)" (1979), in *Je suis né*, ed. Maurice Olender (Paris, 1990), 81–93, esp. 84; Georges Perec, "The Work of Memory" (interview with Franck Venaille), in Perec, *Species of Spaces* (see note 15), 123–29, esp. 124.

den Blick abdriften lassen und die Bordsteinkanten und Türschwellen betrachten.[28] Mit Michel de Certeau könnte man das ‚infra-ordinaire' als eine Kunst des Handelns bezeichnen.[29] Es verfolgt eine Verfremdungs-Taktik, die die gewöhnlichen Umgangsformen mit alltäglichen Räumen unterläuft.[30] In diesem Sinn begreift auch Perec seine ‚infra-ordinaire'-Texte als Übungen des Beobachtens, durch deren proto-ethnologische Einstellung das Vertrauteste fremd wird. Die Topologie von trügerischer Oberfläche und wahrem Untergrund, die Lefebvre noch bemüht, verliert dabei ihre Gültigkeit. In diesem Sinn setzen Perecs ‚infra-ordinaire'-Texte auf minutiöse Beschreibungen des oberflächlich Sichtbaren, die die Infrastruktur alltäglich genutzter öffentlicher Plätze aufzeichnen, wie zum Beispiel die Taktung des Busverkehrs.

Lieux

In einem Interview zur Erinnerungsarbeit erklärt Perec, dass die ‚infra-ordinaire'-Texte wie die autobiografischen Versuche von dem Bedürfnis ausgingen, „de faire le tour de quelque chose pour le situer" („etwas einzukreisen, um es einzuordnen")[31]. Das Schreiben umkreise sowohl im Fall der vergangenen Kindheit als auch im Fall des gegenwärtigen Alltags etwas, das sich nicht greifen und verorten lasse. Während Perecs autobiografische Praxis um die wenigen Erinnerungsfragmente ringt, sammelt das ‚infra-ordinaire' ein, was gewöhnlich als Unwichtiges übersehen wird. Diese Gemeinsamkeit ist in der Zweigleisigkeit von Vor-Ort-Beschreibungen und Erinnerungstexten in *Lieux* angelegt. Autobiografische und ‚infra-ordinaire'-Texte bedingen bzw. stabilisieren sich dabei gegenseitig. Die gegenpolige Schreibstrategie schlägt sich schließlich in der Erzählstruktur des Romans *W ou le souvenir d'enfance* nieder, der 1975, also im gleichen Jahr, in dem Perec *Lieux* aufgibt, erscheint. Während sich viele Erinnerungs-Texte aus *Lieux* in *W ou le souvenir d'enfance* wiederfinden, werden die Vor-Ort-Beschreibungen bzw. die ‚infra-ordinaire'-Texte vereinzelt in Zeitschriften veröffentlicht. Trotz aller Auskopplungsversuche bleibt die Praxis des ‚infra-ordinaire' für Perec aber so stark mit dem Autobiografischen verkoppelt, dass er sie nicht, wie von den ArchitektInnen gewünscht, an einem beliebigen Ort ausführen kann, an dem keine Spuren der eigenen Lebensgeschichte zu finden sind.

28 Vgl. Virilio, Paul: „La défaite des faits", *Cause commune*, Bd. 1 (= Le pourissement des sociétés) (1975), 257–260, hier 260.

29 Vgl. de Certeau, Michel: *L'invention du quotidien. 1. Arts de faire*, hg. v. Luce Giard, Paris 1990.

30 De Certeau zitiert Perec sehr früh als einen taktischen Alltagsexperten. Ebd., 332.

31 Perec, Georges: „Le travail de la mémoire (entretien avec Franck Venaille)", in: Ders.: *Je suis né* (Anm. 13), 81–93, 84. *Je suis né*, Paris 1990 [1979], 81–93, hier 84. (Perec, Georges: „Gedächtnisarbeit (Gespräch mit Franck Venaille)", in: *Geboren 1936*, Berlin/Zürich 2015, 67–76, hier 69.)

structure of the novel *W ou le souvenir d'enfance*, which was published in 1975, the same year in which Perec abandoned *Lieux*. Although many of the memory texts from *Lieux* are also found in *W ou le souvenir d'enfance*, the in-situ descriptions or "infra-ordinaire" texts were published individually in newspapers. Despite all his attempts to decouple it, however, the practice of the "infra-ordinaire" was so powerfully coupled with the autobiographical for Perec that he was not able to demonstrate it, as the architects wished, using the example of a random place where clues of his own life story could not be found.

In *Lieux*, Perec also called the in-situ texts "bombes du temps" (time capsules).[32] Time capsules contain objects that people of a given time considered especially meaningful documents of their own era. Anyone who fills and leaves behind such a capsule is anticipating catastrophic destruction and trying to counter being forgotten by leaving behind a safeguarded clue. If Perec understood his texts as such clues for the future, then he was clearly trying to avoid parts of his life disappearing without a trace for a second time. In the *Lieux* letters, accordingly, he thus sealed not only his own texts but also photographs, café receipts, and other documents that were "susceptibles de faire plus tard office de témoignages" ("capable later on of serving as evidence")[33]. At the architecture conference in 1981, Perec declared that he was writing clues about the present for the future. *Lieux* is thus not about documenting three forms of aging, as Perec himself once claimed.[34] In the "infra-ordinaire" texts, rather, a Jewish author was writing against the fear of future catastrophes and the forgetting that goes hand in hand with them.

At the end of the *Lieux* entry from June 28, 1969, Perec reflected on his memory project and asks himself what can emerge from it. He suspected that the descriptions and memories would merely serve as notes for a new text to be written. From the outset, the author viewed the long parcourse of different views of sites as merely a structure that he calls "métatopique" (metatopical).[35] The individual texts thus become a literary infrastructure that is in this case an infrastructure of the autobiographical. The function of spatial experiences turned into language is not reduced to the metaphorical figuration of a textual space. The autobiographical narrative results rather from describing specific places that are thereby transformed into a memory space. They do not initially function as places of memory but only become such through the work on *Lieux*. Perec left behind clues in his descriptions that can be found in the future as the past. The author suggested that himself in the *Lieux* text from July 21, 1970. In it he regretted that there were no places to preserve the clues of his life even

32 Perec, *Lieux* (see note 14), 104; Perec, "The Street" (see note 27), 56. Perec, "À propos de la description" (see note 1), 236.

33 Perec, *Espèces d'espaces* (see note 27), 109; Perec, "The Street" (see note 27), 55.

34 See ibid., 110; (ibid., 56.)

35 Perec, *Lieux* (see note 14), 104.

Die Vor-Ort-Texte weist Perec in *Lieux* auch als „bombes du temps" („Zeitkapseln")[32] aus. Zeitkapseln enthalten Gegenstände, die in der jeweiligen Gegenwart für besonders aussagekräftige Dokumente der eigenen Epoche gehalten werden. Wer eine solche Kapsel bestückt und hinterlegt, antizipiert eine katastrophale Zerstörung und versucht dem Vergessenwerden durch die Erstellung einer gesicherten Spur entgegenzuwirken. Wenn Perec seine Texte als derartige Spuren für die Zukunft begreift, dann möchte er augenscheinlich verhindern, dass Teile seines Lebens ein zweites Mal spurlos verschwinden. In den *Lieux*-Briefen versiegelt er dementsprechend nicht nur seine Texte, sondern auch Fotos, Café-Rechnungen und andere Dokumente, die „susceptibles de faire plus tard office de témoignages" („die später als Zeugnisse dienen konnten")[33] sind. In diesem Sinn erklärt Perec 1981 auf der Architektur-Konferenz, er schreibe Spuren der Gegenwart für die Zukunft. Es geht in *Lieux* also nicht, wie Perec einmal selbst behauptet, um die Dokumentation dreier Alterungsformen.[34] Mit den ‚infra-ordinaire'-Texten schreibt vielmehr ein jüdischer Autor gegen die Angst vor zukünftigen Katastrophen und das mit ihnen einhergehende Vergessen an.

Am Ende des *Lieux*-Eintrags vom 28. Juni 1969 reflektiert Perec sein Erinnerungsprojekt und fragt sich, was daraus entstehen kann. Er vermutet, dass die Beschreibungen und Erinnerungen lediglich als Notizen für einen neu zu schreibenden Text dienen werden. Den weitschweifigen Parcours der verschiedenen Ortsansichten betrachtet der Autor also bereits von Anfang an als eine bloße Struktur, die er als „métatopique" („Metatopik")[35] bezeichnet. Die einzelnen Texte werden damit zu einer literarischen Infrastruktur, d.h. in diesem Fall zu einer Infrastruktur des Autobiografischen. Die Funktion der versprachlichten Raumerfahrungen reduziert sich dabei nicht auf die metaphorische Figuration eines Textraums. Das autobiografische Narrativ entsteht vielmehr aus der Beschreibung bestimmter Orte, die sich dadurch in einen Gedächtnisraum transformieren. Sie funktionieren nicht von vornherein als Erinnerungsorte, sondern werden erst durch die Arbeit an *Lieux* zu solchen. Perec hinterlässt durch seine Beschreibungen Spuren, die zukünftig als Vergangenes wiederzufinden sind. Das legt der Autor selbst in dem *Lieux*-Text vom 21. Juli 1970 nah. Darin bedauert er, dass es keine Orte gebe, die die Spuren seines Lebens bewahrten, obgleich er die Spuren dieser Orte in sich aufhebe.[36]

32 Perec: *Lieux*, (wie Anm. 14), 104; Perec: „À propos de la description", (wie Anm. 1), 236; Perec: *Espèces d'espaces*, (wie Anm. 27), 109.

33 Perec: *Espèces d'espaces*, (wie Anm. 27), 109. (Perec: *Träume von Räumen*, wie Anm. 27, 71.)

34 Vgl. Ebd., 110. (Ebd., 72.)

35 Perec: *Lieux*, (wie Anm. 14), 104.

36 Vgl. ebd., 188.

though he preserved the clues of these places within him.[36]

Both in *Lieux* and in *W ou le souvenir d'enfance*, Perec imagined moments of a childhood that had, unlike his own, left behind rememberable clues. In both cases, the author dispended with imagining idyllic family scenes. Instead, he described spatial structures. The earlier text is found in a poetologically self-reflexive memory from *Lieux* that Perec wrote on July 21, 1970, while staying in the country in the space parental home of friends. He was writing while sitting on a terrace with a lake view and thinking: If he had spent his childhood in such a place, then his memory of childhood would not have been lost. The tiles in the bathroom, "ce carrelage, à lui seul" (this tiling alone),[37] sufficed to lend roots and tradition to an existence. The blue-edged tiles are mirrored in *W ou le souvenir d'enfance* by a blue-checked tablecloth. A scene is sketched in which the child is helping his mother in the kitchen and then sits down at the kitchen table and does his homework:

> Moi, j'aurais aimé aider ma mère à débarrasser la table de la cuisine après le dîner. Sur la table, il y aurait eu une toile cirée à petits carreaux bleus; au-dessus de la table, il y aurait eu une suspension avec un abat-jour presque en forme d'assiette, en porcelaine blanche ou en tôle émaillée, et un système de poulies avec un contrepoids en forme de poire. Puis je serais allé chercher mon cartable, j'aurais sorti mon livre, mes cahiers et mon plumier de bois, je les aurais posés sur la table et j'aurais fait mes devoirs.
>
> ("I would have liked to help my mother clear the dinner from the kitchen table. There would have been a blue, small-checked oilcloth on the table, and above it, a counterpoise lamp with a shade shaped almost like a plate, made of white porcelain or enamelled tin, and a pulley system with pear-shaped weights. Then I'd have fetched my satchel, got out my book and my writing pad and my wooden pencil-box. I'd have put them on the table and done my homework.")[38]

The entire section from which this is quoted is written in the *conditionnel passé*. That tense is used to express a wish. It seems above all to be the clear spatial structure that the author would not only like to remember but that he also understands as a topic that ensures a memory or as the infrastructure for autobiographic writing. Not coincidentally, the supports of this structure are such ordinary objects as bathroom tiles or a tablecloth. They form the back- and underground of an everyday life that can be remembered.

The image of the child doing his homework at the kitchen table with a checked tablecloth also figures in the scene of writing of *Lieux*. The checked structure

36 See ibid., 188.

37 Ibid., 187.

38 Perec, *W* (see note 4), 99; Perec, *W* (see note 4), 70.

Sowohl in *Lieux* als auch in *W ou le souvenir d'enfance* imaginiert Perec Momente einer Kindheit, die im Gegensatz zu der seinigen erinnerbare Spuren hinterlassen hätte. In beiden Fällen verzichtet der Autor auf der Vorstellung idyllischer Familienszenen. Stattdessen beschreibt er räumliche Strukturen. Der frühere Text findet sich in einer poetologisch selbstreflexiven Erinnerung aus *Lieux*, die Perec am 21. Juli 1970 während eines Land-Aufenthalts in dem großzügigen Elternhaus von Freunden schreibt. Er sitzt beim Schreiben auf einer Terrasse mit Seeblick und denkt: Hätte er seine Kindheit an einem solchen Ort verbracht, dann wären ihm seine Kindheitserinnerung nicht abhandengekommen. Allein die Fliesen im Bad, „ce carrelage, à lui seul",[37] reichten aus, um einer Existenz Wurzeln und Tradition zu schenken. Die blau geränderten Kacheln reflektieren sich in *W ou le souvenir d'enfance* in einer blau karierten Tischdecke. Es wird eine Szenerie entworfen, in der das Kind seiner Mutter in der Küche hilft und danach am Küchentisch seine Hausaufgaben macht:

> Moi, j'aurais aimé aider ma mère à débarrasser la table de la cuisine après le dîner. Sur la table, il y aurait eu une toile cirée à petits carreaux bleus; au-dessus de la table, il y aurait eu une suspension avec un abat-jour presque en forme d'assiette, en porcelaine blanche ou en tôle émaillée, et un système de poulies avec un contrepoids en forme de poire. Puis je serais allé chercher mon cartable, j'aurais sorti mon livre, mes cahiers et mon plumier de bois, je les aurais posés sur la table et j'aurais fait mes devoirs.
>
> (Ich hätte meiner Mutter gern geholfen, nach dem Abendessen den Küchentisch abzuräumen. Auf dem Tisch hätte es ein Wachstuch gegeben mit kleinen blauen Karos; über dem Tisch hätte es eine Hängelampe gegeben mit einem Lampenschirm aus weißem Porzellan oder aus emailliertem Blech fast in Form eines Tellers und ein System von Rollen mit einem birnenförmigen Gewicht. Dann wäre ich meinen Ranzen holen gegangen, ich hätte mein Buch herausgenommen, meine Hefte und meinen Federkasten aus Holz, ich hätte sie auf den Tisch gelegt und ich hätte meine Aufgaben gemacht.)[38]

Der gesamte Abschnitt, dem das Zitierte entstammt, ist im Conditionnel Passé geschrieben. Das Tempus markiert, dass es sich um eine Wunschvorstellung handelt. Es scheint vor allem die klare räumliche Struktur zu sein, an die der Autor sich nicht nur gern erinnern würde, sondern die er als eine Erinnerung garantierende Topik bzw. als eine Infrastruktur für autobiografisches Schreiben begreift. Träger dieser Struktur sind nicht zufällig derartig gewöhnliche Gegenstände wie Badfliesen oder eine Tischdecke. Sie bilden den Hinter- und Untergrund eines Alltags, der erinnerbar ist.

37 Ebd., 187.
38 Perec: *W ou le souvenir d'enfance*, (wie Anm. 4), 99. (Perec: *W oder die Kindheitserinnerung*, wie Anm. 4, 77f.)

returns in form of the graph pad on which Perec draws his table of the timetable for *Lieux*. The structure of the writing paper serves as the infrastructure for future remembering (fig. 1).

Yet the dividing of the white page into squares should not be misunderstood as a poetological motif or a metaphorical poetry. The structured writing pad is a form of prestructuring related to the Oulipian *contrainte* and provides orientation when writing.[39] If the conversation between Perec and the architects on the representation of space had been more productive, this project sketch could have been discussed as the sketch of a textual building. Unfortunately, that did not happen. Nevertheless, Perec repeatedly sought to engage in conversation with sociologists and placed the "infra-ordinaire" in nonliterary contexts. Even if the depiction of the infrastructure of public space was from Perec's perspective related above all to the lack of memories, this deficit is manifested in an observer's position that is unusual not only from the perspective of architects and brings with it special attention to that which is ordinarily overlooked: the "infra-ordinaire."[40]

Translation: Steven Lindberg

39 Perec used such prestructuring again and again, for example, for the novel *La vie mode d'emploi* (*Life, A User's Manual*). The novel tells the individual life stories of the residents of a building. Among other things, Perec established the sequence of the narrative in advance in a table that looks very similar to the plan for *Lieux*.
40 On questions of the sociological or sociocritical dimension of Perec's writings, see Johanna-Charlotte Horst, *Schreibformen: Georges Perecs literarischer Materialismus* (Paderborn, 2023), 11–116.

Das Bild des Kindes, das seine Hausaufgaben am Küchentisch mit der karierten Decke macht, figuriert auch die Schreibszene von *Lieux*. Die Karo-Struktur findet sich in dem karierten Papier wieder, auf das Perec den tabellarischen Zeitplan für *Lieux* zeichnet. Hier dient die Strukturierung der Schreibunterlage als Infrastruktur für zukünftiges Erinnern.

Dabei darf die Aufteilung des weißen Blattes in Quadrate nicht als poetologische Motivik oder metaphorische Poetik missverstanden werden. Die strukturierte Schreibunterlage ist eine dem oulipotischen ‚contrainte' verwandte Form der Vorstrukturierung und dient der Orientierung im Schreiben.[39] Wäre das Gespräch zwischen Perec und den ArchitektInnen zur Repräsentation des Raumes produktiver verlaufen, hätte man diese Projektskizze als Aufriss eines Textgebäuden diskutieren können. Dazu ist es leider nicht gekommen. Perec hat dennoch immer wieder das Gespräch mit SoziologInnen gesucht und das ‚infra-ordinaire' in nicht-literarische Kontexte gestellt. Auch wenn die Darstellung der Infrastruktur öffentlicher Plätze aus Perecs Perspektive vor allem mit dem Mangel an Erinnerungen zu tun hat, schlägt sich dieses Defizit nicht nur aus der Perspektive von ArchitektInnen als eine ungewöhnliche Beobachterposition nieder, die besondere Aufmerksamkeit für das gewohntermaßen Übersehene, das ‚infra-ordinaire', mit sich bringt.[40]

39 Perec verwendet eine solche Vorstrukturierung immer wieder, zum Beispiel für den Roman *La vie mode d'emploi*. In diesem Roman wird erzählt, was sich in den einzelnen Lebensgeschichten der Bewohner eines Hauses ereignet. Unter anderem die Reihenfolge des Erzählten legt Perec vorab in einer Tabelle fest, die dem Plan für *Lieux* sehr ähnlich sieht.

40 Vgl. zu der Frage nach der soziologischen bzw. gesellschaftskritischen Dimension von Perecs Schreiben Horst, Johanna-Charlotte: *Schreibformen. Georges Perecs literarischer Materialismus*, Paderborn 2023, 11–116.

1 Remittance houses, Kozarac, 2020

Erneuter Hausbesuch zu Hause
Revisiting Houses at Home

Ajna Babahmetović

An einem warmen Augustabend des Jahres 2023 sitzen drei Frauen um einen Tisch im Garten eines geräumigen Hauses in Kozarac, einer Kleinstadt in Bosnien-Herzegowina. Sie nippen an bosnischem Kaffee, essen selbstgebackene *Lokums*[1] und trinken rosmarinparfümiertes Wasser. Der Hund läuft im Garten umher, eine Plastikflasche im Maul. Er ist auf der Suche nach einer Stelle, an der er sie öffnen kann, wie sich später herausstellt.

Es war ein ungewöhnlicher Anblick in Kozarac, wo die meisten Häuser verlassen dastehen, die Rollläden geschlossen, die Gärten menschenleer, die Zauntore versperrt, die Fassaden makellos (Abb. 1). Ich war eine der wenigen Personen auf der Straße, noch dazu eine, die fotografierte. Damit erregte ich das Interesse der Frauen. Ich erklärte, ich sei Architektin und interessierte mich für Diaspora-Architektur, worauf eine von ihnen – N., die Besitzerin des Hauses – ausrief: „Nismo mi dijaspora!" (Wir sind keine Diaspora!). Ich versicherte ihr, dass ich den Begriff nicht herabwürdigend meinte, worauf N. erklärte, dass sie tatsächlich im Ausland lebe – also Teil der bosnischen Diaspora sei –, und mich auf eine Tasse Kaffee und ein *Lokum* einlud.[2]

Kozarac hat eine der größten Diaspora-Communities in Bosnien und Herzegowina und ist ein Extrembeispiel für seine „Remittance Landscapes",[3] Siedlungen mit Einfamilienhäusern, die im Ausland lebende und arbeitende Landsleute in der ehemaligen Heimat gebaut haben. Die Besuche ihrer diasporischen BesitzerInnen

1 Bosnisches Teegebäck, nicht zu verwechseln mit der gleichnamigen türkischen Süßigkeit.
2 Feldforschungsnotizen, August 2023, Kozarac.
3 In ihrem 2015 erschienen Buch *The Remittance Landscape: Spaces of Migration in Rural Mexico and Urban USA* analysiert Sarah Lynn Lopez die Transformation ländlicher Gebiete in Mexiko durch die Investitionen ihrer in den USA lebenden Diaspora-Communities. Die als „Remittance Landscapes" bezeichneten Landschaften bilden sich um die von MigrantInnen in ihrer Heimat erbauten Häuser, die dann öffentliche Gebäude und andere Infrastrukturprojekte nach sich ziehen. Es sind Gegenden, die durch Rücküberweisungen (*Remittances*) am Leben erhalten werden und stark davon abhängig bleiben.

On a warm late August eve in 2023, three women gathered around the table in the yard of a spacious yellow house in Kozarac, a small city in Bosnia and Herzegovina. They were sipping on Bosnian coffee, eating homemade *lokums*,[1] and drinking rosemary-infused water. The dog was running around the yard, carrying a plastic bottle in his muzzle. His goal was to find a spot for successfully uncapping the bottle, as I would find out later.

This was an unusual sight in Kozarac, where most of the houses stand quiet with shutters closed, yards empty, fences sealed, and facades intact (fig. 1). I was one of the few people on the street, and what is more, I was photographing, which sparked the women's interest. I explained that I am an architect, interested in diaspora architecture, to which one of them—N., the owner of the house—said loudly, "Nismo mi dijaspora!" (We are not diaspora!). I assured her that my usage of the word was in no way derogatory, after which N. declared that she did indeed usually live abroad—being, therefore, a member of the Bosnian diaspora—and invited me for a cup of coffee and a *lokum*.[2]

Kozarac has one of the largest diaspora communities in Bosnia and Herzegovina and is one of the extreme examples of its remittance landscapes,[3] settlements of single-family houses built in one's native country by people now living and working abroad. The visits by their diasporic owners are reserved for the holidays, summer vacations, weddings, funerals, and commemorations.

1 Type of Bosnian tea biscuits, not to be confused with Turkish Delight.
2 Fieldwork notes, August 2023, Kozarac.
3 In her 2015 book *The Remittance Landscape: Spaces of Migration in Rural Mexico and Urban USA*, Sarah Lynn Lopez analyzed the transformation of the rural areas of Mexico brought about by the investments from its diaspora community living in the United States, which she referred to as the "remittance landscape." These landscapes are formed around houses built by migrants in their home countries, which are then followed by public buildings and other forms of infrastructure projects. These areas, kept alive thanks to remittance payments, remain heavily dependent on them.

beschränken sich auf die Ferienzeiten, den Sommerurlaub, Hochzeiten, Begräbnisse und Gedenkfeiern. Das urbane und soziale Gefüge der Stadt passt sich diesem saisonalen Leben an. Das restliche Jahr über werden die Häuser von vor Ort lebenden BewohnerInnen oder eigens dafür geschaffenen Betrieben erhalten.[4]

N.s Bemerkung „Wir sind keine Diaspora!" macht deutlich, dass die bosnische Diaspora ein kompliziertes und vielschichtiges Phänomen ist. In Jugoslawien begann die Diaspora-Bildung in den 1960er- und 1970er-Jahren mit der Rekrutierung von GastarbeiterInnen durch die westlichen Demokratien und dem Export einheimischer Arbeitskräfte in die blockfreien Bruderstaaten in Afrika und im Nahen Osten.[5] Nach der Eingliederung Kozaracs in die benachbarte Großgemeinde Prijedor und dem sprunghaften Anstieg der Arbeitslosigkeit in Jugoslawien in den 1960er-Jahren gab es in Kozarac fast in jeder Familie jemanden, der im Ausland arbeitete. Die *Gastarbajteri*, wie die ArbeitsmigrantInnen auch in Jugoslawien hießen, wurden nicht in ihre Gastländer integriert und hatten auch in Jugoslawien keine Sicherheiten, galt doch das Recht auf Wohnen dort nur für Mitglieder der Arbeitskollektive.[6] Die ersten „Rücktransfer-Häuser" in Bosnien – und speziell auch in Kozarac – wurden in den 1960er-Jahren von *Gastarbajteri*[7] erbaut.

1992 bis 1995, während des Bosnienkriegs, eskalierte die Diaspora-Bildung. Nach Auflösung der Sozialistischen Föderativen Republik Jugoslawien und der Abhaltung des bosnischen Unabhängigkeitsreferendums 1992 mobilisierten die bosnischen Serben – unterstützt durch die jugoslawische Volksarmee (JNA) und die serbische Regierung – ihre Streitkräfte zum Schutz des serbischen Territoriums. Dies geschah durch verschiedene Formen ethnischer Säuberung. Die vorwiegend muslimische Bevölkerung von Kozarac wurde vertrieben oder getötet – fast alle BewohnerInnen durchliefen das System der Konzentrationslager – und ihre Häuser wurden komplett zerstört. Nach dem 1995

4 Security-Firmen, die Überwachungskameras mit 24-Stunden-Service anbieten, sind zum Beispiel ein äußerst einträgliches Geschäft.

5 Vgl. Dolečki, Jana: „‚Heimat fremde Heimat'. Das Anwerbeabkommen zwischen Österreich und Jugoslawien wurde fünfzig Jahre alt", Übers. Mascha Dabić, in: Buden, Boris/Dokuzović, Lina (Hg.): *They'll Never Walk Alone. The Life and Afterlife of Gastarbeiters*, Wien 2018, 89–101 (dt. Fassung online unter: https://transversal.at/transversal/1017/dolecki/de).

6 Vgl. Sekulić, Dubravka: *Glotzt Nicht so Romantisch! On Extralegal Space in Belgrade*, Maastricht 2011, 36.

7 Aufgrund der Unzulänglichkeiten sowohl der Gastländer als auch Jugoslawiens sind die Rolle des Gastarbeiters wie auch der Begriff selbst heute zu einem tragischen Symbol geworden und haben einen negativen Beigeschmack. Die durch Rücküberweisungen entstandenen Häuser in Bosnien und Herzegowina werden oft immer noch als *gastarbajterske* beschrieben, unabhängig davon, wann und warum ihre BesitzerInnen ins Ausland zogen.

2 Kozarac, 2020

The urban and social fabric of the city adapts to this seasonal living. For the rest of the year, the houses are maintained by the remaining residents or by services created specifically for that purpose.[4]

Indeed, N.'s remark "We are not diaspora!" reveals that the concept of Bosnian diaspora is a complicated and multilayered one. The diaspora formation began in the 1960s and 1970s in Yugoslavia with a program designed to recruit guest workers for Western democracies while exporting the local workforce to Yugoslav nonaligned allies in Africa and the Middle East.[5] After Kozarac lost its municipality status to the neighboring bigger city of Prijedor in the 1960s, and Yugoslav unemployment issues skyrocketed, almost everyone from Kozarac had a family member working abroad. The *gastarbajteri* (guest workers), a term derived from the German *Gastarbeiter*, were not being integrated into the guest countries, nor did they have any security in Yugoslavia, where, for example, the right to housing was reserved for members of working collectives.[6] The first remittance houses in Bosnia, and Kozarac specifically, were built by *gastarbajteri*[7] in the 1960s.

The diaspora formation escalated during the Bosnian War from 1992 to 1995. After the dissolution of the Socialist Federal Republic of Yugoslavia and the Bosnian independence referendum in 1992, Bosnian Serbs, supported

4 For example, security companies, providing surveillance cameras and twenty-four-hour service, are highly profitable businesses.

5 See Jana Dolečki, "'Home, Foreign Home': Commemorating the 50-Year Anniversary of the Signing of the Agreement on Labor Migration between Austria and Yugoslavia,"trans. Tijana Gojić Topolnik, in *They'll Never Walk Alone: The Life and Afterlife of Gastarbeiters*, ed. Boris Buden and Lina Dokuzović (Vienna, 2018), 89–101.

6 See Dubravka Sekulić, *Glotzt Nicht so Romantisch! On Extralegal Space in Belgrade* (Maastricht, 2011), 36.

7 As a symbol of shortcomings from both the guest countries and Yugoslavia, the *gastarbajter* and the word itself have taken on a tragic symbolism and a derogatory meaning. Today the remittance houses in Bosnia and Herzegovina are still often described as *gastarbajterske*, no matter when and why their owners moved abroad.

3 Kozarac, 2020

geschlossenen Friedensabkommens von Dayton begannen die KozaračerInnen ihre Häuser wiederaufzubauen. Heute ist es die Stadt mit den meisten RückkehrerInnen in der Republika Srbska.[8] Mit ihren 8.000 EinwohnerInnen ist sie dennoch weit entfernt von ihrer Vorkriegspopulation von 25.000. Die revisionistische Politik der Republika Srbska, die die ethnischen Säuberungen, die der Staatsgründung vorausgingen, nicht anerkennt, und die insgesamt instabile politische Situation in Bosnien und Herzegowina fördern weiterhin den *Braindrain*.[9]

Meinen ersten Besuch stattete ich Kozarac im Oktober 2016 im Rahmen eines Master Design Studios über die urbane Nachkriegslandschaft in Bosnien und Herzegowina ab. Unter der Leitung der Künstlerin Milica Tomić untersuchte unsere Gruppe den in der Nachbarschaft liegenden Bergbaubetrieb Omarska, der während des Krieges 1992 als Konzentrationslager gedient hatte, und später ohne jedweden Hinweis darauf wieder für den Bergbau reaktiviert wurde. Einige Jahre später, 2019, wählte ich Kozarac als Fallstudie für meine Architektur-Masterarbeit mit dem Titel „Houses at Home: Architecture of Displacement“ und führte dort meine ersten Feldstudien durch. Mein Hauptinteresse galt der Frage, wie sich die

8 Das Recht auf Rückkehr war zwar ein Teil des Daytoner Friedensabkommens, aber die politische Führung von Prijedor führte zunächst die Kriegspolitik fort, versuchte, den Vertriebenen die Rückkehr zu verweigern und die Gegend ethnisch rein zu halten. Das Jahr 1998 wurde von den internationalen Organisationen zum „Jahr der Rückkehr“ erklärt, und es wurden große Summen für die Wiederaufbau der Infrastruktur und für die Unterstützung des ganzen Prozesses durch die lokalen Behörden bereitgestellt. So kamen die KozaračerInnen langsam zurück und fingen an, den Schutt ihrer zerstörten Häuser wegzuräumen. Lokale Internet-Blogs und -Foren förderten zu Beginn des 21. Jahrhunderts weiter den Wiederaufbau der Gemeinschaft und der Gemeinde, doch die Nachwehen des Krieges und die revisionistische Politik der Republika Srbska erschwerten eine permanente Rückkehr.

9 Vgl. Sivac-Bryant, Sebina: *Re-Making Kozarac: Agency, Reconciliation and Contested Return in Post-War Bosnia*, London 2016, 1–21.

by the Yugoslav People's Army (JNA) and the Serbian government, mobilized their forces in order to secure the Serb territory. This was to be achieved through different forms of ethnic cleansing. The mostly Muslim population of Kozarac was either displaced or killed, almost everyone went through the concentration camp system, and their houses were completely destroyed. Following the Dayton Accords, a peace agreement reached in 1995, Kozarčans started rebuilding their houses, and today it is the city with the most returnees in the political entity of Republika Srpska.[8] Still, with its 8,000 inhabitants, the population is a far cry from the over 25,000 residents before the war. The revisionist politics of Republika Srpska, which does not acknowledge the ethnic cleansing that preceded its creation, and the unstable political situation in the whole of Bosnia and Herzegovina fuel the ongoing brain drain.[9]

My first visit to Kozarac was in October of 2016 as part of a master design studio on the postwar urban landscape of Bosnia and Herzegovina. Led by the artist Milica Tomić, our group examined the neighboring Omarska mining complex, once a concentration camp during the 1992 war and later revived for mining without any memorialization efforts. A couple of years later, in 2019, I chose Kozarac as a case study for my master's thesis in architecture, which would be titled "Houses at Home: Architecture of Displacement," and did my first fieldwork. My main interest was how migrants' narratives have manifested through architecture, and the remittance house seemed like a perfect tool.

During the initial fieldwork I conducted, locals told me that they could decipher where the owners of the houses lived abroad, based on the architectural elements of their homes in Bosnia; for example, pseudo chalet style homes were "Swiss" (fig. 2), they told me, while ground-floor houses were owned by "Norwegians" (fig. 3). An intuitive response would be to see this as a defining characteristic of the remittance house—copying and importing different architectural styles. While this may have been of relevance in the past, when the first *gastarbajteri* started building houses in the 1960s and accelerated the introduction of the new modern house as opposed to a traditional

8 The right to return was a part of the Dayton Peace Agreement, yet the official political leadership of Prijedor was continuing with war politics, trying to deny return to the displaced, and trying to keep the area ethnically clean. The year 1998 was declared the "year of the minority returns" by international agencies, and large sums of money were offered for the rebuilding of infrastructure, and as an incentive for local authorities to support the process. Kozaračans started coming back and cleaning up the rubble of their destroyed homes. Local Internet blogs and forums further accelerated the rebuilding of the community and the city in the early years of the twenty-first century, but the aftermath of the war and the revisionist politics of Republika Srpska made a permanent return very difficult.

9 See Sebina Sivac-Bryant, *Re-Making Kozarac: Agency, Reconciliation and Contested Return in Post-War Bosnia* (London, 2016), 1–21.

Geschichte von MigrantInnen in der Architektur manifestiert, und die Rücktransfer-Häuser schienen ein perfektes Beispiel dafür zu sein.

Während der ursprünglichen Feldforschung erzählten mir die Einheimischen, sie könnten aufgrund der Architekturelemente der in Bosnien gebauten Häuser sagen, wo im Ausland deren BesitzerInnen lebten; Häuser im Pseudo-Chalet-Stil gehörten zum Beispiel „Schweizern" (Abb. 2), wogegen einstöckige Häuser „norwegische" Besitzer hatten (Abb. 3). Intuitiv könnte man darin geradezu ein Definitionsmerkmal des Rücktransfer-Hauses sehen: das Kopieren und Importieren verschiedener Architekturstile. Wiewohl das früher von Bedeutung war, als die ersten *Gastarbajteri* in den 1960er-Jahren anfingen, Häuser zu bauen, und damit im ländlichen Raum die Einführung moderner Haustypen anstelle der traditionellen bosnisch-ottomanischen beschleunigten,[10] so ist heute, in Zeiten des Informationsüberflusses, der Import „fremder"[11] Stile keine rein migrantenspezifische Taktik mehr und erst recht keine Novität. Vielmehr sind es der Lebensstil und die Aspirationen seiner BesitzerInnen, von denen das Haus erzählt. Wie Paolo Boccagni und Marta Bivand Erdal zeigen, zeugen die Häuser eigentlich von der selektiven Akkulturation der MigrantInnen an bestimmte Aspekte der in ihrem Gastland herrschenden Mainstream-Architektur, „eher der stückweisen Aneignung bestimmter kultureller Muster denn deren abstrakter Zirkulation."[12]

Später dann fand ich heraus, dass viele vor Ort lebende KozaracerInnen auf die eine oder andere Weise in den Bau und die Erhaltung der Diaspora-Häuser involviert waren. Dazu kommt, dass in einer Kleinstadt jeder jeden kennt. Srdjan Jovanović Weiss fragte sich in Bezug auf die Rücktransfer-Architektur in Kozarac einmal, ob es sich dabei um eine Rückassimilation oder eine Rückkonstruktion – oder beides auf einmal – handelt.[13] Auf jeden Fall war sie nie etwas Passives. Insofern war die „Entschlüsselung" der Herkunft ihrer architektonischen Elemente eine nachträglich erworbene Fähigkeit und keine inhärente.

D. und S. lebten nach dem Krieg viele Jahre lang in Italien. Während sie dort arbeiteten, begannen sie ihr zerstörtes Haus wiederaufzubauen und legten jeden Monat

10 Vgl. Babahmetović, Ajna: „Houses at Home: Architecture of Displacement" (Masterarbeit, Technische Universität Graz 2020), 36.

11 Das Wort „fremd" spiegelt hier ein verbreitetes Sentiment gegenüber rücktransferierten Häusern; sie werden als andersartig, unauthentisch betrachtet und ignoriert (vgl. Anm. 16).

12 Boccagni, Paolo/Erdal, Marta Bivand: „On the Theoretical Potential of ‚Remittance Houses': Toward a Research Agenda across Emigration Contexts", *Journal of Ethnic and Migration Studies* 47, 5 (2021), 12.

13 Srdjan Jovanović Weiss in einem Kommentar zu Ajna Babahmetovićs Online-Lecture „Living Borders", International Architecture Month 2021, online unter: www.youtube.com/watch?v=RRwjtNUURhs (Stand: 30. Jänner 2024).

4 Kozarac, 2023

Bosnian-Ottoman one in rural areas,[10] today, in times of abundant information influx, importing "alien"[11] styles is not a migrant-exclusive tactic, let alone a novelty. Much more than that, it is about the way of living and the aspiration that the house reveals. As Paolo Boccagni and Marta Bivand Erdal point out, the houses actually reveal the migrants' own selective acculturation into particular aspects of the mainstream architecture abroad, "the piecemeal appropriation of specific cultural patterns, more than their abstract circulation."[12]

Later, I would find out that many local Kozarčans were included in various ways in the process of building or maintaining the diaspora houses. Furthermore, in a small city, everybody knows each other. Srdjan Jovanović Weiss once ruminated on the nature of the remittance architecture of Kozarac, questioning if it was retroactive assimilation or retroactive engineering—or most likely both.[13] In any case, it was never a passive affair. Hence, this "deciphering" of the origin of architectural elements was a retroactively acquired skill, rather than an inherent one.

D. and S. lived in Italy for many years after the war. While working there, they started rebuilding their destroyed house, using parts of their Italian paychecks every month. Construction was led by a cousin who lived in Kozarac, with many photos and videos exchanged. It lasted for many years, being built in bits and pieces, depending on the amount of money available at the moment and their current needs. Extralegal ways of

10 See Ajna Babahmetović, "Houses at Home: Architecture of Displacement" (master's thesis, Graz University of Technology, 2020), 36.

11 The word *alien* here echoes a common sentiment toward remittance houses—being othered, ignored, not seen as authentic (see note 16).

12 Paolo Boccagni and Marta Bivand Erdal, "On the Theoretical Potential of 'Remittance Houses': Toward a Research Agenda across Emigration Contexts," *Journal of Ethnic and Migration Studies* 47, no. 5 (2021): 12.

13 Srdjan Jovanović Weiss in a comment on Ajna Babahmetović's online lecture "Living Borders," International Architecture Month 2021, www.youtube.com/watch?v=RRwjtNUURhs (accessed January 30, 2024).

einen Teil ihres Lohns dafür beiseite. Die Bauarbeiten wurden von einem in Kozarac lebenden Cousin beaufsichtigt und zahlreiche Fotos und Videos dafür hin- und hergeschickt. Es dauerte viele Jahre, ging Schritt für Schritt vonstatten, je nach dem Geld, das sie zur Verfügung hatten, und ihren jeweiligen Bedürfnissen. Illegale Baumethoden, die Distanz zwischen Bauenden und Gebautem sowie die Lebensumstände der MigrantInnen – das alles wird in der architektonischen Formsprache dieses Hauses sichtbar (Abb. 4). „Was als informelle gebaute Umwelt betrachtet wird", schreibt die Architektin und Theoretikerin Dubravka Sekulić, „dient als optisches Hilfsmittel zur Sichtbarmachung des Unsichtbaren."[14]

S. und F. lebten bereits seit den späten 1970er-Jahren in Deutschland. Ihr Haus in Kozarac war das Werk eines Architekten, und nach seiner Zerstörung bauten sie es wieder auf – so wie es vorher war, die von einem Profi geplanten Volumen und Elemente respektierend (Abb. 5). Sie fügten lediglich ein zusätzliches Stockwerk für einen weiteren Sohn hinzu, da das erste bereits für den älteren Bruder reserviert war. Beide Söhne lebten in Deutschland. Außerdem nahmen sie einige funktionale Verbesserungen vor, fügten weitere Eingänge, Küchen und Toiletten hinzu, um das Haus möglichst flexibel zu halten. Es sollte in Zukunft nicht nur ihre Söhne beherbergen, sondern auch für alle Unwägbarkeiten eines unsteten Lebens gerüstet sein.

5 Kozarac, 2020

Ich versuchte, die funktionalen Merkmale des „Diaspora-Hauses" zu bestimmen: geräumig und generationenübergreifend, performativ, flexibel, adaptierbar und zukunftsorientiert. Geräumig, weil es imstande sein muss, mehrere Generationen einer Familie aufzunehmen;

14 Sekulić, Dubravka: „Ambiguities of Informality", *dérive* 71 (2022), 37–42, online unter: https://monoskop.org/images/2/2e/Sekulic_Dubravka_2018_The_Ambiguities_of_Informality.pdf (Stand: 30. Jänner 2024).

building, distance between the builders and the built, and the intermittent migrants' way of life are all visible in the formal architectural language of this particular house (fig. 4). As the architect and theorist Dubravka Sekulić writes: "What is considered to be the informal built environment serves as an optical device for seeing the invisible."[14]

S. and F. had been living in Germany since the late 1970s. Before the war, their house in Kozarac had originally been the work of an architect, and even after its destruction, they rebuilt it as it was, respecting the basic volumes and elements designed by a professional (fig. 5). They only added an extra floor for another son, the first floor being reserved for their older son. Both sons lived in Germany. Additionally, they made many functional tweaks to the house, like adding multiple entrances, kitchens, and toilets, making the house as flexible as possible. It was intended not only to house their sons in the future, but also to anticipate all the indubitable uncertainties of an unsettled life.

I tried to define functional characteristics of the "diaspora houses": spacious and intergenerational, performative, flexible, adaptable, and future-oriented. They were spacious because they had to be able to house more generations of the family; performative because they were tools for first-generation migrants to keep their children attached to their roots; flexible and adaptable because they had to be able to quickly accommodate migrants' ever-changing needs; and, finally, future-oriented because of all of the above.[15] Still, in their incredible versatility (figs. 6, 7), the most prominent feature consistently lay in the absence of its owners and in its exclusion from architectural discourse or narratives, simplifying it as a mere nouveau riche, kitschy aesthetic display. In this sense, the house itself was being treated as its migrant owner—othered, excluded, exotified.[16] I choose to read the house as a form of therapy. The void created by displacement, and by the loss of a displaced, caused phantom pain and the house was the cure, an extension of the body. Yet, in my faulty conceptualization, the house jumped between

14 Dubravka Sekulić, "Ambiguities of Informality," *dérive* 71 (2022), 37–42, online at: https://monoskop.org/images/2/2e/Sekulic_Dubravka_2018_The_Ambiguities_of_Informality.pdf (accessed January 30, 2024).

15 See Babahmetović, "Houses at Home" (see note 10), 75.

16 For example, one of the rare mentions in architectural discourse: "Other negative impact[s] are emigrants—gastarbeiter. ... migrants brought new types of construction, characteristic for the landscape in which they lived, the so-called 'gastarbeiter' architecture. There are examples ... built and decorated under the influence of alpine types of objects, which have nothing to do with the landscapes and architectural heritage of the municipality." Marija Maksin-Mičić, "An Approach to Municipality Plan's Development of Regulation in Territorial Arrangement and Construction: A Case Study of Valjevo," *Arhitektura i Urbanizam* 16–17 (2005), 59–61.

6 Kozarac, 2020

performativ, weil es für MigrantInnen der ersten Generation ein Mittel ist, ihre Kinder an die Heimat zu binden; flexibel und adaptierbar, weil es in der Lage sein muss, sich rasch an die ständig wechselnden Bedürfnisse von MigrantInnen anzupassen; und zukunftsorientiert aus allen der oben genannten Gründe.[15] Doch bei all seiner Versatilität (Abb. 6, 7) blieb doch das hervorstechendste Merkmal die Abwesenheit seiner BesitzerInnen und seine Exklusion aus dem architektonischen Diskurs oder Narrativ, die es zu einer bloß neureichen, kitschigen Prahlgeste reduziert. So gesehen wird das Haus wie sein migrantischer Besitzer oder seine Besitzerin behandelt – für fremd erklärt, ausgegrenzt, exotisiert.[16] Ich beschloss, das Haus als eine Art Therapie zu betrachten. Die Leere, die die Entwurzelung und der erlittene Verlust hinterlässt, verursacht

15 Vgl. Babahmetović: „Houses at Home“ (wie Anm. 10), 75.

16 Eine der seltenen Erwähnungen im Architekturdiskurs lautet zum Beispiel so: „Andere negative Einflüsse kommen von Emigranten – Gastarbeitern. [...] Migranten führten neue aus der Gegend, in der sie lebten, stammende Bautypen ein, die sogenannte „Gastarbeiter“-Architektur. Es gibt Beispiele [...] die bis zum Zierrat unter dem Einfluss alpiner Haustypen gebaut wurden, Haustypen, die nichts mit der Landschaft und dem architektonischen Erbe der Stadt zu tun haben.“ Maksin-Mičić, Marija: „An Approach to Municipality Plan's Development of Regulation in Territorial Arrangement and Construction: A Case Study of Valjevo“, *Arhitektura i Urbanizam* 16–17 (2005), 59–61 (Übers. W. P.).

the roles of the lost limb, the prosthetic one, and a reflection in the mirror.[17] It did, however, in every role, render the body whole.

My third fieldwork visit to Kozarac was planned for the summer of 2020 but did not happen because of the coronavirus pandemic. I wanted to experience the mythical summer where the city comes to life and all of the houses are being lived in. The pinnacle of summer in Kozarac is late July, when various manifestations are seen—from commemorations and burial ceremonies for victims of war (whose bones are still being excavated and identified to this day) to weddings.

As Boccagni and Erdal wrote, a methodologically "good enough" study of remittance houses should link people's accounts with the everyday social practices that take place in these spaces. Furthermore, researchers need to take into account the significance of temporality and be motivated and able to return to the exact same dwelling places over time.[18] For this article, I wanted to revisit the houses I had analyzed three years ago, as one of the questions lingered: What is the future—and the present—of Kozarac, its remittance houses, and their owners?

17 The missing limb causes phantom pain—the invisible limb hurts. One therapy for this is to move the remaining limb in front of the mirror, thus creating the illusion that the lost limb is moving.

18 See Boccagni and Erdal, "On the Theoretical Potential of 'Remittance Houses'" (see note 12), 14.

Phantomschmerzen, und das Haus ist das Heilmittel dafür, eine Erweiterung des Körpers. So schwankten die Rollen des Hauses in meiner unvollkommenen Vorstellung zwischen den verlorenen Gliedmaßen, einer Prothese, und der eines Spiegelbilds.[17] In all diesen Rollen aber machte es den Körper ganz.

Mein dritter Feldforschungsaufenthalt in Kozarac sollte im Sommer 2020 stattfinden, fiel aber wegen der Coronapandemie ins Wasser. Ich wollte den mythischen Sommer miterleben, in dem die Stadt zum Leben erwacht und alle Häuser bewohnt sind. Höhepunkt des Sommers in Kozarac ist Ende Juli, eine Zeit zahlreicher Festlichkeiten – von Gedenktagen über Bestattungszeremonien für Kriegsopfer (deren Gebeine bis heute exhumiert und identifiziert werden) bis hin zu Hochzeiten.

Boccagni und Erdal schreiben, eine methodisch „akzeptable" Studie von Rücktransfer- Häusern sollte die Erklärungen ihrer BewohnerInnen mit den Alltagspraktiken verknüpfen, die in diesen Räumen tatsächlich stattfinden. Überdies sollten Forschende die Rolle der Zeit nicht unterschätzen und gewillt und imstande sein, über längere Zeiträume zu den gleichen Häusern zurückzukehren.[18] Für diesen Artikel wollte ich die Häuser, die ich vor drei Jahren analysiert hatte, erneut aufsuchen, da eine Frage noch nicht beantwortet war: Was ist die Zukunft – und Gegenwart – von Kozarac, seiner Rücktransfer-Häuser und deren BesitzerInnen?

Aus unvorhergesehenen Gründen war ich auch im Juli 2023 außerstande, nach Kozarac zu reisen. Ich schaffte es erst Ende August und hoffte das Beste, da es schließlich immer noch Sommer war. Doch es bot sich mir genau das gleiche Bild wie im Herbst 2019. Die Häuser verlassen, die Straßen verstummt. Ganz offensichtlich hatten viele Angehörige der Diaspora schon den ganzen Sommerurlaub aufgebraucht, zumal man ja nur Anspruch auf fünf Wochen hat und die Juliwochen mit dazugehören. Ich hatte also den Sommer erneut versäumt. Aber die Situation war vertraut und fühlte sich natürlich an. Mir kam der Gedanke, dass genau dies die Realität, der Alltag von Kozarac ist – und der Sommer die Störung. Oder war es doch umgekehrt?

In diesem späten August lauschte ich also an einem warmen Abend im Garten dieses geräumigen gelben Hauses bei Kaffee und Lokums den Geschichten seiner Besitzerin N.: „Ich habe in einem Nachbarort eine neue Person für meinen Hund gefunden. Wenn ich hier bin, meist zwei, drei Monate im Jahr, ist der Hund bei mir. Den Rest der Zeit ist er bei dieser anderen Person. Alles andere wäre zu kompliziert." Es war ein passendes Arrangement für N., die in Österreich lebt und in den Winter- und Sommerferien nach Kozarac kommt. Wenngleich schon in Rente,

17 Die fehlende Gliedmaße verursacht Phantomschmerzen. Eine Therapie dafür ist, die noch vorhandene Gliedmaße vor dem Spiegel zu bewegen und so die Illusion zu erzeugen, dass sich die verlorene Gliedmaße bewegt.

18 Vgl. Boccagni/Erdal: „On the Theoretical Potential of ‚Remittance Houses'" (wie Anm. 12), 14.

7 Kozarac, 2023

For reasons unforeseen, in July 2023 I again was not able to visit Kozarac. It was not until the end of August that I arrived there, and I hoped for the best, since it was still summer, after all. I encountered the exact same scene as in autumn 2019. Houses empty, streets quiet. Clearly, many diaspora members had already used up their full summer vacation, as the vacation entitlement typically doesn't exceed five weeks, with these couple of weeks in July counting as part of it. I had again missed the summer. But this was familiar and felt natural. It occurred to me that precisely this is the reality, the everyday life of Kozarac — with summer its glitch. Or was it the other way around?

On that warm late August eve in 2023, while sipping coffee and eating *lokum* in the yard of the spacious yellow house, I listened to N., its owner: "I found a new guy for my dog in the nearby city. I spend time with my dog when I am here, usually two or three months. The rest of the year it is with this other person. Otherwise, it would be too complicated." It is an arrangement that best suited N., who was living in Austria and came to Kozarac during the winter and summer holidays. Although she was retired, her health deterioration tied her to Austria and its superior health-care system. Additionally, her son, daughter, and grandchildren all lived in Austria as well. Her husband had died unexpectedly in 2021, leaving her alone with the issue of the house, its future, and its maintenance.

Approaching the back side of the house revealed that it was much bigger than one may assume judging by its front facade. N. complained about its size. In the backyard, there was a garden with lush tomatoes, cabbage, pumpkins, and a plum orchard. When I complimented it, she said: "Thank God, my neighbor watered it all the time." The house was finished in 2003, which was the peak of the return after the war.[19] The ground floor had been converted from a commercial into a barrier-free residential level in 2014; realizing that the possibility of starting a business in Bosnia was unlikely, N. and her husband had decided to instead prepare for their old age. On the second floor were the apartments for the kids, but the window shutters were down.

19 See note 8.

ist sie wegen ihres schlechter werdenden Gesundheitszustands an Österreich und sein besseres Gesundheitssystem gebunden. Hinzu kommt, dass auch ihr Sohn, ihre Tochter und ihre Enkel in Österreich leben. Ihr Mann ist 2021 überraschend verstorben und ließ sie mit dem Haus, seiner Zukunft und seiner Erhaltung zurück.

Auf der Rückseite des Hauses bemerkte ich, dass es wesentlich größer war, als man aufgrund der Vorderseite vermutet hätte. N. beschwerte sich über die Größe. Hinter dem Haus befand sich ein Garten mit üppigen Tomatenpflanzen, Kohl, Kürbissen und einem Zwetschkenhain. Als ich sie dazu beglückwünschte, sagte sie: „Gottseidank hat sie der Nachbar die ganze Zeit gegossen." Das Haus war 2003, auf dem Höhepunkt der Rückkehr nach dem Krieg, fertig geworden.[19] Die Geschäftsräume im Erdgeschoss wurden 2014 in einen barrierefreien Wohnraum umgewandelt. Nachdem sie erkannt hatten, dass die Möglichkeit, in Bosnien ein Geschäft zu eröffnen, kaum realisierbar war, beschlossen sie, stattdessen für das Alter vorzusorgen. Im ersten Stock lagen die Wohnungen für die Kinder, aber die Rollläden waren heruntergelassen. N. erzählte mir, dass auch die Kinder und Enkel, wenn sie da waren, bei ihr im Erdgeschoss schliefen. Das Obergeschoss benutzt niemand. Nach dem Tod ihres Mannes wurde das Haus zur Last und das Erdgeschoss zu groß. Dennoch hat N. nie in Erwägung gezogen, das Haus aufzugeben. Es war immer noch eine Quelle der Freude und ein Projekt, an dem es ständig weiterzuarbeiten galt. Die beiden anderen Frauen am Tisch waren ihre Nachbarinnen. Eine war, wie sie es selbst ausdrückte, „das seltene Exemplar einer Person, die tatsächlich das ganze Jahr über in Kozarac lebt". Ihre Tochter lebte in der Schweiz. Die dritte Frau redete nicht viel, aber N. sagte, sie lebe in Frankreich.[20]

In diesem August suchte ich die vor Jahren dokumentierten Häuser erneut auf. Bei manchen gab es ein paar prächtig gedeihende Pflanzen im Garten, ein Zeichen, dass die BesitzerInnen oder NachbarInnen kürzlich vor Ort waren (Abb. 8). Dabei kam ich auch am Haus von S. und F. vorbei und hielt neugierig nach irgendwelche Änderungen Ausschau. Ich hatte sie vor meiner Ankunft kontaktiert, aber sie waren Anfang August nach Deutschland zurückgekehrt. Ich sah, dass ebenerdig ein vollkommen neuer Anbau im gleichen weiß-braunen-Farbschema dazu gekommen war. Das ursprüngliche Haus war ein dreistöckiges Gebäude mit einem großen Gästehaus und Waschküche daneben. Der neueste Anbau sah aus, als ob er als Büro gedacht war (Abb. 9). Nach Rückfrage bei S., ob er zum Haus gehöre, sagte sie: „Wie du siehst, gibt es genug Platz für dich, wenn du auf Besuch kommst."[21]

19 Vgl. Anm. 8.
20 Persönliches Gespräch, 26. August 2023, Kozarac.
21 Persönliches Gespräch, 11. September 2023, Graz.

8, 9 Kozarac, 2023

N. told me that even when kids and grandkids were there, they all slept on the ground floor, with her. Nobody used the upper floor. After her husband's death, the house became a burden and the ground floor was too big. Yet N. did not even for a moment contemplate abandoning the house. It was still a source of joy and a project that had to be continuously worked on. The other two women around the table were her neighbors. One was, in her own words, "a rare example of someone who actually lives in Kozarac all year round." Her daughter was living in Switzerland. The third woman did not talk much, but N. said she lived in France.[20]

In August, I revisited the houses I documented years ago. Some had a couple of lush plants in the gardens, indicating either the recent presence of the owners or of their neighbors (fig. 8). I passed by the house of S. and F., curiously inspecting it, looking for changes. I had contacted them before arriving, but they had gone back to Germany at the beginning of August. I noticed that there was a whole new ground floor structure next to their house in the same familiar white-and-brown color scheme. The original house was a three-story building with a big guest and laundry house next to it. The newest addition looked like a possible office space (fig. 9). After asking S. if it belonged to the house, she answered:

20 Personal interview, August 26, 2023, Kozarac.

D. und S. empfingen mich an einem heißen Nachmittag herzlich bei *Loboda*-Burek,[22] Saft und Kaffee. Sie waren im Ruhestand nach Kozarac zurückgekehrt, hatten ihre Zelte in Italien abgebrochen. Vor vier Jahren hatte D. begeistert von den neuen Zubauten erzählt, an denen er gerade arbeitete, unter anderem einem Außengrillplatz. Als ich damals fragte, wann das Haus fertig würde, antwortete er: „Wenn es fertig ist, ist es Zeit zu gehen." Jetzt, vier Jahre später, erkundigte ich mich erneut nach dem Grillplatz, ob er denn fertig sei. „Ja", sagte er, „er ist fertig, aber wir benutzen ihn nie." Die Kinder und Enkel, die alle anderswo leben, waren im Juli zu Besuch, aber sie hatten es nicht geschafft, während der zwei Wochen, in denen sie da waren, auch nur einmal zu grillen. Es lag eine stille Resignation in seinen Worten.[23] Das war vor vier Jahren anders, als das Haus noch Leben und Aufregung bedeutete.[24]

Vielleicht war es der falsche Zeitpunkt, gemahnte die frische Erinnerung an die Opulenz des Sommers daran, wie das Leben sein könnte, wenn es anders verlaufen wäre. Oder es lag einfach am Vergehen der Jahre, am Alter, der langsam schwindenden Fähigkeit, seine Ambitionen voll auszuleben. Vor allem, denke ich, war es die Erkenntnis, dass die Zukunft nicht immer herbeigebaut werden kann. Die Erkenntnis, dass erwachsene Kinder lieber im Erdgeschoss schlafen als in einer Wohnung im selben Gebäude, die nicht ihnen gehört.

Das Rücktransfer-Haus unterscheidet sich ontologisch schließlich nicht groß von jedem anderen Haus.[25] Es ist ein Raum zum Leben, ob er nun mit der Gegenwart des Lebens, seiner Antizipation oder seinem Reenactment verbunden ist. Es ist etwas, das versorgt, gefühlt und von Zeit zu Zeit besucht werden muss. Etwas, das das Leben seiner Besitzerin oder seines Besitzers erzählt, während es vergeht (Abb. 10).

Als ich das Haus von S. und F. fotografierte, näherte sich ein Mann auf einem Motorrad. Nachdem ich kurz erklärt hatte, was ich hier trieb, lud er mich zu einem Glas Cola auf sein nahegelegenes Anwesen ein. Er benötigte die Meinung einer ArchitektIn. A.s in Deutschland lebender Sohn interessierte sich nicht für das von seinem Vater gebaute Haus, obwohl die oberen Stockwerke für ihn vorgesehen waren. Er interessierte sich für ein großes, schönes Grundstück im Zentrum von Kozarac, das A. vor vielen Jahren erworben hatte. Es gab dort viel Grün und ein sehr kleines ebenerdiges Gebäude mit zwei Fenstern, einer

22 *Loboda* ist ein bosnisches Wort für Bergspinat, auch französischer Spinat oder Orach genannt, ein häufig verwendetes Blattgemüse vor dem Aufkommen des Spinats, das immer noch als Warmwetteralternative dazu angebaut wird oder wild im Wald und in den Bergen wächst. Hier habe ich ihn zum ersten Mal gegessen.

23 Persönliches Gespräch, 27. August 2023, Kozarac.

24 Persönliches Gespräch, 24. Dezember 2019, Kozarac.

25 Vgl. Boccagni/Erdal: „On the Theoretical Potential of ‚Remittance Houses'" (wie Anm. 12), 13.

"There is a lot of space for you to visit, as you can see."[21]

D. and S. warmly welcomed me on a hot August afternoon, with a *loboda* pie,[22] juice, and coffee. They had come back to Kozarac in their retirement, leaving their life in Italy behind. Four years ago, D. told me excitedly about new additions to the house he was building at the time, one of them an outdoor grilling space. Back then, when I had asked when the house would be finished, he answered: "When it is finished, it is time to go." Four years later, I asked again about the grilling space, if it was finished: "Yes, yes, it is finished, but we never use it." Children and grandchildren, all living elsewhere, visited in July, yet they did not manage to gather for a barbeque during these two weeks before they left again. There was a quiet resignation lining his words.[23] This was different than four years ago, when the house meant life and excitement.[24]

It was maybe bad timing, the memory of the summer abundance still fresh, reminding one of how life could be if life played out differently. Or it was simply the passing of years in old age with the capacity for exhausting aspirational living slowly diminishing. Mostly, I believe, it was the realization that the future cannot always be built into existence. The realization that grown-up children would much rather sleep down on the ground floor than in an apartment in the same building that is not their own.

The remittance house was, after all, ontologically not so different from any other house.[25] A space for living, be it rooted in the presence of living, its anticipation, or its reenactment. A structure that has to be cared for, felt, and seen from time to time. A structure that has narrated its owner's life, as it happens (fig. 10).

While photographing S. and F.'s house, I was approached by a man on a motorbike. After briefly explaining my intentions, he invited me to join him for a glass of Coke on his property nearby. He needed an architect's opinion. A.'s son, who lived in Germany, was not interested in the house his father had built, though the upper floors were reserved for him. He was interested in a big, beautiful property at the center of Kozarac, which A. had acquired many years ago. There was a lot of greenery and a very small ground-floor structure with a toilet, two windows, and a kitchen. On the edge of the property was a mound that we climbed up on, in order to look out over the neighborhood. A. started telling me where the owners of these empty neighborhood houses were, knowing the

21 Personal interview, September 11, 2023, Graz.

22 *Loboda* is a Bosnian word for the plant called mountain spinach, French spinach, or arrach, used as a leaf vegetable that was common before spinach and still grown as a warm-weather alternative to that crop, also to be found in woods and mountains as a wild plant. This was the first time I had tried it.

23 Personal interview, August 27, 2023, Kozarac.

24 Personal interview, December 24, 2019, Kozarac.

25 See Boccagni and Erdal, "On the Theoretical Potential of 'Remittance Houses'" (see note 12), 13.

10 Kozarac, 2023

Toilette und einer Küche. Am Rand des Grundstücks befand sich ein Erdhügel, den wir erklommen, um einen Blick über die Nachbarschaft zu werfen. A. fing an zu erzählen, wo die BesitzerInnen der leeren Häuser in der Umgebung lebten, konnte die Länder zu jedem von ihnen nennen (er war Dachdecker und hatte auf den meisten Häusern gearbeitet). Dann erklärte er, dass der Hügel von einer vermutlich aus ottomanischer Zeit stammenden Steinmauer begrenzt wird. Auf dem Hügel sollte ein *šadrvan* – ein Gartenpavillon – entstehen. Der Sohn wollte das kleine Gebäude aufstocken, um ein Schlafzimmer zu haben. Es sollte sein eigenes Ferienhaus werden, bescheiden und leicht zu erhalten. Schließlich hätte er daneben noch gern einen Pool gehabt.[26]

Wie viele MigrantInnen der zweiten Generation war für ihn die Rückkehr in die Heimat mit Freizeit und Erholung verbunden. Das Haus sollte ein Ferienhaus werden, und nicht mehr.[27] Das war nicht ganz das, was sich der Vater vorgestellt hatte. Der hatte die oberen Stockwerke ausgebaut, damit sie sein Sohn eines Tages bewohnt, was nun vermutlich nicht mehr der Fall sein würde. Was das Haus allerdings schaffte, war, den Sohn an seine Wurzeln

26 Persönliches Gespräch, 26. August 2023, Kozarac.
27 Vgl. Wagner, Lauren: „Trouble at Home: Diasporic Second Homes as Leisure Space Across Generations", *Annals of Leisure Research* 17, 1 (2014), 13.

countries for each house by heart (he was a roofer and had worked on most of these houses). He then explained that the mound is bordered by a stone wall, probably from the Ottoman period. The mound would be a designated place for a *šadrvan*, or garden pavilion. The son wanted to add a floor for the bedroom on top of the small existing structure and transform it into his own holiday house, leaving it modest and easy to maintain. Eventually, he would like to have a pool next to it.[26]

As many second-generation migrants, returning to the homeland would be connected with leisure and respite. The house would become a holiday home, without being anything more than that.[27] This did not play out exactly as the father had envisioned. He had built the upper floors for his son to occupy one day, which now would most likely not be the case. What the house did accomplish, though, was to tie his son to his roots. The city still existed and the house continued to fulfill its duty. Bodies built houses, and the houses, in return, rendered the body whole. The houses built the city, and the city kept the community—even scattered—together. Despite the country's painful history, as revealed by the many empty houses of Kozarac,

26 Personal interview, August 26, 2023, Kozarac.
27 See Lauren Wagner, "Trouble at Home: Diasporic Second Homes as Leisure Space Across Generations," in "Second Homes," *Annals of Leisure Research* 17, no. 1 (2014), 13.

11 Kozarac, 2023

zu binden. Die Stadt existierte noch, und das Haus erfüllte weiter seine Aufgabe. Körper bauten Häuser, und die Häuser machten im Gegenzug die Körper ganz. Die Häuser bildeten die Stadt, und die Stadt hielt – selbst noch in der Zerstreuung – die Gemeinde zusammen. Trotz der schmerzlichen Geschichte des Landes, wie sie die vielen leeren Häuser in Kozarac bezeugen, bauten sie tatsächlich eine Zukunft herbei.

Wie die Zukunft von Kozarac – mit ihren Rücktransfer-Häusern, ihren BesitzerInnen und deren Familien – genau aussehen wird, ist offen. Der Rücktransfer macht den Bau und die Erhaltung der Häuser möglich, aber diese Häuser binden ihre BesitzerInnen gleichermaßen an ihr Aufenthaltsland wie an ihr Herkunftsland. Dieses unauflösliche Band erfordert das ständige Weiterarbeiten am Haus, anfangs als ein Symbol von Hoffnung und Widerstand, dann als fortwährende Anpassung an die wechselnde Familiendynamik und (un)erfüllte Aspirationen. Dieses Narrativ kann kein Ende haben, denn wie D. auf die Frage, wann sein Haus fertig würde, sagte: „Wenn es fertig ist, ist es Zeit zu gehen."

Übersetzung: Wilfried Prantner

they actually were building a future into existence.

The question of what exactly the future of Kozarac will look like, with its remittance houses, their owners, and their families, remains open. Remittance makes the construction and maintenance of the houses possible. But also, these houses keep the owners tethered to both the country of residence and the country of origin at the same time. This unbreakable bond requires continuous work on the house, initially a symbol of hope and defiance, now constantly adapting to the shifting family dynamics and (un)fulfilled aspirations. There can be no end to the narrative, because, as D. swiftly answered the question of when his house had been finished: "When it is finished, it is time to go."

Unité d’Habitation, Westfassade, Blick von der Avenue de Mazargues © Thomas Meinecke

„Es ist kein Denkmal, das nur in seiner Denkmalhaftigkeit dasteht"
"It's Not a Monument Just Standing There in All its Monumentality"

Thomas Meinecke (TM) im Gespräch mit / in Conversation with Julian Müller (GAM)

Thomas Meinecke ist Schriftsteller, Musiker und DJ. Während seines Studiums der Theaterwissenschaft und Neueren Deutschen Literatur in München gründete er die Literaturzeitschrift *Mode und Verzweiflung*, aus der die Band F.S.K. (Freiwillige Selbstkontrolle) hervorging. Seit 1986 hat er zahlreiche Erzählungen, Hörspiele und Romane veröffentlicht, darunter *Tomboy* (1998), *Lookalikes* (2011) und *Selbst* (2016), und mehrere Literaturpreise gewonnen. 2022 hat Thomas Meinecke seinen Wohnsitz nach Marseille verlegt und bewohnt seitdem eine der 337 Wohnungen in der von Le Corbusier von 1945 bis 1952 entworfenen Unité d'Habitation. Julian Müller hat mit ihm über den Alltag in der historisch bedeutsamen Wohnanlage gesprochen.

GAM: Wir haben uns vor einiger Zeit bei einer Veranstaltung getroffen, und in der Kaffeepause hast du mir erzählt, dass du kürzlich nach Marseille gezogen bist und seitdem in der Unité d'Habitation wohnst. Erzähl mir doch zunächst mal, wie es dich dorthin verschlagen hat …

TM: Das erste Mal gesehen habe ich das Haus, als ich mit meiner Frau, Michaela Melián, auf einer Radtour durch Frankreich war. Wir rasten aus den Calanques-Bergen in die Stadt runter und sahen auf einmal völlig unvorbereitet durch die Bäume hindurch dieses Haus aufblitzen, diese Architektur, die man ja irgendwie schon kannte, weil sie sich so sehr in das allgemeine Bewusstsein eingeschrieben hat. Wir hatten an dem Tag allerdings gar nicht die Zeit und die Muße anzuhalten, weil wir noch eine ziemliche Strecke vor uns hatten. Das war jedenfalls die erste Begegnung mit dem Haus, das ich bis dahin auch nur von Abbildungen kannte. Und vor ungefähr fünfzehn Jahren stand ich dann zum ersten Mal auf dem Dach des Gebäudes. Freunde von uns lebten da, und so kamen wir in das Haus hinein. Und dieses Dach hat uns absolut fasziniert, ja, ergriffen geradezu. Wir standen da oben und hatten Tränen in den Augen. Man spürte irgendwie, dass da etwas erzählt wird von einer besseren Welt, die dann aber doch nicht kommt. Und aus dieser Diskrepanz zwischen dem, was

Thomas Meinecke is an author, musician, and DJ. While studying theater and modern German literature in Munich, he founded the literary magazine *Mode und Verzweiflung*, from which the band F.S.K. (Freiwillige Selbstkontrolle) originated. Since 1986 he has published numerous stories, audio plays, and novels, including *Tomboy* (1998), *Lookalikes* (2011), and *Selbst* (2016), and he has won several literature prizes. In 2022, Thomas Meinecke moved to Marseille and has been living in one of the 337 apartments in the Unité d'Habitation designed by Le Corbusier from 1945 to 1952. Julian Müller spoke with him about everyday life in this historically relevant housing complex.

GAM: We recently met at an event, and during the coffee break you told me that you had just moved to Marseille and have been living in the Unité d'Habitation. First of all, please tell me how you ended up there …

TM: I saw the building for the first time when I was on a bicycle tour of France with my wife, Michaela Melián. We were careening down the hill into the city from the Calanques range and suddenly saw, out of the blue, this building through the trees, this architecture, which was of course quite familiar because it has become so deeply inscribed in the collective consciousness. We were not at leisure to stop that day, for we were short on time, with quite a distance still to go. In any case, that was my first encounter with the building, which until then I had only seen in photographs. And then, about fifteen years ago, I stood on the roof of the structure for the first time. Friends of ours were living there, which is how we were able to enter the building. We were utterly fascinated by this roof; it really captivated us. We were standing up there with tears in our eyes. It felt like something was being said about a better world, about a world that would never come. Arising from this discrepancy between what one sees and what does not actually come to pass was a feeling similar to what we sometimes experience when listening to music with its nonverbal, visionary power. And from that moment on, it was our dream house.

man sieht, und dem, was dann doch nicht eingetroffen ist, ergab sich irgendwie so ein Gefühl, das sich manchmal auch beim Hören von Musik in ihrer nonverbalen, visionären Kraft einstellt. Und von da an war das eigentlich unser Traumhaus.

GAM: Wie seid ihr dann von BesucherInnen, die ergriffen auf dem Dach standen, zu BewohnerInnen des Hauses geworden?

TM: Vor einiger Zeit ist mein Vater gestorben, weswegen ich das Haus meiner Eltern verkauft habe. Lustigerweise gab es auch in meinem Elternhaus eine gewisse Affinität zu dem, was die Unité d'Habitation symbolisiert. Meine Eltern waren Anhänger einer doch sehr französelnden Modernität. Sie hörten gerne französische Pop-Musik und Modern Jazz, wir haben unsere Sommerurlaube an der französischen Riviera verbracht, mein Vater fuhr Citroën DS, es stand auch ein Corbusier-Sessel im Wohnzimmer. Und mit dem Verkauf des Hauses meiner Eltern hatte ich auf einmal mitten in der Pandemie Geld. Und da ich nicht der Typ bin, der mit Geld gerne auf irgendwelchen Märkten rumjongliert, haben meine Frau und ich überlegt, wo wir denn gerne noch wohnen würden. Wir leben ja in einem oberbayerischen Dorf mit 100 EinwohnerInnen, und das ist auch sehr schön dort, aber urban ist es da natürlich nicht. Also sind wir im Kopf verschiedene Städte durchgegangen: Neapel war dabei, Barcelona war dabei, aber eben auch Marseille.

GAM: Aber wie kommt man dann an eine Wohnung in der Unité d'Habitation? Ist das nicht wahnsinnig schwer?

TM: Das war schon ein ziemliches Glück. Die meisten freien Wohnungen gehen ja gar nicht auf den Immobilienmarkt, sondern werden über Mundpropaganda im Haus weitergegeben. Die Leute, die da wohnen, mögen das Haus wirklich sehr gerne und wohnen zum Teil schon in dritter Generation dort. Jedenfalls hatte der Vormieter die Wohnung vor einigen Jahren aus erster Hand übernommen und auch sehr aufwendig renoviert – allerdings nicht immer ganz nach den Vorschriften, die man mit Le Corbusier verbindet. Zum Beispiel hat er die Küche umgebaut. Du musst wissen, dass die Küchen wirklich sehr klein sind. Das hat schon fast etwas Klaustrophobisches. Wenn man dazu bei Le Corbusier nachliest, dann sollte sich „die Frau" seiner Vorstellung nach in dieser Küche nur einmal um sich selbst drehen müssen, um an alles zu gelangen. Aber die Frau war eben auch auf eine Art in der Küche gefangen – so hart muss man es schon sagen. Jedenfalls hat wohl die Frau des Vormieters eine schwarze steinerne Küche – übrigens aus Stuttgart – einbauen lassen, die nicht so ganz nach unserem Geschmack ist. Trotzdem soll es ihr in der Wohnung nicht mehr gefallen haben, so ist zumindest die Legende. Und weil dem neuen Besitzer es wohl peinlich war, die Wohnung nach dieser aufwendigen Renovierung letztlich

GAM: How did you go from being smitten visitors standing on the roof to residents of the building?

TM: My father passed away a while back, which is why I sold my parents' house. Interestingly enough, in my family home there was a certain affinity with that which the Unité d'Habitation symbolizes. My parents had been proponents of a very Frenchified modernity. They enjoyed listening to French pop music and modern jazz, we spent our summer vacations on the French Riviera, my father drove a Citroën DS, and we had a Corbusier armchair in our living room. So when I sold my parents' home, smack-dab in the middle of the pandemic, I suddenly had money. And since I'm not the type of person who likes to throw money around the markets, my wife and I gave some consideration to where else we might like to live. We have been residing in a village with about 100 inhabitants in Upper Bavaria, and while it is very beautiful, there are of course no urban qualities. So we went through various cities in our heads: Naples was one, Barcelona too, and then Marseille.

GAM: But how did you manage to get an apartment in the Unité d'Habitation? Is that not just incredibly difficult?

TM: It really was a stroke of luck. Most of the free apartments never make it to the real-estate market because they are passed along by word of mouth within the community itself. The people living there truly adore the building, and some families have even been there for three generations. In any case, the previous owner had taken over the apartment directly in-house and then carried out extensive renovations—though not always purely according to the provisions associated with Le Corbusier. For example, the previous owner modified the kitchen. It's important to understand that these kitchens really are very small. It almost feels claustrophobic. Reading Le Corbusier's words on the subject, one notices that in his mind "the woman" should only have to turn around once in a circle in order to be able to reach everything in the kitchen. But a woman was also more or less trapped in the kitchen—there is no gentle way to put it. At any rate, it appears that the wife of the previous owner had a black stone kitchen installed—from Stuttgart, by the way—that does not quite fit with our personal tastes. Legend has it that she still didn't want to live in the apartment, even with this kitchen of her choice. Since it apparently embarrassed the new owner that he and his wife could not in fact move in after this extensive renovation work, the apartment was not passed along in-house like usual but rather ended up on the free market. And on the very day the ad went online, I was sitting in front of my computer once again looking for apartments in this building. The whole thing was a giant coincidence. We didn't even travel there to view the apartment—for it was of course at the height of the Covid-19 pandemic—but instead purchased it solely based

gar nicht zu beziehen, wurde die Wohnung nicht im Haus weitergegeben, sondern gelangte auf den freien Markt. Und genau an dem Tag, als die Anzeige online geschaltet wurde, saß ich vor dem Computer und habe mal wieder nach Wohnungen in diesem Gebäude geschaut. Das war alles ein großer Zufall. Wir sind ja nicht mal angereist, um die Wohnung zu besichtigen – es war ja gerade die Hochphase der Covid-19-Pandemie –, sondern haben die Wohnung nur auf Grundlage einer WhatsApp-Führung gekauft. Und seitdem leben wir dort. Es ist aber schon so, dass ich ab und zu im Fahrstuhl gefragt werde, wie es uns da eigentlich hin verschlagen hätte, wie ausgerechnet zwei Deutsche hier eine Wohnung bekommen hätten.

GAM: Du hast gesagt, dass du die Unité d'Habitation bereits kanntest, bevor du zum ersten Mal dort warst. Sie ist, wie du es eben genannt hast, Teil eines allgemeinen Bewusstseins. In deinen Romanen thematisierst du immer wieder das Ikonische, vor allem Ikonen der Popkultur. Nimmst du das Haus auch als eine Ikone wahr?

TM: Wir nehmen das Haus schon als Ikone wahr. Man staunt eigentlich jeden Tag aufs Neue über irgendwelche Löcher und Luftdüsen in den Wänden. Und fragt sich, wo eigentlich die Luft herkommt und wieso man die Nachbarn nie hört. Die Inspiration für Le Corbusiers Bauprinzip der Unité d'Habitation war ja ein Flaschenregal. Das Haus ist also eine Art Regal aus Beton, in dem dann aber Wohnungen aus Holz stecken. Das unterscheidet die Unité d'Habitation in Marseille etwa auch von der in Berlin. Man geht also den ganzen Tag über knarzende Holzdielen, und auch die Fenster sind alle aus Holz, mit ganz alten Beschlägen. Es gibt schon so eine archaische Dorfschmiedhaftigkeit in dem Haus. Und sowas nimmt man schon immer wieder aufs Neue wahr, auch den Einfall des Lichts. Man beobachtet das Haus also schon permanent auf seine Gemachtheit hin und fragt sich dann, was er – also Le Corbusier – sich wohl dabei gedacht hat. Man lebt ja bis zu einem gewissen Grad in einem Denkmodell. In Marseille heißt das Haus auch *la maison du fada*, das Haus des Verrückten. Das war natürlich als Beleidigung gedacht, aber das Haus enthält viele höchst irrationale Momente. Das hat nicht so viel mit einer etwas simplen Vorstellung von Rationalismus zu tun. Das Haus ist eher *soulful*, gerade oben auf dem Dach. Und es ist auch in seiner Programmatik sehr stark am Kind ausgerichtet. Geländer sind beispielsweise auf Wadenhöhe montiert, also für Erwachsene völlig ungeeignet. Und bei den Treppenstufen gibt es in der Mitte so eine Rille, damit sich Kleinkinder darin einhaken und hochziehen können. Und solche Sachen ziehen sich durch das ganze Haus. Der prominenteste Raum auf dem Dach ist der Werkraum des Kindergartens. Es sind wirklich irre Bilder, die man täglich zu sehen bekommt, wie die Kinder in dieser Betonlandschaft rumtoben. Da gibt es bestimmt täglich ein Knie zu verpflastern.

on a WhatsApp tour. And we have been living there ever since. Occasionally someone in the elevator will ask me how we ended up here, that is, how it happened that two Germans succeeded in getting an apartment.

GAM: You mentioned having been familiar with the Unité d'Habitation before you were there for the first time. It is, as you noted earlier, part of our collective consciousness. In your novels, you thematically explore the iconic again and again, especially icons of pop culture. Do you see this building as an icon?

TM: Yes, we do see the building as an icon. Every single day one is amazed at the holes and air vents in the walls. And one wonders where the air is actually coming from and why we never hear the neighbors. Serving as inspiration for Le Corbusier's building principle in designing the Unité d'Habitation was, in fact, a bottle rack. Indeed, the building is almost like a shelf made of concrete, into which apartments made of wood were inserted. This sets the Unité d'Habitation in Marseille apart from its counterpart in Berlin. So all day long you are treading on creaking wooden floorboards, and the windows are all made of wood, with very old fittings. There is a rather archaic village blacksmith feel to the whole building. You never stop noticing such things, including the way the light falls. One is constantly examining the building as to how it was made, and wondering what he—Le Corbusier—might have been thinking. To a certain extent, one is living in a conceptual model. In Marseille, the building is also called "La maison du fada," which means "house of the madman." Of course, this was meant as an insult, but the building really does spawn many highly irrational moments. Yet this has little to do with a rather simplistic concept of rationalism. Rather, the house is soulful, especially up on the roof. And in terms of a programmatic approach, it is strongly geared toward children. For example, the railings are mounted at calf height, making them totally unsuitable for adults. And the stairs have a groove in the middle of the step area to allow toddlers to grab on and pull themselves up. Such details are found all over the building. The most prominent space on the rooftop is the kindergarten crafts room. You see crazy things there daily when the children are running around this concrete landscape. There must be a knee needing a Band-Aid every single day.

GAM: Le Corbusier had a very clear idea of how to tailor his design to day-to-day family life in the building. He integrated everyday processes into the planning process, for instance through the corresponding common areas, the kindergarten, the shopping street, and much more. What is everyday life really like at the Unité d'Habitation today?

TM: The shopping passageways still exist, but today they are used in a very different way than originally planned. The hotel, for example, which is located within the

GAM: Le Corbusier hatte eine genaue Vorstellung, wie das alltägliche, familiäre Zusammenleben im Haus gestaltet sein sollte und hat alltägliche Abläufe im Planungsprozess integriert, z.B. mit entsprechenden Gemeinschaftsbereichen, dem Kindergarten, der Einkaufsstraße und vielem mehr. Wie sieht der Alltag in der Unité d'Habitation heute tatsächlich aus?

TM: Die Einkaufsstraßen gibt es noch, aber die werden heute ganz anders genutzt als geplant. Das Hotel etwa, das sich im Haus befindet, das waren in den ersten Jahren noch Gästeappartements für die BewohnerInnen. In den Wohnungen selbst gibt es nämlich kaum Möglichkeiten, Gäste zu empfangen. Es gibt nur wenige Türen und dadurch auch nur wenige Rückzugsmöglichkeiten in den Wohnungen. Deshalb wurden bis ungefähr 1965 diese Gästewohnungen im Haus genutzt. Dann gibt es heute einen Kunstraum, in dem vor allem Ausstellungen zu Architektur gezeigt werden. In dem Raum standen früher die Waschmaschinen. Es gab dann noch einen Supermarkt, der von außen noch immer erkennbar ist, weil der Schriftzug noch leicht lesbar ist. In dem Raum finden heute auch ab und zu Ausstellungen statt. De facto sind die Läden also nicht leerstehend, aber sie werden einfach anders genutzt. Auf dem Dach ist dann noch das ehemalige Gym, das sich der französische Designer Ito Morabito unter den Nagel gerissen hat. Der macht da aber nur ab und zu mal was, und viele BewohnerInnen sind eigentlich sauer auf ihn. Aber ja, die klassischen Läden gibt es kaum noch. Was es noch gibt, ist eine kleine Konditorei, zugleich Café. Ach ja, es gibt noch das große Restaurant, das sehr beliebt ist, auch weil man da auf dem Balkon zur Meeresseite hin sitzen kann. Und dann gibt es ein paar hippe Läden – das hatte ich schlimmer befürchtet – und ein paar Architekturbüros. Es gibt aber auch Chiropraktiker und eine Buchhandlung, die, weitgehend auf Architektur konzentriert, sehr gut funktioniert. Neben der Buchhandlung gibt es noch einen Merchandising-Shop, in dem

Gemeinschaftsräume in den Erschließungszonen
© Thomas Meinecke

building, originally served as dwellings for guests visiting the residents. This is because the apartments themselves hardly have room enough for welcoming overnight guests. Since there are not many doors, space for being alone in the units is rather limited. That's why these guest apartments were in use until about 1965. Then there is an art space where mostly exhibitions about architecture are shown. There actually used to be washing machines located in this room. Then there was a supermarket, which is even still discernible from the outside, because the lettering remains slightly legible. Today, sometimes exhibitions are shown in this space. As a matter of fact, the stores are not vacant; they're simply used in a different way. Then there is the former gym on the roof, which the French designer Ito Morabito has snapped up, though he only uses it occasionally, so many of the residents are angry with him. Anyways, there are hardly any traditional stores left. Though there is still a small pâtisserie, also serving as a café. And of course there is the big restaurant, which is very popular, not least because you can sit on the balcony with a view of the sea. And there are a few hip stores—I had really expected worse—and several architectural firms. Moreover, there is a chiropractor and a bookstore, the latter being primarily concentrated on architecture and quite well visited. Alongside the bookstore is a merchandising shop, where items are even sold that are only remotely connected to the building and to Le Corbusier. And let's not forget to say that lots of visitors stop by every day, many of whom are specialists, such as art historians or architects.

GAM: So it is a building that is constantly reflecting on itself in one way or another. It sounds as if one cannot help but think of it as an attraction. Or does that effect eventually wear off?

TM: One could get around it if one really wanted. The building also has apartments for students directly facing the loud boulevard without any view of the sea. I would guess that these residents don't see the building as a never-ending attraction. There is the Association des habitants, founded soon after the building was inaugurated. Members pay an annual fee, allowing one to use a few hidden things in the building that are not really considered attractions. For instance, near the stairwells there are a few incognito rooms, like in the film *Being John Malkovich*. There is a small library run by a touching elderly gentleman who is tasked every month with acquiring six or seven new relevant publications. You'll find the new book by Annie Ernaux there, or one by Didier Eribon, as well as lots of children's books. And if you ask when the book you've chosen needs to be returned, he replies, "Well, when you have finished reading it." It's fantastic how anachronistic everything is. There is also a little cinema showing films by Akira Kurosawa or Werner Herzog. There are thirty or forty cinema seats set in a hidden,

Ausblick in Richtung Westen zum Meer © Thomas Meinecke

Utensilien verkauft werden, die im weitesten Sinne mit dem Haus und mit Le Corbusier zu tun haben. Es kommen natürlich, das muss man schon auch sagen, täglich eine Menge BesucherInnen, sehr viel Fachpublikum, KunsthistorikerInnen, ArchitektInnen.

GAM: Es ist also schon ein Haus, das sich permanent auf eine Art und Weise selbst reflektiert. So wie das klingt, scheint man gar nicht umhinzukommen, es eigentlich immer auch als Sehenswürdigkeit zu betrachten. Oder nutzt sich das irgendwann ab?

TM: Man könnte schon drum herum kommen, wenn man das unbedingt wollte. Es gibt ja auch Wohnungen für Studierende, die direkt zum lauten Boulevard raus sind und keinen Ausblick auf das Meer haben. Ich würde mal vermuten, dass die das Haus nicht permanent als Sehenswürdigkeit wahrnehmen. Es gibt auch eine *association des habitants*, die schon bald nach der Einweihung des Hauses gegründet wurde. Da zahlt man pro Jahr einen kleinen Mitgliedsbeitrag, für den man dann auch ein paar versteckte, nicht sehenswürdige Dinge im Haus nutzen kann. Es gibt zum Beispiel bei den Treppenhäusern so ein paar Inkognito-Räume, so wie im Film „Being John Malkowich". Da ist dann eine kleine Bibliothek, die von einem rührenden älteren Herrn geleitet wird, der zur Auflage hat, jeden Monat sechs oder sieben relevante Neuerscheinungen zu erwerben. Da steht dann das neue Buch von Annie Ernaux oder von Didier Eribon und viele Kinderbücher. Und wenn man fragt, wann man das ausgeliehene Buch wieder zurückgeben soll, dann antwortet der, „Naja, wenn Sie es halt ausgelesen haben". Das ist alles toll anachronistisch.

rather plain room. In the Jardin d'hiver, the wintergarden, you'll also find a gathering place. It really is all very touching. Occasionally meetings will be held there, attended by a few legendary people who grew up in the building. And when we also attend, sometimes we hear dumbfounded questions like: "Who are you? And what are you doing here?" So there is certainly a vibrant social life going on for everyone living in the building. But of course there are also Airbnbs, and there is an apartment that is not rented out but is instead reserved for shooting films, because everything inside is still original.

GAM: Please describe to me how the Unité d'Habitation is actually situated in the city. Shouldn't we be imagining the building as Le Corbusier did, like a giant ocean liner stranded in the urban realm?

TM: The building is standing on stilts, of course, surrounded by greenery. It is located in the former park of a small castle from the seventeenth century. So we look down on this little castle. In the nineteenth century, the park was already divided by a wide boulevard, as straight as if drawn by a ruler, which today also runs past the Olympique de Marseille stadium. When soccer games are played there, the clouds of smoke from the Bengal lights reach us here, and you can basically hear every single foul. The neighborhood is rather unique in general. Officially, the building is located within an industrial area, a *zone industrielle*. Surrounding the structure are lots of automotive repair shops and former industrial premises, but also quite a few high-rises which, amusingly enough, have balconies facing the Unité d'Habitation. So the building does appear

Eingangsbereich und Hof, Westseite © Thomas Meinecke

Dann gibt es noch ein kleines Kino, in dem Filme von Akira Kurosawa oder Werner Herzog laufen. Da stehen dann dreißig, vierzig Kinostühle in so einem versteckten, eigentlich auch ziemlich schmucklosen Raum. Im *jardin d'hiver*, dem Wintergarten, gibt es auch einen Versammlungsort für das Haus. Das ist alles ganz anrührend. Dort gibt es ab und an Versammlungen, bei denen auch ein paar legendäre Leute erscheinen, die im Haus schon ihre Kindheit verbracht haben. Und wenn wir da hingehen, werden wir manchmal ganz entgeistert gefragt: „Wer seid ihr denn eigentlich? Was macht ihr denn hier?" Es gibt also durchaus ein reges soziales Leben all derer, die im Haus leben. Aber natürlich gibt es auch Airbnbs, und es gibt auch eine Wohnung, die gar nicht fest vermietet ist und in der immer Filme gedreht werden, weil darin noch alles original ist.

GAM: Beschreib mir mal, wie die Unité d'Habitation eigentlich in der Stadt liegt. Muss man sich das Haus wirklich, wie Le Corbusier es getan hat, als einen riesigen Ozeandampfer vorstellen, der in der Stadt gestrandet ist?

TM: Das Haus steht ja auf Stelzen im Grünen, in einem ehemaligen Park eines kleinen Schlösschens aus dem 17. Jahrhundert. Auf dieses Schlösschen blickt man dann herab. Der Park wurde aber schon im 19. Jahrhundert durchschnitten von einem breiten, wie mit dem Lineal gezogenen Boulevard, der auch am Stadion von Olympique Marseille vorbeiführt. Wenn da Spiele sind, dann reichen die Bengalo-Rauchschwaden bis zu uns, und du kannst im Grunde jedes Foul hören. Insgesamt ist die Gegend schon etwas seltsam. Das Haus steht offiziell in einer *zone industrielle*, also einem Gewerbegebiet. Man hat rund um das Haus sehr viele Autowerkstätten und ehemalige Industriegebäude. Aber auch sehr viele Hochhäuser, die ihre Balkons lustigerweise auf die Unité d'Habitation

to be a compelling urban landmark. And yes, it really is kind of an ocean liner that is stranded there. At the same time, in contrast to many of the surrounding buildings, it is not locked up at all. In the near vicinity there are numerous gated communities. If I want to go to the beach, which is only about a kilometer away, then I have to walk at least two kilometers because of the detour around these gated communities. So for this reason it is a pleasantly mixed area: the soccer fans park along the boulevard in front of the building, two prostitutes on wheels come park under the building, and people from the area let their dogs make a mess in the park. But all this is somehow very likeable, especially because it's not a monument just standing there in all its monumentality. That wouldn't be possible anyway, since nearly 1,000 people are living there.

GAM: You had a text published in a 1981 issue of *Mode & Verzweiflung*, a passage which reads: "We enjoy thinking back on those balmy summer evenings when we sat on our 13th floor balcony, letting our gaze wander to the green outskirts of the city. We had always liked the high-rise buildings."

TM: Back then, that was of course written in an ideological battle against such hippie ideas ...

GAM: ... and one of the most famous lyrics from your band F.S.K. reads, "And we say Yes to the modern world." The Unité d'Habitation itself represented a very loud architectural "Yes" to the modern world. Yet at the same time, this modern architectural world of the time is today a bygone one. What is it like for you, as a decidedly unnostalgic author, to live in a utopia that has already become obsolete?

gerichtet haben. Das Haus stellt also schon einen städtischen Faszinationspunkt dar. Und ja, es ist wirklich so eine Art Ozeandampfer, der da gestrandet ist. Gleichzeitig ist es, im Gegensatz zu vielen anderen Häusern rundherum, überhaupt nicht abgeschlossen. Es gibt im Umkreis eine Menge an Gated Communities. Wenn ich an den Strand gehen will, der eigentlich nur einen Kilometer weg ist, laufe ich mindestens zwei Kilometer, weil ich im Zickzack um diese Gated Communities herum muss. Deswegen ist es schon eine angenehm gemischte Gegend: die Fußballfans parken auf dem Boulevard vor dem Haus, zwei Prostituierte auf Rädern kommen und parken unterm Haus, und die Leute aus der Gegend lassen ihre Hunde den Park verkoten. Aber das ist alles irgendwie sehr sympathisch, weil es eben kein Denkmal ist, das nur in seiner Denkmalhaftigkeit dasteht. Das geht auch gar nicht, weil darin immerhin fast 1.000 Leute wohnen.

GAM: Es gibt einen Text von dir, der 1981 in *Mode & Verzweiflung* erschienen ist, darin heißt es: „Gern denken wir an jene lauen Sommerabende, an denen wir in unserem 13. Stockwerk auf dem Balkon gesessen sind und unsere Blicke bis an den grünen Stadtrand schweifen ließen. Immer haben wir die Hochhäuser schön gefunden."

TM: Das war natürlich damals in einem weltanschaulichen Kampf gegen so Hippie-Ideen geschrieben …

GAM: … und eine der bekanntesten Songzeilen deiner Band F.S.K. lautete „Und wir sagen Ja zur modernen Welt". Die Unité d'Habitation war ja selbst auch ein sehr lautes architektonisches „Ja" zur modernen Welt. Und gleichzeitig ist diese damals gebaute moderne Welt heute bereits eine vergangene. Wie ist das für dich, als dezidiert nicht-nostalgischer Autor, in einer sich doch bereits überholt habenden Utopie zu leben?

TM: True, it really is a bittersweet feeling. Sometimes an old Citroën DS will be standing in front of the building, and it evokes such a feeling of nostalgia about how the future, as it was laid out back then, somehow never came to pass. But does this building nonetheless remain a strong philosophical statement? You know, I like to read Peter Kropotkin or Gustav Landauer. And though things didn't turn out as planned, you still might feel inspired in certain circumstances—even if anarchy certainly never did play out. In fact, a kind of halo hovers above these ideas. But you are so right. Now my father's Corbusier armchair is situated in the apartment, which is somehow a museum of sorts for the progressive ideas of the past. However, it is not this way all over the building. From time to time, the residents show each other their apartments in turn, often with a tinge of pride. So one occasionally finds oneself standing in an apartment that no longer recalls Le Corbusier, for instance because it is filled with Biedermeier furnishings.

GAM: I would like to close by asking what role architecture plays for you as an author. I have the feeling that concrete rooms and places had a much stronger presence in your earlier texts—this is made clear by titles like *Café Adler*, *Interieur*, or *Villa Hammerschmidt*. It appears to me that, over time, this interest in places and spaces has been replaced by an interest in fashion, gender roles, theory, and language. Do you share this assessment, or am I barking up the wrong tree?

TM: I think you're mistaken here. In my upcoming novel, for example, a very concrete site plays a pivotal role. The book deals with Amorbach, as one of Theodor W. Adorno's places of longing. And in Amorbach there are a number of buildings designed by Peter Speeth, one of the few German representatives of revolutionary architecture. And from

Blick auf die Ostfassade vom Jardin de la Magelone © Thomas Meinecke

TM: Ja, es ist wirklich ein bittersüßes Gefühl. Manchmal steht dann so eine alte Citroën DS vor dem Haus, und da könnte man wirklich nostalgisch werden, dass die Zukunft, wie sie da so entworfen wurde, nun irgendwie doch nicht gekommen ist. Aber bleibt dieses Haus nicht dennoch ein starkes philosophisches Statement? Ich lese ja auch gerne Kropotkin oder Gustav Landauer. Und das ist ja auch alles nicht so gekommen, und trotzdem wird man unter Umständen davon beflügelt – auch wenn das mit der Anarchie ja nun wirklich nicht geklappt hat. Trotzdem bleibt so eine Art *halo* um diese Ideen. Aber du hast schon recht, jetzt steht da der Corbusier-Sessel meines Vaters in der Wohnung, die irgendwie so eine Art Museum für die Fortschrittsideen der Vergangenheit ist. Das ist allerdings im Haus nicht überall so. Die BewohnerInnen zeigen sich ja immer mal wieder wechselseitig ihre Wohnungen, durchaus mit gewissem Stolz. Und da steht man dann schon mal in Wohnungen, in denen Le Corbusier nicht mehr wirklich zu erkennen ist, weil sie etwa mit Biedermeier-Mobiliar vollgestellt sind.

GAM: Ich würde dich gerne zum Abschluss fragen, welche Rolle Architektur eigentlich für dich als Autor spielt. Ich habe das Gefühl, dass in deinen frühen Texten konkrete Räume und Orte noch sehr viel präsenter waren – was schon an Titeln wie „Café Adler", „Interieur" oder „Villa Hammerschmidt" deutlich wird –, dass dieses Interesse für Orte und Räume mit der Zeit abgelöst wurde durch ein Interesse an Mode, Geschlechterrollen, Theorie und Sprache. Teilst du diese Einschätzung oder täusche ich mich da?

TM: Ich glaube, da täuscht du dich. In meinem kommenden Roman wird zum Beispiel ein ganz konkreter Ort eine zentrale Rolle spielen. Da wird es um Amorbach gehen, als Sehnsuchtsort von Theodor W. Adorno. Und in Amorbach stehen auch einige Gebäude von Peter Speeth, einem der wenigen deutschen Vertreter der Revolutionsarchitektur. Und von dort lande ich im Roman dann wiederum in Odessa, wo Speeth auch gebaut hat. Es gibt auch einen anderen Roman von mir, *Hellblau*, der in Chicago spielt und in dem Architektur ein ganz zentrales Motiv ist. Das hatte damit zu tun, dass, während ich an dem Roman arbeitete, die Sozialwohnungsblöcke in der South Side von Chicago abgerissen wurden. Das war eine regelrechte Kapitulation vor den Ideen und den Hoffnungen, die mit deren Errichtung zusammenhingen. Deswegen würde ich schon sagen, dass Architektur für mich als Autor eine ganz wesentliche Bezugsebene ist, über die ich etwas erzählen kann.

GAM: Vielen Dank für das Gespräch.

Thomas Meinecke auf seinem Balkon der Unité d'Habitation

there, in the novel, I end up in Odessa, where Speeth had also designed buildings. Another of my novels, *Hellblau*, which is set in Chicago, has architecture as one of its main motifs. This is because the social housing estates on Chicago's South Side were demolished around the time I was writing the novel. That represented an utter capitulation of the ideas and hopes associated with the building of these high-rises. So I actually would say that, for me as an author, architecture is a very essential plane of reference that enables me to tell a story.

GAM: Thank you for the conversation.

Translation: Dawn Michelle d'Atri

Palazzo di Nerone, Napoli, 2023 © Gianluca Piccolo

Lob der Nutzlosigkeit
Neapel und seine Palazzi

In Praise of Uselessness
Naples and Its Palazzi

Luigiemanuele Amabile, Alberto Calderoni

In wenigen Städten finden sich so viele architektonische Charakteristika und Ereignisse auf so engem Raum konzentriert wie im süditalienischen Neapel. Neapels lange Geschichte – einst griechische Polis und römische Kolonie,[1] später Hauptstadt eines Königreiches, das jahrzehntelang von ausländischen Mächten beherrscht und kulturell geprägt wurde, die städtische Neuordnung beim sog. *Risanamento* infolge der Wiedervereinigung der Apenninhalbinsel im späten 19. Jahrhundert – wird auf eine eigene Weise in der Architektur sichtbar. Diese ist nicht so sehr durch Abriss, bauliche Neugestaltung und das Eindringen von neuen Architekturformen und -stilen gekennzeichnet, sondern durch die Koexistenz verschiedenartiger Bauwerke, die einander gegenübergestellt, übereinander geschichtet und ineinander verschachtelt wurden. Wie verwitterte, von der Zeit geformte Felsen, die auf die Erfüllung ihres Schicksals warten, beobachten und berühren sie sich in Neapels Altstadt, bleiben in ihren räumlichen Eigenschaften aber immer lesbar und erkennbar. Betrachtet man die Altstadt als Ganzes, lassen sich einige Eigenheiten feststellen, die weder in anderen italienischen Städten noch in der heutigen Kommerzarchitektur zu finden sind. Einer der auffälligsten Aspekte ist die Fülle an Räumen ohne Funktion, *useless* [nutzlose] oder scheinbar unnötige Räume. Für heutige ArchitektInnen ist es eine Herausforderung, sich eine Architektur vorzustellen, die für die verschiedenen, an den urbanen Transformationsprozessen beteiligten Parteien keinen unmittelbaren praktischen und ökonomischen Nutzen hat.[2] Im Folgenden

1 Vgl. Capasso, Bartolomeo: *Napoli Greco-Romana*, Neapel 1906, Nachdruck 1978.

2 Ein Vorkommnis, das Neapel mit besonderer Härte traf, war das unkontrollierte, der Geschichte zuwiderlaufende Wachstum während des ganzen 20. Jahrhunderts, das mit Billigung einer skrupellosen und nur auf den eigenen Vorteil bedachten politischen Klasse das sorgfältig geplante organische Stadtwachstum ersetzte. Francesco Rosis berühmter Film *Le mani sulla città* (dt. Die Hände über der Stadt, 1963) illustriert diesen historischen Vorgang.

Few cities in history have such a dense concentration of architectural features and events in such a small geographical area as Naples, in the south of Italy. Its long history—from a Greek polis to a Roman colony,[1] then to the capital of a kingdom ruled for centuries by foreign powers, marked by their consequent cultural influences, and finally to the urban reorganization of the late nineteenth century (known as the *Risanamento*) following the reunification of the Italian peninsula—has had a peculiar way of telling itself through the architecture of the city. This was not so much through demolitions, renovations, and the imposition of new tastes and architectural styles, but rather through the juxtaposition of inherently different and specific pieces of architecture and buildings, juxtaposed, superimposed, and interlaced. Like stones sculpted and worn by time, waiting for a destiny to be fulfilled, the buildings of the ancient city—born to meet different demands—observe and touch each other, whilst remaining legible and recognizable in their spatial attributes.

Observing the ancient city in its entirety, it is possible to notice certain peculiarities that cannot be found in other Italian cities or in contemporary mass architectural production. One of the most striking aspects is the apparent abundance of spaces without function, *useless* or seemingly unnecessary. In this sense, it is a real challenge for today's architects to envision an architecture without immediate practical and economic value for the various parties involved in the process of urban transformation.[2] The aim here is not to identify causes or solutions to this

1 See Bartolomeo Capasso, *Napoli Greco-Romana* (1906; repr., Naples, 1978).

2 An event that was particularly felt in Naples, which throughout the twentieth century—contrary to the events of its history, with the approval of an unscrupulous political class and professionals who wanted to make a name for themselves—experienced uncontrolled expansion at the expense of an organic and careful growth of urban space. This historical moment is depicted in the famous movie by Francesco Rosi, *Le mani sulla città* (Hands over the City, 1963).

werden jedoch keine Gründe oder Erklärungen für diese komplexe Thematik gesucht, vielmehr sollen einige Gebäude in Neapels Altstadt betrachtet und als lehrreiche Modelle und Denkanstöße wiederentdeckt werden. Indem sie *uselessness* [Nutzlosigkeit] vor Augen führen, markieren sie eine konzeptuelle Kategorie, die von der zeitgenössischen Architektur offenbar vergessen wurde. Was aber meinen wir mit *uselessness*? Der Begriff mag anti-modern wirken und negativ konnotiert sein, er will aber auf eine proaktive Großzügigkeit in jenem architektonischen Raum hinweisen, in dem die Saat eines möglichen Zukunftsentwurfs angelegt ist. Anders als der italienische Begriff *inutile* [unnütz] ist das Englische *useless* weicher und geschmeidiger und damit besser geeignet, diese neapolitanischen Räume zu beschreiben.

Wenn zutrifft, dass „Dichtung nur fernab von Berechnung und ohne Hast gedeiht“[3], dann sind Neapel und seine Architektur ein ganz eigenes Beispiel für intuitive, offenkundig nicht aus Berechnung entstandene urbane Räume. Neapels Altstadt ist ein unerschöpflicher Katalog architektonischer Möglichkeiten, die sich über Jahrhunderte bewährt haben und BesucherInnen bis heute faszinieren. Ein wiederkehrender architektonischer Typus, der für dieses historische Gefüge charakteristisch ist, ist der Palazzo, der im Folgenden aus der Perspektive seiner *uselessness* analysiert wird.

„Vedi Napoli e poi muori“:[4] Bauen über Bauten

Das antike Zentrum Neapels wurde an einem Hang angelegt, der von Norden nach Süden zum Meer hin abfällt. Seine Hauptachsen – die drei πλατεῖαι, die *decumani* – geben die städtischen Entwicklungslinien in Ost-West-Richtung vor. An sie schließen die *cardini* oder στενωποί an, enge Gassen, die die *decumani* verbinden und kreuzen und dadurch ein städtisches Raster aus Blöcken von ungefähr 35 mal 180 Meter Länge, sogenannten *insulae*, erzeugen. Diese Stadtstruktur besteht bis heute unverändert fort, und bei einem Stadtspaziergang sind auch ihre Grenzen noch zu erkennen. In den Straßen ist die Vergangenheit allgegenwärtig. Neapels Altstadt ist ein Palimpsest, das zu entschlüsseln ist, ein unerschöpflicher Katalog von Lebensweisen, die Jahrhunderte überdauert und sich hier abgelagert haben. Das komplexe Geflecht vielfältiger historischer Einflüsse, die sich in Neapel verweben, hat eine eigene urbane Landschaft geschaffen, die die tiefe Verbundenheit der NeapolitanerInnen mit ihrer Stadt speist.[5]

3 Ordine, Nuccio: *Von der Nützlichkeit des Unnützen*, Deutsch von Martina Kempter, München 2014, 24.

4 Goethes berühmtes „Siehe Neapel und stirb!“, mit dem er die besondere „Lage der Stadt und ihre Herrlichkeiten“ meint, die einen lebensverändernden Eindruck hinterlassen können. Zitiert nach Goethe, Johann Wolfgang von: *Italienische Reise*. Erster und Zweiter Teil (dtv Gesamtausgabe Bd. 25), München 1960, 169 (2. März 1787).

5 Vgl. De Seta, Cesare: *Napoli*, Bari 1981.

complex matter, but to rediscover valuable models to learn from in the observation of some buildings of the ancient city. By showing *uselessness*, they denote a conceptual category that contemporary architecture seems to have forgotten. But what do we mean by this kind of *uselessness*? It is a term that might seem anti-modern with negative connotations, yet seeks to highlight a proactive generosity inherent to architectural space that harbors the seed of a potential projected future. In the English language, the term useless, unlike the Italian term *inutile*, is mild and flexible and therefore better suited to describe these Neapolitan spaces.

If it is true that “only far from calculation it is possible to cultivate poetry,”[3] then Naples and its architecture illustrate peculiarly the process of intuitive and apparently uncalculated urban spaces. An inexhaustible catalogue of architectural possibilities that have stood the test of time and continue to fascinate visitors, the ancient city is characterized by a recurring type within its historical fabric, the palazzo, which is to be analyzed from the perspective of its *uselessness*.

“Vedi Napoli e poi muori”:[4] Building on Buildings

The ancient center of Naples was founded on a slope that descends from north to south toward the sea. Its arteries—the three πλατεῖαι, the *decumani*—guide the city’s development lines from its foundation from west to east. On them are the cardini, στενωποί, narrow streets that connect the *decumani* and form, through their intersection, an urban grid composed of *insulae*—blocks approximately 35 by 180 meters in length. Still today, this urban structure remains unchanged, and its boundaries can be read while strolling through the city. Among the streets, the presence of the past is lingering. The ancient city is a palimpsest to unveil, an inexhaustible catalog of ways of living that have survived and stratified over the centuries. These various imprints of the many historical influences that have intertwined in Naples have created a peculiar urban landscape that defines the citizens’ deep sense of attachment to their city.[5] This stems from a self-awareness (as to a way of being) that consistently entrusts collective identity to the production of the city: instead of fading away with time, these architectural interventions converge, illustrating an idealized manifestation of a collective, industrious spirit. “The Neapolitan firmly believes that he lives in Paradise,”[6] and the entire architecture of the city exudes this superstitious belief.

3 Nuccio Ordine, *L’utilità dell’inutile* (Milan, 2013), 19.

4 “See Naples and die!” as quoted by Johann Wolfgang von Goethe in *Italian Journey*, meaning that nothing compares to the beauty of Naples, and one could consider life complete after experiencing it. Johann Wolfgang von Goethe, *Italian Journey* (Harmondsworth, 1996), 189.

5 See Cesare de Seta, *Napoli* (Bari, 1981).

6 von Goethe, *Italian Journey* (see note 4), 184.

Dies gründet in dem Selbstbewusstsein, das die kollektive Identität durchweg an die Erschaffung der Stadt bindet: Statt im Laufe der Zeit verloren zu gehen, fließen architektonische Interventionen ineinander und verdichten sich zu einer idealisierten Erscheinungsform eines alle verbindenden tätigen Geistes. „Der Neapolitaner glaubt, im Besitz des Paradieses zu sein",[6] und Neapels gesamte Architektur strahlt diese abergläubische Überzeugung aus.

In ihrem gesamten langen Transformationsprozess hat sich Neapels Altstadt unentwegt verändert und ist doch immer wieder zu dem zurückgekehrt, was Bestand hat – eine *anakyklosis* –, die Gelegenheit, einen eigenen Ausdruck zu prägen und zugleich durch fortwährendes Anverwandeln Häuser zu bauen, die gegen unvorhergesehenen Wandel eine gewisse Resilienz zeigen. Mit Ausnahme von Katastrophen, die heute noch sichtbare Spuren[7] in manchen umgestalten Stadtteilen[8] hinterlassen haben, prägt diese Gleichzeitigkeit verschiedener, miteinander verbundener Vergangenheiten die Atmosphäre der Stadt. Dort scheint es geradezu eine biologische Notwendigkeit zu sein, die Stadt immer weiter zu verändern und das bestehende menschliche Erbe umzuarbeiten.

Die Entwicklung der Gebäude in der Altstadt unterliegt selten zentral gesteuerten Initiativen oder Planungskomitees, sondern entspringt häufiger einem kollektiven Willen zur Veränderung, wodurch Neapel zu einem Experimentierfeld für namenlose BauarbeiterInnen und HandwerkerInnen – in gewisser Weise selbst ArchitektInnen – wurde, die aus eigenem Antrieb ihre Lebensbedingungen verbessern wollten. Das Ergebnis war eine unvollständige, scheinbar auch ungesetzliche Ordnung, die aber seit Jahrhunderten nebeneinander existierende Fragmente von exzellenter architektonischer Qualität enthielt. Dennoch ist Kunst, wie Eugène Viollet-le-Duc anmerkt, unabhängig vom Zivilisationsniveau eines Volkes.[9] Auch wenn man bei Neapel heute noch an die Gesetzlosigkeit eines Teils seiner Bevölkerung denkt, bildete sich im Palimpsest des alten Zentrums aus einem „*Kunstwollen*, einem Gestaltungswillen, der von der ‚Technik' des Überlebens in der

6 Goethe, Johann Wolfgang von: *Italienische Reise* (wie Anm. 4), 164 (25. Februar 1787).

7 Die Stadterneuerung während des Risanamento ab 1885, der Zweite Weltkrieg und das Erdbeben von 1980 haben Neapel tiefgreifend verändert. Vgl. Di Mauro, Leonardo/Vitolo, Leonardo: Breve storia di Napoli, Ospedaletto 2006, und Alisio, Giancarlo: *Napoli e Risanamento: Recupero di una struttura urbana*, Neapel 1980.

8 Die Via Marina entlang des Hafens und der Ostteil Neapels wurden einer Reihe von Stadtentwicklungsplänen unterzogen, die für eine Belebung und neue Verbindungen in die Vorstädte sorgen sollten.

9 Vgl. Viollet-le-Duc, Eugène: *La civilisation de l'art*, Paris 1863, in italienischer Übersetzung: *Le civiltà dell'arte*, Rom 2014.

Throughout its long process of transformation, the ancient city has made this incessant change and the consequent cyclical return to what endures—an *anacyclosis*—the occasion to define a peculiar expression, while at the same time building houses through continuous adaptations, demonstrating a certain resilience toward unexpected changes. Except in the cases of some catastrophes, whose traces are still visible[7] in some parts of the city undergoing redevelopment,[8] this condition of contemporaneity between interconnected pasts is what conjures the atmosphere of the city. There, an almost biological necessity prevails to continue the work of modification of the city, reworking the existing human legacy.

The evolution of the buildings in the ancient city often originated not so much from centralized initiatives or planning committees, but rather from a collective will to change, turning Naples into an experimental ground for anonymous builders, craftspeople—in a sense, architects themselves—who autonomously took up the challenge of improving their living conditions. The result was an imperfect order, seemingly outside the law, but containing fragments of architectural excellence that had coexisted for centuries. Nevertheless, as Eugène Viollet-le-Duc reminds us, art remains independent of the level of civilization achieved by a people.[9] While Naples is still remembered today for the lawlessness of some of its population, this artistic tendency unfolded in the palimpsest of the ancient center of the city, through a "*Kunstwollen*, a will to form, distinct from the daily 'technique' of surviving in the urban fabric."[10] Indeed, the natural evolution of the city has often developed outside the boundaries of norms and laws, both as a survival technique and as an architectural culture in its own right. A will to form that has evolved without shared predetermined intentions as if the city were indeed a living, growing organism, more akin to nature than to built works. It was an urban workshop, established from the outset out of informal building practices, where place and life of its inhabitants are inseparable characters of a fixed scene, asserting that "mind takes form in the city; and in turn, urban forms condition mind."[11]

At the heart of this urban configuration lies the Neapolitan palazzo, the fundamental architectural unit

7 The Risanamento urban renewal project from 1885, World War II, and the earthquake of 1980 were all defining moments of transformation of the city. See Leonardo Di Mauro and Leonardo Vitolo, *Breve storia di Napoli* (Ospedaletto, 2006) and Giancarlo Alisio, *Napoli e il Risanamento: Recupero di una struttura urbana* (Naples, 1980).

8 The street along the port, Via Marina, and the eastern part of Naples have been subject to a series of redevelopment plans for activities and new connections with the suburbs.

9 See Eugène Viollet-le-Duc, "La civilisation de l'art", in *Entretiens sur l'architecture* (Paris, 1863).

10 Massimo Cacciari, "Non potete massacrarmi Napoli!" in *La città porosa*, ed. Claudio Velardi (Naples, 1992), 157.

11 Lewis Mumford, *The Culture of Cities* (London, 1938), 5.

urbanen Struktur geschieden ist",[10] diese künstlerische Neigung heraus. Die Stadt hat sich tatsächlich oft jenseits des gesetzlichen und normativen Rahmens weiterentwickelt, sowohl als eine Frage des Überlebens wie als Ausdruck einer architektonischen Kultur. Als Formwille, der sich ohne gemeinsame, vorher festgelegte Absichten herausgebildet hat, so als wäre die Stadt wirklich ein lebendiger wachsender Organismus, eher der Natur verwandt als etwas von Menschenhand Gebautem. Sie entwickelte sich von Anfang an aus informellen Baupraktiken, als urbane Werkstatt, in der Ort und Leben der BewohnerInnen voneinander nicht zu trennende Bestandteile einer festen Szenerie sind – wie zur Bestätigung, dass „der Geist in der Stadt Form annimmt; und umgekehrt urbane Formen den Geist prägen."[11]

Herzstück dieser urbanen Ordnung ist der neapolitanische Palazzo als grundlegende architektonische Einheit, die das Geflecht der Stadt durchzieht. Er stammt von ungenannten Architekten,[12] aber sie haben die Geografie von Neapels Altstadt definiert, indem sie ihr baulich Großzügigkeit eingeschrieben und vermittelt haben. Diese lässt sich an den vielen ungeplanten Freiräumen in der dicht bebauten Stadt ablesen, die sich zu Laboratorien ordnen, in denen sich kollektives Leben und Zusammensein ungezwungen entfalten und ineinander übergehen kann: *androni* [Hauseingänge], Innenhöfe, Treppen, Treppenabsätze, Verbindungsgänge, Terrassen, ummauerte Gärten, kleine Plätze, *fondaci*.[13] Orte, an denen Wandel und Zufall einen Platz haben. Als nutzlose Räume bar jeglichen rationalen oder optimierenden Zwecks scheinen sie nur dazu bestimmt zu sein, ihre zukünftige Transformation zu erleichtern, weil sie sich allem Wollen der EinwohnerInnen gegenüber als offen erweisen. Reiner, unverdorbener Raum, der von jenen, die ihn einst bewohnten, als notwendig empfunden wurde, als unabdingbar für das Gelingen und den Vollzug des Lebens.

10 Cacciari, Massimo: „Non potete massacrarmi Napoli!", in Velardi, Claudio (Hg.): *La città porosa*, Neapel 1992, 157 [dt. im Original].
11 Mumford, Lewis: *The Culture of Cities*, London 1938, 5.
12 Namentlich bekannt und erforscht sind nur wenige, die meisten aus der Zeit des Barocks. Vgl. Blunt, Anthony: *Neapolitan Baroque and Rococo Architecture*, London 1975.
13 „Fondaci" bezeichnet schmale lange mittelalterliche Gassen in einer insula mit offenem Zugang zur Hauptstraße. Hier wurden auch Waren gelagert und gehandelt. Im dicht bevölkerten Neapel wurden die fondaci nach und nach in Wohn- und Geschäftsgebäude umgewandelt. Während des Risanamento wurden sie wegen ihres schlechten Erhaltungszustandes größtenteils beseitigt; heute sind nur noch wenige erhalten. Eine genaue, wenngleich etwas oberflächliche Betrachtung der Lebensumstände im Neapel des ausgehenden 19. Jahrhunderts bietet Serao, Matilde: *Il ventre di Napoli*, Mailand 1884.

composing the city fabric. It was built by nameless architects[12] who defined the geography of the ancient center of Naples by absorbing and transmitting generosity through construction. This is measurable in the high number of open spaces, which appear, as they are unplanned, within the dense built city, configuring themselves as laboratories where collective living, being together, unfolds informally, flowing one within the other: *androni*, courtyards, stairs, landings, corridors, terraces, protected inner gardens, small squares, *fondaci*.[13] Places available to accommodate change and chance. Useless spaces, absolutely devoid of any rationalized or optimizing intent, these spaces seem solely inclined to further facilitate their own future transformation, as they were open to any will of the inhabitants. Units of pure, uncorrupted space, understood as necessary by those who lived in them, mandatory for life to happen and be realized.

Androne, corte, scala: The Palazzo as Primer

"Seen from a height not reached by the cries from below [Naples] lies deserted in the dusk, grown into the rock,"[14] wrote Walter Benjamin and Asja Lacis, observing Naples from the heights of the San Martino hill, where the flat roofs of the palazzi seem to sketch an inscrutable and abstract pattern of forms, as mineral and hostile as a crumbling volcanic stone. The city "is based on an extraordinary harmony between natural and built geography,"[15] almost as if the original geological sediment had found a new layer, similar to the pyroclastic flows of the Vesuvius eruptions,[16] and was stratified into the buildings that make up

12 Few are actually known and studied, and if so, mainly from the late Baroque. See Anthony Blunt, *Neapolitan Baroque and Rococo Architecture* (London, 1975).
13 The term *fondaci* denotes a medieval narrow and elongated street inside an insula with an open entrance to the main street. It was used for the storage of goods and as a trading area. In Naples, over time, they were gradually transformed into residential and commercial buildings due to the high population density. During the *Risanamento*, the fondaci were largely eliminated due to their deteriorating conditions; today only a few examples exist. For a precise and somewhat crude description of living conditions in Naples in the late nineteenth century, see Matilde Serao, *Il ventre di Napoli* (Milan, 1884).
14 Walter Benjamin and Asja Lacis, "Naples" (1924), in Walter Benjamin, *Reflections: Essays, Aphorisms, Autobiographical Writings*, ed. Peter Demetz, trans. Edmund Jephcott (New York and London, 1986), 165.
15 Francesco Venezia, "Il deserto, il corpo, il sottosuolo," in Velardi, *La città porosa* (see note 10), 11.
16 The volcanic eruptions of Mount Vesuvius have been a recurring theme in the pictorial representation of the city and have influenced the architecture of the city, particularly during the Baroque period. See Roberto Pane, *Architettura dell'età Barocca in Napoli* (Naples, 1939) and Gaetana Cantone, *Napoli Barocca* (Bari, 1992).

Palazzo in via Atri, Napoli, 2023 © Gianluca Piccolo

Palazzo in via Atri, Napoli, 2023 © Gianluca Piccolo

Androne, corte, scala.
Der Palazzo als Lehrstück

„Aus der Höhe, wo die Rufe nicht heraufdringen, vom Castell San Martino gesehen, liegt [Neapel] in der Abenddämmerung ausgestorben, ins Gestein verwachsen“[14], schrieben Walter Benjamin und Asja Lacis über den Anblick der Stadt von oben, bei dem sich die Flachdächer der Palazzi zu einem Muster abstrakter Formen vereinen, so mineralisch und abweisend wie bröckelndes Vulkangestein. Die Stadt „beruht auf einer außergewöhnlichen Verbindung von natürlicher und gebauter Geografie“[15], so als hätte das ursprüngliche geologische Sediment durch etwas, das den pyroklastischen Strömen nach den Vesuvausbrüchen[16] vergleichbar ist, eine neue Schicht erhalten, das sich als Gebäude abgelagert und zum historischen Geflecht der Stadt verbunden hat. Einer Stadt, die vor allem aus Häusern und Klöstern besteht.[17]

Im 15. Jahrhundert hat sich der Typus des neapolitanischen Palazzo mit seinen wesentlichen Gestaltungsmerkmalen durchgesetzt und die *insulae* aus der Zeit der Stadtgründung durchdrungen.[18] Der neapolitanische Palazzo zeichnet sich typischerweise durch seine Gedrungenheit und Kompaktheit aus und weist im Zentrum eine freie Fläche auf, die sich nahtlos in das urbane Geflecht einfügt und mit dem umliegenden Straßenraum in ein dynamisches Verhältnis tritt. Diese architektonische Vorkehrung ermöglicht es diesen Bauten, sich flexibel an neue Sitten und Gebräuche seiner BewohnerInnen anzupassen. Es gehört zu ihren baulichen Eigenarten, dass sie auf wichtige Themen wie die der Resilienz und der Selbstregulierung Antworten finden und Jahrhunderte überdauern, ohne bei kleineren Anpassungen an neue Bedingungen ihre Typologie zu verwässern.

Von der Höhe der Straße bis in die Innenräume entfaltet sich der neapolitanische Palazzo als eine Raumfolge, dessen feste Bestandteile kunstvoll umgestaltet werden. Der *androne*, der Torgang, ist ein überdachter Hauseingang mit Gewölbe, der Straße und Innenhof verbindet und den BewohnerInnen als Zugang zu ihren Wohnungen dient. Seine Größe steht oft im Verhältnis zur Gebäudetiefe des Palazzo, d.h., er bemisst sich nach der Entfernung zwischen Straßenfront und Hoffront. Dennoch besteht zwischen der Gesamtgröße des Palazzo und der *androne*

14 Benjamin, Walter/Lacis, Asja: „Denkbilder“, zitiert nach Benjamin, Walter: *Gesammelte Schriften*. Band IV-1, Frankfurt am Main 1980, 309.

15 Venezia, Francesco: „Il deserto, il corpo, il sottosuolo“, in: Velardi: *La città porosa* (wie Anm. 10), 11.

16 Die Ausbrüche des Vesuvs sind ein wiederkehrendes Thema in der bildlichen Darstellung Neapels und haben die Architektur der Stadt vor allem in der Zeit des Barock beeinflusst. Pane, Roberto: *Architettura dell'età Barocca in Napoli*, Neapel 1939, und Cantone, Gaetana: *Napoli Barocca*, Bari 1992.

17 Vgl. Hills, Helen: *Invisible City: The Architecture of Devotion in Seventeenth-Century Neapolitan Churches*, Oxford 2004.

18 Vgl. Ferraro, Italo: *Napoli: Atlante della Città Storica; Centro antico*, Neapel 2002.

the historic fabric of the city. A city mainly consisting of houses and monasteries.[17]

It was in the fifteenth century that the type of the palazzo consolidated in Naples in its fundamental characteristics of arrangement, effectively saturating the *insulae* of the city's foundation.[18] Typically characterized by compactness and density, the Neapolitan palazzi feature a central void that seamlessly integrates into the urban fabric, fostering a dynamic relationship with the surrounding street space. This architectural forethought has enabled these structures to adapt adeptly to the evolving customs and behaviors of their inhabitants. They encapsulate spatial characteristics responding to urgent themes such as resilience and self-adjustment, persisting over centuries without compromising their clear typology in favor of subtle adjustments to accommodate changing conditions.

From street level to interior spaces, the Neapolitan palazzo unfolds as a spatial sequence wherein fixed elements are artfully reconfigured. The *androne*, the entryway, serves as a vaulted covered passageway connecting the street to the courtyard and guiding the inhabitants as they ascend to the house. Its size often corresponds to the structural span of the palazzo, that is, the exact distance between the street front and the courtyard front. Nevertheless, there is no direct correlation between the overall size of the palazzo and the dimensions of the *androne*. In fact, many smaller palazzi allocate only half of their ground floor surface to the entryway.[19] The courtyard, a void within the solid stone construction, serves the dual purpose of providing light and ventilation to lower floors, while facilitating social interactions within the palazzo. These courtyards, distinguished by varying geometries and physical attributes, collectively form an array of private spaces that engage in dialogue, defining a distinctive presence within the urban framework. This resultant space embodies both communal and intimate dimensions.

“Tenement blocks of six or seven stories, with staircases climbing their foundations, appear against the villas as skyscrapers,”[20] Benjamin and Lacis noted, underlying how, in the ancient city, the longing for a vertical extrusion of the floors is a rule that finds no exception. The staircase, a recurring element in palazzi, transcends mere functionality to become an architectural space capable of mediating between the collective and private spheres. By regulating the vertical articulation of facades and harmonizing differences in floor levels, the staircase contributes to the cohesive morphological character of the entire structure.

17 See Helen Hills, *Invisible City: The Architecture of Devotion in Seventeenth-Century Neapolitan Convents* (Oxford, 2004).

18 See Italo Ferraro, *Napoli: Atlante della Città Storica; Centro antico* (Naples, 2002).

19 See the map “Mappa topografica della città di Napoli e de' suoi contorni” (Topographical Map of the City of Naples and Its Surroundings) by Giovanni Carafa Duca di Noja from 1775.

20 Benjamin and Lacis, “Naples” (see note 14), 165.

keine unmittelbare Korrelation. Viele kleinere Palazzi weisen dem Hauseingang sogar nur weniger als die Hälfte der gesamten Erdgeschossfläche zu.[19] Der *corte* [Innenhof] ist eine freie ummauerte Fläche inmitten des Bauwerks und hat die doppelte Funktion, die unteren Stockwerke mit Licht und Frischluft zu versorgen und zugleich die soziale Interaktion zwischen den BewohnerInnen des Palazzo zu erleichtern. Diese Höfe, die sich in Gestalt und baulicher Ausprägung unterscheiden, bilden eine Anordnung von Privaträumen, die miteinander in Dialog stehen und eine charakteristische Präsenz im Stadtgefüge definieren. Das resultierende Raumgefüge verkörpert beide Dimensionen, die des Gemeinschaftlichen und des Privaten.

„Mietskasernen mit sechs und sieben Stockwerken, auf Untergründen, an denen Treppen herauflaufen, erscheinen gegen die Villen als Wolkenkratzer",[20] bemerkten Benjamin und Lacis und unterstrichen damit, dass in der Altstadt der Wunsch nach vertikaler Ausdehnung der Stockwerke vorherrscht. Als ein wiederkehrendes Element in Palazzi ist die *scala* [Treppe] nicht auf ihre bloße Funktion zu reduzieren, sondern wird zum architektonischen Raum, der in der Lage ist, zwischen den Sphären des Öffentlichen und Privaten zu vermitteln. Indem die Treppe den vertikalen Ausdruck von Fassaden reguliert und die Unterschiede zwischen den Stockwerkshöhen ausgleicht, trägt sie zu einem zusammenhängenden morphologischen Charakter des gesamten Gebäudes bei. Üblicherweise als Treffpunkt für die BewohnerInnen konzipiert, ist die Treppe ein Ort, an dem man sich begegnet und Erfahrungen teilt, ehe man sich in die relative Ruhe seiner Wohnung zurückzieht. In ihrer unnötig großzügigen Dimensionierung und der zwecklosen Vergeudung von Wohnraum wird die neapolitanische Treppe, die nur für wenige NutzerInnen gedacht ist, ihrer entscheidenden Funktion, Zugang zu höhergelegenen Stockwerke zu bieten, enthoben und lässt sich als *useless*, als nutzloser Raum par excellence verstehen.

Ist man die Treppe bis oben hinaufgestiegen, erreicht man eine Abfolge von ineinander verschachtelten Räumen, die in weitere, im Inneren des Hauses verborgene Räume eingebettet sind. Die Maße dieser verbundenen Wohnräume hängen von den baulichen Möglichkeiten ab, die in der jeweiligen Bauzeit gegeben waren. Folglich erstreckt sich jeder Raum über die jeweilige Länge des Baus und erzeugt ein ununterbrochenes Kontinuum von Räumen, für die gemischte Nutzungen und Tätigkeiten charakteristisch sind: Man soll durch einen Raum gehen, um den anderen zu erreichen. In diesem dynamischen Setting kann jeder Raum mühelos einer Vielzahl von Funktionen dienen, wodurch eine wandlungs- und anpassungsfähige Umgebung entsteht.

Die von der palazzotypischen Raumfolge *androne-Hof-Treppe* geschaffene Atmosphäre – als „Stufen der

19 Venezia: „Il deserto, il corpo, il sottosuolo" (wie Anm. 15).

20 Benjamin/Lacis: „Denkbilder" (wie Anm. 14), 309.

Typically designated as a meeting place for residents, it serves as a venue for encounters and shared experiences before inhabitants retreat to the relative tranquility of their dwellings. For the gratuitous generosity in the proportions, and for the unnecessary waste of livable space destined to a few passersby, the Neapolitan staircase, taken out of its essential role of bringing walkers to upper floors, can be deemed a *useless* space par excellence.

Having walked up the staircase, the ascent culminates in a succession of rooms nested within rooms, ensconced in the interiors of the house. The dimensions of these interconnected living spaces are dependent upon the structural possibilities prevalent during their respective construction periods. Consequently, each room occupies the entirety of a typical structural span, creating an uninterrupted continuum of spaces characterized by mixed uses and activities: one should cross a room to reach the other one. In this dynamic setting, any room readily accommodates a diverse array of functions, fostering an environment of versatility and adaptability.

The atmosphere conjured by the *androne*-courtyard staircase—as "levels of intimacy"[21] within the palazzo—survives resiliently to this day. While examples of living matter in ongoing evolution, the species of diverse and multiple staircases encountered in the ancient city are a feature that each palazzo embodies in a specific way, based on whether they were built ex novo or as a result of renovations or expansions; and their geometry and spatial configuration can be read according to the evolution of their plan in the historical modifications.[22] Well before the Renaissance—of which very few traces survive in Naples[23]—certain iterations of this typology have birthed some of the city's most captivating structures, driven by the quest for architectural extraordinariness. As a matter of fact, the city's residents have developed the skill to harness and integrate these extraordinary elements into their daily lives.

Ordinary Elements, Exceptional Features: Staircases within the Palazzi

Indeed, the staircase is the physical locus in the Neapolitan palazzo, where private dwelling and communal living intersect. The extraordinariness of these structures represents an exception within the panorama of Italian cities. Yet for Neapolitans, staircases are more than a simple monumental architectural feature to preserve; instead, they serve as both an extension of the city within the courtyard and an extension of the home outside the door.

From the interior, a *domesticating* attitude toward other parts of the building unfolds with precise intrusions,

21 Peter Zumthor, *Atmospheres* (Basel, 2006), 49.

22 See Lidia Savarese, *Il centro antico di Napoli: Analisi delle trasformazioni urbane* (Naples, 1991).

23 See Di Mauro and Vitolo, *Breve Storia di Napoli* (see note 7).

Intimität“[21] innerhalb des Palazzo – besteht allen Widerständen zum Trotz bis heute fort. Wie etwas Lebendiges in einem evolutionären Prozess sind die vielen unterschiedlichen Treppenarten, denen man in Neapels Altstadt begegnet, ein Charakteristikum, das jeder Palazzo auf spezifische Weise verkörpert, je nachdem ob sie neu erbaut wurden oder Resultat von Umbauten oder Renovierungen sind; und die Maße und die Raumkomposition lassen sich vor dem Hintergrund der Evolution ihres Plans durch historische Veränderungen lesen.[22] Noch vor der Renaissance, von der sich in Neapel nur wenige Zeugnisse erhalten haben,[23] brachten Iterationen dieser Typologie einige der faszinierendsten Gebäude der Stadt hervor, deren Entstehen von einem Streben nach architektonischer Außergewöhnlichkeit begünstigt wurde. Tatsächlich haben die NeapolitanerInnen die Fähigkeit entwickelt, diese außergewöhnlichen Elemente in ihr tägliches Leben einzubinden und zu nutzen.

Gewöhnliche Bestandteile, außergewöhnliche Charakteristika: Treppen in Palazzi

Die Treppe ist der Ort im neapolitanischen Palazzo, an dem privates Wohnen und gemeinschaftliches Leben aufeinandertreffen. Diese außergewöhnlichen Gebilde sind eine Ausnahme im Spektrum der italienischen Städte. Doch für die NeapolitanerInnen sind Treppen mehr als nur charakteristische Architekturdenkmäler, die zu bewahren sind; sie sind außerdem sowohl eine Erweiterung der Stadt hinein in den Innenhof als auch eine Erweiterung des Zuhauses bis hinaus vor die Tür.

Mit präzisen Einbauten, Anbauten, angestückeltem Bodenbelag und Mauergips, Pflanzen, Möbeln und allgegenwärtigen Stühlen greift ein *domestizierendes* Verhalten aus dem Inneren heraus auf die anderen Gebäudeteile über: Die Eingriffe, mit denen die BewohnerInnen jahrhundertelang die Monumentalität der Treppen modifiziert haben, waren notwendige Interventionen, um die *Großartigkeit* der Proportionen zu zähmen, ihren Maßstab zu reduzieren, sie mit Blicken erfassbar und mit Händen spürbar zu machen. Die damit vorgenommene *Reduzierung* wird vor allem durch die Veränderung des Raumcharakters bewirkt: In Neapel *demontiert* sich das Monumentale Stück für Stück selbst und wird auf Raumfolgen mit einem menschlichen Maß heruntergebrochen, die Schutz und Richtung geben, leiten, und dadurch werden sinnlich erfahrbare Schwellenräume, Öffnungen und unerwartete Kehren offengelegt, ohne die vorgefasste Absicht zu beeindrucken und in die schwindelerregenden Höhen über der Stadt zu führen.[24] Diese Veränderung des Raumcharakters ergibt sich „aus der langen Geschichte [Neapels] und dem,

21 Zumthor, Peter: *Atmosphären*, Basel 2006, 49.
22 Vgl. Savarese, Lidia: *Il centro antico di Napoli: Analisi delle trasformazioni urbane*, Neapel 1991.
23 Vgl. Di Mauro/Vitolo: *Breve storia di Napoli* (wie Anm. 7).
24 Vgl. Pane, Roberto: *Napoli Imprevista*, Turin 1949.

additions, newly added patches of pavement and wall plaster, plants, furniture, and the ubiquitous chairs: modifications to the monumental state of the staircases, which over the centuries have been injected by the inhabitants with interventions necessary to tame the grandeur of the proportions, reduce its scale, manage it with the eyes, and feel it with the hands. This operation of reduction primarily occurs through the modification of its character: in Naples, the monumental dismantles itself, piece by piece, and is diluted into reassuring spatial sequences that protect and direct, guide, reveal sensual thresholds, openings, and unexpected turns without the predetermined intention to amaze, toward dizzying heights that tower above the city.[24] This modification of character lies “in [the city of Naples's] long history and in what its form is able to express about that history in its constant and progressive definition and adaptation to daily life, ultimately becoming ... an irreplaceable element of our own identity.”[25]

Over the centuries, symmetry has been corrupted by additions and shifts that alter its focus; new elevators, like foreign bodies, cling to the entablatures and ornaments to end onto the landings of the staircases; cantilevered rooms, produced by unknown bricoleurs, generate a complex section, with one prevailing over the other. The eloquence of the building's original appearance is lost and hybridized. The palazzo is the expression of itself, but also of its history, devoid of a single author, instead reflecting a composite outcome of an ongoing process: “In such corners one can scarcely discern where building is still in progress and where dilapidation has already set in. For nothing is concluded.”[26]

This is the case of Palazzo di Nerone, inserted between the two Roman arches from 62 AD incorporated on the *insula*'s exterior walls, which still define an extraordinary threshold space as it has been for more than two thousand years. The palazzo is balanced between two courtyards of different sizes, held together by an unusual staircase, seemingly too monumental. Around these two voids gather different houses in terms of size and surface area, followed by a series of adjacent spaces, enabled by small ramps, uneven pavements, and degraded patinas that inform their character: spaces that resist the constriction of functions that time will eventually incorporate into the building. Access to the apartments is possible through an octagonal staircase, the generosity of its spaces seeming

24 See Roberto Pane, *Napoli Imprevista* (Turin, 1949).
25 Giorgio Grassi, “Il carattere degli edifici,” *Casabella* 722 (2004).
26 Benjamin and Lacis, “Naples” (see note 14), 166.

was ihre Form über diese Geschichte der fortwährenden Neubestimmung und Anpassung an den Alltag auszudrücken vermag, wodurch sie letztlich … ein unverzichtbarer Bestandteil unserer Identität wird."[25]

Über Jahrhunderte wurden Symmetrien durch Anbauten und Perspektivwechsel zerstört; wie Fremdkörper klammern sich neue Aufzüge an das Gebälk und an Ornamente, um an Treppenabsätzen zu enden; von unbekannten *bricoleurs* geschaffene Auskragungen verursachen komplexe Staffelungen, die einander überlagern. Die Beredtheit der ursprünglichen Gebäudegestalt geht verloren und wird hybridisiert. Der Palazzo ist Ausdruck *seiner selbst* wie seiner Geschichte, er hat nicht einen Erbauer, sondern gibt das zusammengesetzte Ergebnis eines fortwährenden Prozesses wieder. „In solchen Winkeln erkennt man kaum, wo noch fortgebaut wird und wo der Verfall schon eingetreten ist. Denn fertiggemacht und abgeschlossen wird nichts."[26]

Dies ist beim Palazzo di Nerone der Fall, der zwischen zwei römischen Bögen aus dem Jahr 62 AD in die Außenmauern der *insula* integriert wurde, die noch immer einen seit mehr als zweitausend Jahren bestehenden außergewöhnlichen Schwellenraum definieren. Es ist ein Palazzo zwischen zwei unterschiedlich großen Höfen, die von einer ungewöhnlichen, fast übertrieben monumental wirkenden Treppe zusammengehalten werden. Um diese beiden freien Plätze gruppieren sich Häuser verschiedener Größe und Grundfläche, gefolgt von einer Flucht von Räumen, die über kleine Rampen und unebene Gehwege zugänglich sind und deren verblichener Putz bröckelt: Räume, die sich funktionalistischen Beschränkungen widersetzen und die durch die *Zeit* schließlich in das Gebäude eingegliedert werden. Zugang zu den Wohnungen gewährt eine oktogonale Treppe, deren bauliche Großzügigkeit die der größeren und berühmteren Barocktreppen wachzurufen scheint.[27] Alles wirkt übereinander geschichtet, und selbst wenn die Originalelemente von den jüngeren unkontrollierten Ergänzungen verfremdet wurden, blieb die Kohärenz des architektonischen Ensembles bestehen und die Form- und Maßverhältnisse wurden bewahrt.

In diesem Beispiel fällt *uselessness* [Nutzlosigkeit] mit der *Möglichkeit von Schönheit* zusammen. Die Abwesenheit eines erkennbaren Nutzens in den Räumen des Palazzo verleitet die Betrachtenden zu der Frage: Hätte man keine kleineren Treppen, schmalere Eingänge und kleinere Höfe bauen können, um höhere Mieteinnahmen zu erzielen

25 Grassi, Giorgio: „Il carattere degli edifici", in *Casabella*, 722, 2004.
26 Benjamin/Lacis: „Denkbilder" (wie Anm. 14), 310.
27 Damit sind die bemerkenswerten, in ihrer Form an Falkenschwingen erinnernde Treppen von Ferdinando Sanfelice gemeint, darunter die Treppen des Palazzo dello *Spagnulo* und des Palazzo Sanfelice im nördlich an die Altstadt anschließenden Rione Sanità. Vgl. Ballabio, Fabrizio: „Snails and Hawkwings", in *AA Files* 69 (2014), 107-117.

to recall that of more famous and imposing Baroque staircases.[27] Everything appears stratified, and even if original elements have been contaminated by recent uncontrolled additions, nothing has managed to weaken the spatial coherence of this architectural object, which preserves proportional relationships in its dimensions and geometries.

In this case, *uselessness* coincides with the possibility of beauty. The absence of apparent utility in the spaces of the palazzo encourages observers to question: Could smaller staircases, narrower entryways, and smaller courtyards have been created to optimize rental income and available surfaces? According to Nuccio Ordine, "value … emerges independently of the ability to produce practical benefits":[28] if it remains true that one of the inherent values of architecture is ultimately its capability to produce environmental beauty in which to develop and live our lives, then the presence of useless spaces within such a dense built context can only signify a quest and longing for beauty. Architecturally, this translates into the creation of generous thresholds to accommodate different lifestyles and a self-imposed spatial syntax. The validation of this proposition lies in the resilience of these architectures to stand the test of time, for when examined today, they do not diminish in emotional power or formal interest.[29]

Free from immediate practical purposes these spaces defy descriptive categories such as functionality, typology,[30] or historiography,[31] but rather can be better described in terms of the atmospheres[32] that are legible through firsthand experience. This practice of observation has provided evidence of a tamed monumentality: the adaptation to generous spaces disarms them of their monumental burden to react to the minor alterations of the inhabitants. Need a wall? Build one. Need support for drying clothes in the sun? Extend some wires: the most essential needs of dwelling over time have contributed to making exceptionality commonplace, with spatial complexity becoming an everyday circumstance; ornament becomes a structuring part of the architectural language, and its absence causes boredom, astonishment, or indifference.

27 Reference is made to the remarkable staircases designed by Ferdinando Sanfelice with a structure resembling the wings of a hawk. Among these are the staircases of Palazzo dello Spagnuolo and Palazzo Sanfelice, located in the Rione Sanità outside the walls of the ancient city of Naples. See Fabrizio Ballabio, "Snails and Hawkwings," *AA Files* 69 (2014): 107–17.
28 Ordine, *L'utilità dell'inutile* (see note 3), 8.
29 See Dirk de Meyer, *Showpiece and Utility: Eighteenth Century Staircases* (Ghent, 2017); Dirk de Meyer, *Showpiece and Utility: More Eighteenth Century Staircases* (Ghent, 2018).
30 See Lidia Savarese, *Il centro antico di Napoli: Modelli "ricostruttivi" di palazzi* (Naples, 2002).
31 See Ferraro, "Architettura e forma urbana: Il Palazzo Napoletano," in Ferraro, *Centro Antico* (see note 18), XLVIII.
32 See Alberto Calderoni, Marianna Ascolese, and Vanna Cestarello, eds., *Anaciclosi: sguardi sulla città antica di Napoli* (Macerata, 2017).

Palazzo in via Paladino, Napoli, 2023 © Gianluca Piccolo

und die Flächennutzen zu optimieren? Laut Nuccio Ordine entsteht Wert „unabhängig davon, ob [er] einen praktischen Nutzen hat."[28] Wenn es zutrifft, dass einer der Werte, die der Architektur innewohnen, letztlich ihre Fähigkeit ist, ein Umfeld der Schönheit zu schaffen, in dem wir leben und uns entwickeln können, dann kann das Vorhandensein von nutzlosen Räumen in einer so dicht bebauten Umgebung nur ein Sehnen und Streben nach Schönheit bedeuten. Architektonisch übersetzt sich dies in die Schaffung von großzügigen Schwellenräumen, um verschiedene Lebensstile und eine selbstauferlegte räumliche Syntax miteinander zu versöhnen. Bestätigung findet diese Aussage in der Resilienz dieser Architekturen, die Zeiten überdauern, denn wenn man sie heute betrachtet, verlieren sie nichts an emotionaler Kraft oder formaler Faszination.[29]

Ohne unmittelbaren praktischen Zweck verweigern sich diese Räume deskriptiven Kategorien wie Funktionalität, Typologie[30] oder Historiografie[31] und lassen sich besser in Konzepten wie dem der Atmosphären[32] beschreiben, die sich durch persönliche Erfahrung erschließen. Diese Betrachtungsweise erbringt den Beweis für eine gezähmte Monumentalität: Ihre Anpassung an großzügige Räume *enthebt* sie von ihrer *monumentalen Last*, auf kleinere Veränderungen durch die BewohnerInnen reagieren zu müssen. Du brauchst eine Wand? Dann bau sie. Du brauchst ein Gestell, um Wäsche in der Sonne zu trocken? Spann ein paar Leinen. Diese grundlegenden Wohnbedürfnisse haben im Laufe der Zeit dazu beigetragen, das Außergewöhnliche *alltäglich* zu machen und die räumliche Komplexität zum täglichen Umstand; das Ornament wird ein Strukturelement der architektonischen Sprache, und seine Abwesenheit erzeugt Langeweile, Erstaunen oder Gleichgültigkeit. „Die Außergewöhnlichkeit einiger von ihnen nimmt sie nicht von dieser Qualität aus, offene Formen, kollektive Gestaltung, die sich in jahrtausendealten Bestand einfügt [...] Portale und Treppen, autonome Zeichen und Architektur werden in bereits bestehende formale Organismen eingebunden."[33] Es ist diese *Nonchalance*, mit der die neapolitanische Architektur ihr Streben nach Großartigkeit regelt, die überrascht und die die Altstadt weiterhin zu einer Notwendigkeit macht. Eine Lektion in Großzügigkeit für eine ortsbezogene und achtsame Designkultur.

28 Ordine: *Von der Nützlichkeit des Unnützen*, 12.
29 Vgl. de Meyer, Dirk: *Showpiece and Utility: Eighteenth-Century Neapolitan Staircases*, Gent 2017; de Meyer, Dirk: *Showpiece and Utility: More Eighteenth-Century Neapolitan Staircases*, Gent 2018.
30 Vgl. Savarese, Lidia: *Il centro antico di Napoli: Modelli „ricostruttivi" di palazzi*, Neapel 2002.
31 Vgl. Ferraro: *Centro Antico*, XLVIII (wie Anm. 18).
32 Vgl. Calderoni, Alberto/Ascolese, Marianna/Cestarello, Vanna (Hg.): *Anaciclosi: sguardi sulla città antica di Napoli*, Macerata 2017.
33 Ferraro: *Centro Antico*, XL (wie Anm. 18).

Palazzo Trabucco, Napoli, 2023 © Gianluca Piccolo

"The extraordinariness of some of them does not exempt them from this quality, open forms, a collective design that integrates with millennia-old permanence ... portals and staircases, autonomous signs and architecture, are inserted into preexisting formal organisms."[33] It is this nonchalance with which Neapolitan architecture governs the aspiration for greatness that surprises and makes the ancient city still necessary. A lesson in generosity for a situated and attentive design culture.

If monumentality implies a display of power—in the case of the palazzo, a manifestation of the families of the aristocracy—the observer prostrates before the architecture. Whether overwhelmed by its scale, struck by the weight and solemnity of its language, or engulfed by its opulence and grandeur, the inhabitants of the palazzi, subverting the performative essence of these spaces, almost ironically seek to neutralize it through a series of strategies that allow the management of proxemic distances between objects. They selectively add elements from the available repertoire: stairs, low walls, various pieces of furniture, chairs that define niches where one can sit and smoke or take advantage of the wind that blows more favorably through the staircases. In architectural terms, however, all the dimensions relate to the foot, the hand, or the arm; the generous heights are not

33 Ferraro, *Centro Antico* (see note 18), XL.

Wenn Monumentalität eine Zurschaustellung von Macht impliziert – im Fall des Palazzo wird sie von Adelsfamilien demonstriert –, dann müssen sich die Betrachtenden der Architektur unterwerfen. Ob sie von den Ausmaßen überwältigt, von der Schwere niedergedrückt, von der feierlichen Sprache zum Schweigen gebracht oder von Opulenz geblendet werden, die BewohnerInnen der Palazzi untergraben das performative Wesen dieser Räume auf geradezu ironische Weise und versuchen diese Wirkungen durch eine Reihe von Strategien zur Bewältigung der proxemischen Distanzen zwischen den Objekten zu neutralisieren. Selektiv fügen sie Elemente aus einem vorhandenen Repertoire hinzu: Treppen, niedrige Mauern, Möbelstücke, Stühle, die Nischen gestalten, um dort zu sitzen und zu rauchen oder den Wind zu genießen, der hier erfrischend durch die Treppenhäuser weht. In architektonischer Hinsicht haben diese Dinge alle ein menschliches Maß, beziehen sich auf den Fuß, die Hand oder den Arm; die großzügigen Höhen sind nicht disproportional, sondern resultieren aus der Tragkraft der gelben Tuffsteinmauern für die oberen Stockwerke und des *Piperno*, einer magmatischen Gesteinsart für den stabileren Unterbau, ergänzt von den auf langen Tragebalken ruhenden Holzböden. Die Massivität der Bauten richtet sich nach den technischen Möglichkeiten und entspricht praktisch dem menschlichen Körper vergleichbaren Maßen.

In besonderer Weise zeigt sich das an dem kleinen Palazzo di Ludovico di Bux, in dem eine Kette von Räumen einen schmalen Hof umschlingt, der so breit ist wie der Palazzoeingang; der Hauptzugang zu den Wohnungen seinerseits ist eine entkernte gotische Kapelle. Nach dem Eingang in der Breite der Spannweite des Gebäudes, die auch der Größe aller Zimmer zur Straßenseite entspricht, erreicht man die erste Treppe durch einen schmalen Zugang, der auf dem Piano nobile, der Beletage endet. Auf dieser Etage beginnt eine versteckte Treppe mit sechs parallelen Armen, die im Laufe der Zeit gebaut wurden, um die noch höheren Etagen zu erreichen und zu bewohnen, die *auf das Gebaute gebaut* wurden. Die Treppe ist gerade, steil und schmal und entspricht proportional dem Hof, zu dem sie gehört. Die kleineren Dimensionen des Palazzo sind eindeutig: Die den nutzlosen Räumen inhärente Großzügigkeit zeigt sich darin, dass Ausblicke und Perspektiven geschaffen und Licht und Luft auch in die dunkelsten Etagen dringen können.

Raum, bestimmungsmäßig das Produkt einer spezifischen Gesellschaft, scheint im neapolitanischen Palazzo einen Wendepunkt zu finden. Offenkundig eine soziale Übereinkunft, die von den BewohnerInnen in dem privaten Hof, der an die Straße angrenzt, zu ihr aber nicht wirklich offen ist, gestaltet wird. Wie der ernste Waldspaziergänger von Adolf Loos[34] wird man sich im Inneren

34 Loos, Adolf: „Architektur", in: Ders.: *Sämtliche Schriften in zwei Bänden*, hg. v. Franz Glück, Wien 1962, 302–318, hier 317.

Palazzo Ludovico di Bux, Napoli, 2023 © Gianluca Piccolo

disproportionate but result from the load-bearing capacity of the yellow tuff walls for the upper floors and piperno for the sturdier bases, complemented by wooden floors supported by long beams. The thickness of the structure is in proportion to the technological possibilities and is effectively commensurate with measurements comparable to the human body.

This is particularly evident in the small Palazzo di Ludovico di Bux, where a concatenation of spaces envelops this narrow courtyard, as wide as its entryway, which is an ancient Gothic chapel gutted to serve as the main entrance to the apartments. After the entryway, as thick as the building's span, which is the size of all the rooms facing the street, the first flight of stairs is reached through a small access point, ending at the noble floor. From this level, a hidden staircase starts, made of six parallel flights, built over time to reach ever higher levels, to inhabit levels *built upon the built*. The staircase is linear and steep, narrow and proportionate to the courtyard it belongs to. The reduced dimensions of the palazzo leave no room for hesitation: the internal generosity of useless spaces unfolds to create views, perspectives, and to allow light and air to enter even the darkest floors.

Space, intended as a product of a specific society, seems to find a breaking point in the Neapolitan palazzo. An apparent social pact managed among the inhabitants in the private space of the courtyard, adjoining the street

der Heiligkeit des häuslichen Raums bewusst. Das gilt auch heute noch: Höfe sind von starken Toren geschützte Inseln und werden von standhaften Torwächtern bewacht, die die Schwellenräume ihres Territoriums schützen, und ihre BewohnerInnen kümmern sich selbsttätig um diese Räume, verschönern sie und gestalten sie nach ihren Wünschen und Vorstellungen. Auch heute noch lassen sich die Treppen „auf einen gemeinsamen Charakter zurückverfolgen, der sich dann manifestiert, wenn der individuelle und der kollektive Ausdruck in der Architektur einander widersprechen.“[35]

Die Benjamin'sche Ambiguität.
Vorhang für den Palazzo

„Porös wie das Gestein [gelber Tuff] ist die Architektur“,[36] schrieben Benjamin und Lacis. „Bau und Aktion gehen in Höfen, Arkaden und Treppen ineinander über. In allem wahrt man den Spielraum der es befähigt, Schauplatz neuer unvorhergesehener Konstellationen zu werden. Man meidet das Definitive, Geprägte. Keine Situation erscheint so, wie sie ist, für immer gedacht“.[37] Neuere neofolkloristische Darstellungen von Neapel, das im vergangenen Jahrzehnt einen – teilweise besorgniserregenden – Tourismusboom erlebt hat, haben eine Art Dogma formuliert, das jene entkräften müssen, die lange in und mit der Stadt gelebt und sie zu ihrem Forschungsgebiet gemacht haben.

Die Porosität besteht weiterhin nur hinsichtlich des Materialaufwands; porös wie der Tuff ist der geschlossene einheitliche Stadtkörper durch die Leichtigkeit seiner Materie definiert. „Bauten werden als Volksbühne benutzt. Alle teilen sich eine Unzahl simultan belebter Spielflächen. Balkon, Vorplatz, Fenster, Torweg, Treppe, Dach sind Schauplatz und Loge zugleich ... Eine hohe Schule der Regie ist, was auf den Treppen sich abspielt.“[38] Während die Stadt poetisch verbrämt und das Theaterhafte der neapolitanischen *Verve* herausgestrichen wird, leidet die Stadt unter diesen idealisierten Darstellungen ihrer Wesensart. Beleg dafür ist der neue städtische Widerstand gegen das unaufhaltsame, von der Lokalpolitik geförderte Anschwellen der Touristenströme, das zur Vertreibung von alten Geschäften und Kunsthandwerkern führt, die dann durch etwas ersetzt werden, das sich in einer Stadt, die eine der letzten Bastionen der *Italianità* zu sein scheint,[39] besser für einen schnelleren und exotischeren Tourismus eignet. Der exotische Blick der TouristInnen auf die verwirrten Gesichter der NeapolitanerInnen, die entsetzt sind über

35 Ferraro: *Centro Antico*, XL (wie Anm. 18).
36 Benjamin/Lacis: „Denkbilder“ (wie Anm. 14), 309.
37 Ebd.
38 Ebd., 310.
39 Jones, Tobias: „The City of Imminent Doom: Why the Coolest, Edgiest TV Shows and Books Are Set in Naples,“ *The Guardian*, 25. September 2023, online unter: www.theguardian.com/artanddesign/2023/sep/25/naples-hand-of-god-elena-ferrante-gomorrah-mixed-by-erry-paradise-devils (Stand: 15. Februar 2024).

but never truly open to the street. In fact, as the somber walker in the forest identified by Adolf Loos,[34] one becomes aware of the sacredness of domestic space. This is still true today: courtyards are islands protected by thick gates, defended by steadfast gatekeepers who protect the threshold of their territory, with inhabitants who self-sufficiently take care of the spaces, embellish them, and shape them in their own image and likeness. "The staircases" still today "exhibit their traceability to a common character, which manifests when individual and collective expression contradict each other in architecture."[35]

The Benjaminian Ambiguity:
Curtain on the Palazzo

"As porous as this stone [yellow tuff] is the architecture"[36] write Benjamin and Lacis. "Building and action interpenetrate in the courtyards, arcades, and stairways. In everything, they preserve the scope to become a theater of new, unforeseen constellations. The stamp of the definitive is avoided. No situation appears intended forever."[37] Recent neofolk representations of Naples subjected to a tourist boom of the last decade—which is in part cause of concern—have defined a kind of dogma forced to be dismantled by those who have lived and experienced the city for a long time and made it territory for research.

Porosity still lives only in terms of material consumption; porous like tuff, the cohesive and uniform body of the city is defined through the subtraction of its matter. "Buildings are used as a popular stage. They are all divided into innumerable, simultaneously animated theaters. Balcony, courtyard, window, gateway, staircase, roof are at the same time stage and boxes. ... What is enacted on the staircases is a high school of stage management."[38] While veiled in poetry and by highlighting the theatricality of Neapolitan verve, the city has suffered from these idealized representations of its character. This is evident from the city's recent resistance to the unstoppable tourist influx favored by local policies, leading to the expulsion of ancient shops and artisans from the city center, replaced by activities more suitable for quick and voracious sightseeing for a city that seems to be one of the last strongholds of Italianness.[39] The exoticist gaze of tourists on the confused faces of the Neapolitans dismayed by the rapidity

34 Adolf Loos: „Architektur“, in: Ders.: *Sämtliche Schriften in zwei Bänden*, hg. v. Franz Glück, Wien 1962, 302–318, esp. 317.
35 Ferraro, *Centro Antico* (see note 18), XL.
36 Benjamin and Lacis, "Naples" (see note 14), 165.
37 Ibid., 165–166.
38 Ibid., 167.
39 Tobias Jones, "The City of Imminent Doom: Why the Coolest, Edgiest TV Shows and Books Are Set in Naples," *The Guardian*, September 25, 2023, www.theguardian.com/artanddesign/2023/sep/25/naples-hand-of-god-elena-ferrante-gomorrah-mixed-by-erry-paradise-devils, accessed February 10, 2024.

die Geschwindigkeit des vor ihren Augen stattfindenden Wandels in ihrer Stadt, ist derselbe wie der von Benjamin und Lacis, als sie die von der gleichen Unausweichlichkeit gekennzeichnete grassierende Armut und das Elend des letzten Jahrhunderts darstellten: „Nichts ist genießbar als das berühmte Trinkwasser."[40]

Benjamin und Lacis betrachten Neapel mit den Augen von faszinierten Reisenden, die von der Lage, in der die Stadt sich befindet, irritiert sind. Das Bild, das sie zeichnen, ist nicht gerade idyllisch, aber es erzählt von der *Normalität* des städtischen Lebens und einer Mischung aus Nutzungen und Räumen, die bis heute fortbesteht. Das Leben entfaltet sich auf den Straßen, den Arterien des komplexen Organismus der Altstadt und auf den Restflächen, die in Plätze umgewandelt wurden;[41] in den Palazzi herrscht ein solides häusliches, von der Außenwelt abgeschirmtes Leben vor. Die genaue Betrachtung der Palazzi offenbart die Koexistenz von Erhabenheit und Normalität, ihre poröse und für den Wandel empfängliche Architektur zeigt, wie sich Alltagsleben und ein Streben nach Üppigkeit harmonisch verbinden. Palazzi stellen konventionelle Vorstellungen von Monumentalität in Frage, indem sie der kontemplative Nutzung von Architektur als heiliger Materie, die nicht berührt und verändert werden darf, entgegenwirken. Weil sie den tiefgreifenden Einfluss normaler BewohnerInnen auf die historische gebaute Umwelt augenfällig machen, regen Palazzi zu einer Neubewertung unseres Verständnisses von architektonischer Bedeutung an und laden dazu ein, die traditionellen Grenzen zu hinterfragen, die die Wahrnehmung des Monumentalen vom Banalen trennen. Nur in den Palazzi entfaltet sich Porosität. *Androne*, *corte*, *scala*: geschützte Sequenzen, die in den sicheren Schoß des Hauses führen und damit die Gerüche und Geräusche, die Stimmen auf der Straße ausschließen. Das Stück ist zu Ende, das Portal ist der Vorhang.

Übersetzung: Sven Koch

40 Benjamin/Lacis: „Denkbilder" (wie Anm. 14), 308.
41 Vgl. Ascolese, Marianna: *Strade di Città*, Syrakus 2022.

with which the city has changed before their eyes is the same as that of Benjamin and Lacis when they portrayed the endemic poverty and misery of the early last century, and characterized by the same inescapability: "Nothing is enjoyable except the famous drinking water."[40]

Benjamin and Lacis observe Naples with the eyes of a fascinated traveler, partly confused by the situation in which the city finds itself. The image they sketch is not comforting, in fact, but it tells of the ordinariness of urban life, a mixture of uses and spaces that still exists today. It is in the streets, the arteries of the complex organism that is the ancient center, and in the residual spaces adapted as squares that life unfolds;[41] in the palazzi, instead, resides a solid domestic life well separated from the outside.

The study of the palazzi reveals the coexistence of grandeur with ordinariness. This architecture, porous and available to change, demonstrates how everyday life intertwines with an aspiration for opulence, resulting in a harmonious proximity. Palazzi challenge conventional notions of monumentality, inhibiting the contemplative use of architecture as sacred matter not to be touched or altered. It encourages a reevaluation of our understanding of architectural significance, highlighting the profound impact of the ordinary inhabitants on the historic built environment, inviting us to question the traditional boundaries that separate the perception of the monumental from the banal.

It is only in the palazzi that porosity unfolds. *Androne, corte, scala*: protected sequences that guide toward the safe womb of the house and at the same time dilute the presence of the street saturated with voices, scents and sounds. The theater closes; the portal is the curtain.

40 Benjamin and Lacis, "Naples" (see note 14), 164.
41 See Marianna Ascolese, *Strade di Città* (Siracusa, 2022).

1 Different K67 settings around the world, 2023. Left to right, top to bottom: 1–2: Belgrade © Matija Zlatanović; 3–5: Berlin © Armin Stocker; 6: Graz © Ena Kukić; 7: Houston © Dijana Handanović; 8: Novi Sad © Igor Vukičević; 9: Sarajevo © Ena Kukić; 10–11: Zadar © Ena Kukić; 12: Ljubljana © Martin Ruge; 13–14: Sarajevo © LIFT; 15: Sarajevo © Dinko Jelečević

Kiosk K67

Ein Denkmal jugoslawischen Alltagslebens
A Monument to Everyday Yugoslav Life

Ena Kukić

Im seltenen Fall eines Produkts, das gleichbedeutend mit seiner Typologie ist, sucht das Auge instinktiv nach einer freundlichen retrofuturistischen Kapsel, wenn es eine Zeitung – oder eigentlich alles Mögliche – von einem Kiosk zu besorgen gilt. So erging es jedenfalls vielen, die die rasche Entwicklung urbanen Lebens in Jugoslawien miterlebten, wo die omnipräsenten K67-Kioske die Alltagsaktivitäten stimulierten, eine Vielfalt an Funktionen im öffentlichen Raum erfüllten: als Zeitungsstände, Fahrscheinschalter, temporäre Büros, Skilifthäuschen, Blumenläden, Schuhreparatur-Pop-ups, Grenzschutzstationen, Imbissbuden – um nur einige zu nennen. Mehr als ein halbes Jahrhundert nach ihrem ersten Erscheinen beherrschen die leuchtend bunten Kioske noch immer vielfach das Straßenbild, nicht nur in Ex-Jugoslawien, sondern in weiten Teilen der Welt, wobei sie manchmal mit neuen Funktionen, manchmal durch ihren Verfall gegenwärtige sozioökonomische und lokale Verhältnisse spiegeln. Mit ihrem überaus menschlichen Maß – eine K67-Einheit hat eine Grundfläche von etwa fünf Quadratmetern bei zweieinhalb Metern Höhe – und ihrem heiteren, farbenfrohen Aussehen – einer markanten Box mit gerundeten Kanten und auskragenden Öffnungen oder Wänden – vermittelten diese Objekte stets eine einladende, nachbarschaftliche Atmosphäre, dienten als Treffpunkte in gemeinschaftlichen Räumen. Mit ihrer modularen Anlage, deren Elemente sowohl als einzelne Einheiten funktionieren wie auch endlos kombinierbar sind, ermöglichten sie kleinen, aufstrebenden Unternehmen während des wirtschaftlichen Aufbruchs in Jugoslawien eine Geschäftspräsenz auf der Straße.

Entworfen vom jugoslawischen Architekten Saša Mächtig,[1] wurde der Kiosk 67 ab 1968 drei Jahrzehnte lang in Masse produziert. Er versuchte, funktionale Flexibilität

1 Saša Mächtig lebt und arbeitet in Ljubljana und wird im heutigen geografischen Kontext oft als slowenischer Architekt bezeichnet. Seine Arbeit ist allerdings eng mit den soziopolitischen Gegebenheiten Jugoslawiens verbunden und auch davon beeinflusst, sodass er mit Recht als „jugoslawischer Architekt" betitelt werden kann.

In the exceptional case of a product becoming synonymous with its typology, the eyes impulsively seek a bright retrofuturist capsule when going to get newspapers—or anything, really—from any kiosk anywhere. This is the case for many who had actively experienced rapidly evolving urban life in Yugoslavia, where omnipresent K67 kiosks generated everyday activity, housing a myriad of functions in public space: newspaper stands, ticket shops, temporary offices, ski-lift booths, flower stalls, shoe repair pop-ups, border patrol stations, fast-food stands—to name but a few. More than half a century after they came to life, these vibrant cubicles still dominate numerous streetscapes, not only in post-Yugoslav geographical space but far and wide throughout the world, reflecting the contemporary socioeconomic currents and local context wherever they stand—sometimes with new functions, other times by their own state of decay. With their rather human scale—a single K67 unit has a footprint of around 5 square meters, at a total height of 2.5 meters—and their friendly, colorful appearance, taking the form of a distinctive fillet-edge box with outward-protruding walls, these objects have consistently conveyed a neighborly and inviting atmosphere, serving as focal points in communal spaces. Functioning like building blocks that can exist as single units or in endless combinations, they allowed small, thriving businesses during the Yugoslav economic awakening to establish a retail presence in the streets.

Kiosk 67 was designed by the Yugoslav architect Saša Mächtig[1] and from 1968 onward mass-produced over three decades. It aimed to address the necessity of functional flexibility in different public environments and also in the workspace.[2] K67 enabled growth through the addition

1 Saša Mächtig is based in Ljubljana, and in today's geographical context, he is often described as a Slovenian architect. However, his work is heavily influenced by and intricately connected to the Yugoslav sociopolitical context, which justifies referring to him as a "Yugoslav architect."

2 See Saša Mächtig, "Fenomeni v urbanskem okolju," *Kontakti* 1 (1977), 4–19.

an verschiedenen öffentlichen Räumen, aber auch in Bezug auf das Raumvolumen herzustellen.[2] Der K67 ermöglichte Wachstum durch Hinzufügung standardisierter Module und reagierte damit auf das politische und ökonomische Klima der 1960er-Jahre, deren Dezentralisierungspolitik den sechs Republiken Jugoslawiens größere Autonomie gewährte und zum Teil Marktkräfte als neues objektives System der Produktionsregulierung zuließ.[3] Dank dieser Reformen, aber auch der raschen Urbanisierung kam es zu einem Aufschwung des privaten Kleinunternehmertums und einem zunehmenden Bedarf an flexiblen und leistbaren Verkaufsräumen.

Mächtigs Ansatz zur Schaffung solcher Räume war stark von seiner Ausbildung an der Architekturfakultät der Akademie der Bildenden Künste in Ljubljana beeinflusst, wo er den berühmten, in den frühen 1960er-Jahren von Edvuard Ravnikar angebotenen B-Kurs besuchte, in dem großer Wert auf experimentelle Forschung und vom Bauhaus inspirierte Gestaltungsprinzipien gelegt wurde. Während dieser Zeit führten Mächtigs Experimente mit der Kreuzung zweier Plastikröhren zur Schaffung des flexiblen Konstruktionssystems K67, das endlose Kombinationsmöglichkeiten standardisierter geometrischer Formen eröffnete. Die Designlandschaft Jugoslawiens war in den

2 Vgl. Mächtig, Saša: „Fenomeni v urbanskem okolju", *Kontakti* 1 (1977), 4–19.
3 Vgl. Rebernjak, Rujana: „Designing Self-Management: Objects and Spaces of Everyday Life in Post-War Yugoslavia", PhD Diss., Royal College of Art, London 2018.

of standardized modular elements and responded to the distinct political and economic climate of the 1960s, where the Yugoslav policy of decentralization gave greater autonomy to the six individual republics and introduced partial market forces as a new, objective system of regulating production.[3] Due to these market reforms, as well as rapid urbanization, small private entrepreneurship began to thrive, and the need for flexible and affordable retail-oriented spaces became prominent.

Mächtig's approach to providing such spaces was heavily influenced by his training at the Architecture Faculty of the Ljubljana Academy of Fine Arts, where he had attended the renowned B-Course taught by Edvard Ravnikar in the early 1960s. The course placed strong emphasis on experimental research and Bauhaus design principles, and it was during this time that Mächtig's experimentation with the intersection of two plastic tubes led to the creation of the K67 flexible construction system capable of endless combinations, all based on standardized geometric forms. The design landscape in 1960s Yugoslavia was already marked by significant processes of industrialization, urbanization, and mass production, which undoubtedly influenced Mächtig's vision of developing an object that taps into both urban and industrial design scales. While previous capsule structures used as newsstands were developed with the logic of tiny houses,

3 See Rujana Rebernjak, "Designing Self-Management: Objects and Spaces of Everyday Life in Post-War Yugoslavia" (PhD diss., Royal College of Art, London, 2018).

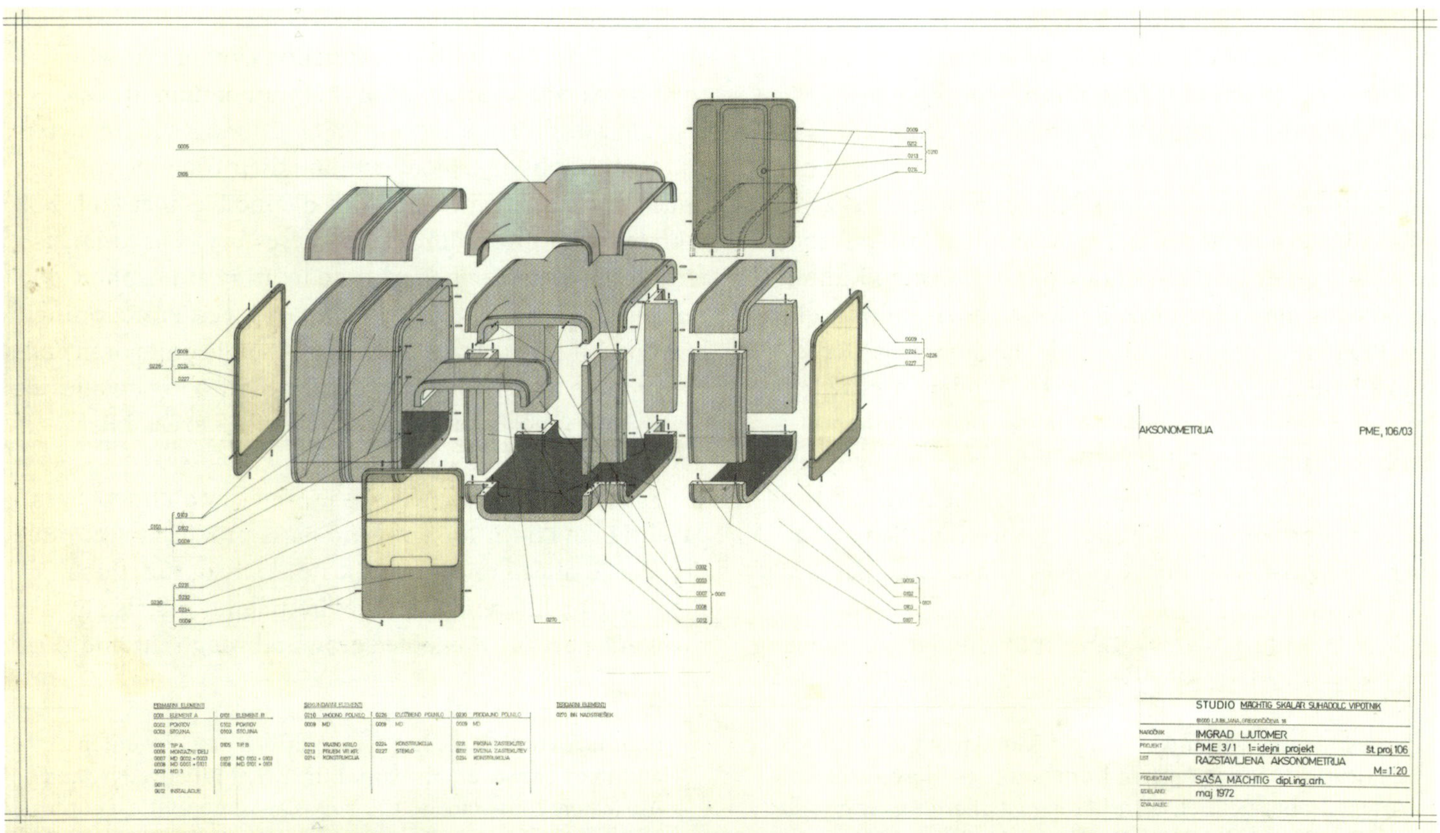

2 Exploded axonometric drawing of the second generation of the K67 from 1972.
© Museum of Architecture and Design (MAO), Ljubljana

1960er-Jahren bereits von einer signifikanten Industrialisierung, Urbanisierung und Massenproduktion gekennzeichnet, die Mächtigs Entwicklung eines Objekts, das sowohl eine urbane als auch eine industriedesignerische Dimension besitzt, zweifellos beeinflusst hat. Während frühere als Zeitungskiosk benutzte Kapselbauten mit der Logik von Tiny Houses entwickelt wurden, war der K67 konzeptuell wie konstruktiv als ein großes Industrieprodukt angelegt.

Mächtigs Materialwahl für den K67 beruhte auf früheren, für seine Diplomarbeit angestellten Forschungen zur Verwendung von verstärktem Polyester und Polyurethan für Bauzwecke. Während der ersten Produktionsjahre wurden die K67-Kioske in einem einzigen Stück gegossen. 1971 wurde das Design jedoch modifiziert und der Kiosk in zwei Teilen gefertigt – eine Änderung, die seinen Transport und seine Installation erleichtern sollte.[4] Sie war Ausdruck einer von vielen PrivatunternehmerInnen geschätzten Qualität: einfache Montage und Wartung. Am Ende bestand die Einheit aus separaten Boden- und Deckenschalen und vier Eckpfeilern (Abb. 2). Diese Komponenten dienten als Träger für sekundäre Elemente wie Türen, Verkaufsfenster, konvexe Fenster und Wandpaneele. Gelegentlich wurden auch – von Mächtig selbst entwickelte – Speziallösungen für bestimmte Funktionen eingeführt (zum Beipiel Adaptionen für die Zubereitung von Fast Food).[5]

Die von einem pragmatischen und dezidiert modernistischen Design geprägten K67- Kioske wurden vielerorts rasch zu einem integralen Bestandteil des Straßenbilds. Ihre lebhaften Farben bildeten einen harmonischen Kontrast zu den brutalistischen Bauten, akzentuierten den öffentlichen Raum. Zwar war Signalrot die häufigste Variante, doch gab es den ursprünglichen K67 auch in Grün-, Gelb- oder Weißtönen. Im Lauf der Zeit wurden einige Exemplare von ihren BesitzerInnen übermalt, um sie besser mit dem darin betriebenen Geschäft zu akkordieren, aber durch die typische skulpturale Form behielt die ursprüngliche K67-Identität immer die Oberhand. Die typologische Einbettung ins Alltagsleben sorgte für eine ständige Interaktion mit der Gesellschaft, machte die Kioske zu einem unvermeidlichen Teil vieler Routinen im öffentlichen Raum und brannte sie tief ins kollektive Gedächtnis ein.

Alles in allem hat die Fabrik Imgrad im slowenischen Ljutomer 7.500 Einheiten produziert, die in weit entfernte Länder geliefert wurden oder sich über ganz Jugoslawien verstreuten. Mit Ausnahme der Antarktis fanden sie wie Weltraum-Kapseln ihren Weg auf jeden Kontinent, wurden in Japan, Kenia, Neuseeland und den Amerikas

4 Vgl. Kinchin, Juliet: „KIOSK K67" in: Stierli, Martino/Kulić, Vladimir (Hg.), *Toward a Concrete Utopia*, Ausst. Kat., New York: The Museum of Modern Art 2018, 149.

5 Vgl. Huber, David: „The Enduring Lives of Sasa Mächtig's Modular Creations", in: *Metropolis*, 23. Februar 2017, https://metropolismag.com/profiles/the-enduring-lives-of-sasa-machtigs-modular-creations (Stand: 1. Juni 2023).

K67 was devised as a large industrial product in terms of both conceptualization and construction.

Mächtig's choice of materials for the K67 was informed by his earlier research into the structural use of reinforced polyester and polyurethane for his graduation project. During the first production years, the K67 kiosks were molded in a single monolithic piece. However, in 1971, the design was modified to divide the structure into two sections, a change made to enhance ease of transport and installation,[4] reflecting a quality that appealed to many private entrepreneurs—the simplicity of assembly and maintenance. Ultimately, the unit consisted of separate ceiling and floor shells, along with four corner posts (fig. 2). These components provided support for secondary elements, such as doors, vending and convex windows, and blind I-panels. Occasionally, special customizations were introduced to accommodate specific functions, developed by Mächtig himself (for instance, adaptations for fast-food preparation).[5]

Characterized by their pragmatic and distinctly modernist design, K67 kiosks rapidly became an integral part of numerous streetscapes. Their vibrant colors created a harmonious contrast to brutalist buildings, placing emphasis on public spaces. While the signal red appearance was the most common variant, the original K67s could also be found in shades of green, yellow, or white. Over time, some of these objects were repainted by their owners to be better aligned with the businesses they housed, but the peculiar sculptural form always ensured the dominance of the original K67 identity. Their typological embeddedness in everyday life facilitated constant interaction with society as a whole, making them an indispensable part of any habits within public space and etching them deep into collective memory.

In total, around 7,500 units were produced by the Imgrad factory in Ljutomer, Slovenia, before being transported to faraway lands or scattered throughout Yugoslavia. Not counting Antarctica, these round-edged, space-age cubes made their way to every continent, having been documented in Japan, Kenya, New Zealand, the Americas, and particularly across Europe. With their distinctive visual identity, K67 kiosks served as emblems of Yugoslavia's physical and ideological metamorphosis from a postwar Eastern Bloc state to a nonaligned utopia that provided a concrete framework for the evolution of the design field.

However, following the violent collapse of the state in the 1990s, and the widespread environmental damage that this breakup entailed, many local kiosks were left abandoned and in a state of decay, today bearing witness

4 See Juliet Kinchin, "KIOSK K67," in *Towards a Concrete Utopia*, ed. Martino Stierli and Vladimir Kulić (New York, 2018), 149.

5 See David Huber, "The Enduring Lives of Sasa Mächtig's Modular Creations," *Metropolis*, February 23, 2017, https://metropolismag.com/profiles/the-enduring-lives-of-sasa-machtigs-modular-creations (accessed June 1, 2023).

gesichtet, vor allem aber in ganz Europa. Mit ihrer starken visuellen Identität fungierten die K67-Kioske als Embleme für die physische und metaphorische Verwandlung Jugoslawiens von einem Ostblockstaat in eine blockfreie Utopie, die einen konkreten Bezugsrahmen für die Entwicklung auf dem Gebiet des Designs bildete.

Das gewaltsame Ende des Staates in den 1990er-Jahren und die vielen Umweltschäden, die der Zusammenbruch mit sich brachte, hatten zur Folge, dass in Jugoslawien viele Kioske aufgegeben wurden oder verfielen und heute an Provinzstraßen und auf Privatgrundstücken Zeugnis von der politischen Vergangenheit der Region ablegen. Einige von ihnen wurden restauriert und für verschiedene Zwecke – z. B. als Bienenstock oder Parkscheinautomat – weiterverwendet, an lokale Identitäten und zeitgenössische Bedürfnisse angepasst. Verfolgt man die Entwicklung renovierter K67-Kioske nach dem Krieg, findet man sie häufig auch in westlichen Ländern, wo sie – nicht nur wegen der geografischen, sondern auch wegen der zeitlichen Distanz und dem Verlust an historischem Wissen – völlig von ihrem ursprünglichen Kontext abgelöst wurden. Beispiele dafür sind etwa ein oranges Exemplar, das in einer trendy Cocktailbar auf dem Mont des Arts in Brüssel als DJ-Kabine genutzt wird, oder ein bunt bemaltes Exemplar für „grief rave"-Events und Minidiscos von Fandangoe Kid in London. Wenn diese retrofuturistischen Gebilde für jüngere Leute im Westen wie außerirdische Expeditionskapseln aussehen, dann weil sie es sind: Ihr jugoslawischer Hintergrund wirkt heute tatsächlich wie eine andere Welt, und ohne adäquate didaktische Aufbereitung[6] sind die K67-Kioske als kulturelles Phänomen nicht wirklich zu fassen. Darin liegt auch die Gefahr einer rein ästhetischen Würdigung. Dabei könnte nämlich übersehen werden, dass diese Kioske auch das Ergebnis sehr konkreter staatlicher Rahmenbedingungen waren, die zum Experimentieren ermunterten, Fortschritt förderten und außergewöhnliches Design in die Öffentlichkeit brachten. Zu einem weitereren Dekontextualisierungseffekt kommt es bei Museumsausstellungen des K67, seiner bloßen Betrachtung als ein besonderes Stück Industriedesign und nicht als Mitakteur im öffentlichen Leben, so dass sein nur im Kontext des geschäftigen urbanen Treibens sich entfaltendes Potenzial nicht voll gewürdigt wird.

Vor dem Hintergrund dieses Gegensatzes – der Betrachtung des K67 als Kunstobjekt und seinem Alltagsgebrauch –, ist es wichtig zu betonen, dass der Kiosk nicht als solches geplant oder produziert wurde. Eigentlich ist er eher so etwas wie ein Auto – ein massenproduzierter großer Gebrauchsgegenstand. Zwei Jahre bevor der K67 im Jahr 1972 so modifiziert wurde, dass man ihn zerlegen konnte, hatte Mächtig die Technikzentrale von General Motors in

6 Ein positives Beispiel dafür ist Dijana Handanović' Forschungs- und Ausstellungsprojekt „Kiosk K67: System for Urban Imagination" am Blaffer Art Museum der University of Houston in Texas, USA, im Januar 2023.

3 K67, Novi Sad
© Igor Vukičević

to the area's political past along provincial roads or on private property. Some have been restored and continue to serve various purposes, such as housing a beehive or an automated parking ticket machine, building upon local identities and adapting to contemporary needs. Following the trajectories of renovated K67s after the war, one often finds the kiosks in Western countries where they have become entirely detached from their original context—due not only to geographical distance but also to the passage of time and the loss of historical knowledge. Such examples include an orange unit used as a DJ booth in a trendy cocktail bar on the historic Kunstberg square in Brussels or a colorfully repainted unit for "grief rave" events and mini disco experiences by The Fandangoe Kid in London. If these retrofuturist structures look like alien expedition pods to younger generations in the West, it is because they are: their Yugoslav background does seem otherworldly now, and without providing adequate didactic material,[6] one cannot fully grasp the K67s' significance as a cultural phenomenon. Therein lies the danger of merely promoting their distinct aesthetics only: one might overlook the fact that these kiosks were also products of a very tangible, state-provided framework that encouraged experimentation,

6 A positive example of such an approach is Dijana Handanović's research project and exhibition "Kiosk K67: System for Urban Imagination" at the University of Houston's Blaffer Art Museum, Texas, USA, in January 2023.

Michigan besucht, was ihn zu neuen Einsichten in industrielle Prozesse und zum Testen von Einzelkomponenten vor ihrem Zusammenbau führte. Diese Erfahrung erwies sich nicht nur als vorteilhaft für die zweite Version des K67, sondern auch für zahlreiche weitere Produkte. Während seines Studiums bei Ravnikar hatte Mächtig auch Bekanntschaft mit dem Werk von Christopher Alexander und Kevin Lynch gemacht. Ihre Ideen beeinflussten besonders seine Auffassung von Kiosken als Knotenpunkte, die die öffentliche Aktivitiät konsolidieren und stimulieren,[7] was dazu führte, dass er seine Designbemühungen erweiterte und die Kioske durch zusätzliches Stadtmobiliar ergänzte. Nach dem Erfolg der K67-Kioske in heimischen Kommunen in den 1970er-Jahren erweiterte Mächtig sein Straßeneinrichtungssortiment um Abfalleimer, Infostände, Recycling-Behälter, öffentliche Telefonzellen und überdachte Bushaltestellen. Die meisten dieser zusätzlichen Objekte wurden erfolgreich in den öffentlichen Raum integriert, sodass eine zusammenhängende Objektfamilie entstand, die sich jeder Person erschloss und eine einheitliche visuelle Identität aufwies, die dazu einlud, mit dem umgebenden Raum zu interagieren. Immer wieder machte Mächtig mit seinem Werk deutlich, dass die Einzelelemente in erster Linie ein integraler Bestandteil eines Ganzen sein sollten – ganz im Einklang mit der Gemeinschaftsorientierung seiner Epoche.

7 Vgl. Huber: „The Enduring Lives“ (wie Anm. 5).

progress, and the accessibility of exceptional design in the public. Another issue of decontextualization comes to the fore when exhibiting K67s in a museum as an artifact, viewing them solely as an individual work of industrial design, rather than as a participant in public life, and thus not fully appreciating their potential, which exists only in the context of the bustling urban outdoors. Considering the dichotomy evident when observing the K67 as an art object in contrast to its everyday use, it is important to know that the kiosk was not envisioned or produced as such. In reality, its nature is more akin to that of a car—a mass-produced, large utilitarian object. Two years before the K67 was updated to be dismantlable in 1972, Mächtig visited General Motors' technical center in Michigan, which led to fresh insights into industrial processes and the approach of individually testing components prior to their assembly. This experience proved beneficial not only for the second edition of K67 but also for numerous products that followed. During his studies under Ravnikar, Mächtig became acquainted with the work of Christopher Alexander and Kevin Lynch. Their ideas notably influenced his perception of kiosks as central nodes that both consolidate and stimulate public activity,[7] leading him to expand his design efforts and complement the kiosks with further public furniture. Following the success of K67 kiosks in local communities in the 1970s, Mächtig augmented his collection of street equipment to include waste bins, information display cabinets, recycling containers, public phone booths, and bus stop shelter systems. Most of these additions were successfully integrated into public spaces, creating a cohesive family of objects that were accessible to everyone and that shared a unified visual identity, inviting the community to connect with the surrounding space. Time and again, Mächtig's work emphasized the significance of each self-sufficient element being firstly an integral part of the whole, reflecting the community-oriented ideology of the era.

Unlike their Western peers, for post-Yugoslav generations in the Balkans, the predominantly decaying appearance of the remaining kiosks in public spaces instantly immerses them in an era of which they have secondhand memories:[8] the era of their predecessors, whose remnants are often considered unwanted heritage in the postwar, essentially ethnonationalist political context. Many such shabby K67s still serve everyday retail needs in the Balkans but exist in sharp juxtaposition to a myriad of contemporary, well-maintained yet generic capsules that now populate public spaces while bearing no connection to the local context (fig. 3). This phenomenon reflects a lack of interest on the part of the establishment in the development—

7 See Huber, "The Enduring Lives" (see note 5).

8 Secondhand or inherited memories are the relationship that the "generation after" bears to the personal, collective, and cultural experiences of those who came before, deeply transmitted by means of the stories, images, and behaviors among which they grew up.

4 K67, Poreč © Museum of Architecture and Design (MAO), Ljubljana

Anders als ihre westlichen AltersgenossInnen werden die postjugoslawischen Generationen auf dem Balkan durch die meist im Verfall begriffenen verbleibenden Kioske im öffentlichen Raum unmittelbar in eine Ära zurückversetzt, die sie nur aus zweiter Hand erinnern:[8] die Ära ihrer Vorfahren, deren Überreste im vorwiegend ethnonationalistischen politischen Kontext der Nachkriegszeit als unerwünschtes Erbe gelten. Viele dieser schäbigen K67-Kioske dienen auf dem Balkan immer noch für Verkaufszwecke, stehen aber in scharfem Kontrast zu einer Fülle zeitgenössischer, gut erhaltener generischer Kapseln, die heute ohne jeglichen Bezug zum lokalen Kontext den öffentlichen Raum bevölkern (Abb. 3). Das spiegelt ein mangelndes Interesse seitens des Establishments an der Entwicklung – oder auch nur Erhaltung – kommunaler Räume und der Bereitstellung führenden Designs für die breite Öffentlichkeit wider. Steht im Museum die neuere Identität des Kiosks als Kunstobjekt im Mittelpunkt, bleibt sein künstlerischer Wert im lokalen öffentlichen Kontext vollkommen ungewürdigt.

Angesichts von über einem halben Jahrhundert Alltagserfahrung mit dem K67 in den unterschiedlichsten sozialen Umgebungen (zuerst in Jugoslawien, dann in den Kriegszeiten der 1990er-Jahre und in der Übergangsperiode danach), ist es wohl nur natürlich, ihn als ein grundlegendes Raumfragment der jugoslawischen kollektiven Erinnerung zu lesen. Gerade in seiner unintendierten Rolle als Ersatzdenkmal für eine bestimmte Ära strahlt der Kiosk am hellsten.[9] Die offensichtlichen architektonischen Symbole der nichtethnischen kollektiven Erinnerung, die sozialistischen Denkmäler – sogenannten Spomeniks – statt, wurden im Grunde sich selbst überlassen und aus dem sozialen Gefüge der neu gebildeten ethnisch und religiös geteilten Gesellschaften Postjugoslawiens ausgeschlossen.[10] Die K67-Kioske bestehen dagegen fort; nicht *trotz*, sondern *wegen* ihres Allerweltscharakters, ihrer Untrennbarkeit vom alltäglichen Leben verkörpern sie weiter die kollektive Identität der Gemeinschaften, in denen sie zum Leben erweckt wurden. Sie sind auch eine

8 Erinnerungen aus zweiter Hand oder ererbte Erinnerungen sind die durch die Geschichten, Bilder und Verhaltens weisen derer, mit denen sie aufgewachsen sind, tief eingeschriebenen Beziehungen nachfolgender Generation zu den persönlichen, kollektiven und kulturellen Erfahrungen ihrer VorgängerInnen.

9 Vgl. Deaver, Jes: „This Is Us: K67, More Than a Memory", in: *Texas Architect Magazine* (2023), online unter: https://magazine.texasarchitects.org/2023/07/03/this-is-us-k67-more-than-a-memory/ (Stand: 4. December 2023).

10 Das ist teilweise auf das vorherrschende politische Klima, zum Teil aber auch auf die typologische und geografische Abgelegenheit dieser Bauwerke zurückzuführen.

or even maintenance—of communal spaces and in the accessibility of forefront design to the broader public. While in a museum environment the kiosk's newer identity as an art object takes center stage, in the local public context the appreciation of its artistic value has been entirely absent.

With more than half a century of everyday user experience in very different social environments, first in Yugoslavia, followed by the war in the 1990s and the postwar transition period, reading K67 as an essential spatial fragment of the Yugoslav collective memory comes naturally. It is in its unintended role of a surrogate monument to a certain era that the K67 kiosk wears the brightest of its colors.[9] The obvious architectural symbols of nonethnic collective identity, the socialist monuments known as Spomeniks, have actually been neglected and excluded[10] from the social fabric of the newly formed, ethnically and religiously divided communities within the post-Yugoslav sociopolitical context. The K67 kiosks, however, endure—not despite but precisely because of their mundane nature, and due to their inseparability from everyday life, continuing to embody the collective identity of the communities in which they were brought to life. They also provide a subtle yet persistent rebuttal to the anti-Yugoslav propaganda that depicts the previous system as single-minded, backward, and a nemesis to private entrepreneurship. Through their mere presence, K67 kiosks evoke the nurturing of the community-building potential of public space, highlighting its coexistence with private and public property, blurring the line between the two, and pointing out the inevitable public responsibilities of private entrepreneurs,

9 See Jes Deaver, „This Is Us: K67, More than a Memory," *Texas Architect Magazine* (2023), available online at: https://magazine.texasarchitects.org/2023/07/03/this-is-us-k67-more-than-a-memory, accessed December 4, 2023.

10 This can be attributed in part to the prevailing political climate, as well as to the typologically and geographically secluded nature of these structures.

subtile und fortwährende Widerlegung der antijugoslawischen Propaganda, die das frühere System als unbeweglich, rückständig und Gegner des freien Unternehmertums hinstellt. Allein durch ihre Präsenz erinnern die K67-Kioske an das gemeinschaftsbildende Potenzial des öffentlichen Raums und heben die Koexistenz von privatem und öffentlichem Eigentum hervor, indem sie die Grenze zwischen ihnen verschwimmen lassen, auf die unvermeidliche öffentliche Verantwortung der privaten KioskbesitzerInnen verweisen und die Synergien zwischen Top-down und Bottom-up-Ansätzen in der Entwicklung öffentlicher Räume in Jugoslawien aufzeigen.

Betrachtet man die Flexibilität und ständige Weiterentwicklung der K67-Kioske im Rahmen ihrer dominanten Identität stellt sich unvermeidlich die Frage nach ihrer Zukunft. Die ständig wachsende Nachfrage nach Notunterkünften in einer kapitalistischen Welt – samt drohendem Technofeudalismus – wurde auf postjugoslawischem Boden, der immer schon eine Brücke zwischen Ost und West bildete, durch die Bedeutung von Migrationsrouten verstärkt. Mit seinen Maßen von 256,5 × 240 × 240 Zentimetern ist ein K67 mit vielen alternativen Unterkünften vergleichbar. Die slowenische Künstlerin und Stadtanthropologin Marjetica Potrč untersuchte bereits 2003 in ihrem Mixed-Media-Projekt „Next Stop Kiosk" das Potenzial des K67 als Behausung. Ausgehend von südamerikanischen Behausungen auf Stelzen und heimlichen Dachsiedlungen in Belgrad beschäftigte sie sich mit den sozialen Anforderungen in beiden Fällen.[11] Anders als in ihrer Ausstellung in der Moderna Galerija in Ljubljana, wo zwei K67-Einheiten zur öffentlichen Betrachtung ausgestellt waren, werden einige Kioske in den Sommermonaten entlang der Dalmatinischen Küstenstraße tatsächlich als Übernachtungsmöglichkeit für StraßenhändlerInnen genutzt. Schon beim Nachdenken über ihre mögliche künftige Nutzung als Behausung kommt einem der krasse Unterschied zwischen der jugoslawischen Wohnungspolitik, die verfassungmäßig ein allumfassendes Wohnrecht garantierte, und den in den Nachfolgestaaten geltenden – oder fehlenden – heutigen Regelungen in den Sinn. Es ist schwer, sich einen K67 als privates Tiny House vorzustellen, weniger wegen der räumlichen Beschränkung, sondern wegen der kommunalen Identität. So wie man bei einem typischen Haus an ein rotes Giebeldach auf einem weißen Quader denkt, so assoziieren viele Menschen geschäftliche Aktivitäten im öffentlichen Raum mit einem durch einen schwachen Sepiafilter gesehenen Plastikwürfel mit gerundeten Kanten – ein Bild, das an ein anderes Zeitalter erinnert, welches diese Gruppe von Menschen einst zusammenführte (Abb. 4).

Übersetzung: Wilfried Prantner

11 Puncer, Mojca: „The Politics of Aesthetics of Contemporary Art in Slovenia and Its Avant-garde Sources", in: *Filozofski Vestnik* 37,1 (2016), 133–156, hier 147.

the kiosk owners, while underscoring the synergy between top-down and bottom-up approaches to developing public spaces in Yugoslavia.

Considering the flexible and ever-evolving nature of K67 kiosks within their dominant identity, one cannot help but wonder about their future. The ever-growing demand for emergency housing in a capitalist world—along with looming technofeudalism—has been amplified by the prominence of migrant routes on the post-Yugoslav soil, which serves as a perpetual bridge between East and West. With its dimensions of 256.5 by 240 by 240 centimeters, a single K67 unit is comparable to many habitation alternatives. Slovenian artist and urban anthropologist Marjetica Potrč embarked on an exploration of K67's potential as a shelter as early as 2003 in her mixed-media project "Next Stop, Kiosk." Drawing inspiration from South American housing on stilts and clandestine rooftop settlements in Belgrade, she sought to address social issues in both contexts.[11] Unlike her exhibition at Moderna Galerija in Ljubljana, where the two K67 units were on display for public contemplation, some kiosks find practical use during the summer months as overnight shelters for street vendors along the Dalmatian magistral road. Even reflecting on their possible housing function in the future brings to mind the stark contrast between Yugoslavia's housing policy, characterized by the all-encompassing right to housing enshrined in its constitution, and the contemporary policies—or lack thereof—in its successor nations. It is difficult to picture a K67 as a tiny, private house—not because of spatial constraints, but due to its distinct communal identity. Much like envisioning a red gable roof atop a white box when thinking of the quintessential house, a rather large group of people associate everyday retail activities in public spaces with the image of a plastic cube featuring rounded edges, enveloped in a slight sepia filter—an image that recalls a different era, one that once brought that group of people together (fig. 4).

11 Mojca Puncer, "The Politics of Aesthetics of Contemporary Art in Slovenia and Its Avant-garde Sources," *Filozofski Vestnik* 37, no. 1 (2016): 133–156, esp. 147.

South Street, Philadelphia, 1968, photograph by Denise Scott Brown; courtesy of Denise Scott Brown

Von Pop lernen
Learning from Pop

Denise Scott Brown

Las Vegas und Los Angeles, Suburbs im Stile von Levittown, der Single-Lifestyle an Houstons Westheimer Strip, Golfresorts, eigene Boating Communities für Freizeitkapitäne, soziale Großwohnprojekte wie die Co-op City in der Bronx, die Kulissen des Wohnens in Seifenopern, in der Fernsehwerbung und bei Anzeigen in Publikumszeitschriften, Reklametafeln und die Route 66 – all das beeinflusst und verändert unsere Architekturvorstellungen. Wenn sich alte Formen überlebt haben, die weitere Entwicklung aber noch unklar ist, sucht man neue Anfänge; dann kann ein klassisches Erbe, eine Kunstbewegung oder eine von Bauingenieuren oder Naturvölkern geschaffene „Architektur ohne Architekten" die Nachblüten einer früheren, von konservativen Gralshütern weitergepflegten Revolution hinwegfegen. Im Amerika der Sechzigerjahre kam zu diesem Grundrezept für künstlerischen Wandel noch eine weitere Zutat hinzu: sozialer Umbruch. Die Stadterneuerung, die ArchitektInnen seit zwei Jahrzehnten mit Aufträgen versorgt und zum Hort für die faden Reste des Modernismus wurde, war nicht nur künstlerisch unfruchtbar, sie wirkte auch in sozialer Hinsicht zerstörerisch. Das Drängen gesellschaftlicher Fragen, die sozial motivierte Kritik an der Stadterneuerung und am Architekten als einem Dienstleister für eine kleine reiche Bevölkerungsschicht – insbesondere die Kritik von Herbert Gans – haben genauso viel dazu beigetragen wie die Pop-KünstlerInnen, unsere Aufmerksamkeit auf die zeitgenössische amerikanische Stadt und ihrer Erbauer zu lenken. Wenn die Architekten des hohen Stils nicht das liefern, was die Leute wollen oder brauchen, wer tut es dann, und was können wir von ihnen lernen?

Bedürfnisse im Plural

Ein Gespür für Bedürfnisse zu entwickeln, ist ein Hauptgrund für die Beschäftigung mit der heutigen Stadt. Dabei ist die erste Lektion für ArchitektInnen, dass es überhaupt Bedürfnisse im Plural gibt. Kein Bauunternehmer oder Immobilienentwickler mit klarem Verstand würde von sich behaupten: Ich baue für die Menschheit. Er baut für einen Markt, eine Bevölkerungsgruppe, die durch Einkommensniveau, Alter, Familienzusammensetzung und Lebensstil genau definiert ist. Schlafstädte, Rentnerorte und Stadthäuser im georgianischen Stil entstehen, weil jemand die Bedürfnisse der Gruppen, die seinen Markt

Las Vegas, Los Angeles, Levittown, the swinging singles on the Westheimer Strip, golf resorts, boating communities, Co-op City, the residential backgrounds to soap operas, TV commercials and mass mag ads, billboards, and Route 66 are sources for a changing architectural sensibility. New sources are sought when the old forms go stale and the way out is not clear; then a Classical heritage, an art movement, or industrial engineers' and primitives' "architecture without architects" may help to sweep out the flowery remains of the old revolution as practiced by its originators' conservative descendants. In America in the sixties an extra ingredient was added to this recipe for artistic change: social revolution. Urban renewal, supplier of work for architects for two decades and a major locus of the soft remains of the Modern movement, was not merely artistically stale, it was socially harmful. The urgency of the social situation, the social critique of urban renewal and of the architect as server of a rich narrow spectrum of the population—in particular the criticism of Herbert Gans—have been as important as the Pop artists in steering us toward the existing American city and its builders. If high-style architects are not producing what people want or need, who is, and what can we learn from them?

Needs, Plural

Sensitivity to needs is a first reason for going to the existing city. Once there, the first lesson for architects is the pluralism of need. No builder-developer in his right mind would announce: I am building for Man. He is building for a market, for a group of people defined by income range, age, family composition and life style. Levittowns, Leisureworlds, Georgian-styled town houses grow from someone's estimation of the needs of the groups who will be their markets. The city can be seen as the built artifacts of a set of subcultures. At the moment, those subcultures which willingly resort to architects are few.

Of course learning from what's there is subject to the caveats and limitations of all behavioristic analysis—one is surveying behavior which is constrained, it is not what people might do in other conditions. The poor do not willingly live in tenements and maybe the middle classes don't willingly live in Levittowns; perhaps the Georgian-styling is less pertinent to the townhouse resident than is the rent.

bilden, entsprechend einschätzt. Die Stadt lässt sich als die baulichen Artefakte gewisser Subkulturen begreifen. Derzeit gibt es nur wenige Subkulturen, die gerne und freiwillig auf die Dienste von ArchitektInnen zurückgreifen.

Aus dem, was da ist, seine Schlüsse zu ziehen, unterliegt selbstverständlich den Beschränkungen und Fallstricken jeder Verhaltensanalyse – man beobachtet nur ein an eine bestimmte Situation gebundenes Verhalten und erfährt nicht, wie sich jemand unter anderen Bedingungen verhalten würde. Arme Leute wohnen nicht gerne in Mietskasernen und die Mittelklasse vielleicht auch nicht gerne in Suburbia; und über die BewohnerInnen von Stadthäusern verrät der georgianische Stil vielleicht weniger als die Höhe des Mietpreises. Gerade eine Zeit des Wohnungsmangels ist ein triftiges Argument gegen eine Analyse von Architekturnutzung, denn ohne eine Alternative können Menschen ein verfügbares Angebot schlecht ablehnen und nicht darin wohnen. Entschärft wird dieses Problem durch den Blick auf vergleichbare Umgebungen, in denen solche Beschränkungen aus irgendeinem Grund nicht greifen. Und tatsächlich existieren Umgebungen, die besser zeigen, wie der Geschmack von Menschen mit knappem Budget aussähe, wenn sie sich weniger einschränken müssten. Es ist die Sphäre der Neureichen, etwa das Hollywood einer früheren Ära oder das heutige Las Vegas, die Häuser von Filmstars, Sporthelden und anderen Gruppen, deren sozialer Aufstieg kometengleich verlief, die zugleich aber gerne an früheren Wertesystemen festhalten.

Eine andere Informationsquelle sind die Kulissen, die in den Massenmedien, Filmen, Seifenopern oder in der Werbung für Konserven und Möbelpolitur verwendet werden. Hier will man zwar keine Häuser verkaufen, sondern etwas anderes, aber die verwendeten Einrichtungen spiegeln wider, was die Käufer von Konserven oder das Publikum von Seifenopern nach Meinung von irgendjemand (vielleicht die Werbeindustrie?) gerne in einem Haus sähen. Selbstverständlich können BeobachterInnen aus der Werbeindustrie ebenso voreingenommen sein wie ArchitektInnen, und es sollte auch nicht vergessen werden, was verkauft wird – muss Konservendosenarchitektur, die erfolgreich Dosen verkauft, so gemütlich aussehen wie mein Zuhause oder so schick wie deines? Aber immerhin ist das eine andere Voreingenommenheit, eine Alternative zur architektonischen Nabelschau, auf die viele Überlegungen hinauslaufen, nämlich auf die Frage: Was hat Le Corbusier gemacht? Auch wenn die Werbeindustrie und die Bauwirtschaft nur wenig über die Bedürfnisse der Ärmsten verraten, bilden sie ein breiteres Bevölkerungsspektrum ab und sind härteren Marktbedingungen ausgesetzt als ArchitektInnen in Stadtplanung und Wohnungswirtschaft, und wenn wir daraus nichts anderes lernen, als dass Architektur für verschiedene Gruppen auch verschieden sein muss, dann ist das schon viel.

Eine weitere alternative Informationsquelle ist der Blick auf das, was Menschen mit den Gebäuden anstellen, sobald sie eingezogen sind – in Suburbia wie in

In times of housing shortage this is a particularly forceful argument against architectural behaviorism since people can't vote against a particular offering by staying away if there is no alternative. To counteract this danger one must search for comparison environments where for some reason the constraints do not hold. There are environments which suggest what economically constrained groups' tastes might be if they were less constrained. They are the nouveau riche environments; Hollywood for a former era, Las Vegas for today, and the homes of film stars, sportsmen, and other groups where upward mobility may resemble vertical takeoff, yet where maintenance of previous value systems is encouraged.

Another source is physical backgrounds in the mass media, movies, soap operas, pickle and furniture polish ads. Here the aim is not to sell houses but something else, and the background represents someone's (Madison Avenue's?) idea of what pickle buyers or soap opera watchers want in a house. Now the Madison Avenue observer's view may be as biased as the architect's, and it should be studied in the light of what it is trying to sell—must pickle architecture look homey like my house or elegant like yours if it is to sell me pickles? But at least it's another bias, an alternative to the architectural navel contemplation we so often do for research; i.e., ask: What did Le Corbusier do? Both Madison Avenue and the builder, although they can tell us little of the needs of the very poor, cover a broader range of the population and pass a stiffer market test than does the architect in urban renewal or public housing, and if we learn no more from these sources than that architecture must differ for different groups, that is a great deal. But an alternative to both is to examine what people do to buildings—in Levittowns, Society Hills, gray areas and slums—once they are in them. Here, costs and availability are less constraining forces since the enterprise is smaller. Also, changes tend often to be symbolic rather than structural, and aspirations can perhaps be more easily inferred from symbols than from structures.

Attention to built sources for information on need does not imply that asking people what they want is not extremely necessary as well. This is an important topic, as is the relation between the two types of survey, asking and looking; but it is not the subject of this enquiry, which is on what can be learned from the artifacts of pop culture.

Formal Analysis as Design Research

A second reason for looking to pop culture is to find formal vocabularies for today which are more relevant to people's diverse needs and more tolerant of the untidinesses of urban life than the "rationalist," Cartesian formal orders of latter-day Modern architecture. How much low-income housing and nineteenth-century architecture has been cleared so some tidy purist architect or planner could start with a clean slate?

Modern architects can now admit that whatever forces, processes, and technologies determine architectural form,

wohlhabenden Bezirken, in gesichtslosen Vierteln oder in Slums. Dabei sind Kosten und Verfügbarkeit nicht so stark einschränkende Faktoren, weil die Eingriffe geringfügiger sind. Zudem sind bauliche Änderungen oft eher symbolischer als struktureller Art, und aus Symbolen lassen sich Erwartungen und Wünsche vermutlich auch leichter ableiten als aus Umbauten.

Die Beachtung der in der Architektur verankerten Information über Bedürfnisse heißt nicht, dass es nicht unerlässlich wäre, Menschen zu ihren Wünschen zu befragen. Das bleibt wichtig, genau wie die Frage nach dem Verhältnis der beiden Arten von Bestandsaufnahme, Fragen und Schauen; aber das ist nicht Thema dieser Überlegungen; das Thema ist vielmehr die Frage, was wir von den Artefakten der Popkultur lernen können.

Formanalyse als Designforschung

Ein zweiter Grund, sich mit der Popkultur zu befassen, ist die Suche nach einer Formensprache für die Gegenwart, die den unterschiedlichen menschlichen Bedürfnissen mehr entgegenkommt und die Unordentlichkeiten des urbanen Lebens besser aushält als die „rationalistischen", cartesianisch-formalen Ordnungen der spätmodernen Architektur. Wie viel Wohnraum für niedrige Einkommen und Bauten aus dem neunzehnten Jahrhundert wurden abgerissen, nur damit ein ordentlicher puristischer Planer oder Architekt bei null beginnen konnte?

Inzwischen können moderne ArchitektInnen einräumen, dass die architektonische Form auch von Vorstellungen über Form geprägt wird, ganz egal welche Einflüsse, Prozesse und Technologien sie sonst noch bestimmen; dass eine Formensprache ebenso Teil von Architektur ist wie Ziegel und Mörtel (oder Kunststoff und Fertigbauteile, wenn man die Zukunft ins Auge fasst); dass Form nicht allein der Funktion entspringt, ihr nicht so neu und unschuldig entsteigen kann wie Venus ihrer Muschel, sondern dass Form *gleichermaßen* Funktion, Einflussfaktoren und Form folgt. Wenn einem die formalen Voreinstellungen bewusst sind, müssen sie nicht in Tyrannei ausarten, so wie es in der Stadterneuerung geschehen ist; und angesichts der Bedeutung der Formensprache für die Architektur darf man sie durchaus analysieren und verbessern, um funktionale Anforderungen zu erfüllen, statt sie gedankenlos und ohne Rücksicht auf ihre Eignung anzuwenden wie den überkommenen Lehrsatz eines nicht mehr maßgeblichen Meisters. Die Formen der Pop-Landschaft sind für uns Heutige so bedeutsam wie die Formen des alten Rom für den Jugendstil, wie Kubismus und Maschinenarchitektur für die frühe Moderne und die Formen der industriellen Midlands und der Dogon für Team 10, das heißt, ungeheuer bedeutsam und bedeutsamer als irgendeine Tiefseetauchkugel, eine Startrampe oder ein Systembaukrankenhaus (und, bei allem Respekt für Reyner Banham, der Santa Monica Pier). Anders als diese korrelieren popkulturelle Formen nicht nur ästhetisch mit unserer gesellschaftlichen Situation, sondern auch

ideas about form determine it as well; that a formal vocabulary is as much a part of architecture as are bricks and mortar (plastics and systems, for futurists); that form does not, cannot, arise from function alone, newborn and innocent as Venus from her shell, but rather that form follows, *inter alia*, function, forces, and form. Formal biases, if they are consciously recognized, need not tyrannize as they have done in urban renewal; and formal vocabularies, given their place in architecture, can be studied and improved to suit functional requirements, rather than accepted unconsciously and unsuitably—some old hand-me-down from some irrelevant master. The forms of the pop landscape are as relevant to us now as were the forms of antique Rome to the Beaux Arts, Cubism and Machine Architecture to the early Moderns, and the industrial Midlands and the Dogon to Team 10, which is to say extremely relevant, and more so than the latest bathysphere, launch pad, or systems hospital (or even, *pace* Banham, the Santa Monica pier). Unlike these, they speak to our condition not only aesthetically, but on many levels of necessity, from the social necessity to rehouse the poor without destroying them to the architectural necessity to produce buildings and environments that others will need and like. The pop landscape differs from the earlier models in that it is also the place where we build; it is our context. And it is one of the few contemporary sources of data on the symbolic and communicative aspects of architecture, since it was untouched by the Modern movement's purist reduction of architecture to space and structure only.

But formal analysis presents a problem. First, since form has for so long been an illegitimate topic, we have lost the tradition of analyzing it, and second, the forms we are dealing with are new and don't relate easily to traditional architectural or planning techniques of analysis and communication. Orthographic projection hardly covers the essence of the Stardust sign, and, although this sign is a block long and has an overpowering visual impact *in situ*, it doesn't show well on a land use map. Suburban space, being automobile space, is not defined by enclosing walls and floors and is therefore difficult to portray graphically using systems devised for the description of buildings.

In fact, space is not the most important constituent of suburban form. Communication across space is more important, and it requires a symbolic and a time element in its descriptive systems which are only slowly being devised.

New analytic techniques must use film and videotape to convey the dynamism of sign architecture and the sequential experience of vast landscapes; and computers are needed to aggregate mass repeated data into comprehensible patterns. Valuable traditional techniques should also be resuscitated by their application to new phenomena; for example, when Nolli's mid-eighteenth-century technique for mapping Rome is adapted to include parking lots, it throws considerable light on Las Vegas. It could also lend itself fairly easily to computer techniques.

Formal analysis should be comparative, linking the

in Bezug auf verschiedene Anforderungen – von der sozialen Forderung nach der Schaffung von Wohnraum für die arme Bevölkerung, ohne sie zu vernichten, bis hin zur architektonischen Forderung, Gebäude und Umgebungen zu gestalten, die von anderen gebraucht und gemocht werden. Die Pop-Landschaft unterscheidet sich insofern von früheren Vorbildern, als sie auch das ist, worin wir bauen; sie bildet unseren Rahmen. Zugleich ist sie eine der wenigen zeitgenössischen Informationsquellen zu den symbolischen und kommunikativen Aspekten von Architektur, weil sie von der modernistischen puristischen Reduktion der Architektur auf nichts als Raum und Konstruktion unberührt geblieben ist. Dennoch bereitet die Formanalyse Probleme. Erstens haben wir, weil die Form so lange ein Tabuthema war, kaum Übung darin, sie zu analysieren; und zweitens sind die Formen, mit denen wir es heute zu tun haben, neu und lassen sich mit den herkömmlichen architektonischen oder planerischen Analyse- und Kommunikationstechniken schlecht beschreiben. Per Orthogonalprojektion ist das Wesentliche des Neonschildes des Stardust-Hotels kaum wiederzugeben, und obwohl das Schild fast einen Straßenzug groß ist und vor Ort eine überwältigende visuelle Wirkung hat, ist auf einem Flächennutzungsplan fast nichts davon zu sehen. Der suburbane Raum, der maßgeblich ein automobiler ist, wird nicht von den Wänden und Etagen darum definiert und ist daher mit Mitteln zur Gebäudebeschreibung grafisch kaum darzustellen. Eigentlich ist Raum auch nicht das Element, das die suburbane Form am stärksten prägt. Wichtiger ist die Kommunikation im Raum, und zu deren Beschreibung sind Systeme erforderlich, die symbolische und zeitliche Elemente berücksichtigen, aber die werden erst allmählich entwickelt.

Neue Analyseverfahren müssen mit Film und Video arbeiten, um die Dynamik der Architektur von Schildern und Zeichen und die sequentielle Erfahrung weiter Landschaften zu vermitteln; und Computer sind nötig, um große Mengen sich wiederholender Daten zu aussagekräftigen Aggregationen hochzurechnen. Auch nützliche traditionelle Verfahren sollten aufgegriffen und auf neue Phänomene angewendet werden; wenn etwa die Methode von Nollis Rom-Plan aus dem 18. Jahrhundert so angepasst wird, dass auch Parkplätze verzeichnet werden können, wirft das ein erhellendes Licht auf Las Vegas. Dafür könnte sich auch recht leicht Computertechnik nutzen lassen.

Die Formanalyse sollte vergleichend sein und die neuen Formen durch Abgleich an den Rest der architektonischen Formtradition anschließen, um sie für die Architektur nutzbar zu machen und uns zu helfen, unsere neue Erfahrung auch von fachlicher Seite her zu begreifen. Mit der Forderung nach einer Formanalyse meine ich nicht, dass die Funktion (das Programm), die Technologien oder Einflussfaktoren (soziale Prozesse in der Stadt oder Umweltökonomik) für die Architektur nicht essenziell sind oder dass ArchitektInnen davon nicht auch künstlerisch angeregt würden. Sie alle sind notwendig, und sie

new forms, by comparison, to the rest of the formal tradition of architecture thereby incorporating them into the architectural discipline and helping us to understand our new experience in the light of our formal training. By suggesting that form should be analyzed, I do not imply that function (the program), technologies, or forces (urban social processes or land economics) are not vital to architecture, nor indeed, that they too can't serve as sources of artistic inspiration to the architect. All are necessary and they work in combination. The others are merely not the subject of this particular enquiry.

The Soup Can and the Establishment

There is an irony in the fact that the "popular" culture and the "popular" landscape are not popular with those who make the decisions to renew the city and rehouse the poor. Here is John Kenneth Galbraith, an important and influential liberal, quoted in *Life* magazine:

"For the average citizen there are some simple tests which will tell him when we have passed from incantation to practical action on the environment. Restriction of auto use in the large cities will be one. Another will be when the billboards, the worst and most nearly useless excrescence of industrial civilization, are removed from the highways. Yet another will be when telephone and electric wires everywhere in the cities go underground and we accept the added charge on our bills.

My own personal test, for what it may be worth, concerns the gasoline service station. This is the most repellent piece of architecture of the past two thousand years.

There are far more of them than are needed. Usually they are filthy. Their merchandise is hideously packaged and garishly displayed. They are uncontrollably addicted to great strings of ragged little flags. Protecting them is an ominous coalition of small businessmen and large. The stations should be excluded entirely from most streets and highways. Where allowed, they should be franchised to limit the number, and there should be stern requirements as to architecture, appearance and general reticence. When we begin on this (and similar roadside commerce), I will think that we are serious."[1]

He does not even mention the need for low-income housing as an urgent environmental problem, and in my opinion he should stick to economics.

But the conventional wisdom which Galbraith expounds is shared by his colleagues, the elderly architectural radicals who man America's fine arts commissions, the "design" departments of HUD and the planning and redevelopment agencies, who plan and build for the larger public and private corporations and have the ear of the city makers. If the public is to be well served by their decisions, these members of the architectural establishment must learn to separate out for a different type of scrutiny their

1 John Kenneth Galbraith: "To My New Friends in the Affluent Society—Greetings," *Life*, March 27, 1970.

gehören alle zusammen. Sie sind nur nicht das Thema dieser speziellen Betrachtung.

Suppendose und Establishment

Es liegt eine gewisse Ironie in der Tatsache, dass die Populärkultur und die „Populärlandschaft" bei jenen, die die Entscheidungen über die Stadterneuerung und die Wohnsituation der Armen treffen, ganz und gar nicht populär sind. So sagt der einflussreiche liberale Wirtschaftswissenschaftler John Kenneth Galbraith in der Zeitschrift *Life*:

„Für den Durchschnittsbürger gibt es ein paar einfache Prüfsteine, die verraten, ob wir uns nicht mehr nur in Lippenbekenntnissen um die Umwelt kümmern, sondern auch in der Praxis. Einer davon ist die Beschränkung der Autonutzung in Großstädten. Ein anderer die Entfernung von Reklametafeln, diesen schlimmsten, nutzlosen Auswüchsen der industriellen Zivilisation, von den Highways. Ein weiterer ist die Bereitschaft, die Zusatzkosten zu übernehmen, wenn in den Städten überall Telefonleitungen und Stromkabel unter die Erde verlegt werden.

Mein persönlicher Prüfstein, auch wenn das vielleicht nicht allzu relevant ist, sind Tankstellen. Tankstellen sind das scheußlichste Stück Architektur der letzten zwei Jahrtausende. Es gibt viel mehr von ihnen als nötig. Meistens sind sie schmutzig. Die dort verkauften Waren sind grässlich verpackt und werden grellbunt zur Schau gestellt. Beinahe jede wird geradezu zwanghaft von zerfetzten Wimpeln an langen Schnüren verziert. Zu ihrem Schutz hat sich eine merkwürdige Koalition aus kleinen und großen Unternehmern zusammengetan. Tankstellen sollten an den meisten Straßen und Highways verboten werden. Wo sie gestattet sind, sollte ihre Anzahl streng begrenzt werden, und ihre Architektur, ihr Aussehen und ihre generelle Unauffälligkeit sollten strengen Vorschriften unterliegen. Wenn wir hier (und bei ähnlichen kommerziellen Bauten an Straßen) anfangen, dann glaube ich, dass wir ernst machen."[1]

Mit keinem Wort erwähnt Galbraith, dass kostengünstiger Wohnraum ein drängendes Problem unserer Zeit ist, und meiner Meinung nach sollte er bei seiner Wirtschaftswissenschaft bleiben. Doch die abgedroschenen Ansichten, die aus Galbraith sprechen, werden von seinen Konsorten geteilt, den ältlichen Architekturradikalen in Amerikas Kunst-am-Bau-Kommissionen, in den „Design"-Abteilungen des Ministeriums für Wohnungsbau und Stadtentwicklung und in den Ämtern für Stadtplanung und -erneuerung, die für große öffentliche und private Unternehmen bauen und planen und das Ohr der Stadtoberen haben. Sollte dieses architektonische Establishment mit seinen Entscheidungen wirklich der Öffentlichkeit dienen wollen, dann müsste es seine Ästhetik von seiner Lieblingsbeschäftigung mit „Umweltverschmutzung" zu trennen lernen und die Dinge etwas anders betrachten. Verschmutztes Wasser und Reklametafeln sind Probleme sehr verschiedener

1 Galbraith, John Kenneth: „To My New Friends in the Affluent Society – Greetings", *Life*, 27. März 1970.

aesthetic from other preoccupations with "environmental pollution." Fouled water and billboards are not of the same magnitude or order of problem. The first cannot be done well, but the second can; particularly if we are given the opportunity to study them for awhile, nonjudgmentally.

When "blighted" neighborhoods are swept away together with billboards and gasoline stations in the name of the avoidance of "visual pollution," the social harm can be irreparable. However, an old aesthetic formula, even though it is shown to be obstructive, will not be relinquished until it is replaced by a new one, since, as we have seen, form depends on form for its making. And, for the architectural establishment, the new vocabulary must have a respectable lineage. Hence, if the popular environment is to provide that vocabulary, it must be filtered through the proper processes for its acceptance. It must become a part of the high-art tradition; it must be last year's avant garde. This is another reason to submit the new landscape to traditional architectural analysis: for the sake of its acceptance by the establishment. They can't learn from pop until Pop hangs in the academy.

Hop on Pop

I have recommended an investigation of the forms of the new, existing city on both social and aesthetic grounds for architects who hope to hone their skills to a sharp new edge. High art has followed low art before and vice versa; in fact, where did the McDonald's parabola and the split-level ranch come from in the first place?

In the movement from low art to high art lies an element of the deferral of judgment. Judgment is withheld in the interest of understanding and receptivity. This is an exciting heuristic technique but also a dangerous one since liking the whole of pop culture is as irrational as hating the whole of it, and it calls forth the vision of a general and indiscriminate hopping on the pop bandwagon, where everything is good and judgment is abandoned rather than deferred. Yet artists, architects, actors, must judge, albeit, one hopes, with a sigh. After a decent interval, suitable criteria must grow out of the new source. Judgment is merely deferred to make subsequent judgments more sensitive.

Note

This text has first been published in *Casabella* 359–360 (December 1971) and was previously reprinted in *Architecture Theory since* 1968, edited by K. Michael Hays (2000).
The reprint in this GAM issue was made possible by the kind permission of Denise Scott Brown.

Größenordnungen und Kategorien. Im ersten Fall gibt es kein richtig, im zweiten schon; vor allem, wenn man die Zeit hat, sich eine Weile unvoreingenommen damit zu befassen.

Werden „problematische" Viertel zusammen mit Reklametafeln und Tankstellen unter dem Vorwand der Beseitigung einer „visuellen Umweltverschmutzung" einfach abgerissen, kann der Schaden für die Gesellschaft irreparabel sein. Allerdings wird eine alte ästhetische Formel, selbst wenn sie nachweislich hinderlich ist, nicht aufgegeben, solange keine neue an ihre Stelle tritt, weil – wie oben gezeigt – sich Form aus der Form heraus entwickelt. Und das architektonische Establishment verlangt von einer neuen Formensprache einen akzeptablen Herkunftsnachweis. Daher muss die popkulturelle Umwelt, soll diese Formensprache aus ihr hervorgehen und akzeptiert werden, durch entsprechende Prozesse gefiltert werden. Sie muss in die hochkulturelle Kunsttradition eingespeist werden; sie muss zur gestrigen Avantgarde werden. Das ist ein weiterer Grund, die neue Pop-Landschaft der traditionellen Architekturanalyse zu unterziehen: damit das Establishment sie akzeptiert. Diese Leute können erst von Pop lernen, wenn er akademische Würden erlangt hat.

Hop on Pop

Ich habe ArchitektInnen, die ihren Fähigkeiten einen neuen zeitgemäßen Schliff geben wollen, geraten, sich sowohl in sozialer wie ästhetischer Hinsicht mit den Formen der neu entstandenen Stadt zu befassen. Schon früher hat sich die hohe Kunst an der niederen orientiert, genau wie umgekehrt; woher stammen der Doppelbogen von McDonald's und die Split-Level-Ranchhäuser denn ursprünglich?

In der Bewegung von der niederen zur hohen Kunst liegt ein Moment des aufgeschobenen Urteils. Man hält sich mit dem Urteilen zurück, um etwas besser aufnehmen und verstehen zu können. Das ist eine spannende heuristische Methode, jedoch nicht ohne Gefahren, weil es genauso irrational ist, die gesamte Populärkultur hochzujubeln, wie sie in Bausch und Bogen zu verdammen, und sie verleitet dazu, ohne Wenn und Aber auf den Pop-Zug aufzuspringen und alles für gut zu befinden und das Urteilsvermögen aufzugeben, statt sich zurückzuhalten. Doch KünstlerInnen, ArchitektInnen, SchauspielerInnen haben Urteile zu fällen, auch wenn sie es hoffentlich zurückhaltend tun. Nach einer angemessenen Zeit müssen den neuen Umständen geeignete Urteilskriterien entwachsen. Das Urteil wird nur aufgeschoben, um danach umso klüger urteilen zu können.

Übersetzung: Sven Koch

Anmerkung

Dieser Text erschien zuerst in *Casabella*, Dezember 1971, S. 359–360 und wurde später nachgedruckt in *Architecture Theory since 1968*, hrsg. von K. Michael Hays, 2000. Der Nachdruck in dieser Ausgabe des GAM erfolgt mit freundlicher Genehmigung durch Denise Scott Brown.

Brescia

Alltäglicher Traum und soziales Experiment
Everyday Dream and Social Experiment

Andrea Canclini

„Da die Architektur direkt in das Alltagsleben eingreift, [...] schafft sie eine dauerhafte Verbindung, die eine solide kritische Grundlage schafft, von der aus man über viele ‚gute Absichten' urteilen kann."[1]

Bis zu Beginn des 19. Jahrhunderts war Brescia eine Stadt, die von Mauern umschlossen war und in einem Quadrat von zwei Kilometern rund 30.000 Einwohner beherbergte. Auf halber Strecke der Straße von Turin nach Venedig, auf der gesamten Nordseite der einzigen großen Ebene Italiens gelegen, wird sie im Norden durch das Alpenvorland und im Süden durch die fruchtbare Ebene und viel Wasser begrenzt. Die Stadt wurde von den Römern auf einer bereits bestehenden Siedlung der zisalpinen Kelten gegründet und später in das Königreich der Langobarden eingegliedert, bevor sie eine autonome Gemeinde wurde. Das Gebiet wurde lange Zeit sowohl vom Herzogtum Mailand als auch von der Republik Venedig beansprucht; es wurde von der Armee Ludwigs XII. während eines der Kriege der Liga von Cambrai zu Beginn des 16. Jahrhunderts belagert, gehörte zu den Besitztümern Napoleons und wurde dann in der ersten Hälfte des 19. Jahrhunderts eine Provinz des *Lombardisch-Venezianischen Königreichs* als Teil des *Kaisertums Österreich*. Ein ziemlich typischer Fall, der die komplexe Geschichte eines Großteils Norditaliens veranschaulicht.

Die Stadt ist fast calvinistisch mit der Verpflichtung ihrer BewohnerInnen zu harter Arbeit, die es ihr ermöglichte, mindestens ein Jahrhundert lang eine der ersten italienischen Industriestädte zu werden,[2] eine Art lokales Black Country, als italienische Hauptstadt der Eisenverarbeitung; fähig, ihre metallurgische Industrie an die Bedürfnisse beider Weltkriege anzupassen, fromm genug,

1 Grassi, Giorgio: „Avant-Garde and Continuity", *Oppositions* 21 (1980), 30.
2 Vgl. Piovene, Guido: *Viaggio in Italia*, Mailand 1957, 142.

"[S]ince architecture enters directly into everyday life ... it creates a permanent bond that provides a firm critical base from which to pass judgment upon many 'good intentions.'"[1]

An Italian city, enclosed within its walls until the beginning of the 19th century, a small square of two kilometers to accommodate its 30,000 inhabitants: this was Brescia for centuries, situated about halfway along the road from Turin to Venice, on the entire northern side of Italy's only great plain: the first Alpine foothills to the north, the fertile plain to the south, and plenty of water. Founded by the Romans on pre-existing settlements inhabited by Cisalpine Celts, the town was later incorporated into the Kingdom of the Lombards before becoming an autonomous commune. The territory was long disputed between the Duchy of Milan and the Republic of Venice, besieged by the army of Louis XII during one of the wars of the League of Cambrai in the early 16th century. It became part of Napoleon's possessions and then, in the first half of the 19th century, a province of the *Lombardisch-Venetianisches Königreich* as part of the *Kaisertum Österreich*. A fairly typical story to illustrate the complex history of much of northern Italy.

The town is almost Calvinist in its commitment to hard work, which allowed it to become, for at least a century, one of the first Italian industrial towns,[2] a sort of local Black Country, as the Italian capital of worked iron; able to adapt its metallurgical industry to support both World Wars, devout enough to offer the Catholic Church Paul VI,[3] the Pope of the Second Vatican Council, the last great reform, the Church being an institution with which the

1 Giorgio Grassi, "Avant-Garde and Continuity," *Oppositions* 21 (1980): 30.
2 See Guido Piovene, *Viaggio in Italia* (Milan, 1957), 142.
3 Pope Paul VI (1897–1978), was the 262nd Bishop of Rome and Pope of the Catholic Church for 15 years, Primate of Italy and 4th Ruler of the Vatican City State from June 21, 1963 until his death on August 6, 1978.

1 Houses in Villaggio Badia and Villaggio Sereno, Brescia, Italy, 2023
Photos: © Andrea Canclini, edited by Stefano Butturini

um der katholischen Kirche Paul VI.,[3] dem Papst des Zweiten Vatikanischen Konzils, die letzte große Reform anzubieten. Dabei ist die Kirche eine Institution, zu der die Stadt immer eine sehr enge Beziehung hatte und die von einfacher und traditioneller Frömmigkeit, aber auch von sozialem Engagement gekennzeichnet war.

In diesem untrennbaren Zusammenhang von Arbeit und Frömmigkeit lassen sich die Bedingungen für die Möglichkeit einer originellen Entwicklung in der Stadtentwicklung der Nachkriegszeit finden, die auf einer typologischen Homogenisierung als wirtschaftlicher, politischer und sozialer Logik beruht. Nach dem Ende des Zweiten Weltkriegs und der Befreiung Italiens vom Faschismus durch die anglo-amerikanischen Streitkräfte wurde der Wiederaufbau Italiens dank dem Marshall-Plan wirtschaftlich erheblich unterstützt. Die Ergebnisse dieser raschen Anpassung des Landes an die neuen politischen, sozialen und wirtschaftlichen Koordinaten werden von vielen Intellektuellen auf radikale Weise anerkannt; Luciano Bianciardis Roman *La Vita Agra*[4] wurde 1962 veröffentlicht. Pier Paolo Pasolinis *Teorema*[5] 1968. Beide beschreiben das Paradoxon, das von der neokapitalistischen Bourgeoisie verkörpert wird, die während des so genannten „italienischen Wirtschaftswunders“[6] entstand, gemäß dem Kanon dessen, was Pier Paolo Pasolini als „anthropologische Mutation“[7] bezeichnete – die präzise, unaufhaltsame und radikale Dynamik des Wirtschaftssystems zwischen

3 Papst Paul VI. (1897-1978), war der 262. Bischof von Rom und 15 Jahre lang Papst der katholischen Kirche, Primas von Italien und vierter Herrscher des Staates Vatikanstadt vom 21. Juni 1963 bis zu seinem Tod am 6. August 1978.

4 Bianciardi, Luciano: *La vita agra*, Mailand 1962. 1965 auf Englisch unter dem Titel *It's a Hard Life* veröffentlicht. [Anm. d. Übers.: Auf Deutsch erschien der Roman 1967 unter dem Titel *Das saure Leben*.]

5 So der Titel des Romans, den Pier Paolo Pasolini zur gleichen Zeit wie das Drehbuch für seinen gleichnamigen Film von 1968 schrieb und der manchmal auch als *Theorem* übersetzt wird.

6 „Italienisches Wirtschaftswunder“ war ein journalistischer Begriff, der häufig verwendet wurde, um die sozioökonomische Leistung Italiens in der Zeit zwischen den frühen 1950er-und den frühen 1960er-Jahren zu beschreiben. Vgl. Cardini, Antonio (Hg): *Il miracolo economico italiano (1958–1963)*, Bologna 2007; Crainz, Guido: *Storia del miracolo italiano*, Rom 1996, Crainz, Guido: *Il paese mancato. Dal miracolo economico agli anni Ottanta*, Rom 2003 und Ginsborg, Paul: *Storia d'Italia dal dopoguerra a oggi. Società e politica 1943–1988*, Turin 1989.

7 „Das bäuerliche und altindustrielle Italien ist zusammengebrochen, es ist nicht mehr da, und an seiner Stelle gibt es eine Leere, die darauf wartet, von einer vollständigen [...] modernisierenden, falsch toleranten, amerikanisierenden [...] Bourgeoisisierung ausgefüllt zu werden. Die daraus resultierende ‚kulturelle‘ Homologisierung betrifft alle: das Volk und die Bourgeoisie, die Arbeiter und die Unterschicht [...] Die Matrix, die alle Italiener hervorbringt, ist nun dieselbe.“ Pasolini, Pier Paolo: „Gli italiani non sono più quelli“, *Corriere della Sera*, 10. Juni 1974, 1.

town has always had a very close relationship, made up of simple and traditional devotion, but also of social commitment.

Within this inseparable context of labor and devotion, it is possible to find the conditions for the possibility of an original evolution in the postwar urban development of the town, based on typological homogenization as an economic, political, and social rationale.

After the end of World War II and the liberation of Italy from Fascism by the Anglo-American forces, Italy's reconstruction received substantial economic aid from the Marshall Plan. The results of this rapid adaptation of the country to the new political, social, and economic coordinates are radically recognized by many intellectuals; Luciano Bianciardi's novel *La vita agra*[4] was published in 1962, Pier Paolo Pasolini's *Teorema*[5] in 1968: both describe the paradox embodied by the neo-capitalist bourgeoisie that emerged during the so-called “Italian economic miracle,”[6] according to the canon of what Pasolini would define an “anthropological mutation,”[7] the precise, inexorable and radical dynamic of the economic system between the 1950s and the 1970s, the transformation, that is, of Italian society in general, into a mass organic to the consumer society.[8] This was an unprecedented social price paid for the postwar economic growth, which both authors see as an intrinsic aspect of the contradictory nature of the mutation, carried out through modernization without civil development.

The symbolic value of the detached or semi-detached house, both in terms of existential redemption as well as individual and social, is immediately apparent.

4 Luciano Bianciardi, *La vita agra* (Milan, 1962), published in English in 1965 as *It's a Hard Life.*

5 The novel (Milan, 1968) that Pier Paolo Pasolini wrote at the same time as the screenplay for his 1968 film of the same name, sometimes translated as *Theorem*.

6 “Italian economic miracle” was a journalistic term commonly used to define the socio-economic performance of Italy in the period between the early 1950s and the early 1960s. See *Il miracolo economico italiano (1958–1963)*, ed. Antonio Cardini (Bologna, 2007), Guido Crainz, *Storia del miracolo italiano* (Rome, 1996), Guido Crainz, *Il paese mancato. Dal miracolo economico agli anni Ottanta* (Rome, 2003), and Paul Ginsborg, *Storia d'Italia dal dopoguerra a oggi. Società e politica 1943–1988* (Turin, 1989).

7 “Peasant and paleo-industrial Italy has collapsed, it is undone, it is no more, and in its place there is a void waiting to be filled by a complete ... modernising, falsely tolerant, Americanising ... bourgeoisisation. The resulting ‘cultural’ homologation affects everyone: the people and the bourgeoisie, workers and the underclass ... The matrix that generates all Italians is now the same.” Pier Paolo Pasolini, “Gli italiani non sono più quelli,” *Corriere della Sera*, June 10, 1974, 1.

8 See also Pier Paolo Pasolini, “Il vuoto del potere in Italia, ovvero ‘La scomparsa delle lucciole’”, *Corriere della Sera*, February 1, 1975, 1.

den 1950er- und 1970er-Jahren, die Verwandlung der italienischen Gesellschaft im Allgemeinen in eine organische Masse der Konsumgesellschaft.[8] Dies war ein noch nie dagewesener sozialer Preis, der für das Wirtschaftswachstum der Nachkriegszeit entrichtet wurde, was beide Autoren als einen immanenten Aspekt der widersprüchlichen Natur der Mutation sehen, die durch die Modernisierung ohne zivile Entwicklung vollzogen wurde.

Der symbolische Wert des Ein- oder Zweifamilienhauses, sowohl in Bezug auf die existenzielle Erlösung als auch auf die individuelle und soziale Entwicklung, ist unmittelbar ersichtlich. Franco Alasia und Danilo Montaldi[9] brachten dies 1960 in ihrer Studie *Milano, Corea. Inchiesta sugli immigrati* zum Ausdruck: „Das Haus beginnt als Betonwürfel, doch was man von außen sieht, sagt nichts aus; das Haus beginnt im Keller. Es ist der Keller, der den Bau des Hauses ermöglicht, denn er wird sofort von einer Familie gemietet, die nicht über das gesamte Geld verfügt, um es selbst zu bauen; eine Familie wohnt im Keller, die Familie des Vermieters im Erdgeschoss: es sind zwei Zimmer und ein Abstellraum oder ein Zimmer mit einer Trennwand. Im nächsten Jahr haben die Einwanderer, wenn es gut läuft, eine erste Etage gebaut, in die sie sofort einziehen werden. Die Mieter aus dem Keller ziehen in das Erdgeschoss und der Keller wird an eine neu angekommene Familie untervermietet."[10]

In einem Artikel mit dem Titel „Der zurückgetretene Pionier: In zehn Jahren 600.000 Einwanderer zwischen Mailand und den Seen", der am 8. September 1963 in *Il Giorno* veröffentlicht wurde, erklärt Giorgio Bocca[11] den Unterschied zwischen dem amerikanischen und dem italienischen Traum: „Die Dörfer/Städte des Streifens (Sesto hat mehr als 80.000 Einwohner) sind für die Einwanderer feindlich und agrarisch, wie es Amerika für die Männer der Eroberung war: die gleichen Entbehrungen, Schandtaten, Leiden und Enttäuschungen; hier, wie im [Fernen] Westen, eine Generation am Rande, die ihre Häuser in der Nacht baut und alles riskiert, was sie besitzt. Doch wer glaubt, dass hier ein neuer Italiener entsteht, selbstbewusst, stolz auf sein eigenes Epos wie der Amerikaner, der irrt wahrscheinlich."[12]

8 Vgl. auch Pasolini, Pier Paolo: „Il vuoto del potere in Italia, ovvero ‚La scomparsa delle lucciole'", *Corriere della Sera*, 1. Februar 1975, 1.

9 Franco Alasia war zusammen mit seinem Lehrmeister Danilo Dolci einer der Hauptvertreter der Bewegung für Gewaltlosigkeit und Pazifismus seit den 1950er-Jahren, während Danilo Montaldi ein antileninistischer libertärer marxistischer Schriftsteller war.

10 Alasia, Franco/Montaldi, Danilo: *Milano, Corea. Inchiesta sugli immigrati*, Mailand 1960, 59.

11 Giorgio Bocca war einer der führenden Journalisten Italiens in der Nachkriegszeit, zunächst radikal antifaschistisch, später Anti-Berlusconi.

12 Bocca, Giorgio: „Il pioniere rassegnato. In dieci anni 600.000 immigrati fra Milano e i laghi", *Il Giorno*, 8. September 1963, 26.

Franco Alasia and Danilo Montaldi[9] articulated this point in their 1960 study *Milano, Corea: Inchiesta sugli immigrati:* "The house starts as a concrete cube, but what you see outside doesn't say anything; the house starts in the cellar. It is the cellar that allows the house to be built because it is immediately rented by a family that does not have all the money to build it themselves; one family lives in the cellar, the landlord's family on the ground floor: it is two rooms and a cubbyhole, or a room with a partition. The next year, if things go well, the immigrant has made a first floor, in which they will immediately move in. The tenants from the cellar will move up to the ground floor and the cellar will be sublet to a newly arrived family."[10]

Giorgio Bocca,[11] in an article entitled "The Resigned Pioneer: In Ten Years 600,000 Immigrants Between Milan and the Lakes", published in *Il Giorno* on September 8th, 1963, gives a brief description of the difference between the American and the Italian dream:

"The villages/towns of the strip (Sesto has more than 80,000 inhabitants) hostile and agrarian for the immigrants, as America was for the men of the conquest: the same privations, infamies, sufferings, and disappointments; here, as in the [Far] West, a generation on the brink, building its homes in the night, risking everything it possessed. But anyone who thinks that a new Italian, confident, proud of his [/her] own epic like the American, will emerge here is probably mistaken."[12]

A way to study the genealogy of the phenomenon of detached and semi-detached houses in postwar Italy, the housing problems of the urban systems that made this typology possible, the methods used to satisfy the desire for urbanization, experienced as a kind of natural right to be realized through the creation of communities based on new forms of everyday life capable of giving shape to this desire, is to address the cooperative system, embodied by the politically alternative "Confcooperative" and "Legacoop".[13] The latter is in fact the confederation of the so-called "red" cooperatives, those of communist and socialist inspiration, while "Confcooperative" is the confederation of the so-called "white" cooperatives, i.e. those expressing the economic and professional Catholic milieu. While "Legacoop" has traditionally focused on social cooperation with corporate growth as a strategic objective,

9 Franco Alasia, together with his master Danilo Dolci, was one of the main exponents of the non-violence/pacifism movement since the 1950s, while Danilo Montaldi was an anti-Leninist libertarian Marxist writer.

10 Franco Alasia and Danilo Montaldi, *Milano, Corea: Inchiesta sugli immigrati* (Milan, 1960), 59.

11 Giorgio Bocca was one of Italy's leading postwar journalists, first radically anti-fascist, later anti-Berlusconi.

12 Giorgio Bocca, "Il pioniere rassegnato. In dieci anni 600,000 immigrati fra Milano e i laghi", *Il Giorno*, September 8, 1963, 26.

13 Mario Taccolini, *A servizio dello sviluppo. L'azione economico-sociale delle congregazioni religiose in Italia tra Otto e Novecento* (Milan, 2004).

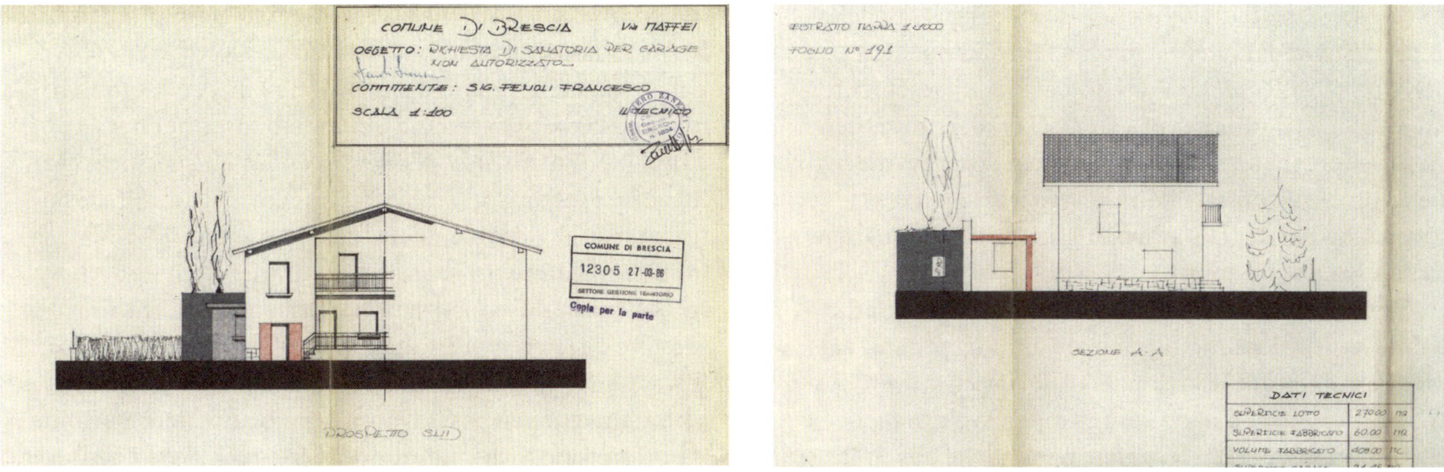

3 © Photos: Andrea Canclini

Eine Möglichkeit, die Genealogie des Phänomens der Ein- und Zweifamilienhäuser im Italien der Nachkriegszeit zu untersuchen, (d.h. die Wohnungsprobleme der städtischen Systeme, die diese Typologie ermöglicht haben und die angewandten Methoden, um den Wunsch nach Urbanisierung zu befriedigen), besteht darin, sich mit dem Genossenschaftssystem zu befassen, das durch die politisch alternativen „Confcooperative“ und „Legacoop“ verkörpert wird.[13] Denn der Wunsch nach Urbanisierung wurde als eine Art natürliches Recht empfunden, das durch die Schaffung von Gemeinschaften verwirklicht werden sollte, die sich auf neue Formen des Alltagslebens stützen, die in der Lage sind, diesem Wunsch Gestalt zu verleihen.

„Legacoop“ bezeichnet den Zusammenschluss der so genannten „roten“ Genossenschaften, d.h. der kommunistisch und sozialistisch inspirierten Genossenschaften, während die „Confcooperative“ den Zusammenschluss der sogenannten „weißen“ Genossenschaften bezeichnet, d.h. der Genossenschaften, die Ausdruck des wirtschaftlichen und beruflichen katholischen Milieus sind. Während sich „Legacoop“ traditionell auf die soziale Zusammenarbeit mit dem Ziel des Unternehmenswachstums konzentriert, verfolgt „Confcooperative“ von jeher eine Art Bergman'scher *Wilde Erdbeeren*-Strategie, bei der die lokale Verwurzelung im Vordergrund steht und gleichzeitig eine territoriale Expansion angestrebt wird. Beide haben neue alltägliche Weltanschauungen hervorgebracht, und ihre Anwesenheit ist nützlich, um zumindest die allgemeinen Merkmale eines spezifischen Falles zu skizzieren, der einmalig und schwer zu wiederholen ist, obwohl er in seiner Definition eines räumlich definierten Alltagslebens einen gewissen Charakter der Universalität aufweist. Dieser Fall ereignete sich in dieser fleißigen, peripheren und frommen Stadt; hier überdeckte eine Art moralisierender Pragmatismus die

13 Taccolini, Mario: *A servizio dello sviluppo. L'azione economico-sociale delle congregazioni religiose in Italia tra Otto e Novecento*, Mailand 2004.

“Confcooperative” has historically adopted a sort of Bergmanian *Wild Strawberries* strategy, prioritizing local rootedness while aiming at territorial expansion. Both gave rise to new everyday *Weltanschauungen* (ideologies), and their presence is useful to outline, at least the general characteristics of a specific case, unique and difficult to repeat, although with a certain character of universality in its definition of a daily life spatially defined. This case occurred in this industrious, peripheral, and devout city; here, a kind of moralizing pragmatism covered up the inherent shortcomings of the settlement model itself: “Either I go to paradise, or I go to jail,” the protagonist of this story, a local Catholic priest, used to say jokingly to his collaborators, convinced of the alternative nature, under certain conditions, between the possibilities offered by Christian eschatology and the civil nomos.

The IACP[14] (Istituto Autonomo Case Popolari, the nation's public body for social dwellings) and INA-Casa[15] (Istituto Nazionale delle Assicurazioni) were, during

14 IACP was a public body founded in 1903 with the aim of promotion, construction, and management of public housing with controlled rents. The Autonomous Institute did not have a single national system, but was divided into several branches, with local headquarters at the municipal, provincial or regional level, depending on local needs.

15 Founded with Law 43 in 1949, called “Piano Ina Casa.” See Paola Di Biagi, *La grande ricostruzione, il piano INA-Casa e l'Italia degli anni Cinquanta* (Roma, 2001). INA-Casa (Istituto Nazione delle Assicurazioni) was used by Amintore Fanfani, the Minister of Labor and Social Security, to fund a national housing plan. In force between 1949 and 1963 to realize public housing throughout the Italian territory, it was a sort of small welfare state intervention, with the Italian National Insurance money used to finance social housing, a sort of Beveridge Report, used by the United Kingdom to establish and finance the welfare state after World War II. Ruled by Adalberto Libera until 1952, Mario Ridolfi, Giorgio Raineri, Roberto Gabetti, Carlo Aymonino, Franco Albini, the BBPR, Enrico Castiglioni, Ignazio Gardella, Figini and Pollini, Ettore Sottsass, Italo Insolera and many others designed several residential projects planned and financed by INA-Casa Institute.

inhärenten Unzulänglichkeiten des Siedlungsmodells selbst: „Entweder komme ich ins Paradies oder ins Gefängnis", pflegte der Protagonist dieser Geschichte, ein lokaler katholischer Priester, scherzhaft zu seinen MitarbeiterInnen zu sagen, überzeugt von der Alternative, die unter bestimmten Bedingungen zwischen den Möglichkeiten der christlichen Eschatologie und dem zivilen Nomos besteht.

Das IACP[14] (Istituto Autonomo Case Popolari, die staatliche Einrichtung für Sozialwohnungen) und das INA-Casa[15] (Istituto Nazionale delle Assicurazioni) waren in den Jahrzehnten nach dem Zweiten Weltkrieg die beiden Hauptakteure des sozialen Wohnungsbaus in Italien. INA-Casa war von Anfang an der nationale Interventionsplan, der die Wohndichte auf etwa 500 EinwohnerInnen pro Hektar begrenzen sollte; eine Zahl, die bereits eine erwartete spezifische Lebensweise definiert, wobei häufig auf ArchitektInnen zurückgegriffen wurde, die bereits in der Designforschung tätig und in der Lage waren, die in der italienischen Kultur konsolidierten Gestaltungstrends zu verkörpern. In Brescia begann INA-Casa seine Tätigkeit 1949 mit dem Bau des ersten Satellitenviertels, dem Lamarmora-Viertel, während es in den späten 1950er und frühen 1960er-Jahren in den westlichen Vororten mit Projekten von Architekten wie Giovanni Muzio und Piero Bottoni aktiv war.

Neben diesen institutionellen Interventionen, die lokale Ergebnisse eines umfassenderen nationalen Planungsprozesses waren, begann ab Mitte der 1950er-Jahre auch der örtliche Pfarrer Ottorino Marcolini (1897–1978)

14 Das IACP war eine öffentliche Einrichtung, die 1903 mit dem Ziel der Förderung, des Baus und der Verwaltung von Sozialwohnungen mit kontrollierten Mieten gegründet wurde. Das autonome Institut verfügte nicht über ein einheitliches nationales System, sondern war in mehrere Zweigstellen unterteilt, die je nach den lokalen Bedürfnissen auf kommunaler, provinzieller oder regionaler Ebene angesiedelt waren.

15 Gegründet mit Gesetz 43 im Jahr 1949, genannt „Piano Ina Casa". Vgl. dazu Paola Di Biagi, *La grande ricostruzione, il piano INA-Casa e l'Italia degli anni Cinquanta*, Rom 2001. INA-Casa (Istituto Nazione delle Assicurazioni) wurde von Amintore Fanfani, dem Minister für Arbeit und soziale Sicherheit, zur Finanzierung eines nationalen Wohnungsbauplans eingesetzt. Dieser Plan, der zwischen 1949 und 1963 in Kraft war, um auf dem gesamten italienischen Staatsgebiet Sozialwohnungen zu errichten, war eine Art kleine Intervention des Wohlfahrtsstaates, bei der die Gelder der italienischen Sozialversicherung zur Finanzierung des sozialen Wohnungsbaus verwendet wurden – eine Art Beveridge-Report, wie ihn das Vereinigte Königreich nach dem Zweiten Weltkrieg zur Errichtung und Finanzierung des Wohlfahrtsstaates verwendet hatte. Unter der Regierung von Adalberto Libera bis 1952 entwarfen Mario Ridolfi, Giorgio Raineri, Roberto Gabetti, Carlo Aymonino, Franco Albini, die BBPR, Enrico Castiglioni, Ignazio Gardella, Figini und Pollini, Ettore Sottsass, Italo Insolera und viele andere mehrere Wohnprojekte, die vom Institut INA-Casa geplant und finanziert wurden.

the decades after World War II, the two main protagonists of social housing in Italy. From the earliest years, INA-Casa was the national intervention plan, set out to limit housing density to around 500 inhabitants per hectare, a number that already defines an expected specific way of life, often relying on architects already engaged in design research and able to embody design trends consolidated in Italian culture. In Brescia, INA-Casa began its activity in 1949 with the construction of Lamarmora, the first satellite district, while in the late 1950s and early 1960s, it was active in the western suburbs with projects designed by architects such as Giovanni Muzio and Piero Bottoni.

Alongside these institutional interventions, local results of a broader national planning process, from the mid-1950s, the local priest Ottorino Marcolini (1897–1978), also began to intervene in the reconstruction of Brescia with the building cooperatives that he himself began to found; with completely different modalities, they were based on the type of housing for one or two families to be built in areas outside the urban fabric without any building capacity yet and outside the urban development plans. The preference for peripheral areas is primarily due to their comparatively lower acquisition costs, as these areas were often zoned for agricultural purposes and typically need to be made developable after purchase. The buildings in these areas are characterized by their simple design and the use of poor quality materials and are always equipped with small private outside areas and spaces, small vegetable gardens, and backyards. It is an initiative with a declared moral character: "Usually," writes Marcolini, "people do not care about moral issues, and so very harmful agglomerations are created, morally and socially ... the family threatens to disintegrate because of the lack of love for the family nest."[16]

It is also from this perspective that it is necessary to frame the peculiar phenomenon constituted by the residential villages built in Brescia on the initiative of Marcolini. A design approach commented on almost exclusively by local politics and chronicles, that is, by the environment that essentially offered the conditions of possibility to this socio-urban phenomenon. Instead, the tools of the epistemological apparatus offered by urban anthropology can be used to outline the ways in which the forms of everyday feeling that these settlements seek and recreate through their configuration of life are reproduced; in particular, these tools can be useful for analyzing both the ways in which the design approach was structured and its relationship to local and national urban policies, the only two levels of Italian urban planning in those decades.

Marcolini was a unique figure, not only in Brescia, but in Italy: certainly, no priest would ever build 25,000 housing units, mostly single and two-family houses, in

16 Ottorino Marcolini quoted in Roberto Busi, *Padre Marcolini: Dalla casa per la famiglia alla costruzione della città* (Rome, 2000), 177.

mit den von ihm selbst gegründeten Baugenossenschaften, in den Wiederaufbau von Brescia einzugreifen; mit völlig unterschiedlichen Modalitäten basierten sie auf der Art von Wohnungen für eine oder zwei Familien, die in Gebieten außerhalb des städtischen Gefüges ohne jegliche Baukapazität und außerhalb der Stadtentwicklungspläne errichtet wurden. Die Bevorzugung von Randgebieten ist in erster Linie auf die vergleichsweise geringeren Erwerbskosten zurückzuführen, da diese Gebiete häufig für landwirtschaftliche Zwecke ausgewiesen waren und nach dem Erwerb in der Regel erst erschlossen werden müssen. Die Gebäude in diesen Gebieten zeichnen sich durch ihre einfache Gestaltung und die Verwendung minderwertiger Materialien aus und sind stets mit kleinen privaten Außenbereichen und -flächen, kleinen Gemüsegärten und Hinterhöfen ausgestattet. Es handelt sich um eine Initiative mit einem erklärtermaßen moralischen Charakter: „Normalerweise", schreibt Marcolini, „kümmern sich die Menschen nicht um moralische Fragen, und so entstehen moralisch und sozial sehr schädliche Agglomerationen [...] die Familie droht zu zerfallen, weil die Liebe zum familiären Nest fehlt."[16]

Unter diesem Blickwinkel ist auch das besondere Phänomen der auf Initiative von Marcolini in Brescia errichteten Wohndörfer zu sehen. Ein Planungsansatz, der fast ausschließlich von der lokalen Politik und den Chroniken kommentiert wird, d.h. von der Umgebung, die diesem sozio-urbanen Phänomen im Wesentlichen die Bedingungen der Möglichkeit bot. Stattdessen können die Werkzeuge des erkenntnistheoretischen Apparats der Stadtanthropologie genutzt werden, um die Art und Weise zu skizzieren, in der die Formen des Alltagsgefühls, welche diese Siedlungen durch ihre Lebenskonfiguration suchen und schaffen, reproduziert werden. Insbesondere können diese Werkzeuge nützlich sein, um sowohl die Art und Weise zu analysieren, in der der Planungsansatz strukturiert war, als auch seine Beziehung zur lokalen und nationalen Stadtpolitik, den beiden einzigen Ebenen der italienischen Stadtplanung in jenen Jahrzehnten.

Marcolini war eine einzigartige Persönlichkeit, nicht nur in Brescia, sondern in ganz Italien: Noch nie hatte ein Priester 25.000 Wohneinheiten, hauptsächlich Ein- und Zweifamilienhäuser, in einer einzigen italienischen Provinz gebaut, fast 30.000 in ganz Norditalien. In der Stadt wurde er als „Ingenieur Gottes" bezeichnet, da er in den Jahren des Wiederaufbaus einen echten privaten Bauplan umsetzte. Marcolini war sofort von den Gründen überzeugt, die in den folgenden Jahrzehnten die italienische Debatte über die Regulierung des Städtebaus bestimmen sollten, als das Wohnungsproblem von einer öffentlichen Angelegenheit zu einem reinen Marktphänomen wurde, wie jedes andere Konsumgut auch. Marcolini selbst pflegte

16 Ottorino Marcolini zitiert in Busi, Roberto: *Padre Marcolini. Dalla casa per la famiglia alla costruzione della città*, Rom 2000.

a single Italian province, almost 30,000 in all of northern Italy. Nicknamed in town "God's Engineer" for some reason, he implemented a real private building plan during the years of reconstruction. Marcolini was immediately persuaded of the reasons that would drive the Italian debate on urban planning regulation in the following decades, when the housing problem would go from being a public issue to being a phenomenon of market dynamics alone, like any other consumer good. Marcolini himself used to ask himself in public: "Housing is a consumer good; we have to give houses that last a generation, who forces us to make them last a thousand years?",[17] directing his work from the outset towards a form of welfare society as an alternative to the welfare state.[18] Decades later, at the national level the ten-year plan established by Law 457 of 1978,[19] whose effects lasted until the early 1990s, followed by the Law 865 of 1971,[20] which had already previously marked the beginning of active and profound public intervention in the real estate sector. In fact, since the early 1990s, public intervention has disappeared not only as a social emergency, but also as a topic of debate. Housing is no longer a public problem: the market alone is responsible for it.

Born into a family where his father Giovanni was an inspector in the Royal Post Office,[21] the first of seven children, Ottorino studied at the local Jesuit college with Giovanni Battista Montini, the future Pope Paul VI, and grew up in the oratory of the *Padri della Pace*, a local confraternity founded in the mid-sixteenth Century.

In October 1916, he took part in World War I as an officer in Carnia; in 1918 he enrolled at Politecnico di Milano, where he obtained a degree in Mechanical Industrial Engineering. After that, he became General Manager of the "Officina del Gas" in Brescia, which had recently been municipalized, before obtaining a second degree in mathematics in Padua in 1924, the year in which he joined the congregation of the *Padri della Pace*. Spiritual assistant

17 Lucio Bregoli, Clotilde Castelli and Antonio Fappani, *Un prete fuori serie. Ottorino Marcolini* (Brescia, 2012), 21.

18 See Tom Avermaete, Mark Swenarton and Dirk van den Heuvel, eds., *Architecture and the Welfare State* (London, 2014).

19 Law 457 was a "framework law" passed in 1978, i.e., a law that summarizes and synthesizes previous regulations in the field of economic and social housing; in fact, it modifies, incorporates, and reorganizes the entire economic and social housing sector.

20 In 1971, Law 865 transformed the Istituto Autonomo Case Popolari (IACP) from being an Economic Public Body to a Non-Economic Public Body with a predominance of public welfare activities, setting objectives that encompassed the entire social housing sector. In fact, there was talk of integrating housing policy, land development, and a unified rent regulation.

21 See Federica Piardi and Lidio Piardi, *Padre Ottorino Marcolini: Il manovale di Dio* (Bergamo, 2018).

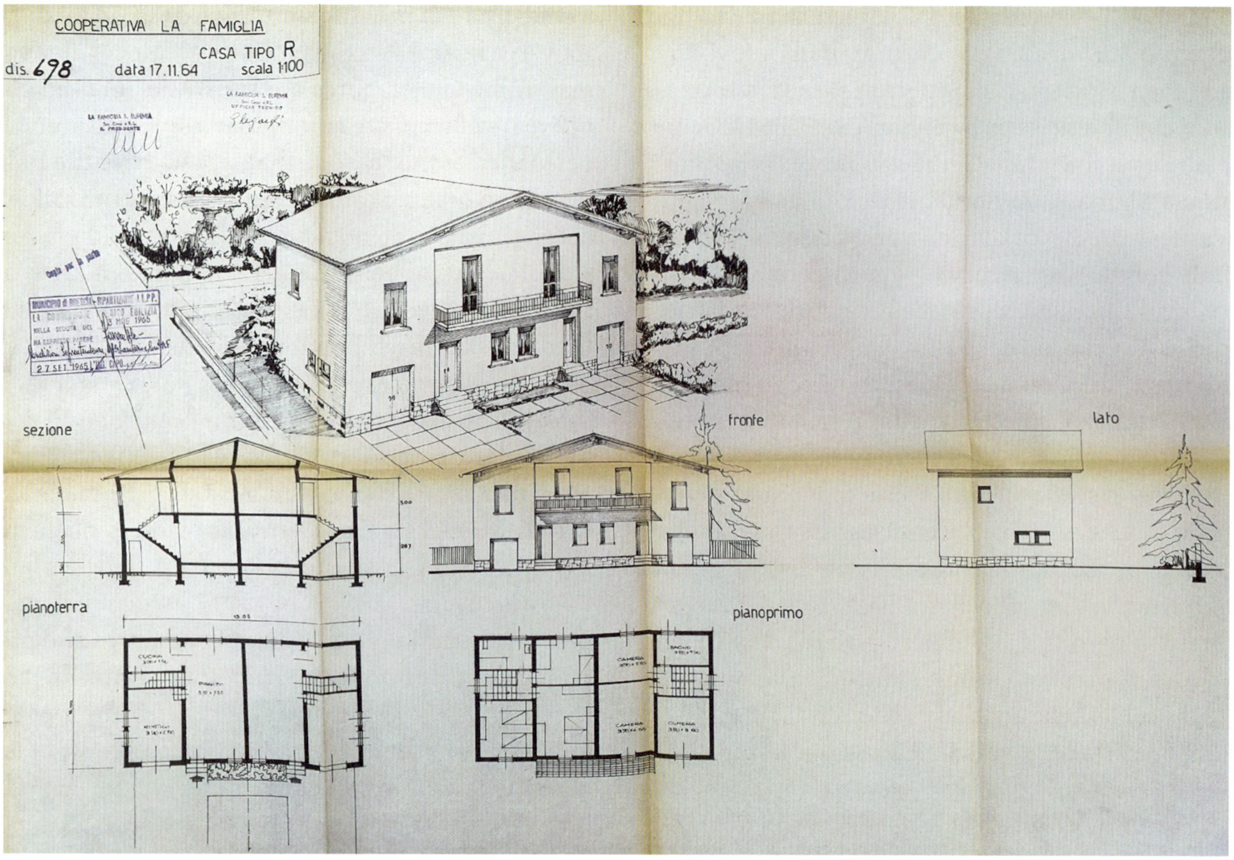

2 House Type R © Photo: Andrea Canclini

sich in der Öffentlichkeit zu fragen: „Wohnen ist ein Konsumgut, wir müssen Häuser bauen, die eine Generation halten, wer zwingt uns dazu, dass sie tausend Jahre halten sollen?“[17] und richtete seine Arbeit von Anfang an auf eine Form der Wohlfahrtsgesellschaft als Alternative zum Wohlfahrtsstaat aus.[18] Jahrzehnte später folgte auf nationaler Ebene der Zehnjahresplan des Gesetzes 457 aus dem Jahr 1978[19], dessen Auswirkungen bis Anfang der 1990er-Jahre andauerten, den das Gesetz 865 von 1971[20] fortsetzte, das bereits zuvor den Beginn einer aktiven und tiefgreifenden öffentlichen Intervention im Immobiliensektor markiert hatte. Seit Anfang der 1990er-Jahre ist

17 Bregoli, Lucio/Castelli, Clotilde/Fappani, Antonio: *Un prete fuori serie. Ottorino Marcolini*, Brescia 2012, 21.
18 Vgl. Avermaete, Tom/Swenarton, Mark/van den Heuvel, Dirk (Hg.): *Architecture and the Welfare State*, London 2014.
19 Das Gesetz 457 war ein 1978 verabschiedetes „Rahmengesetz“, d.h. ein Gesetz, das frühere Vorschriften im Bereich des wirtschaftlichen und sozialen Wohnungsbaus zusammenfasst und synthetisiert; tatsächlich ändert, integriert und reorganisiert es den gesamten Bereich des wirtschaftlichen und sozialen Wohnungsbaus.
20 Im Jahr 1971 wurde das Istituto Autonomo Case Popolari (IACP) durch das Gesetz 865 von einer wirtschaftlichen öffentlichen Einrichtung in eine nichtwirtschaftliche öffentliche Einrichtung umgewandelt, die vorwiegend im Bereich der öffentlichen Wohlfahrt tätig ist und deren Ziele den gesamten sozialen Wohnungsbau umfassen. Es war sogar die Rede davon, die Wohnungspolitik, die Landentwicklung und eine einheitliche Mietpreisregelung zu integrieren.

to the students of the FUCI[22] and of San Vincenzo[23] during World War II he was a volunteer military chaplain with the mountain infantry troops of the Alpine Army Corps in Russia, on the Don and until the retreat after the battle of Nikolayevka (Russia, January 1943); after the armistice, he was imprisoned in the Nazi concentration camp of Hohenstein.[24]

Writer Mario Rigoni Stern[25] recalls how Marcolini was the only officer to volunteer to accompany captured soldiers on the road from the Brenner Pass to Innsbruck

22 The Italian Catholic Federation of University Students (*Federazione universitaria cattolica italiana*), founded in 1896, is a federation of Catholic university student groups. It was one of the cornerstones of the formation of Italian Catholic intellectuals in the 20th century and was also the only recognized Catholic association in universities during the twenty-year Fascist period, in which a large part of the future ruling class of the Christian Democratic Party was formed. In the first decade of the 20th century the FUCI developed an identity and a vision of reality that were considered progressive and too open; this attitude earned some of its adherents the accusation of modernism. From 1925 to 1933, Montini was its national ecclesiastical assistant.
23 The *Società di San Vincenzo De Paoli*, founded locally in the mid-1800s, is still particularly active in assisting and welcoming people in economic and housing need in its dormitories.
24 See Antonio Fappani and Clotilde Castelli, *Il prete di tutti* (Brescia, 1989).
25 Mario Rigoni Stern (1921–2008), was an Italian writer; his novels mainly tell stories of harmony and the relationship with the natural mountain environment.

die öffentliche Intervention nicht nur als soziale Notlage, sondern auch als Thema der Debatte verschwunden. Das Wohnungswesen ist kein öffentliches Problem mehr: Dafür ist allein der Markt zuständig.

Ottorino Marcolini wurde als erstes von sieben Kindern in eine Familie hineingeboren, in der sein Vater Giovanni Inspektor bei der Königlichen Post war.[21] Er studierte am örtlichen Jesuitenkolleg bei Giovanni Battista Montini, dem späteren Papst Paul VI., und wuchs im Oratorium der *Padri della Pace* auf, einer örtlichen Bruderschaft, die Mitte des 16. Jahrhunderts gegründet wurde.

Im Oktober 1916 nahm er als Offizier in Carnia im Ersten Weltkrieg teil und schrieb sich 1918 am Politecnico di Milano ein, wo er einen Abschluss in mechanischem Wirtschaftsingenieurwesen erwarb. Danach wurde er Generaldirektor der „Officina del Gas" in Brescia, die gerade in städtischen Besitz überführt worden war, bevor er 1924 in Padua ein zweites Mathematikstudium absolvierte, in dem Jahr, in dem er der Kongregation der *Padri della Pace* beitrat. Als geistlicher Assistent der Studierenden der FUCI[22] und von San Vincenzo[23] war er während des Zweiten Weltkriegs freiwilliger Militärseelsorger bei den Gebirgsinfanterietruppen des Korps der Alpenarmee in Russland, am Don und bis zum Rückzug nach der Schlacht von Nikolajewka (Russland, Januar 1943); nach dem Waffenstillstand war er im Nazi-Konzentrationslager Hohenstein inhaftiert.[24]

Der Schriftsteller Mario Rigoni Stern[25] erinnert sich, dass Marcolini der einzige Offizier war, der sich freiwillig meldete, um gefangene Soldaten auf dem Weg vom Brennerpass nach Innsbruck ins Konzentrations-lager

21 Vgl. Piardi,Federica/Piardi, Lidio: *Padre Ottorino Marcolini. Il manovale di Dio*, Bergamo 2018.

22 Der 1896 gegründete katholische italienische Universitätsverband (*Federazione universitaria cattolica italiana*) ist ein Zusammenschluss katholischer Universitätsstudentengruppen. Sie war einer der Eckpfeiler der Bildung italienischer katholischer Intellektueller im 20. Jahrhundert und war auch die einzige anerkannte katholische Vereinigung an den Universitäten während der zwanzigjährigen faschistischen Periode, in der ein Großteil der späteren Führungsschicht der Christdemokratischen Partei gebildet wurde. Im ersten Jahrzehnt des 20. Jahrhunderts entwickelte die FUCI eine Identität und Weltsicht, die als fortschrittlich und zu offen angesehen wurden; diese Haltung brachte einigen ihrer Anhänger den Vorwurf des Modernismus ein. Von 1925 bis 1933 war Montini ihr nationaler kirchlicher Assistent.

23 Die *Società di San Vincenzo De Paoli*, die Mitte des 18. Jahrhunderts auf lokaler Ebene gegründet wurde, ist hinsichtlich der Unterstützung und Aufnahme von Menschen in wirtschaftlicher und wohnungsmäßiger Not in ihren Wohnheimen noch immer besonders aktiv.

24 Vgl. Fappani, Antonio/Castelli, Clotilde: *Il prete di tutti*, Brescia 1989.

25 Mario Rigoni Stern (1921–2008) war ein italienischer Schriftsteller, dessen Romane hauptsächlich von Harmonie und der Beziehung zur natürlichen Bergwelt erzählen.

to the concentration camp. Rigoni Stern, his comrade in the Vestone Alpine Regiment at Colle Isarco before September 1943, and then a fellow prisoner in a second concentration camp, remembers Marcolini in 1979 as a character known for the comfort he offered to the soldiers, especially when he talked about home.[26] He would stay with them until the last one, until October 1945, when he wrote, in a private letter to the future mayor of Brescia, Cesare Trebeschi, that he considered the reconstruction of the country essential, and that the destroyed houses would only help to make Italians better people if the new ones did not make them selfish again.[27] He tried, in his own way, to create communities in which he could try to prevent the recurrence of the moral problems he had experienced in Fascist Italian society; for these reasons, in 1953, he founded the cooperative *La Famiglia*, with which he extended his achievements to 14 Italian provinces, creating almost 30,000 homes inhabited by more than 100,000 people.[28] In this, Marcolini was inspired by the model of the American single-family house,[29] a typology he saw described in one of the films produced and distributed in Italy and in more than 150 other countries worldwide by the United States Information Service (USIS),[30] previously part of the US embassies and later as the overseas agency of the US Information Agency (1953–1999);[31] the Italian offices were based in Trieste and were set up to produce hundreds of footages, videos and films by the end of the 1950s to propagate the Marshall Plan in the climate of the Cold War.

Inspired by the postwar American model of life, and by a simplified idea of the Garden City Movement, one of Marcolini's reference models was the French example

26 See Mario Rigoni Stern, "Ci parlò di casa e di pace...," *Giornale di Brescia*, September 13th, 1979.

27 The letter was published in the 2 December 1945 issue of *La Fionda*, an irregular periodical published in Brescia between 1918 and 1947.

28 See Giovanni Gregorini, "La cultura e i problemi dell'industrializzazione bresciana: Giulio Bevilacqua e Ottorino Marcolini," in *A servizio dello sviluppo. L'azione economico-sociale delle congregazioni religiose in Italia tra Otto e Novecento*, ed. Mario Taccolini (Milano, 2004), 191–249.

29 See Laura J. Miller, "Family Togetherness and the Suburban Ideal," *Sociological Forum* 10, no. 3 (1995): 393–418.

30 USIS footage, videos and films are now archived at the Archivio Centrale dello Stato (Central State Archives is the archival institute of the Ministry of Culture responsible for the preservation and knowledge of the memory of the unified Italian state); some of them are posted on their YouTube channel. Particularly interesting is *Case a buon mercato* (Affordable Housing), a short propaganda film about the promotion of the American construction industry as an economic and lifestyle model: www.youtube.com/watch?v=G_MjQ7JCy1I (October 2023).

31 See Simona Tobia, *Advertising America. The United States Information Service in Italy (1945–1956)* (Milan, 2008).

zu begleiten. Rigoni Stern, sein Kamerad im Alpenregiment Vestone am Gossensaß (Colle Isarco) vor September 1943 und ein Mitgefangener in einem zweiten Konzentrationslager, erinnern sich 1979 Marcolinis als einer Persönlichkeit, die dafür bekannt war, dass sie die Soldaten tröstete, vor allem wenn sie von zu Hause sprachen.[26] Er blieb bis zuletzt bei ihnen, bis zum Oktober 1945, als er in einem privaten Brief an den zukünftigen Bürgermeister von Brescia, Cesare Trebeschi, schrieb, dass er den Wiederaufbau des Landes für unerlässlich halte und dass die zerstörten Häuser nur dazu beitragen würden, die Italiener zu besseren Menschen zu machen, wenn die neuen sie nicht wieder zu Egoisten machten.[27] Er versuchte auf seine Weise, Gemeinschaften zu schaffen, in denen er versuchen konnte, die Wiederholung der moralischen Probleme zu verhindern, die er in der faschistischen italienischen Gesellschaft erlebt hatte. Aus diesem Grund gründete er 1953 die Genossenschaft *La Famiglia*, mit der er seine Leistungen auf 14 italienische Provinzen ausdehnte und fast 30.000 Wohnungen schuf, die von mehr als 100.000 Menschen bewohnt wurden.[28] Dabei ließ sich Marcolini vom Modell des amerikanischen Einfamilienhauses inspirieren,[29] einer Typologie, die er in einem der Filme beschrieben sah, die vom United States Information Service (USIS),[30] der früher zu den US-Botschaften gehörte und später als Auslandsvertretung der US-Informationsagentur (1953–1999) in Italien und in mehr als 150 anderen Ländern weltweit verbreitet wurde.[31] Die italienische Niederlassung hatte ihren Sitz in Triest und produzierte bis Ende der 1950er-Jahre Hunderte von Aufnahmen, Videos und Filmen, um im Klima des Kalten Krieges für den Marshallplan zu werben.

Inspiriert vom amerikanischen Lebensmodell der Nachkriegszeit und einer vereinfachten Vorstellung von

26 Vgl. Rigoni Stern, Mario: „Ci parlò di casa e di pace…“, *Giornale di Brescia*, 13. September 1979.

27 Der Brief wurde am 2. Dezember 1945 in *La Fionada* veröffentlicht, einem in unregelmäßigen Abständen publizierten Periodikum, das zwischen 1918 und 1947 in Brescia erschien.

28 Vgl. Gregorini, Giovanni: „La cultura e i problemi dell'industrializzazione bresciana: Giulio Bevilacqua e Ottorino Marcolini“, in: Taccolini, Mario (Hg): *A servizio dello sviluppo. L'azione economico-sociale delle congregazioni religiose in Italia tra Otto e Novecento*, Mailand 2004, 191–249.

29 Vgl. Miller, Laura J.: „Family Togetherness and the Suburban Ideal“, *Sociological Forum* 10, 3 (1995), 393–418.

30 Material, Videos und Filme der USIS sind heute im Archivio Centrale dello Stato (Zentrales Staatsarchiv, das Archivinstitut des Kulturministeriums, das für die Bewahrung und Kenntnis des Gedächtnisses des vereinigten italienischen Staates zuständig ist) archiviert; einige von ihnen sind auf ihrem YouTube-Kanal zu sehen. Besonders interessant ist *Case a buon mercato* (Erschwingliches Wohnen), ein kurzer Propagandafilm über die Förderung der amerikanischen Bauindustrie als Wirtschafts- und Lebensmodell: www.youtube.com/watch?v=G_MjQ7JCy1I (Oktober 2023).

31 Vgl. Tobia, Simona: *Advertising America: The United States Information Service in Italy (1945-1956)*, Mailand 2008.

of the self-building *Castors mouvement coopératif*,[32] a federation of independent associations, which in turn derived from the *cottages sociaux* of the 1928 French *Loi Loucheur*, the first law to provide for economic intervention by the state to promote social housing; he was so convinced of this that in the 1950s he opened his own cement factory, Cementificio Bresciano CemBre, north of the city, to produce the cement needed for the building sites of his cooperatives from the limestone quarried from the hill above. The factory closed in 1971 and remained abandoned for decades; it has now been demolished and turned into a public park. The two types of housing that Marcolini will be offering with his cooperative are quite simple: "Type A," a 70-square-meter one-story house with three rooms and bathrooms, and "Type B," a two-story house with an extra room and a garage with laundry room, both with a 150-square-meter garden:[33] enough to make the city dweller feel uprooted from its environment of original and continue the ordinary rhythm of rural life to which they were used to.

The fact that Brescia grew from 140,000 to 210,000 inhabitants between 1951 and 1982, was thanks to the 20,000 people from the countryside who moved to the four Marcolini villages, an incredibly high number considering that in the period between 1945 and 1953 about 17,000 rooms were built in town. The first to be completed was named "Villaggio Violino," to the west of the town, in 1953; a few hundred meters away, "Villaggio Badia" was built in 1954, while from 1955 onwards a long list of towns in the province followed, starting with Villa Carcina in 1957, Gardone Valtrompia in 1958 and then Chiari and Sarezzo, all small towns near Brescia. There would be dozens of places that would welcome this type of intervention: in the end, there would be 238 cooperatives for 138 villages, spread over almost the whole of Northern Italy, with about 30,000 houses.

The local regulatory context in which Marcolini operates, between the mid-1950s and the mid-1970s, is rather fragmented, although not without effectiveness. At the end of World War II, the master plan for the reconstruction of the municipality of Brescia began its process in 1948;[34] the Municipal Technical Commission to study

32 Michèle Pezzagno, "Padre Marcolini e Padre Zanardini: due esperienze a confronto", in *Atti del Convegno di Studi "Autocostruzione della città: l'edilizia per la famiglia"*, ed. Roberto Busi (Brescia, 2003), 99–110.

33 See Franco Robecchi, *Brescia fra Ricostruzione e Boom: Edilizia e Urbanistica dal 1945 al 1975* (Brescia, 2006).

34 With the Ministerial Decree 485 of March 22, 1946 Brescia was included in the list of cities that had to have a Reconstruction Plan, to repair the war damage to the building heritage. The municipal technical office was supported by a special commission, the plan was presented in March 1947. See Aldo Di Gennaro, Dario Dominico and Maurilio Lovatti, "La ricostruzione edilizia a Brescia (1945–1953)," in *Brescia negli anni della ricostruzione (1945–1949)*, ed. Roberto Chiarini (Brescia, 1981), 243–266.

der Gartenstadtbewegung war eines von Marcolinis Referenzmodellen das französische Beispiel des selbstbauenden *Castors mouvement coopératif*,[32] eines Zusammenschlusses unabhängiger Vereinigungen, der wiederum auf die *cottages sociaux* des französischen *Loi Loucheur* von 1928 zurückgeht, dem ersten Gesetz, das wirtschaftliche Interventionen des Staates zur Förderung des sozialen Wohnungsbaus vorsah. Er war davon so überzeugt, dass er in den 1950er-Jahren eine eigene Zementfabrik, die Cementificio Bresciano CemBre, nördlich der Stadt eröffnete, um den für die Baustellen seiner Genossenschaften benötigten Zement aus dem Kalkstein herzustellen, der auf dem oberhalb gelegenen Hügel abgebaut wurde. Die Fabrik wurde 1971 geschlossen und stand jahrzehntelang leer; heute ist sie abgerissen und in einen öffentlichen Park umgewandelt worden. Die beiden Wohnungstypen, die Marcolini mit seiner Genossenschaft anbieten wird, sind recht einfach: „Typ A", ein 70 Quadratmeter großes, einstöckiges Haus mit drei Zimmern und Badezimmern, und „Typ B", ein zweistöckiges Haus mit einem zusätzlichen Zimmer und einer Garage mit Waschküche, beide mit einem 150 Quadratmeter großen Garten:[33] genug, um den zukünftigen StadtbewohnerInnen das Gefühl zu geben, trotz der Entwurzelung aus ihrer ursprünglichen Umgebung den Rhythmus des Landlebens fortsetzen zu können, an den sie gewöhnt waren.

Wenn Brescia zwischen 1951 und 1982 von 140.000 auf 210.000 EinwohnerInnen wuchs, dann auch dank der 20.000 Menschen, die vom Land in die vier Marcolini-Dörfer zogen, eine unglaublich hohe Zahl, wenn man bedenkt, dass in der Zeit zwischen 1945 und 1953 etwa 17.000 Zimmer in der Stadt geschaffen wurden. Das erste Dorf, das 1953 fertiggestellt wurde, hieß „Villaggio Violino" im Westen der Stadt; einige hundert Meter weiter wurde 1954 „Villaggio Badia" errichtet, während ab 1955 eine lange Liste von Orten in der Provinz folgte, beginnend mit Villa Carcina im Jahr 1957, Gardone Valtrompia im Jahr 1958 und dann Chiari und Sarezzo, alles kleine Städte in der Nähe von Brescia. Es gab Dutzende von Orten, die diese Art von Intervention begrüßen sollten: Am Ende waren es 238 Genossenschaften für 138 Dörfer, die sich über fast ganz Norditalien mit etwa 30.000 Häusern verteilten.

Der lokale Regelungskontext, in dem Marcolini zwischen Mitte der 1950er- und Mitte der 1970er-Jahre tätig ist, ist ziemlich zersplittert, wenn auch nicht ohne Wirkung. Nach dem Ende des Zweiten Weltkriegs wurde 1948 der Masterplan für den Wiederaufbau der Gemeinde

32 Pezzagno, Michèle: „Padre Marcolini e Padre Zanardini: due esperienze a confronto", in: Busi, Roberto (Hg.): *Atti del Convegno di Studi Autocostruzione della città: l'edilizia per la*, Brescia 2003, 99–110.

33 Vgl. Robecchi, Franco: *Brescia fra Ricostruzione e Boom. Edilizia e Urbanistica dal 1945 al 1975*, Brescia 2006.

the reconstruction project, which had already been established in 1945, was chaired by the mayor Guglielmo Ghislandi with vice-president Vittorio Montini, councillor for Public Works and cousin of Giovanni Battista Montini, the future pope Paul VI. The plan was approved by the Ministry of Public Works in 1950, with a validity limited to the following four years. The report lists the damage suffered by buildings as a result of the bombing that took place between February 1944 and April 1945: about 35 percent of the housing stock was destroyed or damaged, about 35,000 rooms out of the 100,000 or so in which the 120,000 or so citizens who make up the population of the urban core lived, out of a total population of about 165,000 in the urban area. The plan sets out the building regulations that any new building must comply with if it is to be included within the boundaries of the real urban core: regulations that are not in force in the areas chosen by Marcolini, which are all outside that perimeter.

The subsequent urban planning instrument began its administrative process in 1957; sent to the Ministry of Public Works for approval, it was rejected with the request to resubmit it within eight months; the second draft, entrusted to Mario Morini, a former professor at Politecnico di Milano, was approved by the City Council in March 1960 and by the General Council of the Ministry of Public Works in November 1960, and it entered into force in 1961. The main flaw of the plan, which left the city at the mercy of unlimited building, even in agricultural and hilly areas, would be partially corrected in later versions, which were implemented in various stages until 1968.

In the meantime, Marcolini had planned, approved, and built most of his main villages. It was only in 1973 that the Municipal Technical Office, with the advice of designers and historians such as Franco Albini, Leonardo Benevolo,[35] Vittoria Calzolari, Franca Helg, and Giorgio Lombardi, prepared the important variant of the urban

35 Leonardo Benevolo's relationship with Brescia is significant; since 1972, he has been the protagonist of one of the most important and successful social housing projects in Italy, that of the San Polo district: 375 hectares on the south-eastern outskirts of the city, today home to about 20,000 people, in a district whose urban planning was carried out by the City Council on the basis of Benevolo's project, based on the idea of nine *unités d'habitation*, each with about 500 dwellings of three different types (high-rise, terraced and row houses), where the City Council, in order to keep prices down, provided the land free of charge on the basis of urban planning agreements. Today, the neighborhood is an integral part of the city, with a metro, bike paths, 20 hectares of parks, schools, and social and community centers. About 20 years ago, an extension of about 2,000 housing units was built, with major interventions by Mauro Galantino. A wide project that includes the possibility of organizing an infraordinary that is completely different from the model of Marcolini. See Leonardo Benevolo, *Brescia, San Polo: un quartiere di iniziativa pubblica* (Rome, 1976).

5 Postcard from Villaggio Badia, Brescia, Italy, 1958

Brescia in Angriff genommen;[34] die bereits 1945 gegründete kommunale technische Kommission zur Untersuchung des Wiederaufbauprojekts wurde vom Bürgermeister und von Vittorio Montini, Stadtrat für öffentliche Arbeiten und Cousin Giovanni Battista Montinis (des späteren Papstes Paul VI.), geleitet. Der Plan wurde 1950 vom Ministerium für öffentliche Bauarbeiten mit einer auf die folgenden vier Jahre begrenzten Gültigkeit genehmigt. Der Bericht listet die Gebäudeschäden auf, die durch die Bombenangriffe zwischen Februar 1944 und April 1945 entstanden sind: Etwa 35 Prozent des Wohnungsbestands wurden zerstört oder beschädigt, d.h. etwa 35.000 der rund 100.000 Zimmer, in denen die etwa 120.000 Einwohner des Stadtkerns lebten, bei einer Gesamtbevölkerung von etwa 165.000 im Stadtgebiet. Der Plan legt die Bauvorschriften fest, denen jedes neue Gebäude entsprechen muss, wenn es innerhalb der Grenzen des eigentlichen Stadtkerns errichtet werden soll: Vorschriften, die in den von Marcolini ausgewählten Gebieten, die alle außerhalb dieses Perimeters liegen, nicht gelten.

Der anschließende städtebauliche Apparat begann 1957 mit dem Verwaltungsprozess. Es wurde dem Ministerium für öffentliche Bauarbeiten zur Genehmigung vorgelegt, von diesem jedoch mit der Aufforderung abgelehnt, es innerhalb von acht Monaten erneut vorzulegen. Der zweite Entwurf, mit dem Mario Morini, ein ehemaliger Professor des Politecnico di Milano, betraut wurde, wurde im März 1960 vom Stadtrat und im November 1960 vom Generalrat des Ministeriums für öffentliche Arbeiten genehmigt und trat 1961 in Kraft. Der Hauptmangel des Plans, der die Stadt der unbegrenzten Bebauung selbst in landwirtschaftlichen und hügeligen Gebieten überließ, wurde in späteren Versionen, die in verschiedenen Phasen bis 1968 umgesetzt wurden, teilweise korrigiert.

In der Zwischenzeit hatte Marcolini die meisten seiner wichtigsten Dörfer geplant, gebilligt und gebaut. Erst 1973 erarbeitete das Technische Büro der Stadt unter der

34 Mit dem Ministerialdekret 485 vom 22. März 1946 wurde Brescia in die Liste der Städte aufgenommen, die einen Wiederaufbauplan zur Beseitigung der Kriegsschäden am baulichen Erbe aufstellen mussten. Das technische Büro der Stadt wurde von einer Sonderkommission unterstützt. Der Plan dafür wurde im März 1947 vorgelegt. Vgl. Di Gennaro, Aldo/Dominico, Dario/Lovatti, Maurilio: „La ricostruzione edilizia a Brescia (1945–1953)“, in: Chiarini, Roberto (Hg): *Brescia negli anni della ricostruzione (1945–1949)*, Brescia, 1981, 243–266.

planning instrument that, with the conception of the new San Polo district, introduced a new policy for the social housing in residential areas, with the main objective of resolving the dynamics of private urbanization on the basis of public planning, finally ending the main season of Marcolini's villages. The subsequent version of 1977, approved by the region in 1980 on the basis of the project drawn up by the municipal technical office with the advice of Benevolo, Calzolari, and Lombardi, further reduced the expansion forecasts mainly by increasing the areas to be allocated to the so-called "urban standards," such as schools, parking lots, parks, sports centers and playgrounds, areas that were not central to Marcolini's interests, replacing them with the sole presence of a church with its oratory as the only public space. In the last decades, every sixth inhabitant of Brescia lived in a Marcolini house.[36]

All of this also found an echo at the national level, so much so that in 1961, it encouraged the parliamentary work of the IX Permanent Commission of Public Works, which in 1962 drafted Law 167 for the acquisition of building land for economic and social housing. In fact, the law drafted by the Commission stated that its aim was to create "socially balanced neighborhoods, where the citizen can achieve the highest degree of freedom and see his [/her] personality strengthened, ... the morality of the fundamental cell of society is strengthened, ... the moral and cultural formation of youth is promoted, ... the peace and serenity of the elderly, ... the productivity of human labor on the one hand and the spiritual elevation of the citizen

36 See Roberto Busi, *Padre Marcolini: Dalla casa per la famiglia alla costruzione della città* (Rome, 2000).

Beratung von PlanerInnen und HistorikerInnen wie Franco Albini, Leonardo Benevolo,[35] Vittoria Calzolari Ghio, Franca Helg und Giorgio Lombardi die wichtige Variante des städtebaulichen Instruments, die mit der Konzeption des neuen Stadtteils San Polo eine neue Politik für den sozialen Wohnungsbau in den Wohngebieten einführte. Sie hatte das Ziel, die Dynamik der privaten Urbanisierung auf der Grundlage der öffentlichen Planung zu lösen, um den Hype um die Marcolini-Dörfer endgültig zu beenden. Die nachfolgende Version von 1977, die 1980 von der Region auf der Grundlage des vom technischen Büro der Gemeinde unter der Beratung von Leonardo Benevolo, Vittoria Calzolari und Giorgio Lombardi ausgearbeiteten Projekts genehmigt wurde, reduzierte die Ausbauprognosen noch weiter, vor allem durch die Vergrößerung der Flächen, die den so genannten „städtischen Standards" zugewiesen werden sollten, wie Schulen, Parkplätze, Parks, Sportzentren und Spielplätze, Bereiche, die nicht im Mittelpunkt der Interessen Marcolinis standen, und ersetzte sie durch die alleinige Präsenz einer Kirche mit ihrem Oratorium als einzigem öffentlichen Raum. In den letzten Jahrzehnten lebte jede/r sechste der EinwohnerInnen Brescias in einem Marcolini-Haus.[36]

All dies fand auch auf nationaler Ebene ein Echo, und zwar so sehr, dass es 1961 die parlamentarische Arbeit der IX. Ständigen Kommission für öffentliche Bauarbeiten anregte, die 1962 das Gesetz 162 über den Erwerb von Bauland für den wirtschaftlichen und sozialen Wohnungsbau ausarbeitete. In dem von der Kommission ausgearbeiteten Gesetz heißt es nämlich, das Ziel bestehe darin, „sozial ausgewogene Stadtviertel zu schaffen, in denen der Bürger ein Höchstmaß an Freiheit erlangen und seine Persönlichkeit gestärkt sehen kann, [...] die Moral der Grundzelle der Gesellschaft gestärkt wird, [...] die moralische und

35 Leonardo Benevolos Beziehung zu Brescia ist bezeichnend: Seit 1972 ist er der Protagonist eines der wichtigsten und erfolgreichsten sozialen Wohnungsbauprojekte Italiens, des Stadtteils San Polo: 375 Hektar am südöstlichen Stadtrand, auf denen heute etwa 20.000 Menschen leben, in einem Viertel, dessen Stadtplanung von der Stadtverwaltung auf der Grundlage von Benevolos Projekt durchgeführt wurde, das auf der Idee von neun Wohneinheiten mit jeweils etwa 500 Wohnungen dreier verschiedener Typen (Hoch-, Zeilen- und Reihenhäuser) basierte, wobei die Stadtverwaltung, um die Preise niedrig zu halten, die Grundstücke auf der Grundlage städtebaulicher Verträge kostenlos zur Verfügung stellte. Heute ist das Viertel ein integraler Bestandteil der Stadt, mit einer U-Bahn, Fahrradwegen, 20 Hektar großen Parks, Schulen sowie Sozial- und Gemeindezentren. Vor etwa 20 Jahren wurde ein Erweiterungsbau mit etwa 2.000 Wohneinheiten errichtet, an dem Mauro Galantino maßgeblich beteiligt war. Ein umfangreiches Projekt, das die Möglichkeit bietet, eine Infrastruktur zu schaffen, die sich vom Modell Marcolini völlig unterscheidet. Vgl. Benevolo, Leonardo: *Brescia, San Polo: un quartiere di iniziativa pubblica*, Rom, 1976.

36 Vgl. Busi, Roberto: *Padre Marcolini: Dalla casa per la famiglia alla costruzione della città*, Rom 2000.

on the other":[37] perhaps the only time that so many moral contents, described as a clear social objective, have been listed in a legislative text, where the ordinary level of people's daily lives is so clearly defined as a desirable sphere.

One of the emblems of the "Italian economic miracle" will therefore be the houses owned by the members of the cooperative, in other words, as the result of an entirely private initiative, in villages to which the municipalities will only later provide essential urban services. Characterized by a very low density, around 100 inhabitants per hectare, the villages are guaranteed the church with its oratory and a bar, in effect forming a small village within the urban fabric, autonomous and somewhat socially self-sufficient.

It was a quick success that convinced his old classmate Montini, who had become Pope in the meantime, to let him organize the return of the last evacuees of World War II to Acilia in 1971, when he was appointed Special Procurator of the Vicariate of Rome: between 1972 and 1973, the San Francesco district in Acilia, a small town on the extreme southwestern outskirts of Rome on the way to the sea, was completed and handed over to the community, about 1,300 families, 6,000 people, in a district initiated 20 years earlier by Pope Pius XII for the same reasons. An all-Catholic model that will also experience moments of some fortunate fame in the immediate future, mainly linked to missionary intervention: the Marcolini village model will be exported on the initiative of another Brescian prelate, Giuseppe Zanardini, a Salesian missionary, in Paraguay on the outskirts of Asunciòn, where 15 villages should be built by 2004 for about 12,000 inhabitants.[38]

Urban sociological thought has undergone considerable changes over the last 50 years. The figure of the militant intellectual, the "social critic," or the *intellectuel engagé*, has often seen its proposals replaced by economic and technical planning tools based on the transformation of the concept of need into the ordinary, more or less given its own space of expression.[39] The focus on what is local and informal, as the basis of the infraordinary, as opposed to what is universal and unitary, on the basis of the conflict between participatory instances and the centrality of decision-making, has also led to this particular emergency, exemplified in the villages, a kind of need to build a new alternative ordinary housing, no longer identifiable with public housing, based as it is on different sources of resources and involving a plurality of actors, all of them private.

All of this is based on an ideological rejection of both the theory and practice of the Modern Movement:

37 See Report of the IX Permanent Commission of Public Works, April 14, 1961.

38 See Bregoli, Castelli and Fappani, *Un prete fuori serie* (see note 17), 37.

39 See Andrea Villani, "Case, quartieri, abitanti, politiche di Antonio Tosi," *Rivista Internazionale di Scienze Sociali* 4 (2006): 617–621.

kulturelle Bildung der Jugend gefördert wird, [...] die Ruhe und Gelassenheit der älteren Menschen, [...] die Produktivität der menschlichen Arbeit einerseits und die geistige Erbauung des Bürgers andererseits".[37] Vielleicht war dies das einzige Mal, dass so viele sittliche Inhalte, die als klares gesellschaftliches Ziel beschrieben werden, in einem Gesetzestext aufgeführt werden, in dem das gewöhnliche Niveau des täglichen Lebens der Menschen so klar als wünschenswerter Bereich definiert ist.

Eines der Wahrzeichen des „italienischen Wirtschaftswunders" werden daher die Häuser sein, die den Genossenschaftsmitgliedern gehören, d.h. das Ergebnis einer rein privaten Initiative in Dörfern, denen die Gemeinden erst später die wesentlichen städtischen Dienstleistungen zur Verfügung stellen werden. Die Dörfer zeichnen sich durch eine sehr geringe Bevölkerungsdichte von etwa 100 EinwohnerInnen pro Hektar aus und verfügen über eine Kirche, ein Oratorium und eine Bar, so dass sie ein kleines Dorf innerhalb des städtischen Gefüges bilden, das autonom und sozial einigermaßen autark ist. Es war ein schneller Erfolg, der seinen alten Klassenkameraden Montini, der in der Zwischenzeit zum Papst gewählt worden war, davon überzeugte, ihn 1971, als er zum Sonderprokurator des Vikariats von Rom ernannt wurde, die Rückkehr der letzten Evakuierten des Zweiten Weltkriegs nach Acilia organisieren zu lassen: Zwischen 1972 und 1973 wurde der Stadtteil San Francesco in Acilia, einer kleinen Stadt am äußersten südwestlichen Stadtrand von Rom auf dem Weg zum Meer, fertiggestellt und der Gemeinschaft übergeben, etwa 1.300 Familien, 6.000 Menschen, in einem Stadtteil, der 20 Jahre zuvor von Papst Pius XII. aus den gleichen Gründen initiiert worden war. Ein rein katholisches Modell, das in naher Zukunft ebenfalls einige glückliche Momente erleben wird, vor allem im Zusammenhang mit missionarischer Intervention: Das Modell der Marcolini-Dörfer wird auf Initiative eines anderen Prälaten aus Brescia, Giuseppe Zanardini, einem Salesianermissionar, nach Paraguay exportiert, in die Umgebung von Asunción, wo bis 2004 fünfzehn Dörfer für etwa 12.000 Einwohner entstehen sollen.[38]

Das stadtsoziologische Denken hat sich in den letzten 50 Jahren stark gewandelt. Die Figur des kämpferischen Intellektuellen, des „Sozialkritikers" oder *intellectuel engagé* wurde häufig von wirtschaftlichen und technischen Planungsinstrumenten abgelöst, die die Inhalte des Bedürfnisbegriffs bereits in das Gewöhnliche ihrer Verfahren transformierten, dem dadurch mehr oder weniger ein eigener Ausdrucksraum gegeben wird.[39] Die Konzentration auf das Lokale und Informelle als Grundlage des

37 Aus dem Bericht der IX. Ständigen Kommission für Öffentliche Bauarbeiten vom 14. April 1961.

38 Vgl. Bregoli/Castelli/Fappani: *Un prete fuori serie* (wie Anm. 17), 37.

39 Vgl. Villani, Andrea: „Case, quartieri, abitanti, politiche di Antonio Tosi", *Rivista Internazionale di Scienze Sociali* 4 (2006), 617–621.

economic planning and spatial planning at both local and national levels are denied as both socio-urban theory and political orientation, as is urban planning based on zoning. The result will not be so different, however, if it is true that this model ultimately leads to a concentration of homogeneous social and functional categories; it is also remarkable how architectural culture will remain largely on the margins of these realizations: buildings will be constructed that are essentially similar, if not identical, differing only in orientation, far from any design research and process.

The denial of any communitarian social value in the certainty that the model proposed and embodied in the belief that private property guarantees better care even for the village itself, if not for the neighborhood and the entire city, seems to be rooted in, and in turn fundamental to, an infraordinary kind of identity. This conviction makes this little house one's home,[40] or to be "roi chez moi."[41]

These were the simple but powerful motives that drove Ottorino Marcolini to develop neighborhoods for tens of thousands of people who arrived in town from the countryside seeking a job. In Brescia too, the *Lumpenproletariat* is urbanized and re-sacralized by the gentrification of Marcolini's version of the single-family detached house, where the original peasant faith is perpetuated as the only constant in its infraordinary life. Brescia, a provincial town, as were the neighboring provinces of Cremona, Mantua and Bergamo, known for a "sad Catholicism, by puritanical blackmail, and its well-thinking bourgeoisie,"[42] as Pasolini writes about Milan, was an ideal testing ground for the reactionary moralism of Marcolini's socio-urban experiment, all aimed at constituting an alternative to the social, collective, democratic and progressive thought that was in some ways dominant at the time.

The "Cooperativa La Famiglia," the operational and economic center of Marcolini's work, closed all its activities in 2014, after several years of serious economic disruption, also due to the hundreds of unsold housing units. The changes that have taken place in the models of management and expectations of everyday life and in the dynamics of social interaction, already foreseen by Bianciardi and Pasolini,[43] have affected this typology, which is increasingly showing its cultural, social, political, and economic limits.

40 Italy shares with most European countries a very high percentage of people living in owner-occupied housing, close to 80 percent.

41 Véronique Fillieux, "L'accession poulaire à la propriété: du paternalisme privé aux mesures législatives", Bollettino dell'Archivio per la storia del movimento sociale cattolico in Italia 3 (2003): 340–365.

42 Pier Paolo Pasolini, "Risposta all'inchiesta di Adele Cambria. Milano o Roma? Due centri storici," *Paese Sera*, November 28th–29th, 1961.

43 See Giovanni Inzerillo, "Milano e la borghesia destinata a non lottare. *Teorema* di Pier Paolo Pasolini e *La vita agra* di Luciano Bianciardi tra letteratura e cinema," *Cuadernos de Filología Italiana* 27 (2020): 241–254.

Ungewöhnlichen im Gegensatz zum Universellen und Einheitlichen, auf der Grundlage des Konflikts zwischen partizipatorischen Instanzen und der Zentralität der Entscheidungsfindung, hat auch zu dieser besonderen Notlage geführt, die in den Dörfern zum Ausdruck kommt, einer Art Notwendigkeit, einen neuen alternativen gewöhnlichen Wohnbau zu errichten, der nicht mehr mit dem öffentlichen Wohnungsbau identifizierbar ist, welcher sich auf unterschiedliche Ressourcen stützt und eine Vielzahl von AkteurInnen einbezieht, die alle privat sind.

All dies beruht auf einer ideologischen Ablehnung sowohl der Theorie als auch der Praxis der Strömung der Moderne: Wirtschaftsplanung und Raumplanung auf lokaler und nationaler Ebene werden als sozio-urbane Theorie und politische Orientierung abgelehnt, ebenso wie die Stadtplanung auf der Grundlage von Zoneneinteilung. Wenn es stimmt, dass dieses Modell letztlich zu einer Konzentration homogener sozialer und funktionaler Kategorien führt, wird das Ergebnis nicht anders sein; bemerkenswert ist auch, wie die architektonische Kultur weitgehend am Rande dieser Realisierungen bleiben wird: Es werden Gebäude errichtet, die im Wesentlichen ähnlich, wenn nicht gar identisch sind und sich nur in der Ausrichtung unterscheiden, fernab jeglicher Entwurfsforschung und -bearbeitung.

Das Bestreiten jeglichen gemeinschaftlichen sozialen Wertes in der Gewissheit, dass das in diesen Eingriffen vorgeschlagene und verkörperte Modell in der Überzeugung wurzelt, dass das Privateigentum eine bessere Versorgung auch für das Dorf selbst, wenn nicht sogar für das Viertel und die ganze Stadt, garantiert, scheint wiederum grundlegend zu sein für eine Art von Identitätsüberzeugung, die dieses kleine Haus zum eigenen Zuhause macht,[40] oder um „roi chez moi“[41] zu sein.

Das waren die einfachen, aber starken Motive, die Ottorino Marcolini dazu brachten, Wohnviertel für Zehntausende von Menschen zu bauen, die auf der Suche nach Arbeit vom Land in die Stadt kamen. Auch in Brescia wird das Lumpenproletariat durch die Gentrifizierung der lokalen Marcolini-Variante des Einfamilienhauses, in dem der ursprüngliche bäuerliche Glaube als einzige Konstante in seinem ungewohnten Leben fortbesteht, urbanisiert und re-sakralisiert. Wie die benachbarten Provinzen Cremona, Mantua und Bergamo ist auch Brescia bekannt für einen „traurigen Katholizismus praktiziert durch puritanische Erpressung und ihr wohlmeinendes Bürgertum“[42].

40 Italien hat mit den meisten europäischen Ländern einen sehr hohen Prozentsatz an Menschen, die in selbst genutztem Wohneigentum leben, nämlich fast 80 Prozent.

41 Fillieux, Véronique: „L'accession poulaire à la propriété: du paternalisme privé aux mesures législatives“, *Bollettino dell'Archivio per la storia del movimento sociale cattolico in Italia* 3 (2003), 340–365.

42 Pasolini, Pier Paolo: „Risposta all'inchiesta di Adele Cambria. Milano o Roma? Due centri storici“, Paese Sera, 28.–29. November 1961.

The crisis of these housing types is to be combined with the demographic changes defined by the aging of the society that gave rise to them, with the social changes triggered by the general crisis of the traditional family as the founding nucleus of society and the related type of pious management of the ordinary, with the progressive change in housing preferences linked to the awareness of the costs inherent in these housing models, and the strong attraction of the city as a productive and working space. All these reasons are also leading to a rethinking of the future of these neighborhoods and to a shift of interest in the now scarce performance of this housing stock, within the framework of a now secularized provincial society that generates, manages, and expresses dimensions of the infraordinary in different ways and spaces.

Brescia war damit ein ideales Versuchsfeld für Marcolinis sozio-urbanes Experiment. Es zielte darauf ab, eine Alternative zum sozialen, kollektiven, demokratischen und fortschrittlichen Denken zu bilden, das zu dieser Zeit in gewisser Weise vorherrschte.

Die „Cooperativa La Famiglia", das operative und wirtschaftliche Zentrum von Marcolinis Arbeit, beendete 2014 nach mehreren Jahren schwerwiegender wirtschaftlicher Störungen, die auch auf die Hunderte von unverkauften Wohnungen zurückzuführen waren, endgültig alle ihre Aktivitäten. Die bereits von Bianciardi und Pasolini vorhergesagten Veränderungen in den Verwaltungsmodellen und Erwartungen des täglichen Lebens sowie in der Dynamik der sozialen Interaktion[43] haben diese Typologie betroffen, deren kulturelle, soziale, politische und wirtschaftliche Grenzen zunehmend in Erscheinung treten.

Die Krise dieser Wohnformen geht mit verschiedenen Faktoren einher: den demografischen Veränderungen, die durch die Überalterung der Gesellschaft, die sie hervorgebracht hat, bestimmt werden; mit den sozialen Veränderungen, die durch die allgemeine Krise der traditionellen Familie als Keimzelle der Gesellschaft und der damit verbundenen Art der frommen Verwaltung des Gewöhnlichen ausgelöst werden; mit der fortschreitenden Veränderung der Wohnpräferenzen, die mit dem Bewusstsein der mit diesen Wohnmodellen verbundenen Kosten einhergehen, und mit der starken Anziehungskraft der Stadt als Produktions- und Arbeitsraum zusammenhängt. All diese Gründe führen auch zu einem Überdenken der Zukunft dieser Viertel und zu einer Verschiebung des Interesses an der inzwischen geringen Leistungsfähigkeit dieses Wohnungsbestands im Rahmen einer mittlerweile säkularisierten Provinzgesellschaft, welche Dimensionen des Ungewöhnlichen auf unterschiedliche Weise und in unterschiedlichen Räumen erzeugt, verwaltet und zum Ausdruck bringt.

Übersetzung: Nikolaus G. Schneider

43 Vgl. Inzerillo, Giovanni: „Milano e la borghesia destinata a non lottare. *Teorema* di Pier Paolo Pasolini e *La vita agra* di Luciano Bianciardi tra letteratura e cinema", *Cuadernos de Filología Italiana* 27 (2020), 241–254.

„L'infra-ordinaire“

Helmut Tezak

„L'infra-ordinaire“

Alltäglich
Selbstverständlich
Allgemein
Gewöhnlich
Banal –
„*L'infra-ordinaire*“
nennt es Georges Perec.

KINO

ANFANG
KURZPARKZONE

EINBAHN

Gösser
ZIMMER

BRUNO

Privatgrund
14

Triester Straße
1

FLEISCH
WURS

LAUFHAUS
NORD
48

HOTEL

Eggenberg
Bruck/Mur
Gösting
Weiz
Graz Ost
Andritz
Mariatrost

TRANS
OCEAN

IN GRAZ

VIX

STOP
6m
Ende

VOLVO

MARTINI

Am Damm

Salis &

SCHWEISSEN

Graz
Stattegg

E NORDSTERN

HERRENKLEIDERFABRIK
ARISTOKRAT
• Anzüge
• Sakkos
• Hosen
• Sportswear
• Maßkonfektion
Großer Kundenparkplatz
DIREKTVERKAUF
Tel. 91 43 50
OPEL

tanz

„Eines der Mittel zur Gestaltung von Wissen ist die Erzählung“
Toni Morrison

… fotografiert, in *Graz* –
entlang der Wiener Straße,
in der Leonhardstraße,
am ehemaligen Schulweg,
entlang der Alten-Post-Straße,
in der Kärntner Straße,
in der Triester Straße,
in der Liebenauer Hauptstraße,
weiter in der Münzgrabenstraße,
in der Mariatroster Straße – auch
an der Theodor-Körner-Straße,
in der Keplerstraße,
am Kalvarienweg
(…)
und sonst wo –
irgendwie überall
– in der Stadt

Vorstellen. Erinnern. Assoziieren.
Denken verläuft sequenzhaft linear –
oder eher gleichzeitig, gewissermaßen räumlich

Der Essay ist ein Bild davon.

Helmut Tezak

1 Pavesi kiosk, Novara, Architect: Angelo Bianchetti, 1947 © Archivio Jan Jacopo Bianchetti

Straßenrand-Spektakel
Zur Architektur der Autogrill-Raststätten

Roadside Spectacle
On the Architecture of Autogrill Roadside Restaurants

Beatrice Azzola

Die italienischen Autobahnraststätten entstanden als kommerzieller Gebäudetyp nach dem Zweiten Weltkrieg parallel zur Ausbreitung großangelegter amerikanischer Verkaufs- und Vertriebsmodelle in Italien. Mit der Hoffnung auf eine Wiederbelebung des Landes nach den Schrecken des Krieges kam auch die Sehnsucht nach einem Leben in Reichtum und Wohlstand auf, von dem das amerikanische Kino erzählte, das vermehrt Einzug in den Alltag der ItalienerInnen hielt. Das Verlangen nach einer Zukunft im Wohlstand zeigt sich auch in der Autobahnarchitektur der Zeit, an der futuristischen und mitunter auch monumentalen Architektursprache, mit der Reisende angelockt und letztlich zum Konsumieren verführt werden sollten. Die *Autogrills* – eine Abwandlung des amerikanischen Begriffs „grillroom" (Grillrestaurant) – sollten trotz ihrer banalen Funktion, der Versorgung von Reisenden mit Speis und Trank, nach etwas Besonderem aussehen. Der Gewöhnlichkeit ihrer Funktion zum Trotz wirkten sie wie in die bukolische italienische Landschaft gepflanzte fantastische Maschinen.

Aufstieg und Untergang des Automobiltraums, der in Italien von den späten 1940er bis in die späten 1970er-Jahre währte, finden ihren Widerhall in der in dieser Zeit entlang der italienischen Autobahnen entstandenen Architektur. Angefangen bei den ersten kleinen Kiosken, deren Baukörper von überdimensionierten Reklameschildern beherrscht wurden, bis zu den Brückengebäuden, die schon durch ihre Form die Aufmerksamkeit der Reisenden auf sich zogen, wird hier die Geschichte der Autobahnarchitektur hin zu ihrer heute typischen Standardisierung nachgezeichnet. Eine Vergleichsanalyse der geschichtlichen Entwicklung amerikanischer und italienischer Autobahnarchitektur zeigt, dass eine dem Verkauf eines Traums dienende Architektur eine visionäre Formsprache mit den alltäglichen Bedürfnissen Autoreisender zu versöhnen vermag.

Heutzutage wird die Einzelhandelsarchitektur zumeist – und manchmal aus gutem Grund – als uninteressant

The emergence of Italian highway service stations as a commercial type began after World War II, in conjunction with the spread of the American large-scale sales and distribution model across Italy. Along with the hope for a rebirth of the country after the horrors of war, a yearning for a life of wealth and prosperity, as recounted by American cinema—a constant presence in the daily lives of Italians—became increasingly widespread. This tension toward a future of prosperity is also seen in the highway architecture of the period, through the futuristic—sometimes monumental—architectonic language used to attract travelers and, ultimately, invite them to buy. The *autogrills*, named such after a derivation of the American term "grillroom," despite their mundane function of providing refreshment to travelers, were designed to look exceptional. Regardless of the infra-ordinariness of their function, they appeared as amazing machines reclined over the Italian bucolic landscape.

The rise and fall of the automotive dream, taking place in Italy between the late 1940s and the late 1970s, manifests itself in the architecture built along Italian highways during those years. Beginning with the first small kiosks, their architectural body dominated by the oversized advertising structures, and moving on to the bridge buildings, whose very forms played the role of attracting the attention of travelers, a path is outlined that would ultimately lead to a standardization, one typical of today's highway buildings. A comparative approach between the history of American and Italian roadside architecture provides insight into how an architectural model based on the selling of a dream, the American dream, allows for a reconciliation between a visionary architectural imagery and the quotidian activities connected to the needs of travelers.

Nowadays, retail architecture is often considered—sometimes with good reason—uninteresting, because it falls victim to the overwhelming power of business strategies. At the same time, the genericness of the "architectural box" is compensated for by the maximal

erachtet, schon weil sie von der überwältigenden Macht von Geschäftsinteressen erdrückt wird. Zudem wird das Generische der „architektonischen Box" durch einen riesigen Kommunikations- und Werbeaufwand kompensiert, der meist wichtiger ist als die architektonische Form. Auch wenn dieses Generische bei NutzerInnen ein Gefühl der Entfremdung auslösen kann, so werden wir bei näherer Betrachtung kommerzieller Straßenrand-Architektur doch entdecken, dass der durch sie vermittelte Eindruck oft komplexer ist. Selbst gewöhnliche Gebäude können so etwas wie ein Heimatgefühl oder auch ein angenehmes Gefühl von Fremdheit hervorrufen. Von Anfang an wurden Restaurants und Geschäfte entlang italienischer Autobahnen zu Touristenzielen, was belegt, dass es dieser Architektur gelingt, einen „Verweilplatz" im Transitraum der Autobahn zu schaffen. Welche Rolle also spielt die Architektur in diesem Prozess der Domestizierung von Nicht-Orten? Was können wir in dieser Hinsicht von diesen außergewöhnlichen Bauten lernen?

Anfänge der Straßenrand-Architektur in Nordamerika: Der Frontscheibenfilm

Das Zusammenspiel von Werbung und Infrastruktur reicht bis ins späte 19. Jahrhundert zurück, als amerikanische Werbeleute begannen, große Reklametafeln neben Straßen und Bahntrassen aufzustellen, um die Aufmerksamkeit der Reisenden zu erregen. Wie Chester H. Liebs in *Main Street to Miracle Mile: American Roadside Architecture* schreibt: Wer mit dem Auto reiste, wurde fortwährend aufgefordert, „zurückzuschalten, einzukehren und zu kaufen."[1] Im Gegensatz zu Zugreisenden gab es bei Autoreisenden viel mehr Bedürfnisse zu befriedigen. Gastronomie- und Mineralölfirmen erkannten sehr rasch, dass sich hier eine neue Geschäftsmöglichkeit bot, packten sie freudig beim Schopf. Tankstellen, Rasthäuser, Motels, aber auch Einkaufszentren, Golfanlagen und Autokinos wurden zur selbstverständlichen Umgebung der Straße. Das heißt, dass Straßen- und Autobahnlandschaften rund um die Wahrnehmung der AutofahrerInnen gebaut wurden und versuchten, ihre Aufmerksamkeit auf sich zu ziehen. Liebs beschreibt diesen Prozess als „Kommerzialisierung der Landschaft": Wenn das Autofenster die neue Kinoleinwand ist, dann sind die Plakatwände und Reklametafeln entlang der Straße die „Werbeclips" im „Frontscheibenfilm".[2]

Diese Kinometapher scheint besonders auf die Zeit nach dem Zweiten Weltkrieg zuzutreffen, als die Werbung eine „kreative Revolution"[3] erlebte. In diesen Jahren boomte besonders der Verkauf von Automobilen und

1 Liebs, Chester H.: *Main Street to Miracle Mile: American Roadside Architecture*, Boston 1985, 5. (Übers. W.P.)
2 Ebda. (Übers. W.P.)
3 Der Begriff bezeichnet eine Ära in der Geschichte der New Yorker Werbebranche, in der eine neue Welle junger WerberInnen einen innovativen, künstlerischen Zugang zu ihrer Tätigkeit einführte.

communicativeness of advertising devices, which often outweigh architectural forms. Even though such genericness may generate a feeling of alienation in its occupants, by studying roadside commercial architecture we will discover that the impression produced is often more complex. Even such ordinary buildings might be able to arouse emotions of domesticity or, sometimes, a pleasant sense of extraneousness. From their first appearance, roadside restaurants and stores on Italian highways would become actual tourist destinations, demonstrating the ability of architectural design to "build a place" that was previously just a location along a route. Then what is the role of architecture in this process of domestication of nonplaces? What can we learn in this regard from the extra-ordinary roadside buildings of the twentieth century?

Origins of Roadside Architecture in North America: The Windshield Movie

The interplay between advertisement and infrastructure dates back to the late nineteenth century, when American advertisers started putting up large billboards beside streets and railroad tracks, to catch the attention of the casual traveler gazing at the landscape. As Chester H. Liebs puts it in *Main Street to Miracle Mile: American Roadside Architecture*, the motorist was constantly invited to "slow down, pull in, and buy."[1] Compared to the railroad traveler, the motorist had many more needs to accommodate. Food and oil companies were fast to appreciate this new opportunity and happily grabbed it. Gas stations, roadside restaurants, motels, but also shopping malls, golf courses, and drive-in theaters became commonplace in the highway environment. This new context meant that road and highway landscapes were being built around the perception of the driver and aimed at attracting their attention. Liebs describes this process as "commercialization of landscape:" if the car window is the new silver screen, then billboards and advertisements along the road are the "commercials" in the "windshield movie."[2]

This cinematic metaphor seems particularly apt when dealing with the period following World War II, during which the "creative revolution"[3] of advertising took place. Notably, the automobile and the television were booming in sales in those same years and were becoming an integral part of the daily life of Americans.[4] The society of consumerism was consolidated and spreading across the globe. In this consumerist society, people become objects, rather than actors—producers or buyers—of consumption and

1 Chester H. Liebs, *Main Street to Miracle Mile: American Roadside Architecture* (Boston, 1985), 5.
2 Ibid.
3 The term refers to a particular time in the history of New York advertisement circles, in which a new wave of young advertisers contributed to shape an innovative, artistic approach to their practice.
4 Mark S. Foster, *A Nation on Wheels: The Automobile Culture in America since 1945* (Belmont, 2003), 65.

Fernsehgeräten, die nun zu einem integralen Bestandteil des amerikanischen Alltagslebens wurden.[4] Die Konsumgesellschaft entstand und verbreitete sich über den Globus. In dieser Konsumgesellschaft werden Menschen zu Objekten, statt Akteure – ProduzentInnen oder KäuferInnen – zu sein. Ja, sie werden sogar selbst zu Waren. Auch Bauten werden zu Objekten, die sich so schnell wie möglich beseitigen lassen sollen, sobald sie keinen Profit mehr abwerfen. In der alten Gesellschaft von ProduzentInnen, wie Zygmunt Bauman in seinem 2007 erschienenen Buch *Consuming Life* schreibt, bedeutet Masse Macht: „Big is beautiful".[5] Selbst wenn ein Produkt den Zweck, für den es entworfen wurde, also seine Funktion nicht erfüllt, wird es lange aufbewahrt, weil sich ein neuer Zweck dafür finden könnte. Das Gleiche gilt für Bauwerke, die so gebaut wurden, dass sie ihre ErbauerInnen überdauerten. In der Gesellschaft von Konsumenten hingegen werden Einzelhandelsgebäude so entworfen, dass sie möglichst schnell modifiziert, zerlegt, neu zusammengestellt und beseitigt werden können, damit sie der – wie Bauman sagt – „Unbeständigkeit der Wünsche und Unstillbarkeit der Bedürfnisse"[6] gerecht werden.

Neon-Alpträume und das Spektakel des Kommerzes

Im Film- und Fernsehzeitalter, also in den 1950er- und 1960er-Jahren, setzte sich unter Intellektuellen allmählich die Vorstellung durch, dass die Repräsentation und das Bild von Objekten über ihre physische Realität obsiegt. In *La Société du Spectacle*[7] definiert der Philosoph und Filmemacher Guy Debord das „Spektakel" als „die Behauptung des Scheins und die Behauptung jedes menschlichen, d. h. gesellschaftlichen Lebens als eines bloßen Scheins".[8] Die Feindseligkeit, mit der Intellektuelle die aufkommende Konsumgesellschaft betrachteten, war auch in der Architekturgeschichte und Architekturkritik verbreitet, sodass kommerzielle Bauten in den Kreisen der Hochkultur und Hochmoderne mehr oder minder unbeachtet blieben. In „Aesthetic Ideology and Urban Design" thematisiert Barbara Rubin die Aversion ihrer ZeitgenossInnen gegen Einkaufsstraßen. Ausgehend von einer „The Real ... The Ideal" betitelten Werbekampagne aus den frühen 1970er-Jahren schildert sie, wie die „reale" Stadt mit Ausdrücken wie „Main-Street-Aufputz [...] Neon-Alptraum [...] würdelose Gebäude [...] die Sonne verdunkelnde Reklametafeln" beschrieben wurde, während die „idealen"

4 Vgl. Foster, Mark S.: *A Nation on Wheels: The Automobile Culture in America since* 1945, Belmont 2003, 65.

5 Bauman, Zygmunt: *Consuming Life*, Cambridge 2007, 29 (dt. *Leben als Konsum*, Übers. Richard Barth, Hamburg 2009, 42.)

6 Ebda., 31 (45).

7 Debord, Guy: *La Société du Spectacle*, Paris 1967.

8 Ders.: *Die Gesellschaft des Spekatels*, Übers. Jean-Jacques Raspaud, Hamburg 1978, 4.

are transformed into commodities themselves. As for the buildings, they become objects to be disposed of as quickly as possible the moment they no longer produce profit. As Zygmunt Bauman writes in his 2007 book *Consuming Life*, "bulk is power" and "big is beautiful" in the old *society of producers*.[5] Even in cases where the produced and possessed object fails the purpose for which it was designed—and thus its function—it is still preserved for the long term in the expectation that a new purpose for it might arise. The same principle can be found in architectural artifacts, made to outlive their builders. In the *society of consumers*, retail buildings are designed to be modified, disassembled, reassembled, and demolished so quickly that they can respond to what Bauman calls an "instability of desires and insatiability of needs."[6]

Neon Nightmares and the Commercial Spectacle

In the era of cinema and television, in the 1950s and 1960s, the idea that the representation and the image of objects were starting to prevail over their physical reality began to take hold among intellectuals. In *La Société du Spectacle*,[7] the French philosopher Guy Debord, also a filmmaker, defines the "spectacle" as "*affirmation* of appearance and affirmation of all human life, namely social life, as mere appearance."[8] The hostility of intellectuals toward the nascent consumer society also permeated architecture history and criticism, while commercial buildings were mostly excluded from the circles of high art and the modern movement. In "Aesthetic Ideology and Urban Design," Barbara Rubin discusses the aversion of her contemporaries to commercial streets. Referring to an advertisement campaign from the early 1970s titled "The Real ... The Ideal," she explains how "the real" city was depicted as "Main Street garnish ... neon nightmares ... graceless buildings ... billboards [that] block out the sun," while "the ideal" rural and suburban environments are "wholesome and beautiful."[9]

Nonetheless, in the 1960s, commercial architecture was beginning to enter architectural history. In 1965, Reyner Banham wrote an article titled "Unrecognized American Architecture: The Missing Motel,"[10] in which he denounced the absence of commercial architecture at that year's exhibition *Modern Architecture, U.S.A.* held

5 Zygmunt Bauman: *Consuming Life*, (Cambridge 2007), 29.

6 Ibid., 31.

7 Guy Debord, *La Société du Spectacle* (Paris, 1967).

8 Guy Debord, *Society of the Spectacle*, trans. Fredy Perlman et al. (Detroit, 1970), 10.

9 Barbara Rubin, "Aesthetic Ideology and Urban Design," *Annals of the Association of American Geographers* 69, no. 3 (1979): 339.

10 The article was originally published in 1965 by the BBC, in the weekly magazine *The Listener*. Of note is the link between commercial architecture and television.

ländlichen und vorstädtischen Gegenden als „gesund und schön" galten.[9]

Dessen ungeachtet betritt die kommerzielle Architektur in den 1960er-Jahren allmählich das Feld der Architekturgeschichte. 1965 schrieb Reyner Banham einen Artikel mit dem Titel „Unrecognized American Architecture: The Missing Motel",[10] in dem er das Fehlen der kommerziellen Architektur in der im selben Jahr abgehaltenen Ausstellung „Modern Architecture, U.S.A." im New Yorker Museum of Modern Art (MoMA) anprangerte.[11] Die meisten ArchitekturkritikerInnen der Zeit hielten sie einer Museumsausstellung nicht für würdig, sondern bevorzugten eher von europäischen Beispielen beeinflusste modernistische Architektur.[12] In *Learning from Las Vegas* wird die Architektur entlang der Highways sehr wohl als Teil der kommerziellen Architektur gesehen, aber auch darauf hingewiesen, dass ArchitektInnen zwar die primitive Volksarchitektur – die „Architektur ohne Architekten"[13] – und die industrielle Gebrauchsarchitektur akzeptiert haben, jedoch nicht die kommerzielle Formensprache.[14] Maria Bottero, die den Fokus auf ihre Konventionen und Anonymität legte, bezeichnete sie 1968 als amerikanische „Pop"-Architektur.[15] Inzwischen wurde die kommerzielle Architektur Amerikas von vielen HistorikerInnen und WissenschaftlerInnen erforscht und als ein Ausdruck der Massenkultur erkannt.

Parabeln, Bumerangs und Kinderträume

In seinem Vorwort zu Alan Hess' Buch *Googie* beschreibt Steven Izenour die Coffeeshops der 1950er-Jahre mit dem Begriff „Alltagsarchitektur". Er erklärt, dass solche Bauten in den 1950er-Jahren noch „ad hoc und ungeplant" entstanden und sogar Raum für Humor hatten, „manchmal eher flüchtig – eine seltsam mit ihrer Umgebung kontrastierende Reklametafel – manchmal etwas dauerhafter –

9 Rubin, Barbara: „Aesthetic Ideology and Urban Design", in: *Annals of the Association of American Geographers* 69, 3 (1979), 339.

10 Der Artikel erschien ursprünglich im Wochenmagazin des BBC *The Listener*. Beachtenswert daran ist die Verbindung zwischen Kommerzarchitektur und Fernsehen.

11 Die Ausstellung im MoMA fand vom 18. Mai bis 6. September 1965 statt.

12 Banham, Reyner: „Unrecognized American Architecture: The Missing Motel", *Landscape* 15, 2 (1965), 4–6.

13 Die von Bernard Rudofsky kuratierte gleichnamige Ausstellung am MoMA in New York fand vom 11. November 1964 bis zum 7. Februar 1965 statt.

14 Venturi, Robert/Scott Brown, Denise/Izenour, Steven: *Learning from Las Vegas: The Forgotten Symbolism of Architectural Form*, Cambridge, MA, 1977, 6 (dt. *Lernen von Las Vegas. Zur Ikonographie und Architektursymbolik der Geschäftsstadt*, Übers. Heinz Schollwöck, Braunschweig/Wiesbaden 1979, 16).

15 Bottero, Maria: „Passato e Presente nell'Architettura ‚Pop' Americana", *Comunità* (1968), 100–113.

at The Museum of Modern Art (MoMA) in New York.[11] Most architecture critics of his time did not consider it worthy of display in a museum, while preferring modernist architecture inspired by European examples.[12] In *Learning from Las Vegas*, roadside architecture is included in the "commercial vernacular," pointing out how architects have accepted the primitive vernacular of "Architecture Without Architects,"[13] as well as industrial vernacular and even space vernacular, but not yet commercial vernacular.[14] In 1968, Maria Bottero called it American "pop" architecture and focused on its conventionality and anonymity.[15] Since then, many historians and scholars have been studying American commercial vernacular architecture, recognizing it as representative of mass culture.

Parabolas, Boomerangs, and the Dreams of Children

In his foreword to the book *Googie* by Alan Hess, Steven Izenour uses the expression "everyday architecture" to describe the coffee shops of the 1950s. He explains how in the 1950s such buildings were still "ad hoc and unplanned," even making space for humor, "sometimes fleeting [humor] —a billboard weirdly juxtaposed with its surroundings—and sometimes a little more permanent—a hot dog stand in the shape of a hot dog."[16] He nostalgically recalls the impression left by roadside commercial buildings of the 1950s in his memory: "Oh, those names! They fly and swoop, dance and jump, rock and roll—Ship's and Chip's, Googie's and Biffs, Bob's Big Boy, and Tiny Naylor's, Smorgyburger, Jump N' Jack and the Celestial Motel. We all grew up with them on roadside strips—east, west, north, south."[17] Everyday buildings, anonymous in their function and their uses, were made original and unique by a new kind of modern architecture that kept the disruptiveness of the modern movement, while dismissing its linguistic purity. The expressive freedom that architects took in designing 1950s commercial architecture allowed for the construction of a mixed language, characterized by "tapered columns, cantilevers, vaults, parabolas and boomerangs."[18] It was the language of the future, evocative of hyper-technologized scenarios, where the car took

11 The exhibition was held at MoMA in New York from May 18 to September 6, 1965.

12 Reyner Banham, "Unrecognized American Architecture: The Missing Motel," *Landscape* 15, no. 2 (1965): 4–6.

13 The exhibition was curated by Bernard Rudofsky and held at MoMA in New York from November 11, 1964, to February 7, 1965.

14 Robert Venturi, Denise Scott Brown, and Steven Izenour, *Learning from Las Vegas: The Forgotten Symbolism of Architectural Form* (Cambridge, MA, 1977), 6.

15 Maria Bottero, "Passato e Presente nell'Architettura 'Pop' Americana," *Comunità* (1968): 100–113.

16 Steven Izenour, foreword to Alan Hess, *Googie: Fifties Coffee Shop Architecture* (San Francisco, 1986), 8.

17 Ibid.

18 Izenour, foreword to *Googie* (see note 16), 7.

ein Hotdogstand in Form eines Hotdogs."[16] Nostalgisch ruft er sich in Erinnerung, welchen Eindruck die kommerziellen Gebäude am Straßenrand auf ihn machten: „Oh, diese Namen! Sie fliegen heran und schnappen zu, tanzen und springen, rocken und rollen – Ship's und Chip's, Googie's und Biffs, Bob's Big Boy und Tiny Naylor's, Smorgyburger, Jump N' Jack und Celestial Motel. Wir alle sind mit ihnen aufgewachsen entlang unserer Straßen, im Osten, Westen, Norden, Süden".[17] In Funktion und Gebrauch anonyme Alltagsbauten wurden durch eine neue Art moderner Architektur, die sich das Disruptive der Moderne bewahrte, aber den Purismus ihrer Sprache verwarf, zu etwas Originellem und Besonderem gemacht. Die Freiheit des Ausdrucks, die sich ArchitektInnen in den 1950er-Jahren beim Entwerfen kommerzieller Architektur nahmen, ermöglichte einen formsprachlichen Mix, der von „konischen Säulen, Auskragungen, Gewölben, Parabeln und Bumerangs"[18] geprägt war. Es war die Sprache der Zukunft, die hypertechnische Szenarien heraufbeschwor, in denen sich alles ums Auto drehte und die Kinder – wie den jungen Steven Izenour beim Betrachten der Coffeeshops – von magischen fernen Welten träumen ließen.

Es ist kein Zufall, dass jener Ort, der überwiegend Kinder als Zielgruppe hat, nämlich Disneyland, von Charles W. Moore 1965 als „wichtigstes Bauwerk im Westen [der USA] während der letzten paar Jahrzehnte"[19] bezeichnet wurde. Unter Bezug auf Moores Vision erklärt John Chase in „The Role of Consumerism in American Architecture", Ziel der kommerziellen Architektursprache sei es, etwas vorzuspiegeln, das sie nicht ist. Sie müsse BesucherInnen ungewöhnliche Erlebnisse bieten und Emotionen wecken, die sonst nirgendwo zu haben sind.[20] Diese Erlebnisse, die Moore schlicht als „öffentliches Leben" bezeichnet, sind in der Konsumgesellschaft nicht gratis, sondern müssen gekauft werden.[21] Chase betont auch den kollektiven, fast rituellen Charakter des Einkaufens. Mit einer optimistischen Haltung gegenüber der Konsumkultur beschreibt er den Erwerb von Dingen an einem öffentlichen Ort als etwas, das Ich-Grenzen auflöst und „eine breitere Sicht der Welt schafft, eine Kosmologie aus Fernsehen, Werbung und Magazinen".[22]

16 Izenour, Steven: Vorwort zu Hess, Allen: *Googie: Fifties Coffee Shop Architecture*, San Francisco 1986, 8.
17 Ebda.
18 Ebda, 7.
19 Moore, Charles W.: *You Have to Pay for the Public Life: Selected Essays of Charles W. Moore*, Cambridge, MA/London 2004, 124.
20 Vgl. Chase, John: „The Role of Consumerism in American Architecture", *Journal of Architectural Education* 44, 4 (1991), 217.
21 Moore, *You Have to Pay for the Public Life* (wie Anm. 19), 126. (Übers. W.P.)
22 Chase, "The Role of Consumerism" (wie Anm. 20), 212. (Übers. W.P.)

center stage, and children—like young Steven Izenour watching the coffee shops—could dream of magical faraway universes.

It seems no coincidence, then, that the very place in the world that targets children the most, Disneyland, was defined by Charles W. Moore in 1965 as "the most important single piece of construction in the [US] West in the past several decades."[19] In "The Role of Consumerism in American Architecture," referring to Moore's vision, John Chase explains how the goal of the commercial vernacular is to pretend to be something it is not. It must offer unusual experiences to its visitors, arousing emotions that cannot be replicated anywhere else.[20] These experiences, which Moore simply calls "public life," are not free in consumerist society, but must be purchased.[21] Chase also emphasizes the collective, almost ritualistic nature of shopping. With an optimistic approach to consumer culture, he talks about how the act of buying objects in a public place dissolves ego boundaries and "creates a larger world view, a cosmology of television, advertising, and magazines."[22]

Commercial Domesticity and the Building as a Sign

In the 1968 article "A Bill-Ding-Board Involving Movies Relics and Space," Robert Venturi describes the building he had designed with Denise Scott Brown for the National Football Hall of Fame competition, in which a huge billboard looms above the actual architecture. In their design, the disconnect between the building and its façade is taken to an extreme. The frontal view prevails over the other viewpoints, with a false-front façade projecting much higher than the volume of the museum itself. After entering the building, the visitor is transported, through the use of lighting and projections, into a different world. The traditionally sacred universe of the museum is not "commercial," as its looks might suggest, but "cultural."[23] The building is a physical representation of the consumerist idea of "architecture as a sign," of the Debordian "image" over "object." However, it is still architectural, reminiscent as it is of the false-front façades of the Wild West.[24]

In *Learning from Las Vegas*, buildings along the Strip all have the same characteristics: they are set back from

19 Charles W. Moore, *You Have to Pay for the Public Life: Selected Essays of Charles W. Moore* (Cambridge, MA and London, 2004), 124.
20 John Chase, "The Role of Consumerism in American Architecture," *Journal of Architectural Education* 44, no. 4 (1991): 217.
21 Moore, *You Have to Pay for the Public Life* (see note 19), 126.
22 Chase, *The Role of Consumerism* (see note 20), 212.
23 Robert Venturi, "A Bill-Ding-Board Involving Movies Relics and Space," *Architectural Forum* (1968).
24 For an overview on false-front façades, see Richard Longstreth, "Compositional Types in American Commercial Architecture," *Perspectives in Vernacular Architecture* 2 (1986): 12–23.

Kommerzielle Heimeligkeit und das Gebäude als Zeichen

In seinem 1968 erschienenen Artikel „A Bill-Ding-Board Involving Movies Relics and Space" beschreibt Robert Venturi das Gebäude, das er zusammen mit Denise Scott Brown im Rahmen des Wettbewerbs für die National Football Hall of Fame entwarf. In ihrem Entwurf überragt eine riesige Werbetafel das eigentliche Gebäude und treibt so die Entkoppelung von Gebäude und Fassade ins Extrem. Die Vorderansicht dominiert die anderen Ansichten, wobei die falsche Frontfassade weit höher ist als der Baukörper des Museums selbst. Nach dem Betreten des Gebäudes wird der/die BesucherIn mittels Beleuchtung und Projektionen in eine andere Welt versetzt. Die traditionell als heilig geltende Welt des Museums ist nicht „kommerziell", wie ihr Aussehen nahelegen könnte, sondern „kulturell".[23] Das Gebäude ist eine physische Umsetzung der konsumfördernden Idee von der „Architektur als Zeichen", der Debord'schen Herrschaft des „Bildes" über das „Objekt". Als Reminiszenz an die falschen Frontfassaden des Wilden Westens ist es allerdings immer noch architektonisch.[24]

Laut *Learning from Las Vegas* weisen die Gebäude am Strip alle die gleichen Merkmale auf: Sie sind vom Boulevard so weit zurückversetzt, dass genügend Raum für Parkplätze davor bleibt, sie aber von der Straße dennoch direkt sichtbar sind, um BesucherInnen anzulocken. Die Hauptfassade verläuft parallel zur Straße und ist aufwändig gestaltet, um möglichst repräsentativ zu erscheinen. Die Seitenfassaden sind ebenfalls stark gestaltet, da sie für das heranfahrende Auto am längsten zu sehen sind. Die Gebäude stehen so weit auseinander, dass sie von sämtlichen Seiten bis auf die Rückseite gut sichtbar sind. Diese Regeln gelten für verschiedene Typologien: Casinos, Motels, Hochzeitskapellen und Tankstellen. In diesem Kontext werden die Gebäude letztlich aus der Sicht von Marketing- und Markenstrategien gesehen: Einzelhandelsimmobilien müssen aus kommerziellen Gründen für schnell fahrende BetrachterInnen erkennbar sein und erscheinen FußgängerInnen daher als zu imposant. Vor allem Tankstellen sind so gestaltet, dass sie universell erkennbar sind; sie erscheinen als „freundlich", weil sie für Autoreisende genau „denen zuhause" gleichen.[25]

Das Heimelige kommerziell genutzter Orte – freundliche Tankstellen, lustige Coffeshops, traumhafte Vergnügungsparks – steht im Widerspruch zu ihrer im späten 20. Jahrhundert aufgekommenen negativen Bezeichnung

23 Venturi, Robert: „A Bill-Ding-Board Involving Movies Relics and Space", *Architectural Forum* (1968).

24 Einen Überblick über Falsche-Front-Fassaden gibt Longstreth, Richard: „Compositional Types in American Commercial Architecture", *Perspectives in Vernacular Architecture* 2 (1986), 12–23.

25 Vgl. Venturi et al., *Learning from Las Vegas* (wie Anm. 14), 35.

the boulevard, permitting enough space for a parking lot in front, but are still directly visible from the road so as to invite visitors. The main façade is parallel to the street and is heavily designed to be the most representative. The side façades exhibit strong connotations as well, since they are the ones that are visible to the passing motorist for the longest period of time. Buildings are far enough apart to allow the view from all sides, except the back, and the visitors reach the building by car. These rules apply to different typologies: casinos, motels, chapels, and gasoline stations. In this framework, buildings are ultimately investigated through the lens of marketing and branding strategies: for commercial reasons, retail buildings need to be noticeable by fast-moving observers, hence appearing overly imposing to the pedestrian passersby. The gasoline station, in particular, is designed to be universally recognizable; it is "friendly" because, to the traveling motorist, it looks just like "the one at home."[25]

The domesticity of commercial places—friendly gasoline stations, humorous coffee shops, dreamy amusement parks—contrasts with the unfavorable epithet of *nonplaces*[26] that they acquired in the late twentieth century. Those *neon nightmares* often seem to arouse pleasant emotions, rather than ones of estrangement or alienation—that could be caused by the impossibility of space appropriation. In *L'Invention du Quotidien*,[27] published in English as *The Practice of Everyday Life*, Michel de Certeau discusses the ability of users to reappropriate spaces governed by power structures, making a distinction between *strategies* and *tactics*. Strategies are used by "a subject with will and power (a business, an army, a city, a scientific institution)," while tactics are the tools of the "weak" for insinuating the space of power. According to Certeau, "every 'strategic' rationalization seeks first of all to distinguish its 'own' place, that is, the place of its own power and will, from an 'environment'."[28] Strategies are therefore founded on *space*, whereas tactics depend on *time* and are "always on the watch for opportunities that must be seized 'on the wing'." Tactics are found in the details of ordinary life; they are familial activities, such as cooking, shopping, or doing handicrafts.[29]

The Future Advertised and the Americanization of Italian Mass Culture

Highway service stations are by their very nature places of the *infra-ordinary*,[30] where only mundane activities

25 Venturi et al., *Learning from Las Vegas* (see note 14), 35.

26 See Marc Augé, *Non-Lieux: Introduction à Une Anthropologie de La Surmodernité* (Paris, 1992).

27 Michel de Certeau, *L'Invention du Quotidien*, vol. I, *Arts de Faire* (Paris, 1980).

28 Michel de Certeau, *The Practice of Everyday Life*, trans. Steven Rendall (Berkeley and Los Angeles, 1984), 35–36.

29 Ibid., xix.

30 See Georges Perec, *L'infra-ordinaire* (Paris, 1989).

„Nicht-Orte".[26] Diese Neon-Alpträume scheinen oft eher angenehme Gefühle hervorzurufen als solche der Entfremdung, die wohl durch die Unmöglichkeit der Aneignung solcher Räume ausgelöst werden. In *L'Invention du Quotidien*[27] spricht Michel de Certeau von der Möglichkeit, sich von Machtstrukturen geprägte Räume anzueignen, und unterscheidet dabei zwischen Strategie und Taktik. Strategien verweisen auf ein „mit Willen und Macht versehenes Subjekt (ein Unternehmen, eine Armee, eine Stadt oder eine wissenschaftlichen Institution)", wogegen Taktiken das Mittel sind, mit dem die „Schwachen" den Raum der Macht infiltrieren. Laut de Certeau ist „jede ‚strategische' Rationalisierung vor allem darauf gerichtet, das ‚Umfeld' vom ‚eigenen Bereich', das heißt vom Ort der eigenen Macht und des eigenen Willens, abzugrenzen".[28] Gründet die Strategie im *Raum*, so ist die Taktik von der *Zeit* abhängig, „immer darauf aus, ihren Vorteil ‚im Fluge zu erfassen'". Taktik ist in den kleinen Dingen des Alltagslebens am Werk, in häuslichen Tätigkeiten wie Kochen, Einkaufen und Handarbeiten.[29]

Zukunft und die Amerikanisierung der italienischen Massenkultur

Raststätten sind ihrem ganzen Wesen nach Orte, die infraordinär[30] sind. Orte, die der Verrichtung banaler Tätigkeiten gewidmet sind. Der Versorgung mit Gütern dienende Gebäude gehören zu einer Kategorie Architektur, der man keine große Aufmerksamkeit schenkt, weil man darin meist nicht lange verweilt. Dennoch haben sich die in den Blütezeiten des Autobahnbaus, den 1950er- und 1960er-Jahren, entlang der Straßen entstandenen Geschäftsgebäude in ihrer Formsprache an den Traumbildern von einer glänzenden Zukunft orientiert.[31] Der Titel der New Yorker Weltausstellung von 1939 lautete „Die Welt von Morgen"[32] und spiegelte damit die allgemeine Begeisterung der Öffentlichkeit für – und ihr Vertrauen in – den technischen Fortschritt wider. In den Vereinigten Staaten, der Heimat der autogerechten Großstadt, hatte sich analog zur italienischen und russischen Avantgarde

26 Vgl. Augé, Marc: *Non-Lieux: Introduction à Une Anthropologie de La Surmodernité*, Paris 1992 (dt. *Orte und Nicht-Orte: Vorüberlegungen zu einer Ethnologie der Einsamkeit*, Übers. Michael Bischoff, Frankfurt am Main 1994)

27 de Certeau, Michel: *L'Invention du Quotidien*, Bd. I, *Arts de Faire*, Paris 1980.

28 de Certeau, Michel: *Die Kunst des Handelns*, Übers. Ronald Voullié, Berlin 1988, 87.

29 Vgl. Ebda., 23.

30 Vgl. Perec, Georges: *L'infra-ordinaire*, Paris 1989 (dt.: *Warum gibt es keine Zigaretten beim Gemüsehändler*, Übers. Eugen Helmlé, Zürich/Berlin 2014).

31 Vgl. Hess, Alan: *Googie Redux: Ultramodern Roadside Architecture*, San Francisco 2004.

32 Zim, Larry/Lerner, Mel/Rolfes, Herbert: *The World of Tomorrow: The* 1939 *New York World's Fair*, New York 1988.

take place. Supply and refreshment buildings belong to that category of architecture to which one may not pay particular attention, not planning to spend much time there. Nevertheless, in the booming days of highways and freeways, the 1950s and 1960s, buildings related to roadside commerce responded, in terms of language and form, to the dreamlike imagery of positive trust in a luminous future.[31] The 1939 New York World's Fair was titled "The World of Tomorrow,"[32] well representing the general fascination of the public with technological development, and their confidence in it. In the United States, home of the motorized metropolis, a mainstream form of futurism had spread in parallel with the Italian and Russian avant-gardes.[33] The architectural style ascribed to this late form of futuristic modernism was named *Googie*, after a coffee shop designed by John Lautner,[34] and it became a symbol of the architectural space age.

Meanwhile, countless roads and highways were stretching across the land on the European continent as well. In Italy, after the reconstruction post–World War II and the Marshall Plan, the American economic model was spreading. In order to increase consumption, heavy investments began to be made in the infrastructure network, particularly telecommunications and transportation.[35] The national television network—Rai—openly promoted consumer culture, by showcasing to its viewers their opportunities to increase individual and family wealth. Once again, spectacle and economy were closely intertwined. In the meantime, also due to the bombing of railways, private transportation had become more widespread, while after the war the Allies had abandoned hundreds of vehicles on Italian territory, which began to be illegally traded. This was also when the quintessential Italian private vehicle, the Vespa, was born. Even in Italian, they still call it a *scooter*, after the small vehicles driven by American paratroopers.[36] It was the beginning of the Americanization of Italian culture.

Origins of Italian Roadside Architecture

The history of Italian service stations began in 1947 on the *autostrada*[37] from Novara to Turin. That is when Mario Pavesi, head of the Pavesi biscuit factory, built the first refreshment point at the Novara tollbooth. Pavesi, a self-made businessman from the confectionary food industry,

31 See Alan Hess, *Googie Redux: Ultramodern Roadside Architecture* (San Francisco, 2004).

32 See Larry Zim, Mel Lerner, and Herbert Rolfes, *The World of Tomorrow: The* 1939 *New York World's Fair* (New York, 1988).

33 See Elizabeth Guffey, "Crafting Yesterday's Tomorrows: Retro-Futurism, Steampunk, and the Problem of Making in the Twenty-First Century," *The Journal of Modern Craft* 7, no. 3 (2014): 252.

34 See Hess, *Googie* (see note 16), 61.

35 See Enrico Menduni, *L'Autostrada del Sole* (Bologna, 1999), 9.

36 See Ibid., 10–22.

37 *Autostrada* is the Italian word for "high-speed toll road."

eine mainstreamtaugliche Form des Futurismus herausgebildet.[33] Der mit dieser Spätform der futuristischen Moderne verbundene Architekturstil wurde nach einem von John Lautner entworfenen Coffeeshop „Googie“[34] getauft und entwickelte sich zu einem Symbol des architektonischen Weltraumzeitalters.

Bald entwickelte sich auch auf dem europäischen Kontinent ein ansehnliches Straßen- und Autobahnnetz. Im Zuge des vom Marshallplan beflügelten Wiederaufbaus nach dem Zweiten Weltkrieg verbreitete sich in Italien auch das amerikanischen Wirtschaftsmodell. Um den Konsum anzukurbeln, wurden enorme Investitionen in die Infrastruktur, insbesondere das Telekommunikations- und Verkehrsnetz, getätigt.[35] Die staatliche italienische Rundfunkanstalt Rai förderte offen die Konsumkultur, indem sie ihren ZuschauerInnen Möglichkeiten aufzeigte, den individuellen Wohlstand oder den der Familie zu mehren. Auch hier waren Spektakel und Ökonomie auf das Engste verquickt. Gleichzeitig nahm auch der Privatverkehr zu. Ein Grund dafür waren die Bombardierungen der Eisenbahnlinien, aber auch der Umstand, dass die Alliierten nach dem Krieg Hunderte Fahrzeuge zurückließen, die dann illegal gehandelt wurden. Es war auch die Zeit, in der das italienische Privatfahrzeug schlechthin, die Vespa, das Licht der Welt erblickte. Bis heute wird sie sogar auf Italienisch „Scooter“ genannt – nach den von den amerikanischen Luftlandetruppen benutzen Kleinfahrzeugen.[36] Mit ihnen begann die Amerikanisierung der italienischen Kultur.

Anfänge der italienischen Straßenrand-Architektur

Die Geschichte italienischer Raststätten begann 1947 an der *autostrada*[37] von Novara nach Turin. In diesem Jahr ließ Mario Pavesi, Chef der Keksfirma Pavesi, bei der Mautstelle Novara den ersten Kiosk bauen. Pavesi, ein Selfmade-Unternehmer in der Süßwarenbranche, wurde mit einer Strategie groß, die eine Veränderung der italienischen Essgewohnheiten zum Ziel hatte. Er versuchte, das erfolgreiche amerikanischen Geschäftsmodell zu imitieren, aber es mit einer bestimmten Auffassung von den Bedürfnissen der ItalienerInnen nach dem Zweiten Weltkrieg zu verbinden: Der Konsum von Süßigkeiten symbolisierte alsbald das Gegenteil der während des Kriegs erlebten Entbehrungen. Auch die Historikerin Simone Colafranceschi meint, dass die erste italienische Autobahnraststätte zum Bewerben von Produkten entstand, die sich die italienische Bevölkerung noch nicht leisten konnte: „1950 waren

made his way into entrepreneurship with a strategy aimed at transforming the eating habits of the Italians. His attempt was to imitate the successful American business model, while combining it with a specific interpretation of the needs of the Italian people after World War II: the consumption of sweets, a voluptuous food, came to symbolize the opposite of the misery and deprivation experienced during the war. The historian Simone Colafranceschi underlines how the first Italian highway service station was born as a tool for the promotion of products that the Italian population still could not afford: “… [I]n 1950, 20 percent of Italian families were poor or indigent. More than half of the population lived in rural municipalities. Only one out of ten apartments had a bathroom, and less than half had running water … more than 47 percent of family spending was destined for food consumption: cars were less than one for every hundred inhabitants.”[38] In 1952, the First Multi-Year Program for the improvement and increase of the high-speed road network, presented by the Italian Ministry of Public Works, financed the construction of new motorways, favoring transport on private vehicles. It was the beginning of the future success of the Italian *autostrade*. In the early 1950s, the economy of the country began to record an increase in net national income, approximately doubled as compared to the previous period, with a consequent change in the lifestyle of middle-class Italians. In 1954, television broadcasts began to air nationally, becoming a new tool for promoting products and spreading the American way of life. The *autogrillroom*, together with the television, became a symbol of the beginnings of consumer society.[39]

Throughout the second half of the twentieth century, hundreds of new service stations sprang up along Italy’s fledgling highway system, representing an opportunity for architects to experiment, as they grappled with nonurban contexts and were therefore free from regulatory ties and the necessity to integrate contemporary buildings within the historic fabric. In the wake of American roadside architecture, a new building typology was born, and with it a futuristic imagery, representative of the enthusiasm for the economic boom and the confidence in the growth of the country. The *autogrill*, a false Anglicism for “roadside restaurant,” became not only a place to stop and refresh, but a tourist destination itself, from which to write enthusiastic postcards, just like the “243 Cartes Postales en Couleurs Véritables à Italo Calvino”[40] that Georges Perec wrote in the magazine *Le Fou Parle*.[41] In its

33 Vgl. Guffey, Elizabeth: „Crafting Yesterday’s Tomorrows: Retro-Futurism, Steampunk, and the Problem of Making in the Twenty-First Century“, *The Journal of Modern Craft* 7, 3 (2014), 252.

34 Vgl. Hess, *Googie* (wie Anm. 16), 61.

35 Vgl. Menduni, Enrico: *L’Autostrada del Sole*, Bologna 1999, 9.

36 Ebda., 10–22.

37 *Autostrada* ist die italienische Bezeichnung für eine mautpflichtige Schnellstraße.

38 Simone Colafranceschi, *Autogrill: Una Storia Italiana* (Bologna, 2007) (translation by the author).

39 See Ibid.

40 The title translates as “Two Hundred and Forty-Three Postcards in Real Colour” (translation by the author). The text was first published in *Le Fou Parle* 8 (October 1978) and later included in the book *L’infra-ordinaire* (1989).

41 Bernard Magné, “De l’Écart à la Trace: Avatars de la Contrainte,” *Études Littéraires* 23, nos. 1–2 (1990): 9–26.

20% der italienischen Familien arm oder mittellos. Mehr als die Hälfte der Bevölkerung lebte in Landgemeinden. Nur eine von zehn Wohnungen verfügte über ein Badezimmer und weniger als die Hälfte über fließend Wasser [...] mehr als 47% des Haushaltsbudgets wurden für Essen ausgegeben. Auf hundert EinwohnerInnen kam nicht einmal ein Auto."[38] 1952 präsentierte das Ministerium für öffentliche Bauten den ersten Mehrjahresplan zur Verbesserung und Erweiterung des Schnellstraßennetzes, was die Finanzierung neuer Autobahnen sicherte und den Privatverkehr begünstigte. Es war der Anfang des künftigen Erfolgs der italienischen *autostrade*. In den frühen 1950er-Jahren kam es zu einem beträchtlichen Anstieg des Nettonationaleinkommens, das sich gegenüber der Vorperiode nahezu verdoppelte und zu einer Veränderung des Lebensstils der italienischen Mittelschicht führte. 1954 begann das Fernsehen landesweit zu senden und wurde zu einem neuen Instrument der Produktwerbung und der Verbreitung des amerikanischen Lebensstils. Der *auto-grillroom* wurde neben dem Fernsehen zu einem Symbol der aufkeimenden Konsumgesellschaft.[39]

Während der gesamten zweiten Hälfte des 20. Jahrhunderts schossen an Italiens neuem Autobahnnetz Hunderte neuer Raststätten aus dem Boden und boten ArchitektInnen eine Möglichkeit zu experimentieren, da sie es dabei mit nichturbanen Kontexten zu tun hatten und so von regulatorischen Fesseln und der Notwendigkeit zur Einpassung zeitgenössischer Gebäude in eine historische Umgebung befreit waren. Im Gefolge der amerikanischen Straßenrand-Architektur entstand eine neue Bautypologie und mit ihr eine futuristische Formensprache, die die Begeisterung für den Wirtschaftsaufschwung und das Vertrauen in das nationale Wachstum widerspiegelte. Der *Autogrill*, ein falscher Anglizismus, wurde nicht nur zu einer Rast- und Versorgungsstation, sondern zu einem eigenständigen Touristenziel, von dem man begeisterte Ansichtskarten schrieb – so wie die Italo Calvino gewidmeten „243 Cartes Postales en Couleurs Véritables",[40] die Georges Perec in der Zeitschrift *Le Fou Parle* veröffentlichte.[41] In seiner banalen Funktion – Versorgung mit Teibstoff und Lebensmitteln – und seinem Status als Nicht-Ort – einem anonymen Knoten in einem Netz mit Hunderten anderen – war der *Autogrill* ein Ort, der infraordinär war. Dieser Alltagscharakter wurde jedoch durch die architektonische Repräsentation eines märchenhaften Lebensstils auf den Kopf gestellt. In den staunenden Augen italienischer Autoreisender stammten diese Gebäude direkt aus der Zukunft.

38 Colafranceschi, Simone: *Autogrill: Una Storia Italiana*, Bologna 2007. (Übers. W.P.)
39 Vgl. ebd.
40 Deutsch: „Zweihundertdreiundvierzig Postkarten in Echtfarbendruck." Der ursprünglich in *Le Fou Parle* 8 (Oktober 1978) veröffentlichte Text wurde später in *L'infra-ordinaire* (1989) aufgenommen.
41 Magné, Bernard: „De l'Écart à la Trace: Avatars de la Contrainte", *Études Littéraires* 23, 1–2 (1990), 9–26.

ordinariness of use—food and fuel supply—and its nonplace status—an anonymous node in a network of hundreds—the *autogrill* was a place of the infraordinary. However, the quotidian trait was overturned through the architectural representation of a fabulous lifestyle. To the eyes of the wide-eyed Italian motorist, those buildings appeared to have come from the future.

The Trip across the Atlantic and the First Italian Service Stations

In June 1959, Angelo Bianchetti, the architect commissioned by Pavesi to design the new *autogrills* took a trip to the United States, together with Mario Pavesi, to study American service stations.[42] In an article titled "Le Oasi dell'Autostrada,"[43] Bianchetti describes the ones he visited, also citing some of the Italian examples on which he had worked. In the caption to the picture of the Ronco Scrivia *autogrill*, the building is described as *fiabesco*, which means "fairytale-like."[44] Once again, the imagery is dreamy, childlike in the recalling of *fables*, reminiscent of magical or future worlds. The "oases" in the title also remind of the Las Vegas leisure fantasy, with its fountains and gardens in the desert. In the field of highway architecture, there have been various exchanges between Italy and the United States. Particularly notable is the similarity between the Lainate service station—built in 1958—and the Theme Building at the Los Angeles International Airport—built in 1961—also noted by the *Autogrill* marketing department which used it for an advertising campaign in 2009.

In a 1941 article, Angelo Bianchetti and Cesare Pea described their vision of advertising architecture as diverging from what has been defined as "traditional" architecture: "Although in antiquity famous artists such as Raphael, Leonardo, or Bernini dealt with the creation of pavilions, or temporary decorative structures on the occasion of religious or political celebrations, it was not until the nineteenth century, with the emergence of the first universal exhibitions, that artists were able to fully address the new problem: no longer the classical canons of architecture and decoration, but the search for new and freer means of expression had to be the basis of this research. Imagination aided by symbolism and the allegorical spirit and supported by a new technique and new construction methods, created the basis for advertising construction."[45]

Angelo Bianchetti is the architect of the first Pavesi kiosk, built in 1947 on the Turin-Novara *autostrada*. From its beginnings as a small confectionery store, the

42 See Archivio Jan Jacopo Bianchetti.
43 The title translates as "The Oases of the Highway" (translation by the author).
44 Angelo Bianchetti, "Le Oasi dell'Autostrada," *Quattroruote* (January 1, 1960): 90–97.
45 Angelo Bianchetti and Cesare Pea, "Architettura Pubblicitaria," *Casabella Costruzioni* 159–60, no. XIX (1941): 96–97 (translation by the author).

2 Pavesi pavilion, Lainate, Architect: Angelo Bianchetti, 1958 © Archivio Jan Jacopo Bianchetti

Die Reise über den Atlantik und die ersten italienischen Raststätten

Im Juni 1959 unternahm Angelo Bianchetti, der von Pavesi mit dem Entwurf der neuen *Autogrills* beauftragte Architekt, zusammen mit seinem Auftraggeber eine Reise in die Vereinigten Staaten, um die amerikanischen Raststätten zu studieren.[42] In einem Artikel mit dem Titel „Le Oasi dell'Autostrada"[43] beschrieb Bianchetti die von ihm besuchten Raststätten, ging aber auch auf die italienischen ein, an denen er arbeitete. In der Bildlegende zum *Auto-grill* Ronco Scrivia wird das Gebäude als „fiabesco", als „märchenhaft" beschrieben.[44] Die Bildsprache ist also auch hier träumerisch, kindlich in der Beschwörung von Märchen, an Zauber- und Zukunftswelten erinnernd. Die „Oasen" aus dem Titel lassen auch an das Freizeitparadies Las Vegas mit seinen Springbrunnen und Gärten mitten in der Wüste denken.

Auf dem Gebiet Autobahnraststättenarchitektur

building was transformed and expanded over the years, seeing the addition of a bar, restaurant, and later tourist-market and motel. It was eventually demolished to make way for one of those bridge buildings which later became a symbol of the *Autogrill* brand. In the kiosk in Novara (fig. 1), as well as in the 1958 pavilions in Lainate (fig. 2) and Ronco Scrivia (fig. 3), Bianchetti demonstrated the ability, acquired through his long experience in fair exhibition design,[46] to reconcile architectural design with the use of advertising signs and removable structures. In 1948, he had designed, with Cesare Pea, the Palazzo delle Nazioni at the Milan Trade Fair, a building with a bridge-like structure under which cars and pedestrians transited. This experience would later be useful in the design of the Pavesi bridges,[47] opened between 1959 and 1972, starting with the bridge *autogrill* of Fiorenzuola d'Arda, which Bianchetti

42 Archivio Jan Jacopo Bianchetti.
43 Deutsch in etwa: „Die Oasen der Autobahn"
44 Bianchetti, Angelo: „Le Oasi dell'Autostrada", *Quattroruote* (1. Jänner 1960), 90–97.

46 See Laura Greco, *Architetture autostradali in Italia: Progetto e costruzione degli edifici per l'assistenza ai viaggiatori* (Rome, 2016), 54.
47 See Laura Greco, *Angelo Bianchetti: Gli Autogrill* (Milan, 2022).

3 Pavesi pavilion, Ronco Scrivia, Architect: Angelo Bianchetti, 1958 © Archivio Jan Jacopo Bianchetti

fanden zwischen Italien und den Vereinigten Staaten mehrere Austauschprozesse statt. Besonders auffällig ist die Ähnlichkeit der 1958 erbauten Raststätte Lainate mit dem 1961 errichteten Theme Building am internationalen Flughafen Los Angeles, was auch von der *Autogrill*-Marketingabteilung bemerkt wurde, die es 2009 für eine Werbekampagne verwendete. In einem 1941 erschienenen Artikel beschrieben Angelo Bianchetti und Cesare Pea ihre Idee einer werbenden Architektur im Unterschied zur sogenannten „traditionellen" Architektur. „Zwar haben sich berühmte Künstler wie Raphael, Leornardo oder Bernini auch schon in älteren Zeiten anlässlich religiöser oder politischer Festivitäten mit der Schaffung von Pavillons oder temporären Zierbauten beschäftigt, doch erst im 19. Jahrhundert mit dem Aufkommen der ersten Weltausstellungen konnten sich Künstler dem neuen Problem voll und ganz zuwenden: Nicht mehr der klassische Kanon der Architektur und der Dekoration, sondern die Suche nach neuen und freieren Ausdrucksmitteln bildete die Grundlage dieses Unterfangens. Einbildungskraft gepaart mit Symbolismus und dem Geist der Allegorie, gestützt von neuer Technik und neuen Konstruktionsmethoden,

himself called a "transatlantic docked astride the highway."[48] Although one can sense the American dream in the background of Bianchetti's words, the construction of bridge restaurants in the United States remained a limited experience,[49] while it became a widespread typology for the flagship restaurants of Italian food companies along the *autostrade*.

Pavesi, Motta, and Alemagna: Architecture and Brand Identity

In a period of strong transformation, Pavesi was not the only one putting in place innovative entrepreneurial strategies to make his way into this sector: Angelo Motta and Gioacchino Alemagna soon became valid competitors, capable of interpreting the volatile Italian economic situation. During the post–World War II economic boom, the three food companies Pavesi, Motta, and Alemagna competed for control as service providers on Italian high-speed roads. Starting with the architectural languages chosen

48 Greco, *Architetture Autostradali in Italia* (see note 46), 100.
49 See ibid., 91.

schufen das Fundament für werbende Bauwerke."[45]

Angelo Bianchetti ist der Architekt des 1947 an der *autostrada* Turin-Novara errichteten ersten Pavesi-Kiosks. Von seinen Anfängen als kleiner Süßwarenladen wurde das Gebäude im Lauf der Jahre immer weiter um- und ausgebaut; es erlebte den Anbau einer Bar, eines Restaurants und später dann eines Touristenmarkts sowie eines Motels. Am Ende wurde es abgerissen, um Platz für eines jener Brückengebäude zu schaffen, die zum Markenzeichen von *Autogrill* wurden. Im Kiosk in Novara (Abb. 1) wie auch in den 1958 erbauten Pavillons in Lainate (Abb. 2) und Ronco Scrivia (Abb. 3) bewies Bianchetti seine durch langjähriges Messe-Ausstellungsdesign[46] erworbene Fähigkeit, architektonische Gestaltung mit der Verwendung von Reklame- und beweglichen Bauelementen zu verbinden. 1948 hatte er zusammen mit Cesare Pea den Palazzo delle Nazioni auf der Mailänder Messe entworfen, ein Gebäude mit einer brückenartigen Konstruktion, unter der Autos durchfahren und FußgängerInnen durchgehen konnten. Diese Erfahrung kam ihm später beim Entwurf der zwischen 1959 und 1972 eröffneten Pavesi-Brücken zugute.[47] Die erste war das *Autogrill*- Brückenrestaurant in Fiorenzuola d'Arda, das Bianchetti selbst als „über der Autobahn angedockten Transatlantikliner bezeichnete.[48] Doch auch wenn Bianchettis Worte auf den amerikanischen Traum verweisen, so blieb der Bau von Brückenrestaurants in den Vereinigten Staaten doch überschaubar.[49] Dagegen wurden Brückenbauten entlang der *autostrade* zu einer verbreiteten Typologie für Flagship-Restaurants italienischer Gastrounternehmen.

Pavesi, Motta und Alemagna: Architektur und Markenidentität

In dieser von starken Veränderungen geprägten Zeit war Pavesi nicht der einzige, der mithilfe innovativer Unternehmensstrategien in diesem Sektor zu reüssieren versuchte: Angelo Motta und Gioacchino Alemagna wurden bald ernstzunehmende Konkurrenten, die die volatile Wirtschaftslage in Italien ebenfalls zu deuten verstanden. Während des wirtschaftlichen Aufschwungs nach dem Zweiten Weltkrieg kämpften also mit Pavesi, Motta und Alemagna drei Gastrounternehmen um die Vorherrschaft als Raststättenbetreiber auf den italienischen Schnellstraßen. Von der Wahl der Architektursprache bis zum Angebot der Dienstleistungen lassen sich dabei verschiedene Strategien bei der Entwicklung des jeweiligen

45 Bianchetti, Angelo/Pea, Cesare: „Architettura Pubblicitaria", *Casabella Costruzioni* 159–60, 19 (1941), 96–97. (Übers. aus dem Engl. W.P.)

46 Vgl. Greco, Laura: *Architetture autostradali in Italia: Progetto e costruzione degli edifici per l'assistenza ai viaggiatori*, Rom 2016, 54.

47 Vgl. Greco, Laura: *Angelo Bianchetti: Gli Autogrill*, Mailand 2022.

48 Greco, *Architetture autostradali in Italia* (wie Anm. 46), 100.

49 Ebda., 91.

4 Pavesi Autogrill, Fiorenzuola d'Arda, Architect: Angelo Bianchetti, 1959 © Archivio Jan Jacopo Bianchetti

to represent the company and the choices of service offered, one can recognize the different strategies for the construction of the company's corporate image. Pavesi and Motta challenged each other at the grand scale of highway bridges. As Laura Greco writes, the bridges were transformed into food and beverage machines, as they are designed for large numbers of people and offer homogeneous services throughout the territory, thus pushing the two companies toward an industrial dimension. Pavesi's bridges, proper *Autogrills*, as Mario Pavesi held the rights to the name, presented no functions at their base other than entry and are therefore kept light on the ground. In the *Mottagrill*, some quick-service dining functions are provided at the foot of the building, which is thus more articulated in its side elements.[50] The architecture of the Pavesi roadside restaurant is characterized by a marked use of contemporary technologies, particularly steel, which Bianchetti was familiar with. The imagery of the first Pavesi *autogrills* is visionary, with large steel structures supporting headers bearing the brand name of the company (fig. 4). For this era of Italian motorway architecture, Colafranceschi (2007) uses the term "heroic age."[51] While Bianchetti's bridges for Pavesi are characterized by a strong, massive image, those of Motta are usually more transparent, with steel and glass façades, and they do not have as large of advertising structures as Pavesi's. In general, Motta buildings tend to be characterized by their architectural forms, rather than by the movable elements of advertising, as we can see, for example, in the Somaglia store (fig. 5) or the Cantagallo bridge (fig. 6), in which the very movement of the building's roof seems to form a Motta "M."

The architectural language of Alemagna instead contrasts with the sensationalist approach of Pavesi

50 Ibid., 91–96.

51 Colafranceschi, *Autogrill* (see note 38).

1

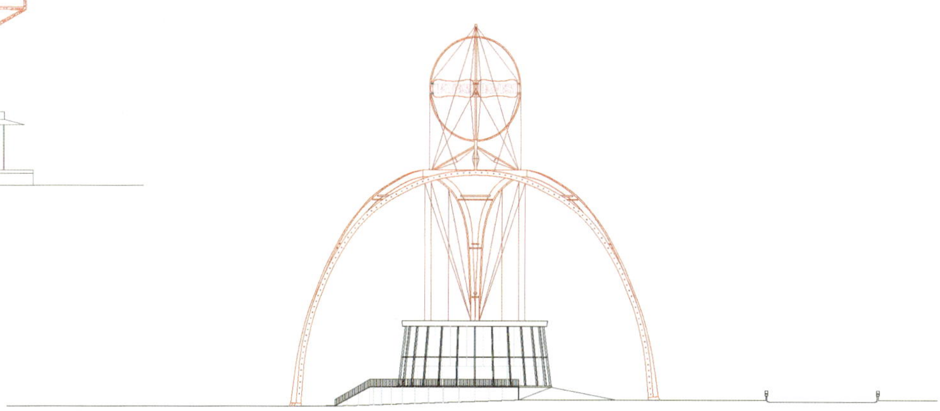

3

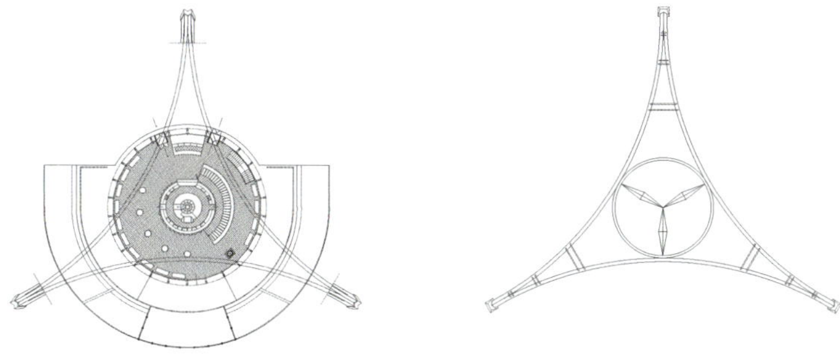

4

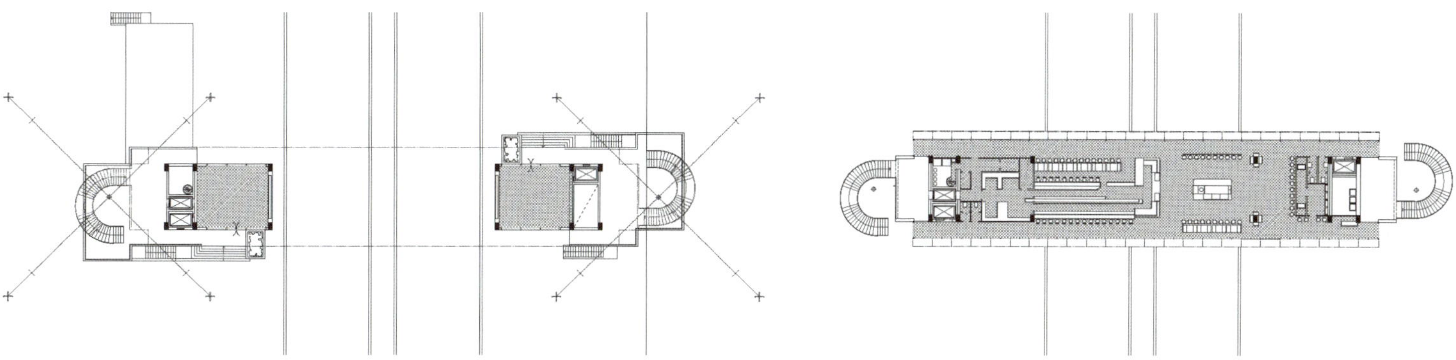

Drawings by Elena Colletti and Michal Kilarski

Firmenimages ausmachen. Pavesi und Motta wetteiferten miteinander im großen Format der Brückenrestaurants. Die Brücken wurden, wie Laura Greco schreibt, in Speise- und-Getränke-Maschinen verwandelt, da sie für große BesucherInnenzahlen gedacht waren und im ganzen Land die gleichen Dienstleistungen anboten, was beide Unternehmen in Richtung Industrialisierung trieb. Bei den Pavesi-Brücken, den eigentlichen *Autogrills*, für die Mario Pavesi die Namensrechte besaß, beherbergten die Brückenköpfe keine andere Funktion als den Eingang, sodass die Unterbauten leicht ausfielen. In den *Mottagrills* hingegen wurden zu ebener Erde einige Schnellimbissleistungen angeboten, weshalb die Seitenteile ausgeprägter waren.[50] Die Architektur der Pavesi-Raststätten fällt durch eine prononcierte Verwendung zeitgenössischer Techniken, insbesondere Stahlkonstruktionen auf, womit sich Bianchetti gut auskannte. Die Formensprache der ersten Pavesi-*Autogrills* ist visionär, mit mächtigen Stahlkonstruktionen, die Schilder mit dem Firmenlogo tragen (Abb. 4). Colafranceschi bezeichnet diese Ära der italienischen Autobahnarchitektur als „heroisches Zeitalter".[51] Sind Bianchettis Pavesi-Brücken durch ein starkes, kompaktes Bild geprägt, so sind die von Motta meist transparenter, mit Glas-und-Stahl-Fassaden und ohne die bei Pavesi üblichen großen Konstruktionen für die Werbung. Tendenziell sind die Motta-Gebäude eher durch die architektonische Form als durch austauschbare Werbemittel gekennzeichnet, wie man etwa am Pavillon in Somaglia (Abb. 5) oder an der Brücke in Cantagallo (Abb. 6) sieht, wo schon die Form des Daches das Motta-„M" nachzubilden scheint.

Die Architektursprache von Alemagna wiederum setzt sich von der Effekthascherei sowohl von Pavesi als auch von Motta ab. Hier lag der Fokus auf rasch errichtbaren, im großen Stil reproduzierbaren Bauten. Die Alemagna-Raststätte hieß *Autobar* und war eine abgespeckte Version des *Autogrill*, meist mit rechteckigen Formen und aus vorgefertigten Teilen. Selbst das Angebot in den Allemagna-Raststätten war reduziert und beinhaltete zum Beispiel keine Bedienung. Bis heute werden Gebäude dieser Art in den *Autogrill*-Entwurfsteams informell als „Alemagnas" bezeichnet. Weder Pavesi und Motta noch Alemagna betrieben die mit den Raststätten verbundenen Tankstellen. Letztere wurden vielmehr als Lizenzbetriebe der großen Mineralölgesellschaften Agip, ESSO, BP usw. geführt. Vor allem an den Agip-Tankstellen wurde auch ein Speiselokal – das sogenannte *Risoragip* – und, falls vorhanden, auch eines Motels namens *Motelagip* betrieben.[52] Diese Gebäude glichen eher dem Alemagna-Typus, insofern sie der Logik konstruktiver und typologischer Standardisierung folgten.

50 Ebda., 91–96.
51 Colafranceschi, *Autogrill* (wie Anm. 38).
52 Vgl. Deschermeier, Dorothea: *Impero ENI: l'Architettura Aziendale e l'Urbanistica di Enrico Mattei*, Bologna 2008.

5 Mottagrill, Somaglia Ovest, Architect: Melchiorre Bega, 1959–1960 © Archivio Fotografico Autostrade per l'Italia

and Motta. The choice was to focus on the design of quickly buildable structures, reproducible on a large scale. The Alemagna roadside restaurant was called *Autobar*, a much more stripped-down version of *autogrill*, featuring orthogonal lines and prefabricated elements. Even the service provided on the Alemagna premises is more streamlined and does not include, for example, table service. Even today, within the *Autogrill* architecture and design team, the buildings in this category are informally referred to as "Alemagnas." Pavesi, Motta, and Alemagna did not manage the fueling facilities in the rest areas, which were instead held under concession by the oil companies Agip, ESSO, BP, and others. In the Agip gas stations, in particular, it was the same fuel supply company that also managed the food service building—called *Ristoragip*—and, if provided, the motel, which was called *Motelagip*.[52] Such buildings were more similar to the Alemagna type, in that they responded to the logic of constructive and typological standardization.

Epilogue: The End of the Dream

The dream began to vanish around the 1970s, when the idea of large highway buildings for the rest areas was challenged by difficulties in maintenance and by the changed use of highway facilities.[53] The end of the Italian economic boom marked the closing of the heroic era of highway architecture, which shifted toward construction speed and economization. In 1977, the three companies Pavesi, Motta, and Alemagna merged into Autogrill S.p.A. In 2022, the Autogrill Group controlled 231 service stations on Italian *autostrade*, operated mainly under concession. Nowadays, the duration of the concessions and the pressing need to comply with corporate budgets—also due to the large fees imposed by the highway concessionaires—force the architecture and design departments of the company to make limited interventions on existing buildings and to contain investments in new construction projects.

Back in the United States, during the 1960s and 1970s, the faith of Enlightenment in a bright future governed by

52 See Dorothea Deschermeier, *Impero ENI: l'Architettura Aziendale e l'Urbanistica di Enrico Mattei* (Bologna, 2008).
53 See Greco, *Architetture Autostradali in Italia* (see note 46).

Epilog: Das Ende des Traums

Um die 1970er-Jahre, als die Idee von Raststätten in Form riesiger Bauten an der Autobahn aufgrund von Wartungsproblemen und einer veränderten Nutzung der Autobahninfrastruktur fragwürdig wurde, begann der Traum zu verblassen.[53] Das Ende des italienischen Wirtschaftsaufschwungs beendete auch das heroische Zeitalter der Autobahnarchitektur, die sich nun in Richtung Baugeschwindigkeit und Ökonomisierung entwickelte. 1977 fusionierten die drei Unternehmen Pavesi, Motta und Alemagna zur Autogrill S.p.A. 2022 kontrollierte die Autogrill-Gruppe 231 vorwiegend in Lizenz betriebene Raststationen an italienischen *autostrade*. Heute zwingen die Dauer der Pachtverträge und die – auch wegen der von den Autobahngesellschaften verlangten hohen Pachten – knappen Konzernbudgets die Architektur und Entwurfsabteilungen des Unternehmens zu beschränkten Eingriffen in die bestehende Gebäude und zur Zurückhaltung bei Investitionen in neue Bauvorhaben.

In den Vereinigten Staaten war der Glaube an eine strahlende, von der Hypereffizienz von Maschinen regierte Zukunft bereits in den 1960er-Jahren allmählich verblasst und kam dann endgültig ans Ende, als die Wirtschafts- und Ölkrise der 1970er die Autoträume der breiten Bevölkerung platzen ließ. Schon in den 1980er-Jahren wich der optimistische Futurismus der ersten Jahrhunderthälfte einem nostalgischen Gefühl für eine „Zukunft, die es nie gab."[54] Die 1984 von der Smithsonian Institution gezeigte Ausstellung „Yesterday's Tomorrows: Past Visions of the American Future" markiert den Beginn einer später als Retrofuturismus bezeichneten künstlerischen Bewegung, die die Zukunftsvorstellungen vergangener ZeitgenossInnen wiederzuerwecken sucht. Angesichts der New Yorker Weltausstellung von 1939 – „The World of Tomorrow" – entbehrt der Ausstellungstitel von 1984 zwar nicht einer gewissen Ironie, er bringt aber gut auf den Punkt, dass der während der vorangegangenen Jahrzehnte herrschende kollektive Optimismus an sein Ende gekommen ist.

Die fantastischen Highway-Bauten, die in den 1950er- und 1960er-Jahren entlang der Straßen Kaliforniens entstanden, erzählen ebenso wie die heroischen Autobahngebäude der Nachkriegszeit in Italien von einer galaktischen Zukunft, in der alle Rädchen reibungslos ineinandergreifen. Unterdessen haben die Marketingstrategien des Einzelhandels und strenge Budgetvorgaben dazu geführt, dass der ambitionierte architektonische Entwurf heute nur mehr in den Rissen und Ritzen eines profitorientierten Bauwesens stattfinden kann. Um an dessen Oberfläche zu kratzen, können ArchitetktInnen lediglich versuchen, sich wie die Schwachen mit Taktiken des Alltags, Taktiken des Infraordinären, gegenüber den Mächtigen zu behaupten.

Übersetzung: Wilfried Prantner

53 Vgl. Greco, *Architetture Autostradali in Italia* (wie Anm. 46).

54 Vgl. Guffey, „Crafting Yesterday's Tomorrows" (wie Anm. 33).

6 Model of the Mottagrill, Cantagallo, Architect: Melchiorre Bega, 1959–1960 © Università IUAV di Venezia, Archivio Progetti, fondo Melchiorre Bega. Photo: Agenzia Publifoto

the hyperefficiency of machines had begun to fade, only to finally come to an end when the economic recession and the oil crisis shattered the automotive dreams of the general public. By the 1980s, the optimistic Futurism of the first half of the century would give way to a nostalgic form of sensitivity toward a "future that never was."[54] In 1984, the Smithsonian's exhibition *Yesterday's Tomorrows: Past Visions of the American Future* marked the beginning of an artistic movement that would later be called Retrofuturism, which aims to rediscover the images of the future prefigured by the inhabitants of the past. The title of the exhibition seems ironic when compared with that of the 1939 New York World's Fair, "The World of Tomorrow," but it well represents the end of the collective feeling of optimism that had characterized the previous decades.

The fantastical roadside architecture of California in the 1950s and 1960s, like the heroic highway buildings that had arose in Italy after the war, told a story of a full galactic future in which everything works thanks to the perfect cogwheel of the machine. Instead, retail marketing strategies and budget compliance have forced architectural design to creep, as a glittering residue, into the cracks of a profit-driven building system. The architect, like the weak against the powerful, can now only try to scratch its surface using the tactics of the everyday, of the *infra-ordinary*.

54 See Guffey, "Crafting Yesterday's Tomorrows" (see note 33).

Der ruhende Verkehr im Stadtraum
Eine darstellende Untersuchung seiner raumbildenden Wirkung am Beispiel Graz

Stationary Traffic in Urban Space
A Graphic Survey of Its Space-Forming Effect by Example of Graz

Svenja Hollstein

In jedem Stadtbild gibt es Objekte, die mit gestalterischem Anspruch bewusst im Stadtraum platziert werden, wie zum Beispiel Sitzbänke, Brunnen oder Wartehäuschen.[1] Gleichzeitig gibt es auch Objekte ohne ästhetischen Anspruch, deren Form und Positionierung ausschließlich durch ihre Funktion bestimmt sind, wie Stromkästen, Müllcontainer oder Hydranten. Auch diese haben einen ästhetischen Einfluss auf die Wahrnehmung des Stadtraums. Neben solchen kleineren baulichen Elementen städtischer Infrastruktur beeinflusst aber besonders der ruhende Verkehr unsere Wahrnehmung. Er ist im Gesamtbild nahezu statisch und beansprucht oft große Flächen im Stadtraum. Dabei wird er ähnlich wie Mülltonnen potenziell als störend empfunden. Diesen störenden Einfluss des ruhenden Verkehrs verdeutlicht zum Beispiel die provokante Plastik des Künstlers Wolf Vostell aus dem Jahr 1969. Sie zeigt einen PKW, der aus Beton gegossen auf einem Parkplatz an der Domstraße in Köln platziert wurde und damit mehrfach für Kritik sorgte: „Was wäre, wenn das jeder machen würde? Wie sähe Köln in einem Jahr aus?" lauteten die Reaktionen auf die Kunstaktion, die in einem Film dokumentiert wurden.[2] Diese Kritik stand jedoch im Widerspruch zur Realität, da das Stadtbild zu dieser Zeit bereits massiv von ruhendem Verkehr geprägt war und bis heute ist.

Der nach wie vor bestehende ästhetisch störend empfundene Einfluss auf die städtische Raumwahrnehmung

1 Vgl. Lampugnani, Vittorio Magnago: *Bedeutsame Belanglosigkeiten. Kleine Dinge im Stadtraum*, Berlin 2023.

2 „Vostell und andere oder Lippenstifte für Vietnam," Köln 1969. Regie: Paul Karalus.

In every urban setting there are objects that have been purposely set in urban space with good design in mind, such as benches, fountains, or bus shelters.[1] At the same time, there are objects without any claim to aesthetics, with their form and positioning determined solely by their actual function, such as electricity boxes, garbage bins, or fire hydrants. Yet they, too, have an aesthetic influence on the perception of urban space. Alongside such smaller structural elements in urban infrastructure, stationary traffic influences our perception most especially. In terms of overall appearance, it is almost static, and often takes up large areas of urban space. Yet it has the potential to be seen as disruptive, similar to garbage bins. Stationary traffic's disruptive influence is quite clearly illustrated by a provocative sculpture that Wolf Vostell made in 1969. Cast in concrete, it embodies an automobile on Domstraße in Cologne, near the cathedral, and has thus often attracted criticism: "What if everyone made a sculpture like that? What would Cologne look like in a year?" Thus were the reactions to this art project, which was documented in a film.[2] However, such criticism starkly contrasts with reality, for at that time the urban setting was already heavily characterized by stationary traffic, as it still is today.

While current research work on the fundamental question of how stationary traffic impacts ecology, economy, traffic, and society as a whole mentions its ongoing aesthetically disruptive influence on the perception of

1 See Vittorio Magnago Lampugnani, *Bedeutsame Belanglosigkeiten: Kleine Dinge im Stadtraum* (Berlin, 2023).

2 "Vostell und andere oder Lippenstifte für Vietnam," Cologne, 1969. Directed by Paul Karalus.

1 Ruhender Verkehr, Schießstattgasse, Graz

wird in aktuellen Forschungsarbeiten zur grundsätzlichen Frage des Einflusses des ruhenden Verkehrs auf Ökologie, Ökonomie, Verkehr und Gesellschaft zwar erwähnt, aber nicht weiter vertieft.[3] So weist zum Beispiel Volker Blees 2021 in seiner Studie über die Nutzung des öffentlichen Straßenraums durch parkende Kraftfahrzeuge in Darmstadt-Arheilgen darauf hin, dass „vor allem dort, wo das Parken den Straßenraum dominiert, die Aufenthalts- und ästhetische Qualität des öffentlichen Raums gemindert wird".[4] Vor diesem Hintergrund ist es von Bedeutung, diesen bisher wenig beachteten Aspekt der städtischen Raumwahrnehmung genauer zu untersuchen. Es gilt, die Faktoren zu analysieren, die für den als störend empfundenen Einfluss verantwortlich sind, und darauf aufbauend gestalterische Ansätze zu erforschen, die diesen Einfluss reduzieren können.

3 Zur architekturhistorischen Betrachtung siehe Wegerhoff, Erik: *Automobil und Architektur. Ein kreativer Konflikt*, Berlin 2023.

4 Blees, Volker: „Fehlnutzung des öffentlichen Straßenraumes durch parkende Kraftfahrzeuge. Fallstudie am Beispiel Darmstadt-Arlheilgen", Arbeitsberichte Fachgruppe Mobilitätsmanagement, 013, Hochschule RheinMain, Wiesbaden 2021. Siehe u.a: Knierim, Bernhard: *Ohne Auto leben: Handbuch für den Verkehrsalltag*, Wien 2017; Shen, Tong/Hua, Kun/ Liu, Jiapung: "Optimized Public Parking Location Modelling for Green Intelligent Transportation System Using Genetic Algorithms", in: *IEEE Access* 7 (2019); Bendiks, Stefan/Degros, Aglaée: *Traffic Space. Public Space*, Zürich 2019; Brinkmann, Ulrich: *Vorsicht auf dem Wendehammer! Die Staße als Element des Städtebaus*, Berlin 2023.

urban space, the subject is not explored in any great depth.[3] For example, Volker Blees notes in his 2021 study on the occupying of public street space by parked cars in the Arheilgen neighborhood of Darmstadt that "especially in places where parking dominates the street space, the qualities of stay and aesthetics in public space are diminished."[4] Against this backdrop, it is important to examine this aspect of the perception of urban space in more detail, for it has received little attention to date. We need to analyze the factors that are responsible for the perceived disruptive influence and, building on this, research design approaches that are able to mitigate this problem.

In order to understand the spatial effect of stationary traffic, it is first of all imperative to view it impartially as

3 For the architectural-historical analysis see Erik Wegerhoff, *Automobil und Architektur: Ein kreativer Konflikt* (Berlin, 2023).

4 Volker Blees, "Fehlnutzung des öffentlichen Straßenraumes durch parkende Kraftfahrzeuge: Fallstudie am Beispiel Darmstadt-Arlheilgen," Arbeitsberichte Fachgruppe Mobilitätsmanagement, 013, Hochschule RheinMain, Wiesbaden, 2021. See among others: Bernhard Knierim, *Ohne Auto leben: Handbuch für den Verkehrsalltag* (Vienna, 2017); Tong Shen, Kun Hua, and Jiapung Liu, "Optimized Public Parking Location Modelling for Green Intelligent Transportation System Using Genetic Algorithms," *IEEE Access* 7 (2019); Stefan Bendiks and Aglaée Degros, *Traffic Space: Public Space* (Zurich, 2019); Ulrich Brinkmann, *Vorsicht auf dem Wendehammer! Die Staße als Element des Städtebaus* (Berlin, 2023).

Um die räumliche Wirkung des ruhenden Verkehrs zu verstehen, ist es zunächst wichtig, diesen vorurteilsfrei als Objekt im Raum zu betrachten.[5] Als solches kann schließlich ein Vergleich mit anderen Objekten im Raum dabei helfen, den Einfluss des ruhenden Verkehrs besser zu verstehen. Gemäß Josef Franks undogmatischem Ansatz – „Man kann alles verwenden, was man verwenden kann",[6] – wird im Folgenden der ruhende Verkehr mit Möbeln im Innenraum verglichen, um seine Wirkung auf die Raumwahrnehmung zu ergründen.[7]

In seinem Artikel „Rum och inredning" [„Raum und Einrichtung"] beschrieb Josef Frank 1934 die Auswirkungen von Möbeln auf die Raumwahrnehmung. Er betonte darin, dass diese im Wesentlichen von der Form des Raumes abhängt, die von den ihn begrenzenden Flächen und Wänden bestimmt wird und nicht von dessen Möblierung.[8] Wenn die eigentliche Form des Raumes jedoch aufgrund der Möblierung nicht klar wahrgenommen werden kann, kann diese die Raumwahrnehmung indirekt beeinflussen. Dies geschieht nach Frank, wenn die Begrenzungslinien des Raumes aufgrund der Möblierung, nicht in ihrer ganzen Ausdehnung oder wenigstens ohne wesentliche Unterbrechungen sichtbar sind.[9]

Um die Wirkung des ruhenden Verkehrs in dieser Hinsicht zu untersuchen, wird in Abbildung 1 ein exemplarischer Straßenraum auf Augenhöhe dargestellt. Die Positionierung und die Aneinanderreihung der Fahrzeuge führen dazu, dass der ruhende Verkehr die unteren Begrenzungslinien des Straßenraumes vollständig verdeckt.

5 Wie schon Denise Scott Brown 1971 in „Learning from Pop" festhielt: „Judgment ist withheld in the interest of understanding and receptivity." Siehe dazu den Abdruck von Denise Scott Browns Essay in dieser GAM-Ausgabe auf den Seiten 76–82.

6 Frank, Josef: „Der Geschnas fürs G'mut und Gschnas als Problem", in: *Bau und Wohnung*, Ausstellungskatalog, Stuttgart 1927, 48–57.

7 Um diesen Vergleich zu ziehen, muss auch der Stadtraum mit einem anderen Entwurfsaspekt, nämlich dem Innenraum, verglichen werden. Der Vergleich zwischen Innen- und Stadtraum basiert darauf, dass die Baukörper, die den Stadtraum gemeinsam mit der Bodenfläche begrenzen, mit den Wänden eines Innenraums verglichen werden, die letztendlich den Raum formen. Insbesondere um 1900 erschienen mehrere Entwurfshandreichungen, die sich ausführlich mit dem gestalterischen Potenzial der Form eines Stadtraums auseinandersetzten und zusammen die wohl größte stadträumliche Wissenssammlung darstellen. Tatsächlich beziehen sich auch aktuelle Publikationen, die sich mit der Form und Gestalt von Stadträumen beschäftigen, immer wieder auf diese über 100 Jahre alten Werke. Auch für die folgende Untersuchung können aus diesen Handbüchern neue gestalterische Ansätze zur Anordnung des ruhenden Verkehrs abgeleitet werden, um dessen störenden Einfluss zu mindern.

8 Vgl. Frank, Josef: „Rum och inredning", *Form* 30, 10 (1934), 218.

9 Vgl. ebd.

an object in space.[5] In so doing, a comparison with other objects in space can ultimately help us to better understand the influence of stationary traffic. According to Josef Frank's undogmatic approach—"One can use everything that can be used,"[6]—stationary traffic will be compared with furniture in interior space in the following, with the aim of exploring its effect on spatial perception.[7]

In his 1934 article "Rum och inredning" (Rooms and Interiors), Josef Frank described the effects of furnishings on the perception of space. He emphasized that the effects are essentially dependent on the dimensions of the space, which are in turn determined by the delimiting surfaces and walls and not by the furnishings.[8] However, if the actual dimensions of the space cannot be discerned due to the furnishings in the room, then this can indirectly influence spatial perception. According to Frank, this happens when, due to the presence of furnishings, the room's lines of delimitation are not fully visible, or at least not without significant interruptions.[9]

So as to research the effect of stationary traffic in this respect, Figure 1 presents a typical example of street space at eye level. Due to the positioning and the sequence of vehicles, the street space's lower lines of delimitation are totally concealed by the stationary traffic. The actual form of the space is thus no longer clearly perceptible, hence stationary traffic becomes space-forming in this sense. One might even argue that it divides the original space between the structures into three separate spaces. However, such a development should be avoided, according to Frank, if one wants to create a pleasant spatial

5 As Denise Scott Brown already put down on paper in her 1971 essay "Learning from Pop": "Judgment is withheld in the interest of understanding and receptivity." On this, see the reprint of Denise Scott Brown's essay in this GAM issue on pages 76–82.

6 Josef Frank, "Der Geschnas fürs G'mut und Gschnas als Problem," in *Bau und Wohnung*, exh. cat. Deutscher Werkbund (Stuttgart, 1927), 48–57.

7 To make this comparison, it is important to likewise contrast urban space with another design aspect, namely, interior space. The comparison between interior and urban space is based on the building structures that delimit the urban space together with the ground surface being contrasted with the walls of an interior space, which ultimately give the space its form. Around the year 1900 in particular, several design manuals were printed that extensively investigated the design-related potential of the form taken by urban space; together, these works represent what is likely the largest collection of urbanistic knowledge available. In fact, current publications dealing with the form and design of urban spaces repeatedly refer back to these volumes that are over a hundred years old. For the current study as well, new design approaches to structuring stationary traffic could be derived from these manuals, with the aim of reducing its disruptive influence.

8 See Josef Frank, "Rum och inredning," *Form* 30, no. 10 (1934), 218.

9 See ibid.

Die eigentliche Form des Raumes ist somit nicht mehr klar wahrnehmbar, und der ruhende Verkehr wird in diesem Sinne raumbildend. Man könnte sogar argumentieren, dass er den ursprünglichen Raum zwischen den Baukörpern in drei separate Räume aufteilt. Eine solche Entwicklung sollte jedoch im Hinblick auf ein angenehmes Raumempfinden nach Frank vermieden werden, da raumbildende Möbel die Klarheit des Raumes „zerstören".[10] Mit dieser architektonischen Betrachtung des ruhenden Verkehrs lässt sich erklären, warum dieser vermutlich als ästhetisch störend empfunden wird. Das Reduzieren des ruhenden Verkehrs ist daher nicht nur aus ökologischen, ökonomischen und verkehrstechnischen Gründen relevant, sondern auch aus architektonischer Sicht.

Trotz dieser bereits bestehenden Forderungen, den ruhenden Verkehr zu verringern, ist er immer noch fester Bestandteil aktueller Stadtplanungen. Laut Stellplatzverordnung muss nach wie vor ein gewisser Prozentsatz an Parkmöglichkeiten pro Wohneinheit vorgesehen werden. Aber auch wenn die in bestehenden Forschungen untersuchten alternativen Verkehrskonzepte die Nachfrage langfristig reduzieren können oder technologische Entwicklungen eines Tages dazu führen könnten, dass der ruhende Verkehr tatsächlich aus dem Stadtbild verschwindet, bleibt die Frage, was mit den für den ruhenden Verkehr vorgesehenen Flächen geschehen soll. Diese werden vermutlich nicht frei bleiben, sondern von anderen Stadtmöblierungen besetzt, wie es derzeit zum Beispiel durch die sogenannten Schanigärten geschieht.[11] Dass auch diese dem ruhenden Verkehr möglicherweise folgenden Möblierungen eine ebenso raumbildende Wirkung besitzen könnten, steigert die Relevanz einer Untersuchung der räumlichen Wirkung (Abb. 2). Denn die derzeit scheinbar unvermeidbare Existenz des ruhenden Verkehrs bedeutet nicht, dass sein als störend empfundener Einfluss auf die Raumwahrnehmung akzeptiert werden muss.

Deswegen sollen im Folgenden Herangehensweisen untersucht werden, die die raumbildende Wirkung des ruhenden Verkehrs als Möblierung vermindern. Dafür schlug Frank bereits einen ebenso speziellen wie simplen Ansatz vor: Er stellte das Möbelstück auf „Füße", hoch genug, um die Begrenzungslinie zwischen Boden und Wand darunter erkennen (oder zumindest erahnen) zu können (Abb. 3). Andernfalls würde die auf dem Boden stehende „Kiste" jede Raumwirkung „zerstören".[12]

10 „Man sollte sich davor hüten, Architektur mit Möbeln zu schaffen und dadurch die Klarheit des Raumes zu zerstören. Um angenehm zu wirken, muss der Raum selbst klar wahrgenommen werden, d.h. alle seine Begrenzungslinien (im gewöhnlichen prismatischen Raum sind es insgesamt zwölf) sowie die Flächen, die die Größe des Raumes anzeigen (Boden und Decke), müssen in ihrer ganzen Ausdehnung oder ohne wesentliche Unterbrechungen sichtbar sein." (Aus dem Schwedischen übersetzt mit ChatGPT) Ebd.

11 Siehe zum Beispiel Abb. 6.

12 Ebd.

experience, because space-forming furniture "destroys"[10] the clarity of a room. Such an architecture-inspired consideration of stationary traffic makes it possible to explain why it is presumably felt to be aesthetically disruptive. A reduction of stationary traffic thus makes sense not only for reasons of ecology, economics, and traffic, but also from an architectural point of view.

10 "One must be careful not to create architecture with furniture and thereby destroy the clarity of the room. The room itself needs to be clearly perceived in order to have a pleasant effect, meaning that all of its lines of delimitation (in a typical prismatic room there are twelve in total), along with the surfaces that indicate the size of the room (floor and ceiling), must be visually graspable in their entirety or at least without major discontinuity." Ibid.

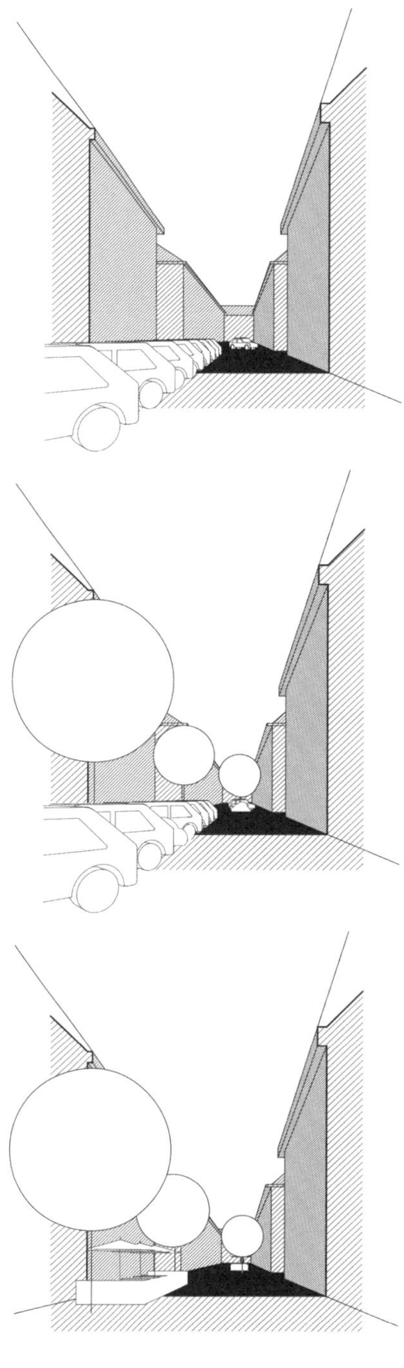

2 Mögliche Entwicklung der Flächen des ruhenden Verkehrs

Dieser ebenso einfache wie effektive Entwurfsansatz ist jedoch nur schwierig auf den ruhenden Verkehr zu übertragen, und stellt somit keine zufriedenstellende Entwurfslösung dar, um dessen raumbildende Wirkung zu verringern (Abb. 4). Das Automobil selbst kann nicht durch solche Hilfsmittel verändert werden. Daher wird im Folgenden nicht nach der vollständigen Vermeidung der raumbildenden Wirkung des ruhenden Verkehrs gesucht, sondern nach Möglichkeiten, sie zu reduzieren. Konkret wird untersucht, ob durch eine gezielte Anordnung die Begrenzungslinien zumindest teilweise freigelegt werden können, um die Form des Raumes besser zu erahnen und so, nach Frank, eine angenehme Raumwahrnehmung zu generieren. Damit stellt sich die Frage, ob es Mittel

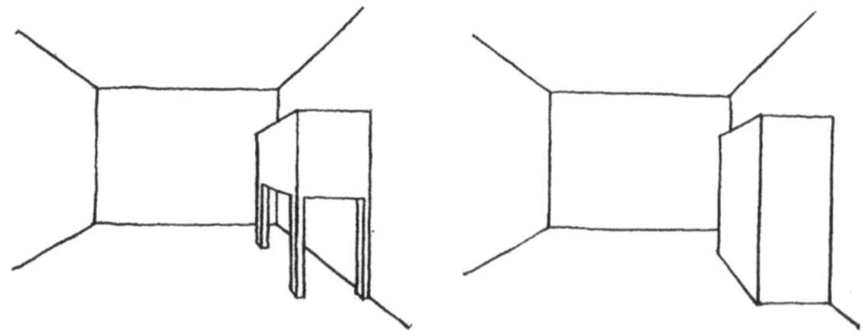

3 Möblierung ohne und mit raumbildender Wirkung nach Josef Frank aus: Frank, Josef: Rum och inredning, in: *Form* 30, 10 (1934), 218.

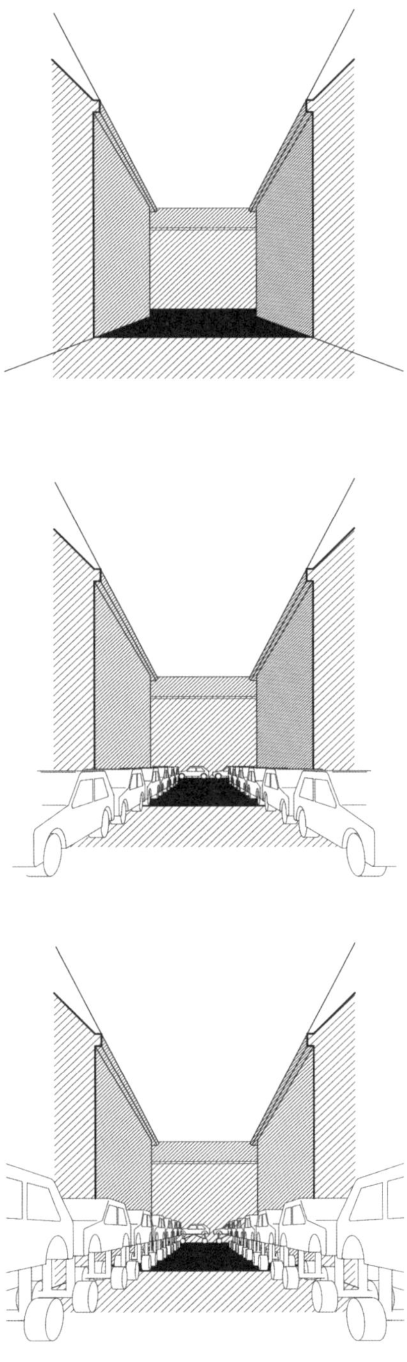

4 Entwurfsansatz nach Josef Frank zur Vermeidung der raumbildenden Wirkung des ruhenden Verkehrs

Despite these already existing demands to reduce stationary traffic, it still remains an integral part of present-day urban planning. According to the Graz's parking space ordinance, a certain number of parking spaces must be provided per residential unit in any case, depending on the number of inhabitants. Yet even if the alternative traffic concepts being examined in current research are able to reduce demand in the long run, or if technological developments might one day lead to stationary traffic even disappearing from the cityscape altogether, the question remains as to what will happen to the areas earmarked for stationary traffic. Most likely they would not remain open spaces but rather be occupied by city furnishings, as is presently seen in the case of the so-called *Schanigärten*, which is what tables and chairs set up on the sidewalk in front of cafés or restaurants are called in Austria.[11] The need for a study on the spatial effect of stationary traffic is further bolstered by the fact that these furnishings, which could be regarded as paralleling stationary traffic, may also have an equally space-forming effect (fig. 2). Indeed, the present seemingly unavoidable existence of stationary traffic does not imply that its perceived disruptive influence on spatial perception must be accepted.

For this reason, in what follows we will examine approaches to diminishing the space-forming effect of stationary traffic when viewed as furnishings. Frank already suggested a strategy that is as unique as it is simple: he placed the piece of furniture on "feet," high enough to be able to identify (or at least intuit) the line of delimitation between floor and wall beneath it (fig. 3), else the "box" positioned on the floor would "destroy" any spatial effect.[12] However, it is difficult to transfer this simple and effective design approach to stationary traffic, thus it is not a satisfactory design solution for minimizing the space-forming effect of the traffic situation (fig. 4). The automotive vehicle itself cannot be altered through such means. This is why the following passages will present ideas for reducing the space-forming effect of stationary traffic, rather than trying to eliminate it altogether. More concretely, it will

11 See, for example, fig. 6.
12 Ibid.

Räumlich signifikante Stadträume in Graz.
5–6 Gerade Straße: Villefortgasse

7–8 Gekrümmte Straße: Münzgrabenstraße

9–10 Platz: Felix-Dahn-Platz

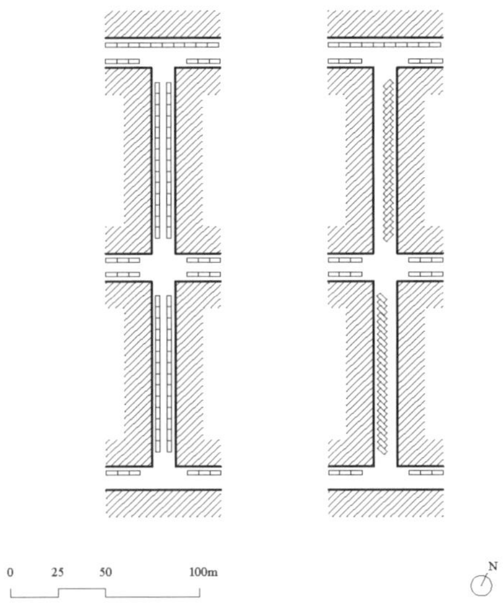

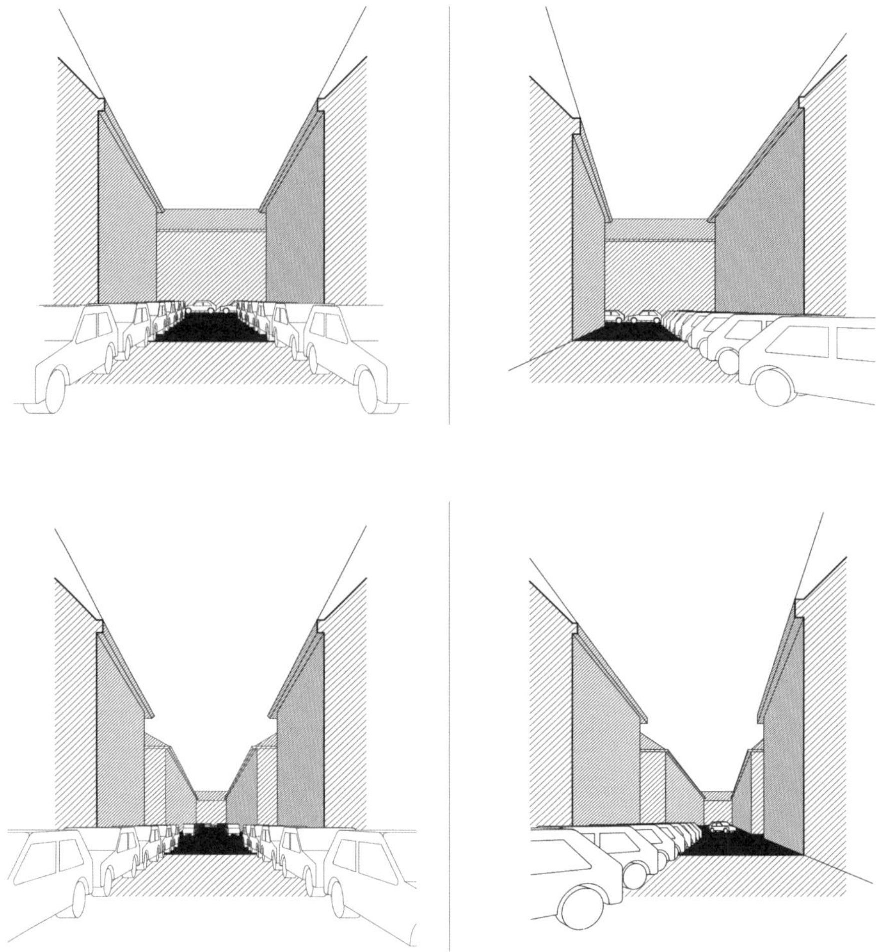

11
Gerade Straße, Grundriss
Links: Zweiseitiges Längsparken (Ist)
Rechts: Einseitiges Schrägparken (Entwurf)

12
Gerade Straße, Schnittperspektive
Links: Zweiseitiges Längsparken (Ist)
Rechts: Einseitiges Schrägparken (Entwurf)

und Wege gibt, den ruhenden Verkehr bewusst zu gestalten, oder ob sein störender Einfluss einfach zu akzeptieren ist, ähnlich wie Blumenvasen auf einem Esstisch, die ungeachtet ihrer Platzierung das Gespräch mit dem Gegenüber immer behindern.[13]

Die Untersuchung dieser Fragen erfolgt anhand von drei räumlich signifikanten Stadträumen in Graz: der geraden Villefortgasse, der gekrümmten Münzgrabenstraße und dem Felix-Dahn-Platz (Abb. 5–10). In diesen Beispielen werden verschiedene Anordnungen des ruhenden Verkehrs grafisch dargestellt, um zu prüfen, inwiefern alternative Platzierungen des ruhenden Verkehrs die Raumwahrnehmung des Stadtraumes verändern, selbst wenn die eigentliche Form des Raumes unverändert bleibt.

Gerade Straße: Villefortgasse

Die erste Untersuchung (Abb. 11–12) widmet sich der Untersuchung der Villefortgasse und vergleicht den aktuellen Zustand des Längsparkens auf beiden Seiten einer geraden Einbahnstraße (56 Parkplätze) und die Möglichkeit des Schrägparkens auf einer Seite (50 Parkplätze). Beim Vergleich zwischen dem Ist-Zustand und einem alternativen Entwurfsansatz fällt zunächst auf, dass im Ist-Zustand beide unteren Begrenzungslinien durch den ruhenden Verkehr verdeckt werden, während bei dem

13 Vgl. Gurlitt, Cornelius: *Handbuch des Städtebaues*, Berlin 1920, 391.

be examined whether a targeted arrangement of cars might allow lines of delimitation to be made visible, at least partially, in order to allow the shape of the space to be better discerned and, as per Frank, to engender a pleasant perception of space. This gives rise to the question of whether there are means and ways of consciously designing stationary traffic, or whether its disruptive influence must simply be accepted, similar to a vase with flowers on a dining-room table, which, regardless of how it is positioned, inevitably interferes with the conversation between two people.[13]

These questions are addressed based on the example of three spatially significant urban spaces in Graz: the straight Villefortgasse, the curved Münzgrabenstraße, and the square Felix-Dahn-Platz (fig. 5–10). These examples visually present different arrangements of stationary traffic, so as to examine how alternative placements of stationary traffic might change the spatial perception of urban space, even if the actual shape of the space remains the same.

A Straight Street: Villefortgasse

The first study (figs. 11–12) is dedicated to the investigation of Villefortgasse. It compares the current state of parallel parking on both sides of a straight, one-way street (fifty-six parking spaces) and examines the possibility of angle

13 See Cornelius Gurlitt, *Handbuch des Städtebaues* (Berlin, 1920), 391.

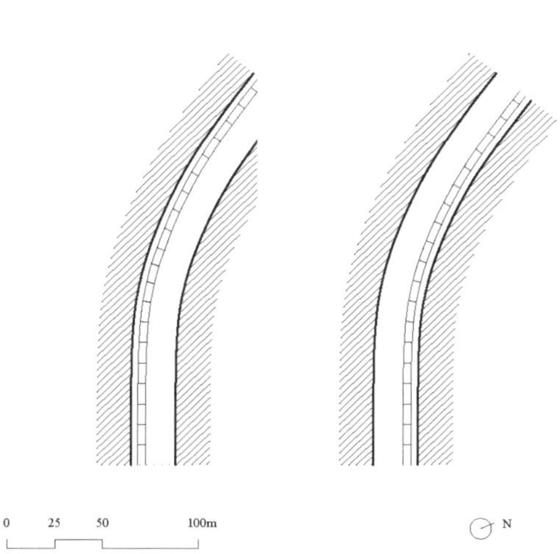

13
Gekrümmte Straße, Grundriss
Links: Parken auf konkaver Straßenseite
Rechts: Parken auf konvexer Straßenseite

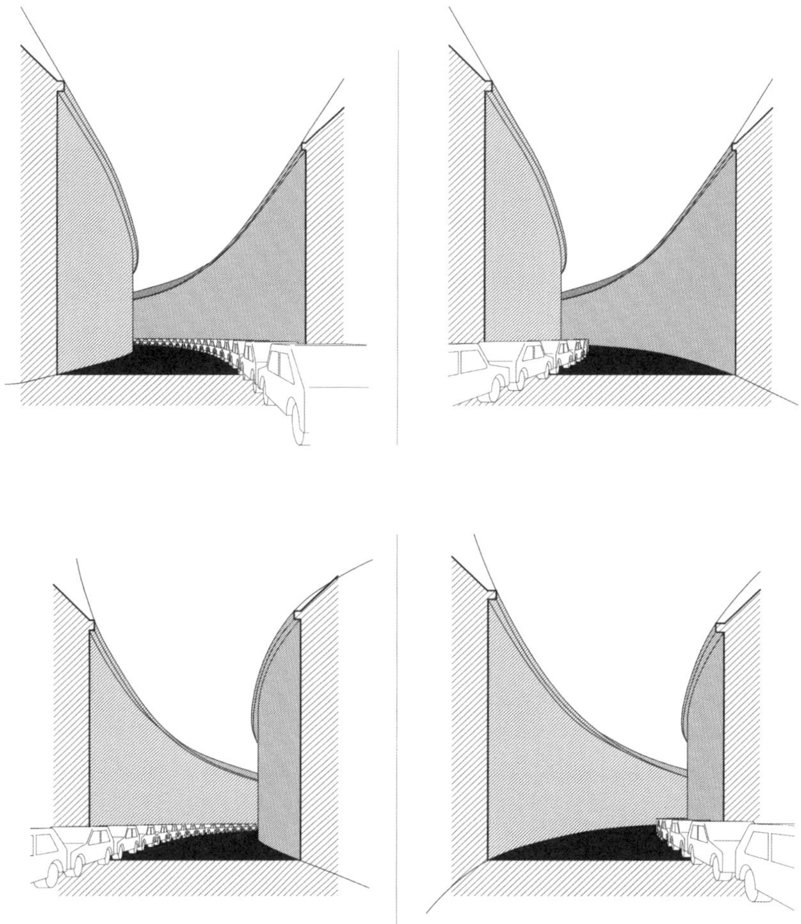

14
Gekrümmte Straße, Schnittperspektive
Links: Parken auf konkaver Straßenseite
Rechts: Parken auf konvexer Straßenseite

neuen Entwurfsansatz nur eine Seite verdeckt wird. Dies führt dazu, dass die räumliche „Klarheit“ auf der rechten Abbildung höher ist als auf der linken Abbildung. Neben der Verbesserung der Raumwahrnehmung hat diese Anordnung auch das Potenzial, besonders bedeutende Gebäude vor dem ruhenden Verkehr zu schützen und deren Eingänge wieder sichtbar zu machen. Darüber hinaus kann das Einführen von Versprüngen, wie in diesem Beispiel veranschaulicht, dazu beitragen, einen Straßenraum in mehrere Abschnitte zu zerlegen und diese durch das Blickziel des ruhenden Verkehrs räumlich zu begrenzen und damit die Raumwirkung zu erhöhen.[14] Der Versprung in der Straßenführung kann aber auch zur Verkehrsberuhigung beitragen. Neben den räumlichen Vorteilen einer Umstrukturierung des ruhenden Verkehrs erscheint es daher sinnvoll, auch die praktischen Auswirkungen näher zu betrachten und sie in Einklang zu bringen, um fundierte Entwurfsentscheidungen treffen zu können.

Gekrümmte Straße: Münzgrabenstraße

Im Gegensatz zur Villefortgasse wird in der Münzgrabenstraße bereits nur auf einer Seite geparkt. Daher konzentriert sich diese Untersuchung darauf (Abb. 13–14), zu ermitteln, ob es eine Seite gibt, die zu bevorzugen ist. Hierzu ist es zunächst erforderlich, die unterschiedliche

parking on one side of the street (fifty parking spaces). When comparing the current situation with an alternative design approach, it is first of all noticeable that in the current situation both lower lines of delimitation are concealed by stationary traffic, whereas in the new design approach only one side is concealed. This means that more spatial “clarity” is evident in the right figure than in the left one. Besides improving the perception of space, this arrangement holds the potential to spare particularly important buildings from stationary traffic by making their entrances visible again. Moreover, an introduction of offset positioning, as this example illustrates, can contribute to a partitioning of street space into several sections, using the visual target of stationary traffic to delimit these sections, thus heightening the spatial effect.[14] Offsetting the alignment of the street can also serve the purpose of traffic calming. In addition to the spatial advantages of restructuring stationary traffic, it seems sensible to take a closer look at the related practical effects and to harmonize them, thus enabling sound design decisions to be made.

A Curved Street: Münzgrabenstraße

In contrast to Villefortgasse, parking in Münzgrabenstraße is already only permitted on one side. This study is thus focused on determining whether one side or the other is

14 Vgl. Fischer, Theodor: *6 Vorträge über Stadtbaukunst*, München 1920, 23.

14 See Theodor Fischer, *6 Vorträge über Stadtbaukunst* (Munich, 1920), 23.

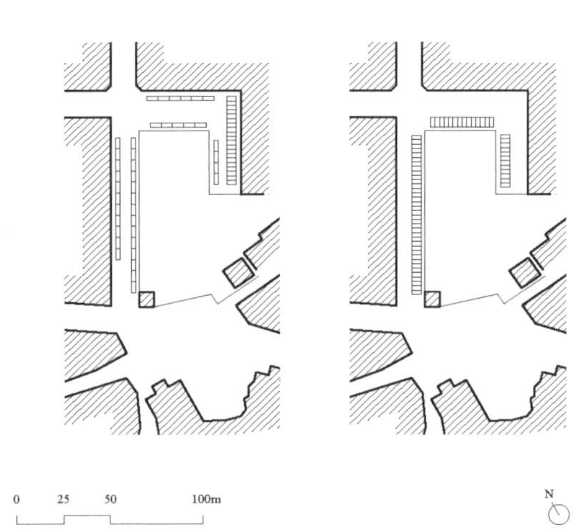

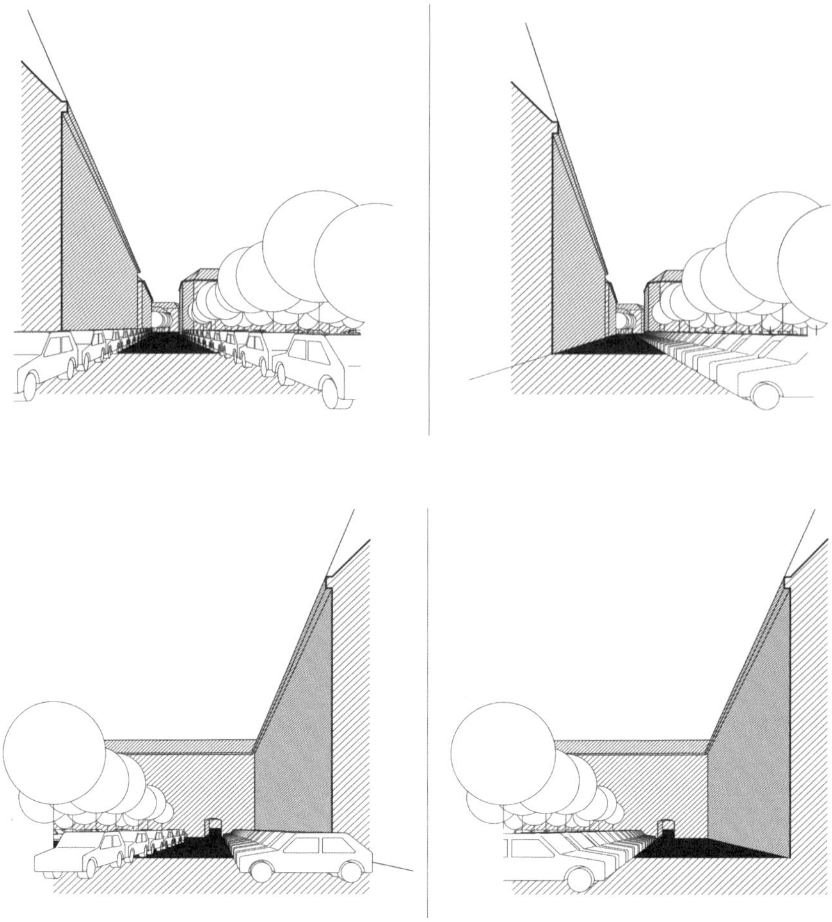

15
Platz, Grundriss
Links: Zweiseitiges Längs- und Senkrechtparken (Ist)
Rechts: Einseitiges Senkrechtparken (Entwurf)

16
Platz, Schnittperspektive
Links: Zweiseitiges Längs- und Senkrechtparken (Ist)
Rechts: Einseitiges Senkrechtparken (Entwurf)

räumliche Wirkung zwischen der konkaven und der konvexen Seite zu erläutern. Karl Henrici wies in seinem Aufsatz „Langweilige und Kurzweilige Straßen" von 1893 darauf hin, dass „die konkave Wandung dem Auge [...] in größerer Ausdehnung [erscheint] als die gerade und konvexe Wandung, sie führt zu Kurzweiligkeit. Die konvexe Seite ist nur auf kurze Strecken und in verstärkter Verkürzung zu sehen [...]".[15] Die Raumkanten auf der konkaven Seite sind für die BetrachterInnen also vollständig sichtbar, während auf der konvexen Seite nur ein Bruchteil überblickt werden kann. Wenn also der ruhende Verkehr als störend empfunden wird, erscheint es naheliegend, ihn auf der konvexen Seite anzuordnen, da in diesem Fall auch der ruhende Verkehr nicht im Ganzen wahrgenommen werden kann. Darüber hinaus bleibt die gesamte konkave Raumkante sichtbar, wodurch wiederum die Wahrnehmung der eigentlichen Form und Gestalt des Raumes verbessert wird.

Platz: Felix-Dahn-Platz

In der dritten und letzten Untersuchung wird der Felix-Dahn-Platz betrachtet (Abb. 15–16), auf dem bislang das Parken auf beiden Seiten der Straße praktiziert wurde. In diesem Entwurfsansatz wird – ähnlich wie in der

15 Henrici, Karl: „Langweilige und kurzweilige Strassen" [1893], in: *Beiträge zur praktischen Ästhetik im Städte Bau. Eine Sammlung von Vorträgen und Aufsätzen*, München 1904, 90.

more favorable (figs. 13–14). To this end, it is first necessary to elucidate the different spatial effects of the concave and the convex sides of the street. Karl Henrici, in his essay "Langweilige und Kurzweilige Straßen" (Boring and Pleasant Streets) from 1893, points out that "the concave wall [appears] to the eye ... to be more extensive than the straight and convex wall; it conveys a more pleasant feel. The convex side can only be seen across short distances and with increased foreshortening ..."[15] The edges of the space on the concave side are therefore fully visible to the viewers, while only a fraction of the edges are discernible on the convex side. So if stationary traffic is perceived as disruptive, then it stands to reason that it should be allotted to the convex side, for in this case the stationary traffic cannot be perceived in its entirety. What is more, the whole concave edge of the space remains visible, which in turn enhances perception of the space's actual shape and form.

A Square: Felix-Dahn-Platz

The third and final study considers Felix-Dahn-Platz (figs. 15–16), where, to date, parking is permitted on both sides of the street. This design approach examines—similar to Villefortgasse—the spatial effect of parking on only one side of the square when it is set perpendicularly to the

15 Karl Henrici, "Langweilige und kurzweilige Strassen" (1893), in *Beiträge zur praktischen Ästhetik im Städte Bau: Eine Sammlung von Vorträgen und Aufsätzen* (Munich, 1904), 90.

Villefortgasse – untersucht, welchen räumlichen Effekt es hat, wenn das Parken auf nur einer Seite senkrecht zur Fahrtrichtung erfolgt, wodurch tatsächlich zwei Parkplätze gewonnen werden. Ebenso wie bei der gekrümmten Straße unterscheiden sich die Seiten der an den Platzwänden entlanglaufenden Straße. Während die eine Seite an der durch die Baukörper definierten Raumkante liegt, schließt die andere Seite an den Platz oder Park an. Um den Raum nach den Grundsätzen von Frank nun klarer wahrnehmbar zu gestalten, wird der ruhende Verkehr nicht entlang der raumbegrenzenden Wände, sondern entlang der Platzseite positioniert. Dies ermöglicht die Freilegung sämtlicher Platzraumkanten und führt zu einer Verbesserung der Raumwahrnehmung. Die raumbildende Wirkung des ruhenden Verkehrs geht dabei nicht verloren, sie ordnet sich jedoch den eigentlichen Raumkanten des Platzes unter. Die nichtsdestotrotz raumbildende Wirkung hat darüber hinaus zur Folge, dass die ruhigen Bereiche des Platzes und der Bereich der Bewegung, d.h. der eigentliche Verkehrsraum, deutlicher voneinander abgegrenzt werden, was ihre jeweilige Funktion und Wahrnehmung verstärkt.

Fazit

Der ruhende Verkehr beeinflusst als raumbildende Möblierung die Klarheit des Raumes und beeinträchtigt dadurch dessen Raumwahrnehmung. Die vorliegenden Untersuchungen zeigen jedoch, dass in Bezug auf den ruhenden Verkehr aktives Gestaltungspotenzial besteht. Durch die Identifizierung der Faktoren, die den ästhetisch störend empfundenen Einfluss des ruhenden Verkehrs verursachen, können gezielte Gestaltungsansätze entwickelt werden, um diesen Einfluss zu mindern. Die raumbildende Wirkung des ruhenden Verkehrs, die durch die Verdeckung der räumlichen Begrenzungslinien entsteht, kann bereits durch alternative und bewusste Anordnungen der Parkflächen reduziert werden.[16] Der Aufwand für diesen gestalterischen Ansatz ist dabei äußerst gering: Bodenmarkierungen und die Umverteilung von Straßenschildern könnten das Problem bereits lösen. Der hier dargestellte Entwurfsansatz ließe sich also einfach und schnell realisieren, ohne dass dabei auf Stellplätze verzichtet werden müsste. Es gibt also keinen Grund, warum man bei aktuellen Parkraumplanungen nicht auch den räumlichen Einfluss des ruhenden Verkehrs miteinbeziehen und bewusst gestalten sollte.

direction of travel, which actually creates two parking spaces. As with the curved street, the sides of the street running along the walls of the square are not the same. While one side is bordered by the delimiting buildings at the edge of the space, the other is adjacent to the square or park. In order to make the space more clearly perceptible according to Frank's principles, in the study the stationary traffic is not positioned along the space-defining walls, but rather along the side of the square. Hence, all the edges of the square are exposed, which leads to an improved perception of the space. The space-forming effect of the stationary traffic is not lost, yet it is subordinated to the actual edges of the square. Moreover, the space-forming effect that arises all the same means that the quiet areas of the square and the area of movement, that is, the actual traffic area, are more clearly delimited from each other, which serves to reinforce their respective function and perceptibility.

Conclusion

Stationary traffic seen as space-forming furnishings influences the clarity of a space and thus impairs perception of this space in the process. However, the current study demonstrates that there is active design potential when it comes to stationary traffic. By identifying the factors that exert an aesthetically disruptive influence on the perception of stationary traffic, targeted design approaches can be developed in order to minimize this impact. The space-forming effect of stationary traffic that arises when lines of delimitation are no longer visible can already be reduced by pursuing alternative and conscious arrangements of parking spaces.[16] This design approach involves precious little effort: ground markings and a redistribution of road signs could already solve the problem. Hence, the design approach put forth here lends itself to easy and expedient implementation, without having to give up parking spaces in the process. Thus, nothing stands in the way of taking the spatial influence of stationary traffic into account and consciously designing it in the context of present-day parking space planning.

Translation: Dawn Michelle d'Atri

16 Ausgehend von diesem ersten Ansatz wäre es interessant, der Frage nachzugehen, wie sich die Flächen des ruhenden Verkehrs anders gestalten ließen. Beispielsweise könnte untersucht werden, ob der ruhende Verkehr als raumbildende Möblierung bewusst eingesetzt werden könnte, um eventuell unterbrochene Raumkanten fortzusetzen, wie es bereits Karl Henrici mittels Alleen und Laternenreihen vorschlägt. Vgl. ebd., 88.

16 Based on this initial approach, it would be interesting to pursue the question of how stationary traffic areas could be designed in a more favorable way. For example, one could analyze whether it might be possible to purposely introduce stationary traffic as space-forming furniture in order to continue any potentially interrupted room edges, as Karl Henrici already proposed doing with the use of boulevards and rows of lanterns. See ibid., 88.

Bartheken-Grundriss- und Schnittbeispiele, Zeichnung von Hans-Jürgen Meier-Menzel, in:
Mayr, Otto/Hierl, Fritz: *Handbuch für den Hotelbau*, München 1962, 136.

Liquor License: An Ethnography of Bar Behavior
Sherri Cavan

Intro: Julian Müller

Was macht eine Bar als konkreten Raum aus? Und was tun Menschen in solchen Räumen, in denen es nicht in erster Linie um den Austausch von Argumenten, das Erteilen von Anweisungen oder um religiöse Bekehrung geht? Derartige Fragen stehen im Zentrum eines Buches, das im Jahr 1966 erschienen ist und den Titel *Liquor License. An Ethnography of Bar Behavior* trägt. Es handelt sich dabei um die Doktorarbeit der amerikanischen Soziologin Sherri Cavan, die lange Zeit in Vergessenheit geraten war, vor einiger Zeit jedoch wiederentdeckt wurde.[1] Betreut wurde die Arbeit von Erving Goffman, dem vielleicht berühmtesten Vertreter einer Soziologie des Alltags. Wie diesem ging es auch Cavan darum, alltägliche Verhaltensweisen in alltäglichen Räumen zu beschreiben. Zu diesem Zweck besuchte sie zwischen 1963 und 1965 mit einem Notizbuch ausgerüstet verschiedene kalifornische Bars, um die barspezifische Ordnung der Interaktion besser zu verstehen. In einer biographischen Notiz beschrieb Cavan ihr Forschungsvorhaben wie folgt: „Ich schlug vor, das normale Trinkverhalten zu untersuchen, indem ich beobachtete, was die Leute in Bars, Cocktail-Lounges, Tavernen, Saloons und Nachtclubs so taten. Ich las fast alles, was über diese sozialen Einrichtungen aus historischer und kulturvergleichender Sicht geschrieben worden war, und verbrachte dann mehr als zwei Jahre mit meinen Beobachtungen in einhundert Lokalen mit Ausschanklizenz in San Francisco. Dabei habe ich gelernt, systematisch Notizen zu machen, die Beobachtungen zu kategorisieren und Beziehungen zwischen den Kategorien sowie zwischen Kategorien und Theorien festzustellen."[2]

Im Rahmen ihrer teilnehmenden Beobachtung entdeckte Cavan Orte, an denen ganz eigene Regeln des sozialen Verkehrs herrschten. Es waren Räume, in denen das kultiviert wurde, was sie an einer Stelle „tiny talk" nennt. Räume, in denen Begegnungen viel leichter begannen, aber auch viel abrupter enden konnten, als man es üblicherweise gewohnt war. Einen besonderen Fokus legt Cavan

1 Vgl. Felsch, Philipp: *Der lange Sommer der Theorie. Geschichte einer Revolte 1960–1990*, München 2015, 232ff.

2 Sherri Cavan: „Becoming an Ethnographer", in: Meadow, Kathryn P./Wallace Ruth A. (Hg.): *Gender and the Academic Experience. Berkeley Women Sociologists,* Lincoln/London 1994, 57–70, hier 63f.

What defines a bar as a concrete place? And what do people do in such places that are not primarily about exchanging arguments, giving instructions, or religious conversion? Such questions are the focus of a book published in 1966 under the title *Liquor License: An Ethnography of Bar Behavior*. It was the dissertation of the American sociologist Sherri Cavan, which had fallen into oblivion for a long time but was rediscovered some time ago.[1] It had been supervised by Erving Goffman, perhaps the most famous representative of a sociology of everyday life. Like him, Cavan too was concerned with describing everyday behaviors in everyday spaces. To that end, she visited various bars in California from 1963 to 1965, taking a notebook with her, in order to understand better the bar-specific order of interaction. In a biographical note, Cavan described her research project as follows: "I proposed to study normal drinking behavior by observing what people did in bars, cocktail lounges, taverns, saloons, and nightclubs. I read almost everything that had been written on these social institutions from a historical and cross-cultural perspective, then spent more than two years making observations in one hundred licensed establishments in San Francisco. I learned to make notes in a systematic fashion, to organize observations into conceptual categories, to see relationships between the categories, and between categories and theories."[2]

As part of her participant observation, Cavan discovered places with their very own rules of social interaction. They were spaces where what she calls "tiny talk" was cultivated. Spaces in which encounters began much more easily but could also end much more abruptly than one was ordinarily accustomed to. Cavan focused especially on the spatial arrangement of bars. In the chapter "Space and Spatial Properties," excerpts from which follow, she asks about the interrelationship of space and social behavior by reconstructing spatial movements, measuring distances between guests, and describing how the guests demarcate

1 See Philipp Felsch, *Der lange Sommer der Theorie: Geschichte einer Revolte, 1960–1990* (Munich, 2015), 232–234.

2 Sherri Cavan, "Becoming an Ethnographer," in *Gender and the Academic Experience: Berkeley Women Sociologists*, ed. Kathryn P. Meadow Orlans and Ruth A. Wallace (Lincoln, NE, 1994), 57–70, esp. 63–64.

auf die räumliche Ordnung von Bars. In dem Kapitel „Space and Spatial Properties“, das im Folgenden in Auszügen abgedruckt ist, fragt sie nach dem Wechselverhältnis von Raum und sozialem Verhalten, indem sie Sitzordnungen analysiert, räumliche Bewegungen rekonstruiert, Abstände zwischen verschiedenen Gästen misst und beschreibt, wie die Gäste mithilfe von Gegenständen wie Barhockern, Gläsern und Aschenbechern ihren eigenen Bereich – in der Soziologie spricht man an dieser Stelle von „Territorien des Selbst“ – abstecken.

All diese Beobachtungen Cavans verdanken sich einem spezifischen historischen wie kulturellen Entstehungskontext. Sie erforschte, darauf weist sie selbst hin, Räume der amerikanischen Mittelschicht der 1960er-Jahre mit entsprechenden Rollenerwartungen und Geschlechterklischees. Cavans Beschreibungen lassen sich daher nicht ohne Weiteres auf die Gegenwart übertragen. Was man aber noch heute von Sherri Cavan lernen kann ist, mit welcher Ernsthaftigkeit und Präzision sich alltägliche Räume und Verhaltensweisen beschreiben lassen, die wir alle kennen, über die wir uns aber wegen ihrer Alltäglichkeit nur selten Gedanken machen.

Der folgende Text ist ein Auszug aus *Liquor License. An Ethnography of Bar Behavior*. Er liegt in dieser GAM-Ausgabe erstmals in deutscher Übersetzung vor. Der englische Originaltext wurde mit freundlicher Genehmigung von Adam Cavan abgedruckt.

their own area with the aid of objects such as bar stools, drinking glasses, and ashtrays—in sociology one speaks of “territories of the self.”

All of Cavan’s observations are indebted to the specific historical and cultural context in which they were made. She studied, as she herself pointed out, spaces of the American middle class of the 1960s with the role expectations and gender stereotypes that went along with them. Cavan’s descriptions cannot therefore simply be applied to the present. What one can still learn from Sherri Cavan today, however, is the seriousness and precision with which one can describe everyday spaces and behaviors that we all know but seldom think about, probably because they are too ordinary.

The following text is excerpted from *Liquor License: An Ethnography of Bar Behavior*. It has been translated into German for the first time. The original text is being reprinted with the kind permission of Adam Cavan.

Translation: Steven Lindberg

Raum und raumbezogene Ordnungen
Space and Spatial Proprieties

Sherri Cavan

Die meisten öffentlichen Bars in San Francisco bieten ihren Gästen Sitzplätze, sowohl direkt am Tresen als auch an tresenfernen Tischen oder in Sitznischen. Das Verhältnis von Tresenplätzen zu jenen an davon entfernten Tischen unterscheidet sich abhängig von der Lokalität: Manche haben nur wenige nicht am Tresen befindliche Sitzplätze, in anderen gibt es viel mehr Plätze im Raum als unmittelbar am Tresen. Zudem bieten manche Bars keine Sitzgelegenheiten außer am Tresen, in anderen dient der Tresen nur der Bestellung und der Ausgabe von Getränken und verfügt über keine Sitzplätze.

In most public drinking places in San Francisco, there are usually seating facilities available for the patrons both along the physical bar and at tables and booths away from the bar. The ratio of bar seating facilities to non-bar seating facilities varies among establishments: in some there may be few if any facilities away from the bar and in others there may be many more places to sit away from the bar than there are along its length. There are, of course, some establishments that have no seating facilities away from the bar and others that have only a service bar and hence no seating facilities along the bar.

Wo der Anteil an Tresenplätzen im Vergleich zu tresenfernen Sitzgelegenheiten hoch ist, sind Erstere überwiegend nebeneinander angeordnet; ist das Verhältnis umgekehrt, sind die meisten oder sogar sämtliche Tresensitze einander gegenüber gelegen: Die Gäste sehen sich ins Gesicht. Während eine Anordnung mit gegenüberliegenden Sitzplätzen Gruppen im Allgemeinen räumlich erkennbar trennt und Gruppenmitglieder teilweise oder vollständig einander zugewandt zusammensitzen, ist das bei der seitlichen Anordnung nicht so. Hier sitzen Gäste aus jeder der über Sitzplätze verfügenden Gruppen nebeneinander, und der Abstand zwischen den Mitgliedern zweier Gruppen ist nicht größer als der Abstand zwischen Gästen aus einer Gruppe.

Im Vergleich zu einer gegenüberliegenden sind bei einer seitlichen Sitzanordnung die Gruppengrenzen viel unklarer und leichter zu überwinden. Hier neigen die Gruppen dazu, instabil zu sein, Begegnungen (*encounters*) sind fließender, eine Gruppe vermischt sich mit der anderen, Begegnungen verschmelzen, und Gäste, die ursprünglich zu keiner Gruppe oder Begegnung gehört haben, entwickeln große Nähe zu beiden Seiten. Im Allgemeinen sind Tresengäste offener füreinander und begegnen sich leichter, wenn sie sich auf seitlich angeordneten Sitzgelegenheiten über den Raum verteilen. Folglich knüpfen einander unbekannte Gäste mit höherer Wahrscheinlichkeit Kontakt, wenn sie nebeneinander am Tresen sitzen, als wenn sie vom Tresen entfernt sitzen.

Sowohl die vagen Gruppengrenzen als auch die allgemeine Nähe zueinander tragen zur größeren Offenheit der Tresengäste und zur gesteigerten Erwartung bei, dass sich zwischen einander unbekannten Gästen Kontakt ergibt. Nach Erikson bestimmen die Grenzen eines Systems die Fluktuation seiner Bestandteile, was es dem Ganzen erlaubt, ein bestimmtes Muster an Zusammenhalt und Stabilität zu bewahren.[3] Bei vagen Grenzen sind also auch Zusammenhalt und Stabilität der Bestandteile jeder Gruppe geringer, und man kann annehmen, dass die Gruppen sich eher vermischen. Zugleich ist der Abstand zwischen den Gästen am Tresen im Durchschnitt meist geringer als zwischen Gästen an Tischen und in Sitznischen, und insofern der räumliche Abstand zwischen Personen und die Wahrscheinlichkeit ihrer Kommunikation in einem negativen Verhältnis stehen, wäre ein solcher Kontakt eher am Tresen zu erwarten als davon entfernt.[4]

Kontaktabstand

Generell ist eine Distanz von drei Barhockern der maximale Abstand, den Gäste zu überwinden bereit sind, um sich einem anderen anzunähern und eine Begegnung

Where the ratio of bar seating to non-bar seating facilities is high, the dominant arrangement is lateral; in the reverse case, the dominant arrangement is largely or totally contrapositional: the patrons are face-to-face. While contrapositional seating generally demarcates groups by separating them spatially from each other and orienting their members in a partial or fully face-to-face arrangement, this is not true of lateral seating. Here the members of any seated group are abreast of each other and the distance separating the members of different groups is no greater than the distance separating the patrons within groups.

Boundaries of any group in a lateral seating arrangement are much less clear and easier to cross than those of a group in a contrapositional arrangement. Where the dominant seating arrangement is lateral, there is a tendency for groups and their encounters to be much more fluid, group merging into group, encounter merging into encounter, and patrons who were originally a part of neither group nor encounter being in close proximity to both. In general, the mutual openness of bar patrons and their encounters is heightened when patrons are spatially distributed in a lateral seating arrangement. Consequently, contact is more likely between unacquainted patrons seated along the bar than among those seated away from the bar.

Both the vagueness of group boundaries and general proximity contribute to the heightened openness of bar patrons and the heightened expectation that contact between the unacquainted will take place. At Erikson notes, the boundaries of a system control the fluctuation of its component parts, permitting the whole to retain a definite pattern of consistency and stability.[3] Thus, where such boundaries are vague, there is less consistency and stability of the component parts of each group, and one would expect that groups would be more likely to merge. At the same time, the average distance between patrons at the physical bar is typically less than between patrons seated away from the bar, and insofar as there is an inverse relationship between the physical distance separating persons and the likelihood of communication between them, such contact would be expected to be more prevalent along the bar than away from it.[4]

Contact Distance

As a general rule, a distance of three bar stools is the maximum distance over which patrons will make overtures as preludes to encounters. When three stools separate unacquainted patrons, overtures may well be made, but when the distance is four or more stools, they generally are not.

3 Vgl. Erikson, Kai T.: „Notes on the Sociology of Devicance“, in: *Social Problems* 9 (1962), 308.

4 Vgl. Barnlund, Dean C. /Harland, Carroll: „Propinquity and Prestige and Determinates of Communication Networks“, in *Sociometry* 26 (1963), 468.

3 See Kai T. Erikson, "Notes on the Sociology of Deviance," *Social Problems* 9 (1962), 308.

4 See Dean C. Barnlund and Carroll Harland, "Propinquity and Prestige and Determinates of Communication Networks," *Sociometry* 26 (1963): 468.

einzuleiten. Wenn zwischen einander unbekannten Gästen drei Barhocker stehen, kann einer den anderen noch gut ansprechen, doch mit vier und mehr Hockern Abstand ist das im Allgemeinen nicht der Fall. Will *ego* zu *alter* Kontakt aufnehmen, wird er oder sie in der Regel auf den dritten Hocker überwechseln, nicht selten auch auf den zweiten und von hier die Begegnung einleiten.

Vier Barhocker zwischen Gästen entsprechen durchschnittlich 2,5 bis 3 Meter Abstand. Zur Einleitung einer Begegnung über diese Distanz ist die Stimme so weit zu erheben, dass sie für die meisten anderen Gäste ebenso hörbar ist wie für die angesprochene Person. So eine Einleitung kann eine Art allgemeine Feststellung sein, die dem oder der anderen die Möglichkeit eröffnet, darauf zu reagieren oder auch nicht, einen aber auch selbst für die Reaktion jedes anderen Gastes öffnet, der oder die vielleicht darauf antwortet, auch wenn er oder sie aus irgendeinem Grund nicht die erwünschte beteiligte Person der Begegnung ist.[5]

Begegnungen mit einem Anfangsabstand von drei Barhockern zwischen den Beteiligten lassen sich über diese Distanz auch aufrechterhalten, aber im Allgemeinen geschieht das nicht. Gäste am Tresen verteilen sich für gewöhnlich so, dass jeder zumindest einen Hocker Abstand vom anderen hält. Wenn drei Barhocker voneinander entfernte Gäste eine Begegnung begonnen haben, ist die Wahrscheinlichkeit, dass sich ein neu eintretender Gast zwischen ihnen niederlässt, höher, als wenn nur zwei Hocker zwischen ihnen stehen. So kommt es häufig vor, dass, wenn *alter* eine Erwiderung zu *egos* Eröffnungsbemerkung vorbringt und wenn er oder sie die Begegnung über die erfolgte Antwort hinaus fortsetzen möchte, entweder unmittelbar vor oder während dieser Antwort auf den zweiten Hocker wechselt, um die Begegnung vor der unbeabsichtigten Beendung durch einen dazwischentretenden neuen Gast zu schützen.

Es sei angemerkt, dass mit verbalen Erwiderungen auf allgemeine Feststellungen der typische Abstand für Begegnungen aufgehoben werden kann. Nach solchen Feststellungen kann ein Austausch auch über größere Abstände als vier Hocker stattfinden. Wenn die Begegnungen jedoch länger andauern, wollen die Beteiligten den Abstand zwischen sich voraussichtlich verringern, so wie in folgendem Beispiel:

Ein Mann mittleren Alters begann Songs aus alten Filmen der 1930er-Jahre zu summen, dem Anschein nach nur für sich, aber laut genug, dass alle am Tresen Sitzenden es hörten. Ein anderer Mann, der ungefähr fünf Barhocker entfernt saß (und von dem ersten Mann durch einen weiteren Gast getrennt war), fing an, die Songtitel

5 Zumindest im gesellschaftlichen Kontext Amerikas betrachtet man einen Abstand zwischen 1,3 und 1,7 Meter als neutrale Distanz für ein nichtpersönliches Gespräch, während ein Abstand zwischen 2,5 und 6 Meter eher für die Ansprache einer Gruppe als eines Einzelnen geeignet ist. Vgl. Hall, Edward: *The Silent Language*, Greenwich 1961, 163–164.

If ego desires to contact alter seated four stools away, he will typically move to the third stool, and not infrequently to the second, and from there begin the encounter.

Four bar stools represent, on the average, between eight and ten feet of space separating the patrons. To start an encounter over this distance means that one's voice must be raised to the point at which it would be audible to most of the other patrons present as well as to the other participant in the conversation. Such a remark might well take on the character of a declaration, giving the other the option to respond or not as well as opening oneself to the response of any other patron who might choose to respond but who, for some reason, might not be desired as a participant in an encounter.[5]

Encounters that begin with a distance of three bar stools separating the participants may be maintained over this distance, but generally they are not. Bar patrons customarily space themselves out along the bar whenever possible in such a way that each is separated from the other by at least one stool. When patrons separated by three stools are carrying on an encounter, the probability that an entering patron will locate himself between them is much greater than when there are only two stools between them. Thus what frequently occurs is that, when alter proffers a counter-remark to ego's opening remark, if ego desires to continue the encounter beyond his subsequent reply, he will move to the second stool either immediately prior to or during his reply to alter's counter-remark, to protect the encounter from an inadvertent termination caused by the intrusion of a new patron.

It might be noted that verbal responses to declarations are one way in which the typical distance for encounters may be rendered inapplicable. Interchanges following declarations may take place over distances exceeding four bar stools. If the encounters are prolonged, however, the participants are likely to reduce the distance between them, as in the following example:

A middle-aged man began humming songs from 1930 vintage movies, apparently to himself but loud enough for everyone in the bar to hear. A second man, seated about five stools away (and separated from the first man by another patron), began guessing the names of the songs, and after a few minutes the two began talking about old movies. The conversation continued for about five minutes, and then the second man moved over to sit by the first, the encounter between them continuing for almost an hour longer.

If ego and alter are seated two stools apart, an encounter may not only begin from this location but may be

5 In American society, at least, between four and a half and five feet separating individuals is considered neutral distance, appropriate to nonpersonal discourse, while from eight to twenty feet is more appropriate to addressing a group rather than an individual. See Edward T. Hall, The Silent Language (Greenwich, Conn.: (Greenwich, Conn., 1961), 164.

zu raten, und nach ein paar Minuten begannen die beiden ein Gespräch über alte Filme. Dieses Gespräch dauerte etwa fünf Minuten, dann setzte sich der zweite Mann neben den ersten, und die Begegnung der beiden dauerte noch fast eine Stunde.

Wenn *ego* und *alter* zwei Hocker voneinander entfernt sitzen, kann eine Begegnung von dieser Sitzposition aus nicht nur beginnen, sondern auch eine Weile ohne Änderung des Abstands aufrechterhalten werden, es sei denn, eine beteiligte Person gibt der anderen einen Drink aus. Dann obliegt es dem oder der Eingeladenen, auf den Hocker neben dem oder der Spendierenden zu wechseln. Sitzen spendierende und eingeladene Person in einem Abstand von zwei Hockern, stellt der Barkeeper das Getränk für gewöhnlich fast vor den freien Hocker neben dem Spendierenden und platziert dieses nur leicht in die Richtung der eingeladenen Person, sodass diese ihren Platz ohne Weiteres verlassen und sich auf den Hocker neben dem Spendierenden setzen kann. Wenn *alter* und *ego* schon zu Beginn ihrer Begegnung nur einen Hocker voneinander getrennt sitzen und *ego* einen Drink ausgibt, ist *alter* nur dann verpflichtet, auf den Hocker neben *ego* zu wechseln, wenn ein neu eintretender Gast die Begegnung mit hoher Wahrscheinlichkeit unabsichtlich unterbricht. In Bars, in denen üblicherweise weniger Gäste am Tresen sitzen, als es Barhocker gibt, oder in Zeiten mit wenigen Gästen (etwa morgens, nachmittags oder spätabends unter der Woche) können die beiden ihre Begegnung aber auch mit einem Hocker Abstand zwischen sich fortsetzen, selbst wenn ein Drink spendiert wird.

Unter anderen Bedingungen – sei es hinsichtlich der Art der Bar oder der Zeit – ist die Einladung auf einen Drink mit der Verpflichtung des oder der Eingeladenen verbunden, auf den Hocker neben die spendierende Person zu wechseln, selbst wenn beide nur einen Barhocker voneinander entfernt sitzen.

Bei Begegnungen von Menschen verschiedenen Geschlechts obliegt es dem Mann, den Platz zu wechseln, selbst wenn die erste Bemerkung von ihm kam und auch wenn er der Frau das Getränk spendiert hat. Wenn zum Beispiel ein Mann und eine Frau drei Hocker voneinander entfernt sitzen und die Frau mit einer Bemerkung die Begegnung einleitet, dann wird der Mann in der Regel auf den zweiten Hocker wechseln und, außer im Fall eines Annäherungsversuchs, seine Position nicht mehr ändern. Ähnliches gilt, wenn der Abstand zwei Hocker beträgt und der Mann die Frau auf einen Drink einlädt: Auch dann wird er den Platz wechseln und nicht die eingeladene Frau.

Bei gleichgeschlechtlichen Begegnungen mit einem Hocker Abstand zwischen den Beteiligten kann einer von ihnen auf den Nachbarhocker wechseln, auch wenn keine Einladung erfolgt ist, es aber sehr wahrscheinlich ist, dass sich ein neuer Gast dazwischensetzt. Bei verschiedengeschlechtlichen Begegnungen, die nicht als amouröse Annäherungsversuche gedeutet werden sollen, bleibt der Abstand von einem Hocker meist ungeachtet aller

maintained for a time without any change in distance, unless one participant buys the other a gift drink. Then it is incumbent upon the recipient to move to the stool adjacent to the donor. When two stools apart, if ego buys alter a gift drink, usually the bartender sets the drink almost before the stool adjacent to the donor, just slightly toward the side of the recipient, permitting the latter to move with ease from his present location to the stool next to the donor. But if ego and alter are separated by only one stool from the onset of their encounter and ego buys alter a gift drink, alter has an obligation to move to the stool adjacent to ego only during those times when the probability of inadvertent discontinuance of the encounter by an entering patron is great. Thus in bars that are usually populated by fewer patrons than there are seats along the bar, or during times when few patrons are present (such as mornings, midafternoons or weekday nights), the two may continue an encounter separated by one stool, even when a gift drink is purchased.

In other circumstances, in terms of either the general nature of the establishment or the time, even when there is only one stool separating the two participants, the purchase of a gift drink carries with it an obligation for the recipient to move to the stool adjacent to the donor.

In cross-sex encounters, the obligation for changing location is the male's, even when he was not the one to make the initial remark and even when he is the donor of a gift drink to the famale [sic]. For example, in a situation where a male and a female are located three stools apart and the female makes the opening remark beginning an encounter, the male addressed will typically move to the second stool and, with the exception of pickups, this position will not be changed. Similarly, if they are separated by two stools and the male purchases a gift drink for the female, he will be the one to change positions, rather than the female who was the recipient of the drink.

In same-sex encounters where the participants are separated by one stool and no gift drink is purchased, one of them may choose to move to the adjacent stool when the probability of intrusion by another patron is great. However, in cross-sex encounters that are not expected to be read as pickups, unless the participants have begun the encounter from adjacent stools in the first place, a one-stool separation between them is usually maintained throughout the course of the encounter, no matter what the contingencies are. Adjacent stools typically represent a nose-to-nose distance of about eighteen inches when the participants are facing straight ahead and somewhat less if they are facing each other. Such distance is in American society indicative of some degree of intimacy for those involved,[6] and hence even in the public drinking place it may be too close for casual cross-sex conversation.

6 Ibid., 163.

möglichen Zufälle über die gesamte Begegnung gewahrt, wenn die Begegnung nicht von vornherein auf nebeneinanderstehenden Hockern begann. In letzterem Szenario ergibt sich in der Regel ein Abstand von 45 Zentimetern von Kopf zu Kopf, wenn die Beteiligten geradeaus blicken, und etwas weniger, wenn sie sich ins Gesicht sehen. Im gesellschaftlichen Kontext Amerikas ist das der Abstand, der den Beteiligten eine gewisse Intimität ermöglicht;[6] eine solche Distanz mag sogar in öffentlichen Bars für eine lockere Unterhaltung zwischen Personen verschiedenen Geschlechts zu nahe sein. Verschiedengeschlechtliche Begegnungen sind daher oft anfälliger für eine unabsichtliche Beendigung durch einen Dritten, der sich auf einen dazwischenliegenden Hocker setzt, als gleichgeschlechtliche.

Ein Mann und eine Frau, zwischen denen ein freier Hocker stand, hatten sich ungefähr zwanzig Minuten unterhalten. Eine weitere Frau kam herein und setzte sich zwischen die beiden.

Der Mann sah die neue Frau an, blickte auf seinen Drink und versuchte dann, vorne an der neuen Frau vorbei die erste Frau anzusehen, aber das gelang ihm augenscheinlich nicht. Danach sah er wieder auf seinen Drink, fuhr sich durchs Haar und wirkte unschlüssig, wie er den Kontakt zur ersten Frau wiederaufnehmen konnte. Währenddessen war die erste Frau offenbar sehr damit beschäftigt, in ihrem Drink zu rühren, doch als sie aufsah, begann die Frau, die neu dazugekommen war, ein Gespräch mit ihr. Fünf Minuten später erhob sich der Mann, um auf die Toilette zu gehen, und als er zurückkam, nahm er wieder im Abstand von zwei Hockern zur ersten Frau Platz.

Anders als bei gleichgeschlechtlichen Begegnungen, bei denen ein Platzwechsel ohne weiteren Kommentar erfolgen kann, geht man bei zwanglosen Begegnungen zwischen den Geschlechtern mit einem Hocker Zwischenraum davon aus, dass der Mann, dem der Platzwechsel obliegt, die Frau um Erlaubnis fragt, wenn er einen unbeabsichtigten Abbruch der Begegnung vermeiden und den Platz wechseln möchte.

Wenn eine Begegnung, deren Beteiligte schon vor der Aufnahme nebeneinander oder nur durch einen Hocker getrennt saßen, beendet werden soll, so stehen beiden mehrere Möglichkeiten offen: sich vorübergehend vom anderen entfernen (etwa auf die Toilette, zu einem Zigarettenautomaten oder zur Jukebox gehen) oder sich dauerhaft wegbegeben (etwa wenn man seine Sachen vom Tresen einsammelt und sich woanders hinsetzt oder die Bar verlässt), in ein abschließendes Schweigen verfallen oder sich förmlich verabschieden. Nach einer Veränderung der Position der Beteiligten im Raum haben beide allerdings nicht mehr dieselbe Macht, die Begegnung zu beenden. Bewegt sich eine beteiligte Person im Laufe der Begegnung zur anderen hin, ist sie verpflichtet, die Begegnung so lange aufrechtzuerhalten, wie die andere Person das

6 Vgl. ebd., 163.

Thus cross-sex encounters in public drinking places are often more vulnerable than same-sex encounters to inadvertent termination by the intrusion of a third person sitting down on an intervening stool.

A man and a woman had been talking for about twenty minutes, with one stool between them. Another woman came in and sat down between the two.

The man looked at the new woman, looked down at his drink, then tried to look at the first woman around the front of the new woman, but this appeared to be unsuccessful. He then looked down at his drink again, smoothed his hair, and appeared to be somewhat at a loss as to how to reestablish contact with the first woman. During this time the first woman was apparently very involved in stirring her drink, and when she looked up, the new woman engaged her in conversation. The man left about five minutes later to go to the bathroom and when he returned, he relocated two stools away from the first woman.

Unlike the same-sex encounter, where nothing need be said if positions are to be changed, the general expectation that casual cross-sex encounters are maintained over a one-stool separation requires that, if a change is desired to prevent inadvertent discontinuance of the encounter, the male (whose obligation it is to make the change) request the female's permission to do so.

Where an encounter is begun by participants who were in the first place seated on adjacent stools or separated by one stool, if either party wishes to terminate the encounter, he is at liberty to do so by a variety of means: by moving away from the other party either temporarily (as by going to the bathroom, the cigarette machine, or the juke box) or permanently (as by gathering his goods from the bar and relocating somewhere else or leaving the establishment altogether); by means of terminal silence; or by means of ceremonial goodbyes. But once the relative positions of the participants have been altered, control over the termination of the encounter is no longer equally distributed between them. If one participant moves closer to another during an encounter, he is bound to maintain that encounter as long as the other desires. Whatever the reason involved in the move, he who has moved has in effect surrendered his right to terminate the encounter and granted control over the course of the interaction to the other. He may terminate the encounter if he must (or is willing to) leave the establishment entirely, but this is, in general, the only exception, and it requires that he who is to leave ceremonially excuse himself.[7]

Spatial moves during the course of an encounter typically are read as expressions of the extent of the mover's

7 Erving Goffman has suggested that what may be established when spatial changes are made between patrons is a participation unit rather than an interaction unit. Reduction of the distance between those already in interaction may in this sense characterize the inception of a "with" or an "in-the-company-of" relationship, and it may be this feature, rather than the interaction as such, that is binding.

wünscht. Aus welchem Grund die Bewegung auch zustande gekommen ist, jene Person, die sich bewegt hat, hat das Recht aufgegeben, die Begegnung zu beenden, und der anderen die Kontrolle über den weiteren Verlauf der Interaktion übertragen. Sie kann die Begegnung beenden, wenn sie die Bar verlassen muss (oder sich dazu entschließt), aber das ist im Allgemeinen die einzige Ausnahme, und sie verlangt, dass der oder die Gehende sich förmlich entschuldigt.[7]

Das Verändern der Position im Raum während einer Begegnung wird zumeist als Ausdruck dafür verstanden, wie sehr sich die Person, die die Position wechselt, auf die Begegnung eingelassen hat, und die mit dem Positionswechsel verbundene Übertragung des Rechts, die Begegnung zu beenden, an die andere beteiligte Person gibt dieser Anlass zu glauben, dass der so verstandene Ausdruck ehrlich gemeint ist. Wenn *ego* also während der Begegnung näher an *alter* heranrückt, kann das damit stillschweigend bekundete Engagement für die Begegnung *alter* gestatten, sich auch selbst stärker in die Begegnung einzubringen oder entsprechend auszudrücken – weil der Positionswechsel *alter* versichert, dass das Gegenüber die Interaktion nicht plötzlich beenden wird.

Weil diejenige Person, die den räumlichen Abstand zwischen sich und der anderen Person ändert, sich zur Aufrechterhaltung der Begegnung bekennt, bis die andere Person sie beenden möchte, und weil es bei verschiedengeschlechtlichen Begegnungen dem Mann obliegt, den Abstand zu ändern, ist ersichtlich, dass Frauen im Prinzip davon befreit sind, sich zu solchen Begegnungen zu bekennen. Während sich die Frau womöglich durch ihre Anwesenheit in dieser Umgebung einer willkürlichen Annäherung durch alle anwesenden Männer aussetzt, kann sie, wenn sie will, in den meisten Fällen jede Begegnung jederzeit beenden, ohne dass sie sich entschuldigen oder einen förmlichen Grund nennen müsste.[8] Gleichzeitig ist zu beobachten, dass bei verschiedengeschlechtlichen Begegnungen Frauen nie als Erste mehr als ein beiläufiges Interesse bekunden müssen und daher nie in die Situation kommen, mehr Interesse zu zeigen als der Mann.

Der Tresen

Nicht zuletzt weil die Erwartung vorherrscht, dass der Kontakt zwischen Unbekannten am Tresen wahrscheinlicher ist als abseits von ihm, bildet er in einer Bar oft den sozialen Anziehungspunkt. Hier sind stets die meisten

7 Erving Goffman hat vorgeschlagen, dass das, was etabliert wird, wenn zwischen zwei Gästen räumliche Veränderungen stattfinden, eher eine Partizipationseinheit ist als eine Interaktionseinheit. Die Verringerung des Abstands zwischen zwei bereits interagierenden Personen mag in diesem Sinne den Anfang einer Beziehung des „Mit“ oder des „In-Begleitung-von“ markieren, und es mag diese Eigenschaft sein, die stärker als die Interaktion bindend wirkt.

8 Die bedeutendste Ausnahme ist, wenn ihr während einer Begegnung ein Drink spendiert wurde.

involvement, and the concommitant concession of the right to terminate the encounter to the other provides grounds for the other to believe that the expression so read is sincere. Thus when ego, during the course of an encounter, moves closer to alter, ego's tacitly expressed commitment to the encounter may subsequently permit alter to generate or express a greater involvement in the encounter as well—alter having been assured by the move, as it were, that ego will not suddenly terminate the interaction between them.

Since he who alters the spatial distance between himself and the other commits himself to the encounter until the other desires to terminate it, and since in cross-sex encounters the obligation for changing spatial distance is the male's, it can be seen that women are essentially exempted from committing themselves to such encounters. Thus while the woman in the public drinking place may, by her presence in the setting, open herself indiscriminately to the overtures of all males who are present, in most circumstances she may at any time terminate any ensuing encounter at her pleasure, with neither ceremony nor excuse[8]. At the same time, it can also be seen that in such cross-sex encounters, females need never be the first to express more than casual involvement and hence need never be in the position of having shown more interest than will subsequently be shown by the male.

The Physical Bar

In part, at least, because of the expectation that contact between the unacquainted is greater along the bar than away from it, the physical bar is typically the focal point of the public drinking place. It is here that at any given time the maximum concentration of patrons will be found (except for nightspots). Whether or not an establishment provides an abundance of seats away from the bar, and very frequently whether the entering patrons are alone or with others, locating in the vicinity of the bar is generally preferred to locating away from it.

Women are the notable exception to this generalization. Public drinking places vary in their official policy toward women. Some establishments categorically exclude women from the premises, maintaining the bar as an exclusively male domain. In some establishments, although women may be permitted access, in no circumstances may they sit at the bar, whether they are alone or in the company of another woman or in the company of a man; in other establishments, women accompanied by a male escort may sit at the bar, but not if they are accompanied by another female. In still other establishments it is only the solitary female who is excluded from sitting at the bar, while in many others there is no official policy about where women may locate themselves.

8 The notable exception is when she has been made the recipient of a gift drink during the course of an encounter. This will be treated in the next chapter.

Gäste versammelt (die Ausnahme sind Nachtbars). Ein Platz nahe am Tresen wird im Allgemeinen einem Platz abseits von ihm vorgezogen, unabhängig davon, ob eine Bar über viele tresenferne Sitzplätze verfügt oder nicht, und sehr oft auch unabhängig davon, ob Gäste allein oder in Begleitung kommen.

Die bemerkenswerte Ausnahme von dieser Regel bezieht sich auf Frauen. Öffentliche Bars unterscheiden sich in ihrer Haltung Frauen gegenüber. Manche lassen grundsätzlich keine Frauen zu, hier ist der Tresen ausschließlich Männern vorbehalten. Manche Bars gestatten Frauen den Zutritt, lassen sie aber unter keinen Umständen am Tresen sitzen, egal ob allein oder in Begleitung einer Frau oder eines Mannes. In anderen Bars dürfen Frauen in Begleitung eines Mannes am Tresen sitzen, aber nicht in Begleitung einer Frau. Schließlich gibt es Bars, in denen alleinsitzende Frauen nicht am Tresen geduldet werden. Viele andere Bars wiederum machen keine Vorgaben, wo Frauen Platz nehmen dürfen. Doch selbst wenn eine Bar keine Regelungen zur Platzierung von Frauen trifft, tendieren Frauen im Allgemeinen dazu, sich nicht an den Tresen zu setzen, egal ob es für sie dort Sitzplätze gibt oder nicht.

Am Tresen waren mehrere Plätze frei. Eine ältere Frau kam mit mehreren Paketen herein und ging zu einem der Tische auf der anderen Seite der Bar. Sie trank etwas und ging dann.

Als wir reinkamen, waren nur sieben andere Gäste da. In Türnähe saß ein ungefähr sechzigjähriger, gut gekleideter Mann am Tresen.

Vermutlich mehr als vier Plätze von ihm entfernt saßen drei junge Männer in Freizeitkleidung. Neben ihnen war ein Hocker frei, dann kam ein Paar mittleren Alters, sie im Pelzmantel. An einem Tisch saß eine junge, etwa fünfunddreißigjährige, gut angezogene Frau. Sie saß dort allein, bis wir ungefähr eine Stunde später gingen.

Zwei Frauen mittleren Alters betraten die Bar, ließen den Blick über den Tresen streifen (dort waren mehrere Hocker unbesetzt) und entschieden sich für einen Tisch.

Als ich eintrat, waren etwa fünfundvierzig Personen im Raum; die meisten Barhocker am Tresen und die meisten Tische und Nischen waren besetzt. Zwei Mittvierzigerinnen kamen herein, und eine sagte: „Oh, schau, da sind zwei." Sie deutete auf zwei nebeneinanderstehende Barhocker. Doch dann wirkten sie und ihre Begleiterin etwas unschlüssig und ließen den Blick über die Tische schweifen. Schließlich entdeckten sie einen freien Tisch, doch gerade als sie dorthin wollten, nahmen ihn drei Männer in Beschlag. Die Frauen machten enttäuschte Gesichter und fanden sich anscheinend schweren Herzens mit den Tresenplätzen ab.

Je nachdem, wie sehr der Tresen in einer Bar als sozialer Anziehungspunkt fungiert, lassen sich Frauen also oft in der Bar antreffen, aber nicht am Tresen. Während sie vielleicht allein aufgrund ihrer Anwesenheit in dieser Umgebung als offen für geselliges Beisammensein

But even when the establishment itself has no official policy concerning the proprieties of female seating, there is a general tendency for women to locate away from the physical bar whether or not there are seating facilities available to them there.

There were a number of empty seats along the bar. An elderly woman with some bundles came in and walked to one of the tables on the far side of the room. She had one drink and then left.

There were only seven people present when we entered. Along the bar, near the door, was a well dressed man who appeared to be in his mid-sixties.

Over about four seats from him were three young men in casual sports clothes. Next to them was one empty stool and then a well-dressed middle-aged couple, she in a fur coat. At one of the tables was a single woman, around thirty-five years old, nicely dressed. She sat there by herself until we left, about an hour later.

Two middle-aged women came in, looked down the bar (where there were a number of empty stools) and then moved to a table.

There were about forty-five persons present when I arrived; most of the stools along the bar and the tables and booths were occupied. Two women in their mid-forties came in and one said, "Oh, there are two here," indicating two adjacent bar stools. Then she and her companion looked bewildered and began glancing around at the tables. Finally they spotted an empty table, but just as they started over toward it three men took it. The women looked a bit disappointed and apparently resigned themselves to sitting at the bar.

Thus to the extent that the physical bar is the center of social gravity of the public drinking place, women may frequently be found to be in the bar, but not of it. While they may be defined as open to overtures of sociability by their mere presence in the setting, their actual spatial location within the bar is often such that the probability of being contacted is lessened.

Once all the available seats around the physical bar have been taken, persons entering the bar may freely move between the occupied stools to stand at the bar and order, and then to stand behind those who are seated while they consume their drinks. Even in establishments where there are tables or booths remaining empty, one can often find patrons standing two or more deep around the bar. And, just as the lateral seating arrangement heightens the mutual openness of bar patrons and their encounters by minimizing the distance between them, so does the clustering of patrons around the bar increase the likelihood that sociability among the unacquainted will ensue.

Patrons do locate at tables when the seats along the bar are all occupied. When there are no available stools, a cross-sex couple will usually move to the bar area together only when there is someone there whom they can greet by name: an acquaintance seated at the bar, one standing behind those who are seated, or even one

eingeschätzt werden, nehmen sie in der Bar oft eher solche Plätze ein, die eine Anbahnung von sozialen Kontakten weniger wahrscheinlich machen.

Sobald alle verfügbaren Tresenplätze belegt sind, können Gäste, die neu in die Bar kommen, einfach zwischen die Hocker treten, bestellen, sich dann hinter die Sitzenden stellen und ihre Getränke konsumieren. Sogar in Bars mit freien Tischen oder Sitznischen finden sich oft Gäste, die in zweiter oder dritter Reihe am Tresen stehen. Und so wie eine seitliche Anordnung der Tresenplätze die gegenseitige Offenheit der Gäste dort begünstigt und durch den geringen Abstand Begegnungen erleichtert, so erhöht die Versammlung von Gästen am Tresen die Wahrscheinlichkeit, dass sich zwischen einander Unbekannten geselliger Umgang entwickelt.

Gäste lassen sich an Tischen nieder, wenn alle Sitzplätze am Tresen belegt sind. Gibt es keine freien Barhocker, wird ein verschiedengeschlechtliches Paar nur dann gemeinsam in den Tresenbereich gehen, wenn es dort jemanden per Namen begrüßen kann: eine am Tresen sitzende bekannte Person, eine hinter den Sitzenden stehende bekannte Person oder auch eine hinter dem Tresen arbeitende, solange diese mit Namen begrüßt werden kann. Doch wenn es für eine Frau keinen „berechtigten Grund" gibt, am Tresen zu stehen – also wenn das neu hinzugekommene Paar dort niemanden per Namen kennt –, wird es sich im Allgemeinen an einen Tisch setzen; wenn in der Bar nicht bedient wird, wird der Mann anschließend an den Tresen gehen, bestellen und die Getränke zum Tisch bringen.

Dass ein „berechtigter Grund" notwendig ist, wenn sich ein verschiedengeschlechtliches Paar einen Platz in Tresennähe sucht, wenn keine Tresensitzplätze zur Verfügung stehen, hängt damit zusammen, dass Frauen dazu neigen, den Tresenbereich zu meiden. Aber selbst in Bars, in denen Frauen am Tresen sitzen können und es auch tun, ist das Stehen am Tresen noch einmal etwas ganz anderes.

Eine Frau stand neben ihrer am Tresen sitzenden Begleiterin. Der Barmann kam zu ihnen, deutete zum anderen Tresenende und sagte: „Da drüben sind zwei freie Plätze". Zwei Gruppen von Männern befanden sich ebenfalls in diesem Bereich, aber sie wurden nicht von dem Barmann auf die freien Plätze hingewiesen.

Dazu passen auch die Antworten zweier Männer auf die Frage, ob Frauen am Tresen erlaubt sein sollten:

„Auf alle Fälle. Vor allem den schönen. Aber nur zu den Besuchszeiten. Es ist doch immer ein Genuss, wenn man sieht, wie sich eine schöne Frau ladylike benimmt.

Da halte ich es mich Charles McCabe, der meinte: ‚Erlaubt, aber nicht gern gesehen.' Eine clubartige Bar ist was Feines. Frauen sehen in einer Sitznische einfach besser aus, als wenn sie am Tresen stehen."[9]

Während Gäste dazu neigen, sich zunächst einen

9 The Question Man: „Should Women be Allowed in Bars?", *San Francisco Chronicle*, 6. Juni 1964.

standing behind the bar if he can be greeted by name. But if there is no "justifiable reason" for a female to stand at the bar—that is, if the newly entered couple know no one there by name—they will usually go to one of the tables; if there is not a waitress in the establishment, the man will then go to the bar and order, bringing the drinks back to the table.

The necessity of a "justifiable reason" for a cross-sex couple to locate in the vicinity of the bar when there are no seats available along its length is related to the general tendency of women to shun the bar area. But even in establishments where women can and do choose to sit at the bar, for them to stand at the bar is something else again.

One woman was standing beside her female companion, who was seated at the bar. The bartender came down to them and said, "There's some seats down there," indicating the far end of the bar. Two groups of men were situated in the same way, but the bartender said nothing to them about available seats.

In the same vein, when asked if women should be allowed in bars, two male respondents made the following statements:

"By all means. Particularly the pretty ones. But only during visiting hours. A pretty woman conducting herself in a ladylike manner is a delight to behold. But they don't belong standing at a bar.

I go along with what Charles McCabe said. 'Allowed but not condoned.' A club type of bar is a fine thing. Women look better sitting back in a booth than standing at a bar."[9]

Again, while there is a decided tendency for patrons to occupy the bar seats first, in those establishments where the non-bar-seating facilities are in excess of those along the bar, it is relatively rare that patrons of either sex will stand at the bar if there are seats available away from the bar. However, in establishments where the ratio is reversed and the number of bar-seating facilities exceeds the number of away from the bar, male patrons, either singly or in groups, will frequently cluster around the physical bar even when there are tables or booths available for their use.

In the L________ there are four or five times more seats available away from the bar than there are along the bar. A number of entering male groups of two and three members who came in when the bar-seating facilities were fully occupied went automatically to the tables. There was little if any clustering around the bar at any time.

In the S________, there are 16 bar stools and three small tables, each with two chairs, across from the bar (a distance of about five feet). Around 1 A.M. the bar had begun to empty, but by 1:30 it began to fill again, mostly with young men. A little before 2 A.M. there were about twenty-five persons crowded around the bar, many

9 The Question Man, "Should Women be Allowed in Bars?", *San Francisco Chronicle*, June 6, 1964.

Tresenplatz zu suchen, ist es in Bars, in denen es mehr tresenferne Sitzplätze gibt als Plätze am Tresen, relativ selten, dass sich Gäste beiderlei Geschlechts an den Tresen stellen, wenn woanders noch freie Sitzplätze verfügbar sind. In Bars, in denen es umgekehrt mehr Plätze am Tresen als abseits davon gibt, sammeln sich männliche Gäste, einzelne wie Gruppen, häufig um den Tresen, selbst wenn Tische oder Sitznischen frei sind.

Im L_____ gibt es etwa vier bis fünf Mal mehr Sitzplätze an Tischen als am Tresen. Mehrere Gruppen von Männern, die zu zweit oder dritt hereinkamen, als alle Tresenplätze besetzt waren, gingen automatisch an die Tische. Zu keiner Zeit gab es größere Ansammlungen am Tresen.

Im S_____ gibt es 16 Barhocker und drei kleine, dem Tresen im Abstand von ungefähr 1,5 Meter gegenübergelegene Tische mit je zwei Stühlen. Gegen 1:00 begann sich die Bar zu leeren, aber ab 1:30 füllte sie sich wieder, zumeist mit jungen Männern. Kurz vor 2:00 befanden sich etwa 25 Personen in Tresennähe, und weil es keine freien Hocker mehr gab, standen viele, obwohl die drei Tische alle unbesetzt waren.

Darüber hinaus bleiben Gäste in Bars mit mehr Sitzgelegenheiten abseits des Tresens gar nicht in der Bar, wenn sie weder am Tresen noch woanders einen Sitzplatz finden; dagegen verlassen Gäste selten eine Bar, die mit mehr Sitzplätzen am Tresen als anderen Sitzplätzen ausgestattet ist, nur weil gerade kein Platz frei ist. [...]

Zusammenfassend lässt sich sagen, dass die Merkmale und die praktischen Kontingenzen der konkreten Raumsituation in einer Bar zu einer unterschiedlichen Verteilung der Gäste im Raum und manchmal auch zu einer unterschiedlichen Verteilung der Aktivitäten führen. Die Verteilung im Raum kann entweder die Offenheit der Gäste füreinander fördern oder sie von einer Kontaktaufnahme abschirmen, und manchmal vergrößert sie auch die Distanz zwischen einzelnen Gruppen oder Aktivitäten und reduziert so die Möglichkeit, dass Gruppen oder Aktivitäten störend aufeinander einwirken. Anders als die Begegnungen und das Verhalten in der Bar kann der Raum also etwas sein, über das sich die Anwesenden unschlüssig sind. Aber wenn die erwartete und die tatsächliche Raumnutzung in der Bar über den Moment hinaus Konsequenzen hat, treten diese Konsequenzen, anders als die Folgeerscheinungen vieler ernsthafterer Umgebungen, nicht automatisch ein. Vielmehr verlangen sie nach aktiver Mitwirkung seitens der Anwesenden. Wem seine Anwesenheit in dieser Umgebung nicht egal ist (etwa jenen, die „ernsthaft trinken“ wollen, oder die, die zu einem besonderen Anlass und als Teil einer speziellen Gruppe anwesend sind), die müssen nach dem Eintreten besondere Aufmerksamkeit darauf verwenden, wo sie sich einen Platz suchen und wie sie sich gruppieren, genauso wie alle, die ihr Engagement für eine laufende Begegnung bekennen möchten, dies auch aktiv tun müssen.

Übersetzung: Sven Koch

standing because there were no empty stools, although all three tables were vacant.

In addition, in establishments where there is an excess of non-bar seating facilities, patrons who can find neither bar nor non-bar seating accommodations may not stay at all, although it is rare for patrons to leave establishments where the ratio of bar to non-bar facilities is reversed simply because there are no seats available. (...)

In summary, the proprieties and the practical contingencies associated with space in the public drinking place result in a differential spatial distribution of patrons and sometimes a differential distribution of activities. This differential spatial distribution may either heighten the mutual openness of patrons or insulate them from contact, and in some cases it may maximize the distance between separate groups or activities and hence reduce the possibility for disparate groups or activities to disrupt one another. Thus space, unlike encounters and comportment within the public drinking place, may be a matter of concern for those present. But if the expected and actual use of space in the bar has implications beyond the immediate moment, unlike the consequential features of many more serious settings, these implications are not automatic contingencies. Rather they require active work on the part of the persons present. Those who are not indifferent about their presence in the setting (such as those present for “serious drinking” or those who are there as a part of a special group and for a special occasion) must take particular care with respect to where they locate and how they arrange themselves once they have entered, just as those who would express any commitment to an ongoing encounter must actively work at doing so.

This text has first been published in Sherri Cavan's monograph *Liquor License: An Ethnography of Bar Behaviour* (Aldine Publishing Company, 1966). The reprint in this GAM issue was made possible by the kind permission of Adam Cavan.

Dieser Textauszug erschien erstmals in *Liquor License: An Ethnography of Bar Behavior*, Aldine Publishing, 1966. Der Nachdruck in dieser GAM-Ausgabe erfolgt mit freundlicher Genehmigung durch Adam Cavan.

“City of the Dead”

Kairos Stuckwerkstätten
Cairo’s Stucco Workshops

Luc Merx

Das mittelalterliche islamische Zentrum Kairos war stark verdichtet. Die Toten wurden nicht innerhalb der Stadtmauer, sondern außerhalb begraben, dadurch entstanden im Laufe der Zeit riesige Nekropolen. Das Gebiet westlich der Stadt war nicht für die Bestattung der Toten geeignet, weil es dort regelmäßig Hochwasser durch die Überschwemmungen des Nils gab. Östlich der Stadt fehlte Platz, weil das Niltal dort durch die steilen Felswände von Mokatam begrenzt wird. Die Gräberfelder „Al Qarafa“ oder „City of the Dead“ genannt, sind dementsprechend im Norden und Süden der Altstadt konzentriert. Mausoleen, Medressen und Koranschulen wechseln sich hier mit einfachen Familiengräbern ab. Im Laufe der Zeit entstand eine riesige Nekropole. Kairo ist inzwischen weitergewachsen. Der ehemalige Stadtrand und somit auch die beide Nekropolen liegen jetzt im Zentrum der Stadt. Während die umliegenden Gebiete immer stärker verdichtet wurden, war die systematische Besiedlung der Nekropolen tabu. Nichtsdestotrotz werden die Nekropolen schon seit dem 18. Jahrhundert gewerblich genutzt und zunächst temporär, dann auch permanent bewohnt. Die Zahl der Menschen, die sich dort inzwischen niedergelassen haben, wird auf 300.000 geschätzt.

„City of the Dead“, die zweite Fotoserie zu Kairos Stuckwerkstätten, beschäftigt sich mit der informellen Nutzung der Nekropolen durch Stuckateure. Vernachlässigte Familiengräber werden besetzt und als Stuckwerkstatt umgenutzt. Das Innere der Gräber und deren Außenwände dienen als Showroom. Die Fotos dokumentieren die Werkstätten am Westrand der südlichen City of the Dead. Sie sind ein Beispiel für die gewerbliche Nutzung der Nekropolis. Die Stuckateure haben sich dort zunächst vor allem angesiedelt, weil sie sich um den Bau, um die Pflege und um die Restauration der Gräber gekümmert haben. Inzwischen ist ein Großteil ihrer Aufträge aber profan. Die meisten Stuckateure arbeiten hauptsächlich im Wohnungsbau. Die Ästhetik der Werkstätten steht dementsprechend im Kontrast zu den umgebenden Grabstätten.

The medieval Islamic center of Cairo was extremely dense. The dead were buried outside the city walls, not inside, which gave rise to giant necropolises over time. The area west of town, however, was not suitable for burials because the Nile regularly flooded there. And to the east there was not enough space, because the Nile valley is delimited by the steep cliff faces of the Mokatam hills. It follows that the burial grounds called “Al Qarafa” or “City of the Dead” are situated to the north and the south of Cairo’s old town. Here, mausoleums, madrasas, and Koran schools alternate with simple family tombs. Over time, a giant cemetery emerged. In the meanwhile, the population of Cairo has grown. What used to be the urban periphery, and thus also the two necropolises, is now the middle of town. Although the adjacent areas became more and more dense, a systematic colonization of the necropolises was not permitted. Nonetheless, the necropolises have been used in commercial ways since the eighteenth century, and also for housing, first temporarily and then permanently. The number of people now dwelling there is estimated at about 300,000 residents.

This second photographic series on Cairo’s stucco workshops, “City of the Dead”, created shortly before the coronavirus pandemic, deals with the informal use of the necropolises by stucco plasterers. Neglected family plots are occupied and used as stucco workshops. The inside of these tombs and their exterior walls serve as a showroom. The photos document the recently demolished workshops at the western edge of the southern “City of the Dead,” which had been an example of the commercial use of the necropolises. The stucco plasterers had originally settled there mainly because they were responsible for building, maintaining, and restoring the tombs. Eventually, however, most of their commissions were of a secular nature. Most plasterers worked primarily in building housing. The aesthetics of the workshops thus strongly contrasted with the surrounding burial grounds. In lieu of the traditional Islamic ornamentation predominating there,

Anstelle der traditionellen islamischen Ornamentik, die dort vorherrscht, sind die Wände hier übersäht mit den für Kairo charakteristischen historistischen Ornamenten. Die Fotos sind aus dem Interesse an historischem Handwerk entstanden. Noch funktionieren die Kairoer Werkstätten, indem Wissen von einer Generation auf die nächste weitergegeben wird. Die Ausführung ist zwar oft nicht präzise und die Qualität leidet unter schlechtem Werkzeug und Material, aber das Handwerk ist lebendig. Durch den Mangel an Präzision und fehlendes Verständnis für den Kontext der Ornamente entstehen dabei oft bizarre Lösungen. Man kann diese als Scheitern lesen, interessanter ist es aber, die improvisierte neue Deutung von historischen Fragmenten als Modell für eine lokale zeitgenössische Architektur und als Beitrag einer neuen Ästhetik zu verstehen.

the walls were covered in ancient ornaments so typical of Cairo. These photographs were based on an interest in historical artisanship. Knowledge of craftsmanship is still passed down from one generation to the next in present-day Cairo. These skilled crafts and trades are alive and well, despite the execution sometimes lacking in precision or the quality suffering from poor tools and materials. Such a lack of precision coupled with little understanding of the ornaments' context gives rise at times to bizarre solutions. While this might be interpreted as failure, it is more compelling to see the improvised reinterpretation of historical fragments as a model for local contemporary architecture, and as a contribution to a whole new aesthetic.

Translation: Dawn Michelle d'Atri

الورشة الفنية لجميع ديكورات الجبس
GRC+GRB

FONA
WITH FONA

AutorInnen
Authors

Luigiemanuele Amabile ist wissenschaftlicher Mitarbeiter (Postdoc) an der Universität Neapel Federico II, wo er zum Thema Designpädagogik von Design Studios arbeitet. Seit 2017 unterrichtet er dort im Forschungskollektiv A402 verschiedene Design Studios. Neben seinem Lehrauftrag an der Universität Parma ist er seit 2021 auch Redaktionsmitglied der Architekturzeitschrift *Stoà*.

Luigiemanuele Amabile is a postdoctoral researcher at the University of Naples Federico II, focusing on the pedagogy of the architectural design studio. Since 2017, he has taught in several architectural and urban design studios within the research unit A402. He is an adjunct lecturer at the University of Parma and, since 2021 also a member of the editorial team of the architecture journal *Stoà*.

Beatrice Azzola ist Architektin und Doktorandin am Politecnico di Milano. Im Rahmen ihrer Dissertation forscht sie zur Architektur von Raststationen und deren disziplinären Wechselwirkungen zwischen Architektur, Landschaft und Werbung. Bevor sie als Wissenschaftlerin tätig wurde, hat sie in Architekturbüros in Italien, Portugal und der Schweiz gearbeitet.

Beatrice Azzola is an architect and a PhD candidate at Politecnico di Milano. In her dissertation, she explores roadside architecture and the disciplinary interferences between architecture, landscape, and advertisement. Before becoming an academic researcher, she worked in architecture firms in Italy, Portugal, and Switzerland.

Ajna Babahmetović hat in Graz Architektur studiert und in ihrer Masterarbeit räumliche Ausprägungen von Migration erforscht. Die Ergebnisse dieser Arbeit wurden auf publizistischen Plattformen wie *Failed Architecture* und *Drawing Matter* veröffentlicht. Sie ist aktuell als Universitätsassistentin am Institut für Grundlagen der Konstruktion und des Entwerfens (KOEN) der TU Graz beschäftigt.

Ajna Babahmetović studied architecture in Graz, graduating on spatial manifestations of migrations. Her master's thesis findings appeared on publication platforms such as *Failed Architecture* and *Drawing Matter*. She is currently a research associate and teaching fellow at the Institute of Construction and Design Principles (KOEN) at TU Graz.

Alberto Calderoni ist Assistenzprofessor (RTdB) für Entwerfen an der Universität Neapel Federico II, wo er das Forschungsprojekt „DT2" koordiniert, das sich mit der Pädagogik von Architekturstudios befasst. Er ist Mitbegründer des Forschungskollektivs A402, deren Arbeiten ausgezeichnet und veröffentlicht wurden, und seit 2021 Chefredakteurder Zeitschrift *Stoà*.

Alberto Calderoni is Assistant Professor of Architectural Design at the University of Naples Federico II, where he is the coordinator of "DT2", a research project focused on architectural design studio pedagogy. He is a co-founder of A402, a design research unit, whose projects have been awarded and published. Since 2021 he's the editor-in-chief of the journal *Stoà*.

Andrea Canclini ist Dozent für Architectural Humanities an der School of Architecture der Lancaster University. Zuvor lehrte er am Politecnico di Milano und als Gastprofessor an der Beirut Arab University. Er hat Architektur und Philosophie studiert und am Politecnico di Torino im Fach Architekturgeschichte promoviert. Er ist Mitglied des Editorial Boards von *Khōrein* und forscht zu den kulturellen Grundlagen der modernen und zeitgenössischen Architektur.

Andrea Canclini is a lecturer in Architectural Humanities at the School of Architecture at Lancaster University. Previously, he lectured at Politecnico di Milano and was a Visiting Professor at Beirut Arab University. He holds degrees in Architecture and Philosophy and a PhD in History of Architecture from Politecnico di Torino. He is a member of the Editorial Board of *Khōrein* and researches the cultural basis of modern and contemporary architecture.

Matthias Castorph ist Professor für Entwerfen im Bestand und Denkmalpflege an der TU Graz. Er hat an der TU München Architektur studiert und wurde an der Universität Kaiserslautern promoviert. Castorph ist in München Partner im Architekturbüro Lehmann, Tabillion & Castorph Architektur Stadtplanung Gesellschaft mbH.

Matthias Castorph is a professor of Design in Existing Structures and Architectural Heritage Protection at TU Graz. He studied architecture at TU München and completed his doctorate at the University of Kaiserslautern. He is a partner at the architecture firm Lehmann, Tabillion & Castorph Architektur Stadtplanung Gesellschaft mbH in Munich.

Sherri Cavan war von 1965 bis 2003 Professorin für Soziologie an der San Francisco State University und Ko-Direktorin der Erving Goffman Archives, einer webbasierten Sammlung von kritischen Schriften und biografischen Materialien. Zu ihren wichtigsten akademischen Publikationen zählen *Liquor License: An Ethnography of*

Bar Behavior (1966), *Hippies of the Haight* (1972), *20th Century Gothic: America's Nixon* (1979) und „Becoming an Ethnographer" (1994).

Sherri Cavan was a Professor of Sociology at San Francisco State University from 1965 to 2003 and co-director of the Erving Goffman Archives, a web-based collection of critical studies and biographical materials. Her scholarly publications include *Liquor License: An Ethnography of Bar Behavior* (1966), *Hippies of the Haight* (1972), *20th Century Gothic: America's Nixon* (1979), and "Becoming an Ethnographer" (1994).

Michael Heinrich ist Architekturfotograf in München. Nach der Fotografenausbildung an der Bayerischen Staatslehranstalt studierte er Architektur an der TU München. Seit 2003 gibt er Fotoseminare an verschiedenen Universitäten, Hochschulen und Architektenkammern.

Michael Heinrich is an architectural photographer based in Munich. After completing his training as a photographer at the Bayerische Staatslehranstalt, he studied architecture at the Technical University of Munich. Since 2003, he has been giving photography seminars at various universities, colleges, and chambers of architects.

Svenja Hollstein forscht zum Möglichkeitsraum der Form und Gestalt von Raumkörpern sowie zum sensiblen Weiterbauen von bestehenden städtischen Strukturen. Seit 2021 ist sie als Dozentin am Institut für Entwerfen im Bestand und Denkmalpflege der TU Graz tätig. Zuvor arbeitete sie an den Lehrstühlen „Stadtbaukunst und Entwerfen" und „Raumgestalt und Entwerfen" an der TU Kaiserslautern.

Svenja Hollstein investigates the potential space of the form and shape of spatial bodies and the sensitive development of existing urban structures. Since 2021, she has been a lecturer at the Institute of Design in Existing Structures and Architectural Heritage Protection at TU Graz. Prior to that, she worked at the Chair of Urban Art and Design and the Chair of Spatial and Architectural Design at TU Kaiserslautern.

Johanna-Charlotte Horst ist Akademische Rätin a.Z. am Institut für Allgemeine und Vergleichende Literaturwissenschaft an der LMU München. Sie studierte AVL, Nordische Philologie und Kunstgeschichte in München und Paris und und wurde zu Georges Perecs literarischem Materialismus promoviert. Zu ihren Forschungsschwerpunkten zählen u.a. das Alltägliche in der Literatur, Oulipo, Formen der Geschichtsschreibung, und feministische Theorien. Sie schreibt regelmäßig für das Feuilleton der *FAZ* und der *SZ*.

Johanna-Charlotte Horst is assistant professor at the Department of Comparative Literature at LMU Munich. She studied Comparative Literature, Nordic Philology, and Art History in Munich and Paris and holds a PhD on Georges Perec's literary materialism. Her research interests include the everyday in literature, Oulipo, forms of historiography, and feminist theories. She is a regular contributor to the *FAZ* and *SZ*.

Ena Kukić beschäftigt sich sowohl in der Praxis als auch in der akademischen Forschung mit dem räumlichen Rahmen des kollektiven Gedächtnisses. Derzeit promoviert sie über Erinnerungsarchitektur am Institut für Gebäudelehre in Graz und unterrichtet außerdem Gestalten und Entwerfen sowie Modellbau am KOEN-Institut. Ihre Arbeit wurde international ausgestellt, publiziert und mit Preisen ausgezeichnet.

Ena Kukić explores the spatial framework of collective memory in both practice and academic research. Currently pursuing a PhD on memorial architecture at the Institute of Design and Building Typology in Graz, she also teaches design and model making at the Institute of Construction and Design Principles (KOEN) at TU Graz. Her work has been exhibited, published, and recognized with awards on an international scale.

Thomas Meinecke ist Schriftsteller, Musiker und DJ. Während seines Studiums der Theaterwissenschaft und Neueren Deutschen Literatur in München gründete er die Literaturzeitschrift *Mode und Verzweiflung*, aus der die Band F.S.K. hervorging. Er ist Autor zahlreicher Erzählungen, Hörspiele und Romane, darunter *Tomboy* (1998), *Lookalikes* (2011) und *Selbst* (2016), und hat mehrere Literaturpreise gewonnen.

Thomas Meinecke is an author, musician, and DJ. While studying theater and modern German literature in Munich, he founded the literary magazine *Mode und Verzweiflung*, from which the band F.S.K. originated. He is the author of numerous short stories, radio plays, and novels, including *Tomboy* (1998), *Lookalikes* (2011), and *Selbst* (2016), and has won several literary awards.

Luc Merx arbeitet als Architekt an der Schnittstelle zwischen Architektur, Design und Kunst. Im Forschungsprojekt „Rokokorelevanz" untersucht er Parallelen zwischen der Gestaltung des 18. Jahrhunderts und dem Einfluss der Digitalisierung auf die heutige Entwurfspraxis. Er ist Teil des Gründungsteams der Felsbergakademie und der Felsberg Future Laboratories und unterrichtet aktuell an der Maastricht Academy of Architecture und an der TU Kaiserslautern.

Luc Merx works as an architect at the nexus of architecture, design, and art. As part of the research project "Rokokorelevanz," he investigates parallels between 18th-century design and the influence of digitalization on today's design practice. He is part of the founding team of the Felsberg Academy and the Felsberg Future Laboratories and currently teaches at the Maastricht Academy of Architecture and TU Kaiserslautern.

Julian Müller ist Soziologe. Er ist derzeit Gastprofessor an der Staatswissenschaftlichen Fakultät der Leuphana Universität Lüneburg. Von 2022 bis 2023 arbeitete er im Rahmen einer Gastprofessur an der Fakultät für Architektur der TU Graz. In seiner Forschung beschäftigt er sich u.a. mit soziologischer und politischer Theorie, mit einer Soziologie des Alltags sowie mit dem Wechselverhältnis von Architektur und Gesellschaft.

Julian Müller is a sociologist. He is currently a visiting professor at the Faculty of Political Science at Leuphana University Lüneburg. From 2022 to 2023, he worked as a visiting professor at the Faculty of Architecture at Graz University of Technology. His research interests include sociological and political theory, sociology of everyday life, and the interrelationship between architecture and society.

Denise Scott Brown ist Architektin, Stadtplanerin, Theoretikerin und Autorin. Als Lehrende hatte sie Architektur- und Planungsprofessuren an den Universitäten von Pennsylvania, Harvard, UCLA, UC Berkeley und Yale inne. Ihre Publikationen *Learning from Las Vegas* (1972; überarbeitete Ausgabe 1977, mit Robert Venturi und Steven Izenour) und *Learning from Levittown* (1970; mit Robert Venturi) sind architektonische Standardwerke, die eine neue Sicht auf bislang unbeachtete räumliche Aspekte von Städten entwickelten. Ihre architektonischen Forschungsarbeiten und ihre Hochschullehre kennzeichnen sie als eine der einflussreichsten Architektinnen des 20. Jahrhunderts.

Denise Scott Brown is an architect, planner and urban designer, theorist, and writer. She held architecture and planning professorships at the Universities of Pennsylvania, Harvard, UCLA, UC Berkeley, and Yale. Her publications *Learning from Las Vegas* (1972; revised edition 1977, with Robert Venturi and Steven Izenour) and *Learning from Levittown* (1970 with Robert

Venturi) have become canonical works that developed a new perspective on previously overlooked spatial aspects of cities. Her architectural research and teaching mark her as one of the most influential architects of the 20th century.

Helmut Tezak beschäftigt sich seit 1976 mit Fotografie und arbeitet seit 1981 an der Architekturfakultät der TU Graz als Fotograf. Zu seinen veröffentlichten Arbeiten zählen „ArchiGschnas" (TU Graz, 1982/2022), *Dakar* (Edition Camera Austria, 1984), *3Orte* (Neue Galerie Graz, 1987), *Peripherie Graz* (Leuschner & Lubinsky, 1990), *Chinesisch* (Verlag Droschl, Graz 1992), „Graz" (*GAM.08*, Springer, 2012), „Fresh Evidence" (Marenzi Galerie Leibnitz, 2012), oder „When I Paint My Masterpiece" (Kunstwerkstatt Lienz, 2017).

Helmut Tezak has been involved with photography since 1976 and has been working as a photographer at the Faculty of Architecture at TU Graz since 1981. Among his published works are „ArchiGschnas" (TU Graz, 1982/2022), *Dakar* (Edition Camera Austria, 1984), *3Orte* (Neue Galerie Graz, 1987), *Peripherie Graz* (HDA Graz, 1990), *Chinesisch* (Verlag Droschl, Graz 1992), „Graz" (*GAM.08*, Springer, 2012), „Fresh Evidence" (Marenzi Galerie Leibnitz, 2012), or „When I Paint My Masterpiece" (Kunstwerkstatt Lienz, 2017).

Buchrezensionen
Book Reviews

Buchrezensionen
Book Reviews

Lernen von Latour. Wo Soziologie auf Architektur trifft

Latour for Architects
Albena Yaneva
Oxford: Routledge, 2022
Englisch, 154 Seiten

„Es gibt immer ein wenig Philosophie in der Architektur und viel Architektur in der Philosophie" – mit diesem Zitat von Bruno Latour beginnt die Publikation *Latour for Architects*, die bei Routledge erschienen ist und von Albena Yaneva, Professorin für Architekturtheorie an der Universität Manchester und ehemalige Doktorandin von Latour, verfasst wurde. Das Buch ist in neun Kapitel unterteilt, welche die unterschiedlichen Ideen und methodischen Ansätze des Soziologen beleuchten und anhand konkreter Beispiele im Zusammenhang mit Architektur und Stadtforschung vorstellen. Über ein Dutzend Illustrationen im Buch basieren auf klassischen Diagrammen und Figuren aus den Schlüsselwerken von Latour, die für ein Designpublikum neu interpretiert wurden. Die Publikation ist im Open Access auch zum Download verfügbar.

ArchitektInnen beziehen sich bei ihrer Suche nach innovativen Entwurfsideen und einem kritischen Rahmen für ihre Entwurfspraxis häufig auf philosophische Strömungen. Bruno Latour (1947–2022), den The Guardian als „einen der einflussreichsten Denker unserer Zeit" bezeichnete, bietet hier eine neue und pragmatische Perspektive für die Untersuchung sozialer Phänomene. Der französische Soziologe und emeritierte Professor der Pariser Universität SciencesPo ist vor allem für seine Akteur-Netzwerk-Theorie (ANT) und eine Reihe von Büchern bekannt, darunter *We Have Never Been Modern* (1991), *Laboratory Life* (1979) und *Science in Action* (1987).

In der Fachwelt gilt Bruno Latour als faszinierend und umstritten zugleich. Er kritisiert nicht nur das Selbstverständnis der Moderne, Natur/Wissenschaft auf der einen und Kultur/Gesellschaft auf der anderen Seite klar zu trennen, sondern argumentiert, dass eine solche Trennung in der Praxis nie stattgefunden habe und wir daher nie wirklich „modern" waren. Gleichzeitig sei die Wissenschaft nicht inhärent objektiv, sondern von sozialen, politischen und religiösen Faktoren abhängig, die ihre Objektivität in Frage stellen. Die Wissenschaft wird zum Beispiel von Regierungen finanziert, deren Produkte auf dem Markt verkauft werden, welche wiederum ethische Bedenken aufwerfen. So befinden wir uns in einer Welt der Hybride, die die Grundlagen der Moderne in Frage stellen.

Als relevantes Beispiel für ArchitektInnen präsentiert Albena Yaneva die Neuerrichtung des Bahnhofs von Birmingham, dessen Fassade auf Grund der Blendungsthematik durch Sonnenlicht im Laufe des Baus völlig neu konzipiert werden musste. Die Autorin zeigt, welchen Einfluss die dadurch notwendigen technischen Lösungen auf die Architektursprache des Gebäudes hatten, die wiederum die Ikonographie von Birmingham neu definierte und dazu führte, dass politische Versprechen nicht eingelöst werden konnten. Gerade im disziplinären Feld der Architektur offenbart sich, wie stark Gestaltungsanspruch, Umwelt, Politik, Wirtschaft, Technologie, Ökologie, und rechtliche Gegebenheiten miteinander verwoben sind. Der/die ArchitektIn wird zum Hybriden und ist selbst in einem hybriden Netzwerk tätig, in dem, so Latour, eine ständige Übersetzung (*translation*) notwendig ist.

Parallel dazu stellt Latour die seit Pierre Bourdieu übliche Praxis in Frage, Handlungen (*actions*) durch das Prisma der Gesellschaft (*society*) zu bewerten und definiert somit die Aufgabe der Soziologie völlig neu. So lassen sich beispielsweise Größe, Stil und Form eines bestimmten Gebäudes nicht durch eine Reihe von sozialen und politischen Faktoren oder Werten und Überzeugungen erklären. Vielmehr agieren wir in einem hybriden Netzwerk, in dem sich die vermeintliche Dualität von Objekt und Subjekt sowie Natur und Gesellschaft vollständig auflöst. Latour zufolge befindet sich das Soziale (*the social*) in ständiger Bewegung, und um es zu verstehen müssen wir seinen AkteuerInnen (*actants*) und ihren spezifischen Anliegen und Technologien folgen. Die Lebensrealitäten werden demnach aktiv von miteinander verbundenen AkteurInnen konstruiert, einschließlich SoziologInnen selbst, die um eine Definition ringen.

An dieser Stelle kommt Latours Akteur-Netzwerk-Theorie (ANT) ins Spiel, die die Trennung zwischen dem Objektivem und Subjektivem zugunsten des Konzepts der Vermittlung (*mediation*) vollständig verwirft. Nach dieser Theorie zeugen Objekte und Technologien nicht von einer rein objektiven Realität, sondern sind selbst gesellschaftsprägend. Es findet eine Verlagerung von der Welt der Tatsachen (*matters of fact*) zu der Welt der Belange (*matters of concern*) statt. Als Beispiel führt Latour das glorreiche Scheitern des Aramis Personal Rapid Transport Projektes oder die Besonderheit des Berliner Schlüssels an. Anstatt Objekte auf ihre scheinbar verborgene soziale oder politische Bedeutung zu reduzieren, folgt er ihrer eingeschriebenen Funktion (*programme*) nach und ergründet so die wechselseitigen Beziehungen zwischen Menschen (*humans*) and Nicht-Menschen (*non-humans*). Letztere sind aktive und stimmberechtigte Teilnehmer am sozialen Leben und können als Werkzeuge, Tiere, Technologien, Mikroben, Paragrafen, Flüsse usw. in Erscheinung treten.

Diese Orientierung am Objekt zeigt sich nach Ansicht der Autorin auch in der heutigen Architekturpraxis (*architecture in the making*), die weniger auf der Figur des Stararchitekten als Mastermind beruht, sondern sich vielmehr in entstehenden Modellen ablesen lässt. Dabei steht weder das Modell noch der Modellbauer im Vordergrund. Vielmehr findet eine aktive und wechselseitige Vermittlung (*mediation*) zwischen dem Objekt und dem Subjekt statt, die von unausweichlichen individuellen Bindungen (*attachments*) gesteuert wird. Besonders augenscheinlich zeigt dies Albena Yanelva's Experiment zusammen mit dem der Moderne kritisch gegenüberstehenden Architekten Rem Koolhaas, einen Monat lang ohne Styropormodelle zu arbeiten. Die MitarbeiterInnen von OMA waren nicht in der Lage, in ihrer täglichen architektonischen Arbeit auf dieses Medium zu verzichten, sodass das Experiment frühzeitig abgebrochen werden musste.

In einem weiteren Kapitel wird Latour's Konzept der Kosmopolitik (*cosmo-politics*) besprochen, das angesichts der ökologischen Krise eine neue Bedeutung erhält. Er fordert uns auf, die modernistische Vorstellung einer passiven und kontrollierbaren Natur aufzugeben und sie stattdessen durch lokale AkteurInnen mit spezifischem Wissen gemeinsam zu gestalten. In Latours Kunstfigur „Gaia" offenbart sich Natur als aktiv, schutzbedürftig, ortsansässig und notfalls auch feindlich dem Menschen gegenüber. Hier zeigt sich eine objektorientierte Politik, indem Menschen über gemeinsame Belange (*matters of concern*) zusammenfinden. Die Themen werden in Bezug auf die nicht-menschliche (*non-human*) Welt erörtert und diese anschließend aktiv von innen heraus gestaltet. Die Herausforderung in Latour's „neuem Klimaregime" (*new climatic regime*) liegt für Albena Yaneva in der Darstellung der natürlichen und klimatischen Prozesse. Sie argumentiert, dass gerade ArchitektInnen und DesignerInnen in der Lage sind, mit visuellen Mitteln die Eingriffe in die Natur bzw. in Gaia zu veranschaulichen und damit ein Bewusstsein für deren Ausmaß und die Dringlichkeit eines pro-aktiven Vorgehens zu schaffen.

Die Philosophie von Latour kann uns helfen, über die heutige Welt nachzudenken und bietet einen konzeptionellen Rahmen in Theorie und Praxis, um sich mit den Gegebenheiten von Architektur und Design auseinanderzusetzen. Der bodenständige (*down-to-earth*) Ansatz Latours zeigt sich in einer pragmatischen und objektorientierten Herangehensweise an die Soziologie und bietet Werkzeuge, um unsere Gesellschaft im Zeitalter des Anthropozäns neu zu überdenken. „Latour for Architects" skizziert dabei neue Konzepte and Methoden in der Architektur- und Stadtforschung, wie beispielsweise die Kartierung (*mapping*) von Architekturkontroversen oder die Anwendung der Akteur-Netzwerk-Theorie. Diese ermöglichen es, die Vielfalt des urbanen Lebens nachzuzeichnen und zu messen, ohne dass das Spezifische durch das Allgemeine oder das Konkrete durch das Abstrakte ersetzt wird. Dabei entsteht weniger eine neue Form von Architektur, sondern vielmehr eine neue Sichtweise auf sie. ArchitektInnen interagieren in einem hybriden Netzwerk und wachsen über ihre klassische Rolle als EntwerferInnen hinaus. Diese Fähigkeit wird nicht zuletzt im Kontext der Klimakrise von zentraler Bedeutung für die Zukunft der Architekturpraxis sein.

Johannes Bernsteiner

Learning from Latour: Where Architecture Meets Sociology

"There is always a little bit of philosophy in architecture and a lot of architecture in philosophy"—this quote by Bruno Latour prefaces the Routledge publication *Latour for Architects*, written by Albena Yaneva, professor of architectural theory at the University of Manchester and a former doctoral student of Latour's. The book is divided into nine chapters, which shed light on the sociologist's different ideas and methodological approaches, presenting Latour's work through concrete examples that are related to architecture and urban research. More than a dozen illustrations in the volume are based on classic diagrams and figures from Latour's key works, now reinterpreted for a new design audience. The publication was released as open access and is available for download.

When searching for innovative design ideas and a critical framework for their design practice, architects often take recourse to philosophical currents. Bruno Latour (1947–2022), whom *The Guardian* has called "one of the most influential thinkers of our age," offers a new and pragmatic perspective on the analysis of social phenomena. The French sociologist and professor emeritus at the university Sciences Po in Paris is primarily known for his actor-network theory (ANT) and for a series of books, including *We Have Never Been Modern* (1991), *Laboratory Life* (1979), and *Science in Action* (1987).

In the professional world, Bruno Latour is considered fascinating and controversial at the very same time. He was prone to criticize not only modernity's tendency to clearly separate nature/science on the one hand and culture/society on the other, but he also argued that such divisions never actually took place in practice, and that we were thus never truly "modern." At the same time, he felt that science has never been inherently objective, instead being dependent on social, political, and religious factors that call its objectivity into question. For example, science is funded by governments whose products are sold on the market, a fact that in turn raises ethical concerns. Hence, we find ourselves in a world of hybrids that challenge the foundations of modernism.

Citing an example relevant to architects, Albena Yaneva presents the reconstruction of the Birmingham train station, which boasts a facade that had to be totally redesigned during the building process due to the problem of sun-related glare. The author demonstrates the influence that the necessary technical solutions had on the architectural language of the building, which in turn redefined the iconography of Birmingham and meant that political promises could not be kept. Especially in the disciplinary field of architecture it became apparent how strongly design requirements, the environment, politics, the economy, technology, ecology, and legal conditions are interwoven. Architects become hybrid creatures and are themselves engaged in a hybrid network, one in which, according to Latour, constant translation is needed.

Parallel to this, Latour challenges a practice common since Pierre Bourdieu, that of evaluating actions through the prism of society and thus utterly redefining the task of sociology. For example, the size, style, and shape of a particular building cannot be explained by a variety of social and political factors or values and beliefs. Instead, we operate in a hybrid network, where the purported duality of object and subject, and of nature and society, completely dissolves. In Latour's mind, the social is in constant motion, and in order to understand it, we must follow its actants and their specific concerns and technologies. Hence, the realities of life are actively constructed by interconnected actants, including the sociologists themselves who are striving to arrive at a definition.

This is the point at which Latour's actor-network theory comes into play, which completely overturns the idea of separating the objective and the subjective in favor of the concept of mediation. According to this theory, objects and technologies do not attest to a purely objective reality but instead are themselves formative for society. Taking place here is a shift from the world of matters of fact to the world of matters of concern. Latour cites the example of the spectacular failure of the Aramis personal rapid transit project or the special nature of the Berlin Key. Instead of reducing objects to their seemingly hidden social or political significance, he follows their inscribed function (program) and explores in this way the reciprocal relationships between humans and non-humans. The latter are active and vocal participants in social life and can make an appearance as tools, animals, technologies, microbes, clauses, rivers, and so forth.

The author feels that this orientation toward the object is likewise seen in today's architectural practice (architecture in the making), which, rather than being focused on the figure of the starchitect as mastermind, is actually evident in the models created. In the foreground here, however, is neither the model nor the model-maker. Instead, there is an active and reciprocal mediation between the object and the subject, one that is controlled by ineluctable individual attachments. This is made particularly apparent by Albena Yanelva's collaboration with Rem Koolhaas, an architect who is quite critical of modernism; it was a joint experiment that entailed working a full month without Styrofoam models. Since the collaborators at OMA were not able to do without this medium in their everyday architectural work, the experiment came to a premature end.

In another chapter, Latour's concept of cosmo-politics is discussed, and it attains new meaning in the face of the ecological crisis. He calls on us to abandon the modernist idea of nature being passive and controllable, suggesting that we instead shape it collaboratively through local actants who possess special knowledge. Latour's fictional character "Gaia" reveals nature as being active, in need of protection, locally focused, and, as need be, also hostile toward humans. Arising here is an object-oriented type of politics, where people come together through matters of concern. Topics are discussed in relation to the non-human world and then actively designed from the inside out. In Albena Yaneva's view, the challenge inherent to Latour's "new climatic regime" lies in the representation of natural and climatic processes. She argues that architects and designers are in a special position to harness visual means in order to illustrate interventions in nature or in Gaia, and thus to foster awareness for the related magnitude and the urgency of taking a proactive approach.

Latour's philosophical ideas can help us to contemplate today's world, offering a conceptual framework, in theory and practice, for discussing the reality of architecture and design. His down-to-earth attitude is reflected in a pragmatic and object-oriented approach to sociology and offers tools for rethinking our society in the age of the Anthropocene. Indeed, the volume *Latour for Architects* sketches new concepts and methods in research on architecture and urbanism, such as the mapping of architectural controversies or the application of actor-network theory. These new concepts and methods make it possible to trace and measure the diversity of urban life, yet without replacing the specific with the general, or the concrete with the abstract. Created in this way is not a new form of architecture, but rather a new way of looking at it. Architects interact in a hybrid network and grow above and beyond their traditional role as designers. This ability will be of pivotal importance for the future of architectural practice, most especially in the context of the environmental crisis.

Johannes Bernsteiner
Translation: Dawn Michelle d'Atri

Into the Clouds

Konrad Wachsmann's Television: Post-architectural Transmissions
Mark Wigley
Sternberg Press, 2020
Englisch, 400 Seiten

Das Netzfieber hat uns wieder mal erfasst – und das zu Recht. Mark Wigleys Bericht über Konrad Wachsmann bietet eine facettenreiche Geschichte über Architektur, Medien und darüber, wie sich utopische Ambitionen hinsichtlich der Auflösung der Architektur selbst in den Jahrzehnten nach dem Zweiten Weltkrieg über internationale Netzwerke verbreiteten. *Konrad Wachsmann's Television: Post-architectural Transmissions* erschien 2020 als elfter Band der von Nikolaus Hirsch und Markus Miessen herausgegebenen Reihe Critical Spatial Practice. Die Reihe insgesamt ist als Testgelände für Ideen rund um die Fachdisziplin Architektur gedacht, und die Bandbreite der Themen reicht von der Energiepolitik über Landrechte der indigenen Bevölkerung bis zu einer neuen Untersuchung der Arbeit und des Lebens einzelner ArchitektInnen aus dem 20. Jahrhundert. Wigleys Buch zählt offenkundig zur letztgenannten Kategorie. Doch die zahlreichen Ebenen des Buches gehen über Konrad Wachsmann als Individuum hinaus. Denn während das Buch auf einer Ebene tatsächlich ein gründlich recherchierte intellektuelle Geschichte des nomadenhaften, in Deutschland geborenen Architekten ist, handelt es sich auf einer anderen dabei um eine Untersuchung der, konzeptionellen wie realen, Beziehungen zwischen Gebäuden und televisuellem Raum und ein methodologisches Statement über das Verfassen transnationaler Geschichten. Netzwerke durchdringen das Werk, vom thematischen Inhalt bis zum verwendeten Archivmaterial. Und obwohl dieses Material viele in der Geschichtsschreibung der modernen Architektur bereits vertraute Gesichter beleuchtet (was die Frage aufwirft, warum gerade dieser Akteur und diese Netzwerke jetzt untersucht werden sollten), ist Wigleys Arbeit in einer zunehmend elektronisch geprägten Welt ein zeitgemäßer Hinweis für ArchitektInnen.

Das Buch selbst ist klein und erlaubt eine relativ schnelle Lektüre, die sich über vierhundert Seiten im Taschenformat erstreckt. Wigley, der ein halbes Jahr lang an der Akademie der Künste in Berlin recherchierte und Fakten zusammentrug, hat das Buch in zwölf prägnante Kapitel gegliedert. Jedes Kapitel ist um eines von Wachsmanns Projekten herum aufgebaut, sei es für ein Gebäude oder ein anderes Medium, und reich mit Archivbildern illustriert; manche Projekte erstrecken sich über mehrere Kapitel. Gemeinsam bieten sie eine mehr oder weniger chronologische Darstellung von Wachsmanns Leben und Werk. Wigley beginnt mit den architektonischen Details, für die Wachsmann bekannt ist. Die ersten drei Kapitel schildern die Aufmerksamkeit des Architekten für die materielle Realisierung der Architektur in ihren Gelenken (und durch diese), einschließlich seiner Entwürfe für ein standardisiertes Gelenk, die zur Grundlage des Space Frame werden sollten. Das bekannteste Beispiel ist Wachsmanns umfassendes Air Force Hangar-Projekt für das U.S.-amerikanische Militär in den frühen 1950er Jahren, in dem Wachsmann den Raumrahmen erstmals konzipierte und in dem Wände (und wohl auch Menschen) in einer massiv dimensionierten, scheinbar schwebenden horizontalen Struktur verschwanden. Wie die meisten von Wachsmanns Projekten wurde der Hangar nie gebaut. Dennoch lebte er in verschiedenen Medien weiter, indem er in Zeichnungen, Modellen, Ausstellungen und in Wachsmanns eigenen Vorträgen die Runde machte. Kapitel 4 widmet sich diesem Nachleben und der Verbreitung von Wachsmanns Ideen durch Publikationen und Seminarveranstaltungen in den 1950er-Jahren, von Deutschland über Japan bis nach Israel. Das Kapitel unterstreicht auch Wachsmanns zunehmend radikalere Auffassung von Architektur: Um sich an eine neue elektronische Welt anzupassen – eine Welt, die durch Technologien wie Radio, Fernsehen und Flugzeuge bereits erheblich verändert wurde –, musste die Architektur selbst demontiert und neu gestaltet werden. Wigley schildert den Einfluss Wachsmanns auf eine Generation radikaler ArchitektInnen, die in den 1960er Jahren zu Ruhm gelangten, darunter die Metabolisten in Japan und Archigram im Vereinigten Königreich sowie die feinkörnigen Mechanismen, mittels derer dieser Einfluss weitergegeben wurde.

Die folgenden Kapitel thematisieren andere im Lauf der Jahre, auf Papier, als Modelle und auf Bildschirmen, umgesetzte Projekte. Wachsmanns rätselhafte perspektivische Zeichnung eines sich windenden Netzes umfasst drei dieser Kapitel; die Zeichnung, die Wigley als den „extremsten Versuch des Architekten beschreibt, die kaum greifbare Post-Architektur elektronischer Netze zu erfassen“ (169), entstand 1951 und begleitete, oder „verfolgte“, Wachsmann für den Rest seiner Laufbahn. Der Platz, den sie im Buch einnimmt, legt nahe, dass die Zeichnung und ihre mehrdeutige Raumauffassung auch Wigley verfolgt haben. Die ausführliche Untersuchung des Lebens der Zeichnung in wechselnden Medien über drei Jahrzehnte hinweg, veranschaulicht Wachsmanns eigene Bemühungen, sich ständig mit seinen eigenen Experimenten auseinanderzusetzen, sowie seine eigenen wechselnden Bemühungen, zu verstehen, zu erklären und zu vermitteln, was elektronischer Raum im 20. Jahrhundert sein könnte.

Kapitel 8 untersucht Modelle der Teamarbeit, die in den 1960er Jahren an der University of Southern California entwickelt wurden, einschließlich Wachsmanns Ambitionen in Bezug auf antihierarchischen Wissensaustausch innerhalb von und zwischen Institutionen. Die Kapitel 9 und 10 indes befassen sich mit Wachsmanns nicht realisiertem Projekt für das California City Civic Center, das von 1965 entworfen wurde. Sowohl die Teamwork-Modelle als auch das Civic Center veranschaulichen den „soziotechnischen Optimismus“ (310) von Wachsmanns Arbeit: Der überaus offene, horizontale Raum des Civic Centers wurde durch eine 111 Fuß (etwa 33,8 Meter) hohe Fernsehantenne in der Mitte des Gebäudes ausgeglichen, die das Engagement der Bürger steigern sollte, indem sie die Aktivitäten des Stadtrats direkt an lokale Fernsehgeräte übertrug. Die letzten beiden Kapitel betreffen Wachsmanns Akzeptanz des Fernsehens als wahres Medium des „Post-Architekten“, da Wachsmann selbst in der Hauptsendezeit im Fernsehen auftrat und in den frühen 1970er Jahren einen detaillierten Plan für seine eigene Fernsehsendung über Gebäude entwarf. Das von Wachsmann in einem vierhundertseitigen Manuskript ausgearbeitete Programm sollte sowohl Bildungseinrichtungen als auch die Öffentlichkeit über Fernsehnetzwerke miteinander verbinden. Außerdem sollte es durch Videokassetten und Dias verbreitet werden. Hier äußert sich Wigley am deutlichsten zur Rolle des Fernsehens für Wachsmann: Am Ende seiner Karriere war „das Fernsehen zu Wachsmanns eindeutigem Paradigma der Post-Architektur geworden“ (363), zu einem Versprechen einer friedlichen, egalitären Gesellschaft, in der Informationen frei durch elektronische Netzwerke fließen. Das Fernsehen ersetzte somit den nebulösen und doch materiell begrenzten Raumrahmen und implizierte zugleich eine televisuelle Utopie, eine „einzige transnationale globale Gesellschaft, die überall durch ‚universelle Fragen‘ angesprochen werden könnte“ (351).

Wachsmanns Fernsehen signalisiert für Wigley die Ankunft einer möglichen techno-utopischen Zukunft, in der Gebäude lediglich Knotenpunkte im elektronischen Raum sind. Wigley begreift das Fernsehen also als das zentrale Element in Wachsmanns gesamtem Werk, auch wenn es die diesem zugrunde liegende Idee ist, wie eine Technologie die menschliche Umwelt verändern kann, auch ohne dass die Menschen sich dessen bewusst sind, auf die er am Ende aufmerksam macht. Der Geist des Medientheoretikers Marshall McLuhan, der nie explizit genannt wird, aber in Diskussionen über unsichtbare Umwelten, Medien als Botschaften und Anti-Architektur immer wieder erwähnt wird, schwebt über diesem Buch. Der Verweis bleibt implizit (vielleicht aufgrund der problematischeren Aspekte von McLuhans Werk), äußert sich aber dennoch zur Zirkulation von Ideen in den Netzwerken der Nachkriegszeit. *Konrad Wachsmann's Television* baut auf Wigleys Untersuchung eben dieser Netzwerke in seinem Artikel „Network Fever“ auf, der 2001 in *Grey Room* veröffentlicht wurde. In diesem Artikel war Wachsmann einer von vielen, die von der Begeisterung von einer zunehmend vernetzten, elektronischen Welt erfasst wurden, während McLuhan, Buckminster Fuller, Jaqueline Tyrwhitt und Constantinos Doxiadis sich die Hauptrollen teilten. In dem Buch konzentriert sich das Narrativ auf eine Figur: Wachsmann. Dennoch vermitteln die jedem Kapitel vorangestellten Archivbilder und die in den Endnoten zitierten Korrespondenzen eine Ehrfurcht vor den Nachkriegsnetzwerken, in denen sich Wachsmann bewegte. Sowohl die Bilder als auch die Korrespondenz zeigen enge Verbindungen zu bekannten Namen - Walter Gropius, Buckminster Fuller, Mies - und wie Wachsmann selbst durch diese Interaktionen aufgebaut wurde. Diese Rückkehr zu einer architektonischen Elite der üblichen Verdächtigen ist nicht immer erhellend. Wigley geht jedoch ausführlich auf die Teams von Studierenden ein, die für und mit Wachsmann arbeiteten und zu seinem Denken beitrugen, aber auch auf Wachsmanns eigenen festen Glauben an Kooperation. Aus diesem Grund nennt Wigley den Architekten im gesamten Buch nur „Wachsmann“ und vermeidet jedwelche Personalpronomen, um den Architekten als ein Ideenkollektiv und nicht als einzelnen Autor darzustellen, der für sein Genie gefeiert wird. Das gelingt nur teilweise, sprich es bleibt ein hagiografisches Element, doch die Betonung der Zusammenarbeit ist deutlich.

Konrad Wachsmann's Television ist ein kleines, gut lesbares, äußerst informatives Buch, in dem jede Endnote und Bildunterschrift Aufmerksamkeit verdient. Die Kombination von Material aus Wachsmanns persönlichem Archiv mit publiziertem Material bildet seine Interaktionen auf einer feinkörnigen Ebene ab und hebt die zwischenmenschlichen und institutionellen Netzwerke hervor, in denen Wachsmann tätig war. Das Buch handelt vordergründig von einem Medium – dem Fernsehen – und der damit verbundenen Forderung nach einer Entmaterialisierung der Architektur, zeigt aber zugleich, wie Ideen rund um dieses Medium in anderen materiellen Formen (in Ausstellungen, Zeitschriften, Büchern, Vorträgen, Modellen) verbreitet wurden und über welche Kanäle diese Ideen international zirkulierten. Das Immaterielle und das Materielle prallen im gesamten Buch aufeinander: Selbst Wachsmanns letztes Projekt für eine elektronisch übertragene Fernsehserie endet als gedrucktes Manuskript. Wigleys abschließendes Argument, dass Architekten die Rolle elektronischer Informationsnetzwerke bei der Strukturierung der gebauten Umwelt auch weiterhin weitgehend ignorieren, ist wichtig. Das Buch leistet einen wichtigen Beitrag, indem es Konrad Wachsmanns Engagement für eben diese Themen in ebenso knapper wie detaillierter Form schildert.

Katie Filek
Übersetzung: Nikolaus G. Schneider

Into the Clouds

Network fever is upon us once again—and rightly so. Mark Wigley's account of Konrad Wachsmann offers a layered story of architecture, media, and how utopian ambitions for the dissolution of architecture itself traveled across international networks in the decades following World War II. *Konrad Wachsmann's Television: Post-architectural Transmissions* was published in 2020 by the Sternberg Press as the eleventh volume in the Critical Spatial Practice series, edited by Nikolaus Hirsch and Markus Miessen. The series as a whole is intended as testing ground for ideas around the discipline of architecture, with topics ranging from energy politics to Indigenous land rights to re-examining the work and lives of individual architects from the twentieth century. Wigley's book falls, evidently, into the latter category. Yet the book's many layers take it beyond Konrad Wachsmann as an individual: while on one level the book is indeed a deeply researched intellectual history of the nomadic German-born architect, on another it is both an examination of relationships—conceptual and real—between buildings and televisual space, and a methodological statement on the writing of transnational histories. Networks pervade the work, from thematic content to archival material employed. And while that same material highlights many faces already familiar in the historiography of modern architecture (prompting the question, why examine this particular actor and these particular networks, now?), Wigley's work is nonetheless a timely note to architects, in an increasingly electronic world.

The book itself is small, a relatively quick read spread across four hundred pocket-sized pages. Researched and assembled by Wigley over half a year at the Akademie der Künste in Berlin, the book is organized into twelve concise chapters. Each chapter is constructed around a Wachsmann project, whether for a building or a different medium, and richly illustrated with archival images; certain projects extend over several chapters. Together they offer a roughly chronological account of Wachsmann's life and work. Wigley begins with the architectural details for which Wachsmann is well known: the opening three chapters lay out the architect's attention to the materialization of architecture in (and through) its joints, including his designs for a standardized joint that would become the basis of the space frame. The noted example is Wachsmann's Air Force Hangar project for the United States military in the early 1950s, an expansive project in which Wachsmann first conceptualized the space frame and in which walls (and arguably humans) disappeared within a massively scaled, seemingly floating horizontal structure. Like most of Wachsmann's projects, the hangar was never built. Yet it continued its life in various media, circulating in drawings, models, exhibitions, and in Wachsmann's own lectures. Chapter 4 pays attention to this afterlife and to the travel of Wachsmann's ideas through publications and seminar workshops in the 1950s, from Germany to Japan to Israel. The chapter equally underlines Wachsmann's increasingly radical notion of architecture: that in order to adapt to a new electronic world—a world already significantly altered by technologies such as the radio, television, and airplanes—architecture itself had to be dismantled, and reimagined. Wigley thus highlights Wachsmann's influence on a generation of radical architects about to rise to fame in the 1960s, including the Metabolists in Japan and Archigram in the United Kingdom, alongside the fine-grained mechanisms through which this influence was transmitted.

The subsequent chapters address other projects implemented over the years—on paper, as models, and on screens. Wachsmann's enigmatic perspective drawing of a twisting net occupies three of those chapters: the drawing, which Wigley describes as the architect's "most extreme attempt to capture the barely tangible post-architecture of electronic nets," (169), was created in 1951 and accompanied—or "haunted"—Wachsmann for the rest of his career. The space it occupies in the book suggests the drawing and its ambiguous spatial invocation have haunted Wigley as well. The lengthy examination of the drawing's life in shifting media over three decades demonstrates Wachsmann's own efforts to continually grapple with his own experiments, and his own shifting efforts to understand, explain, and convey what electronic space might be in the twentieth century.

Chapter 8 examines models of teamwork developed at the University of Southern California in the 1960s, including Wachsmann's ambitions for anti-hierarchical knowledge exchange within and between institutions. Chapters 9 and 10 meanwhile focus on Wachsmann's unrealized project for the California City Civic Center, designed from 1965–1972. Both the teamwork models and Civic Center demonstrate the "socio-techno-optimism" (310) of Wachsmann's work: the exceedingly open, horizontal space of the Civic Center was balanced by a 111-foot-tall TV antenna at the building's center, aiming to increase citizen engagement by broadcasting city council activity directly to local televisions. The final two chapters address Wachsmann's embrace of television as the "post-architect's" true medium, as Wachsmann himself appeared on prime-time television and created a detailed plan for his own television program on buildings in the early 1970s. Elaborated by Wachsmann in a four-hundred-page manuscript, the latter would connect both educational institutions and the public through televisual networks. It would continue to circulate through video cassettes and slides. Here Wigley is most explicit about the role of television for Wachsmann: by the end of his career, "television had become Wachsmann's unambiguous paradigm of post-architecture" (363), a promise of a peaceful egalitarian society in which information flowed freely through electronic networks. Television thus replaced the nebulous yet materially bounded space frame to imply a televisual utopia, a "single transnational global society that could be addressed everywhere by 'universal questions'" (351).

Wachsmann's television, for Wigley, signals the arrival of possible techno-utopian futures in which buildings are merely nodes within electronic space. Wigley thus positions the television as central to all of Wachsmann's work, although it is the underlying idea—how a technology can transform human environments, even without human awareness—that he calls attention to in the end. The ghost of media theorist Marshall McLuhan hovers over the book, never explicitly named yet referenced through discussions of invisible environments, media as messages, and anti-architecture. The reference remains implicit (perhaps due to the more problematic aspects of McLuhan's work), yet nonetheless speaks to the circulation of ideas in post-WWII networks. *Konrad Wachsmann's Television* builds on Wigley's examination of those same networks in his article "Network Fever," published in *Grey Room* in 2001. In that article, Wachsmann was one among a cast of many caught up in the excitement of an increasingly connected, electronic world, while leading roles were shared by McLuhan, Buckminster Fuller, Jaqueline Tyrwhitt, and Constantinos Doxiadis. In the book, the narrative centers on one character: Wachsmann. Yet the archival images that precede each chapter and correspondence quoted in the endnotes nonetheless convey a reverence for the postwar networks in which Wachsmann moved. Both images and correspondence highlight close connections to well-known names—Walter Gropius, Buckminster Fuller, Mies—and how Wachsmann himself was built up through these interactions. This return to an architectural elite of the usual suspects is not always enlightening. Wigley does however take care to detail the student teams who worked for and with Wachsmann and who contributed to his thinking, along with Wachsmann's own deep belief in cooperative work. To this same end, Wigley refers to the architect only as "Wachsmann" throughout the book, avoiding any personal pronouns in an effort to present the architect as a collective of ideas rather than an individual author being celebrated for his genius. This is only partly successful—there is still an element of hagiography—yet the emphasis on collaboration is clear.

Konrad Wachsmann's Television is a small, readable, yet densely packed book in which each endnote and image caption merits attention. The combination of material from Wachsmann's personal archive with published material maps his interactions at a granular level, emphasizing the interpersonal and institutional networks in which Wachsmann operated. The book is ostensibly about one medium—television—and a related call for architecture's dematerialization, yet at the same time reveals how ideas around that medium traveled in other material forms (in exhibitions, periodicals, books, lectures, models) and the channels through which those ideas circulated internationally. The immaterial and material collide throughout the book; even Wachsmann's final project for an electronically transmitted television series ends as a printed manuscript. Wigley's final argument—that is, that architects continue to largely ignore the role of electronic information networks in structuring the built environment—is important. The book makes a significant contribution through its mapping, in concise detail, of Konrad Wachsmann's dedication to those same themes.

Katie Filek

Eine Wolke mit Ankern

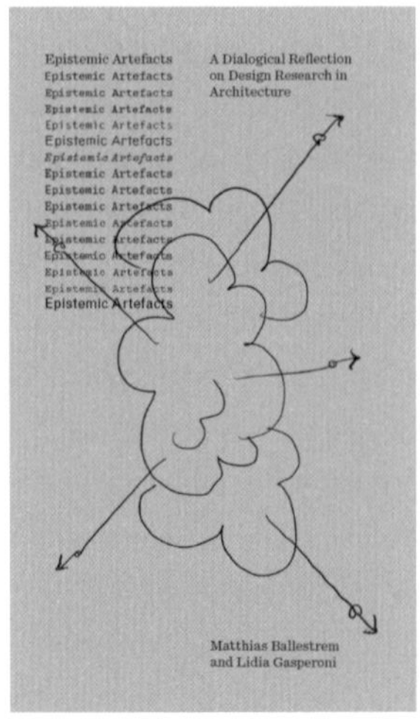

Epistemic Artefacts: A Dialogical Reflection on Design Research in Architecture
Matthias Ballestrem and Lidia Gasperoni
Baunach: AADR – Art Architecture Design Research, 2023
Englisch, 191 Seiten

Matthias Ballestrem, Leiter des „Bauhaus Earth Fellowship Program" in Potsdam und zuvor Professor für Architektur und Experimentelles Entwerfen an der HafenCity Universität Hamburg, und Lidia Gasperoni, wissenschaftliche Mitarbeiterin am Fachgebiet für Architekturtheorie der TU Berlin, beschäftigen sich als Forschende und Lehrende intensiv mit designbasierter Forschung in der Architektur und vor allem mit der Frage, wie entsprechende Doktoratsprogramme entwickelt werden können. Beide waren in diesem Zusammenhang am internationalen Programm CA^{2}RE+ im Rahmen der Erasmus+ Strategischen Partnerschaften sowie den CA^{2}RE-Konferenzen beteiligt. Ballestrem ist zudem Mitbegründer des *Programms Entwurfsbasierter Promotion* (PEP) an der TU Berlin, das darauf abzielt „Promotionen im Entwurf, auf der Basis von Entwurfsresultaten und mit dem Entwurf als Werkzeug zu fördern und dafür wissenschaftliche Verfahren und Bewertungskriterien anzubieten."[1]

1 www.pep.tu-berlin.de/bewerbung (Stand: 17. September 2023)

Gasperonis fachliche Schwerpunkte sind – neben der Architekturtheorie – Medientheorie und Ästhetik. 2022 fungierte sie als Herausgeberin des Buches *Experimental Diagrams in Architecture* von DOM Publishers.

Mit der Publikation *Epistemic Artefacts. A Dialogical Reflection on Design Research in Architecture*, die 2023 bei AADR erschienen ist, präsentieren Ballestrem und Gasperoni einen intensiven gedanklichen Austausch zum Thema der designbasierten Forschung, ausgehend von der Aufzeichnung eines Gesprächs, das im Mai 2021 geführt wurde. Auf Basis des Transkripts dieser Aufzeichnung entstand eine weiterführende schriftliche Korrespondenz, die den Kern der Publikation bildet. Dieser schlussendlich auf gut 60 Seiten abgedruckte Text wird nur durch kurze Überschriften strukturiert, die jeweils den Fokus der folgenden Passage vorwegnehmen.

Die gewählte Dialogform ergibt sich somit einerseits aus der Genese des Textes, entspricht andererseits aber auch dem Inhalt: Ballestrem und Gasperoni gehen davon aus, dass wesentliche Aspekte im Zusammenhang mit designbasierter Forschung bisher zu wenig diskutiert wurden. Namentlich interessiert sie die Rolle des architektonischen Artefakts als *epistemisches Objekt* und in weiterer Folge die Frage, wie das diesen *epistemischen Artefakten* eingeschriebene Wissen zugänglich gemacht werden kann. Im Dialog werden hier Übereinstimmungen und Unterschiede deutlich, vor allem aber die Vielschichtigkeit des Themas: Diskutiert wird das Verhältnis von Forschung *durch* Gestaltung und Forschung über Gestaltung genauso wie das Zusammenspiel des akademischen Bereichs mit der beruflichen Praxis von PlanerInnen. Die Vorstellung, was ein architektonisches Projekt in diesem Zusammenhang ausmacht, wird dabei zusehends nebulös, während sich andererseits dennoch deutlich Anknüpfungspunkte für den Diskurs abzeichnen, was Ballestrem zum treffenden Bild des architektonischen Projekts als „cloud with anchors“(S. 52) inspiriert. Eine Zeichnung dieser Metapher ziert auch das Cover des Buches.

Fokussiert wird im Zusammenhang mit diesen Überlegungen die Möglichkeit einer entwurfsbasierten Dissertation im Bereich der Architektur, illustriert anhand einiger Beispiele aus dem oben genannten *Programm Entwurfsbasierter Promotion*: Helga Blocksdorf versucht im Rahmen ihres Dissertationsprojekt *seismische Punkte* ihrer Entwürfe anhand von Modellen sichtbar zu machen. Marta Fernández Guardado entwickelte eine spezielle Form der perspektivischen Zeichnung, um die Relation von gebautem Raum, der Möblierung und der BenutzerInnen ganzheitlich zu erfassen und so die konkreten Lebensumstände und Alltagsrituale umfassend zu analysieren und in weiterer Folge als Grundlage für architektonische Entwürfe heranzuziehen. Hier stellt sich nicht nur die Frage nach konkreten wissenschaftlichen sowie künstlerischen Ansätzen und Methoden, sondern auch nach der Möglichkeit einer Bewertung: Soll schlussendlich die Qualität eines Entwurfs oder die Qualität der dem Entwurf innewohnenden Wissensinhalte beurteilt werden oder die Qualität der Vermittlung dieser Wissensinhalte?

Den Dialog als textlichen Kern des Buches, abgedruckt ausschließlich auf den ungeraden Seiten, reichern Ballestrem und Gasperoni auf den gegenüberliegenden, geraden Seiten mit Anmerkungen an, beigesteuert von einer illustren Runden von fünfzehn WissenschaftlerInnen und GestalterInnen aus dem Kontext der Auseinandersetzung mit designbasiertem Entwerfen. Zu Wort kommen hier TeilnehmerInnen des PEP ebenso wie arrivierte ForscherInnen und Hochschullehrende, vornehmlich aus dem europäischen Raum. Diese Kommentare bieten teilweise eine Ergänzung und Vertiefung der jeweiligen Passage von Ballestrems und Gasperonis Gespräch, teilweise beinhalten sie auch Einsprüche und Widersprüche. Aus dem Dialog wird so mitunter ein Stimmengewirr, das sich an den neuralgischen, *seismischen* Punkten des Textes verdichtet. Die Inspiration für dieses Format mit integrierten Kommentaren lieferte die Publikation *Architectures of Embodiment*, 2020 erschienen und herausgegeben vom Künstler/Forscher Alex Artega, der u.a. auch Kommentare zu Textstellen in *Epistemic Artefacts* beisteuert.

Dem Hauptteil des Buches, dem kommentierten Dialog, ist ein Nachwort angeschlossen, in dem Marcelo Stamm, Professor an der School of Architecture der Virginia Tech, eine Definition des Begriffs *epistemisches Artefakt* versucht und eine Typologie der verschiedenen Arten epistemischer Artefakte entwickelt. Der Bogen spannt sich hier von Werkzeugen, die Stamm als *instrumentelle epistemische Artefakte* („instrumental epistemicartefacts“, S. 139) definiert, bis hin zum *absoluten Artefakt* („absolute artefact“, S. 143), dem Kunstwerk als solchem. Wittgensteins Konzept der Familienähnlichkeit folgend beschreibt Stamm noch zahlreiche weitere Formen epistemischer Artefakte, die teilweise nur als theoretische Spekulation existieren, wie etwa *transformative, generative, translatorische, didaktische* und *anarchische epistemische Artefakte* („transformative, generative, translational, didactic, and anarchic epistemic artefacts“, S. 155). Das Nachwort wir so zur spekulativen Typologie aller denkbaren epistemischer Artefakte in Form eines *Familienalbums* mit teilweise sehr eigentümlichen und einigen *verschollenen* Verwandten. Dieser faszinierende Schlussteil ist aufgrund seines geringen Umfangs von knapp zwölf Seiten aber nur eine Skizze und würde sich die Weiterentwicklung zu einem umfangreicheren eigenständigen publizistischen Projekt verdienen. Im Kontext von *Epistemic Artefacts* wirkt er zudem als bloßes Anhängsel ohne wirklichen Anschluss an den Hauptteil, der eine systematische und definitorische Sicht auf den Begriff *epistemisches Artefakt* vermeidet.

Insgesamt gelingt Matthias Ballestrem und Lidia Gasperoni mit *Epistemic Artefacts* eine vielschichtige und facettenreiche Darstellung des Themas *designbasierte Forschung*, wobei sich das Wagnis der ungewöhnlichen Form eines mit Kommentaren versehenen Dialogs gelohnt hat: Das Buch als *epistemisches Artefakt* vermittelt sein Wissen nicht nur auf der inhaltlichen, sondern auch auf der formalen Ebene und bietet dabei zahlreiche Anknüpfungspunkte für weitere Diskussionen und Projekte. Es ist im besten Sinn selbst eine *Wolke mit Ankern*.

Stefan Fink

A Cloud with Anchors

Matthias Ballestrem, director of the Bauhaus Earth Fellowship Program in Potsdam and previously a professor of architecture and experimental design at the HafenCity University Hamburg, and Lidia Gasperoni, a research associate in the field of architectural theory at the Technical University of Berlin (TU Berlin), deal in a research and teaching capacity intensively with design-based research in architecture. A particular focus is placed on the question of how related doctoral programs can be developed. In this context, both were involved in the international CA²RE+ program as part of the Erasmus+ strategic partnerships and in the CA²RE conferences. Moreover, Ballestrem is the founder of the Program for Design-Based Doctorate (PEP) at the TU Berlin, which encourages students "to earn doctorates in design that are founded on design results and to use design as a tool, offering scientific procedures and evaluation criteria to this end."[1] Gasperoni's areas of expertise are—aside from architectural theory—media theory and aesthetics. In 2022, she served as editor of the book *Experimental Diagrams in Architecture* released by DOM Publishers.

With the book *Epistemic Artefacts: A Dialogical Reflection on Design Research in Architecture*, published in 2023 by AADR, Ballestrem and Gasperoni are presenting an intensive conceptual exchange on the topic of design-based research, taking a conversation conducted and taped in May 2021 as a point of departure. Extensive written correspondence evolved from the transcript of this recording, which forms the core of the publication. The main body of text ultimately covers about sixty pages and is lent structure only by short headers that anticipate the focus of the passage to follow.

The chosen dialogical form thus arises through the genesis of the text on the one hand, while also corresponding to the content on the other. Ballestrem and Gasperoni operate on the assumption that vital aspects related to design-based research have hitherto received too little attention in discourse. They are specifically interested in the role of the architectural artefact as an *epistemic object* and, further, in the question of how the knowledge inscribed in this *epistemic artefact* can be made accessible. The dialogue clearly reveals congruencies and distinctions, but most of all the intricate nature of the topic: discussed here is the relationship between research *through* design and research *on* design, as well as the synergy between academia and the professional activity of planners. Becoming increasing vague in the process is the notion of what, in this context, an architectural project actually is; at the same time, connecting discursive factors become evident, a fact that inspires Ballestrem to coin the phrase "cloud with anchors" (p. 52) for visualizing such an architectural project. A drawing of this metaphor graces the cover of the book.

The focus in connection with these considerations is on the possibility of writing a design-based dissertation in the field of architecture. Several examples are given from the aforementioned Program for Design-Based Doctorate. For example, Helga Blocksdorf attempts to make *seismic points* visible through model-building in the scope of her dissertation project. Marta Fernández Guardado has developed a special form of perspectival drawing in order to capture the relation between built space, furniture, and users in a holistic manner; this enables her to comprehensively analyze concrete living conditions and everyday rituals, subsequently using it as a basis for architectural designs. Here, the question arises not only of concrete scientific and artistic approaches and methods, but also of how feasible it is to make an evaluation: Ultimately, is it the quality of a design or the quality of the knowledge content inherent in the design that should be assessed, or rather the quality of how this knowledge content is communicated?

Ballestrem and Gasperoni augment the book's dialogue, which forms its textual core and is printed solely on odd-numbered pages, with annotations printed on the opposite, even-numbered pages. The latter material originates from an illustrious panel of fifteen scholars and designers who are involved with design-based activity. PEP participants are given a chance to speak here, as are established researchers and university faculty members, primarily from a European context. At times this commentary serves to supplement and lend depth to the respective passage in Ballestrem and Gasperoni's conversation, while at others it also contains objections and contradictions. The dialogue thus occasionally becomes a babel of voices, densifying at neuralgic, *seismic* places within the text. The inspiration for this format featuring integrated comments goes back to the publication *Architectures of Embodiment*, published in 2020 and edited by the artist and researcher Alex Artega, who is one of those adding comments to passages of text in *Epistemic Artefacts*.

The main body of the publication, the commentated dialogue, is complemented by an epilogue, in which Marcelo Stamm, a professor at Virginia Tech's School of Architecture, ventures a definition of the term *epistemic artefact* and develops a typology of the different kinds of epistemic artefacts. Here, the range spans from tools that Stamm defines as "instrumental epistemic artefacts" (p. 139) to the "absolute artefact" (p. 143), which would be an artwork as such. Following Wittgenstein's concept of family resemblance, Stamm describes numerous other forms of epistemic artefacts, which sometimes exist only as theoretical speculation,

1 www.pep.tu-berlin.de/bewerbung (accessed September 17, 2023)

for instance "transformative, generative, translational, didactic, and anarchic epistemic artefacts" (p.155). The epilogue thus becomes a speculative typology of all conceivable epistemic artefacts; it takes the form of a *family album* with relatives who are at times very peculiar or even *missing*. Yet this fascinating conclusion to the book is little more than a sketch due to its limited scope of only about twelve pages and could have easily deserved more attention in being developed as a comprehensive publication project in its own right. In the context of the book *Epistemic Artefacts*, it seems like a mere appendage, without any real connection to the main body of text, which avoids a systematic and definitional view of the term *epistemic artefact*.

Overall, in *Epistemic Artefacts* Matthias Ballestrem and Lidia Gasperoni succeed in delivering a multilayered and many-faceted presentation of the topic *design-based research*. Their gamble with employing an uncommon form of dialogue augmented by commentary has paid off: this book as an *epistemic artefact* conveys its knowledge not only through content but also through form, thus offering numerous points of reference for further discussion and other projects. The book itself is a *cloud with anchors* in the very best sense.

Stefan Fink
Translation: Dawn Michelle d'Atri

Ein architektonischer Wegweiser zum Umbau

Adaptive Reuse in Architecture: A Typological Index
Liliane Wong
Basel: Birkhäuser, 2023
Englisch, pp.224

Im Mai 2023 erschien im Birkhäuser Verlag *Adaptive Reuse in Architecture. A Typological Index* von Liliane Wong. Sie ist Professorin und Vorsitzende der Fakultät für Innenarchitektur an der Rhode Island School of Design. Das während der Corona-Pandemie geschriebene Buch untersucht Formen der adaptiven Um- und Nachnutzung von Gebäuden der letzten fünf Jahrzehnte und schlägt dafür eine Typologie vor, die sowohl die einstigen als auch die neu behausten Funktionen der besprochenen Bauten in einem tabellarischen Verzeichnis nachvollziehbar macht und sich als Klappenumschlag des Buchs auch auseinanderfalten und studieren lässt.

Das Konzept der Umnutzung von Gebäuden ist eine Konstante der Menschheitsgeschichte, dennoch beschränkt sich Wong auf den Zeitraum seit den 1970er Jahren um dadurch auf wesentliche gesellschaftliche Ereignisse und ihre baulichen Auswirkungen zu fokussieren. Der Begriff „adaptive reuse" wurde 1973 in das Merriam-Webster Dictionary aufgenommen, zur tatsächlich exponentiellen Zunahme von Adaptive-Reuse-Projekten kam es aber erst im 21. Jahrhundert. Wong veranschaulicht das in ihrem typologischen Ansatz der eine Liste von fünfzig Bauwerken in die größeren thematisch-funktionalen Zusammenhänge Energie, Produktion, Landwirtschaft, Verkehr, Religion und neues Kulturerbe gliedert. Diese typologische Ordnung nach dem ursprünglichen Nutzungszusammenhang sortiert die Projekte zugleich in die sechs Hauptkapitel des Buches. Diese werden jeweils mit einem Einführungstext von Wong eingeleitet, der einen Rückblick auf jeweilige technische und gesellschaftliche Umwälzungen seit den 1970er Jahren wirft. Dabei erklärt sie auch die nutzungstechnischen Aspekte dieser sechs funktionalen Betrachtungszusammenhänge und macht plausibel, warum bestimmte Bauwerke ab dem 21. Jahrhundert besonders viele Umnutzungen erfahren. So wurden etwa Gebäude aus den Bereichen der Landwirtschaft, der Religion oder der Produktion altersbedingt oder durch Paradigmenwechsel obsolet oder sie konnten aufgrund der rasanten technologischen Entwicklung nicht entsprechend angepasst werden.
Im Verkehrssektor führten diese Fortschritte beispielsweise zu leerstehenden innerstädtischen Bahnhöfen und Gleisanlagen, da diese nicht an die längeren und effizienteren Züge angepasst werden konnten und somit attraktive, zentrumsnahe Flächen für Umnutzungen bereitstellten.

Faltet man die Klappenbroschüre des Buchs auseinander, findet man eine tabellarische Übersicht zu den Umbauprojekten im Buch, mit zweimal 25 Gebäude-Icons und Informationen zu Jahr, Planenden und Ort. Neben dieser Sortierung nach dem Nutzungszusammenhang und seiner Beziehung zum technologischen Wandel, spielt Wongs violette Umschlaggestaltung auch auf Daniel Bells Buch *The Coming of Post-Industrial Society: A Venture in Social Forecasting* (1973) an, auf den sich Wongs typologische Sortierung zum post-industriellen Umbau stützt. Hier werden auch die neuen Nutzungen der umgebauten Bauwerke tabellarisch markiert – manche auch mit Mehrfachnennung von: Kultur, Bildung,

Krankenhaus, Infrastruktur, Büro, Wohnen, Einzelhandel, Freizeit und Gedenkstätte. Unter den Projekten befinden sich vor allem vielfach und ausführlich publizierte Projekte bekannter Architekten wie das Caixa Forum (Madrid), La Fábrica (Sant Just Desverns), Eremitani Civic Museum (Padua) oder das TWA Hotel (New York). Neben diesen prominenten Projekten helfen ein Rückblick und ein Ausblick sowie die jeweiligen kapitelzugehörigen Essays ein Verständnis für die Projektsammlung zu entwickeln und machen den Zusammenhang aus konkreter Auswahl und historischen Ereignissen plausibel, auf den die Umbauten jeweils reagierten. Jedes der sechs Kapitel wird durch ein Diagramm eingeleitet, welches ein für die Umnutzung der Typologien relevantes Phänomen in Abhängigkeit der Zeit darstellt und den Zeitpunkt des Umbaus der jeweiligen Projekte markiert. Hier werden Hypothesen über die Beziehungen zwischen dem Weltgeschehen und der gebauten Umwelt aufgestellt: So wird beispielsweise die Art der Energieerzeugung mit Energieträgen wie Erdöl, Kohle oder Gas (1950-2025) mit dem Oregon Museum of Science (Portland) oder dem Wiener Gasometer (Wien) in Verbindung gebracht oder auch der Umbau von Bauwerken wie dem Museé d'Orsay (Paris) mit der Entwicklung höherer Betriebsgeschwindigkeiten der wichtigsten Verkehrsträger (1750–2020) verknüpft. Darauffolgende Essays erläutern die jeweiligen geschichtlichen Hintergründe und Aspekte des sozialen, kulturellen und geopolitischen Kontextes. So werden im Kapitel Religion die gesellschaftlichen Entwicklungen und Ereignisse aufgeschlüsselt, die sie hier aber im Laufe der Jahrhunderte zu den damit verbundenen Umnutzungen und Anpassungen von Kirchen und Klöstern beschreibt. Im Kapitel Energie beschreibt Wong zugleich die Entwicklung des Umweltschutzes, der sich seit den 1970er Jahren fortlaufend breiter im öffentlichen Bewusstsein verankert und dabei den Bogen von Ressourcen und nicht nachwachsenden Rohstoffen bis hin zur aktuellen Ölkrise durch den russischen Angriff auf die Ukraine spannt. Diese Erläuterungen führen zu einer Liste thematisch relevanter Umbauprojekte, in der weit mehr Beispiele aufgeführt sind als die im Buch näher erläuterten Projekte. Diese werden nach ihrer ursprünglichen Nutzung sortiert und auf einer Doppelseite mit Schwarz-Weiß-Axonometrie oder entsprechendem Schnitt sowie Gebäudedaten, Text und Foto genauer illustriert. Das Buch schließt mit einem ausführlichen Anhang, sodass die Liste der Projekte noch einmal mit Literaturhinweisen zu jedem Kapitel, sowie einer alphabetischen Liste aller im Buch erwähnten Projekte ergänzt wird. Diese umfangreichen Informationen schließen Wongs Diskurs ab und sollen dem Leser Anregungen und Hinweise für eigene Recherchen geben.

Das Buch schlüsselt *Adaptive Reuse* im Kontext der exponentiellen Zunahme von Umnutzungsprojekten im 21. Jahrhundert nachvollziehbar und umfassend auf. Es betont dabei auch den kritischen Hinweis, Umnutzungsprojekte nicht losgelöst von ihrem zeitgeschichtlichen Kontext zu betrachten und die nun bestehende Nutzung als Ausgangspunkt zu nehmen, um deren Entwicklung mit den gesellschaftlichen, ökonomischen, technischen und nicht zuletzt politischen Hintergründen und Visionen zu verknüpfen. Allerdings wird dieser umfassende Zusammenhang nicht in allen Teilen des Buches deutlich, da es zwischen den Essays und den 50 Projekten keine direkten Verknüpfungen gibt. Auch sind nur wenige „unbekanntere" Bauten unter den fünfzig Projekten – etwa das bemerkenswerte Rosa Parks House Project (Berlin/Providence/Neapel) oder die Fahrradstation Süd am Hauptbahnhof Karlsruhe. Diese ergänzen aber die Hochglanzprojekte um Wongs Argumentation für ein erweitertes Verständnis der adaptiven Umnutzung zu verdeutlichen. Dennoch stellt sich eine gewisse Diskrepanz zwischen den textlich umfassenden Erläuterungen und der sehr knappen grafischen Dokumentationen der fünfzig Projekte ein. Die Umnutzung wird nur durch eine schwarze schematische Einfärbung in den Piktogrammen dargestellt und mit einem Foto des Ist-Zustands dokumentiert. Diese relativ geringe zeichnerische Information überrascht im Verhältnis zu den ausführlichen Aufsätzen doch. Auch wenn der Buchtitel nur einen „typologischen Index" verspricht – mehrfache Umbauten oder Umnutzungen werden damit grundsätzlich ausgeschlossen, da sie grafisch nicht ins gewählte Darstellungsschema integrierbar sind und daher jedes Umbauprojekt auf einen extrem vereinfachten Vorher-Nachher-Stand reduziert. Im Verhältnis zum sonstigen Umfang und zur Informationsdichte fallen diese Kritikpunkte an den Zeichnungen vielleicht weniger ins Gewicht, da das Buch dennoch einen ebenso beeindruckenden wie hochaktuellen Überblick über Um- und Nachnutzungsprojekten des letzten halben Jahrhunderts gibt und diese nicht nur technisch, sondern eben auch kulturell und zeitgeschichtlich aufzuschlüsseln vermag. Ein besonderes Potential der künftigen Entwicklung von adaptiven Umnutzungen sieht Wong in der Entstehung einer neuen Form des „New Heritage", welche auf der in den 1970er Jahren vorgenommenen Neubewertungen von kulturellem baulichem Erbe beruht. Dabei legt sie großen Wert dieses neue Erbe nicht unabhängig von ihrem gebauten Kontext zu lesen und stellt mit der vorgenommenen Projektauswahl die vielseitigen Möglichkeiten und thematische Vielschichtigkeit von *Adaptive Reuse* im 21. Jahrhundert dar.

Liliane Wong verknüpft die zentrale architektonische Zukunftsaufgabe „Adaptive Reuse" mit ebenso vielfältigen Nutzungszusammenhängen, wie sie dabei auch kulturelle, soziale, technische und mediale Einflüsse auf diesen Themenkreis nachvollziehbar macht. Innerhalb dieses Beziehungsfelds können wir als Architektinnen und Architekten Verantwortung übernehmen, durchaus optimistisch und undogmatisch: „With the secure knowledge that adaptive reuse has served different purposes over thousands of years, foresight that includes reuse is the way forward." (S. 237)

Maike Gold

An Architectural Guide to Adaptive Reuse

In May 2023, the book *Adaptive Reuse in Architecture: A Typological Index* by Liliane Wong was published by Birkhäuser Verlag. Wong is a professor and the chair of the Department of Interior Architecture at the Rhode Island School of Design. Written during the coronavirus pandemic, the volume examines forms of the adaptive reuse and continued use of buildings over the last five decades. To this end, she is the first to introduce a typology that gives a good overview (in table form) of both the former and the new rehoused functions of the discussed buildings, which can even be unfolded and studied as a flap cover of the book.

The idea of reusing buildings has been a constant throughout human history, yet Wong limits her focus to the last fifty years in order to better explore special societal events and the effects they have had on architecture. Though the term "adaptive reuse" was accepted into Merriam-Webster's Dictionary in 1973, the actual exponential increase in adaptive reuse projects was not seen until the twenty-first century. Wong illustrates this through a typological approach that divides up a list of fifty architectural structures into the usage contexts of energy, manufacturing, agriculture, transportation, religion, and new cultural heritage. This typological order according to the original context of use serves to arrange the projects into the six main chapters of the book. Introducing each chapter is a text by Wong that looks back on the technical and social revolutions playing out from the 1970s to the present day. She also explains the usage-related aspects of the six functional featured contexts, making plausible why certain architectural structures are subjected to reuse particularly often in the twenty-first century. For example, buildings from the areas of agriculture, religion, or manufacturing have become obsolete due to age or paradigm shifts, or it has proven impossible to adapt them to the rapid technological development accordingly. In the transportation sector, such advancements have for instance led to vacant inner-city train stations and railway tracks, because they could not be adapted to the longer, more efficient trains and thus have provided attractive areas for reuse close to the city center.

Unfolding the book's cover flaps, we find a tabular overview of the rebuilding projects featured in the volume, with each flap presenting twenty-five building icons accompanied by information about the respective year, planners, and site. Besides this arrangement according to context of use and its relationship to technological change, Wong's purple cover design alludes to Daniel Bell's *The Coming of Post-Industrial Society: A Venture in Social Forecasting* (1973), on which Wong's typological sorting of postindustrial rebuilding is based. The new utilizations of the converted buildings are spotlighted in the table, some even with multiple mentions of their cultural, educational, hospital, infrastructural, office, residential, retail, leisure, and memorial use. Among the fifty projects are, notably, widely and extensively publicized ones by well-known architects, such as the Caixa Forum (Madrid), La Fábrica (Sant Just Desvern), Eremitani Civic Museum (Padua), and the TWA Hotel (New York). Complementing these prominent projects are chapters titled "Looking Back" and "Looking Ahead," along with the essays assigned to the various sections, thus helping to cultivate understanding for the collection of projects and to make plausible the connection between the concrete selection and the historical events to which each conversion was responding. Each of the six chapters is introduced by a diagram rendering visible a time-dependent phenomenon relevant to the reuse of the typologies, which thus flags the point in time each project was rebuilt. Hypotheses about how world events and the built environment were interrelated during the last fifty years are put forward here: for example, the type of energy production through energy carriers like petroleum, coal, or gas (1950–2025) is associated with the Oregon Museum of Science and Industry (Portland) or the Wiener Gasometer (Vienna); or the conversion of structures like the Museé d'Orsay (Paris) with the development of higher operating speeds for the most vital modes of transport (1750–2020). Further essays elucidate the respective historical backgrounds and the aspects related to social, cultural, and geopolitical context. Detailed here, for instance in the chapter about religion, are developments and events in society, such as describing the related reuse and adaptation of churches and monasteries over the centuries. In the chapter on energy, Wong simultaneously touches on the development of environmental protection, which has been steadily affecting public consciousness since the 1970s, spanning from resources and nonrenewable raw materials to the current oil crisis caused by the Russian attack on Ukraine. These remarks lead to a list of thematically relevant rebuilding projects that contains many more examples than the projects detailed more closely in the book. Sorted according to their original use, the projects in the book are illustrated more thoroughly on a double-page spread featuring black-and-white axonometric renderings or the specific section, along with building data, text, and photos. The volume concludes with a extensive appendix, so that the list of projects is supplemented once again by literary references to each chapter, as well as by an alphabetical list of all projects mentioned in the book. This comprehensive information rounds off Wong's discourse and is meant to give readers suggestions and ideas for their own research.

The book comprehensibly and comprehensively breaks down adaptive reuse in face of the exponential increase of reuse projects in the twenty-first century. In the process, it emphasizes the critical point that reuse projects cannot be viewed in isolation from their contemporary-historical context, and that the existing use should be taken as a point of departure for linking their development with social, economic, and technical backgrounds and visions—and, not least, with political ones. However, this wide-ranging connection is not apparent in all parts of the book, for there are no direct links between the essays and the fifty projects. Also, there are but few "less famous" buildings among the projects—two such examples are the remarkable Rosa Parks House Project (in Berlin, Germany, Providence, Rhode Island, USA, and Naples, Italy) and the Fahrradstation Süd (Bicycle Station South) at Karlsruhe's main train station in Germany. These examples serve to complement the high-gloss projects, so as to underscore Wong's argument for a broader understanding of adaptive reuse. Nonetheless, a certain discrepancy arises between the quite thorough textual explanations and the very concise graphic documentation of the fifty projects. Reuse is only rendered in the pictograms through black schematic coloration and documented with a photo of the current project state. This relatively minimal amount of graphic information is surprising when one considers how elaborate the essays are. Even if the book title promises only a "typological index," various rebuilding or reuse measures are actually fundamentally excluded because they do not lend themselves to being integrated into the chosen graphic presentation style, hence reducing every rebuilding project to an extremely simplified state of before and after. Considering the broad scope and high density of information in the book as a whole, such criticism of the drawings is perhaps rather insignificant. Indeed, the volume offers an impressive and highly topical overview of reuse and continued use projects of the last half century, and it is able to break these projects down in terms of not only technology but also culture and contemporary history. Wong sees particular potential for the future development of adaptive reuse in the emergence of a novel form of "new heritage," which is based on the reassessment of cultural built heritage pursued in the 1970s. The author deems it vital to avoid interpreting this new heritage independently of its built context; and she presents, through the projects selected, the multifaceted possibilities and complexity of adaptive reuse in the twenty-first century.

Liliane Wong links the main architectural task of the future, "adaptive reuse," with equally multilayered contexts of use, making transparent the cultural, social, technical, and mediatic influences on this topic. Within this field of relations, we as architects can assume responsibility in quite an optimistic and undogmatic way: "With the secure knowledge that adaptive reuse has served different purposes over thousands of years, foresight that includes reuse is the way forward" (p. 237).

Maike Gold
Translation: Dawn Michelle d'Atri

Vergleichende Grundrissstudien *de luxe*. Europäischer Wohnbau der Nachkriegszeit

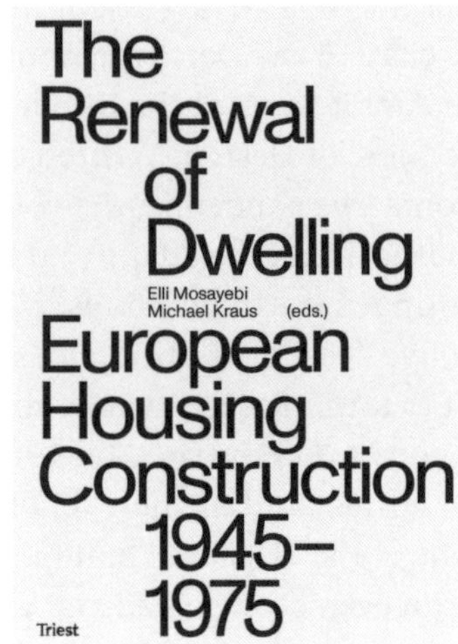

The Renewal of Dwelling—European Housing Construction 1945–1975
Elli Mosayebi, Michael Kraus (Hrg.)
Zürich: Triest 2023
Englisch, 396 Seiten

Die HerausgeberInnen Elli Mosayebi und Michael Kraus nehmen uns im 2023 erschienenen Sammelband *The Renewal of Dwelling* mit auf eine Reise durch die europäische Wohnbaulandschaft der Nachkriegsjahre. Der Umstand, dass der Großteil aller Wohnbauten in Europa in diesen 30 Jahren entstand, gab Anstoß zur intensiven Auseinandersetzung mit den baulichen Erneuerungen dieser Ära. Vorangegangen ist dem Buch eine umfangreiche, vergleichende Studie, die im Rahmen von Mosayebis Professur für Entwerfen und Wohnungsbau an der TU Darmstadt in den Jahren 2012 bis 2018 entstanden ist. In dieser Studie wurden vielfältige Projekte in verschiedenen europäischen Städten untersucht. Die Sammlung wird in sieben Kapiteln abgebildet, in denen jeweils ein Katalog mit Wohnbauprojekten einem Essay gegenübergestellt wird.

Bei ihrer Wohnungssuche konzentrierten sich die HerausgeberInnen auf Städte, die im internationalen Diskurs in der *zweiten Reihe*[1] (S. 7) stehen. Mussten die großen Metropolen Europas eindringlicher die Ideale einer Avantgardebewegung verkörpern, so treffen wir bei dieser Auswahl auf vielschichtigere, autonomere Ansätze, die Erfindungsreichtum, Pragmatismus und Kontextbezug aufzeigen: Porto, Lyon, Köln, Oslo, Zagreb und Athen, sowie die englischen Städte Leeds, Liverpool, Manchester und Sheffield wurden bereist und mit zahlreichen Beispielen zu einem wohnbaulichen Panorama versammelt. Gemeinsam war den Städten die Wohnungsnot aufgrund starker Kriegszerstörungen, hoher Zuwanderungszahlen und Migrationsbewegungen, zu der komplexe politische und nationale Rahmenbedingungen hinzukamen.

Im Zuge von Forschungsseminaren im universitären Austausch, erfolgte die Sammlung und Zusammenstellung von tausenden Dokumenten aus Archiven, Planungsbehörden, Museen sowie aus dem Privatbesitz von ArchitektInnen. Das heterogene Material der Projekte wird, dem Gedanken eines Archivs folgend, gleichberechtigt nebeneinander im Katalogteil des Buches gezeigt. Hier findet man Originalpläne, Skizzen, Zeitungsartikeln, Fotografien und kurze Beschreibungstexte. Die Pläne der Gebäude wurden – um eine bessere Les- und Vergleichbarkeit zu gewährleisten – alle neu gezeichnet.

Sechs vergleichende Kategorien, denen die Wohnhäuser zugeordnet sind, dienen als Prisma, um besondere Merkmale der Wohnbauarchitekturen herauszuheben, Übereinstimmungen und Unterschiede zu verdeutlichen bzw. auch grenzüberschreitende Verbindungen zwischen den verschiedenen Projekten herzustellen: mit „Large dimensions and the human scale", „Refined materials", „The garden in the façade", „Two entrances", „The hidden skeleton" und „Tall building in the city" (S. 9 ff.) werden die typischen Themen und Qualitätsansprüche der versammelten Beispiele auf einprägsame, gemeinsame Nenner gebracht.

So lädt zum Beispiel die Kategorie *Zwei Eingänge* ein, sich mit einem besonderen räumlichen Aspekt der bürgerlichen Wohnung auseinanderzusetzen. Bei dieser gab es getrennte Zugänge für Bewohner und Personal. Während solche räumlichen Lösungen in den 1970er-Jahren auf Grund von Effizienzgründen und gesellschaftlichen Veränderungen endgültig verworfen wurden, gab es in einer früheren Phase durchaus noch eine Reihe von Projekten, bei denen am bürgerlichen Wohnideal festgehalten wurde. Von der Flexibilität, die diese Wohnungen aufweisen, profitieren ihre NutzerInnen noch heute. Das macht diese Entwürfe zu einer wertvollen Referenz, wenn es auch in der aktuellen Wohnungsfrage vermehrt darum geht, den diversen Anforderungen und Vorlieben unterschiedlicher Zielgruppen gerecht zu werden.

Versteckter Skelettbau untersucht den ambivalenten Zugang, den es zum industriell vorgefertigten Wohnungsbau gab. Aufgrund seiner wirtschaftlichen Vorteile und der kürzeren Bauzeit gewann er zwar rasch an Popularität, die gestalterischen Qualitäten wurde aber nur in wenigen Fällen übersetzt. Vielmehr war es gang und gäbe, den Skelettbau hinter Putz und Ziegel zu verstecken, um die Häuser weiter als Massivbauten anmuten zu lassen. Während man noch am tradierten, materiellen Erscheinungsbild festhielt, wurde das Potential für größere Fassadenöffnungen sehr wohl genutzt. Ein sehr schönes Beispiel ist das *Wohnhaus Kemikalijain Zagreb* (S. 284 ff.) vom bedeutenden Architekten Drago Galić aus dem Jahr 1956 – eine ausgeklügelte Lösung für die Eckparzelle eines Blocks im historischen Stadtzentrum. Getreu seiner modernistischen Überzeugung passte Galić die *freischwebende Platte* dem Rahmen der Blockrandbebauung an. Wie schon bei seinem GNO-VPZ Wohnblock (S. 306 ff.) – ein Projekt mit inhaltlicher Nähe zu Le Corbusiers Unité d'Habitation – beweist der Architekt, wie er seine internationalen Referenzen kreativ überwunden hat, um den konkreten sozialen und städtischen Bedingungen gerecht zu werden.

Die thematische Zuordnung *Hohes Gebäude in der Stadt* widmet sich Wohnbauten mit bis zu zwanzig Stockwerken. Mit ihnen wurden nicht nur neue Baumaterialien und Ingenieurleistungen demonstriert. Sie standen auch für eine Haltung des *Urbanismus durch Dichte*. Die Wohnbauten sind multifunktional gedacht und nehmen in den Sockelgeschossen Gewerbe und Büros auf. Gleichzeitig sind sie auch als Kritik an den wenig urbanen Gartenstadtsiedlungen in Randlagen zu verstehen. Und das, obwohl die Wohnungsgrößen vor allem in der frühen Phase auf Grund der höheren Baukosten vorwiegend klein ausfielen und kein probates Angebot für Familien darstellten.

Die Essays, die den Katalog ergänzen, kreisen um zwei Themenbereiche: einerseits wird der Frage nachgegangen, wie der Staat den Wohnungsmarkt regulierte (Lyon, England, Zagreb und Athen), andererseits wird die private Wohnung und ihre Entwicklung detailliert unter die Lupe genommen (Oslo, Köln, Porto). Beispielsweise bespricht Panayotis Tournikiotis in seinem Aufsatz über Athen (S. 374 ff.) ausführlich das griechische Ausnahmemodell *Antiparochi*. Es bedeutet soviel wie *Prinzip der Gegenseitigkeit* und bezeichnet eine private Vereinbarung zwischen Grundeigentümern und Bauträgern. Die Firmen erbringen die Arbeitsleistung, der Eigentümer liefert das Grundstück und bekommt dafür nach der Bebauung mit einem vier- bis sechsgeschoßigen Mehrfamilienhaus – *der Polykatoikia* – selbst eine moderne, komfortable Wohnung. Der Staat engagierte sich äußerst zurückhaltend in der Wohnungsfrage, schuf aber einerseits die Voraussetzungen, die diese privaten Initiativen überhaupt erst ermöglichten und verfasste andererseits eine strenge, präzise Bauordnung, die den Hintergrund für das wichtigste Wohnbaumodul Athens bildete.

Die norwegische Politik stützte sich wiederum auf drei Einrichtungen, um der massiven Wohnungsknappheit zu begegnen. Anne-Kristine Kronborg erörtert in ihrem Essay (S. 270 ff.) den neuen institutionellen Rahmen für die Produktion, Verteilung und Verwaltung

1 Dt. Übersetzungen der Autorin.

von Wohnraum, der eigens dafür entwickelt wurde. Die Hauptrolle übernahmen dabei die staatliche Wohnungsbank, die Gemeinden und die Wohnbaugenossenschaften. Letztere unterstützten auch eine von Fachleuten initiierte Studie über den norwegischen Wohnbaustandard, deren Ergebnisse ernüchternd ausfielen. Die katastrophalen Resultate waren der Anlass, um gemeinsam mit dem Architekten Jens Selmer eine äußerst erfolgreiche, bald ikonische Drei-Zimmer-Wohnung zu entwickeln. Das vorherrschende Familienbild der Kernfamilie, mit dem erwerbstätigen Mann und der Hausfrau und ihrer Arbeit in der Wohnung, fand hier ihre architektonische Entsprechung.

Mosayebi erwähnt in einem Interview[2] die Schriftstellerin Ursula K. Le Guin. Diese schreibt vom „Finden, Sammeln und Ordnen von Dingen, die vielleicht auf den ersten Blick nicht zusammengehören“. Das lässt sich einerseits gut auf das Entwerfen übertragen, es war aber wohl auch für diesen Sammelband eine wesentliche Inspiration. Die *vergleichenden Grundrissstudien* (S. 6) – ein Begriff, den die HerausgeberInnen in Anlehnung an die vergleichende Literaturwissenschaft vorschlagen, um die grenzüberschreitende Idee ihrer Recherche zu unterstreichen – zeichnen ein fein nuanciertes Bild über komplexe Rahmenbedingungen und ihre räumliche Manifestation. Genau hier ist die eindrucksvolle Leistung des Buches zu finden. Ein großes Spektrum an Projekten und Geschichten wird zu einem vielschichtigen Mosaik zusammengefügt. Es zeigt eine Vielzahl an gestalterischen Querverbindungen auf und leitet zu unvermuteten Vergleichen an. Die ebenso dichte, wie gestalterisch und inhaltlich anspruchsvolle Zusammenstellung untermauert die Intention des Buches: es führt uns weg von einer *Erzählung der Defizite* (S. 15), hin zu einer analytischen und zugleich inspirierenden Lesart und von dort aus weiter zu einem visionären, kreativen und lustvollen Umgang mit den Wohnbauten dieser Zeit.

Elisabeth Koller

2 Koeberle, Susanne: „Die Erneuerung des Wohnens“, swiss-architects.com, 16. Februar 2023, online unter: www.swiss-architects.com/de/architecture-news/gefunden/die-erneuerung-des-wohnens (Stand: 11. Dezember 2023).

Comparative Floor Plan Studies Deluxe: Postwar European Housing

In the 2023 anthology *The Renewal of Dwelling*, the editors Elli Mosayebi and Michael Kraus take us on a journey through the housing landscape of Europe from the postwar years. The fact that the majority of all European residential buildings originate from these thirty years inspired this intensive exploration of the architectural innovations of this era. Serving as groundwork for the book was a comprehensive comparative study, conducted from 2012 to 2018 as part of Mosayebi's professorship in design and housing at the Technical University of Darmstadt. In this study, a diverse selection of projects in various European cities was studied. The compilation is rendered in seven chapters, each juxtaposing a catalogue of housing projects with an essay.

In determining which housing units to study, the editors focused on cities that, in international discourse, are in the "second tier" (p. 7). While the great metropolises of Europe were called upon to more emphatically embody the ideals of an avant-garde movement, the selection featured here falls on approaches that are in turn more eclectic and autonomous, ones that demonstrate inventiveness, pragmatism, and contextual relevance. The authors traveled to the cities of Porto, Lyon, Cologne, Oslo, Zagreb, and Athens, as well as to the British cities of Leeds, Liverpool, Manchester, and Sheffield, collecting numerous examples so as to create a panorama of housing. Common to all cities were circumstances like housing shortages due to significant wartime destruction, high levels of immigration, and migration flows, besides the complex political and national parameters.

In the scope of research seminars involving academic discussion, thousands of documents from archives, local planning authorities, museums, and the private collections of architects were collected and compiled. In line with the concept of archiving, the projects' heterogenous material is shown in the catalogue section of the book adjacently and on equal footing. Here we find original plans, sketches, newspaper articles, photographs, and short descriptive texts. The plans of all buildings were newly drafted without exception—in order to guarantee better readability and also comparability.

Six comparative categories, to which the residential buildings were assigned, serve as prisms for highlighting special features of the housing architecture, for illustrating similarities and differences, and also for identifying connections spanning the boundaries between the different projects: typical topics and quality standards found in the compiled examples—such as "Large dimensions and the human scale," "Refined materials," "The garden in the façade," "Two entrances," "The hidden skeleton," and "Tall building in the city" (pp. 9 ff.)—are presented as easily remembered common denominators.

The category "Two entrances," for example, invites us to explore a special spatial aspect of middle-class apartments, which were designed with separate entrances for residents and hired help. Although such spatial solutions were dismissed for good in the 1970s due to reasons of efficiency and also changing values within society, in an earlier phase there certainly was a series of projects that indeed upheld the bourgeois housing ideal. Today's residents are still benefiting from the flexibility that these apartments offer. This alone makes these designs a valuable point of reference, even if the current issue of housing is increasingly concentrated on doing justice to the different requirements and wishes of various target groups.

"The hidden skeleton," in turn, examines the ambivalent approach taken toward residential construction using industrially prefabricated elements. Due to its economic advantages and shorter construction period, this approach rapidly gained in popularity, but its design qualities were rarely translated. Rather, it was common practice to hide the skeleton construction behind plaster and brick, so as to keep the buildings looking solid. Though the traditional material appearance was retained, the potential for larger facade openings was certainly exploited. A quite lovely example is the residential building Kemikalijain Zagreb (pp. 284 ff.) by the renowned architect Drago Galić from the year 1956—a clever solution for the corner plot of a block in the historic downtown area. True to his modernist convictions, Galić adapted the "free-floating slab" (p. 333) to the frame of the perimeter block development. As was the case with his GNO-VPZ residential block (pp. 306 ff.)—a project similar in terms of content to Le Corbusier's Unité d'Habitation—the architect demonstrates how he creatively transcended his international points of reference in order to do justice to the specific social and urban conditions.

The theme of "Tall building in the city" is devoted to residential buildings with up to twenty stories. At the time, these structures demonstrated more than just new construction materials and engineering feats. Indeed, they stood for a stance of "urbanism through density." The residential buildings were conceived to be multifunctional and make room for retail space and offices on the ground floor. At the same time, they can be interpreted as a critique of the less urban garden city estates built in peripheral areas. And this despite the apartment sizes being mainly small, especially in early phases, due to higher construction costs, which did not make them a suitable option for families.

The essays augmenting the catalogue revolve around two thematic areas: on the one hand, the question is pursued of how the state regulated the housing market (Lyon, England, Zagreb, and Athens), while, on the other, private apartments and their development are closely examined (Oslo, Cologne, Porto). For example, Panayotis Tournikiotis, in his essay about Athens (pp. 374 ff.), offers a detailed discussion of the unique Greek model called *Antiparochi*, which basically means "principle of reciprocity" and denotes a private agreement between the landowners and the property developers. The companies provide the work, while the owner supplies the land and—after a four- to six-story apartment building, the *Polykatoikia*, has been constructed—receives a modern, comfortable apartment in return. The state was extremely reluctant to get involved in the housing issue, yet it created the conditions that made these private initiatives possible in the first place, and it also drew up strict, precise building regulations that provided a framework for the most important residential construction module in Athens.

Norwegian politics, in turn, set its sights on three facilities in an aim to counter the massive shortage of housing. Anne-Kristine Kronborg discusses in her essay (pp. 270 ff.) how a new institutional framework was specially developed for the production, distribution, and administration of housing space. The leading role here was played by the state housing bank, the municipalities, and the housing cooperatives. The latter supported a study, initiated by specialists in the field, about the state of Norwegian housing construction, which produced sobering results. Such a disastrous outcome led to the development of a highly successful and eventually iconic three-room apartment, designed together with the architect Jens Selmer. The prevailing picture of a nuclear family, with the man holding a job to support the family and the woman in the role of housewife, found its architectural equivalent in this design.

In an interview, Mosayebi mentions the author Ursula K. Le Guin,[1] who writes about the "finding, collecting, and organizing of things that perhaps, at first glance, do not belong together." This can of course be easily applied to the act of designing, but it was surely also an inspiration for this anthology. The "comparative floor-plan studies" (p. 6)—a concept proposed by the editors in reference to comparative literature meant to emphasize the cross-border focus of their research—paint a finely nuanced picture of such complex framework conditions and their spatial manifestation. It is precisely here that the considerable merit of the book is most evident. Diverse projects and stories are compiled to form a multilayered mosaic, giving rise to a wealth of creatively significant cross-connections and leading to unexpected comparisons, but that is not all. Equally convincing is the dense yet design- and content-related ambitious embodiment of the book's intention—moving away from a "narrative of deficits" (p. 15) and toward an analytical and simultaneously very inspiring reading of the visionary, creative, and pleasurable qualities of residential buildings from this era.

Elisabeth Koller
Translation: Dawn Michelle d'Atri

1 Susanna Koeberle, "Die Erneuerung des Wohnens," *Swiss-Architects*, available online at: www.swiss-architects.com/de/architecture-news/gefunden/die-erneuerung-des-wohnens (accessed March 16, 2023).

Im Human Whirlpool der Großstadt

In einer Welt von Fremden. Eine Anthropologie der Stadt
Rolf Lindner
Berlin: Matthes & Seitz, 2022
Deutsch, 290 Seiten

Wer abends nach einem Glas Wein dem süßen Gift des Kulturpessimismus nicht widerstehen kann, der oder dem sei die Lektüre von *In einer Welt von Fremden* dringend als Antidot empfohlen. Das Buch von Rolf Lindner, einem der profiliertesten Vertreter der Stadtforschung im deutschsprachigen Raum, steigt mit einer historischen Szene ein: Im Mai 1889 hielt der deutsche Reichskanzler Otto von Bismarck eine Rede, in der er sich über die Anziehungskraft Berlins wunderte. Warum eigentlich strömten die Leute massenhaft in die Großstadt, wo sie es in den Provinzen doch mitunter viel komfortabler hätten? Mit seinem Buch stellt Lindner diese Frage nach der Attraktivität der Großstadt erneut, tut das aber anders als Bismarck nicht etwa besorgt oder kritisch, sondern eher verständnisvoll und heiter.

In einer Welt von Fremden kann als Summe des wissenschaftlichen Schaffens Lindners bezeichnet werden, der nach einer Dissertation über Reklame, diversen Aufsätzen zu Subkulturen und Großstadtphänomenen, zuletzt einer Fallstudie zu Berlin vor allem durch seine beeindruckende Abhandlung über die Entstehung der Stadtforschung im Umfeld der *Chicago School of Sociology* bekannt wurde. Viele dieser Fäden nimmt er auch in diesem Buch wieder auf, und doch heißt ‚Summe' nicht, dass man ein streng systematisches Werk erwarten sollte. Lindner weiß nur zu gut, dass sich die Großstadt als Untersuchungsgegenstand bis zu einem gewissen Grad der Systematisierung widersetzt. Er misstraut daher auch allzu selbstsicheren und vereindeutigenden Ansätzen der Stadtforschung, ganz gleich, ob sie funktionalistisch, netzwerkanalytisch oder verhaltensökonomisch inspiriert sind. Ähnlich wie schon Georg Simmel, für den der „rasche und ununterbrochene Wechsel äußerer und innerer Eindrücke" das Wesensmerkmal der Großstadt war, geht Lindner stattdessen impressionistisch vor.

Ebenso wie uns die Stadt mit einem Zuviel an Eindrücken, an Verkehr, Lärm und Leuchtschriften überfordert, konfrontiert uns auch Lindner mit immer neuen Anspielungen, Lektürehinweisen und Bezügen zur Literatur, Kunst, Soziologie und Populärkultur. Es sind gerade die Nebenbemerkungen und diversen Fundstücke, die den Reiz der Lektüre ausmachen. So lernen wir etwa eine frühe Ethnografie der Straße mit einem feinen Gespür für alltägliche Gangarten aus der Feder von August Endell kennen oder werden auf den Unterschied zwischen dem Regen auf dem Land und dem städtischen Regen aufmerksam gemacht. Dieser verfinstere nicht den Himmel, sondern verwandle die Stadt umgekehrt in ein Spiegelkabinett aus funkelnden Straßen und Pfützen. Heutige Leserinnen und Leser dürften dabei allerdings weniger die Gemälde Lesser Urys vor Augen haben, sondern eher an Flächenversiegelung und Lichtverschmutzung denken. Lindner verschweigt derartige Nebenfolgen urbaner Lebensweise zwar nicht, bleibt aber doch spürbar fasziniert von der leuchtenden Großstadt um 1900. Dass das Leben auch nachts stattfinden kann, sei schließlich eine welthistorisch kaum zu überschätzende, nunmehr alltägliche Erfahrung. Die moderne Großstadt steht daher in der Tradition der Aufklärung als Projekt einer allmählichen Ent-Finsterung der Welt; gleichzeitig sind in den Städten aber eben auch all jene schummrig beleuchteten Nachtlokale entstanden, die als Gegen-Orte zu den seit der Aufklärung stetig steigenden Ansprüchen an Selbstdisziplin und rationale Lebensführung fungieren.

Gerade diesen zwielichtigen Orten gilt das Interesse Lindners – den Varietés, Tanzlokalen und Vergnügungsstätten. Der *Berliner Prater* etwa ist ein solcher Ort, an dem sich die Stadt wie im Brennglas beobachten lasse. Ähnlich wie es Rem Koolhaas für *Coney Island* behauptet hat, hält auch Lindner diese frühen Vergnügungsparks für Laboratorien und Testserien späterer Großstädte. Nicht nur zeigen sich hier technische Innovativität, unternehmerischer Größenwahn und ungebrochener Optimismus in verdichteter Form, hier kann man auch prototypische Formen des städtischen Zusammenlebens entdecken. Allein ein Fahrgeschäft wie der *Human Whirlpool* (auf Deutsch: *Teufelsrad*) ist eine perfekte soziologische Parabel auf die moderne Großstadt: Dort treffen Menschen aufeinander, die gleichzeitig Konkurrenten und doch auch auf Kooperation angewiesen sind, dort wirken Kräfte von außen, die permanent Unberechenbarkeit erzeugen, sodass das Ganze auf den ersten Blick chaotisch wirken mag, aber eben doch auch einer gewissen Ordnung gehorcht. Vor allem aber verlangt der *Human Whirlpool* im Kleinen das, was die Stadt im Großen verlangt: eine gewisse Gelassenheit im Umgang mit Fremden. Und das ist alles andere als trivial.

So eklektisch die Beispiele Lindners auch scheinen mögen, sie werden stets auf die zentrale Frage nach dem Zusammenleben von Fremden bezogen. Lindner erinnert uns daran, dass die Anonymität der Großstadt einst ein Freiheitsversprechen war. Die Angst vor Entfremdung war entsprechend weniger groß als die konkrete Furcht vor Aufsicht auf den Gutshöfen. Und wenn man liest, wie sich Georg Simmel noch 1908 darüber wunderte, dass bis zum Aufkommen öffentlicher Verkehrsmittel Menschen „überhaupt nicht in der Lage waren, sich minuten- bis stundenlang gegenseitig anblicken zu können oder zu müssen, ohne miteinander zu sprechen", wird einem klar, wie jung viele jener urbanen Verhaltensweisen sind, die so selbstverständlich erscheinen und uns längst in Fleisch und Blut übergegangen sind. Die Großstadt wurde zu einer Art Trainingslager, um dort das einzuüben, was Erving Goffman „civil inattention" nannte. Es ist das genuin Zivile dieser Form von Gleichgültigkeit, das Lindner uns vor Augen führen will.

Im Untertitel verspricht dieses Buch daher auch eine *Anthropologie der Stadt*. Nicht nur fragt Lindner, was Menschen in Städten tun und wie Städte das Verhalten der Menschen prägen, er möchte darüber hinaus das in den Blick nehmen, was er als das „Ethos einer Stadt" bezeichnet. Damit soll ein spürbares und wirksames Imaginäres einer jeweiligen Stadt bezeichnet sein, das nicht an konkrete Bewohner gebunden ist. Eher handelt es sich um einen bestimmten Tonus oder Habitus einer Stadt, um kollektiv-implizites Wissen, das sich aus tradierten Ereignissen, Bildern, Sprichworten und medialen Repräsentationen speist. So instruktiv dieses Konzept ist, so schwer dürfte es sich allerdings in Forschung umsetzen lassen. Zu groß – das wird auch im Buch selbst deutlich – ist die Gefahr der *misplaced concreteness*. Jedes herangezogene Beispiel droht dieses Implizite zu verfehlen. Hinzu kommt, dass gerade diese scheinbar spezifischen städtischen Atmosphären längst der Kommodifizierung und dem Wettbewerb anheimgefallen sind und zunehmend beliebig werden – oder gibt es überhaupt noch Fußballstadien, in denen „You'll Never Walk Alone" nicht gespielt wird?

Lindner weiß um derartige Entwicklungen und hat dennoch ein ungebrochenes Vertrauen in die Großstadt, in ihr zivilisatorisches und emanzipatorisches Potential. Wenn er von „Großstadt" spricht, ist damit fast immer Berlin, Chicago, Paris, London oder New York gemeint. Das ist der Auswahl seines Materials, dem Zuschnitt auf die Zeit um 1900 und auch seinen lebenslangen Forschungsinteressen geschuldet. Wir lesen nur wenig von Lagos, Xiong'an oder Kiew und müssen diese Städte beim Lesen daher selbst mitdenken. Und auch wenn Graz im Buch nicht explizit erwähnt wird, so dürften besonders die Ausführungen zum Phänomen der *second city* für Grazer Leserinnen und Leser von Interesse sein. Es liege bisweilen ein besonderer Reiz gerade in den zweitgrößten Städten eines Landes, der auf eine Mischung aus Minderwertigkeitsgefühl gegenüber der Hauptstadt, provinziellem Stolz, unprätentiöser Entspanntheit und Überlegenheit in bestimmten Bereichen zurückzuführen ist.

Julian Müller

In the Human Whirlpool of the Metropolis

For those who cannot resist the sweet poison of cultural pessimism after enjoying an evening glass of wine, the book *In einer Welt von Fremden* (*In a World of Strangers*) may just well be the perfect antidote. Penned by Rolf Lindner, one of the most prominent representatives of urban research in the German-speaking world, the publication starts off with a historical scene: in May 1889, Otto von Bismarck, chancellor of the German Empire, gave a speech in which he pondered the appeal of Berlin. Why were people flocking to the metropolis when their life in the countryside was often much more comfortable? Lindner, in his book, reposes this question of how attractive large cities really are, though he takes a different tack than Bismarck — not worried or critical, but rather sympathetic and sunny.

Indeed, *In einer Welt von Fremden* can be viewed as a sum of Lindner's scholarly work to date. After his dissertation on advertising, various essays about subcultures and metropolitan phenomena, and, most recently, a case study on Berlin, Lindner is known above all for his impressive treatise on the emergence of urban research in the context of the Chicago school of sociology. Many of these threads are woven into the current book as well, yet "sum" by no means implies that we should expect a strictly systematic work. Lindner is all too aware of that fact that the metropolis, as an object of study, defies systematization to a certain degree. He thus harbors some distrust of overly self-assured and nonambiguous approaches to urban research, regardless of whether inspired by functionalism, network analysis, or behavioral economics. Similar to Georg Simmel, who saw the "swift and uninterrupted change of outer and inner stimuli" as the essential feature of the metropolis, Lindner takes an impressionistic approach.

Just as cities overwhelm us with too many impressions, with traffic, noise, and neon signs, Lindner also confronts us with ever-new allusions, recommended reading, and references to literature, art, sociology, and popular culture. It is precisely these side notes and various findings that make the book so fascinating to read. For example, we are introduced to an early street ethnography with a keen sense of everyday gaits from the hand of August Endell, or we are made acquainted with the difference between rain in the countryside and urban rain. The latter, we learn, does not darken the sky but instead transforms the city into a hall of mirrors composed of gleaming streets and puddles. However, today's readers are more likely to have land sealing and light pollution in mind than the paintings of Lesser Ury. Though Lindner does not conceal such aftereffects of urban life, he certainly remains fascinated by the luminous metropolis around 1900. Life playing out at night is, after all, an everyday experience today that assumes a place in world history that can hardly be overestimated. The modern metropolis thus stands in the tradition of the Enlightenment as a project of gradual global un-darkening. Yet the cities have also been fertile ground for all of those dimly lit nightclubs serving as counter-places to the demands for self-discipline and a rational lifestyle that have ever been increasing since the Enlightenment.

Lindner's interest is focused on these very sketchy places—the variety shows, dance halls, and entertainment venues. Berlin's Prater is one such locale, where the city can be observed as if in a burning glass. Similar to Rem Koolhaas's comments on Coney Island, Lindner also considers these early amusement parks to be laboratories and pilots for later metropolises. Prototypical forms of urban cohabitation can be discovered here, alongside technical innovation, entrepreneurial megalomania, and enduring optimism, all in densified form. A perfect sociological parable of the modern metropolis is found in funfair rides like the Human Whirlpool: here people meet who are competitors and yet also dependent on cooperation, and there are forces at play that constantly foster unpredictability, so that at first glance everything seems chaotic though it is actually subject to a specific order. Most of all, however, the Human Whirlpool requires on a small scale that which the city demands on a large scale: a certain sense of composure in dealing with strangers. And this is anything but trivial.

As eclectic as Lindner's examples may seem, they always relate to the pivotal question of a cohabitation of strangers. Lindner reminds us that the anonymous nature of the metropolis once held the promise of freedom. The fear of alienation was in the end less intense than the concrete fear of supervision on the farming estates. And when we read about how, in 1908, Georg Simmel was surprised that, until the advent of public transportation, people "were never put in a position of having to stare at one another for minutes or even hours on end without exchanging a word," then it becomes clear how recent such urban behavior actually is, though it seems so natural to us, having long since become second nature. The metropolis has become a kind of training camp for practicing what Erving Goffman called "civil inattention." It is the genuinely civil nature of this form of indifference that Lindner is trying to bring home to us.

The subtitle of this book hence speaks of an "Anthropology of the City." Lindner goes beyond merely considering what people in cities do and how cities shape the behavior of the inhabitants; he additionally brings into focus what he terms the "ethos of a city." His aim here is to describe a tangible and effective imaginary of a particular city that is not tied to specific inhabitants. Instead, reference is made here to a certain tone or habitus of a city, to implicit collective knowledge cultivated by traditional events, images, dictums, and media representations. As instructive as this concept may be, it would surely be hard to implement in a research context. The danger of "misplaced concreteness" is simply too great, as the book itself so aptly illustrates. Each example given threatens to miss this implicity. What's more, such specific urban atmospheres have long since been commodified and are thus becoming more and more arbitrary. Or are there any football stadiums where "You'll Never Walk Alone" is not played?

Lindner is aware of such developments and yet still has unabated trust in the metropolis, in its civilizational and emancipatory potential. When speaking of the "metropolis," he almost always means Berlin, Chicago, Paris, London, or New York, owing to his selection of material, his focus on the period around 1900, and also his lifelong research interests. There is precious little mention of cities like Lagos, Xiong'an, or Kyiv, so we must imagine these cities ourselves while reading. And even if Graz is not explicitly mentioned in this book, readers based in Graz will surely be interested in the material related to the phenomenon of the "second city." At times, there is even a special charm to a country's second-largest city, which can be attributed to a combination of various factors, such as a sense of inferiority as compared to the capital, provincial pride, an unpretentious, relaxed feel, and superiority in certain other areas.

Julian Müller
Übersetzung: Dawn Michelle d'Atri

Data Center als demokratische Infrastrukturen

Servermanifest. Architektur der Aufklärung: Data Center als Politikmaschinen
Niklas Maak
Hatje Cantz Verlag, 2022
Deutsch, 112 Seiten

„Was in Serverfarmen passiert, ist ein Problem für die Demokratie." (S. 25) Dies ist wohl einer der Schlüsselsätze im 2022 erschienenen Buch *Servermanifest. Architektur der Aufklärung: Data Center als Politikmaschinen* von Niklas Maak. Das Buch handelt im Wesentlichen von der Steuerung und Ausbeutung aller BürgerInnen durch die Digitalriesen und den einhergehenden Verlust der Verantwortung des Staates. Niklas Maak verurteilt deutlich die Monopolstellung bestimmter Konzerne und die Abschöpfung personenbezogener Daten und weist auf das fehlende Bewusstsein der Nutzenden hin. Die daraus resultierende gesellschaftliche Entmachtung ist eine zunehmende Bedrohung für die Demokratie – welche sich am deutlichsten in der boomenden Typologie des Data Centers zeigt.

Niklas Maak, Feuilleton Redakteur der *FAZ*, Architekturkritiker und Gastprofessor für Architektur an der Städelschule Frankfurt präsentiert ein Manifest in zehn Kapiteln, in denen er Data Center sowie den Umgang mit Daten im Allgemeinen nicht nur architektonisch, sondern auch historisch, ökologisch und politisch in den Blick nimmt. Er bietet eine Art Aktionsplan an, einen revolutionären Richtungswechsel im zukünftigen Umgang mit den Gebäuden, aber im Besonderen mit deren Inhalt – den Daten. Das Servermanifest selbst ist gerahmt von einem Vorwort der europäischen Digitalexpertin Francesca Bria und einem Interview mit Karsten Spengler, Direktor bei ARUP, hier mit der Planung von Rechenzentren betraut. Im letzten Teil des Buches werden Zukunftsvisionen von Studierenden für einen ganz anderen Umgang und zugleich menschennäheren Zugang zu Data Centers gezeigt.

„Serverfarmen sind die wichtigste neue Bautypologie des 21. Jahrhunderts. Sie sind in der digitalen Welt, was früher Schlösser waren: der Sitz der Macht.“ (S. 19) Maak ist überzeugt davon, dass wir es hier mit der folgenreichsten und erfolgreichsten Typologie für das digitale Zeitalter zu tun haben. Die enorme Macht der datenbesitzenden Firmen wird durch die Architektur nicht sichtbar. Vielmehr kommt Maak (wie auch ich in meiner Dissertation[1]) zu der Überzeugung, dass Data Center bewusst als flache, möglichst anonyme und unauffällige Hallen in der Peripherie, versteckt werden. „Sie sollen das Gegenteil von Architektur sein: Nichts sagen, nichts verraten, keine Angriffsflächen bieten.“ (S. 20) Währenddessen bildet sich die Verschiebung der Macht auch in den Städten ab, wo keine Bauten des digitalen Zeitalters – egal ob vom Staat oder der Wirtschaft – sichtbar sind, und die Innenstädte zwar bürgerfreundlicher und grüner werden, sich dafür aber inhaltlich leeren. Maak kommt zu dem Schluss, dass die Digitalisierung die Stadt in eine elementare Strukturkrise, in einen „Ruinenpark“ (S. 20) treibt.

Niklas Maak hat zuvor auch durch andere Veröffentlichungen auf die Wichtigkeit des Themas sowie auf die enormen ökologischen Auswirkungen dieser neuen Architekturform aufmerksam gemacht: „Bisher reizte die Architekten die Bauaufgabe Serverfarm wenig, [...]. Vielleicht wäre es aber nötig, gerade an den Hochschulen die Aufmerksamkeit von Ingenieuren und Architekten auf die Riesenkisten [...] zu lenken und ihr Design nicht auf künstlerische Ummantelungen zu beschränken, wenn man nicht will, dass einem die sogenannte Cloud irgendwann als unschöne Rußwolke entgegenkommt.“[2] Auch im vorgestellten Buch geht Maak auf den enormen Energieverbrauch von Data Centers ein und stellt einen Zusammenhang zur gewollten Unsichtbarkeit und zum fehlenden öffentlichen Bewusstsein her. „[...]; man will den Usern kein schlechtes Gewissen machen.“ (S. 23) Denn wer will schon an den Stromverbrauch oder an die CO_2 Emissionen beim alltäglichen Videocall denken.

Das Thema riesiger Serverfarmen und digital vernetzter Städte scheint Niklas Maak seit einigen Jahren und auf vielen Ebenen zu beschäftigen, so hat er im Jahr 2020 den Roman *Technophoria*[3] veröffentlicht, wo er in teils poetischer Lesart über die Ambivalenzen des digitalen Zeitalters schreibt. Kurzgefasst: Ein zuerst von der Smart City euphorisierter Protagonist, stirbt zuletzt einsam in einer Serverhalle.

Der globale Trend der immer weiterwachsenden Datenmenge ist für den Moment unumkehrbar, somit gilt es einen nachhaltigen und bewussten Umgang besonders für das Dateneigentum zu finden. Um nicht den größten kollektiven Schatz der digitalen Gesellschaft – die Daten selbst – wenigen globalen Internetunternehmen zu überlassen, fordert Francesca Bria dazu auf, dass wir dringend die digitale Souveränität zurückerlangen müssen, was bedeutet, dass der technogische Fortschritt, die Technologie und die Daten im Dienst der Gesellschaft stehen müssen. „Städte und deren Bewohnerinnen und Bewohner, nicht Firmen sollten die in Städten produzierten Daten besitzen, die sie dann zur Verbesserung öffentlicher Dienste und zur Verwirklichung weiterer Maßnahmen verwenden können.“ (S. 11) In diesem Sinne schlägt Niklas Maak einen öffentlichen Ort vor, eine Art Centre Pompidou, ein Hybridgebäude aus Rathaus, Bibliothek, Museum, Bildungseinrichtung und Data Center, wo BürgerInnen verstehen, wo sich unsere Daten befinden, aber auch wie beispielsweise künstliche Intelligenz und die Digitalisierung funktionieren. Der konzeptuelle Schlüssel im zukünftigen Umgang mit Data Center und Daten liegt u.a. darin ihnen eine öffentliche und sichtbare Ebene hinzuzufügen.

Der Autor weist selbst darauf hin, dass es ihm nicht um eine umfassende Kulturgeschichte des Data Centers geht. Trotz oder gerade wegen der gewählten Textform gelingt es ihm aber verdichtet und sehr prägnant alle themenrelevanten Aspekte aufzugreifen, um den Handlungsbedarf im zukünftigen Umgang mit Daten herauszustellen und dessen weitreichende Implikationen auch für nichtfachkenntliche LeserInnen begreifbar zu machen. Der politische Blickwinkel und fordernde Handlungsbedarf in Bezug auf Daten und Data Center nimmt ein besonders großes Gewicht ein. Deutlich wird dabei auch seine persönliche Sichtweise – eine durchaus kritische Haltung gegenüber den Veränderungen und Herausforderungen des Digitalen Zeitalters. Anlass zur Sorge, wenn wenige Hightech-Unternehmen die gesamte digitale Welt kontrollieren, gibt es auf jeden Fall. Die Forderung, dass ein Teil Daten wieder öffentliches Gut, also zu „Common Data“ (S. 56) wird, stellt der Autor konsequent durch sein lesenswertes Manifest und führt Barcelona als Modell vor, wo Francesca Bria die digitale Bürgerbeteiligungsplattform *Decidim* eingerichtet hat. Sein Denkansatz eines „Civic Centers des digitalen Zeitalters“ bzw. eine „Serverfarm als Ort der politischen Aktivierung“ (S. 71) bietet ungeheures Potential für einen revolutionären Richtungswechsel. Wie Architektur als kritisches und kreatives Medium der Aufklärung eingesetzt werden kann, gelingt besonders im Zusammenspiel

1 Neubauer, Katharina: *Datenspeichergebäude. Im Spannungsfeld gesellschaftlicher Bedeutung und architektonischer Präsenzlosigkeit*. Berlin 2022.

2 Maak, Niklas: „Auch das Internet hat einen Auspuff“, *FAZ*, 13. Januar 2018, 9.

3 Maak, Niklas: *Technophoria*, München 2020.

mit den studentischen Entwurfsprojekten, die bildhaft demonstrieren, wie Daten räumlich erfahrbar werden. Bleibt zuletzt also die Frage: Wie genau diese Visionen in die Praxis zurückgeführt werden können, an einen Tisch mit den notwendigen AkteurInnen – aus Politik, Architektur und Wirtschaft?

Katharina Neubauer

Data Centers as Democratic Infrastructures

"What happens in server farms is a problem for democracy" (p. 25). This is surely one of the key phrases in Niklas Maak's *Server Manifesto: Data Center Architecture and the Future of Democracy* from 2022. The book essentially deals with the control and exploitation of all citizens through digital giants and the concomitant loss of responsibility on the part of the state. Niklas Maak clearly condemns the monopoly position of certain corporations and the culling of personal data, while pointing out users' lack of awareness. The social disempowerment resulting from this process is an increasing threat to democracy—as is most clearly reflected by this booming data center typology.

Niklas Maak, who is the *FAZ*'s feuilleton editor, as well as an architecture critic and guest professor in architecture at the Städelschule Frankfurt, offers a manifesto in ten chapters, examining data centers along with the general treatment of data not only from an architectural perspective, but also in terms of history, ecology, and politics. He presents an action plan of sorts, signifying a revolutionary change in direction when it comes to future dealings with these buildings, and most especially with their content—the data itself. The server manifesto itself is framed by a foreword by the European digital expert Francesca Bria and by an interview with Karsten Spengler, director of Arup Germany, who is well acquainted with the planning of computing centers. In the last section of the book, visions of the future in the eyes of students are presented, showing us a completely different approach to data centers, one that is decidedly more human.

"Server farms are the most important new building typology of the twenty-first century. They are to the digital world what castles used to be in medieval times: the seat of power" (p. 18). Maak is convinced that we are here dealing with the most momentous and successful typology of the digital age. The enormous power of such data-owning companies is not evident through architecture alone. In fact, Maak is of the conviction (as am I in my dissertation[1]) that data centers are purposely camouflaged as flat, highly anonymous and inconspicuous halls in peripheral areas. "They are meant to be the opposite of architecture: saying nothing, betraying nothing, offering no surface for attack" (p. 20). Meanwhile, the shift in power is also evident in cities, where no buildings of the digital age are visible, neither governmental nor from the private sector; and the downtown areas are becoming more citizen-friendly and green, though empty in terms of content. Maak comes to the conclusion that digitalization is "driving the city into an elementary structural crisis," turning it into a "park of ruins" (p. 20).

In earlier publications, Niklas Maak has also pointed out how crucial this topic is, calling attention to the enormous ecological effects of this new form of architecture. "Up to now, architects have not been particularly interested in the task of building server farms, ... But maybe it is necessary to direct the attention of engineers and architects, especially those at universities, to these giant boxes ... and to avoid limiting their design to artistic wrappings if one cares about not having the so-called cloud become an ugly cloud of soot somewhere down the line."[2] In the book under review here, too, Maak considers the enormous energy expenditure of data centers and establishes a connection to their deliberate invisibility and to the lack of public awareness, for one doesn't want to make users feel guilty (p. 23). After all, who wants to think about power consumption or CO_2 emissions during everyday video calls?

The topic of giant server farms and digitally networked cities appears to have fascinated Niklas Maak for several years now, on various different levels. For example, in 2020 he released the novel *Technophoria*,[3] where he writes about the ambivalence inherent to the digital age, sometimes in a poetic way. To sum up the plot: a protagonist, initially euphoric about the smart city, ultimately faces a solitary death in a server hall.

The global trend toward an evergrowing volume of data is presently irreversible, which means that it is necessary to arrive at a sustainable and conscious approach, especially to dealing with data ownership. Francesca Bria asserts that we must urgently regain digital sovereignty so that the greatest collective treasure of digital society—the data itself—does not remain in the hands of just a few global Internet companies. This means that technological progress, technology itself, and the data must be all in the service of society. "Cities and citizens, not companies, ought to own the data produced in cities and should be able to use the said data to improve public services and put their policies into action" (p. 10). In this regard, Niklas Maak suggests establishing a public site, a kind of Centre Pompidou as a hybrid building with a city hall, library, museum, educational facility, and data center, where citizens understand where our data is stored, but also how artificial intelligence and digitalization work. Conceptually, the key to dealing with

1 Katharina Neubauer, *Datenspeichergebäude: Im Spannungsfeld gesellschaftlicher Bedeutung und architektonischer Präsenslosigkeit* (Berlin, 2022).

2 Niklas Maak, "Auch das Internet hat einen Auspuff," *FAZ*, January 13, 2018, p. 9.

3 Niklas Maak, *Technophoria* (Munich, 2020).

data centers and with data in the future lies in giving them a state that is public and visible.

The author himself points out that he is not pursuing a comprehensive cultural history of data centers. Despite the chosen text form, or perhaps because of it, he nonetheless succeeds in addressing all relevant aspects of the topic in a condensed and highly concise manner, with the aim of highlighting the need for action as to the future handling of data, and of making its far-reaching implications comprehensible even for readers who may be unfamiliar with the subject. The political vantage point and the call for action in relation to data and data centers plays an especially important role. Evident here is the author's personal perspective—a rather critical stance toward the changes and challenges of the digital age. There is certain a reason to be concerned when just a few high-tech companies control the entire digital world. The demand that part of this data should once again become "data commons" (p. 56) is resolutely presented by the author in this manifesto of his that is well worth reading; he cites Barcelona as a model, where Francesca Bria has established a digital participation platform called Decidim. His conceptual approach of a "civic center of the digital age" (p. 71) or "the server farm as a place of political activation" (p. 70) offers incredible potential for a revolutionary shift in direction. The possibility of employing architecture as a critical and creative medium of enlightenment is particularly successful in interplay with the student design projects, which visually demonstrate how data can be experienced spatially. So just one question remains: How exactly can these visions be put back into practice, at a table with the necessary players—from the realms of politics, architecture, and business?

Katharina Neubauer
Übersetzung: Dawn Michelle d'Atri

Architektur von den Produktions-bedingungen her denken

Material Reform:
Building for a Post-Carbon Future
Material Cultures (Summer Islam, Paloma Gormley, George Massoud) und Amica Dall
London: Mack, 2022
English, pp. 144

Der Titel dieser Rezension spielt auf Hermann Czechs rhetorische Frage an, ob „Architektur von der Konsumtion her"[1] gedacht werden könnte. Czech kommt zu dem Schluss, dass sich auch ein konsumorientiertes Architekturschaffen mit Fragen der Produktion beschäftigen muss, um nicht in einer Selbstvergessenheit gegenüber den der Architektur eigenen Herstellungstechniken zu enden. Ebendiese Herstellungstechniken basieren auf enorm ressourcenintensiven Prozessen, die weitestgehend unbeachtet ablaufen. Das britische Architekturkollektiv „Material Cultures" holt diese Prozesse vor den Vorhang.

Dabei gibt der 2022 herausgegebene schmale Band *Material Reform* seinen LeserInnen viel zu denken. Denn wie der Untertitel schon verrät geht es um nichts Geringeres als um das Bauen in einer postfossilen Zukunft. Die in Großbritannien praktizierenden ArchitektInnen Summer Islam, Paloma Gormley und George Massoud haben die Plattform Material Cultures gegründet, um sich dieser Herausforderung anzunähern. Im Zentrum ihrer Arbeit steht eine Architektur aus regenerativen Materialien. Deren Bedingungen und Möglichkeiten loten sie in gebauten Projekten ebenso wie in Forschung und Lehre aus. Die vorliegende Publikation erfolgte in Zusammenarbeit mit Amica Dall, einem Gründungsmitglied des bekannten Architekten- und Künstlerkollektivs Assemble. Zur visuellen Ausgestaltung wurde die Fotografin Jess Gough hinzugezogen, ihre ganzseitig abgedruckten Fotografien begleiten die Lektüre. Im Vorwort verweist Charlotte Malterre-Barthes – bekannt durch die Initiative „A Moratorium on New Construction"[2] – eindringlich auf den intrinsischen, historischen Zusammenhang zwischen Umweltzerstörung und kapitalistischen Praktiken der Akkumulation. Sie konfrontiert die vorgeblich unschuldige „neutrality of design"[3] mit einer Realität, die sich bei genauerer Betrachtung der globalen Produktions- und Lieferketten heutiger Baumaterialien auf vielen Ebenen als problematisch herausstellt. Die AutorInnen dieses Buches vertreten daher eine Position, die fortlaufend neuen Ökolabels und technologisch fortschrittsgläubigen Lösungen kritisch gegenübersteht, da diese gängige Praxismodelle tendenziell perpetuieren und Gewissen beruhigen anstatt sich der mühsameren Frage, wie substanzieller kultureller Wandel aussehen könnte, zu widmen. Dafür legen die AutorInnen den Grundstein für eine reformierte Baubranche, die auf zirkulärem Denken und regenerativen Materialien basiert. Wir werden dazu aufgefordert, die Produktionsbedingungen in unseren Überlegungen zu Form und Wesen der Architektur

1 Czech, Hermann: *Ungefähre Hauptrichtung. Schriften und Gespräche zur Architektur*, Wien 2021, 93.

2 Vgl. https://stopconstruction.cargo.site/ (Stand: 29.09.2023)

3 Malterre-Barthes, Charlotte: „Preface", in: Material Cultures/Rogers, Louis (Hg.): *Material Reform. Building for a Post-Carbon Future*, London 2022, 10.

zu berücksichtigen, um sich jenem „Halbbewusstsein, das sich von der eigenen Produktion distanziert“[4] entgegenzustellen.

Material Cultures schlüsseln die Komplexität des Themas durch die Struktur des Buches in zugänglicher und angemessener Form auf. Den Hauptteil des Buches bildet eine Anthologie kurzer Texte, die je für sich gelesen werden können und zugleich gemeinsam eine übergeordnete Erzählung bilden, die von den materiellen und gesellschaftlichen Implikationen des Bauens handelt. Dabei wird die verhängnisvolle Beziehung zwischen der zeitgenössischen Bau- und Planungspraxis und umweltschädigenden Formen der Ressourcenextraktion sorgfältig herausgearbeitet. Die inzwischen wohlbekannte Kritik[5] an einem Nachhaltigkeitsbegriff, der seine Aufmerksamkeit ausschließlich auf die Energieeffizienz beim Betrieb von Gebäuden lenkt, wird hier erneut und sehr nuanciert formuliert. Über die Beschreibung von Missständen bis hin zu konkreten Überlegungen für eine Reform unserer Beziehung zur gebauten und natürlichen Umwelt wird so ein inhaltlich umfassender Bogen gespannt. Die „klassischen“ Grenzen des Architekturdiskurses werden dabei immer wieder überschritten. Denn der Anspruch, die Architekturpraxis grundlegend anders zu denken macht einen ernsthaften Blick in benachbarte Disziplinen unumgänglich. Das sorgfältig und kompakt aufbereitete Fachwissen aus den Feldern der Ökologie, Landwirtschaft oder Materialwissenschaft ermöglicht es den jeweils individuellen Betrachtungswinkel zu kontextualisieren. Eindrücklich argumentieren Material Cultures für die Notwendigkeit eines architektonischen Bewusstseins, das imstande ist, die Stoffflüsse und Arbeitsbedingungen von der Rohstoffgewinnung über die Errichtung bis zur möglichen Transformation oder dem Abriss eines Gebäudes und darüber hinaus zu berücksichtigen.

Eine wesentliche Qualität liegt hier in der klaren Sprache des umsichtigen AutorInnen-Kollektivs. Nüchtern vorgetragene Thesen und Ansätze treten auf samtenen, aber mit scharfen Krallen besetzten Pfoten. So verschaffen sie sich Zugang zu unseren Gehörgängen, und machen auf die möglicherweise unangenehmen Wahrheiten aufmerksam, mit denen wir uns als ArchitektInnen auseinandersetzen müssen. Material Cultures setzen mit ihrer Kritik bei den Herstellungsprozessen an, in welche das Bauen – und damit auch das Machen von Architektur – unausweichlich eingebunden sind. Besonders deutlich wird das etwa im Kapitel „Oil Vernacular“, in dem die absurden Widersprüche zwischen hoch energieeffizienten Gebäuden und den zur Errichtung notwendigen energieintensiven Praktiken der Ressourcenextraktion beschrieben werden. Jedoch belassen es Material Cultures nicht bei einer bloßen Kritik am Status Quo. Vielmehr stellen sie den Anspruch, die Reform der gängigen materiellen Praxis aktiv voranzutreiben. Als praktizierende ArchitektInnen zeigen sie, wie qualitativ hochwertige Architektur unter dem weitgehenden Verzicht auf die ressourcenintensiven Erfolgsbaustoffe des 20. Jahrhunderts (Beton, Stahl und petrochemische Produkte) realisiert werden kann. Die Bauten von Material Cultures versuchen mit dem Einsatz von regenerativen Materialien und kurzen Transportwegen das Auslangen zu finden. Die so geänderten Rahmenbedingungen können als produktive Einschränkungen verstanden werden, die einen reichhaltigen Möglichkeitsraum für das Machen von Architektur eröffnen. Um eine Skalierung dieser Art des Bauens zu ermöglichen ist allerdings ein Bewusstseinswandel bei allen an der Wertschöpfungskette beteiligten erforderlich, in dessen Zentrum eine Erweiterung des Bezugsrahmens steht. Denn für die Beurteilung architektonischer Qualität darf nicht bloß der Einfluss eines Gebäudes auf seinen unmittelbaren Errichtungsort berücksichtigen werden. Ebenso bedarf es einer Sorge um die Auswirkungen auf jene Regionen und Landschaften, von denen die zur Errichtung erforderlichen Ressourcen entnommen werden. In diesem Zusammenhang werden die in den heutigen Stoffflüssen noch immer vorhandenen Spuren kolonialistischer Praxis thematisiert: Die Importrouten des heutigen Großbritannien, welche für die Beschaffung von Bauprodukten am globalen Markt dienen, haben ihren Ursprung wenigstens zum Teil in den alten Handelsrouten des ehemaligen Empire.

Eine Vielzahl der Textbeiträge beschäftigt sich mit der Landnutzung und den Produktionsmöglichkeiten in Großbritannien. Die AutorInnen zeigen wie im Baustoff-Sektor lokale Wertschöpfungsketten errichtet werden können, die auf ressourcenintensive globale Transportrouten weitestgehend verzichten. Neben einer Behandlung der in großen Mengen vorkommenden mineralischen Stoffe Lehm und Naturstein, für die es im kleineren Umfang schon etablierte und funktionierende Produktionsketten gibt, nimmt das Potenzial einer behutsam skalierten Kultivierung von nachwachsenden Baustoffen eine wesentliche Rolle in der Argumentation von Material Cultures ein. Ausführlich wird so auch die realistische Möglichkeit einer effektiven Senkung der Treibhausgasemissionen mittels der langfristigen Kohlenstoffbindung in gesunden Böden sowie in Getreide und Bäumen, respektive den Baumaterialien Stroh und Holz, beschrieben. Zukunftsweisend ist, wie ein agroforstwirtschaftliches und gemeinwohlorientiertes Landmanagement hier zusammen mit baulicher Praxis gedacht wird. Die vielschichtigen Überlegungen für ein qualitätsvolles Zusammenleben treffen sich auf befruchtende Weise mit strategischen Ansätzen zur makroökonomischen Ausgestaltung der gebauten Umwelt. Übergeordnetes Ziel ist eine ökologische Alphabetisierung[6], die von einem umfassenden Wissen um die

4 Czech: *Ungefähre Hauptrichtung* (wie Anm. 1), 101.

5 Vgl. z.B. Iturbe, Elisa: “Architecture and the Death of Carbon Modernity”, *Log* 47 (2019), 10–23.

6 Material Cultures/Rogers, Louis (Hg.): *Material Reform. Building for a Post-Carbon Future*, London 2022, 141.

Beschaffenheit lokal verfügbarer Baustoffe ausgeht und die es ermöglicht die unterschiedlichen Lebenszyklen der beim Bauen verwendeten Materialien zu berücksichtigen.

Die Stringenz der Argumentation ist beeindruckend, denn sie lässt für einen Moment vergessen, welche enormen Ansprüche hier an das bestehende gesellschaftliche und wirtschaftliche System gestellt werden. Auf Ebene der Praxis gilt es die komplexe Frage rechtlicher Grundlagen und Normierungen so zu verhandeln, dass strukturelle Barrieren schrittweise abgebaut werden und positive Anreize für eine ökologisch verantwortungsbewusste Baukultur geschaffen werden. Denn wir kommen nicht umhin „die Wechselwirkung zwischen Technik und Natur angesichts der gegenwärtigen gesellschaftlichen Bedingungen neu zu denken“[7]. Die Herausforderung liegt in diesem Spannungsfeld wohl darin, eine ausgewogene Haltung zu finden, die es erlaubt Veränderungen in ihrer historischen Kontinuität zu verstehen. So ist die architektonische Kultur reich von qualitätsvollen Gedanken, Gebäuden und Phänomenen, die darauf warten identifiziert und neu bewertet zu werden. Die AutorInnen zeigen in dieser Frage eine mutige und inspirierende Haltung und liefern somit zugleich Anstoß, Beitrag und umfassenden Wissensstand für die wichtige Diskussion um emanzipierte Formen architektonischer Praxis.[8]

Thomas Sommerauer

7 Moravánszky, Ákos: *Stoffwechsel. Materialverwandlung in der Architektur*, Basel 2018, 213.
8 Malterre-Barthes, Charlotte: „Preface“, (wie Anm. 3), 10.

Thinking Architecture Based on Conditions of Production

The title of this review is a play on Hermann Czech's rhetorical question as to whether architecture can be considered from the perspective of consumption.[1] Czech arrives at the conclusion that consumer-oriented architecture must also deal with questions of production so as to avoid ending up oblivious to the production techniques inherent to architecture. These very production techniques are based on processes that consume an enormous amount of resources, a fact that goes largely unnoticed. The British architecture collective Material Cultures brings these processes into the light.

The handy volume *Material Reform*, published in 2022, gives its readers a great deal to think about. As the subtitle reveals, it deals with nothing less than the building of a post-carbon future. The architects Summer Islam, Paloma Gormley, and George Massoud, who all practice primarily in the United Kingdom, established Material Cultures with the aim of addressing this challenge. At the heart of their work is an architecture made of regenerative materials, whose conditions and possibilities are explored in built projects, as well as in research and teaching. The publication reviewed here was developed in collaboration with Amica Dall, one of the founding members of the critically acclaimed architect and artist collective Assemble. The photographer Jess Gough provided the visual structure for the book, with her full-page shots accompanying the text. In the foreword, Charlotte Malterre-Barthes—known for her initiative “A Moratorium on New Construction”[2]—emphatically points to the intrinsic historical connection between environmental destruction and capitalist practices of accumulation. She confronts the purportedly blameless “neutrality of design”[3] with a reality that, upon closer examination of the global production and supply chains of today's building materials, turns out to be problematic on various levels. The authors of this volume thus take a position that is ever-critical of new eco-labels and of solutions that exclusively put faith in technological progress, because they tend to perpetuate such established models of practice and salve one's conscience instead of addressing the more difficult question of what form substantive cultural change might take. To this end, the authors lay the foundation for a reformed building sector based on circular thinking and regenerative materials. We as readers are encouraged to consider, when reflecting on the form and nature of architecture, the conditions of production, so as to confront such “semiconsciousness that distances itself from its own production.”[4]

Through the structure of the book, Material Cultures breaks the complexity of the topic down in an accessible and appropriate way. The main section of the volume is comprised of an anthology of short texts, each of which can be read individually while still being seen as part of an overall narrative dealing with the material and societal implications of building. Here, the calamitous relationship between contemporary building and planning practices and environmentally damaging forms of resource extraction is fleshed out in detail. The now well-known critique[5] of sustainability as a concept, with its focus trained exclusively on energy efficiency in a building operations context, is rephrased here in a highly nuanced way. A comprehensive span of content is covered, from descriptions

1 Hermann Czech, *Ungefähre Hauptrichtung: Schriften und Gespräche zur Architektur* (Vienna, 2021), 93.
2 See https://stopconstruction.cargo.site/ (accessed November 19, 2023).
3 Charlotte Malterre-Barthes, “Preface,” in *Material Reform: Building for a Post-Carbon Future*, ed. Material Cultures and Louis Rogers (London, 2022), 10.
4 Czech, *Ungefähre Hauptrichtung* (see note 1), 101.
5 See, for example, Elisa Iturbe, “Architecture and the Death of Carbon Modernity,” *Log* 47 (2019), 10–23.

of shortcomings to concrete ideas about reforming our relationship to built and natural environments. The "classical" bounds of architectural discourse are thus overstepped again and again, for the aim of thinking about architectural practice in a different way makes it imperative that neighboring disciplines are seriously considered as well. Thanks to carefully and compactly prepared specialist knowledge from the fields of ecology, agriculture, and the science of materials, it is possible to contextualize each individual point of view. Material Cultures argues convincingly for the necessity of cultivating an awareness of architecture that is capable of taking into account material flows and working conditions in a wide variety of contexts, such as the extraction of raw materials, construction, and the possible transformation or demolition of a building.

The book appeals with the clear language used by its thoughtful author collective. Soberly elaborated theses and approaches are presented in a gentle way, though tinged with a cutting edge. Taking this tack, the authors compel us to listen and draw attention to the potentially unpleasant truths that we as architects have to face. In their critique, Material Cultures first addresses manufacturing processes to which building—and thus also the making of architecture—is inevitably linked. This is particularly evident in the chapter "Oil Vernacular" describing the absurd inconsistencies between highly energy-efficient buildings and the ecologically problematic procedures of resource extraction so necessary for constructing the latter. However, instead of stopping at a mere critique of the status quo, Material Cultures aspires to actively promote the reform of the conventional use of materials. As practicing architects, they show how qualitatively valuable architecture can be realized while widely eschewing the resource-intensive, successful building materials of the twentieth century (concrete, steel, and petrochemical products). Buildings designed by Material Cultures aim to make do with the use of regenerative materials and short transportation routes. Such changed framework conditions can be seen as productive restrictions that make way for a rich space of potentiality for creating architecture. However, in order to widen the scope for this way of building, a shift in awareness is necessary among all those involved in the value chain, as it is central to change the system of reference we are using to evaluate our built and unbuilt environment. Indeed, when assessing architectural quality, more needs to be taken into account than just the building's influence on its immediate surroundings. Of equal importance is its impact on those regions and landscapes from which the resources required for construction have been taken. Addressed in this context are the traces of colonialist practice still evident in today's material flows: the import routes of present-day Great Britain, which serve to procure construction products on the global market, go back, at least in part, to the old trade routes of the former empire.

Quite a few of the text contributions deal with the use of land and the production facilities in Great Britain. The authors show how it is possible to establish local value chains in the building materials sector while hardly relying on resource-intensive global transportation routes. Playing an essential role in Material Cultures' line of argumentation is not only an examination of the mineral materials of clay and natural stone, which are found in abundance and for which established and functioning production chains already exist on a smaller scale, but also the potential of a carefully scaled cultivation of renewable building materials. Described in detail is thus the realistic possibility of effectively reducing greenhouse gas emissions through long-term carbon capture in healthy soils, as well as in grains and trees, or through the building materials of straw and wood. The concept presented here of combining land management based on an agroforestry oriented to the common good with an empathic architectural practice is substantially forward-looking. Complex ideas about valuable ways of cohabitation prolifically meet strategic approaches to macroeconomically frame the production of our built environment. The overarching goal is "ecological literacy,"[6] which presupposes comprehensive knowledge of locally available building materials and which makes it possible to consider the different life cycles of the materials used in the construction process.

The compelling nature of the argumentation is impressive, for it temporarily allows us to forget what enormous demands are being placed here on existing social and economic systems. In terms of practice, it is necessary to negotiate the complex issue of legal foundations and standardization in such a way that structural barriers can be removed step by step and positive incentives for an ecologically responsible building culture created. We cannot, in fact, avoid reconsidering "the interaction between technology and nature in the light of current social conditions."[7] The challenge, it seems, lies in arriving at a balanced stance that enables changes to be seen with their historical continuity in mind. Thus, architectural culture is rich in high-quality ideas, buildings, and phenomena that are just waiting to be sensitively identified and newly assessed. In this respect, the authors take a courageous and inspiring approach—and, accordingly, deliver impetus, input, and comprehensive knowledge to the vital discussion on emancipated forms of architectural practice.[8]

Thomas Sommerauer
Translation: Dawn Michelle d'Atri

6 Material Cultures and Louis Rogers, eds., *Material Reform: Building for a Post-Carbon Future* (London, 2022), 141.
7 Ákos Moravánszky, *Metamorphism: Material Change in Architecture* (Basel, 2017), 212.
8 See Malterre-Barthes, "Preface" (see note 3), 10.

Faculty News

Inhaltsverzeichnis
Contents

Faculty

Awards

Research

Publications

Events/Projects

Discourse

Exhibitions

International Cooperations

Faculty

„Vom Potenzial von Widersprüchlichkeiten“

Lisa Yamaguchi (LY) im Gespräch mit
Petra Eckhard und Daniel Gethmann (GAM)

© GAM.Lab, TU Graz

Lisa Yamaguchi besetzt seit März 2023 die Professur für Integral Architecture an der TU Graz. Seit 2019 ist sie Partnerin im Architekturbüro Dreisterneplus ***+ in München.

GAM: Lisa, herzlich willkommen an der Architekturfakultät der TU Graz. Wir freuen uns sehr, dass du als neu berufene Professorin für Integral Architecture bei uns bist. Du kommst aus München, bist seit 2019 Partnerin im Architekturbüro Dreisterneplus ***+. Wie hängt die Tätigkeit hier mit der Tätigkeit in deinem Büro zusammen?

LY: Erstmal vielen Dank, ich freue mich auch sehr, hier zu sein. Die Tätigkeit hier hängt mit der Tätigkeit im Büro so zusammen, dass unsere Arbeit im Büro von einer Arbeitsmethodik geprägt ist, die ich auch hier in der Lehre weitergeben und vermitteln möchte.

GAM: Worin besteht diese Methodik?

LY: Aus einem sehr intensiven Entwurfsprozess, der im Team erfolgt. Wir treffen uns wöchentlich in Entwurfsteams, zwei Leute aus der Geschäftsleitung und ein oder zwei ArchitektInnen, die dann in erster Linie daran arbeiten. Alle vier Wochen treffen sich die GeschäftsführerInnen mit dem/der jeweiligen ProjektleiterIn, so dass wir immer eingebunden sind und gleichzeitig auch mitsprechen. Das ist sozusagen das offensichtlichste, einfachste Mittel, in einen Dialog zu treten. In einem solchen Dialog steckt auch die Möglichkeit der Dialektik, dass man unterschiedliche Sichtweisen zur Sprache bringt und diskutiert, sowie aussprechen und vermitteln kann, was man meint. Auf diese Weise versuchen wir letztendlich, Lösungen zu finden, die vielleicht auf den ersten Blick nicht einfach sind, aus unserer Sicht aber eine Komplexität oder Tiefe erzeugen von der wir glauben, dass sie zu guter Architektur führt.

GAM: Spannend! Und im Sinne der Dialektik legt ihr Wert darauf, dass es im Dialog Widersprüche gibt?

LY: Ja, das liegt im Wesen der Architektur und natürlich auch in der oftmals sehr komplexen Aufgabenstellung, die nie eindeutig ist. Erst im Aushandeln mit anderen Beteiligten, die vielleicht andere Dinge wichtiger finden als man selbst, findet man eine Lösung, die eben bestenfalls kein Kompromiss ist, sondern Neues entstehen lässt. Für mich ist das der fruchtbare Moment in dem Prozess, in dem man merkt, dass man am Ende etwas findet, was richtig Spaß macht, obwohl man vielleicht zu Beginn nur Probleme gesehen hat.

GAM: Könntest du das an einem Beispiel aus der täglichen Arbeit zeigen?

LY: Ein Beispiel, das ich dazu immer mal heranziehe, ist der Fassadenentwurf vom „Stadthaus an der Sendlinger Straße“ in München. Wir haben an dieser Einkaufsstraße auch einen Haupteingang zu einem Passagensystem entworfen, das auch gleichzeitig ein Bürobau ist. Der Bauherr hat sich gewünscht, dass die Bürofassade, die sich zwischen historischen, verputzten Fassaden einfügt, nach den heutigen technischen Anforderungen ausgestaltet ist, dass dort durch viel Glas viel Licht hineinkommt. Das war für uns ein Widerspruch: Wie fügen wir uns einerseits in diese steinerne Identität ein und schaffen es trotzdem, viel Licht und Durchlässigkeit zu generieren? Wir haben aus dieser grundsätzlichen Widersprüchlichkeit eine Fassade entwickelt, die aus einem Betonformstein geformt ist und so gemauert werden kann, dass einerseits ein mauerartiger Charakter entsteht, der auch in der Schrägsicht mit einer gewissen Plastizität in der Fassade tatsächlich so zusammenwächst, dass er als steinern und massiv wahrgenommen wird, aber eben gleichzeitig dieses Aufgebrochene und auch Großzügige vom Innenraum her erzeugt, was sich der Bauherr gewünscht hat.

GAM: Wie bringst du diesen entwerferischen Ansatz aus dem Büro an die Universität? Wie kann die Übersetzung in die Lehre und Forschung gelingen?

LY: Der eine Ansatz, den ich jetzt versuche, ist, dass es mir tatsächlich um das Gespräch geht. Ich versuche, eine Gesprächskultur zu entwickeln, die sich bei Studierenden aus meiner Erfahrung gar nicht so leicht von selbst herstellt. Gerade deswegen ist es mir wichtig, dass wir im Studio eine Atmosphäre erzeugen, die dann vielleicht irgendwann mal so wird, als würden wir zusammen in einem Büro arbeiten und dass sich die Studierenden in das Gespräch auch selbst einbringen. Also zu versuchen, in einen Diskurs zu kommen, ist das Eine. Der andere Ansatz, den ich versuche, ist, schon im Keim der Aufgabenstellung ein Potenzial für Widersprüchlichkeiten zu erzeugen. Und ich versuche, mit bestimmten Übungen Entwurfsmethoden zu provozieren, die diese Widersprüchlichkeit auch zulassen und in Überlagerung bringen.

GAM: Worum geht es in deinem aktuellen Entwurfsstudio an der TU Graz?

LY: Mein aktuelles Entwurfsstudio heißt „Reinventing Munich", die Studierenden sollen einen Stadtteil von München neu erfinden. Ganz konkret wird das südliche Bahnhofsviertel in München behandelt. Wie andere Bahnhofsviertel in größeren Städten Europas ist es ein ziemlich multikulturelles, quirliges Viertel mit vielen Hotels und einem hohen ImmigrantInnenanteil. Die Goethestraße, um die es konkret geht, ist das Zentrum der türkischen Gemeinde und wenn man München kennt, weiß man, dass das eigentlich das untypischste Viertel der Stadt ist – weniger aufgeräumt, wie man es sonst von München kennt. Deswegen hat es auch in dem ganzen Stadtteilgefüge seine besondere Berechtigung, steht gleichzeitig aber aktuell unter einem enormen Entwicklungsdruck. Die Gebäude, die da gebaut wurden, sind nach dem Krieg schnell hochgezogen worden. Das heißt, es ist keine Architektur, die typisch für München ist, sie könnte überall stehen, ist monofunktional ausgerichtet und mittlerweile auch in die Jahre gekommen.

GAM: Worin besteht dann der Bezug zur Neuerfindung der Stadt München in dieser Gegend?

LY: Die ersten Gebäude, die da jetzt neu gebaut werden, sind hauptsächlich Bürogebäude, die alle Nachhaltigkeit verkörpern, was ja einerseits vollkommen richtig und gut ist. Auf der anderen Seite meine ich aber auch zu beobachten, dass das aktuell auch das gängige und einzige Narrativ ist, mit dem eben diese Gebäude auch in die Öffentlichkeit getragen werden. Also wenn schon neu bauen, dann eben aus Holz, sehr transparent und mit viel Grün. So sieht nachhaltige Architektur aus. Und da stelle ich mir die Frage gerade für diesen Ort, den ich sehr gut kenne: ist das jetzt die undiskutierte Antwort für diesen Ort oder wie transformiert sich dieser Stadtteil? Ich komme aus einer Schule, die sehr kontextbezogen gearbeitet hat – da möchte ich Fragen der Identität, der Permanenz, der Überlagerung von unterschiedlichen Geschichten an diesem Ort erforschen. Daraus ergibt sich die Aufgabenstellung, die ich den Studierenden gebe. Was ist an diesem Ort zu finden, welche Geschichten können sich daraus in der Überlagerung entwickeln?

GAM: Das Integrale kommt bei dir insofern auf verschiedenen Ebenen vor – einerseits über den Kontext und andererseits über die Methode des Dialogs mit den Studierenden?

LY: Ja, genau. Mir geht es um das Gesamtheitliche, nicht um das Nebeneinander von möglichst vielen Dingen technischer Natur, die vielleicht viel können, aber doch keine kohärente Ganzheitlichkeit erreichen.

GAM: Gibt es dann auch einen Dialog mit den Leuten aus dem Viertel dort?

LY: Noch nicht, ich bin gerade dabei, das zu versuchen. Es gibt schon einen Verein mit vielen Initiativen. Mittlerweile sind auch Kulturschaffende und ein Theater da. Ich muss mal schauen, wie weit ich da komme.

GAM: Dein integraler Ansatz scheint einer zu sein, der sich stark auf die Integration von Kontexten bezieht und gleichzeitig auch versucht, den Entwurf nicht nur als Einzelarbeit, sondern unter Berücksichtigung vieler anderer Aspekte zu entwickeln. Integral ist allerdings – wie so vieles im Architekturdiskurs – ein ziemlicher Modebegriff. Die einen sagen, wir müssen uns, wenn wir über Integral Architecture sprechen, eher in Richtung Nachhaltigkeit des Bauens ausrichten, die anderen warnen vor der nächsten Krise der Bauindustrie, die sich bereits bemerkbar macht. Was ist deiner Meinung nach notwendig, um in der Architekturausbildung auf diese Szenarien zu reagieren?

LY: Erstmal möchte ich versuchen, die Krise im Positiven umzudeuten. Ich empfinde das als die zentrale Aufgabe unserer Zeit, die Krise ernst zu nehmen und zu versuchen, mit jedem unserer Entwürfe auf dieses wichtige Thema zu reagieren. Ich verstehe diese Zeit des Paradigmenwechsels als eine Zeit des Umdenkens, in der eine Dynamik entsteht, die Dinge anders zu machen, als man sie die letzten Jahrzehnte gemacht hat. Und das begreife ich auch ein Stück weit als Chance. Ganz grundsätzlich glaube ich trotzdem in der Architekturausbildung nach wie vor an die „Kernkompetenz der ArchitektInnen", die sich mit Raum, mit Körperhaftigkeit, mit Nutzbarkeit der Atmosphäre, mit Häusern für Menschen befasst. Darüber hinaus glaube ich, dass auch das Entwerfen als eine weitere Kernkompetenz von ArchitektInnen eigentlich ein wunderbares Tool für alle möglichen Fragestellungen ist. Im Moment sehe ich eine große Chance darin, dass baukulturell ein Umdenken hin zu einer Umbaukultur stattfindet, dass man vielleicht ein Stück weit das Arbeiten mit dem Bestehenden trainiert, also mit Dingen, die schon vorhanden sind, und dass man lernt, zu beobachten, zu sammeln, zu vergleichen, neu zusammenzusetzen. Ich versuche das in einzelnen Entwurfsübungen konkret umzusetzen, also im weitesten Sinne mit den Werten des Bestehenden zu arbeiten, zum Beispiel in Form von Umbaumaßnahmen oder durch das Bauen mit wiederverwendeten Bauteilen. Es können aber auch Geschichten sein, die man findet und weitererzählt oder das Arbeiten mit assoziativen Werten von Architektur. Zuletzt glaube ich, dass das Entwerfen mit Referenzen gerade jetzt eine wichtige Hilfe sein kann, damit wir im Hinblick auf die großen Aufgaben, vor denen wir stehen, nicht aus der Geschichte fallen.

GAM: Du hast ja jetzt knapp zwei Jahre Zeit, diese Vorhaben umzusetzen, das ist ja durchaus eine lange Zeitspanne für eine Gastprofessur. Worauf können wir uns in den nächsten zwei Jahren freuen?

LY: Das Ziel ist auf jeden Fall eine Publikation, die nicht nur eine Sammlung von Entwürfen ist, die die Studierenden in den letzten zwei Jahren gemacht haben, sondern die im besten Fall auch die von mir gerade beschriebenen Methoden in Form von Entwurfsprozessen ablesbar macht. Und da erhoffe ich mir, aus jedem Semester ein Stück weit zu lernen und meinen Ansatz weiter zu präzisieren, damit das irgendwann eine gesamtheitliche Geschichte ergibt. Spannend wäre, wenn dieses Vorhaben, das ich beschrieben habe, anhand von Referenzen und einer Offenlegung der Arbeit – mit was habe ich gearbeitet, was waren meine Fundstücke, was hat mich interessiert – dann zu Entwürfen führen würde und man innerhalb von diesen Bildern ablesen kann, wie diese Entwürfe entstanden sind.

GAM: Wie bekommt ihr diese Fundstücke in die Hand? Ist es ein Text, sind es Bilder, oder ist es ein konkretes Objekt von dem jeweiligen Ort?

LY: Wir hoffen durch eine Exkursion, über das Reisen, das Beobachten – mit fremdem Blick auf eine neue Stadt gerichtet – etwas zu finden. Da geht es schon darum, auch Skurriles zu beobachten; Fundstücke sollte man sich auch selber, im Hinblick auf seine eigene Interpretation der Aufgabe hin, suchen.

GAM: Wie werden die Fundstücke dann im Entwerfen verwendet?

LY: Es gibt zahlreiche spezielle Themen, die sich im Entwurfsprozess ergeben. Man redet ja gerade viel über das „Narrativ" – nicht nur in der Architektur – und darüber, dass es sehr wichtig wird, eine Geschichte zu erzählen – in Form von Bildern, auch über Social Media. Bezogen auf die Architektur bin ich immer auf der Suche nach dem, was man Poesie nennt, die ja auch eine Form der Erzählung ist; nicht in Form der schnellen, offensichtlichen Magazinabbildung, sondern von etwas, das mehr Tiefe entwickelt und vielschichtiger ist. Wenn wir dazu einen Link hinbekämen, wäre ich glücklich.

GAM: Danke für das Gespräch!

"On the Potential of Contradictions"

Lisa Yamaguchi (LY) in Conversation with Petra Eckhard and Daniel Gethmann (GAM)

Lisa Yamaguchi has held the professorship for Integral Architecture at the Faculty of Architecture of Graz University of Technology since March 2023. She has been a partner in the architectural office Dreisterneplus ***+ in Munich since 2019.

GAM: Lisa, welcome to the Faculty of Architecture at Graz University of Technology (TU Graz). We are delighted to have you with us as the newly appointed professor of integral architecture. You're from Munich, and you've been a partner in the architecture firm Dreisterneplus ***+ since 2019. In what way is your work here at TU Graz related to your architectural practice?

LY: Well, first of all, thank you very much; I am also very pleased to be here. My role at the university is closely related to the work at the firm in the sense that it is characterized by a working methodology that I would like to pass on and impart in my teaching here.

GAM: What does this methodology consist of?

LY: It involves a very intense design phase conducted as a team. Each week we meet in design teams, comprising two people from the management and one or two architects, who then work primarily on the design. Every four weeks, the managing partners meet with the respective project lead, ensuring that we are fully involved and, at the same time, have a say in the process. In a way, this is the most obvious and straightforward means of entering into a dialogue. Such discourse also holds the potential for taking a dialectic approach to raising and discussing differing points of view, as well as expressing and communicating our intentions. This is how we ultimately attempt to reach decisions, which, at first glance, may not be simple; but from our point of view, they create the complexity or depth that we believe leads to good architecture.

GAM: That's fascinating! And in terms of dialectics, would you say that contradictions are an integral part of the dialogue?

LY: Yes, that lies in the nature of architecture and, of course, in an often highly complex task, one that is never clear-cut. Only through negotiation with others involved, who perhaps find certain things to be more important, does one find a solution that, ideally, is not a compromise but rather allows for something new to emerge. In my eyes, that's the fruitful moment in the creative process, when you realize that, in the end, you'll discover something really fun, although you may have only seen problems at the beginning.

GAM: Could you give an example from your work in the firm?

LY: The façade design of the "Stadthaus an der Sendlinger Straße" in Munich is an example I always like to reference. Along this high street, we also designed a main entrance to a passageway that doubles as an office building. The client requested that the office front, which is nestled between historical, plastered façades, be designed following today's technical requirements, that plenty of light comes in through lots of glass. We found this to be a challenge: How do we fit into this stone identity yet still manage to generate a high level of light and transparency? Based on this fundamental contradiction, we developed a façade that is shaped by a precast concrete block and can be masoned in such a way that, on the one hand, a brick-like structure is created which, even when viewed from an angle, actually coalesces with a certain plasticity in the façade so that it is perceived as stone-like and solid, but at the same time creates this open and generous interior, which is what the client wanted.

GAM: So how do you bring this approach to design from the practice to the university? In what ways can it be translated into teaching and research?

LY: One approach I'm currently exploring is the importance of initiating conversation. I'm trying to develop a culture of conversation, which is something that, in my experience, doesn't always evolve on its own with students. So I feel it's important to create an environment in the studio that might one day resemble working together in a practice, where the students themselves get involved in that exchange. In other words, trying to enter into discourse is one idea. Another approach I am pursuing involves generating the potential for contradictions in the very essence of the task. And I try to provoke the use of design methods through specific exercises that enable this dialectic and that ultimately make them overlap.

GAM: What is your current design studio at TU Graz about?

LY: My latest design studio is titled "Reinventing Munich," in which the students are asked to reinvent a district of Munich, specifically the area around the southern railway station. Like other station districts in larger European cities, it is a fairly multicultural, bustling district with plenty of hotels and a high concentration of immigrants. The Goethestraße, which happens to be the subject of the project, is the center of the Turkish community, and if you know Munich, then you'll realize that it is, in fact, the most atypical neighborhood of the city—less neat than Munich is usually known to be. That's why it has a special status in the fabric of this whole district, yet at the same time it is currently under enormous pressure to be developed. The buildings constructed there had been quickly erected just after the Second World War, meaning that it is not architecture unique to this city; indeed, it could be found anywhere, and it is starting to age.

GAM: So how does this tie in with the reinvention of the city of Munich in this particular district?

LY: The first new buildings being constructed there are mainly office buildings, all embodying sustainability, which, on the one hand, is fair and reasonable. Yet on the other hand, I also think this is the common and currently only narrative used to describe these buildings. So, if new buildings are to be erected, then it would be better if they were made of wood, highly transparent and with abundant greenery. That's what sustainable architecture looks like. And that is where I ask myself the question, particularly for this place, which I happen to know very well: Is this the uncontested solution for this site, or how is this part of town being transformed? I come from a university that placed a lot of emphasis on context—that is why I want to explore issues of identity, permanence, and the overlapping of past narratives in this place, hence the task I gave to the students. Which stories can be found here, and what can be developed from them through superimposition?

GAM: In that sense, the integral occurs at different levels in your work—on the one hand, through the context and, on the other, through dialogue with the students.

LY: Yes, exactly. I am interested in the whole picture, not in the juxtaposition of as many things of a technical nature as possible, which may be able to do much but do not achieve coherence overall.

GAM: Will there also be a dialogue with the people from the neighborhood there?

LY: No, not yet. I'm in the process of attempting to initiate this. There is already an association there with numerous initiatives. Also, cultural workers and a theater. I'll have to see how far I can get.

GAM: Your integral approach seems to be one that strongly refers to the integration of contexts and, at the same time, tries to develop the design not only as an individual work but also taking many other aspects into account. Integral, however, happens to be—like so much in architectural discourse—quite a fashionable term. Some might say that when we refer to integral architecture, we have to orient ourselves more toward the sustainability of building. In contrast, others warn of the next crisis in the building industry, a crisis that is already making itself felt. What do you think is necessary to respond to these scenarios in architectural education?

LY: First of all, I would like to try to reinterpret the said crisis positively. In my view, a central task of our time involves taking this issue seriously and attempting to respond to it through each of our designs. I understand this paradigm shift as a time of reconsideration, in which momentum is developing toward doing things differently than how they have been done for the last few decades. I regard this to be an opportunity to a certain extent. Fundamentally, however, I still believe in the "core competence of architects" in architectural education, which is concerned with spaces, physicality, the usability of the environment, and houses for people. Furthermore, I think that design—as another core competence of architects—is a wonderful tool for all kinds of questions. At the moment, I see great potential in rethinking building culture toward a culture of redevelopment, in training people to work with the preexisting, that is, with what is already there, and in learning to observe, collect, compare, and reassemble. This is something I try to put into practice in individual design exercises, in order to, in the broadest sense, work with the values of the existing, for example, in the form of reconstruction measures or by building with reused components. Yet it can also be stories you find and retell or one's work with the associative values of architecture. Lastly, I believe that designing alongside references can be a far-reaching tool right now to ensure that we don't forget the past when it comes to the big tasks we are facing.

GAM: You now have almost two years to realize these projects, which is quite a long time for a visiting professorship. What can we look forward to in the coming two years?

LY: In any case, the goal is a publication and one that is not just a compilation of the designs that the students have produced over the last two years but which, in the best case, also illustrates the methods I have just described in the form of design processes. And I hope to learn a bit more each semester and further refine my approach so that it will eventually result in a holistic narrative. It would be very exciting if this project I have described were to lead to designs based on references and disclosure of the work—that is, what did I work with, what were my findings, what provoked my interest—and if one could read within these images how these designs came about.

GAM: How do you obtain these found items? Is it a text, pictures, or a specific object from that particular place?

LY: We hope to encounter something through an excursion, by traveling, observing—looking at a new city with a foreign eye. The idea is to observe the bizarre, yet you should also look for found objects yourself in terms of your understanding of the task at hand.

GAM: How are these found objects then used in the design?

LY: Many specific themes arise in the design process. Right now, there is a lot of talk—not only in architecture—about the importance of telling a story, of a "narrative" in the form of images but also via social media. In terms of architecture, I always find myself looking for the poetic, which is also a form of narrative, not in the way of the quick, obvious magazine illustration, but of something that develops more depth and is multilayered. If we could get a link to that, I would be very happy.

GAM: Thank you for the interview!

Gastprofessur Hannes Peer

Im Sommersemester 2023 war der Architekt Hannes Peer am Institut für Gebäudelehre zu Gast und leitete gemeinsam mit Hans Gangoly, Tobias Gruber, Elisabeth Koller und Eva Sollgruber das Master Studio „Skulptur (Raum)". Die Entwurfsaufgabe bestand in der Konzeption eines „Handwerkapartments" in Graz – eines Arbeits- und Wohnraumes für eine/n BildhauerIn – mit dessen Entwurf Gegensatzpaare wie Privat und Öffentlich oder Wohnen und Arbeiten räumlich neu verhandelt werden sollten. Dafür zur Disposition standen die ersten beiden Etagen des bestehenden Hochhauses am Grazer Dietrichsteinplatz. Den entwurfsmethodischen Leitfaden für den Umbau der bestehenden Bausubstanz bildeten Motive des Unfertigen, Bruchstückhaften und Zirkulären: ähnlich wie in der Bildhauerei wurde die bestehende Masse entwerferisch geformt, durchbohrt und ausgehöhlt, und mit neuen Elementen ergänzt. Neben der Auseinandersetzung mit dem baulich Bestehenden, war das Erforschen der Arbeitsweise ausgewählter KünstlerInnen konzeptueller Ausgangspunkt für die Entwürfe. Künstlerische Arbeiten, Texte und Interviews lieferten die Motive für eine räumliche Entsprechung. Die Ergebnisse der Lehrveranstaltung – Entwurfsartefakte wie Modelle, Bilder, Zeichnungen, Pläne, Skizzen und Texte – zeichnen den jeweiligen Entwurfsprozess nach und verdeutlichen in ihrer Zusammenschau die räumlich atmosphärische Dichte der entstandenen Projekte.

Hannes Peer ist Architekt und Interior Designer mit Sitz in Mailand. Die Arbeiten seines Studios „Hannes Peer Architecture" sind vielfach publiziert und ausgezeichnet und umfassen eine breite Palette an nationalen und internationalen Projekten aus dem Bereich Wohnen, Büro und Einzelhandel. Die Lehrveranstaltung startete mit einer Exkursion nach Mailand, in der Studierende Einblicke in den Büroalltag und das Arbeitsumfeld Hannes Peers bekamen. Während der Besichtigung ausgewählter architektonischer Referenzen wurden Oberflächenbeschaffenheiten sowie Verarbeitungstechniken unterschiedlicher Baustoffe und Materialien akribisch studiert. Diese Auseinandersetzung mit der Bauhandwerkstradition Mailands war für die Studierenden Inspiration und entwerferische Grundlage zugleich.

Eva Sollgruber

© IGL, TU Graz

Visiting Professor Hannes Peer

During the summer semester of 2023, the architect Hannes Peer was a guest at the Institute of Design and Building Typology and, alongside Hans Gangoly, Tobias Gruber, Elisabeth Koller, and Eva Sollgruber, led the master studio "Skulptur (Raum)." The design task consisted of developing a concept for a "craftsperson's apartment" in Graz comprising a space for a sculptor to work and live in, where binaries, such as private and communal or living and working, were to be spatially renegotiated. Both floors of the existing high-rise building at Dietrichsteinplatz in Graz were made available for this purpose. The design methodology guiding the conversion of the existing building fabric drew on motifs of the inchoate, fragmentary, and circular: in a manner analogous to sculpture, the existing mass was molded by design, pierced, hollowed out, and augmented by new elements. Along with an analysis of the existing structure, investigations into the working practices employed by selected artists provided the conceptual starting point for the designs.

Works of art, texts, and interviews supplied the motifs for a spatial equivalent. The results of the course—design artifacts such as models, photos, plans, sketches, and texts—trace the respective design process and, when viewed together, illustrate the spatial and atmospheric density of the resulting projects.

Hannes Peer is an architect and interior designer based in Milan. The works of his studio, "Hannes Peer Architecture," have been widely published and awarded and include a broad range of national and international projects in the residential, office, and retail sectors. The course started with an excursion to Milan, where students were given insight into Hannes Peer's day-to-day office life and working environment. During the visit, surface textures and processing techniques of different building materials were meticulously studied. This examination of Milan's building tradition served both as inspiration and as a design basis for the students.

Gastprofessur Julian Müller

Im Sommersemester 2023 war der Soziologe Julian Müller zu Gast am Institut für Entwerfen im Bestand und Denkmalpflege. Die Einladung zur Gastprofessur verfolgte das Ziel, den bereits bestehenden interdisziplinären Austausch zwischen Architektur und Soziologie zu vertiefen. So wurden in der Lehrveranstaltung „Kontextanalyse" die Herausforderungen jedweder Form von Kontextbestimmung und Kontextualisierung diskutiert, mit denen nicht nur die Architektur, sondern auch andere Fächer zu tun haben. Entsprechend wurden auch Texte aus der Soziologie, der Literaturwissenschaft oder der Nachrichtentheorie besprochen und auf Fragen der Architektur bezogen.

Vor allem aber wurde das Sommersemester dazu genutzt, Methoden aus dem Bereich der qualitativen Sozialforschung, insbesondere der Ethnographie, vorzustellen. Nicht nur in der Lehrveranstaltung „Site Repair", vor allem im gemeinsam mit Matthias Castorph veranstalteten Workshop „Camp Steinhaus" wurden derartige Methoden an Günther Domenigs Steinhaus am Ossiacher See, einem der jüngsten Denkmäler Österreichs, praktisch erprobt. Um sich mit diesem Gebäude und seiner Umgebung nicht nur beiläufig, sondern konzentriert auseinandersetzen zu können, fand der einwöchige Workshop in den Räumen des Steinhauses sowie auf dem unmittelbar angrenzenden Campingplatz, der ebenfalls Gegenstand der Forschung war, statt. Ziel war es, sich mit den Mitteln der Architekturethnographie über einen längeren Zeitraum mit einem einzigen Gebäude bzw. Ort auseinanderzusetzen und dieses bzw. diesen mithilfe unterschiedlicher Techniken – Skizzen, Beobachtungsprotokolle, dichte Beschreibungen, Interviews, Foto- und Videographien etc. – zu erforschen.

Darüber hinaus war Julian Müller an der Organisation und Durchführung der Graz Architecture Lectures 2023 beteiligt, die unter dem Titel „The Infraordinary" unterschiedliche Positionen zum Alltäglichen in der Architektur versammelten.

Julian Müller

© Julian Müller

Visiting Professor Julian Müller

In the summer semester of 2023, the sociologist Julian Müller was a guest in the Institute of Design in Existing Structures and Architectural Heritage Protection. The invitation to the visiting professorship sought to amplify the preexisting interdisciplinary exchange between architecture and sociology. Hence, the course "Context Analysis" addressed the challenges inherent to any attempt at context assessment and contextualization encountered not only in architecture but also in other disciplines. As a result, texts from the fields of sociology, literary studies, and news theory were discussed and put in relation to questions from the discipline of architecture.

Above all, however, the summer semester saw the introduction of methodologies based on qualitative social research, in particular ethnography. These methods were tested in practice not only in the course "Site Repair," but also in the workshop "Camp Steinhaus," organized with Matthias Castorph and held at Günther Domenig's Steinhaus on Lake Ossiach, one of Austria's most recently listed monuments. In order to engage with the building and its surroundings in a manner not merely en passant but also nuanced as well, the one-week workshop took place in the rooms of the Steinhaus as well as at the neighboring campsite, which also served as a subject of research. The aim was to engage with a single building or location over an extended period using the methods of architectural ethnography, and to investigate it using a range of techniques: sketches, observation protocols, thick descriptions, interviews, photography, videography, etc.

In addition, Julian Müller was involved in hosting the Graz Architecture Lectures 2023, which brought together different positions on the everyday in architecture under the title "The Infraordinary."

Awards

TU Graz-Absolvent Dinko Jelečević gewinnt den Young Talent EU Mies Award 2023

© KOEN, TU Graz

Für seine Masterarbeit „VALTER – Vraca Forum Sarajevo" ist Dinko Jelečević, Absolvent der Architekturfakultät der TU Graz, am 29. Juni 2023 mit dem Young Talent EU Mies Award ausgezeichnet worden. Die von Petra Petersson am Institut für Grundlagen der Konstruktion und des Entwerfens (KOEN) betreute Abschlussarbeit sieht die Wiederbelebung der Festungsanlage und des Gedächtnisparks von Vraca durch eine adaptive Wiederverwendungsmethode vor. Der Ort, der in vier verschiedenen Epochen des 20. Jahrhunderts als Festung, Hinrichtungsstätte, Gedenkstätte und Militärstützpunkt genutzt wurde, soll schließlich die Form und Funktion eines öffentlichkeitsorientierten Forums annehmen.

Aus der Projektbeschreibung: „Unter Berücksichtigung des historischen Kontextes der Anlage sowie ihrer geostrategischen Position an der Grenzlinie zwischen der Föderation Bosnien und Herzegowina und der Republika Srpska, sowie des vorherrschenden politischen Narrativs, das die Stätte als unerwünschtes Erbe betrachtet, war es möglich, ihr räumliches und emanzipatorisches Potenzial zu nutzen. Da die Festung seit ihrer Entstehung mehrmals baulich umgestaltet wurde, war es für den Entwurf einerseits notwendig, alle Veränderungen zu bewerten und sämtliche

Interventionen in Betracht zu ziehen sowie gleichzeitig einen ganzheitlichen Entwurfsansatz zu entwickeln, in dem neue Schichten hinzugefügt werden konnten. Das Projekt erforscht das Vraca-Palimpsest indem es räumliche Elemente mit historischen Ereignissen kontextualisiert und eine neue Schicht vorschlägt, die mit ihrer Forumstypologie eine Plattform für das Verständnis der umstrittenen Vergangenheit und die Schaffung einer partizipativen Gesellschaft der Zukunft ermöglicht."

Die EU Mies Awards würdigen seit 2001 herausragende Leistungen europäischer ArchitektInnen und gilt als renommiertester Architekturpreis der Europäischen Union. 2016 wurden die Awards um die Kategorie des „Young Talent EU Mies Award" erweitert. Der von der Fundació Mies van der Rohe ausgelobte Preis richtet sich an AbsolventInnen aus den Bereichen Architektur, Stadtplanung und Landschaftsarchitektur in Europa und anderen Teilen der Welt und wird alle zwei Jahre vergeben. Dinko Jelečevićs Gewinnerprojekt sowie die Projekte aller FinalistInnen werden noch bis November 2023 im Rahmen des Ausstellungsprogramms der Architekturbiennale in Venedig im Palazzo Mora zu sehen sein.

Petra Eckhard

© Dinko Jelečević

© Dinko Jelečević

TU Graz Graduate Dinko Jelečević Wins the Young Talent EU Mies Award 2023

In recognition of his master's thesis "VALTER—Vraca Forum Sarajevo," Dinko Jelečević, a graduate of the Faculty of Architecture at TU Graz, was awarded the "Young Talent EU Mies Award 2023" on June 29, 2023. Supervised by Petra Petersson at the Institute of Construction and Design Principles (KOEN), the graduate thesis proposes the revitalization of a multilayered historic site in Sarajevo through an adaptive reuse methodology. Used as a fortification, execution site, memorial complex, and military base during four different eras in the twentieth century, the site will ultimately take up the shape and function of a public-oriented forum typology.

According to the project description: "Taking into account the historical context of the site and its geostrategic position along the borderline between the Federation of Bosnia and Herzegovina and Republika Srpska, as well as the prevailing political narrative that considers the site to be undesirable heritage, it was possible to harness its spatial and emancipatory potential. Being that the fortress has been structurally altered a number of times since its creation, it proved necessary for the design, on the one hand, to assess all changes and to consider any interventions and, on the other, to develop a holistic design approach to which new layers could be added. The project explores the Vraca palimpsest by contextualizing spatial elements with historical events and proposing a new layer that, with its forum typology, enables a platform for understanding its contested past and for creating a participatory society of the future."

The EU Mies Awards have been honoring outstanding achievements by European architects since 2001 and are regarded as the most prestigious architecture prize within the European Union. In 2016, the awards were expanded to include the category "Young Talent EU Mies Award." The prize, offered by the Fundació Mies van der Rohe, is aimed at graduates in the fields of architecture, urban planning, and landscape architecture in Europe, as well as in other parts of the world, and is bestowed every two years. Dinko Jelečević's winning project, along with the projects of all the finalists, was on display through November 2023 at Palazzo Mora as part of the exhibition program of the Venice Architecture Biennale.

GAD Awards PreisträgerInnen mit Jury und Sponsoren © GAM.Lab, TU Graz

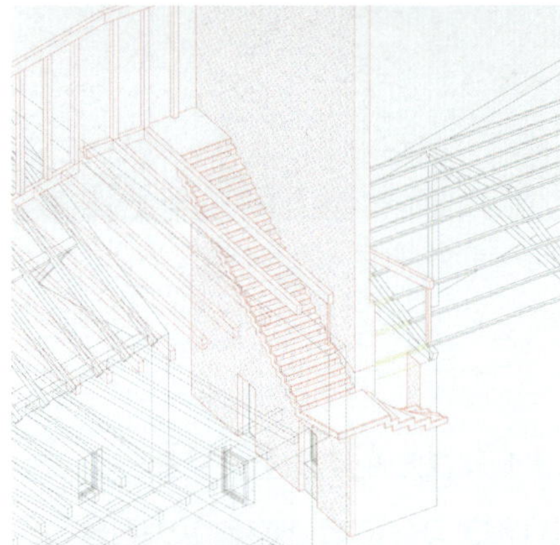

© Beatrice Raith

GAD Awards 2023

Beatrice Raith, Anna-Maria Jäger, Marie-Theres Schwaighofer, Theresa Schleinitz, Valentin Moser, Angelika Hinterbrandner, Nera Džanić und Dennis Baumgartner sind die PreisträgerInnen der GAD Awards 2023. Die Gewinnerprojekte zeigen, wie der Prozess des Weiterbauens, kooperative Stadtteilentwicklung, eine realpolitische Vision des Wohnens, die Rekultivierung von ländlichem Leerstand, frauengerechtes Wohnen, oder aber das Bauen mit Pappmaché gelingen könnte. Die feierliche Preisverleihung fand am 19. Oktober 2023 im HS I der Alten Technik statt.

Der von der Steiermärkischen Landesregierung, Abteilung 16 – Verkehr und Landeshochbau gestiftete erste Preis wurde an Beatrice Raith für ihr Projekt „Die wachsenden Häuser von Wetzelsdorf" verliehen. Die Masterarbeit, betreut von Alex Lehnerer am Institut für Raumgestaltung, thematisiert das situative Entstehen von Architektur, das Immer-Weiter-Bauen. Dieser Prozess wird anhand von einem Einfamilienhaus im Grazer Stadtbezirk Wetzelsdorf veranschaulicht und in Form von vier Heften, die vier Erzählungen beinhalten, aufbereitet. Die diesjährige Jury, bestehend aus Ulrike Tinnacher (tinnacher.studio, Wien), Paul Preissner (Paul Preissner Architects, Chicago) und Pier Paolo Tamburelli (baukuh, Mailand/TU Vienna), befand das Projekt „in einer tieferen konzeptionellen Weise beeindruckend, weil es etwas programmatisch Großes tat, und zwar durch eine Vielzahl von situativ konstruierten Momenten eines Hauses. Diese Momente sind nicht sequenziell, sondern hätten in beliebiger Reihenfolge ausgeführt werden können, dennoch waren sie additiv, um eine andere Beziehung zum ursprünglichen Haus zu schaffen, und zwar in einer freigeistigen Art, die ein wenig an Aktionskunst erinnert." (Paul Preissner).

Den zweiten Preis der GAD Awards teilten sich Anna-Maria Jäger und Marie-Theres Schwaighofer mit dem Projekt von Theresa Schleinitz. Von Aglaée Degros am Institut für Städtebau betreut, beschäftigt sich das Diplomprojekt von Anna-Maria Jäger und Marie-Theres Schwaighofer mit dem Thema der chancengerechten und regenerativen Stadt(teil)entwicklung im Kontext des von Zuwanderung geprägten Grazer Stadtbezirks Gries und spezifischer mit der künftigen Entwicklung der 2014 stillgelegten Rösselmühle. Die Arbeit skizziert die Transformation der Mühle hin zu einem gemeinwohlorientierten Projekt,

© Anna-Maria Jäger, Marie-Theres Schwaighofer

das sich durch eine hohe Nutzungsdichte und vielfältigen Grün- und Freiräumen im Sinne einer gerechteren und gesellschaftlich vielfältigen Stadt auszeichnet. Die Jury würdigte die Auseinandersetzung mit einem „sehr komplexen städtischen Problem aus unterschiedlichen Blickwinkeln" sowie die „präzisen städtebaulichen und architektonischen Interventionen" (Pier Paolo Tamburelli).

Theresa Schleinitz Masterarbeit, die ebenfalls mit dem 2. Preis ausgezeichnet wurde, entstand am Institut für Gebäudelehre und wurde von Eva Sollgruber betreut. Die Arbeit fordert einen Systemumbau bestehender baulicher und gesellschaftlicher Strukturen, der explizit die Lebensrealität von Frauen* berücksichtigt und eine sichere und leichter zugängliche, diversere Welt für alle Menschen zum Ziel hat. Konkret wird ein Bestandsgebäude zu einem Haus für Frauen* umgestaltet, das als Alternative zu monofunktionalen Wohntypologien, einen Beitrag zur Sichtbarmachung drängender feministischer Forderungen an die Architektur leisten kann. Zitat aus dem Jurystatement: „Das Projekt schafft einen neuen feministischen häuslichen Raum, der nicht monoprogrammiert ist, sondern der in Bezug auf das was in ihm geschieht, abwechslungsreich und vielfältig ist, dabei Teile des Bestandsgebäudes entfernt und umbaut. Es ist sanft und aggressiv zugleich." (Paul Preissner)

Der diesjährige Hollomey Reisepreis ging an Valentin Moser, der sich in seiner von Andreas Lechner am Institut für Gebäudelehre betreuten Masterarbeit mit dem Leerstand im ländlichen Raum und dessen Rekultivierung durch Beteiligung regionaler AkteurInnen befasst. „Das Projekt wurde ausgezeichnet, da es sich nicht nur mit dem Leerstand am Land beschäftigt, sondern diesen mit hybriden Nutzungen überlagert und erweitert.
Es bildet mit einem mutigen Neubau und einem sensiblen Umgang mit dem Bestand ein bemerkenswertes und vielseitiges Ensemble." (Ulrike Tinnacher)

Angelika Hinterbrandner Projekt zu Alexander Kleins innovativer Entwurfsmethodik aus den 1930er-Jahren wurde mit dem Tschom Wohnbaupreis ausgezeichnet. Die von Daniel Gethmann am Institut für Architekturtheorie, Kunst- und Kulturwissenschaften betreute Masterarbeit legt den Grundstein für eine Neuinterpretation der Kleinschen Ansätze eines Neuen Standards im Wohnungsbau durch die

© Theresa Schleinitz

© Valentin Moser

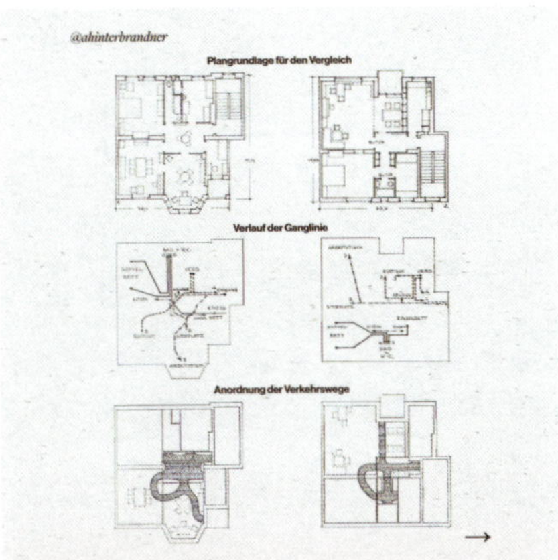

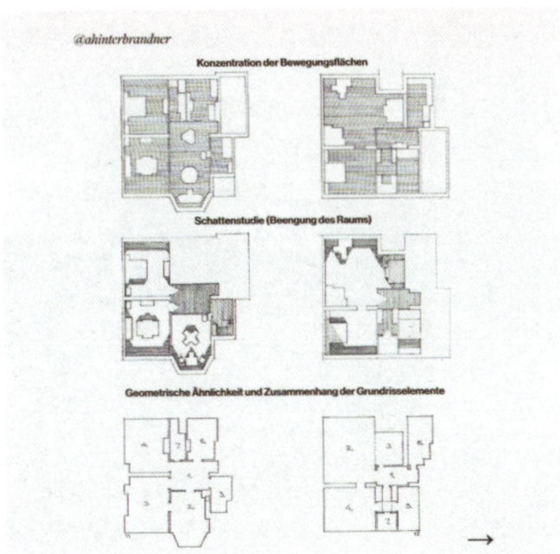

© Angelika Hinterbrandner

sozioökonomische Reflektion der Bedingungen in denen Kleins Ansatz entstand. Laut Jury leistet das Projekt als theoretische und historische Forschung einen wichtigen Beitrag im Bereich des Wohnens, und zeigt, „welches Potenzial in der Wiederentdeckung einiger Erfahrungen der Vergangenheit liegen kann." (Pier Paolo Tamburelli)

Die von der Kammer der ZiviltechnikerInnen für Steiermark und Kärnten gestiftete Anerkennung für ressourcenschonende und klimagerechte Architektur wurde an Nera Džanićs Projekt „Pappmaché. From Paper to Sustainable Architecture Material" vergeben. Die am Institut für Architektur und Medien von Milena Stavrić betreute Masterarbeit untersucht die Herstellung eines neuen, papierbasierten Verbundmaterial durch umweltfreundliche und nachhaltige Verfahren, die zu biologisch abbaubaren und wiederverwendbaren Produkten führen. Der entstandene Verbundstoff beweist immenses Potential zu einem ästhetisch und funktional relevanten Teil der Innenraumgestaltung zu werden. „Es ist ein sehr fokussiertes Projekt, das sich im Detail mit dem Produkt Papier und seinem nachhaltigen Einsatz als architektonisches Material beschäftigt. Wir würdigen den experimentellen und unkonventionellen Zugang dieser Arbeit." (Ulrike Tinnacher)

Der Sachpreis in Form eines marokkanischen Teppichs, gestiftet von Gebhart Blazek (Berber Arts), wurde als besondere Anerkennung an Dennis Baumgartner verliehen. Seine Arbeit, betreut von Andreas Lechner am Institut für Gebäudelehre, beschäftigt sich mit der Haunoldmühle im Steyrtal und nimmt den Leerstand durch die Linse der kulturellen Kunstwissenschaft und Denkmalpflege in den Blick. Der Entwurf der typologischen Umnutzung in eine Eventlocation erfolgte laut Jury „in einem freigeistigen Sinne, indem nicht nur der Verfall des historischen Projekts romantisiert wird, sondern völlig neue Objekte innerhalb des Gebäudes produziert werden, die einerseits den Verfalls in seiner Originalität fixieren und andererseits die Ungenauigkeiten der historischen Struktur bewahren." (Paul Preissner)

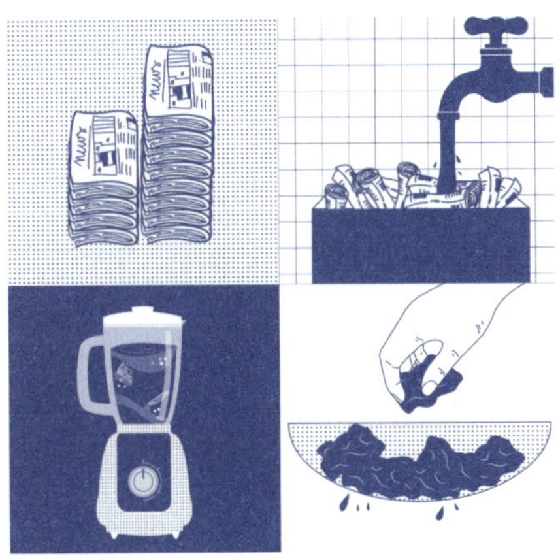

© Nera Džanić

© Dennis Baumgartner

In diesem Jahr wurde das Rahmenprogramm der feierlichen Preisverleihung der Grazer Architektur Diplompreise durch „Drei Standpunkte der Architektur" ergänzt. Dabei präsentierten die diesjährigen Jurymitglieder Ulrike Tinnacher, Paul Preissner und Pier Paolo Tamburelli ihren persönlichen Zugang zur Disziplin und sprachen über aktuelle Projekte aus Forschung und Baupraxis. Das Ausstellungskonzept wurde vom Institut für Raumgestaltung unter der Leitung von Alex Lehnerer entwickelt. Alle nominierten und ausgezeichneten Projekte sind über https:// gad-awards.tugraz.at online zugänglich.

Petra Eckhard

• Beatrice Raith, Anna-Maria Jäger, Marie-Theres Schwaighofer, Theresa Schleinitz, Valentin Moser, Angelika Hinterbrandner, Nera Džanić, and Dennis Baumgartner are the winners of the GAD Awards 2023. The prizewinning projects show how the processes of building-on, cooperative district development, a vision of housing based on realpolitik, the recultivation of vacant buildings in the countryside, housing suitable for women, and building with papier-mâché can succeed. The awards celebration was held on October 19, 2023, in HS I in Alte Technik.

The first prize, endowed by the regional government of Styria, Department 16 Transport and Building Construction, went to Beatrice Raith for her project "Die wachsenden Häuser von Wetzelsdorf" (The Growing Houses of Wetzelsdorf). The subject of her master's thesis, supervised by Alex Lehnerer at the Institute of Spatial Design, is the situational creation of architecture: always-building-on. This process is illustrated using the example of a single-family home in the Wetzelsdorf district of Graz and presented in the form of four booklets with four stories. This year's jury, consisting of Ulrike Tinnacher (tinnacher.studio, Vienna), Paul Preissner (Paul Preissner Architects, Chicago), and Pier Paolo Tamburelli (baukuh, Milan/ TU Vienna), found the project "impressive in a deeper, conceptual way, because it did something programmatically ambitious, namely, working with many situationally constructed moments of a building. These moments are not sequential and could have been executed in any order; nevertheless, they add up to create a different relationship to the original building and do so in a free-spirited way that is somewhat reminiscent of action art." (Paul Preissner).

The second-place prize of the GAD Awards was shared by Anna-Maria Jäger, Marie-Theres Schwaighofer, and Theresa Schleinitz for her project. Supervised by Aglaée Degros at the Institute of Urbanism, this diploma thesis by Anna-Maria Jäger and Marie-Theres Schwaighofer addresses the theme of equal-opportunity, generative urban (district) development in the context of the Gries district of Graz, which has been influenced by immigration, and specifically with the future development of the Rösselmühle, which has been defunct since 2014. The work sketches the transformation of the mill into a community-oriented project distinguished by high density of use and diverse green and open spaces in the spirit of a fairer and socially diverse city. The jury praised its approach to a "very complicated problem from different perspectives" and "precise urban-planning and architectural interventions" (Pier Paolo Tamburelli).

Theresa Schleinitz's master's thesis, which was also awarded the second-place prize, was written at the Institute of Construction and Design Principles and was supervised by Eva Sollgruber. Her thesis calls for a renovation of existing architectural and social structures that explicitly addresses the reality of the lives of women and sets the goal of a safer, more accessible, and more diverse world for all people. Specifically, an existing building is redesigned as a house for women that, as an alternative to monofunctional building types, can increase the visibility of urgent feminist demands of architecture. A quote from the jury's statement: "The project creates a new feminist domestic space that is not monoprogrammed but instead flexible and diverse with regard to what happens within it, with parts of the existing building removed or rebuilt. It is at once gentle and aggressive." (Paul Preissner)

This year's Hollomey Travel Prize has been awarded to Valentin Moser, whose master's thesis, supervised by Andreas Lechner at the Institute of Construction and Design Principles, concerns vacant buildings in the countryside and how to recultivate them by involving local parties. "The project received a prize not just because it concerns vacant buildings in the countryside but also because it overlays hybrid uses that broaden them. With a bold new building and a sensitive approach to the existing fabric, it results in a remarkable and diverse ensemble." (Ulrike Tinnacher)

Angelika Hinterbrandner's project on Alexander Klein's innovative design method from the 1930s was awarded the Tschom Housing Prize. Her master's thesis, supervised by Daniel Gethmann at the Institute of Architectural Theory, Art History, and Cultural Studies, lays the cornerstone for a reinterpretation of Klein's approaches to a new standard in housing construction by reflecting on the socioeconomic conditions under which Klein's approach was developed. According to the jury, the theoretical and historical research of the project make an important contribution to the field of housing and show "the potential that can lie in rediscovering some past experiences." (Pier Paolo Tamburelli)

The prize that the Chamber of Civil Engineers of Styria and Carinthia awards to recognize resource-conserving and climate-just architecture has been conferred on Nera Džanić's project "Papier-mâché: From Paper to Sustainable Architecture Material." Her master's thesis, supervised by Milena Stavrić at the Institute of Architecture and Media, studies the production of a new, paper-based composite material in environmentally friendly and sustainable processes to create biodegradable and reusable products. The resulting composite materials shows immense potential to become and aesthetically and functionally relevant part of interior design. "It is a very focused project that examines in detail paper as a product and its sustainable use as an architectural material. We recognize this project's experimental and unconventional approach." (Ulrike Tinnacher)

A nonmonetary prize in the form of a Moroccan carpet donated by Gebhart Blazek (Berber Arts) was awarded to Dennis Baumgartner as a special recognition. His thesis, supervised by Andreas Lechner at the Institute of Construction and Design Principles, concerns the Haunoldmühle in the Steyr Valley and examines vacant buildings through the lens of cultural and art studies and historical preservation. According to the jury, the typological conversion into an event location was designed "in a freethinking sense, in that it not only romanticizes the decrepitude of the historical project, but also produces entirely new objects within the building, which, on the one hand, retain the decay in its originality and, on the other, preserve the imprecision of the historical structure." (Paul Preissner)

This year, the accompanying program for the GAD Awards ceremony was supplemented by "Three Standpoints of Architecture," in which the members of this year's jury—Ulrike Tinnacher, Paul Preissner, and Pier Paolo Tamburelli—presented their personal approach to the discipline and discussed current projects in their architectural research and practice. The concept for the exhibition was developed by the Institute of Spatial Design under the supervision of Alex Lehnerer. All of the nominated and prizewinning projects are accessible online at https:// gad-awards.tugraz.at.

„Stadt, Anger, Fluss". Herbert Eichholzer Architekturförderungspreise 2023

Daniel Gethmann, Elke Kahr, Eva Hierzer, Günther Riegler © GAM.Lab, TU Graz

i.V. Gregor Klepatsch, Siri Dacar, Theresa Hammerl, Daniel Lučić © GAM.Lab, TU Graz

Das diesjährige Wettbewerbsthema der Herbert Eichholzer Architekturförderungspreise widmete sich unter dem Titel „Stadt, Anger, Fluss: Erinnerungskultur und Zukunft am Grünanger" der Entwicklung von Konzepten, Strategien und Sichtweisen für eine zukünftige Entwicklung des Grazer Grünangers, einem im historischen Kontext des Zweiten Weltkriegs entstandenes Arbeitslager. Seit den 1960er-Jahren wurde der Grünanger in ein gering dicht bebautes Wohngebiet mit ein- bis zweigeschoßigen Gebäuden umfunktioniert. Heute befindet sich das Areal in der Nähe des neu gestalteten Naherholungsgebiets am Fluss Mur und ist von dicht bebauten Siedlungs- und Stadtstrukturen umringt.

Das GewinnerInnenprojekt von Klara Schmidt und Siri Dacar konzentriert sich auf das Freilegen der Zeit- und Informationsschichten des Areals und die Sichtbarkeit von Geschichte im Stadtraum. Die diesjährige Jury, bestehend aus Daniel Gethmann (akk, TU Graz), Tom Kaden (IAT, Architektur und Holzbau, TU Graz) und Eva Hierzer (NOW Architektur, Graz), begründeten ihre Entscheidung wie folgt: „Das Projekt überzeugt durch eine klare Vision und Strategie im bewussten Umgang mit der Geschichte des Ortes und seinem Kontext, ohne im klassischen Sinne neu zu bauen. Es zeigt eine Art Prozessperspektive zur Schaffung einer neuen Erinnerungskultur. Eingriffe werden mit Rücksichtnahme auf die bestehende BewohnerInnenschaft und den Gebäudebestand vorgenommen. Das Projekt positioniert sich klar in seiner Haltung, bietet Stoff zur Diskussion und regt zum Nach- und Weiterdenken an."

Der zweite Preis des „Eichholzer Architekturförderungspreises" wurde an Pia Pollak und Fabian Steinberger verliehen. Ihr Projekt motiviert durch mehrere gezielte Interventionen die soziale Interaktion der BewohnerInnen des Wohngebiets. Dort werden bestehende Strukturen genutzt, stellenweise adaptiert und ergänzt. Durch punktuelle Sanierungsmaßnahmen wird das Abtragen bestehender Gebäude verhindert. Der Fokus des Projektes liegt auf der Kommunikation zwischen BewohnerInnen und Umgebung. „Wenige, behutsame Eingriffe wie Marktplatz, Gemeinschaftszentrum und der Erhalt des bestehenden Jugendzentrums," so die Jury, „öffnen das Quartier nach außen und fördern die Kommunikation über die Bearbeitungsgrenzen hinaus."

Das Projekt von Ingo Candussi, Theresa Hammerl und Daniel Lučić wurde im Rahmen der diesjährigen „Eichholzer Architekturförderungspreise" mit dem Anerkennungspreis ausgezeichnet. Ihr Entwurf sieht trotz einer Verdopplung der Bebauungsdichte einen sensiblen Umgang mit den Außenflächen und Baukörperpositionen vor, um öffentliche Flächen zu erhalten und ruhige, gefasste, semiprivate

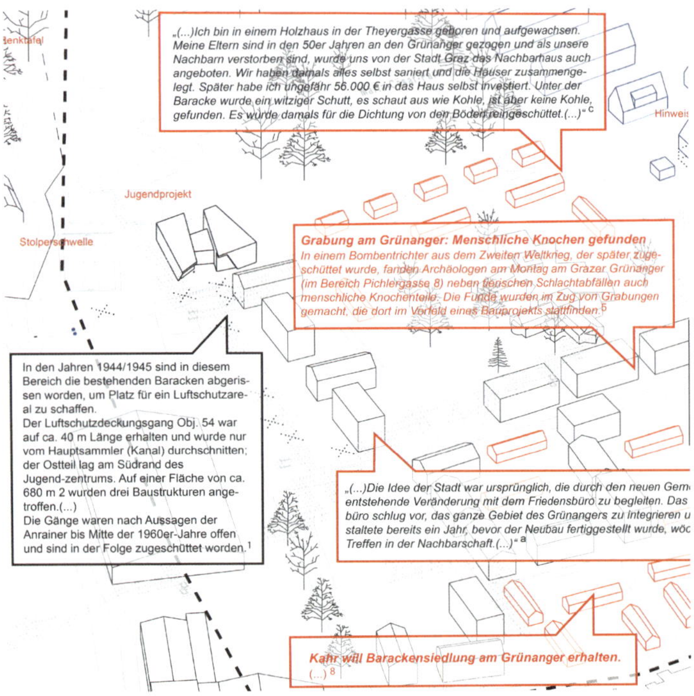

© Klara Schmidt, Siri Dacar

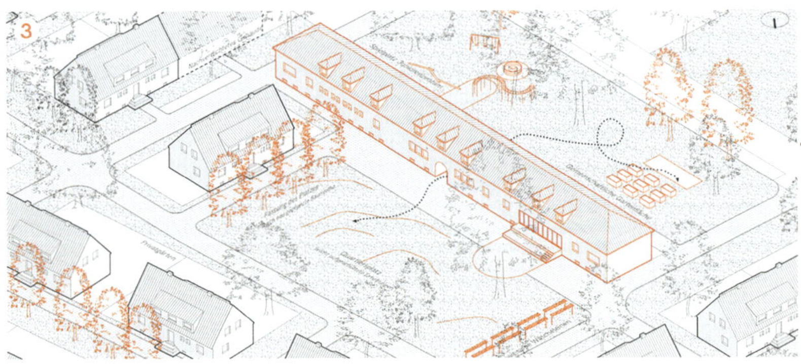

© Pia Pollak, Fabian Steinberger

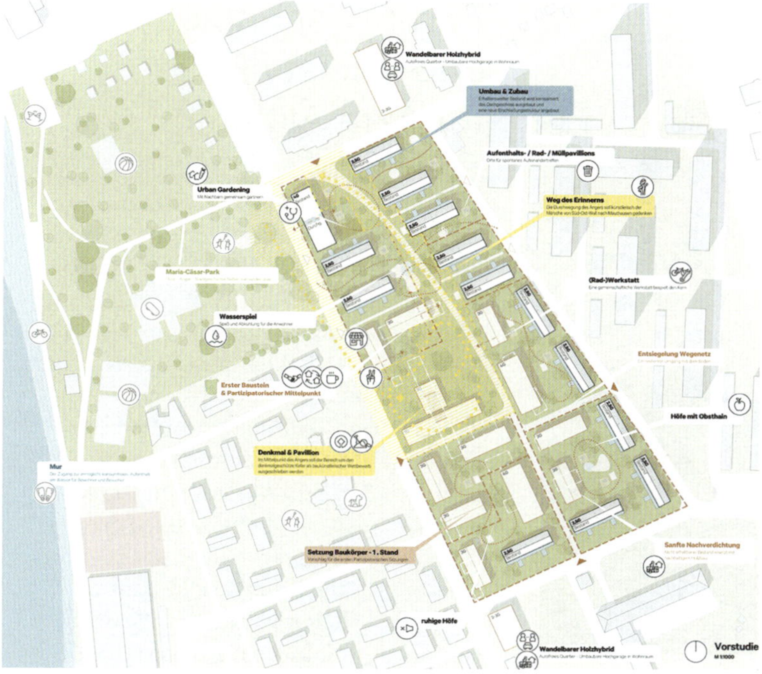

© Ingo Candussi, Theresa Hammerl, Daniel Lučić

Bereiche zu generieren. Die BewohnerInnen und deren Partizipation steht neben der geschichtlichen Aufarbeitung im Vordergrund des Projektes. Ein Weg des Erinnerns, der durch das Quartier führen soll, ruft die Geschichte des Ortes sensibel ins Gedächtnis. Die Jury betonte „die behutsame, phasenweise Entwicklung des Quartiers unter Einbeziehung der ansässigen BewohnerInnen" und das Potential des Entwurfs „für ein heterogenes lebendiges Quartier".

Vergeben wurden die von der Stadt Graz und der Fakultät für Architektur ausgeschriebenen Preise im Rahmen einer Preisverleihung am 23. November 2023, an der auch Bürgermeisterin Elke Kahr und Stadtrat Günther Riegler mitwirkten. Mit dem Herbert Eichholzer Architekturförderungspreis, der seit 1992 zweijährlich vergeben wird, bringen die Stadt Graz und die Technische Universität Graz ihre tiefe Verbundenheit mit Herbert Eichholzer und seinem Wirken als wichtiger Vertreter der Architekturmoderne der Zwischenkriegszeit und des Widerstands gegen den Nationalsozialismus zum Ausdruck. Ausgerichtet und organisiert wurde die Preisverleihung in diesem Jahr von der Professur für Architektur und Holzbau (IATh).

Annalena Arminger

"City, Meadow, River": Herbert Eichholzer Awards 2023

The competition theme for this year's Herbert Eichholzer Awards, under the title "Stadt, Anger, Fluss: Erinnerungskultur und Zukunft am Grünanger" (City, Meadow, River: Culture of Remembrance and the Future at the Grünanger), was to come up with concepts, strategies, and viewpoints for the future development of the Grünanger in Graz, a labor camp built in the historical context of World War II. Since the 1960s, the Grünanger has been repurposed as a small, densely built residential area with one- and two-story buildings. The site, located near a redesigned greenbelt recreational area on the Mur River, is now surrounded by high-density housing developments and urban structures.

The prizewinning project by Klara Schmidt and Siri Dacar concentrates on revealing the temporal and informational layers of the site and making history visible in urban space. This year's jury, consisting of Daniel Gethmann (akk, TU Graz), Tom Kaden (IAT, Architektur und Holzbau, TU Graz), and Eva Hierzer (NOW Architektur, Graz), justified their decision as follows: "The project is convincing with a clear vision and strategy for a deliberate approach to the history of the place and its context without rebuilding in the classic sense. It presents a kind of processual perspective on creating a new culture of memory. The interventions took into account the existing residents and building fabric. The project adopted a clear stance, offered material for discussion, and provided stimuli for continuing reflection."

The second prize of the Herbert Eichholzer Awards was given to Pia Pollak and Fabian Steinberger. Their project uses several targeted interventions to motivate social interaction among the residents of the neighborhood. Existing structures were used and, in some cases, adapted and supplemented. Focused renovation measures prevented demolition of existing buildings. The project focused on communication between residents and their surroundings. "A few modest interventions such as the market square, community center, and preservation of the existing youth century open," according to the jury, "the neighborhood to the outside and encourage communication beyond the boundaries of the project."

The project of Ingo Candussi, Theresa Hammerl, and Daniel Lučić received the Recognition Award of this year's Eichholzer Awards. Despite doubling the building density, their design offers a sensitive approach to outdoor areas and the placement of building volumes to preserve public areas and generate serene, framed, semiprivate areas. The residents and their participation are at the forefront of the project alongside the historical reappraisal. A path of remembrance leading though the neighborhood is intended to bring the history of the place to mind. The jury emphasized "the modest, phased development of the neighborhood that integrates local residents" as well as the design's potential "for a heterogenous, lively neighborhood."

The announced prizes were awarded by the City of Graz and the Faculty of Architecture during a ceremony on November 23, 2023, in which Mayor Elke Kahr and City Councilman Günther Riegler also participated. The Herbert Eichholzer Award, which has been awarded biannually since 1992, the City of Graz and TU Graz, express their profound bond with Herbert Eichholzer and his work as an important representative of modern architecture in the interwar period and the resistance to National Socialism. The award was arranged and organized this year by the Chair of Architecture and Timber Construction (IATh).

Förderpreis des Forums Technik und Gesellschaft für Azra Alibabić

Für ihre Diplomarbeit „Ein Raum. Für Frauen. In Karatschi“ wurde Azra Alibabić, Absolventin der Architekturfakultät der TU Graz im Rahmen der Förderpreise des Forums Technik und Gesellschaft der Sonderpreis „IngenieurINNEN gestalten 2023“ verliehen.

Azra Alibabićs Diplomarbeit widmet sich der Sichtbarmachung des unsichtbar Gemachten und der gesellschaftspolitischen Position stigmatisierter Gruppen in Karatschi, Pakistan. Die Arbeit präsentiert einen Entwurf für das Bilquis Edhi Zentrum, ein Frauenhaus im Norden Karatschis, das aktuell 1.600 Frauen und 150 Kindern Zuflucht und Schutz vor Zurückweisung, Gewalt und Diskriminierung bietet und von Wohlfahrtsorganisationen betrieben wird. Die simple Konstruktion aus Ziegelbauweise und Kalkputz vereint unterschiedliche architektonische Interventionen, die die Wohnqualität im Zentrum verbessern sollen: Sie richtet ihre Baukörper nach innen um Privatsphäre zu ermöglichen. Hohe Windtürme sorgen nicht nur für Durchlüftung, sondern agieren auch als Sichtschutz. Höfe, Rahmen und Öffnungen in den Erschließungsflächen schaffen Blickbeziehungen. Ein Bepflanzungskonzept erhöht die Attraktivität von Gemeinschaftsflächen und fördert Aktivitäten und sozialen Austausch. Regional verfügbare Materialien und lokale Arbeitskräfte leisten einen wesentlichen Beitrag zur Nachhaltigkeit auf unterschiedlichen Ebenen.

Die Auszeichnung, die das gesellschaftliche Potential technischer Forschung in den Mittelpunkt rückt, wird aus den Erlösen des „Ball der Technik“ finanziert, einer Kooperationsveranstaltung der TU Graz, der FH JOANNEUM, alumniTUGraz 1887, der Kammer für ZiviltechnikerInnen für Steiermark und Kärnten sowie der HochschülerInnenschaft der TU Graz.

Annalena Arminger

Azra Alibabić © GAM.Lab, TU Graz

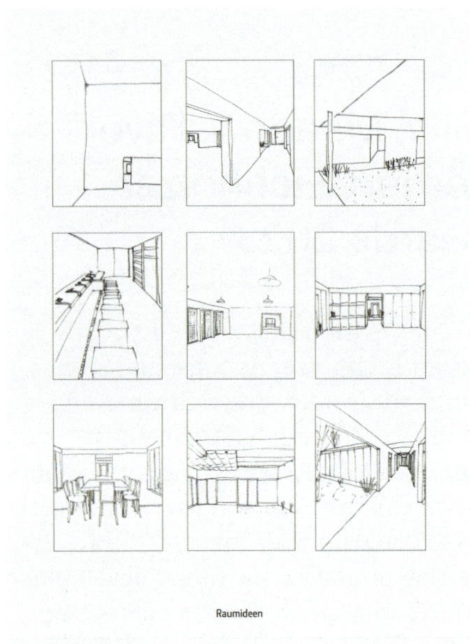

© Azra Alibabić

Forum Technology and Society Prize for Azra Alibabić

For her diploma thesis “Ein Raum. Für Frauen. In Karatschi.” (One Space. For Women. In Karachi.), Azra Alibabic, a graduate of the Faculty of Architecture at TU Graz, was awarded the special prize “IngenieurINNEN gestalten 2023” as part of the advancement awards presented by the Forum Technology and Society.

Azra Alibabic’s diploma thesis is committed to bringing to light the sociopolitical position of stigmatized groups in Karachi, Pakistan. The thesis presents a design for the Bilquis Edhi Centre, a women’s shelter in northern Karachi run by charitable organizations that offers refuge and protection from rejection, violence, and discrimination to 1,600 women and 150 children. The simple construction of brick and lime plaster combines various architectural interventions intended to enhance the quality of living in the center: the design directs the structures inward to offer seclusion; high wind towers facilitate ventilation and act as privacy screens; courtyards and openings in the circulation areas create visual connections; a landscaping concept serves to increase the appeal of communal areas and to promote activities and social exchange. Regionally available materials and local labor are to strengthen the community and contribute to sustainability.

The award, which focuses on the social potential of technical research, is financed from the proceeds of the “Ball der Technik,” a cooperative event organized by TU Graz, FH JOANNEUM, alumniTUGraz 1887, the Chamber of Civil Engineers for Styria and Carinthia, and the Student Union of TU Graz.

WettbewerbsteilnehmerInnen und Jury © KOEN, TU Graz

Manuel Bordos, Phillip Rabl © KOEN, TU Graz

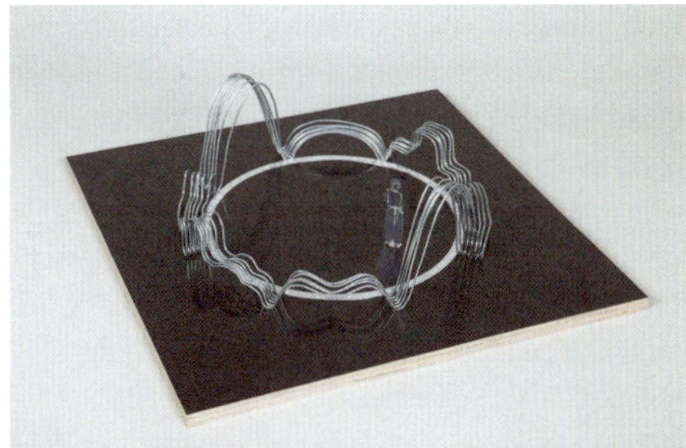

Martin Kern, Manuel Rammerstorfer, Lisa Theurl © KOEN, TU Graz

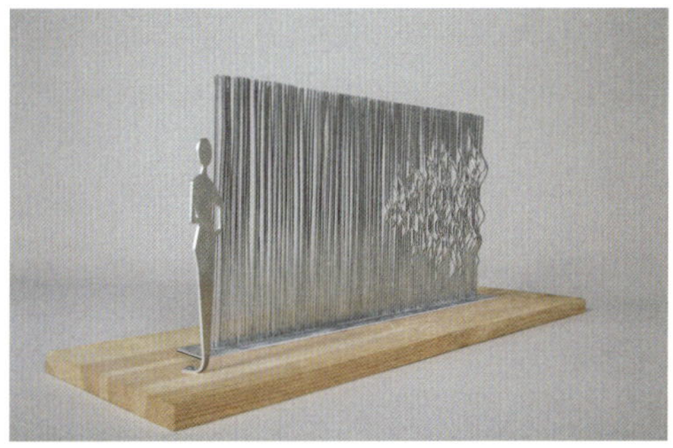

Clemens Cresnar, Dominic Janisch © KOEN, TU Graz

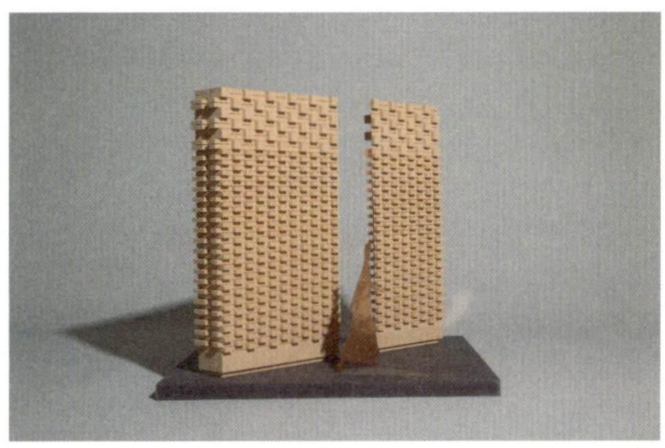

Christoph Bamberger, David Pöll © KOEN, TU Graz

Wettbewerb Erinnerung bauen. Pionierinnen der TU Graz

In Zusammenarbeit mit dem Alumni-Frauennetzwerk („WomenUniverse") der TU Graz fand im Sommersemester 2023 ein KOEN-Modellbauseminar statt, dessen Ziel es war, ein Denkmal zu entwerfen, das den ersten Absolventinnen der TU Graz gewidmet ist. Das Seminar bot den Studierenden den geeigneten Rahmen, um über Erinnerungskultur, Aktivismus und den historischen Status von Frauen an der Universität nachzudenken und dieses Thema mit den Mitteln der Architektur zu bearbeiten. In der von Ena Kukić und Barbara Gruber geleiteten Lehrveranstaltung, wurde auch die Idee eines Gestaltungswettbewerbs aufgegriffen und umgesetzt. Eine fünfköpfige Jury hatte schließlich die Aufgabe, das Siegerprojekt zu küren. Insgesamt wurden vier Preise vergeben: Der erste Preis ging an das Projekt von Manuel Bordos und Phillip Rabl, dessen Denkmal individuell an jede Absolventin anpassbar ist. Das Projekt besteht aus mehreren Ebenen, die jeweils im gleichen Abstand voneinander stehen. Durch die Kombination der Schichten und verschiedenen Farben entsteht ein vielschichtiges, abstraktes Portrait, das die komplexen und vielseitigen Leistungen der Absolventinnen würdigen soll. Die BetrachterInnen werden dazu eingeladen, die verschiedenen Schichten zu erkunden und den Weg der jeweiligen Absolventin nachzuvollziehen. Das abstrakte Portrait kann erst am perspektivischen Ursprung in seiner Gänze erkannt und verstanden werden.

Den zweiten Preis teilen sich Martin Kern, Manuel Rammerstorfer und Lisa Theurl mit Clemens Cresnar und Dominic Janisch sowie mit Christoph Bamberger und David Pöll. Während ersterer unter dem Motto des gemeinsamen Diskurses über Frauen in der Technik bzw. an der TU Graz ein Monument entwarf, das diesen Diskurs auf niederschwelliger und informeller Ebene fördert, bezog sich der Entwurf von Clemens Cresnar und Dominic Janisch auf das bemerkenswerte Erbe, das die Technikerinnen der Universität hinterlassen haben und zeigt die akademischen Leistungen, die von Frauen an der Technischen Universität ab 1811 erbracht wurden. Christoph Bamberger und David Pölls Monument symbolisiert den Erfolg der ersten Absolventinnen durch einen konkreten Durchbruch in einer Mauerstruktur. Die Schnittfläche des Durchganges besteht aus Kupfer und stellt gleichzeitig den Schriftträger für einen Text dar, der von den Leistungen der ersten Absolventinnen berichtet.

Petra Eckhard

Building Memory Competition: Women Pioneers of TU Graz

In association with the alumni women's network ("WomenUniverse") of TU Graz, a KOEN model-building seminar took place during the summer semester of 2023 with the aim of designing a memorial dedicated to the first women graduates of TU Graz. The seminar provided the students with a suitable backdrop to reflect on the culture of remembrance, activism, and the historical status of women at the university and to address this topic by means of architecture. In the course led by Ena Kukić and Barbara Gruber, the idea of a design competition was also taken up and implemented. Ultimately, a jury of five had the task of selecting the winning project. In total, four prizes were awarded. The first prize went to the project by Manuel Bordos and Phillip Rabl, whose memorial can be individually modified for each graduate. Each plane of the monument is equidistant from the others. The interaction of the layers and their different colors creates a multifaceted, abstract portrait that pays tribute to the complex and manifold achievements of the graduates. The viewer is invited to explore the different layers and trace the path of each graduate. Only by looking at the perspective origin of the abstract portrait can it be recognized and understood in its entirety.

The second prize was jointly won by Martin Kern, Manuel Rammerstorfer, and Lisa Theurl; Clemens Cresnar and Dominic Janisch; and Christoph Bamberger and David Pöll. In the first project, Martin Kern, Manuel Rammerstorfer, and Lisa Theurl designed a monument under the motto of a communal discourse about women in technology or a monument for TU Graz, thus promoting this discourse on a low-threshold and informal level. The design by Clemens Cresnar and Dominic Janisch, in turn, drew on the remarkable legacy left by women technicians at the university and shows the academic achievements made by women at the University of Technology starting in 1811. Christoph Bamberger and David Pöll's monument, lastly, symbolizes the success of the first women graduates employing a concrete breakthrough in a wall structure. The cut surface of the passage is made of copper and, at the same time, represents the text carrier for a narrative recounting the achievements of the first women graduates.

GewinnerInnen und Jury © KOEN, TU Graz

Skizzenbuchpreis

Im Zuge des Sommerfests der Architekturfakultät wurde der alljährliche KOEN-Skizzenbuchpreis an Studierende des ersten Studienjahres vergeben. Die Skizzenbücher werden bereits zu Beginn des Architekturstudiums als essenzielles Werkzeug eingeführt und begleiten die Auseinandersetzung mit Architektur als fortlaufenden Prozess. Die Bücher erfassen und strukturieren Gedanken in bildlicher und schriftlicher Form und werden schließlich zu Chroniken der individuellen Entwurfsprozesse und des studentischen Lebens im ersten Studienjahr. Eingereicht werden konnten Skizzenbücher und Hefte der ersten beiden Semester, die während der Lehrveranstaltungen „Konstruieren", „Gestalten und Entwerfen" sowie während der Exkursion nach Mailand mit Handskizzen gefüllt wurden. Die GewinnerInnen freuten sich über Architekturpublikationen, gesponsert vom HDA – Haus der Architektur, und über neue, noch unbefüllte Skizzenbücher, gesponsert von Kaspar Harnisch.

GewinnerInnen: Daniel Unterrainer (1. Preis), Dide Denisa (2. Preis), Kateryna Kalinichenko (2. Preis), Alina Karen (2. Preis), Damian Bobeica (3. Preis), Hana Hamidović (3. Preis), Borbála Kiszely (3. Preis), Stefan Krenn (3. Preis)

Shortlisted: Dania-Dumitrita Berinde, Emma Eichholzer, Janka Enikő Dénes, Maja Krishnan, Nele Liß, Anna Mayr, Anna Moretti, Thomas Neuhofer, Leonardo Novaković, Theresa Sackl-Gutruf, Lewin Schrag, Ana-Maria Szentpeteri-Blaj, Oskar Traut

Lisa Obermayer

Sketchbook Prize

The annual KOEN Sketchbook Prize was awarded to first-year students at the Faculty of Architecture's summer exhibition. The sketchbook has been used from the very beginning as an integral element of the architectural studies program. It reflects one of our primary concerns: the understanding that the making of architecture is a process. The books record and structure thoughts in both visual and written form and ultimately become chronicles of individual design processes and student life in the first year of study. The submissions included notebooks from the first two semesters, filled with hand-drawn sketches during the courses "Construction," "Form and Design," and throughout the excursion to Milan. The winners were delighted to receive architectural publications sponsored by the House of Architecture (HDA) and new, as of yet unfilled sketchbooks sponsored by Kaspar Harnisch.

Winners: Daniel Unterrainer (1st prize), Dide Denisa (2nd prize), Kateryna Kalinichenko (2nd prize), Alina Karen (2nd prize), Damian Bobeica (3rd prize), Hana Hamidović (3rd prize), Borbála Kiszely (3rd prize), Stefan Krenn (3rd prize)

Shortlisted: Dania-Dumitrita Berinde, Emma Eichholzer, Janka Enikő Dénes, Maja Krishnan, Nele Liß, Anna Mayr, Anna Moretti, Thomas Neuhofer, Leonardo Novaković, Theresa Sackl-Gutruf, Lewin Schrag, Ana-Maria Szentpeteri-Blaj, Oskar Traut

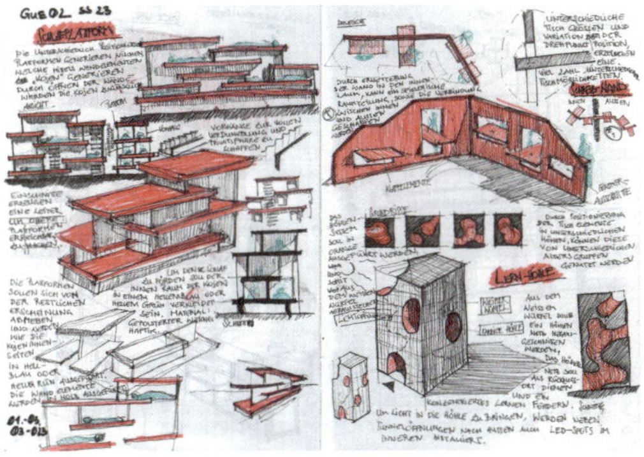

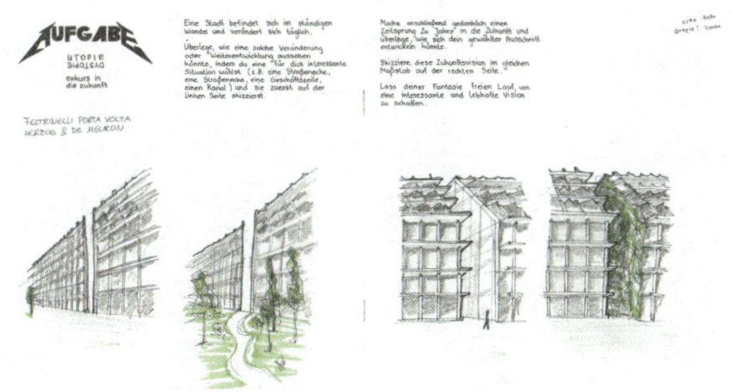
AUFGABE
UTOPIE
BURGBAD
Exkurs in die Zukunft

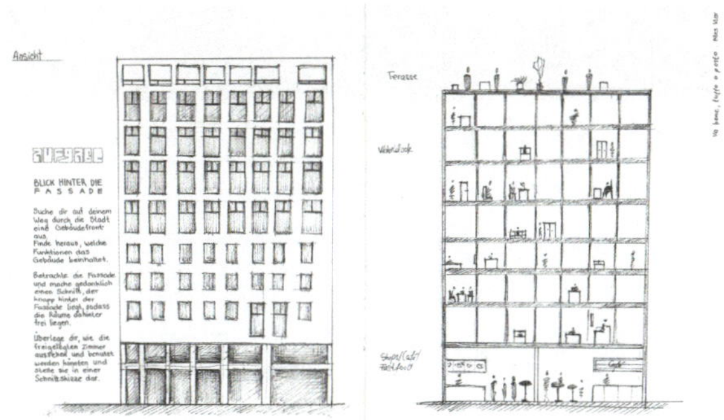

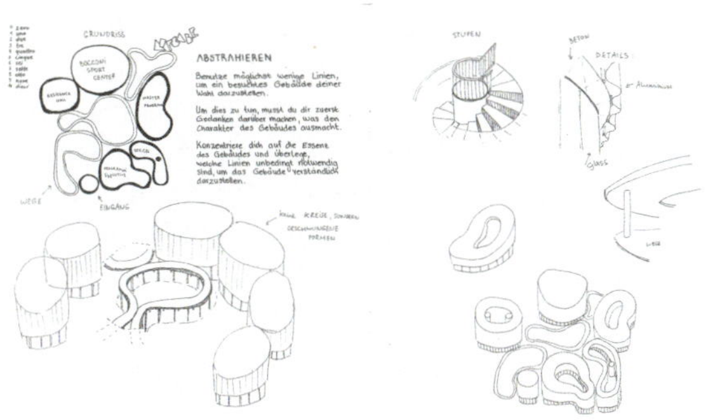

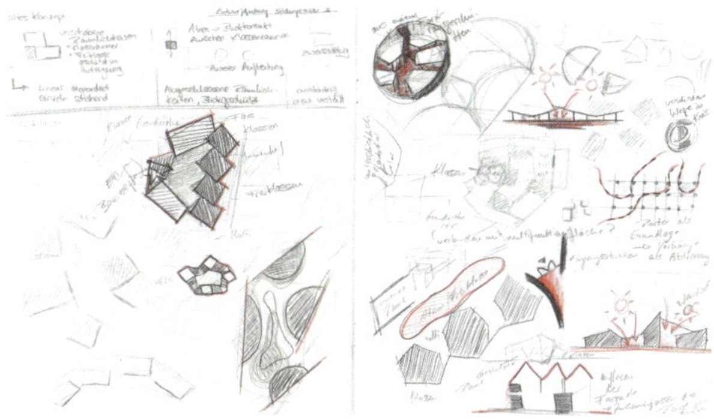

AUFGABE
UTOPIE
BURGBAD

stadtübung
Imbissstände
Christmas edition
OH MY DOG
Imbissstand

L. Kopp, M. Borodos, P. Rabl, D. Racan, M. Tammerle, T. E. Ewerz, P. Weber, V. Angerer, U. Hahn, B. Cody
© ige, TU Graz

Wettbewerb Seestadt Aspern 2030

Der Wettbewerb Seestadt Aspern 2030 wurde in Kooperation zwischen der ARE – Austrian Real Estate GmbH, dem Institut für Gebäude und Energie der TU Graz und der Universität für angewandte Kunst Wien durchgeführt. Die Seestadt Aspern ist eines der größten Stadtentwicklungsgebiete Europas im 22. Wiener Gemeindebezirk, in dem hochwertige Wohnräume und Arbeitsplätze geschaffen werden. Ein mehrstufiger Entwicklungsprozess gab den Studierenden die Möglichkeit, im Zuge ihrer Lehrveranstaltungen zwei Baufelder zu gestalten. Dabei handelt es sich um zwei konkrete und reale Bauvorhaben: Das im südöstlichen Teil der Seestadt gelegene Baufeld J6 und das in zentraler Lage gelegene Baufeld F7. Die Wettbewerbsbeiträge sollten sich abhängig von der besuchten Lehrveranstaltung mit „Renewable Aesthetics“ oder Umweltzertifizierungen befassen und versuchen, die vorausgesetzten Kriterien zu erfüllen. Dabei sollte ein Gebäudeensemble mit gemischter Nutzung entworfen werden. Das Hauptaugenmerk der Lehrveranstaltungen im Sommersemester lag in der Thematik „Outdoor Comfort and Microclimate“.

Wettbewerbsergebnisse:

Kategorie: Bachelor, TU Graz
1. Preis: „In Casa Commune“, Verena Heckmann, Sandra Karner, Stella Elena Maxones, Lisa-Marie Sohneg
2. Preis: „In Natura“, Amir Babikir, Phil Eiberger, Laura Juch, Muris Tihak
3. Preis: „Szél“, Elena Kropek, Simon Strasser, Mara Tolpeit, Sára Anna Tóth

Kategorie: Master, TU Graz
1. Preis: „Aspern Energy Rock“, Max Bonecker, Laura Thießen
2. Preis: „Vortex“, Manuel Breksler, Caio Matos
3. Preis: „Healthy Tower“, Philipp Frank, Felix Waltritsch

Kategorie: Master, die Angewandte
1. Preis: „Ecotopia Parkview“, Olja Radovanovic, Tomaz Roblek, Zubin Tan
2. Preis: „Dynamic Manifold“, Kyrylo Dmytrenko, Melika Hadjarzadeh, Omar Mohamed Abdelhady
3. Preis: „Energy Design Aspern“, Orkhan Hasanov

Brian Cody

Competition Seestadt Aspern 2030

The competition Seestadt Aspern 2030 was held as a joint venture involving ARE – Austrian Real Estate GmbH, the Institute of Buildings and Energy at TU Graz, and the University of Applied Arts Vienna. Seestadt Aspern is one of Europe's largest urban development areas in Vienna's 22nd district, in which high-quality living and working spaces are being created. A multistage development process afforded the students the opportunity to design two building plots as part of their courses. Two concrete and tangible building projects are involved: Site J6, located in the southeastern part of Seestadt, and the centrally located Site F7. Depending on the course attended, the competition entries were to address "Renewable Aesthetics" or environmental certifications in an attempt to meet the required criteria. In doing so, a building ensemble of mixed uses was to be designed. The main emphasis of the courses in the summer semester centered on "Outdoor Comfort and Microclimate."

Competition results:

Category: Bachelor, TU Graz
1st prize: "In Casa Commune," Verena Heckmann, Sandra Karner, Stella Elena Maxones, Lisa-Marie Sohneg
2nd prize: "In Natura," Amir Babikir, Phil Eiberger, Laura Juch, Muris Tihak
3rd prize: "Szél," Elena Kropek, Simon Strasser, Mara Tolpeit, Sára Anna Tóth

Category: Master, TU Graz
1st prize: "Aspern Energy Rock," Max Bonecker, Laura Thießen
2nd prize: "Vortex," Manuel Breksler, Caio Matos
3rd prize: "Healthy Tower," Philipp Frank, Felix Waltritsch

Category: Master, University of Applied Arts Vienna
1st prize: "Ecotopia Parkview," Olja Radovanovic, Tomaz Roblek, Zubin Tan
2nd prize: "Dynamic Manifold," Kyrylo Dmytrenko, Melika Hadjarzadeh, Omar Mohamed Abdelhady
3rd prize: "Energy Design Aspern," Orkhan Hasanov

© Studio Herzig/EIGNER Bauunternehmung GmbH

ITE-Projekt „Concrete Lightweight Ceiling“ gewinnt Architekturpreis Beton 2023

Für die Entwicklung einer 160m² großen gewichtsreduzierten Stahlbetondecke über einer Tiefgarageneinfahrt in Nördlingen (DE) wurde das Projektteam des Instituts für Tragwerksentwurf (ITE) mit dem deutschen Architekturpreis Beton 2023 ausgezeichnet. Das ITE ist verantwortlich für Entwurf, Geometrieentwicklung sowie die statisch-konstruktive Bearbeitung. Das Projekt überzeugte die Jury mit einer materialoptimierten, ressourcenschonenden und ungewöhnlichen Art der Konstruktion.

Das optimierte Dach besteht aus 168 gedruckten Betonsegmenten, die auf der Baustelle zu 48 länglichen Aussparungskörpern gefügt und positioniert wurden. Durch den 3D-Druck, sowie der Verwendung einer zementreduzierten Betonrezeptur für den Vergussbeton konnten 35 Prozent CO_2eq gespart werden. Ebenso erfolgreich verlief in weiterer Folge die Positionierung der Schalkörper, das Einbringen der Bewehrung sowie die Betonage der Konstruktion. „Diese Arbeit zeigt,“ so die Jury, „dass die Zukunft im Drucken von Beton liegen kann. Mit wertvollem Material wird bewusst und sparsam umgegangen. Hier wird Beton dort eingesetzt, wo er unbedingt notwendig ist.“

ITE-Projektteam: Georg Hansemann, Christoph Holzinger, Alexander Dumps, Robert Schmid, Andreas Trummer, Stefan Peters
In Zusammenarbeit mit: Labor für Konstruktiven Ingenieurbau: Bernhard Freytag, Christine Steinmetz, Baumit GmbH, EIGNER Bauunternehmung GmbH, Engelsmann Peters GmbH, Märker Transportbeton
ArchitektInnen des Gesamtbauwerkes: Lattke Architekten, Augsburg
BauherrIn: Stadt Nördlingen

Georg Hansemann

ITE project “Concrete Lightweight Ceiling” Wins Architekturpreis Beton 2023

For the development of a 160m² weight-reduced reinforced concrete ceiling over an underground car park entrance in Nördlingen (DE), the project team of the Institute of Structural Design (ITE) was awarded the German prize for concrete architecture (Architekturpreis Beton 2023). The ITE team, which was responsible for the design, geometry development, structural analysis as well as bending tests, was able to convince the jury with a material-optimized, resource-saving, and unusual type of construction.

The optimized ceiling consists of 168 printed concrete segments and was joined and positioned into 48 elongated recess bodies on the construction site. Through the use of 3D printing and a cement-reduced concrete formula for the grouting concrete, 35 percent CO_2 eq could be saved. The innovation of the reinforced concrete floor lies not only in the significant CO_2 reduction but also in the load-bearing capacity and usability of the design. According to the jury, “this work shows that the future can lie in printing concrete. Valuable material is used consciously and sparingly. Here, concrete is used where it is absolutely necessary.”

ITE-Project team: Georg Hansemann, Christoph Holzinger, Alexander Dumps, Robert Schmid, Andreas Trummer, Stefan Peters
In cooperation with: Labor für Konstruktiven Ingenieurbau: Bernhard Freytag, Christine Steinmetz, Baumit GmbH, EIGNER Bauunternehmung GmbH, Engelsmann Peters GmbH, Märker Transportbeton
Architects of the entire building: Lattke Architekten, Augsburg
Client: Stadt Nördlingen

Milica Tomić, Claudia Unger © GAM.Lab, TU Graz

Kunstpreis der Stadt Graz 2022 für Milica Tomić

Am 9. Oktober 2023 wurde Milica Tomić der Kunstpreis der Stadt Graz 2022 verliehen – eine Auszeichnung ihres künstlerischen Schaffens, welche den Medien Video, Film und Performance zugeordnet werden kann und mittels derer sie komplexe politische oder historische Themen aufgreift. Dabei bilden Recherche und Analyse wesentliche methodische Ansätze, um Fragen zu politischer Gewalt, ökonomischen Hintergründen und gesellschaftlicher Amnesie zu erforschen, aufzudecken und in die öffentliche Diskussion zu rücken. Die Jury fasste in ihrer Begründung Milica Tomićs Œuvre folgendermaßen zusammen: „Das Verharren in Konventionen, egal ob in politischen oder religiösen, wird dabei als eines der Übel unserer Koexistenz kritisiert. Tomić, die meist selbst als Protagonistin in ihren Videoarbeiten auftritt, analysiert die allgemeinen sozio-psychischen Dynamiken, die eine Gesellschaft bestimmen, meist an ihrer eigenen Person oder anhand ihr sehr nahestehenden Menschen. Identitätssuche und Kontextverschiebungen von Privatheit zu Öffentlichkeit und umgekehrt machen Milica Tomićs Arbeit so unentrinnbar – man wird teilweise unangenehm adressiert und auf diese Weise aus der typischen Komfortzone des Publikums geworfen."

Milica Tomić lehrt seit 2014 an der Fakultät für Architektur der TU Graz, wo sie das Institut für Zeitgenössische Kunst (IZK) leitet. Zudem ist sie im Offspace „Annenstrasse 53," aktiv. Der Kunstpreis der Stadt Graz wird seit 1986 alle zwei Jahre an bildende KünstlerInnen in Würdigung und Anerkennung ihres Gesamtwerks verliehen.

Art Prize of the City of Graz 2022 for Milica Tomić

On October 9, 2023, Milica Tomić was awarded the Art Prize of the City of Graz 2022—an award honoring her artistic practice, which can be assigned to the media of video, film, and performance and through which she captures complex political or historical topics. In her art, research and analysis are essential methodological approaches in order to investigate, unearth, and bring to public debate issues related to political violence, economic underpinnings, and social amnesia. In their statement, the jury summarized Milica Tomić's oeuvre as follows: "Refusing to question conventions, whether political or religious, is criticized as one of the evils of our coexistence. Tomić, who usually appears as a protagonist in her video works, analyzes the general socio-psychological dynamics that determine a society, mostly on her own person or based on people very close to her. Identity search and context shifts from private to public and vice versa make Milica Tomić's work so inescapable—one is sometimes uncomfortably addressed and, in this way, thrown out of the typical comfort zone."

Milica Tomić has been teaching at the Faculty of Architecture at TU Graz since 2014, where she heads the Institute of Contemporary Art (IZK). She is also active in the offspace "Annenstrasse 53,." The Art Prize of the City of Graz has been awarded every two years since 1986 to a visual artist in appreciation and recognition of their overall artistic work in the field of visual arts.

Petra Eckhard

Ehrung für Barbara Herz

Barbara Herz, ehemalige Leiterin des Dekanats für Architektur und Vorsitzende des Arbeitskreises für Gleichbehandlungsfragen der Technischen Universität Graz, wurde am 6. November 2023 mit der Erzherzog Johann Medaille ausgezeichnet. Mit dieser Ehrung, von TU Graz Rektor Horst Bischof, Senatsvorsitzender Annette Mütze und Vorsitzender des Universitätsrats Christa Neuper überreicht, würdigte die TU Graz ihr Wirken im 2004 gegründeten Büro für Gleichstellung und Frauenförderung, das zahlreiche Initiativen für Gleichstellung, Diversität und Frauenförderung etablierte, darunter die öffentliche Kinderbetreuungseinrichtung „Nanoversity" oder das Technikkennenlernprogramm für Oberstufenschülerinnen FEM in TECH, das junge Frauen für technische Berufe begeistern soll.

Barbara Herz leistete vier Jahrzehnte lang Pionierarbeit im männlich geprägten technischen Umfeld. Die ausgebildete Chemotechnikerin, die an der Donau-Universität Krems Hochschul- und Wissenschaftsmanagement studiert hat, leitete von 2000 bis 2022 das Dekanat der Fakultät für Architektur „mit Fürsorge und Weitblick" und füllte es, so Vizerektorin Andrea Hoffmann in ihrer Laudatio, „mit Struktur und Leben".

Petra Eckhard

Honoring Barbara Herz

Barbara Herz, former Head of the Dean's Office of the Faculty of Architecture and Chair of the Office for Gender Equality and Equal Opportunity at TU Graz was awarded the Erzherzog Johann Medal on November 6, 2023. With this award, bestowed by Rector Horst Bischof, Senate Chair Annette Mütze, and Chair of the University Council Christa Neuper, TU Graz recognized Barbara Herz's achievements within the Office for Gender Equality and Equal Opportunity (founded in 2004) in advancing gender equality and diversity through important initiatives such as the establishment of the open childcare facility "Nanoversity" or FEM in TECH, a program aimed at inspiring female high school students to pursue careers in technology.

Barbara Herz spent four decades doing pioneering work in a male-dominated technical environment. The trained chemical engineer, who studied university and science management at the University for Continuing Education in Krems, headed the Dean's Office in the Faculty of Architecture "with care and foresight" from 2000 to 2022 and, according to Vice-Rector Andrea Hoffmann in her laudatory speech, she "filled it with structure and life."

Barbara Herz © Lunghammer, TU Graz

Das Unaufgeregte und dennoch Kultivierte: Zur Ehrung von Franz Riepl

Am 8. Mai 2023 wurde dem Architekten und ehemaligen Professor Franz Riepl das Große Ehrenzeichen des Landes Steiermark in Anerkennung seiner bedeutenden Rolle in der Architektur verliehen. Gewürdigt wurde seine Arbeit, die lange Zeit eine entscheidende Lücke in der Baukultur füllte, indem er bodenständige und gleichzeitig typologisch kraftvolle Architektur entwickelte und lehrte – stets mit dem Ziel, Häuser zu gestalten, die dem Menschen und ihrem Standort gerecht werden. Während seiner 20-jährigen Professur für Ländliches Bauen an der TU Graz setzte er sich für eine bescheidene Architektur ein, die harmonisch mit ihrer Umgebung interagiert. Er lehrte das Entwerfen von Architektur im größeren baugeschichtlichen Kontext und befürwortete dabei gleichzeitig die Aufgabenstellung einer zeitgemäßen Synthese.

Seine Überzeugung, dass Architektur einen Rahmen für das Gefühl von Geborgenheit schaffen sollte, scheint aktueller denn je und spiegelt sich in seiner Grundhaltung wider: „Das Unaufgeregte und Kultivierte ist meine Grundhaltung", so Riepl über seine Vorstellung einer Architektur „ohne Schockwirkung". Die Zeitlosigkeit, die seinen Bauten innewohnt, gewinnt zunehmend an Bedeutung, wie auch die Wahrnehmung, dass die Architektur als Ausdruck von Gemeinwohl weit über die eingeschriebenen Funktionalitäten hinauswirken kann und so eine besondere Form der Nachhaltigkeit erfüllt. Ein guter Moment, um Riepls Haltung in seinem von Albert Kirchengast und Hans Kolb herausgegebenen Buch *Über Architektur* (Muery Salzmann, 2015) erneut nachzuvollziehen.

Klaus K. Loenhart

The Unexcited yet Cultivated: Honoring Franz Riepl

On May 8, 2023, the architect and former professor Franz Riepl was awarded the Grand Decoration of Honour of the Province of Styria in recognition of his significant role in architecture. He was celebrated for his work, having long filled a crucial gap in building culture by developing and teaching down-to-earth yet typologically powerful architecture—invariably aiming to design houses that do justice to both the people and their location. Over the course of his twenty-year professorship for rural building at TU Graz, he advocated a modest architecture that interacts harmoniously with its surroundings. In addition to teaching the design of architecture in a broader architectural context, he also championed the task of contemporary synthesis.

Franz Riepl's conviction that architecture should establish a framework for a sense of security seems more pertinent than ever and is reflected in his fundamental approach. "The calm and cultivated is my guiding principle," Riepl comments regarding his architectural vision "without shock effect." The timelessness inherent in his buildings is becoming increasingly significant, as is the realization that architecture, as an expression of the common good, can have an impact far beyond its designated functionalities, thus fulfilling a unique form of sustainability. A good moment to revisit Riepl's stance is in his book *Über Architektur* (Muery Salzmann, 2015), edited by Albert Kirchengast and Hans Kolb.

LH Christopher Drexler, Franz Riepl, LH-Stv. Anton Lang © Land Steiermark/ Frankl

Research

Dissertationen | Dissertations

Aus: „Gradjevinski vjesnik“ Nr. 116: Dušan Smiljanić, Pavillon „Jugoslawien“, Kasindo, 1937.

Siniša Cvijić (2023)
„Funktionalismus in der modernen Architektur in Bosnien und Herzegowina in der Zwischenkriegszeit“

Institut für Architekturtheorie, Kunst- und Kulturwissenschaften | Institute of Architectural Theory, Art History and Cultural Studies

1. Gutachterin | 1st reviewer:
Maja Roso Popovac
2. Gutachter | 2nd reviewer:
Miroslav Malinović

Die Arbeit stellt die erste umfassende Untersuchung der Rezeption des Funktionalismus in der Architektur von Bosnien und Herzegowina zwischen den Weltkriegen dar. Anhand von eingangs analysierten Prinzipien des internationalen Funktionalismus (zum Beispiel umschlossener Raum, modulare Regelmäßigkeit, Vermeidung aufgesetzter Dekoration) wird deren spezifische Umsetzung in verschiedenen Typologien dargestellt. Im politischen und historischen Kontext von Bosnien und Herzegowina als integralem Bestandteil des Königreichs der Serben, Kroaten und Slowenen/Jugoslawien (1918–1941) werden die wirtschaftlichen, soziologischen und kulturellen Bedingungen der Entstehung funktionalistischer Gebäude unter besonderer Berücksichtigung der theoretischen Positionen seiner Architekten erläutert. Die Dissertation belegt, dass eine Kombination verschiedener historischer Umstände erst nach 1929 zu einer signifikanten Entwicklung des Funktionalismus in Bosnien und Herzegowina führte. Zudem weist sie nach, dass der Funktionalismus in der Architektur von Bosnien und Herzegowina allmählich akzeptiert wurde und dass er sich zunächst auf die äußere Form und erst danach auf Inhalt und Konstruktion auswirkte und schließlich die für den Funktionalismus charakteristische sozial engagierte Architektur hervorbrachte.

• This is the first comprehensive study of the reception of functionalism in the architecture of Bosnia and Herzegovina between the world wars. It uses the examples of the principles of international functionalism that are analyzed at the outset (e.g., enclosed space, modular regularity, the avoidance of applied decoration) to present its concrete implementation in different typologies. In the political and historical context of Bosnia and Herzegovina as an integral component of the Kingdom of the Serbs, Croats, and Slovenes/Yugoslavia (1918–41), the economic, sociological, and cultural conditions for the creation of functionalist buildings are explained with particular reference to the theoretical positions of its architects. This dissertation demonstrates that a combination of various historical circumstances led to a significant evolution of functionalism in Bosnia and Herzegovina only after 1929. It also shows that functionalism in the architecture of Bosnia and Herzegovina gained acceptance gradually and influenced first the external form and only later the content and construction, ultimately producing the socially engaged architecture characteristic of functionalism.

Kheder Shadman (2023)
„Stadtplanung und soziale Nachhaltigkeit. Planungsprozess der öffentlichen Parkanlagen im Wohnumfeld"

Institut für Städtebau | Institute of Urbanism

1. Gutachter | 1st reviewer:
Grigor Doytchinov
2. Gutachter | 2nd reviewer:
Jens S. Dangschat

Öffentliche Parkanlagen im Wohnumfeld als Teil der kommunalen Infrastruktur können einen wertvollen Beitrag zur Lebensqualität der EinwohnerInnen, vor allem in den Stadtteilen mit sozioökonomischen Herausforderungen, leisten. Mit dieser Forschungsarbeit wird eine wesentliche Schnittstelle der Stadtplanung und Stadtsoziologie tangiert, bei der soziologische Themenstellungen wie soziale Vielfalt, Verständigung und Aushandlung von (Nutzungs)Konflikten, Wohlbefinden und Zugehörigkeit, dem Planungsprozess für öffentliche Parkanlagen im Wohnumfeld und seinen AkteurInnen zugeordnet werden, um eine sozial nachhaltige(re) Planung zu konkretisieren.

Ausgehend von der Forschungsfrage, „Welche Schritte in der Planungsarbeit können die soziale Nachhaltigkeit der öffentlichen Parkanlagen im Wohnumfeld begünstigen?", wird in der vorliegenden Arbeit die Zielsetzung verfolgt, die Sensibilität der PlanerInnen und anderer am Planungsprozess beteiligten AkteurInnen hinsichtlich Implementierung von Postulaten der sozialen Nachhaltigkeit im Planungsprozess zu fördern.

Die Informationen aus der Literaturrecherche, der leitfadenunterstützten Befragung von ParknutzerInnen, der Recherche und Dokumentation der lokalen Medien sowie Interviews mit Fachpersonen wurden unter Anwendung von Methoden der Diskurs- und Inhaltsanalyse zur Beantwortung der Forschungsfrage herangezogen. Die vier angeführten Datenquellen wurden durch den Methodenmix „Triangulation" aufeinander bezogen und unter Berücksichtigung des relationalen Raumkonzepts und objektiven Planungsansätzen ausgewertet. Die relationale Raumtheorie geht davon aus, dass über die öffentlichen Parkanlagen als institutionalisierte Räume Verteilungsprinzipien, Einschlüsse und Ausgrenzungen organisiert werden.

Die Ergebnisse der Forschungsarbeit liefern ein breites Bild des Planungsprozesses, das sich von der Prozesssteuerung durch die Politik und PlanerInnen bis hin zur Rolle der einzelnen PlanungsakteurInnen spannt und die Funktionsweise der Postulate der sozialen Nachhaltigkeit in den öffentlichen Parkanlagen mit den beteiligten AkteurInnen verknüpft. Ein kommunikatives Planungsverfahren, das sich in der Planungskultur vor Ort durch Merkmale wie Konsensbildung, Teilhabechancen, Abwägung und Aktivierung kennzeichnet, kann die Planung von sozial nachhaltigen Parkanlagen effektiver begünstigen.

• Public parking facilities in residential areas as part of communal infrastructure can make a valuable contribution to the quality of life of residents, above all in parts of the city facing socioeconomic challenges. This research project touches on an essential intersection of urban planning and urban sociology in which sociological themes such as social diversity, mutual understanding and negotiation of conflicts (over use), well-being and belonging, the planning process for public parks in residential areas, and the parties participating in them are categorized in order to make socially (more) sustainable planning more concrete.

Starting out from the question, "What steps in planning can benefit the social sustainability of public parks in residential areas?" the present work pursues the objective of sensitizing planners and others involved in the planning process to encouraging the implementation of postulates of social sustainability in the planning process.

Information from research on the literature, guideline-supported surveying of park users, research and documentation of local media, and interviews with experts were employed using methods of the analysis of discourse and content to answer the research question. The four data sources cited were related to one another through the mix of methods known as "triangulation" and evaluated with regard to the relational concept of space and objective planning approaches. The relational theory of space assumes that public parks are organized as institutionalized spaces according to principles of distribution, inclusion, and exclusion.

The results of this research project provide a broad picture of the planning process, ranging from control of the process by way of politicians and planners to the role of individuals involved in the planning, and connects the way postulates of social sustainability in public parks function to the concerned parties. A communicative process in a local planning culture characterized by features such as consensus building, opportunities to participate, assessment, and activation can more effectively benefit the planning of socially sustainable parks.

Marco Scherz (2024)

„Life Cycle Assessment-Based Procurement of Buildings Using The Systemic Know-Why Planning Process"

Institut für Tragwerksentwurf – Nachhaltiges Bauen | Institute of Structural Design – Sustainable Construction

1. Gutachter | 1st reviewer:
Alexander Passer
2. Gutachter | 2nd reviewer:
Alexander Hollberg

Der Gebäudesektor hat einen enormen Anteil an den weltweiten Treibhausgasemissionen (THG-Emissionen) und ist daher auch für den anhaltenden Rückgang des verbleibenden THG-Budgets verantwortlich. Die jüngste Richtlinie der Europäischen Union (EU) über das öffentliche Beschaffungswesen schlägt vor, dass Aufträge für die Beschaffung von Gebäuden auf der Grundlage der Lebenszykluskostenrechnung (engl. Life Cycle Costing, LCC) unter der Berücksichtigung externer Umweltauswirkungen vergeben werden sollen. Ziel der Dissertation ist es, ein Kostenmodell für die Beschaffung von Gebäuden zu entwickeln, welches künftig eine verpflichtende Anwendung der Ökobilanz (engl. Life Cycle Assessment, LCA) ermöglicht und die umweltbezogene Qualität von Gebäuden bei der Vergabeentscheidung berücksichtigt. Mit der Methode der ökologischen Lebenszykluskostenrechnung (engl. Environmental Life Cycle Costing, eLCC) werden gebäudebezogene THG-Emissionen, d.h. graue und betriebliche THG-Emissionen, monetarisiert und in Form von externen Kosten in die Angebotspreise von abgegebenen Angeboten integriert. Zusätzlich wird ein THG-Emissions-Bonus/Malus ermittelt, um Paris-kompatible (engl. Paris-compatible cost, PCC) Kostenszenarien zu berechnen, die als Vergabekriterium im Gebäudebeschaffungsprozess herangezogen werden. Durch die Kombination der Know-Why-Methode und des Gebäudezertifizierungssystems der Deutschen Gesellschaft für Nachhaltiges Bauen (DGNB) wird ein systemisches Planungsprozessmodell entwickelt. Mit der Anwendung des Prozessmodells können Wechselwirkungen zwischen Planungsmaßnahmen, d.h. Synergien und Zielkonflikte, identifiziert und Auswirkungen auf Projektziele, wie z.B. optimierte umweltbezogene Gebäudequalität oder andere Nachhaltigkeitsaspekte, analysiert werden. Die Dissertation schließt die Forschungslücke eines fehlenden Kostenmodells für einen ökologischeren Gebäudebeschaffungsprozess in Österreich. Durch die Entwicklung der vorgestellten Modelle, das THG-Emissions-Bonus/Malus-System für den Gebäudebeschaffungsprozess und das hierarchische, referenzbasierte Know-Why-Modell für den Planungsprozess, wurden die Grundlagen für weitere Umsetzungsschritte eines ökologischeren Gebäudebeschaffungsprozesses in Österreich geschaffen.

• The building sector accounts for an enormous share of global greenhouse gas (GHG) emissions and, therefore, is also responsible for the continuing decrease in the remaining budget of GHG emissions. The latest European Union directive on public procurement proposes that building contracts should be awarded according to life cycle costing (LCC), under consideration of environmental externalities. The dissertation's objective is to develop a cost model for the procurement of buildings that enables mandatory applications of life cycle assessment (LCA) in the future and considers the environmental quality of buildings in the award decision. The environmental life cycle costing (eLCC) method monetizes building-related GHG emissions, that is, embodied and operational GHG emissions, and integrates them as external costs into the bid prices of submitted bids. Moreover, a GHG emissions bonus/malus has been determined in order to calculate Paris-compatible cost scenarios for use as an award criterion in the building procurement process. By combining the know-why method and the building certification system of the German Sustainable Building Council, a systemic planning process model has been developed. With the application of the process model, interactions among planning measures, that is, synergies and trade-offs, can be identified, and impacts on project goals, such as optimized environmental building quality or other sustainability aspects, analyzed. The dissertation fills the research gap of a missing cost model for a more environmentally friendly building procurement process in Austria. By developing the presented models—the LCA-based bonus/malus system for the building procurement process and the hierarchical reference-based know-why model for the planning process—the basis for steps in further implementing a more environmentally friendly building procurement process in Austria has been laid.

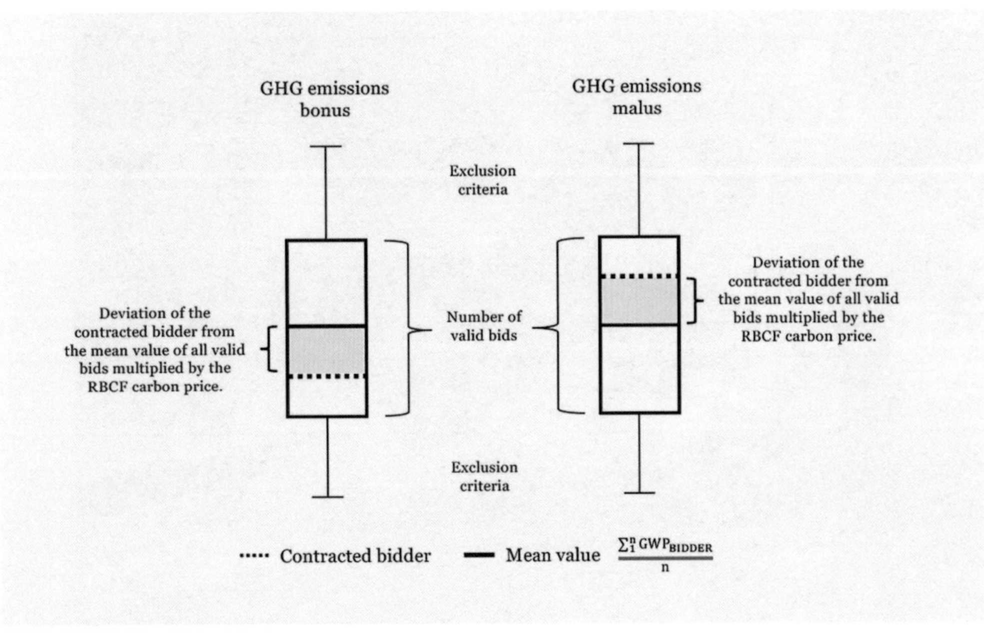

© IAT, TU Graz

Circular Standards

Institut für Architekturtechnologie | Institute of Architecture Technology

Die sich schnell ändernden Umstände unter denen wir unsere gebaute Umwelt schaffen, lassen einen großen und schnell umzusetzenden Bedarf an Änderungen für das Bauwesen erwarten. Auch wenn die Gegenwart herausfordernd ist, bietet sie gleichzeitig viel Raum für Kreativität und neue Visionen. Seit Oktober 2023 werden am Institut für Architekturtechnologie Möglichkeiten für eine kreislaufgerechte Baukonstruktion erforscht – mit dem Ziel, kreislaufgerechte „standardisierte“ Hochbaudetails zu entwickeln. Unter dem Titel „Circular Standards“ bietet das Projekt für ArchitektInnen die Gelegenheit, diese Art zu Bauen im (technischen) Detail neu zu denken und anhand einer gemeinsamen Sprache in Form von „Standarddetails“ in eine mögliche Umsetzung zu überführen. Entdeckt und wertgeschätzt wird dabei das Potenzial von Gebäudebestand im Sinne seiner Weiternutzung als anthropogenes Bauteil-/Baustofflager. Zudem werden „innovative“ und „neue“ Konstruktionen entwickelt, welche u.a. aktuelle Füge- und Verbindungstechniken und (De-) Montageprozesse auf die Probe stellen. Die Basis dafür ist eine Überprüfung der derzeit gebräuchlichen Standardkonstruktionen auf ihre Kreislauffähigkeit. Zudem sollen Potentiale und Hindernisse bei der Etablierung solcher kreislauffähigen Details festgestellt werden. Der Projektgegenstand betrifft den kreislauforientierten Neubau als auch die zukunftsorientierte Sanierung von Bestandsgebäuden.

• The rapidly changing conditions under which we create our built environment point to a great need for rapidly implemented changes in building. Although the present poses challenges, it also leaves a great deal of room for creativity and new visions. Since October 2023, research has been conducted at the Institute of Architecture Technology into the possibilities of recycling-oriented construction with the goal of developing “standardized” building details. Under the title “Circular Standards,” this project for architects offers an opportunity to reconsider the (technical) details of this kind of building and to use a common language in the form of “standard details” to find possibilities to implement them. In the process, we discover and appreciate the potential of the existing building fabric in the sense of continuing to use anthropogenic stores of building parts and materials. In addition, “innovative” and “new” constructions are being developed that, among other things, put current joining and connecting technologies and (dis)assembly processes to the test. To that end, currently common standard constructions are being evaluated in terms of “recyclability.” In addition, the potentials for and obstacles to establishing such circulation-oriented details will be determined. The project addresses both recycling-oriented new construction and forward-looking renovation of existing buildings.

Projektdauer | Project duration:
Oktober 2023–September 2024

Finanzierung | Funding:
Österreichische Forschungsförderungsgesellschaft (FFG) | Austrian Research Promotion Agency (FFG)

Projektteam | Project team:
Institut für Architekturtechnologie | Institute of Architecture Technology:
Marisol Vidal (Projektleitung | Project leader), Matthias Lang-Raudaschl, Clemens Berlach, Saša Ritonja, Viktoriia Mikhaleva

ParisBuildings

Institut für Tragwerksentwurf – Nachhaltiges Bauen | Institute of Structural Design – Sustainable Construction

Das Projekt „ParisBuildings. Transition of the Procurement Process Towards Paris Compatible Public Buildings“ analysierte die gebäudebezogenen Treibhausgas (THG)-Emissionen in Österreich und erforschte darüber hinaus Möglichkeiten, diese im Einklang mit den Pariser Klimazielen zu reduzieren. Der Fokus lag auf öffentlichen Gebäuden, um Klimaschutzmaßnahmen in den öffentlichen Beschaffungsprozess zu integrieren. Frühzeitige Berücksichtigung von Nachhaltigkeitsaspekten in der Planung ist entscheidend für THG-Emissionsreduktionen. Ein im Projekt entwickeltes Prozessmodell für den öffentlichen Gebäudebeschaffungsprozess (THG-Emissions-Bonus/Malus-System) monetarisiert die Umweltqualität von Gebäuden, um diese bei Vergabeentscheidungen zu berücksichtigen. Im Rahmen von zwei Stakeholder-Workshops waren VertreterInnen von Industrie und Verwaltung eingeladen, ihre Perspektiven und Erfahrungen in die laufende Forschung einzubringen.

Während nationale Berichte nur direkte Betriebsemissionen als Gebäudeemissionen ausweisen, zeigen die Projektergebnisse, dass eine Betrachtung des Gebäudebereichs als Handlungsfeld (unter Berücksichtigung sowohl der Betriebsemissionen als auch der grauen THG-Emissionen aller Gebäudetypen) zu deutlich höheren gebäudebezogenen THG-Emissionen führt. Graue Emissionen machen einen erheblichen Anteil aus. Strategien zur Verringerung der grauen Emissionen auf Material- und Gebäudeebene könnten bis 2050 zu erheblichen Reduzierungen führen. Die Integration erneuerbarer Energien im Betrieb von Gebäuden ist für die THG-Reduktionsziele entscheidend.

Das österreichische Vergaberecht bietet Möglichkeiten für Klimaschutzmaßnahmen, jedoch gibt es Barrieren wie mangelndes Bewusstsein und Widersprüche zwischen Beschaffungs- und Planungslogik. Die Integration von Ökobilanz und Lebenszykluskostenberechnung im öffentlichen Beschaffungswesen wird durch verschiedene Hindernisse erschwert. Ein im Rahmen des Projekts entwickeltes Prozessmodell mit internen CO_2-Preisinstrumenten könnte Anreize für umweltfreundlichere Entscheidungen schaffen. Die Projektergebnisse schlagen einen CO_2-Preiskorridor vor, um die Lücke zwischen aktuellen und Paris-kompatiblen

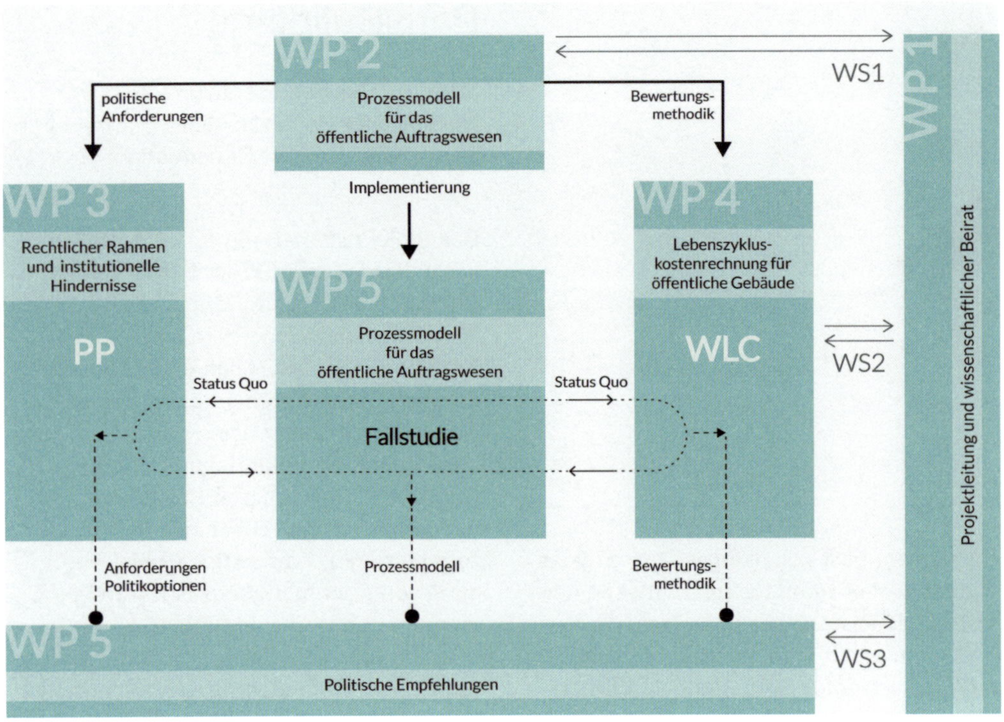

THG-Emissionsreduktionsmaßnahmen zu schließen. Zur Umsetzung des THG-Emissions-Bonus/Malus-Systems sind klare Richtlinien und eine gute Datenbasis erforderlich.

Um die Umsetzung von Maßnahmen voranzutreiben, wurden im Rahmen des Projekts Handlungsempfehlungen für Entscheidungstragende in der öffentlichen Gebäudebeschaffung entwickelt, sowie ein Leitfaden für die nachhaltige Beschaffung von öffentlichen Gebäuden erstellt.

• The "ParisBuildings: Transition of the Procurement Process Towards Paris Compatible Public Buildings" project analyzed building-related emissions of greenhouse gases (GHGs) in Austria and also explored opportunities to reduce them to meet the Paris climate goals. It focused on public buildings in order to integrate climate-protection measures into public procurement processes. Early consideration of issues of sustainability in planning is crucial to reducing GHG emissions. A model developed in this project for the procurement process for public buildings—LCA [Lifecycle analysis]-based bonus/malus system—valuated the environmental quality of buildings so that it can be considered in the procurement process. In two stakeholder workshops, representatives of industry and government were invited to contribute their perspectives and experiences to our ongoing research.

While national reports show only direct operating emissions as building emissions, the results of our project show that looking at the area of the building as a field of action (considering both operating emissions and the gray GHG emissions of all building types) points to considerably higher building-related GHG emissions. Gray emissions represent a significant share. Strategies on the materials and building level to reduce gray emissions could result in substantial reductions by 2050. The integration of renewable energies into building operations is crucial to achieving GHG-reduction goals.

Austrian procurement law offers opportunities for climate-protection measures, but there are barriers and a lack of awareness, as well as contradictions between the logic of procurement and that of planning. Various obstacles make integrating the ecological balance sheet and calculating lifecycle costs in public procurement are made considerably more difficult. A model developed as part of this project could create incentives for more environmentally friendly decisions by means of internal CO_2 price instruments. The results of the project propose a CO_2 price corridor to close the gap between current GHG-emissions reductions and the Paris climate goals. Implementing the LCA-based bonus/malus system requires clear guidelines and a good foundation of data.

To encourage the implementation of such measures, the project has developed recommended courses of action for decision makers in public procurement in construction as well as a guideline for sustainable procurement for public buildings.

Projektdauer | Project duration:
2019–2023

Finanzierung | Funding:
Austrian Climate Research Programme (ACRP) 11th Call for Proposals – 2019

Projektteam | Project team:
Alexander Passer (Projektleitung | Project leader), Institut für Tragwerksentwurf–Nachhaltiges Bauen | Institute of Structural Design—Sustainable Construction

ProjektpartnerInnen | Project partners:
Science, Technology, and Society Unit (TU Graz)
Wegener Center für Klima und Globalen Wandel (Universität Graz)

makingAchange

Institut für Tragwerksentwurf – Nachhaltiges Bauen | Institute of Structural Design – Sustainable Construction

„makingAchange“ ist ein Kooperationsprojekt zwischen Wissenschaft und Schule. Gemeinsam mit dem Bundesministerium für Bildung, Wissenschaft und Forschung lud das Climate Change Center Austria (CCCA) alle Schulen der Sekundarstufe in Österreich ein, sich am Projekt „Klimawandel und Nachhaltigkeit“ zu beteiligen. Ziel war es, einen Beitrag zur Transformation der Gesellschaft zu leisten und die Themen Klimaschutz und Nachhaltigkeit im schulischen Umfeld und im Alltag als selbstverständlich zu integrieren und wahrzunehmen. Die am Projekt teilnehmenden SchülerInnen wurden ermutigt, sich eigenständig mit dem Thema auseinanderzusetzen und Lösungen zu finden. Eines der angebotenen Bildungsformate, die CO_2-Bilanzierung, wurde von der TU Graz (Nachhaltiges Bauen) mitbetreut. Die CO_2-Bilanzierung von „makingAchange“ ermöglichte es den teilnehmenden Schulen, über drei Projektjahre durch Datenerhebungen und Emissionsberechnung die größten Emissionsquellen ihres Schulbetriebs zu identifizieren und in einem nächsten Schritt daraus die effektivsten Klimaschutzmaßnahmen abzuleiten. Bei einer Aktualisierung der Bilanz in regelmäßigen Abständen, kann in Zukunft die Wirksamkeit von gesetzten Klimaschutzmaßnahmen gemessen werden.

Im Rahmen von online-Workshops mit SchülerInnen und Lehrpersonen wurden Grundlagen der CO_2-Bilanzierung vermittelt, und den SchülerInnen Wissen und Werkzeuge zur Verfügung gestellt, um selbstständig eine CO_2-Bilanzierung ihrer Schule durchführen zu können. Darüber hinaus wurden auch Maßnahmen-Workshops abgehalten, um auf der CO_2-Bilanz aufbauend die Entwicklung von Emissionsreduktionsmaßnahmen und -zielen zu unterstützen. Während der Projektlaufzeit wurde die CO_2-Bilanzierung gemeinsam vom Zentrum für globalen Wandel und Nachhaltigkeit der Universität für Bodenkultur Wien (BOKU) und der Arbeitsgruppe Nachhaltiges Bauen der Technischen Universität Graz (TU Graz) betreut. Für die Zeit nach Projektende wurde eine Kooperation mit der TU Graz Organisation TUit gestartet, um eine Weiterführung der CO_2-Bilanzierung zu garantieren.

Beim gemeinsamen Abschlussfest des Projekts „makingAchange“ am 22. September 2023 an der BOKU Wien wurden noch einmal alle „makingAchange“-Formate vorgestellt und die daraus entwickelten Projekte der TeilnehmerInnen präsentiert.

• “makingAchange” is a cooperative project between scientists and schools. Together with the Austrian Federal Ministry of Education, Science, and Research, the Climate Change Center Austria (CCCA) invited all secondary schools in Austria to participate in the “Climate Change and Sustainability” project. Its goal was to contribute to transforming society and to integrate the themes of climate protection and sustainability into schools and daily life as a matter of course. Students participating in the project were encouraged to engage with the theme independently and find their own solutions. One of the educational formats on offer—CO_2 balancing—was co-supervised by TU Graz (Working Group Sustainable Construction). The CO_2 balancing of “makingAchange” enabled participating schools during the project’s three-year span to identify their largest sources of operation emissions by collecting data and calculating emissions in order to, in the next step, determine the most effective measures for climate protection. Updating the balance at regular intervals in the future will measure the effectiveness of the climate measures established.

Online workshops with students and teachers taught the basics of CO_2 balancing to give students the knowledge and tools to achieve CO_2 balancing at their school on their own. In addition, measure workshops were held to support the development of emission-reduction measures and goals on the basis of the CO_2 balance. Over the course of the project, CO_2 balances were supervised jointly by the Center for Global Change and Sustainability (BOKU) and the Working Group Sustainable Construction at TU Graz. A cooperation with TU Graz, it was launched for the period after the project’s end to ensure that CO_2 balancing will continue.

At the joint closing ceremony, held at BOKU Vienna on September 22, 2023, all of the formats and participants’ projects developed were presented once again.

Projektdauer | Project duration:
2020–2023

Finanzierung | Funding:
Bundesministerium für Bildung, Wissenschaft und Forschung

Projektteam | Project team:
CCCA (Projektkoordination | Project coordination)
Helga Kromp-Kolb (Projektleitung | Project leader)
TU Graz: Institut für Tragwerksentwurf – Nachhaltiges Bauen (Projektleitung | Project leader at TU Graz: Alexander Passer)
Universität Innsbruck
BOKU
Universität Graz
Universität Wien
IIASA

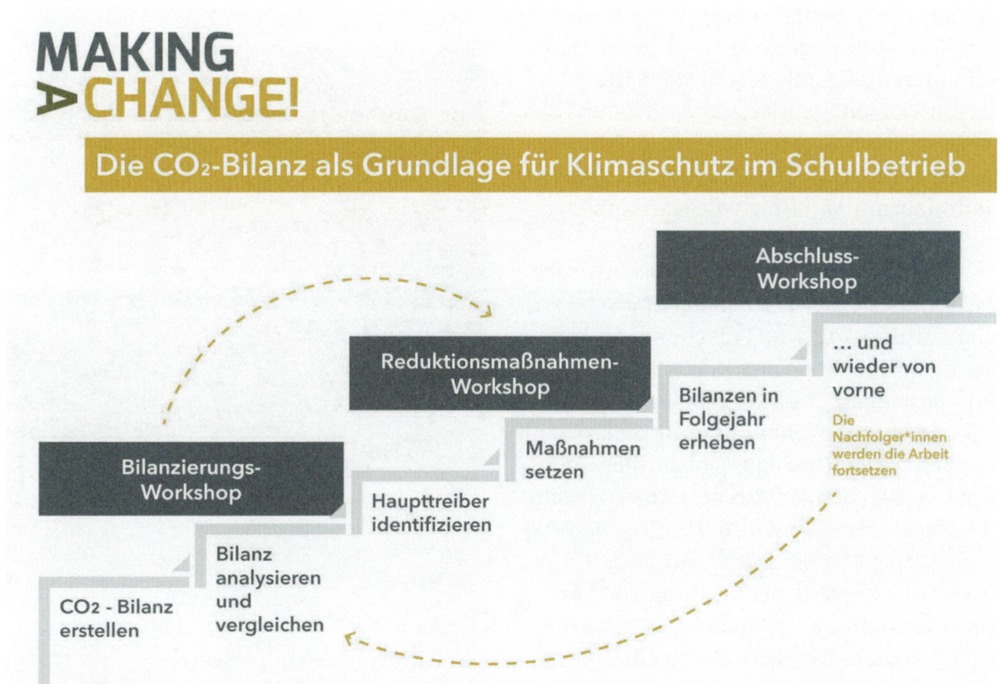

© NHB, TU Graz

Komuna Maro

Institut für Zeitgenössische Kunst | Institute of Contemporary Art

Die Vorstellung des Ozeans als eine leere Weite, die von menschlicher Kultur und Urbanisierung unbeeinflusst bleibt, entspricht nicht der Realität – im Zuge der Entwicklung von Rechtsmechanismen und Technologien zur Verwaltung, Beaufsichtigung, Durchquerung und Ausbeutung von Meeresgebieten sind die Weltenmeere zunehmend mit den Aktivitäten des Menschen verwoben. Auf dieser Annahme basierend, untersucht das künstlerische Forschungsprojekt „Komuna Maro" („Gemeinsames Meer" auf Esperanto) die Netzwerke mariner Gemeinschaften, Technologien und Infrastrukturen der Nordadria. Dabei geht es darum, versteckte Machtdynamiken aufzudecken, neue „Kartographien" zu erstellen und alternative Narrative für die Region zu präsentieren. Gemeinsam mit ausgewählten KünstlerInnen folgt das Kernprojektteam des Instituts für Zeitgenössische Kunst (IZK) verschiedenen menschlichen und nicht-menschlichen AkteurInnen, die am, in der Nähe von, im und mit dem Adriatischen Meer leben, um deren unterschiedliche Erfahrungen zu dokumentieren und diversen Wissensformen über diesen gemeinsamen Lebensraum eine Stimme zu geben. Gleichzeitig werden sich die ForscherInnen mit weiter entfernten – wissenschaftlichen, geopolitischen und rechtlichen – Diskursen und komplexen räumlichen Daten auseinandersetzen. In Form von offenen Diskussionen und Workshops, mehrsprachigen Pamphleten, Radiosendungen, performativen Wanderausstellungen und kollaborativen digitalen Landkarten werden diese verschiedenen Sichtweisen „von unten" und „von oben" verbunden und überlagert, um eine alternative, facettenreiche, transnationale und multimediale Kartographie der Nordadria zu erstellen.

Methodisch wird die analytische Phase des Projekts experimentell-geografische und anthropologische Forschung mit kollaborativer künstlerischer Praxis vereinen. Auf diese Phase folgt eine spekulative Erkundung möglicher Zukunftsszenarien, einschließlich Überlegungen zu alternativen Gesetzgebungen für die nordadriatische Region, neuen Formen der Bewirtschaftung von Meeresressourcen und Ideen für das Hacken, die Wiederverwendung und Vergemeinschaftung bestehender maritimer Technologien. Die Besonderheit des Projekts liegt im Einsatz von künstlerischer Forschung als Mittel, um einen kollektiven und transdisziplinären Prozess des Neukartierens und Neuinterpretierens eines gemeinsamen maritimen Raums – unseres gemeinsamen Ozeans – zu orchestrieren und zu dokumentieren.

• The notion of the ocean as a blank expanse unaffected by human culture and urbanization does not align with reality—with the development of legal mechanisms and technologies for governing, monitoring, traversing, and exploiting marine spaces, the world's seas have become increasingly interconnected with human activities. Based on this assumption, the artistic research project Komuna Maro (Common Sea in Esperanto) investigates the networks of marine communities, technologies, and infrastructures of the North Adriatic. The project's objectives are to uncover hidden power dynamics, create new "cartographies," and present alternative narratives for the region. The core project team from the Institute of Contemporary Art accompanied by a group of selected artists, follow various human and nonhuman actors living at, near, in, and with the Adriatic Sea to document different experiences and give voice to diverse forms of knowledge about this shared habitat. Simultaneously, the researchers engage with more distant—scientific, geopolitical, and legal—discourses and complex spatial data. In the form of open discussions and workshops, multilingual pamphlets, radio broadcasts, performative traveling exhibitions, and collaborative digital maps, these different views "from below" and "from above" connect and overlap to provide an alternative, multifaceted, transnational, and multimedia cartography of the North Adriatic.

In terms of methodology, the analytical phase of the project intertwines experimental geographic and anthropological research with collaborative artistic practice. This phase is followed by a speculative exploration of possible future scenarios, including considerations about alternative legislation for the North Adriatic region, novel forms of cultivating ocean resources, and ideas for hacking, repurposing, and commoning existing maritime technologies. The distinctiveness of the project lies in its utilization of artistic research as a means to orchestrate and document a collective and transdisciplinary process of remapping and reimagining a shared marine space—our Common Sea.

Projektdauer | Project duration:
Oktober 2023 – September 2027

Finanzierung | Funding:
Program for Arts-based Research (PEEK) of the Austrian Science Fund (FWF)

Projektteam | Project team:
Ana Jeinić (Projektleitung | project leader, IZK), Ana Dana Beroš (IZK), and Milica Tomić (IZK)

ProjektpartnerInnen | Project partners:
Elizabeth Johnson (Durham University, Department of Geography, UK)
Nancy Couling (Bergen Arkitekthøgskole, NO)
Lucija Ažman Momirski (Univerza v Ljubljani, Fakulteta za arhitekturo, SI)
TBA21–Academy/Ocean Space (Venice, IT)
Drugo more (Rijeka, HR)

© Matija Kralj Štefanić

© Martin Grabner

Zentrum für Aktive Mobilität

Institut für Städtebau | Institute of Urbanism

Der Klimawandel und andere gesellschaftliche Herausforderungen bedürfen einer weitgehenden Veränderung unseres Mobilitätssystems. Vor diesem Hintergrund richteten die Universität Graz und die Technische Universität Graz im Spätsommer 2023 ein interuniversitäres Zentrum für Aktive Mobilität ein. Aktive Mobilität bedeutet den Einsatz von physischer Energie, um von einem Ort zum anderen zu kommen. Dazu gehören das Zufußgehen oder das Radfahren, aber auch andere Mobilitätsformen, die auf reiner Muskelkraft basieren, wie zum Beispiel das Skateboardfahren oder das Inlineskaten.

Das Zentrum soll neue wissenschaftliche Erkenntnisse, Entscheidungsgrundlagen und Lösungen für aktive Mobilität im handlungsfeldübergreifenden Kontext zwischen Mobilität, Klima und Umwelt, Raum, Gesundheit und Wirtschaft erarbeiten. Durch den intensiven Austausch mit der Stadt Graz und dem Land Steiermark wird eine praxisnahe Forschung gewährleistet und sichergestellt, dass die Ergebnisse rasch eine breite Berücksichtigung in der Praxis finden. Die Personen, die dem Zentrum ein Gesicht geben, sind Nina Hampl (Institut für Umweltsystemwissenschaften, Karl-Franzens-Universität Graz), Aglaée Degros (Leiterin Institut für Städtebau, TU Graz), Eva Schwab (stv. Leiterin stdb, TU Graz) und Barbara Holler (Universitäts-Projektassistentin stdb, TU Graz). Die Finanzierung der Stellen erfolgt durch das Land Steiermark und die Stadt Graz auf fünf Jahre.

• Climate change and other social challenges demand far-reaching changes to our mobility system. Against that backdrop, the University of Graz and TU Graz established in the late summer of 2023 an interuniversity Center of Active Mobility. Active mobility means employing physical energy to get from one place to another. That includes walking and cycling, as well as other forms of mobility based solely on muscle power, such as skateboarding and inline skating.

The center is intended to work out new scientific insights, principles for decision making, and solutions to active mobility in the overarching context between mobility, climate and environment, space, health, and the economy. The intensive interchange between the State of Styria and the City of Graz will permit practical research and ensure the results are quickly and widely put into practice. The people who lend a face to the center are Nina Hampl (Department of Environmental Systems Sciences, University of Graz), Aglaée Degros (head, Institute of Urbanism (stdb), TU Graz), Eva Schwab (deputy head, stdb, TU Graz), and Barbara Holler (university project assistant, stdb, TU Graz). The positions have been funded for five years by the State of Styria and the City of Graz.

Projektdauer | Project duration:
2023–2028

Finanzierung | Funding:
Stadt Graz
Land Steiermark

Projektteam | Project team:
Aglaée Degros, Eva Schwab, Barbara Holler (Institut für Städtebau, TU Graz)

ProjektpartnerInnen | Project partners:
Nina Hampl (Institut für Umweltsystemwissenschaften, Universität Graz)

Fußverkehrsstrategie Steiermark 2030+

Institut für Städtebau | Institute of Urbanism

„Nur einen Spaziergang entfernt" – so lautet das übergreifende Motto der neuen Fußverkehrsstrategie des Landes Steiermark, die in einem mehrmonatigen Prozess gemeinsam mit der TU Graz entstanden ist. Neben sozialwissenschaftlichen Ansätzen bildeten auch räumlich-planerische Ansätze und Analysen die Basis für eine profunde Auseinandersetzung mit dem Gehen als Fortbewegungsart. Aus den Recherchen und Untersuchungen konnten wesentliche Ansätze zur Verbesserung öffentlicher Räume in Ortskernen der Steiermark abgeleitet werden. Die damit einhergehende Attraktivierung von Ortszentren führt zu mehr Lebendigkeit und fördert aktive Bewegung sowie sozialen Zusammenhalt. Neben der Schaffung von fußverkehrsfreundlichen Strukturen in kompakten Orten mit Nutzungsvielfalt, der Anbindung an öffentliche Verkehrsmittel, der Einbindung von BürgerInnen in Planungskonzepte und einer klimagerechten Infrastruktur liegt ein weiterer Schwerpunkt auf einem prozessualen Startpunkt für eine institutionalisierte Begleitung und Förderung. Ziel ist es, Gemeinden zu motivieren, sich um neue und bestehende Fußwege zu kümmern und Grün- und Aufenthaltszonen gendergerecht und inklusiv zu gestalten. Nationale und internationale Beispiele zeigen die unterschiedlichen Möglichkeiten infrastruktureller Verbesserungen. Das Zusammenführen von städtebaulich-planerischen Aspekten mit den vielfältigen Bedürfnissen von Menschen in unterschiedlichen Alters- und Lebensphasen ermöglichte eine ganzheitliche transdisziplinäre Perspektive, die der zuständigen Abteilung des Landes Steiermark nun als Werkzeug zur Beurteilung und den umsetzenden Gemeinden als Leitfaden und Inspiration dient.

• "Just a stroll away" that is the general motto of the new pedestrian traffic strategy of the State of Styria, which was developed together with TU Graz in a process lasting several months. In addition to approaches from the social sciences, spatial planning approaches, and analyses formed the basis for a profound engagement with walking as a form of locomotion. Essential approaches to impression public spaces in the town centers of Styria were derived from research and studies. Making town centers more attractive in this way increases vitality and encourages active movement and social cohesion. In addition to creating pedestrian-friendly structures in compact places with diversity of use, connections to public transportation, integration of residents into planning concepts, and climate-just infrastructure, another focus was on a starting point for the process of accompanying and supporting them through institutions. The goal is to motivate municipalities to pay attention to new and existing footpaths and to design green spaces and recreation zones to be gender-sensitive and inclusive. National and international examples show different possibilities for infrastructural improvements. Bringing together urbanist and planning aspects with the diverse needs of people of different ages and in different phases of life permits a broad, transdisciplinary perspective that will now serve the responsible department of the State of Styria as an assessment tool and the implementing communities as a guideline and inspiration.

Projektdauer | Project duration:
2022–2023

Finanzierung | Funding:
Amt der Steiermärkischen Landesregierung, Abteilung 16 | Office of the Styrian Government, Department 16

Projektteam | Project team:
Institut für Städtebau | Institute of Urbanism:
Prof. Aglaee Degros, Anna Bagaric, Sabine Bauer, Philipp Flachhuber, Carola Hilgert, Carina Mazelle, Markus Monsberger

ProjektpartnerInnen | Project partners:
STS-Unit, Günter Getzinger, Franziska Häller, Katharina Mikula

© stdb, TU Graz

Jigmey Lodey, Helmut Woschitz, Carmen Auer, Tsering Lanzom, Vera Schabbon © akk, TU Graz

to map the Hrab ensemble. This was followed by the documentation of the Namdo ensemble, located about an hour's walk from Tsa. During this period, it was also finally possible to visit and photographically record the Yangtse Monastery near the border with Tibet. On the way back, the opportunity arose to survey the Mehkhim ensemble, which lies in a remote location on the eastern slope of the Tara Valley.

The trip concluded this year's fieldwork, and the team returned to Dunai after a three-day descent. Aside from the good preparation and communication with local protagonists, the results of this year's measurements reveal that the use of 3D laser scanning technology enables buildings to be surveyed quickly and precisely. This can significantly reduce the time required for on-site mapping operations, which is a great advantage, especially in hard-to-reach areas such as Dolpo.

Buddhistische Architektur im westlichen Himalaya: Feldforschung in Upper Dolpo 2023

Institut für Architekturtheorie, Kunst- und Kulturwissenschaften | Institute of Architectural Theory, Art History and Cultural Studies

Die zweite Feldforschung des FWF-Forschungsprojekts konnte vom 23. Mai bis 8. Juli 2023 erfolgreich durchgeführt werden. Gemeinsam mit acht Einheimischen, einem Pferd und elf Maultieren startete das Projektteam der TU Graz – Carmen Auer, Helmut Woschitz und Vera Schabbon – in Dunai in Lower Dolpo. Nach vier Tagen Fußmarsch erreichten sie das Taraptal, wo digitale Vermessungen der Klosteranlagen von Shipchok und dem Ribo Bhumpa Gompa durchgeführt wurden. Nach fünf Tagen Arbeit ging es das Tal weiter aufwärts, um den Dorftempel von Kagar ("Kagar Labrang") und einen kleinen, privaten Tempel („Zur Gompa") sowie die umliegenden Gebäudestrukturen zu vermessen. Danach führte der Weg weiter nach Norden, über den Jyanta-La (5221m) bis ins Dorf Tsa im Nangkhongtal, um das Ensemble von Hrab zu vermessen. Im Anschluss wurde das Ensemble von Namdo dokumentiert, das etwa eine Stunde Fußmarsch von Tsa entfernt liegt. In dieser Zeit war es außerdem endlich möglich, das Kloster von Yangtse nahe der Grenze zu Tibet zu besuchen und fotografisch zu dokumentieren. Auf dem Rückweg ergab sich außerdem die Gelegenheit, das Ensemble von Mehkhim zu vermessen, das abgelegen auf der östlichen Hangseite des Taraptals liegt.

Damit war die diesjährige Feldarbeit abgeschlossen und wir erreichten nach drei Tagen Abstieg wieder Dunai. Die Ergebnisse der diesjährigen Messungen zeigen, dass – neben der guten Vorbereitung und der Kommunikation mit lokalen AkteurInnen – der Einsatz der 3D-Laserscan-Technologie eine schnelle und genaue Gebäudevermessung ermöglicht. Dadurch kann der Zeitaufwand für die Vermessungsarbeiten vor Ort erheblich verkürzt werden, was gerade in schwer zu erreichenden Gegenden wie Dolpo ein großer Vorteil ist.

• The second field research of the FWF research project was successfully conducted from May 23 to July 8, 2023. Alongside eight locals, a horse, and eleven mules, the project team of TU Graz—Carmen Auer, Helmut Woschitz, and Vera Schabbon—set off from Dunai in Lower Dolpo. After a four-day trek, they reached the Tarap Valley, where digital surveys of the Shipchok and Ribo Bhumpa Gompa monasteries were carried out. After five days of work, the group further ascended the valley to survey the village temple of Kagar ("Kagar Labrang") and a small, private temple ("Zur Gompa"), as well as the surrounding building structures. Thereafter, the route led northward over the Jyanta-La (5,221 meters in elevation) and into the village of Tsa in the Nangkhong valley in order

Projektdauer | Project duration:
2022–2025

Finanzierung | Funding:
Der Wissenschaftsfonds | Austrian Science Fund (FWF)

Projektteam | Project team:
Institut für Architekturtheorie, Kunst- und Kulturwissenschaften: Anselm Wagner (Projektleitung | project head), Carmen Auer (Forschungsleiterin | principal investigator), Holger Neuwirth, Vera Schabbon, Natalie Resch

ProjektpartnerInnen | Project partners:
Institut für Ingenieurgeodäsie und Messsysteme | Institute of Engineering Geodesy and Measurement Systems, TU Graz: Peter Bauer, Helmut Woschitz

© Janosch Schallert, Native Media GmbH/Concrete 3D GmbH

Stahlbetonleichtbau-expertise für den Werkhof in Bludenz

Institut für Tragwerksentwurf | Institute of Structural Design

Beauftragt durch Tomaselli Gabriel Bau GmbH, Baumit GmbH und gbd ZT GmbH Dornbirn war das Institut für Tragwerksentwurf maßgeblich an der Planung eines 717m^2 Flachdachs in Stahlbetonleichtbauweise für den Werkhof in Bludenz beteiligt. Das Team des Instituts, das für den Entwurf des Dachtragwerks mit einer freien Spannweite von 14 Metern sowie für die Entwicklung der Printstrategie der 3D-gedruckten Aussparungskörper verantwortlich war, brachte so seine Expertise in der Umsetzung der neuartigen Bauweise bei der bislang weltweit größten Konstruktion dieser Art ein. Das Bauvorhaben wurde mit Jahresbeginn 2023 fertiggestellt und steht stellvertretend für den Einsatz des 3D-Betondrucks als vielversprechende Möglichkeit, filigrane und nachhaltige Tragwerke in Stahlbetonleichtbauweise zu errichten. Die „Grazer Stahlbetonleichtbauweise" auf Grundlage gedruckter Schalungen wurde an der TU Graz im Rahmen eines FFG-Forschungsprojektes entwickelt und ausgiebig erprobt. Zentrales Element sind dabei 3D-gedruckte Schalkörper welche als verlorene Schalung im Bauteil verbleiben. Somit kann die Betonkubatur von Ortbetonkonstruktionen drastisch minimiert werden und eine massive Platte mit Rechteckvollquerschnitt zu einer querschnittsoptimierten Kassettendecke transformiert werden. Neben dem Kräfteverlauf spielten insbesondere auch das Gewicht und die Formstabilität während des Druckprozesses und der Betonage auf der Baustelle eine große Rolle, um zum einen den Transport und die Manipulation vor Ort zu erleichtern, und zum anderen Verformungen oder Brüche der Schalkörper ausschließen zu können. Im Bauprojekt konnten durch den konsequenten Einsatz der 3D-Drucktechnologie 24 Prozent CO_2eq eingespart werden. Neben dem Beton, der durch die Aussparungskörper eingespart wurde, konnte durch die Reduktion des Eigengewichtes der Struktur auf einen Anteil des Bewehrungsstahls verzichtet werden. Somit konnten allein durch das Deckentragwerk 33to CO_2eq vermieden werden.

• The Institute of Structural Design was commissioned by Tomaselli Gabriel Bau GmbH, Baumit GmbH, and gbd ZT GmbH Dornbirn to play a critical role in the planning of a flat roof of 717 sq. m. in lightweight reinforced-concrete construction for the Werkhof in Bludenz. The institute's team responsible for designing the supporting structure for the roof with an open span of fourteen meters and for developing a printing strategy for 3D printed void bodies brought its expertise to implementing a new construction method for the largest construction of this kind thus far anywhere in the world. The building project was completed at the beginning of 2023 and illustrates the promising possibilities of using 3D concrete printing for filigree and sustainable load-bearing light construction of reinforced concrete. "Graz light construction of reinforced concrete" is based on printed formwork and was developed and extensively tested at TU Graz as part of a research project funded by the Austrian Research Promotion Agency (FFG). One of its central elements is the use of 3D printed formwork that remains in the construction element as lost shuttering. The cubic volume of in-situ concrete constructions can thus be drastically minimized, and a solid slab of rectangular full cross-section can be transformed into a coffered ceiling of optimized cross section. In addition to the flow of forces, the weight and stability of form also play an important role during the printing process and the in-situ pouring of the concrete, simplifying, first, transportation and manipulation on site and, second, preventing deformations or cracks in the shuttering. The project's rigorous use of 3D printing technology reduced CO_2eq by 24 percent. In addition to the concrete saved by the void bodies, the weight of the structure could be reduced, and some of the rebar left out. The load-bearing structure for the roof alone saved 33 metric tons of CO_2eq.

Projektdauer | Project duration:
Februar 2022 – März 2023

Finanzierung | Funding:
Stadt Bludenz, WERIT Handels GmbH Österreich, Bludenz

Projektdauer: | Project duration
Februar 2022 – März 2023

Finanzierung | Funding:
Stadt Bludenz, WERIT Handels GmbH Österreich, Bludenz

Projektteam | Project team:
Atelier Ender, Nüziders
BAUMIT GmbH
Concrete 3D, Nüziders
gbd ZT GmbH, Dornbirn
Institut für Tragwerksentwurf: Georg Hansemann, Christoph Holzinger, Robert Schmid, Andreas Trummer, Stefan Peters
Stadt Bludenz
Tomaselli Gabriel Bau, Nüziders
WERIT Handels GmbH Österreich, Bludenz

ReCon

Institut für Architekturtechnologie |
Institute of Architecture Technology

Herkömmliche Klettverschlüsse, wie sie z.B. oft bei Kinderschuhen verwendet werden, dienen als Untersuchungsgegenstand und Inspiration, um eine kreislauffähige und beschädigungsfreie Befestigung von (kurzlebigeren) Baukomponenten an Beton- und Holzbauteilen zu ermöglichen. Das Forschungsteam des Institutes für Architekturtechnologie (IAT) arbeitet hierzu interdisziplinär und mit BauingenieurInnen, PapiertechnikerInnen, SoftwareentwicklerInnen und ElektrotechnikerInnen zusammen. Das Projektziel ist die Definition und Verifikation eines resilienten und intelligenten Klettverbindungssystems, das sich aus industriellen Klettkomponenten, Rohbaustoff-Klettkomponenten sowie aus Digitalisierungs- und Sensortechnologien zusammensetzt. Hierzu werden Anwendungsfälle festgelegt, auf bautechnischer, papiertechnischer und elektrotechnischer Ebene Konzepte entwickelt, deren Potential abgeschätzt und ausgewählte Konzepte im Labor oder durch digitale und elektrotechnische Ausführung verifiziert.

In Zusammenarbeit mit dem Labor für Konstruktiven Ingenieurbau der TU Graz konnte bereits „Klettbeton" hergestellt werden. Dieser kann mit 3D-gedruckten Gegenstücken, welche am IAT konstruiert und in Zusammenarbeit mit dem Institut für Architektur und Medien der TU Graz hergestellt wurden, verbunden werden und zeigt vielversprechende erste Ergebnisse auf. Parallel dazu entwickelte das Institut für biobasierte Produkte und Papiertechnik der TU Graz „Klettpapier" und untersucht die Verbindung im Kontext von Papierwerkstoffen, wobei Falttechniken, ähnlich dem Wellenkarton, Anwendung finden. Darüber hinaus wurden am IAT gemeinsam mit dem Institut für Softwaretechnologie der TU Graz „Schlaufenkomponenten" anhand komplexer Nähmuster mit einer Stickmaschine erstellt. Diese sollen auf Basis der Schlaufen herkömmlicher Klettkomponenten eine Verbindung mit „Klettbeton" und „Kletthol" ermöglichen. Mit den Projektpartnern NET-Automation GmbH und axtesys GmbH wird die Digitalisierung von Bauteildaten für Kreislaufwirtschafsprozesse im Bauwesen thematisiert. Wobei Basisdaten und umfassendere Daten abgebildet werden sollen, die während Umbau- oder Rückbaumaßnahmen relevante Informationen bereitstellen.

• Traditional hook-and-loop closures—like those often used for children's shoes, for example—serve as an object of study and inspiration for fastening (shorter-lived) construction components of concrete and wood that are recyclable and do not cause damage. The research team of the Institute of Architecture Technology (IAT) has been doing interdisciplinary work on this with structural engineers, paper technicians, software developers, and electrical engineers. The goal of the project is to define and verify a resilient and intelligent hook-and-loop fastening system composed of industrial hook-and-loop components, hook-and-loop from raw materials, and digitizing and sensor technologies. Potential uses are being determined, concepts for structural, paper, and electronic technology developed, their potential assessed, and selected concepts verified either in the laboratory or by digital and electronic implementation.

In collaboration with the Laboratory for Structural Engineering of TU Graz, "hook-and-loop concrete" has already been produced. It can be combined with 3D printed counterparts constructed at the IAT and produced in collaboration with the Institute of Architecture and Media of TU Graz, and the initial results are very promising. In parallel with this, the Institute of Bioproducts and Paper Technology of TU Graz has developed "hook-and-loop paper" and is studying the connection in the context of paper materials, in which folding technologies similar to corrugated cardboard are used.

In addition, together with the Institute of Software Technology of TU Graz, "loop components" have been produced at the IAT using complex sewing patterns and an embroidering machine. Based on the loops of traditional hook-and-loop components, this should make it possible to combine "hook-and-loop concrete" and "hook-and-loop wood." With project partners NET-Automation GmbH and axtesys GmbH, the theme of digitizing data on construction parts for architectural processes in the circular economy is being addressed. Basic data and more comprehensive data will be illustrated to provide relevant information for their future remodeling or deconstruction.

© IAT, TU Graz

Projektdauer | Project duration:
November 2022–April 2025

Finanzierung | Funding:
Österreichische Forschungsförderungsgesellschaft (FFG) | Austrian Research Promotion Agency (FFG)

Projektteam | Project team:
Institut für Architekturtechnologie |
Institute of Architecture Technology
(Projektleitung | Project leaders):
Marisol Vidal, Matthias Lang-Raudaschl
Clemens Berlach, Saša Ritonja, Selina Haingartner, Toni Levak, Ernst Alexander Dengg

ProjektpartnerInnen | Project partners:
Labor für Konstruktiven Ingenieurbau |
Laboratory for Structural Engineering:
Bernhard Freytag, David Danner
Institut für biobasierte Produkte und Papiertechnik | Institute of Bioproducts and Paper Technology: Ulrich Hirn, Cemile Sözeri, Thomas Harter
NET-Automation GmbH: Gernot Theuermann, Christian Zuber
axtesys GmbH: Peter Treitler, Leonie Haas

Joining Cards

Institut für Architekturtechnologie |
Institute of Architecture Technology

Im Falle mehrfacher Nutzungswechsel ermöglicht der Innenausbau fortlaufend eine Anpassung an neue Bedürfnisse und Anforderungen. Großes Potential besitzt in diesem Kontext die Anwendung von Karton und Papierwerkstoffen als nachwachsender und wiederverwendbarer Baustoff. Trotz ihrer Bautauglichkeit, die u.a. durch die Demonstrationsgebäude des japanischen Architekten Shigeru Ban oder durch internationale Forschungsprojekte wie „BAMP! – Bauen mit Papier" belegt wurde, werden diese Werkstoffe weiterhin meist nur bei temporären Bauwerken oder in weniger bedeutenden Anwendungsgebieten eingesetzt. Daraus folgend bestand das übergeordnete Projektziel von „Joining Cards" in einer möglichst breiten, erstanwendungsübergreifenden und somit langlebigen Anwendung von Baukomponenten aus Papierwerkstoff. Als dahingehend wesentliche Forschungslücke und Untersuchungsgegenstand bestanden konstruktive Konzepte eines rückbaufähigen Fügens zu Innenausbausystemen und die Evaluierung in gebauten 1:1 Untersuchungsmodellen.

Wie die Ergebnisse des abgeschlossenen Forschungsprojekt zeigen, eignen sich Papierwerkstoffe für eine Anwendung bei nicht tragenden und rückbaubaren Innenwänden, aber auch für Unterdecken- und Fußbodensysteme, wobei bestehende Produkte im Bereich von Decken und Fußböden bereits gute Eigenschaften hinsichtlich einer Rückbaubarkeit erfüllen (können). Zudem verbessert die (rückbaubare) Kombination von Metallkomponenten mit Papierwerkstoffen an der Fügestelle die mechanischen Eigenschaften und führt zu besseren (De-)Montageprozessen bei weniger Beschädigung der Einzelteile. Für weiterführende Forschungsvorhaben wurde darüber hinaus festgestellt, dass für die CO_2-Speicherung in Gebäuden, eine Anwendung von z.B. Strohbauplatten in Innenausbausystemen großes Potential besitzt.

• When its use changes many times, remodeling an interior can continuously adapt it to new needs and requirements. The use of cardboard and paper as renewable and reusable building materials has great potential in this context. Although their suitability for construction has been proven by the demonstration buildings of the Japanese architect Shigeru Ban and by international research projects such as "BAMP! —Building with Paper," among others, in most cases, these materials continue to be employed only for temporary structures or less important purposes. Consequently, the overriding goal of the "Joining Cards" project is to use paper as a construction material for more than just first-use applications and hence for long-lived use. Crucial research gaps thus far, as well as potential objects of study, included construction concepts for deconstructable joints for interior finishing systems and the evaluation of 1:1-scale study models.

As the results of the completed research project show, building materials of paper are suited to application for non-load-bearing and deconstructable interior walls but also for drop-ceiling and floor systems where existing ceiling and floor products are (potentially) already well suited to deconstruction. Moreover, the (deconstructable) combination of metal components with paper construction materials in joints improves mechanical properties and results in better (dis)assembly processes with less damage to individual parts. In addition, it was determined for future research projects that, for example, the use of structural straw boards in interior finishing systems has great potential for CO_2 storage.

© IAT, TU Graz

Projektdauer | Project duration:
November 2021–April 2023

Finanzierung | Funding:
Österreichische Forschungsförderungsgesellschaft (FFG) | Austrian Research Promotion Agency (FFG)

Projektteam | Project team:
Institut für Architekturtechnologie |
Institute of Architecture Technology
Roger Riewe (Projektleitung | Project leaders),
Matthias Lang-Raudaschl, Toni Levak
Bernd Hausegger, Lukas Gschweitl, Martin Boleš, Carina Kurz, Christoph Haidacher, Georgios Triantafyllidis, Alexander Gündera, David Schlegl

Publications

Towards Territorial Transition

Matthias Armengaud/Aglaée Degros/
Radostina Radulova-Stahmer (Hg.|eds.)
Zürich: Park Books, 2023
Englisch, 240 Seiten, gebunden |
English, 240 pages, hardcover
ISBN 978-3-03860-305-4
CHF 39,00 | CHF 39.00

Towards Territorial Transition stellt räumliche Strategien, Konzepte und Ansätze vor, um in Architektur und Stadtplanung in großem Maßstab und grenzüberschreitend Entwicklungen in Richtung Dekarbonisierung und ökologischer Wende zu gestalten. Die Autorinnen und Autoren betrachten dabei die Wechselwirkungen zwischen ökologischen, ressourcenbezogenen Systemen und Landschaften und erforschen die Potenziale, um den dramatischen Bedrohungen durch den Klimawandel und einer daraus möglicherweise folgenden sozialen Krise zu begegnen. Das Buch enthält u.a. Beiträge von Aglaée Degros und Matthias Armengaud, ein Gespräch mit Anita Berrizbeitia, Panos Mantziaras sowie einen Fotoessay von Anna Positano.

Sechs Begriffe der territorialen Wende – Territorium, Maßstab, Transition, Ressource, Plattform, Ungewissheit – werden vorgestellt und mit räumlichen Strategien visualisiert, die an der École nationale supérieure d'architecture Versailles und an der Technischen Universität Graz erarbeitet wurden. Darüber hinaus wird eine Auswahl transnationaler Projekte der territorialen Transition vorgestellt, wie beispielsweise „Luxembourg in Transition“ (Luxemburg/Frankreich), „Grand Genève“ (Schweiz/Frankreich) oder „Top Noordrand“ (Belgien/Niederlande).

Die Publikation wurde im Rahmen einer Roadshow auch auf der Biennale in Venedig (16. September 2023) präsentiert und im Anschluss mit Ingrid Taillandier (ITAR Architectures), Anna Positano (Studio Campo) und Bento Architecture (Kuratoren des belgischen Pavillons auf der Biennale) diskutiert.

Aglaée Degros ist Architektin und Stadtplanerin sowie Gründerin des Büros Artgineering in Brüssel. Seit 2016 ist sie Professorin am Institut für Städtebau der TU Graz, das sie auch leitet.

Radostina Radulova-Stahmer ist Architektin und Universitätsassistentin am Institut für Städtebau der TU Graz.

• *Towards Territorial Transition* presents new spatial strategies, concepts, and approaches for shaping large-scale and transnational developments in architecture and urban design toward decarbonization and ecological transition. The contributions investigate interactions between ecological and resource-related systems and landscapes. They explore potential solutions to address and deal with the dramatic threats posed by climate change and the social crisis that may emerge.

The book introduces six basic terms of territorial transition—Territory, Scale, Transition, Resource, Platform, and Uncertainty—and visualizes them with spatial strategies elaborated at the École nationale supérieure d'architecture Versailles and at Graz University of Technology. Moreover, it presents a selection of transnational projects of territorial transition, such as "Luxembourg in Transition" (Luxembourg/France), "Grand Genève" (Switzerland/France), and "Top Noordrand" (Belgium/Netherlands).

The publication *Towards Territorial Transition* was presented as part of a road show, including at the Venice Biennale (September 16, 2023), where it was subsequently discussed by Ingrid Taillandier (ITAR Architectures), Anna Positano (Studio Campo), and Bento Architecture (curators of the Belgian Pavilion at the Venice Biennale).

Aglaée Degros is an architect, urban designer and founding principle of Artgineering, a design firm based in Brussels. She is also a professor and head of the Institute of Urbanism, TU Graz.

Radostina Radulova-Stahmer is an architect and university assistant at the Institute of Urbanism, TU Graz.

WELTEN

Anne Femmer/Florian Summa/
Alexander Barina (Hg.|eds.)
Graz: Verlag der TU Graz, 2023 |
Publishing Company of Graz University of Technology, 2023
Deutsch, 287 Seiten, gebunden |
German, 287 pages, hardcover
ISBN 978-3-85125-934-6
ISBN 978-3-85125-935-3 (E-Book)
EUR 25,00 | EUR 25.00

WELTEN ist eine katalogartige Sammlung aller Studierendenarbeiten, die im Rahmen der Gastprofessur SUMMACUMFEMMER – Integral Architecture von 2020 bis 2022 an der TU Graz entstanden sind. So unterschiedlich die Arbeiten sind, so sehr sind sie miteinander verwandt durch ihre Bindungen an das Vorhandene, Fassbare, Sichtbare. Die Dokumentation gibt Einblick in rund 60 Arbeiten aus den Bachelor- und Master-Lehrveranstaltungen.

Anne Femmer ist Architektin und Gründerin des Architekturbüros SUMMACUMFEMMER. Von 2020–2022 leitete sie die Professur Integral Architecture an der TU Graz.

Florian Summa ist Architekt und Gründer des Architekturbüros SUMMACUMFEMMER. Von 2020–2022 leitete er die Professur Integral Architecture an der TU Graz.

• *WELTEN* is a catalogue-like collection of all student works created as part of the visiting professorship "SUMMACUMFEMMER – Integral Architecture" at TU Graz from 2020 to 2022. As different as the works are, they are related to each other through their ties to the existing, the tangible, the visible. The documentation provides an insight into around 60 works from the Bachelor's and Master's courses.

Anne Femmer is an architect and founder of SUMMACUMFEMMER. From 2020–2022 she led the visiting professorship Integral Architecture at TU Graz.

Florian Summa is an architect and founder of SUMMACUMFEMMER. From 2020–2022 he led the visiting professorship Integral Architecture at TU Graz.

Ein Pavillon für die Kunst im Salzburger Mirabellgarten und sein Architekt Karl Mayr

Anselm Wagner
Salzburg-Wien: Verlag Müry Salzmann
Deutsch, 112 Seiten, broschiert |
German, 112 pages, softcover
ISBN 978-3-99014-243-1
EUR 25,00 | EUR 25.00

Der Ausstellungspavillon im Salzburger Zwergelgarten wurde 1950 anlässlich einer großen Retrospektive des Nazi-Bildhauers Josef Thorak errichtet, welche die gesamte Parkanlage westlich des Mirabellgartens einbezog.

Erstmals wird das Gebäude nun einer architekturhistorischen Analyse unterzogen: Im Zentrum steht dabei der Architekt des Pavillons, Karl Mayr (1902–1979), der als preisgekrönter Holzmeister-Schüler einen der bedeutendsten modernen Sakralbauten Oberschlesiens schuf, sich dann in den Dienst Hitlers stellte und nach dem Krieg als Stadtplaner und VdU-Politiker im Salzburger Landtag wirkte.

In Wort und Bild macht dieses Buch die wechselvolle Geschichte des Pavillons und seines Planers erlebbar. In ihr bündeln sich wie in einem Brennglas die postfaschistische Restauration nach 1945, die Kulturpolitik der Besatzungsmacht USA und die Architektur der „alten Sachlichkeit", welche das Baugeschehen der Mozartstadt bis weit in die 1960er Jahre prägte.

Heute dient der „Zwergelgartenpavillon" der Galerie der Stadt Salzburg als Sommerquartier. KünstlerInnen schätzen sein schlichtes, atmosphärisches Interieur und seine zentrale Lage.

Anselm Wagner ist Universitätsprofessor und Leiter des Instituts für Architekturtheorie, Kunst- und Kulturwissenschaften an der TU Graz.

• The exhibition pavilion in the Zwergelgarten in Salzburg was built in 1950 on the occasion of a large retrospective of the Nazi sculptor Josef Thorak, which occupied the entire park west of the Mirabellgarten.

The building is analyzed here for the first time in terms of the history of architecture: It centers on the pavilion's architect, Karl Mayr (1902–1979), a prizewinning student of Clemens Holzmeister, who created one of the most important modern sacred buildings in Upper Silesia, then served Hitler, and after the war worked as an urban planner and as a politician of the Verband der Unabhängigen (Federation of Independents) in the Salzburg Landtag.

This book, through text and images, allows readers to experience the pavilion's and its planner's eventful history. As if through a magnifying glass, it focuses on the postfascist restoration after 1945, the cultural politics of the occupying power of the United States, and the architecture of "Old Objectivity," which characterized the urban planning of the city of Mozart well into the 1960s.

The "Zwergelgarten Pavilion" now serves as the summer home of the Galerie der Stadt Salzburg. Artists appreciate its simple, atmospheric interior and its central location.

Anselm Wagner is a university professor and head of the Institute of Architectural Theory, Art History and Cultural Studies at TU Graz.

Ziegelgitter in der Steiermark. Form, Funktion und Konstruktion – Ursprung, Zustand und Zukunft

Hasso Hohmann
Graz: Verlag der TU Graz | Publishing Company of Graz University of Technology, 2022
Deutsch, 304 Seiten, gebunden |
German, 304 pages, hardcover
ISBN 978-3-85125-908-7
EUR 39,00 | EUR 39.00

Die Hauslandschaften der Steiermark werden seit dem 19. Jahrhundert stark von fantasievoll gestalteten Ziegelgittern an Heustadeln geprägt. Sie waren zur Durchlüftung des Heus im Herbst notwendig, damit Kondensatfeuchtigkeit bei Luftbewegungen aus dem Heu transportiert werden konnte. Erstaunlich ist der Gestaltungswille, die Kreativität und die Kraft dieser oft in Nachbarschaftshilfe entstandenen Gebäude. Seit etwa 1950 führen andere Wirtschaftsformen zur Funktionslosigkeit dieser oft prächtigen Bauten. In den letzten 50 Jahren wurden mehr als die Hälfte von ihnen samt ihren Gittern abgetragen und sind seitdem undokumentiert verschwunden. Nur Umnutzungen können den noch bestehenden Ziegelgitterbauten eine nachhaltige Zukunft geben. Manche der Beispiele, die zur anonymen Volksbaukunst gezählt werden, sollten als besondere Zeugnisse einer vergehenden Kultur unter Denkmalschutz gestellt werden. Diese Publikation versammelt, dokumentiert und bespricht einige der besonders interessanten Beispiele von Ziegelgittern, die, nach technischen Gesichtspunkten und Themenbereichen gruppiert, die Bandbreite der Variationen aufzeigt.

Hasso Hohmann ist Architekt und lehrte bis zum Wintersemester 2022 am Institut für Entwerfen im Bestand und Denkmalpflege.

• Since the nineteenth century, the landscape of Styria has been strongly influenced by the imaginatively designed brick grids on hay barns. They were necessary to aerate the hay in autumn so that condensate moisture could be transported out of the hay when the air moves. The nonprofessional masons' strong will to design and their strength of creativity in conceiving these brick grids, which were often built with the help of neighbors, are astounding. Since about 1950, other forms of economy have rendered these magnificent buildings inoperable. In the last fifty years, more than half of the buildings, including the brick grids, have been removed, often disappearing without a trace or any documentation. Only adaptations can give the still-existing brick grid buildings a sustainable future. There are some good examples of this in the book. Many of the examples must be counted among anonymous folk architecture. Some should be placed under monument protection as special testimonies of a passing culture. The rest should at least be photographed and well documented. This publication attempts to capture and discuss in detail some of the particularly interesting brick grids. The examples are grouped according to technical aspects and subject areas and thus also show the range of variations.

Hasso Hohmann is an architect who taught at the Institute of Design in Existing Structures and Heritage Protection until the winter semester of 2022.

Frühe Brücken. Zug- oder druckbeanspruchte Konstruktionen, kreative, innovative und interessante Brücken

Hasso Hohmann
Graz: Verlag der TU Graz | Publishing Company of Graz University of Technology, 2021
Deutsch, 303 Seiten, gebunden |
German, 303 pages, hardcover
ISBN 978-3-85125-832-5
EUR 39,00 | EUR 39.00

Das Buch *Frühe Brücken* untersucht zug- oder druckbeanspruchte Brücken sowie Mischformen nach unterschiedlichen Gesichtspunkten wie Statik oder Material, ordnet diese nach Bauzeit und dokumentiert Indizien für formale Gestaltungsvorlieben der örtlichen Bevölkerung. Geschmiedete Kettenbrücken gab es spätestens ab 67 n. Chr. in China. In dieser Publikation erstmals maßstäblich erfasst wird eine 136 Meter lange Kettenbrücke von 1430 nahe Lhasa, die 1950 von Chinesen abgetragen wurde. Die Publikation zeigt außerdem lebende Brücken aus Nordostindien und Japan, Gras- oder andere Faserhängebrücken sowie Kragstein-Brücken in der Alten und der Neuen Welt. Frühe Hängebrücken, die aus unzähligen dünnen geschmiedeten Drähten Anfang des 19. Jh. im Schweizer Freiburg gefertigt wurden, können als Vorläufer der Stahlseilbrücken gelten.

Hasso Hohmann ist Architekt und lehrte bis zum Wintersemester 2022 am Institut für Entwerfen im Bestand und Denkmalpflege.

• The book *Frühe Brücken* (Early Bridges) examines bridges subjected to tensile or compressive stress, as well as mixed forms, according to various aspects such as statics or material, classifies them as to construction time, and documents evidence of formal design preferences in the local population. Forged chain bridges have been in use in China since 67 AD at the latest. In this publication, a 136-meter-long chain bridge from 1430 near Lhasa, which was demolished by the Chinese in 1950, is recorded to scale for the first time. In addition, the publication shows living bridges from northeast India and Japan, grass and other fiber suspension bridges, as well as corbel bridges in the Old and New Worlds. Early suspension bridges, made from countless thin, forged wires in the early nineteenth century in Fribourg, Switzerland, can be considered the forerunners of steel cable bridges.

Hasso Hohmann is an architect who taught at the Institute of Design in Existing Structures and Heritage Protection until the winter semester of 2022.

Institut für Gebäudelehre. Jahrbuch 21/22

Hans Gangoly (Hg.|ed.)
Graz: Verlag der TU Graz, 2023 | Publishing Company of Graz University of Technology, 2023
Deutsch, 400 Seiten, kartoniert |
German, 400 pages, paperback
ISBN 978-3-85125-945-2
ISBN 978-3-85125-946-9 (E-Book)
EUR 35,00 | EUR 35.00

Das Entwerfen – die Kernkompetenz von ArchitektInnen und Architekturstudierenden – steht auch im vierten Jahrbuch des Instituts für Gebäudelehre im Mittelpunkt. Die insgesamt sechs Entwurfslehrveranstaltungen werden in zwei Abschnitte – Master und Bachelor – unterteilt und anhand von Erläuterungstexten und ausgewählten Studierendenprojekten kapitelweise vorgestellt. Die Masterkurse spannen den Bogen von den ausdrucksstiftenden Gestaltungsmöglichkeiten des Bauhandwerks (Masterstudio „Putzpoesie") über entwurfsmethodische Strategien des Umbaus von Leerstand („Education of an Architect") bis hin zu den Entwicklungspotenzialen einer Stadt als hochverdichteter, multifunktionaler Lebensraum („Oase Stadt").

Im Bachelor-Entwerfen werden spezifische Gebäudetypen wie ein Eckhaus, ein Pavilion oder eine Lückenbebauung mit konkreten Nutzungsprogrammen verknüpft. Bauaufgaben wie städtisches Wohnen an der Ecke zur alten Remise („15 Ecken – ein Haus"), ein niederschwelliges Lokal im Augarten („Chiringuito Familiar"), und ein Therapie- und Wohnort in der Schillerstraße („Shelter") werden im Grazer Stadtraum verortet. Neben diesen Beiträgen zur Entwurfslehre versammelt die Publikation auch eine Auswahl an ausgezeichneten Masterarbeiten.

Hans Gangoly ist Architekt, Universitätsprofessor für Gebäudelehre und leitet das gleichnamige Institut an der TU Graz.

• Designing—the core competence of architects and students of architecture—is again the focus of the fourth yearbook of the Institute of Design and Building Typology. The six events on teaching design are presented in two sections—Master's and Bachelor's—and subdivided into chapters with explanatory texts and selected student projects. The master's courses span an arc from the expressive design possibilities of the craft of building (Masterstudio "Putzpoesie") by way of strategies of design methods for converting vacant buildings ("Education of an Architect") to the potentials for developing a city as a high-density, multifunctional living space ("Oasis City").

In designing for the Bachelor's program, specific building types such as a corner building, a pavilion, or a building that fills a gap are tied to specific programs for their use. Architectural briefs such as urban housing on a corner with a former coach house ("15 corners—one building"), an accessible restaurant in the Augarten park ("Chiringuito Familiar"), and a site for therapy and housing on Schillerstrasse ("Shelter") are located in the urban space of Graz. In addition to these contributions to the teaching of design, the publication also includes a selection of outstanding master's theses.

Hans Gangoly is an architect, university professor, and head of the Institute of Design and Building Typology at TU Graz.

Basic Living. Kooperatives Wettbewerbsverfahren

Schriftenreihe des Instituts für Wohnbau
TU Graz Andreas Lichtblau (Hg.|ed.)
Graz: Verlag der TU Graz, 2022 | Publishing Company of Graz University of Technology, 2022
Deutsch, 447 Seiten, kartoniert |
German, 447 pages, paperback
ISBN 978-3-85125-878-3
EUR 70,00 | EUR 70.00

Im städtischen Umfeld findet sich in den Themen, der Verteuerung des Wohnraums und der zunehmenden Individualisierung und Entsolidarisierung der Gesellschaft, ein gemeinsamer Nenner, der als jeweils mitentscheidender Faktor auftritt: die Dichte. Dieser Zusammenhang lässt sich auf den physikalischen Grundwert des Verhältnisses zwischen Masse und Raum zurückverfolgen, differenziert sich allerdings in zwei Formen aus, deren Abhängigkeit voneinander jedoch nicht eindeutig definiert werden kann: räumliche und soziale Dichte.

Eine gewisse räumliche Dichte bildet die Grundvoraussetzung, damit sich soziale Nähe einstellen kann. Sind die Distanzen zu groß, wird die Chance für ein soziales „Aufeinandertreffen" gering. Ein „Zuviel" an räumlicher Dichte bewirkt aber, dass Menschen freiwillig in die Isolation gehen, sich zurückziehen, wenn sie sich „zu sehr" beengt fühlen. Das durch zu hohe räumliche Dichte hervorgerufene Gefühl des „crowding" bewirkt klaustrophobische Effekte und physischen sowie psychischen Stress.

Andreas Lichtblau ist Architekt, Universitätsprofessor für Wohnbau und leitet das gleichnamige Institut an der TU Graz.

• In an urban environment, the themes of rising housing costs, and the increasing individualization and lack of solidarity in society have a common denominator that is a deciding factor in each case: density. This connection can be traced back to the value of the physical land and the ratio of people and space but is also distinguished in two forms whose interdependence cannot be clearly defined: spatial and social density. A degree of spatial density is a precondition of social proximity. If distances are too large, the opportunity for social "meeting" is minimal. An "excess" of spatial density can cause people to isolate themselves voluntarily, withdrawing when they feel "too cramped." The feeling of "crowding" provoked by excessive spatial density has claustrophobic effects and causes physical and psychological stress.

Andreas Lichtblau is an architect, university professor, and head of the Institute of Housing at TU Graz.

Architekturführer Graz

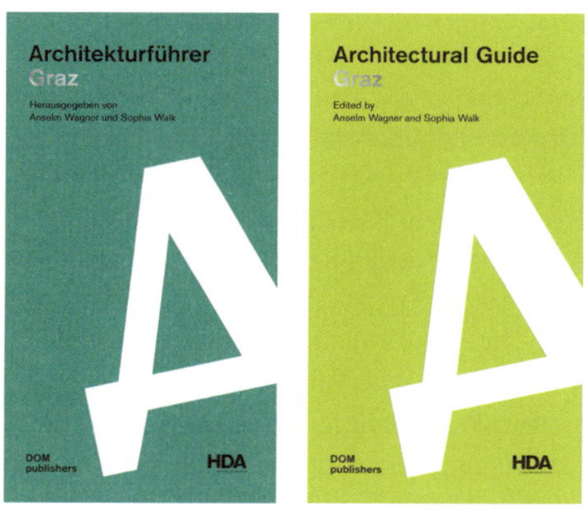

Zweite, aktualisierte und erweiterte Auflage | Second revised and expanded edition
Anselm Wagner/Sophia Walk (Hg.|eds.)
Berlin: DOM publisher, 2023
Deutsch, 496 Seiten, broschiert | German, 496 pages, softcover
ISBN 978-3-86922-894-5
EUR 48,00 | EUR 48.00

Die aktualisierte und um 60 Bauwerke erweiterte zweite Auflage des *Architekturführers Graz* behandelt alle relevanten Gebäude vom 12. bis zum 21. Jahrhundert. Zwölf Touren führen zu über 300 Bauten, Straßenzügen und Plätzen.

Die Texte wurden von Studierenden der Architektur am Institut für Architekturtheorie, Kunst- und Kulturwissenschaften der TU Graz erarbeitet. Ergänzend zur vor fünf Jahren erschienenen, mittlerweile vergriffenen ersten Auflage wurden aktuelle Neubauten wie z.B. der *Green Tower* in Reininghaus oder die Volksschule Puntigam, aber auch viele weitere Bauwerke des 20. Jahrhunderts, die sich vor allem in den Außenbezirken von Graz befinden, aufgenommen. Renommierte FachexpertInnen geben in vertiefenden Schwerpunkttexten Einblicke in die Hintergründe des Baugeschehens und betten sie in einen kunst- und kulturgeschichtlichen Kontext ein. Auch in der zweiten Auflage des Architekturführer finden sich etliche Entdeckungen, die noch nie publiziert worden sind, wie z.B. das expressionistische Heizhaus im Landeskrankenhaus Graz-Süd von Hugo Pohlhammer.

Die Übersetzung ins Englische, die eine Subvention der Stadtbaudirektion Graz möglich machte, übernahmen Dawn Michelle d'Atri, John Wheelwright und Amy Klement. Die grafische Umsetzung besorgten Elvira Fatkhutdinova und Anna Söllinger.

Anselm Wagner ist Universitätsprofessor und Leiter des Instituts für Architekturtheorie, Kunst- und Kulturwissenschaften an der TU Graz.

Sophia Walk war bis September 2021 Universitätsassistentin am Institut für Architekturtheorie, Kunst- und Kulturwissenschaften an der TU Graz.

• The revised second edition of Architekturführer Graz, expanded to include sixty buildings, covers all relevant buildings from the twelfth to the twenty-first centuries. Twelve tours lead to more than 300 buildings, streets, and squares.

The texts have been compiled by architecture students at the Institute of Architectural Theory, Art History, and Cultural Studies of TU Graz (akk). The first edition, published five years ago and now out of print, has been supplemented by recent buildings such as the Green Tower in Reininghaus and the Volksschule Puntigam but also includes many additional buildings from the twentieth century, primarily in outer districts of Graz. Renowned experts have provided in-depth texts that offer insights into the backgrounds of construction processes and embed them in an art and cultural-historical context. The second edition of this architectural guide also includes a number of discoveries never to have been published before, such as the Expressionist boiler house in the Graz-Süd provincial hospital by Hugo Pohlhammer.

The translations into English, made possible by a grant from the Building Department of the City of Graz, were carried out by Dawn Michelle d'Atri, John Wheelwright, and Amy Klement. The graphic design was done by Elvira Fatkhutdnova and Anna Söllinger.

Anselm Wagner is a university professor and head of the Institute of Architectural Theory, Art History and Cultural Studies at TU Graz.

Sophia Walk was a university assistant at the Institute of Architectural Theory, Art History and Cultural Studies at TU Graz until September 2021.

Monoglott Reiseführer Schwarzlsee

Institut für Entwerfen im Bestand und Denkmalpflege (TU Graz)/Michael Hafner/Matthias Castorph/ Julian Müller (Hg.|eds.)
Graz: EnBeDe Eigenverlag, 2023
Deutsch, 44 Seiten, broschiert | German, 44 pages, softcover
ISBN 978-3-200-09626-4
EUR 5,00 | EUR 5.00

Der *Monoglott Reiseführer Schwarzlsee* entstand im Sommersemester 2023 am Institut für Entwerfen im Bestand und Denkmalpflege unter der Leitung von Matthias Castorph und Michael Hafner und liefert Tipps, Must-sees und To-dos rund um den Schwarzlsee in der Peripherie im Süden von Graz. Das Freizeitgelände erstreckt sich rund um einige Badeteiche, die einst für den Kiesabbau angelegt wurden. Es ist ein Ort, der keiner klaren Logik folgt, sondern sich durch pluralistische Gestaltung und architektonisch stilistische Vielfalt auszeichnet. In Kapiteln wie „Kunst und Kultur", „Verkehrswege und Geschichte", „Speisen und Getränke", „Aktivitäten" oder „praktischen Hinweisen" versucht er, dem Wesen dieses speziellen Ortes in Form eines klassischen Reiseführers vorurteilsfrei näherzukommen. Die Publikation ist am Institut für Entwerfen im Bestand und Denkmalpflege erhältlich.

AutorInnen: Marlies Andic, Šejma Balčinović, Angelina Frey, Nazyktere Musliu, Kerstin Neuhold, Timon Oswald, Fabienne Papst, Alexander Rothbart, Ivana Sandalj-Kovačević, Marie Theres Schlederer, Markus Helmut Schmoltner, Anna Schoissengeyer, Vanessa Steger, Julia Westreicher
Umschlaggestaltung: Lena Leander Kaschnig

Matthias Castorph ist Architekt, Stadtplaner, Universitätsprofessor für Entwerfen im Bestand und Denkmalpflege und leitet das gleichnamige Institut an der TU Graz.

Michael Hafner ist Universitätsassistent am selben Institut.

Julian Müller ist Soziologe und arbeitete von 2022–2023 im Rahmen einer Gastprofessur ebenfalls am Institut für Entwerfen im Bestand und Denkmalpflege.

• The *Monoglott Reiseführer Schwarzlsee* was produced during the summer semester of 2023 at the Institute of Design in Existing Structures and Architectural Heritage Protection under the direction of Matthias Castorph and Michael Hafner and offers tips, must-sees, and to-dos around Lake Schwarzl in Graz's southern periphery. This recreation area extends around several bathing beaches that were once used for gravel extraction. It is a place that does not follow any clear logic but is rather characterized by pluralistic design and a diversity of architectural styles. In chapters such as "Art and Culture," "Roads and History," "Food and Drink," "Activities," and "Practical Hints," this book seeks to approach the essence of this special place without prejudice in the form of a classic travel guide. The publication can be purchased at the Institute of Design in Existing Structures and Architectural Heritage Protection.

Authors: Marlies Andic, Šejma Balčinović, Angelina Frey, Nazyktere Musliu, Kerstin Neuhold, Timon Oswald, Fabienne Papst, Alexander Rothbart, Ivana Sandalj-Kovačević, Marie Theres Schlederer, Markus Helmut Schmoltner, Anna Schoissengeyer, Vanessa Steger, Julia Westreicher
Cover design: Lena Leander Kaschnig

Matthias Castorph is an architect, urban planner, university professor, and head of the institute of Design in Existing Structures and Architectural Heritage Protection at TU Graz.

Michael Hafner is assistant professor at the same institute.

Julian Müller is a sociologist and was a visiting professor at the Institute of Design in Existing Structures and Architectural Heritage Protection in 2022–2023.

50 Species-Towns

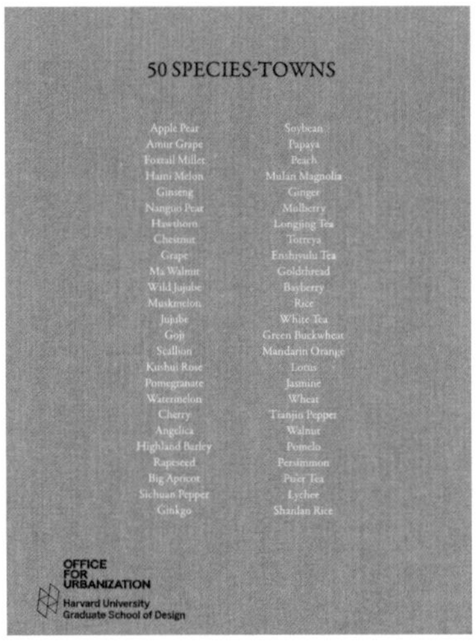

Charles Waldheim with Office for Urbanization/ Charles Gaillard/Mariano Gomez-Luque/Mercedes Peralta/Seok Min Yeo/Boya Zhang
Cambridge, MA: Harvard University Graduate School of Design, 2021
Englisch, 726 Seiten, gebunden | English, 726 pages, hardcover
ISBN 978-1-73404-803-2
ISBN 1734048034
EUR ca. 261,00 | EUR ca. 261.00

Die rasante Urbanisierung Chinas erfolgte auf Kosten der landwirtschaftlich-geprägten ländlichen Gebiete. *50 Species-Towns* stellt ein Alternativmodell für die Modernisierung der Landwirtschaft und für eine Agrarorientierung in der Planung neuer Städte vor. Dieses Modell stützt sich auf den enormen Reichtum kulinarischer Vielfalt und historischer Kulturarten und -sorten, die in ganz China zu finden sind. Den Entwurf prägen dabei die 50 bedeutendsten, am meisten geschätzten und am stärksten vom Aussterben bedrohten Arten. Aufbauend auf dem Integrationsmodell „Eine Stadt, eine Kultursorte" stellt der Vorschlag 50 kleinmaßstäbliche landwirtschaftliche Neustädte in China vor. Dabei steht jede Stadt im Zusammenhang mit einer einzigen, spezifischen historischen Pflanzenart und dem dazugehörigen agrarökologischen System, dem ein hoher kulinarischer und kultureller Wert beigemessen wird. Das Ziel der Publikation ist es, die widersprüchlichen Anforderungen der landwirtschaftlichen Modernisierung, wirtschaftlichen Integration und der Verbesserung der Lebensqualität in Einklang zu bringen und gleichzeitig die außergewöhnliche kulinarische Kultur Chinas zu bewahren. Neben diversen weiteren Beiträgen kuratierte die Co-Autorin Mercedes Peralta die Fotoportfolios, die die visuellen Erzählstränge des Buches miteinander verweben. Zusätzlich entwickelte sie Studien, die eine umfangreiche historische Zeitleiste mit landwirtschaftlichen Bildern sowie eine Reihe von Zeichnungen programmatischer Aktivitäten enthalten, die das ländliche Leben und kulturelle Erbe in den Mittelpunkt stellen.

Mercedes Peralta ist Universitätsassistentin am Institut für Architektur und Landschaft an der TU Graz.

• China's rapid urbanization has come at the expense of its agricultural countryside. *50 Species-Towns* presents an alternative model for agricultural modernization and agrarian new-town planning in China. This model is informed by the extraordinary wealth of culinary diversity and heritage crops found across China. The most significant of these, the fifty most cherished and most vulnerable to loss, shape the proposal. Building upon the "one town, one crop" model of economic integration, the proposal imagines fifty small-scale agricultural new towns across China. Each is conceived in relation to a single, specific heritage crop and associated agroecological system deemed to be of significant culinary and cultural value. *50 Species-Towns* aspires to reconcile the conflicting demands of agricultural modernization, economic integration, and enhanced quality of life while maintaining China's extraordinary culinary culture. Among various contributions, coauthor Mercedes Peralta has curated the photography portfolios that intricately weave the book's visual narrative. Additionally, she has developed studies illustrating a broad historical timeline of agricultural imagery, encompassing a series of drawings of programmatic activities that highlight rural life and cultural heritage.

Mercedes Peralta is an university assistant at the Institute of Architecture and Landscape at TU Graz.

L. Eder, F. Helal, A. Hagner, A.Wickenhauser, E. Hasa, D. Ecker, R. Piotrowski, B. Kolarevic, J.-C. Horst © GAM.Lab, TU Graz

Graz Architecture Lectures 2023: „The Infraordinary“

Die diesjährigen Graz Architecture Lectures, die am 20. und 21. April in der Halle der Kronesgasse 5 abgehalten wurden, stellten das Thema „The Infraordinary“ in den Mittelpunkt. Der Titel spielt auf einen Kunstbegriff des französischen Schriftstellers Georges Perec an. Das Infraordinäre ist dabei als Gegenbegriff zum Extraordinären zu verstehen und bezeichnet nicht einfach nur abwertend das Ordinär-Gewöhnliche, sondern ausdrücklich das Nicht-Außergewöhnliche. Also all jene Nebensächlichkeiten, an denen wir zumeist vorbeisehen. Auf die Architektur übertragen, sollten so alltägliche Formen architektonischer Praxis ebenso in den Blick geraten wie vermeintlich banale Architekturen, alltägliche Gebrauchsweisen außergewöhnlicher Architektur sowie Zwischenformen von Sehenswürdigem und Nicht-Sehenswürdigem. In sieben Vorträgen wurde nach der Tragfähigkeit des Begriffs des Infraordinären und seiner Verwendung in der Architektur gefragt.

Eröffnet wurde die Veranstaltung von Lisa Eder und Fekry Helal, die ihr Projekt *Alltag* vorstellten, ein regelmäßig erscheinendes Journal, in dem verschiedene Beiträge aus den Bereichen der Fotografie, der Literatur, der Grafik sowie der Wissenschaft versammelt werden, die sich der Beschreibung und Dokumentation von Alltagsphänomenen und Alltagspraktiken verschrieben haben.

Alexander Hagner plädierte in seinem Vortrag „Objekt & Prozess“ dafür, Architektur nicht einfach nur als fertiges Objekt zu beurteilen, sondern in erster Linie als Prozess zu verstehen. Am Beispiel u.a. von „Vinzirast-Mittendrin“, einem von Hagner verantworteten Wohnprojekt, in dem ehemalige Obdachlose und Studierende gemeinsam unter einem Dach leben, zeigte er, wie wichtig für den Erfolg eines solchen Projekts das gemeinsame Tun und vor allem der gemeinsam gelebte Alltag während des Bauprozesses ist.

Im Anschluss veranschaulichte die Wiener Architektin Anna Wickenhauser in ihren „Weiteren Befragungen zur sichtbaren Welt“, wie Unauffälliges auch Werk sein kann. Die Beispiele aus ihrer Entwurfspraxis (u.a. „Brunnenhaus Maria Siebenbrünn Türnitz“ und „Hauptplatz & Rochusplatz Stadtschlaining“) illustrierten ihren subtilen Umgang mit historischer Bausubstanz und mit deren zeitgemäßer Veralltäglichung.

Mit der raumpolitischen Dimension des Alltäglichen setzte sich Elisavet Hasa auseinander. Die Mitgründerin des Forschungs- und Designkollektivs „Fatura Collaborative" berichtete in ihrem Vortrag über die informelle Besetzung und Ad-hoc-Umnutzung von Wohnungen und Geschäftslokalen in Gesundheitseinrichtungen, wie sie durch Solidaritätsinitiativen während der Wirtschaftskrise zwischen 2010–2020 in Athen stattfanden.

Dea Ecker und Robert Piotrowski nahmen in ihrem Vortrag die Idee des Banalen zum Ausgangspunkt und illustrierten anhand eigener Büroprojekte das gestalterische Potenzial, das sich aus gewöhnlichen Nutzungen und unspektakulären Bauelementen entfalten kann. Exemplifiziert wurde dieser Ansatz u.a. durch die Verwendung industrieller Förderbänder oder handelsüblicher Entwässerungsrohre, die durch neu zugewiesene Funktionen zu Designelementen wurden und die weitere Entwicklung des Entwurfs mitbestimmten.

Branko Kolarević identifizierte in seinem Vortrag „Architectures of Change" die Kategorie der Zeit als infraordinäres Element im architektonischen Entwurf adaptiver Architektur. Während er die Technologien dieser responsiven Strukturen und interaktiven Systeme dem „Extraordinären" zuschreibt, den zentralen Aspekt der Transformation (*change*) im „Ordinären" verortet, definiert er die Zeit als „infraordinäres" Element, das diesen Diskurs der Veränderung grundlegend steuert. Illustriert wurde diese These anhand von Beispielen aus seinem Buch *Building Dynamics: Exploring Architecture of Change* (2015, gemeinsam mit Vera Parlac).

Den Abschluss machte die Literaturwissenschaftlerin Johanna-Charlotte Horst, die Einblicke in das literarische Werk George Perecs gewährte und dabei insbesondere auf Interferenzen von Literatur und Architektur hinwies. Nicht nur widmete sich Perec wiederholt der Beschreibung alltäglicher Räume, Straßen und Plätze, umgekehrt lässt sich immer wieder eine architektonisch-räumliche Struktur als narrative Strategie seiner Romane ausmachen. Die Architektur taucht bei ihm mithin als Gegenstand wie auch als literarische Methode auf.

Moderiert wurde die Veranstaltung von Petra Eckhard (GAM.Labor, TU Graz) und Daniel Gethmann (akk, TU Graz). Die vorliegende Ausgabe von GAM führt die Diskussion weiter.

Petra Eckhard, Julian Müller

© CH Studio

• The focus of this year's Graz Architecture Lectures, held on April 20 and 21 in the hall of Kronesgasse 5, was placed on the concept of "The Infraordinary." The title alludes to the term *L'infra-ordinaire*, coined by the French writer Georges Perec. In this context, the "infraordinary" is to be understood as an antithesis to the "extraordinary" and refers not simply to the ordinary in a pejorative sense but explicitly to the non-extraordinary. In other words, to all those trivial spaces that we usually overlook or ignore. When applied to the field of architecture, the infraordinary encompasses everyday forms of architectural practice, supposedly banal architectures, quotidian usages of extraordinary architecture and intermediate forms of that which is worth seeing and that which is not. The seven lectures addressed questions related to the viability of the concept of the infraordinary and its use in architecture.

The lecture series was opened by Lisa Eder and Fekry Helal, who introduced their journal *Alltag (Everyday Life)*—a periodical collecting contributions from the fields of photography, literature, the graphic arts, and the humanities that document everyday phenomena and practices.

In his lecture entitled "Object & Process," Alexander Hagner (gaupenraup +/-) argued for architecture to be evaluated first and foremost as a process rather than a finished object. Using the example of VinziRast-mittendrin in Vienna, a communal housing project where students and formerly homeless persons live under one roof, Hagner illustrated the importance of joint efforts during the construction process, which was critical to the project's success.

The third lecture, given by the Viennese architect Anna Wickenhauser, illustrated how the seemingly unremarkable can manifest itself as a work of architecture. Selected projects from her design practice—Brunnenhaus Maria Siebenbrünn Türnitz and Hauptplatz & Rochusplatz Stadtschlaining—exemplified her subtle treatment of historical elements and their contemporary transfiguration into an aesthetic of the mundane.

Elisavet Hasa dealt with the spatial-political dimension of the everyday. In her lecture, the co-founder of the research and design collective Fatura Collaborative shared insights from her research on the informal occupation and ad hoc transformation of apartments and business premises into healthcare facilities, as created through solidarity initiatives during the economic crisis between 2010 and 2020 in Athens.

Dea Ecker and Robert Piotrowski took the notion of the banal as a starting point in their lecture and illustrated the design potential that can unfold from ordinary usage and unspectacular building elements. This approach was exemplified through some of their projects, in which rather unspectacular structural elements, such as industrial conveyor belts or commercially available drainage pipes, were given a new function, thus turning into design elements that helped determine the further development of the design.

In his lecture "Architectures of Change," Branko Kolarević identified the category of time as an infraordinary element in the architectural design process of adaptive architecture. While ascribing the technologies of these responsive structures and interactive systems to the "extraordinary" and situating the central aspect of transformation (change) in the "ordinary," he defines time as an "infraordinary" element that fundamentally guides this discourse of change. This assertion was illustrated by examples from his book *Building Dynamics: Exploring Architecture of Change* (2015, coauthored with Vera Parlac).

Finally, the literary scholar Johanna-Charlotte Horst concluded the Graz Architecture Lectures by sharing her research on the literary work of George Perec, highlighting, in particular, the interferences between literature and architecture. Not only was Perec repeatedly engaged in the description of everyday spaces, rooms, streets, and squares, but he also made use of architectural-spatial structures as a narrative strategy in his novels. Thus, architecture appears in his work as both an object and a literary method.

The event was hosted by Petra Eckhard (GAM.Labor, TU Graz) and Daniel Gethmann (akk, TU Graz). This edition of GAM continues the discussion.

Ringvorlesung „Architectural Research“

Die Ringvorlesung „Architectural Research“ stellt im Rahmen der Grazer Doctoral School Architektur innovative und kreative Forschungsfragen zur Diskussion.
Im Wintersemester 2023/24 präsentierten vier ReferentInnen ihre Arbeiten zur Architekturforschung, der geplante fünfte Vortrag in der Reihe von Salvatore Pisani, Kunst- und Architekturhistoriker an der Johannes Gutenberg-Universität Mainz musste leider entfallen.

Alexander Passer, Professor für Nachhaltiges Bauen an der TU Graz, stellte in seinem Vortrag die Notwendigkeit heraus, im Bauwesen einen allgemeinen Standard zur Berechnung der Life Cycle Analysis für den gesamten Bausektor zu etablieren, um zu einer verlässlichen Einschätzung der Umweltkennzahlen zu gelangen. Dieser Schritt sollte nach seiner Auffassung mit einer Integration des Themas der Nachhaltigkeit in die Studienpläne von Architektur und Bauingenieurwissenschaften einher gehen, was zu einer Verbindung von Erkenntnissen aus der Forschung mit der Lehre genutzt werden könnte.

Robert Jan van Pelt, Architekturhistoriker von der Universität Waterloo in Kanada, sprach in der Ringvorlesung über sein langjähriges Forschungsprojekt zu Baracken, einer für das Verständnis des 20. Jahrhunderts zentralen Bauform, die bislang im Kanon der Architektur noch weitgehend ausgelassen wird. Einer solchen Geringschätzung der Baracken durch die überkommene Architekturforschung begegnete van Pelt mit einer Darlegung ihrer konstruktiven Geschichte, sowie dem Hinweis, dass die sozialgeschichtliche Relevanz der Baracke für Flüchtlings- und Lager-Architektur ihre Integration in das baukulturelle Erbe der Zeigeschichte unumgänglich macht.

Lisa Yamaguchi, Professorin für Integral Architecture an der TU Graz und Geschäftsführerin des Architekturbüros Dreisterneplus ***+ in München, begründete in ihrem Vortrag die Auffassung, dass der architektonische Entwurf eine eigene Erkenntnismethode zwischen den rationalen Methoden der Naturwissenschaften und der Kunstproduktion entfaltet. Das Entwerfen als Methode sieht sich komplex strukturierten Problemen gegenüber, bei denen keine Aussicht auf eine einzige richtige Lösung besteht, sondern vielmehr die Pluralität der Lösungsoptionen zu einer Offenlegung der Entwurfsprozesse führen sollte, um aus deren Bericht das Ergebnis nachvollziehbar und überprüfbar zu machen.

Ana Maria Durán Calisto von der Yale School of Architecture, die seit über zwanzig Jahren mit ihrem Ehemann Jaskran Kalirai das Architekturbüro Estudio A0 in Quito, Ecuador, leitet, stellte ihre langjährigen Forschungsarbeiten zu indigenen Prinzipien der Nachhaltigkeit in der Landwirtschaft Lateinamerikas vor. Im Gegensatz zu westlichen Ölkonzernen oder monokulturellen Agrarproduzenten, die die Amazonasregion in Ecuador als vermeintlich unbesiedelten Landschaftsraum ausbeuten, betont sie die reiche kulturelle Geschichte der Region, die aufgrund einer jahrtausendealten Landwirtschaftstradition sich auch in größeren, miteinander vernetzten, urbanen Agglomerationen im Amazonasbecken zeigt, welche gegenwärtig von der Archäologie wiederentdeckt werden. Ihr Vortrag machte deutlich, wie wichtig es für die Architekturforschung werden kann, die indigenen Beiträge zum Wissen über ökologische Zusammenhänge anzuerkennen und wertzuschätzen.

Daniel Gethmann

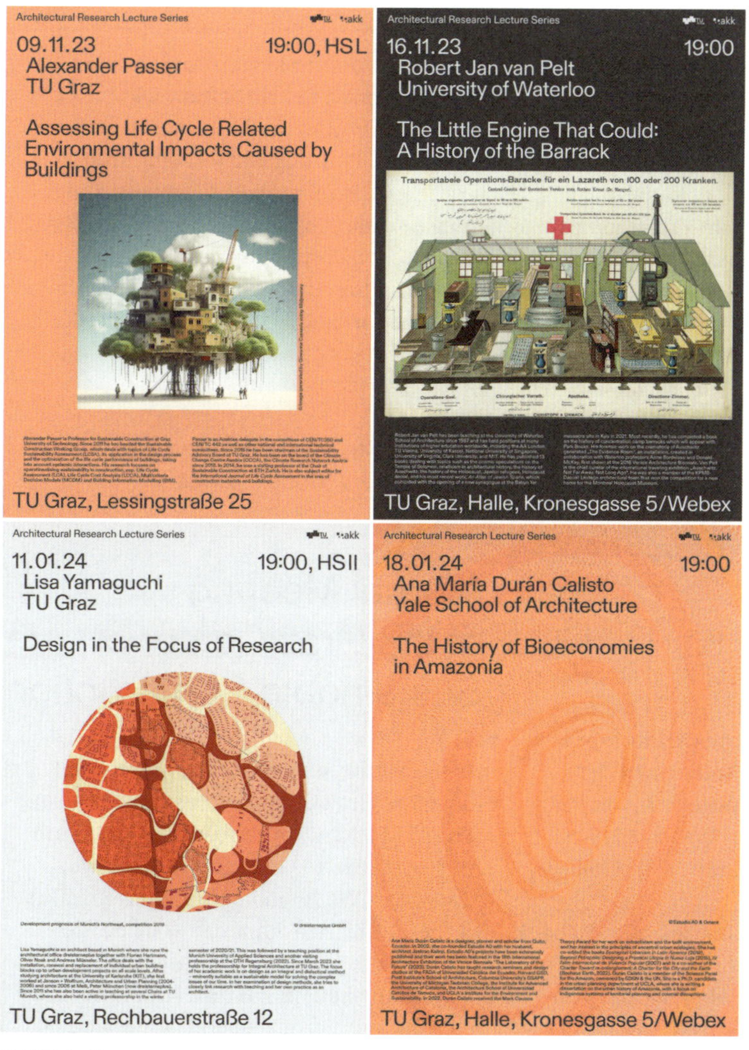

© CH Studio

Lecture Series “Architectural Research”

The “Architectural Research” lecture series puts innovative and creative research questions up for discussion as part of the Graz Doctoral School of Architecture.
In the winter semester of 2023/24, four speakers presented their works on architectural research; the planned fifth lecture in the series by Salvatore Pisani, historian of art and architecture at the Johannes Gutenberg University Mainz, unfortunately, had to be canceled.

In his lecture, Alexander Passer, Professor of Sustainable Building at TU Graz, emphasized the necessity of establishing a general standard for calculating life-cycle analysis for the entire building sector to ensure reliable estimates of environmental indexes. In his view, this step should be part of integrating the theme of sustainability into curricula for architecture and civil engineering, which could be used to connect insights from research to theory.

Robert Jan van Pelt, architectural historian at the University of Waterloo in Canada, spoke in the lecture series about his long-standing research project on barracks, an architectural form central to an understanding of the twentieth century but has largely been left out of the canon. Van Pelt counters such scant regard for barracks in traditional architectural research by presenting the history of their construction and by noting that the social-historical relevance of barracks for refugee and camp architecture makes their integration into the historical legacy of architectural culture indispensable.

In her lecture, Lisa Yamaguchi, Professor of Integral Architecture at TU Graz and partner of the architecture firm Dreisterneplus ***+ in Munich, substantiated the view that the architectural design unfolds its own epistemic method between the rational methods of the natural sciences and the production of art. Designing as a method faces complexly structured problems in which there is no prospect for a single correct solution, but rather a plurality of solution approaches should lead to a disclosure of the design processes in order to make the result comprehensible and verifiable from their report.

Ana María Durán Calisto of the Yale School of Architecture, who for more than twenty years has been running the architectural firm Estudio A0 in Quito, Ecuador, with her husband, Jaskran Kalirai, presented her years of research into indigenous principles of sustainability in Latin American agriculture. In contrast to Western oil companies and monocultural farmers who exploit the Amazon region of Ecuador as supposedly unsettled country-side, she emphasizes the rich cultural history of the region, which, thanks to a millennia-old agricultural tradition, is also found in large, networked urban agglomerations in the Amazon basin that are currently being rediscovered by archaeologists. Her lecture made it clear how important it is for architectural research to recognize and appreciate indigenous contributions to knowledge about ecological contexts.

Urs Hirschberg, Werner Sobek © GAM.Lab, TU Graz

Jahresversammlung des Graz Center of Sustainable Construction

Als eines der sechs Research Center der TU Graz, veranstaltete das Graz Center of Sustainable Construction (GCSC) am 15. November 2023 ein Symposium zur Frage „Wie können wir Klimaneutralität in der gebauten Umwelt erreichen?“. Die Teilnehmenden der Präsentationen und moderierten Workshops, die im Hörsaal II der Alten Technik abgehalten wurden, kamen von Bund, Land, Gemeinden, Interessenvertretungen, Bauwirtschaft, Industrie, Bauplanung und Forschung. Die TU Graz war mit den Fakultäten Architektur, Bauingenieurwesen, Mathematik, Physik und Geodäsie und dem Vizerektorat vertreten. Zu den internationalen Gästen aus dem Scientific Board zählten Ingeborg M. Rocker (Georgia Tech), Anya Vollpracht (RWTH Aachen) und Werner Sobek (Universität Stuttgart).

Projektideen und Forschungsansätze aus verschiedenen Handlungsfeldern wurden in Form von Kurzpräsentationen und Pitches vorgestellt. Diese folgten der dreistufigen Hierarchie des GCSC: (i) Nachfrage reduzieren, (ii) Verwendung CO_2-armer Materialien/Lösungen und (iii) Kompensation der verbleibenden Emissionen. Anschließend wurden Strategien, Maßnahmen und Hindernisse am Weg zur Klimaneutralität in acht moderierten Workshop-Gruppen diskutiert.

Die Podiumsdiskussion mit VR Michael Monsberger, Ingeborg M. Rocker, Anya Vollpracht und Werner Sobek wurde von IAM-Institutsleiter Urs Hirschberg moderiert. Die Bandbreite an vorgestellten Projekten und Forschungsvorhaben spiegeln die Vielfalt an Lösungswegen zur Klimaneutralität wider und verdeutlichen, dass alle Interessengruppen eine gleichermaßen wichtige Rolle bei der Erreichung der Klimaziele spielen. Innerhalb der offenen Diskussionen im Rahmen der Workshops wurde der inhaltliche Bogen weit gespannt: von der Notwendigkeit einer besseren Integration von Forschung und Praxis, ökonomischen Anforderungen, angemessenen Lehrinhalten, Digitalisierung, Motivation der Unternehmen etwas zu ändern, Planungssicherheit durch gesetzliche Rahmenbedingungen, Hindernisse bei der Umsetzung fundierter, wirtschaftlicher Lösungen sowie Normen als Erfolgsfaktor oder Stolperstein. Ebenfalls gut angenommen wurde die Möglichkeit für Networking und Erfahrungsaustausch in den Pausen und am Abend.

Marcella Ruschi Mendes Saade,
Stefan Peters, Doris Arthofer

Annual Meeting of the Graz Center of Sustainable Construction

As one of the six research centers of TU Graz, the Graz Center of Sustainable Construction (GCSC) organized a symposium on November 15, 2023, on the question “How Can We Achieve Climate Neutrality in the Built Environment?” The participants in the presentations and moderated workshops held in Lecture Hall II in Alte Technik came from federal, state, and municipal governments, interest groups, construction, industry, building planning, and research. The TU Graz was represented by the Faculties of Architecture, Civil Engineering, Mathematics, Physics, and Geodesy and by the vice rector. The international guests form the Scientific Board included Ingeborg M. Rocker (Georgia Tech), Anya Vollpracht (RWTH Aachen), and Werner Sobek (Universität Stuttgart).

Ideas for projects and approaches to research from various fields were introduced in the brief presentations and pitches. They followed the three-step hierarchy of the GCSC: (i) Reduce demand, (ii) employ low-CO_2 materials/solutions, and (iii) compensate for the remaining emissions. Strategies, measures, and obstacles on the path to climate neutrality were then discussed in eight moderated workshop groups. The panel discussion with Vice Rector Michael Monsberger, Ingeborg M. Rocker, Anya Vollpracht, and Werner Sobek was moderated by Urs Hirschberg, the head of the Institute of Architecture and Media. The spectrum of projects and research presented reflected the diversity of paths to climate neutrality and make it clear that all interest groups play an equally important role in meeting climate goals. The open discussions in the workshops covered a broad arc of subjects: from the need to integrate research and practice better, economic requirements, suitable subjects for teaching, digitization, motivating companies to change something, planning safety by means of regulation, obstacles to implementing well-founded economic solutions and standards as both a factor in success and potential stumbling block. The opportunity to network and exchange experiences during the breaks and in the evening was also well received.

T. Zillner, M. Monsberger, S. Formanek, M. Fechner, K.-U. Hoffer, H. Hoff, T. Weiss, A. Passer, T. Levak, A. Knotzer, H. Warmuth, D. Weigel © Petra Blauensteiner, ÖGUT

„Highlights der Bauforschung“. Klimaneutrale Sanierung

Unter dem Titel „Highlights der Bauforschung“ wurden am 16. Oktober 2023 in der Kronesgasse 5 aktuelle Ergebnisse der angewandten Bauforschung mit Fokus auf nachhaltige Lösungen für klimaneutrale Gebäude und Quartiere präsentiert. Diese sollen die Mission der „Klimaneutralen Stadt“ des BMK unterstützen und die Umsetzung klimaneutraler Pionierstädte und Quartiere auf nationaler Ebene ermöglichen und beschleunigen.

Eröffnet wurde die Kooperationsveranstaltung des Bundesministeriums für Klimaschutz, Umwelt, Energie, Mobilität, Innovation und Technologie (BMK), des Innovationslabors RENOWAVE und der Fakultät für Architektur der TU Graz durch Theodor Zillner (BMK), Michael Monsberger (Vizerektorat für Infrastruktur und Nachhaltigkeit, TU Graz) und Susanne Formanek (Innovationslabor RENOWAVE). Der erste Vortrag von Kai-Uwe Hoffer (Stadtbaudirektion Graz) thematisierte klimaneutrale Quartiersentwicklungen am Beispiel Smart City in Graz. Holger Hoff (Universität Graz) und Alexander Passer (NHB, TU Graz) stellten integrierte Dekarbonisierungsstrategien im Bausektor vor, die Österreich auf dem Weg zur Klimaneutralität unterstützen sollen. Herausforderungen und Chancen im Feld der Gebäudesanierung, sowie innovative Technologien wie z.B. Multifunktionsfassaden, wurden von Tobias Weiss (AEE Intec) präsentiert. Anknüpfend an technologische Lösungen, folgte ein Vortrag von Toni Levak und Matthias Lang-Raudaschl (IAT, TU Graz) zu „Piezo-Klett“ – piezoelektrischen Klettanwendungen zur Energieversorgung aktiver Sensorik im Bauwesen, in der Klettverbindungen als Verbindungssystem als auch als Energieerzeuger

Anwendung finden sollen. Armin Knotzer (AEE INTEC) stellte in seinem Vortrag die Gemeinde Stanz auf dem Weg zur Plusenergiegemeinde, im Kontext der klimaneutralen Quartiersentwicklung vor. Das Strategiepapier zur Bauforschung 2024–2027 des BMK wurde von Hannes Warmuth (BMK) erläutert. Abschließend stellte Dagmar Weigel (FFG) die Ausschreibung „Technologien und Innovationen für die Klimaneutrale Stadt" vor. Moderiert wurde die Veranstaltung von Miriam Fechner (ÖGUT).

Alexander Passer, Christine Rossegger

"Highlights of Architectural Research": Climate-Neutral Redevelopment

On October 16, 2023, under the title "Highlights of Architectural Research," current results of applied architectural research with a focus on sustainable solutions for climate-neutral buildings and neighborhoods were presented at Kronesgasse 5. It was intended to support the BMK's mission of the "climate-neutral city" and enable and accelerate the implementation of climate-neutral pioneer cities and neighborhoods on a national level.

This cooperative event of the Austrian Federal Ministry for Climate Action, Environment, Energy, Mobility, Innovation, and Technology (BMK), the RENOWAVE innovation laboratory, and the Faculty of Architecture of TU Graz was opened by Theodor Zillner (BMK), Michael Monsberger (Vice Rector of Infrastructure and Sustainability, TU Graz), and Susanne Formanek (RENOWAVE innovation laboratory). The first lecture, by Kai-Uwe Hoffer (Building Department of the City of Graz), addressed climate-neutral neighborhood development using the example of Smart City in Graz. Holger Hoff (Universität Graz) and Alexander Passer (NHB, TU Graz) presented integrated decarbonization strategies in the building sector intended to support Austria on the path to climate neutrality. Challenges and opportunities in the field of building refurbishment and innovative technologies such as multifunctional façades were presented by Tobias Weiss. Continuing the theme of technological solutions, the next lecture by Toni Levak and Matthias Lang-Raudaschl (IAT, TU Graz) addressed the "Piezo-Klett"—piezoelectric hook-and-loop applications for energy supply of active sensor technology in the building industry in which hook-and-loop joints can be used in connector systems in a way that also produces energy. In his lecture, Armin Knotzer (AEE INTEC) presented the Municipality of Stanz, which is on the path to become an energy-plus municipality in the context of climate-neutral neighborhood development. The BMK strategy paper on architectural research from 2024 to 2027 was explained by Hannes Warmuth (BMK). Finally, Dagmar Weigel (FFG) presented the call for proposals "Technologies and Innovations for the Climate-Neutral City." The event was moderated by Miriam Fechner (ÖGUT).

Digital Design Reconsidered

In der Woche vom 18. bis zum 23. September fand an der TU Graz die 41ste eCAADe Konferenz statt. Nach 2003 war es bereits das zweite Mal, dass diese traditionsreiche Konferenz über Lehre und Forschung im Bereich des computerunterstützten architektonischen Entwerfens in Graz abgehalten wurde. Wie schon 2003 waren wieder Wolfgang Dokonal, Ass.Prof. am Institut für Städtebau, und Urs Hirschberg, Leiter des Instituts für Architektur und Medien (IAM), gemeinsam als Conference-Chairs für die Organisation verantwortlich, unterstützt vom Organisationsteam am IAM rund um Claudia Schörghofer, Albert Wiltsche und Alexander Grasser-Parger.

Das Motto der Konferenz, „Digital Design Reconsidered", stellte den Bezug zur Konferenz von 2003 her, die damals unter dem Motto „Digital Design" gestanden hatte. Das Thema gab den WissenschaftlerInnen aus aller Welt Gelegenheit, nicht nur über aktuelle Forschungsergebnisse zu berichten, sondern auch über die veränderte Rolle, welche digitale Werkzeuge im architektonischen Entwurfsprozess spielen, zu reflektieren. Aus 465 Abstracts wurden im zweistufigen Peer-Review-Verfahren schließlich 178 Papers zur Publikation und Präsentation ausgewählt. An der Konferenz teilgenommen haben über 250 Personen aus allen Kontinenten. Obwohl es eine in der Anzahl beschränkte Möglichkeit gab, online vorzutragen, und obwohl sämtliche Vorträge auch frei zugänglich im Internet per Stream miterlebt werden konnten, ließen es sich die allermeisten TeilnehmerInnen nicht nehmen, nach Graz zu reisen und vor Ort teilzunehmen.

Urs Hirschberg, Milena Stavrić © IAM, TU Graz

Zum Auftakt am Montag und Dienstag gab es Workshops zu unterschiedlichen Themen, von Mittwoch bis Freitag fand die eigentliche Konferenz statt, wobei sich die TU Graz ein weiteres Mal als Veranstaltungsort bewährte: Die Hörsäle, die Aula, das Foyer im Tiefparterre der alten Technik und die Mensa auf der Dachterrasse der Stremayrgasse 16 boten bei strahlendem Herbstwetter einen abwechslungsreichen Rahmen sowohl für die Vorträge als auch für den angeregten Austausch in den Pausen. Besondere Höhepunkte im Programm waren die Keynotes von Karolin Schmidbaur (Coop Himmelb(l)au/Universität Innsbruck), Kristina Schinegger and Stefan Rutzinger (soma/Universität Innsbruck), Milena Stavrić (TU Graz), Fabian Scheurer (design2production/Hochschule München) und Fabio Gramazio (gramaziokohler/ETH Zürich).

Ein Empfang im Rathaus, das Conference Dinner im Schlossbergrestaurant und der abschließende High Voltage Event in der Hochspannungshalle rundeten das Programm ab. Für Wolfgang Dokonal, der im Oktober 2023 in Pension ging, war die Konferenz, nach über 30 Dienstjahren an der Architekturfakultät, auch ein äußerst gelungener Abschied.

Urs Hirschberg

© KOEN, TU Graz

• In the week of September 18 to 23, the forty-first eCAADe conference was held at TU Graz. This was the second time, following 2003, that this storied conference on theory and research in the field of computer-aided design in architecture was held in Graz. As in 2003, Wolfgang Dokonal, assistant professor at the Institute of Urbanism, and Urs Hirschberg, head of the Institute of Architecture and Media (IAM), acted as conference chairs and were responsible for organizing it, supported by the IAM team around Claudia Schörghofer, Albert Wiltsche, and Alexander Grasser-Parger.

The motto of the conference, “Digital Design Reconsidered,” refers to the motto of the conference in 2003: “Digital Design.” This theme gave scholars from all over the world an opportunity not only to report on the results of their current research but also to reflect on the changed role that digital tools play in the process of architectural design. In a two-stage peer-review process, from 465 abstracts 178 papers were ultimately selected for publication and presentation. More than 250 people from all continents participated in the conference. Even though a limited number of online sessions were offered, and although all of the talks could be experienced through live streaming on the Internet, the vast majority of the participants preferred to travel to Graz and participate in situ.

It began on Monday and Tuesday with workshops on a variety of themes; the conference proper was held from Wednesday to Friday, for which TU Graz once again proved to be an exquisite venue: The lecture halls, the auditorium, the foyer on the lower ground floor of Alte Technik, and the cafeteria on the roof terrace of Stremayrgasse 16 in glorious autumn weather offered a diverse framework for the presentations as well as for the animated exchange during the breaks. Particular highlights of the program were the keynotes by Karolin Schmidbaur (Coop Himmelb(l)au/University of Innsbruck), Kristina Schinegger and Stefan Rutzinger (soma/University of Innsbruck), Milena Stavrić (TU Graz), Fabian Scheurer (design2production/Munich University of Applied Sciences), and Fabio Gramazio (gramaziokohler/ETH Zürich).

A reception in the town hall, the conference dinner in the Schlossberg restaurant, and the final high-voltage event in the Hochspannungshalle rounded out the program. For Wolfgang Dokonal, who retired in October 2023, the conference was an extremely successful farewell after thirty years of service to the Faculty of Architecture.

Am KOEN zu Gast

Auch dieses Jahr lud das Institut für Grundlagen der Konstruktion und des Entwerfens (KOEN) zur Veranstaltungsreihe „Am KOEN zu Gast“ ArchitektInnen ein, um Studierenden einen Einblick in ihren Werdegang und aktuellen Projekten zu bieten. Anhand von Vorträgen und Podiumsgesprächen wurde die gegenseitige Bedingtheit von Konstruktion und Entwurf untersucht. Durch Kommunikation zwischen Studierenden, Lehrenden und ArchitektInnen wurde Architektur ausgehend vom Entwurf bis hin zur Umsetzung diskutiert. Die Gäste stellten ihr Architekturbüro und eine Auswahl an Projekten vor. Im Anschluss eröffneten Petra Petersson und Armin Stocker durch ein moderiertes Gespräch die Fragerunde. Im Zuge dessen konnten Studierende in einen Dialog mit praktizierenden ArchitektInnen treten und ihnen sowohl projektbezogene als auch allgemeinere Fragen stellen. Die von Armin Stocker konzipierte Veranstaltungsreihe wurde aufgezeichnet und für ein breiteres Publikum digital übertragen. Durchgeführt wurde die Veranstaltung von Petra Petersson, Armin Stocker, Robert Anagnostopoulos und dem KOEN-Team.

Vortragende und GesprächspartnerInnen:
Heidi Pretterhofer
(PRETTERHOFER ARQUITECTOS, Wien)
Nina Kuess
(KUESS Architektur, Lieboch)
Eva Kuß (coabitare, Graz)
Marc Benjamin Drewes (marc benjamin drewes ARCHITEKTUREN
Barbara Poberschnigg
(STUDIO LOIS, Innsbruck)
Lina Streeruwitz
(StudioVlayStreeruwitz, Wien)
Alexander Gebetsroither
(Edelaar Mosayebi Inderbitzin Architekt*innen, Zürich)
Žiga Kreševič (transform, Maribor)

Victoria Michaela Pirker, Armin Stocker

• The Institute of Construction and Design Principles (KOEN) once again invited architects to the event series "Am KOEN zu Gast" to present their careers and current projects to students. Lectures and panel discussions looked at how construction and design condition each other. Through communication between students, teachers, and architects, architecture was discussed from design to implementation. Guests presented their own architecture firm and a selection of projects. Then Petra Petersson and Armin Stocker opened the question round with a moderated conversation. Students were able to participate in a dialogue with practicing architects and ask both project-related and more general questions. This event series, conceived by Armin Stocker, was recorded and broadcast digitally to a wider audience. The event was organized by Petra Petersson, Armin Stocker, Robert Anagnostopoulos, and the KOEN team.

Lecturers and panelists:
Heidi Pretterhofer
(PRETTERHOFER ARQUITECTOS, Wien)
Nina Kuess
(KUESS Architektur, Lieboch)
Eva Kuß (coabitare, Graz)
Marc Benjamin Drewes (marc benjamin drewes ARCHITEKTUREN
Barbara Poberschnigg
(STUDIO LOIS, Innsbruck)
Lina Streeruwitz
(StudioVlayStreeruwitz, Wien)
Alexander Gebetsroither
(Edelaar Mosayebi Inderbitzin Architekt*innen, Zürich)
Žiga Kreševič (transform, Maribor)

© Institut Vierzehn

Institut Vierzehn: Wir malen uns einen Raum

Im Zuge eines Workshops vom 03. bis 04. Dezember 2022 bekannte das Institut Vierzehn und alle Teilnehmenden Farbe. Einem leerstehenden Einfamilienhaus im Grazer Bezirk St. Peter wurde von 19 Architekturstudierenden noch einmal Leben eingehaucht. Durch kollektives Probieren, Experimentieren und freies Arbeiten entstanden Farbkonzepte für acht Räume. Dabei stand das Tun, und weniger das Denken über das Tun, im Vordergrund. Nach anfänglichem Input eines Malers wurden diverse Interventionen in Eigeninitiative durchgeführt. Dabei entstanden beispielsweise blaue oder fragmentiert-kolorierte Räume, Räume mit Schattenspiel oder perspektivischen Farbwirkungen. Im Fokus des Workshops stand das Handwerk und das eigenständige Lernen im Kollektiv.

Institut Vierzehn

Institut Vierzehn: Painting Ourselves a Room

In the course of a workshop on December 3–4, 2022, Institute Vierzehn and all participants took a stand in color. A vacant single-family home located in the St. Peter district of Graz received one last breath of life through nineteen architecture students. Collective experimentation and independent work resulted in color concepts for eight rooms. In doing so, the emphasis was more on doing and less on thinking about doing. Following the initial input by a painter, various interventions were carried out on the participants' own initiative. This led, for example, to blue or fragmented-colored rooms, rooms with shadow play, or perspectival color effects. The workshop was focused on craftsmanship and independent learning as a collective.

Discourse

Pop-Up Fakultätscafé

Seit Jänner 2023 etabliert sich das Pop-Up Fakultätscafé als beliebter neuer Treffpunkt am Campus der Alten Technik, um sich beim gemeinsamen Kaffeetrinken auszutauschen. Die mobile Espressobar, die bereits im Foyer und im Innenhof temporär eingerichtet und in Kooperation mit dem Baristaservice „Espressomobil" umgesetzt wurde, schafft damit ein neues institutsübergreifendes Format der Vernetzung. Als neuer, flexibler Raum eröffnet er Studierenden, Lehrenden und anderen Fakultätsangehörigen die Möglichkeit für niederschwelligen Austausch über fakultäts- oder architekturrelevante Inhalte. Zukünftig soll das Pop-Up Fakultätscafé in häufigeren Intervallen stattfinden und von Studierenden organisiert und betrieben werden.
Wir freuen uns auf weitere gemeinsame Kaffeepausen und spannende Gespräche.

Andrea Schmallegger

Pop-Up Faculty Café

Since January 2023, the pop-up Faculty Café has established itself as a popular new meeting place on the Alte Technik campus for interchanges over coffee. The mobile espresso bar that has been set up temporarily in the foyer and inner courtyard and run in cooperation with the barista service "Espressomobil" provides a new cross-institution format for network. As a new, flexible space, it offers students, teachers, and other faculty members the opportunity for uncomplicated exchange on subjects relevant to the faculty and to architecture. In the future, the pop-up Faculty Café will operate on a more regular basis while being organized and run by students. We are looking forward to more coffee breaks together and fascinating conversations.

© GAM.Lab, TU Graz

Z.A. Ilgün, C. Marchi, M.F. Frühwirt, E. Schwab, S. Joeris, P. Kubin, P. Lucena Ventura, A. Degros
© GAM.Lab, TU Graz

© CH Studio

PHD Days 2023

Der erste PHD DAY des Jahres fand im WS 2022/23 unter der Leitung von Aglaée Degros (Institut für Städtebau, TU Graz) statt. Die sechs DissertantInnen präsentierten ihre Forschungsthemen und -ergebnisse, die einen inhaltlichen Bogen von Digitalisierung über Ökologie bis hin zu Partizipation spannten: Es präsentierten Carlos Marchi („Digital Architectonics and Environmental Urbanism"), Stephan Joeris („Der 6. Sinn der Architektur"), Max Florian Frühwirt („Today's Kyou-machiya – 今日の京町家 (Kyou no Kyou-machiya)"), Petra Kubin ("Gründerzeitliche Innenhöfe in Graz"), Zeliha Asya Ilgün ("Living Architecture for Honeybees") und Patricia Lucena Ventura („The Sensitive City—The Micropolitical Transformation of Territories"). Die Forschungsarbeiten wurden im Anschluss an die Vorträge in einem von Aglaée Degros geleiteten Feedback-Board, dem u.a. auch Eva Schwab (stdb, TU Graz), Antje Senarclens de Grancy (akk, TU Graz), Milena Stavrić (IAM, TU Graz) und Günter Getzinger (Institute of Interactive Systems and Data Science) angehörten, zur Diskussion gestellt.

Der zweite PHD DAY des Jahres wurde am 4. Juli 2023 unter der Organisation und Leitung des Instituts für Gebäude und Energie (ige, TU Graz) abgehalten. Die 20-minütigen Vorträge der fünf teilnehmenden DissertantInnen präsentierten aktuelle Forschungsfragen aus unterschiedlichen Themenfeldern, die im Anschluss in Feedbackrunden kommentiert und in vertiefenden Gesprächen diskutiert wurden. Zur Diskussion gestellt wurden u.a. Themen wie die Untersuchung der Tragfähigkeit von Stampflehmkonstruktionen (Iveta Šarmanová: „Earthern Structures – Numerical and Experimental Examination of Load-Bearing Rammed Earth Structures") oder die historische Aufarbeitung von Bauplanungsprozessen im zweiten Weltkrieg (Lavinia Munteanu: „Der Generalplan OST als Instrument der Vernichtung am Beispiel des ‚volksdeutschen Gebietes Hegewald'"). Weitere Dissertationsprojekte thematisierten u.a. hochtechnisierte Fassadenmaterialien (Toni Levak: „The Building Envelope as a Self-Sufficient Energy Source/Sensor Technology"), eine Untersuchung des CO_2-Budgets aus österreichischer Perspektive (Nicolas Bernard Jean Alaux: „Identifiction of Future Trajectories for Carbon Budget Complaint Buildings: An Austrian Perspective"), sowie den Einfluss von privaten BauträgerInnen auf die Architektur von Wohngebäuden (Amra Muminović: „Influence of Private Property Developers on the Architecture of Residential Buildings"). Neben betreuenden ProfessorInnen zählten auch interessierte Studierende, Universitätsangestellte sowie weitere DissertantInnen der Doctoral School Architektur zu den Gästen beider Veranstaltungen.

Mario Stefan (stdb),
Carmen Feyrsinger (ige)

S. Peters, D. Gethmann, A. Wagner, B. Cody, L. Munteanu, I. Šarmanová, N.B.J. Alaux, A. Muminović, T. Levak © ige, TU Graz

• The first PHD DAY of the year was held in the winter semester of 2022/23 under the direction of Aglaée Degros (Institute of Urban Design, TU Graz). Each of the six doctoral students presented their research topics and findings, which ranged from digitalization to ecology to participation: Carlos Marchi ("Digital Architectonics and Environmental Urbanism"), Stephan Joeris ("Der 6. Sinn der Architektur"), Max Florian Frühwirt ("Today's Kyou-machiya—今日の京町家 [Kyou no Kyou-machiya]"), Petra Kubin ("Gründerzeitliche Innenhöfe in Graz"), Zeliha Asya Ilgün ("Living Architecture for Honeybees"), and Patricia Lucena Ventura ("The Sensitive City: The Micropolitical Transformation of Territories"). Following the presentations, the research projects were put up for discussion in a feedback board led by Aglaée Degros, which included Eva Schwab (stdb, TU Graz), Antje Senarclens de Grancy (akk, TU Graz), Milena Stavrić (IAM, TU Graz), and Günter Getzinger (Institute of Interactive Systems and Data Science).

The second PHD DAY of the year was held on July 4, 2023, and was organized and led by the Institute of Buildings and Energy (ige). The twenty-minute presentations given by the five participating doctoral students thematized current research questions from various subject areas, which were then commented on in feedback rounds and discussed in in-depth talks. Among the topics up for discussion was the investigation of the load-bearing capacity of rammed earth structures (Iveta Šarmanová, "Earthern Structures: Numerical and Experimental Examination of Load-Bearing Rammed Earth Structures") or the historical analysis/assessment of construction planning processes during the Second World War (Lavinia Munteanu, "Der Generalplan OST als Instrument der Vernichtung am Beispiel des 'volksdeutschen Gebietes Hegewald'"). Other dissertation projects focused on topics such as high-tech facade materials (Toni Levak, "The Building Envelope as a Self-Sufficient Energy Source/Sensor Technology"), an investigation into the CO_2 budget from an Austrian perspective (Nicolas Bernard Jean Alaux, "Identification of Future Trajectories for Carbon Budget Complaint Buildings: An Austrian Perspective"), and the impact that private property developers have on residential architecture (Amra Muminović, "Influence of Private Property Developers on the Architecture of Residential Buildings"). Guests at both events included supervising professors, interested students, university staff, and other PhD students from the Doctoral School of Architecture.

© CH Studio

M. Peralta, D. Ajanović, M. Tomić, N. Sarafijanović, N. Sanjta, B. Khalil © IZK, TU Graz

IZK Research Days

Anlässlich der IZK Research Days stellten Mitglieder des Instituts ihre Forschungsarbeiten vor. Ziel dieser Veranstaltung war es, einen anregenden Austausch an Ideen, Wissen und Praktiken zu initiieren und die vielfältigen Projekte, die im Wirkungsbereich des Instituts für Zeitgenössische Kunst (IZK) stattfinden, in einem größeren Zusammenhang zu diskutieren. Die IZK-Research Days umfassten die Präsentationen von Budour Khalil („Unbecoming Architecture“), Amel Bešlagić („Highway Prijedor Banja Luka“), Barbara Seyerl („Regaining Agency: Investigating Methods of Activism in Posthumanism“), Anousheh Kehar („With Fire, Living as Guests on Unceded Homelands of the Maidu, Miwok, North Fork Mono, Patwin, Wintun, …“), Ahmad Darkhabani („Exhibiting as a Deconstructive Form of Reality“), Rose-Anne Gush („The Chambers of the Hands, the Vaults of the Head, Forbidden Rooms: Notes on Art, Form and the Unevenness of Global Capitalist Modernity“), Lina Ramadan („Arab Women Solidarity: Rethinking Mid-Twentieth Century Arab Art“), Nelly Sanjta („Divergence of Space. Ideological Embeddedness in the Built Environment“), Džana Ajanović („Vraca: Site of Horror, Site of Honor“), Philipp Sattler („Monument, Mountain, Mine“), Mercedes Peralta („Architecture as Body of Material Landscapes“), Milica Tomić („Art as Undirected Investigation“), Nour Shantout („How to Do Research Where ‚Research‘ Is A Dirty Word?“), Farnoosh Namaziyan („Repealing the Walls: An Architectural Practice in Iran After 2022“), und Ren Aldridge („Resisting Femicide: Physically and Aurally Stitching Together Community-Based Strategies“).

• For the IZK Research Days, members and affiliates of the Institute of Contemporary Art (IZK) presented their research. This event aimed to create an inspiring exchange of ideas, knowledge, and practices and to connect the rich and diverse projects being conducted within the remit of the institute. The IZK Research Days included the following presentations: Budour Khalil, (“Unbecoming Architecture”); Amel Bešlagić, (“Highway Prijedor Banja Luka”); Barbara Seyerl, (“Regaining Agency: Investigating Methods of Activism in Posthumanism”); Anousheh Kehar, (“With Fire, Living as Guests on Unceded Homelands of the Maidu, Miwok, North Fork Mono, Patwin, Wintun, …”); Ahmad Darkhabani, (“Exhibiting as a Deconstructive Form of Reality”); Rose-Anne Gush, (“The Chambers of the Hands, the Vaults of the Head, Forbidden Rooms: Notes on Art, Form and the Unevenness of Global Capitalist Modernity”); Lina Ramadan, (“Arab Women Solidarity: Rethinking Mid-Twentieth Century Arab Art”); Nelly Sanjta, (“Divergence of Space: Ideological Embeddedness in the Built Environment”); Džana Ajanović, (“Vraca: Site of Horror, Site of Honor”); Philipp Sattler, (“Monument, Mountain, Mine”); Mercedes Peralta, (“Architecture as Body of Material Landscapes”); Milica Tomić, (“Art as Undirected Investigation”); Nour Shantout, (“How to Do Research Where ‘Research’ Is a Dirty Word?”); Farnoosh Namaziyan, (“Repealing the Walls: An Architectural Practice in Iran After 2022”); and Ren Aldridge, (“Resisting Femicide: Physically and Aurally Stitching Together Community-Based Strategies.”)

Rose-Anne Gush, Philipp Sattler

Vortragsabend „Positionen zum Entwerfen im Bestand“

Am 10. Oktober 2023 lud das Institut für Entwerfen im Bestand und Denkmalpflege (EnBeDe, TU Graz) das zweite Mal zum Vortragsabend „Positionen zum Entwerfen im Bestand.“ Die geladenen Gäste – Claudia Cavallar aus Wien, Peter Haimerl aus München und Marco Zünd von Buol und Zünd aus Basel – erläuterten ihre architektonische Haltung und persönliche Entwurfsentscheidungen im Umgang mit Bestand anhand realisierter Projekte.

Unter dem Motto „make do and mend“ zeigte Claudia Cavallar die Umkleiden und WC-Anlagen im Museum für angewandte Kunst in Wien und thematisierte Fragen rund um den Umgang mit den verschiedenen Bauphasen und Veränderungen des Museums. Dabei illustrierte sie, wie gesellschaftliche Veränderung im Gebauten sichtbar wird und dass sich die Unterbrechung des Alltags, die ein Museum vollzieht, sogar in Nebenräumen architektonisch übersetzen lässt.

Der Vortrag von Peter Haimerl setzte sich mit seinem Entwurf der Erweiterung um einen Konzertsaal für das Haus Marteau in Lichtenberg auseinander und machte deutlich, inwiefern die Geschichte eines Ortes von den Bestandsgebäuden als Akteure mitgestaltet wird und wie sein Entwurf an diese Geschichte anknüpft.

„Taking on the baton“ – den Staffelstab weitertragen – bildet für die Projekte von Buol und Zünd die zentrale Entwurfshaltung, die nicht den Kontrast sucht, sondern die Homogenität zwischen Bestehendem und Neuem. Anhand eines Fabrikumbaus in Basel demonstrierte Marco Zünd, wie sich aus einer bestehenden Struktur eine Logik für das Neue, in diesem Fall großzügige Wohnungen, ableiten lässt.

Ein kleiner Apero im Anschluss bot Anstoß zum weiterführenden Gespräch mit den Vortragenden und zur eigenen Verortung im Feld der unterschiedlichen Positionen.

Christina Aschauer

Lecture Evening "Positions on Designing in Existing Structures"

On October 10, 2023, the Institute of Design in Existing Structures and Architectural Heritage Protection (EnBeDe, TU Graz) hosted the second lecture evening on "Positions on Designing in Existing Structures." The invited guests—Claudia Cavallar from Vienna, Peter Haimerl from Munich, and Marco Zünd of Buol und Zünd from Basel—elaborated on their architectural approach and personal design decisions when dealing with existing structures using examples of built projects.

Under the motto "make do and mend" Claudia Cavallar presented the changing rooms and washrooms in the Museum of Applied Arts, Vienna, and addressed questions about the museum's phases of construction and changes. She illustrates how social change becomes visible in the buildings and how the interlude in daily life that the museum provides can be translated into architecture even in its auxiliary spaces.

Peter Haimerl's lecture examined his proposal to expand a concert hall for the Haus Marteau in Lichtenberg, illustrating the extent to which the history of a place is shaped by the existing buildings as actors and how his design ties in with this history.

"Taking on the baton" is the central design attitude for Buol and Zünd's project, seeking not contrast but rather homogeneity between the existing and the new. Using the example of a factory conversion in Basel, Marco Zünd demonstrated how one can derive from an existing structure the logic for a new building, in this case spacious apartments. A small aperitif afterward provided an opportunity to continue the discussion with the presenters and find one's own place within the field of the different positions presented.

© EnBeDe, TU Graz

Bar Limarutti © EnBeDe, TU Graz

EnBeDe-Ortstermin: Bar Limarutti und Galerie Konzett

Am 7. Juni 2023 lud das Institut für Entwerfen in Bestand und Denkmalpflege (EnBeDe, TU Graz), vertreten durch Institutsleiter Matthias Castorph und Michael Hafner, zu einem Ortsbesuch in die Grazer Innenstadt. Anlass dafür waren zwei Architekturen, die als Beiträge der Grazer Schule in Vergessenheit geraten waren: Norbert Müllers Galerie Konzett in der Engen Gasse und die ehemalige Weinbar Limarutti in der Prokopigasse. Ziel dieses Ortstermins war es, die aus dem Jahre 1990 stammenden architekonischen Beiträge Müllers für einen Nachmittag zu reaktivieren. Die ehemalige Kunstgalerie Konzett, ein architektonisches Cuvée aus Grazer Schule und Carlo Scarpa, entstand unter der Mitarbeit von Wolfgang Wimmer. Nach der Schließung der Galerie wurde das Geschäftslokal die letzten Jahre nur als Lager genutzt. Für den Ortsbesuch machten die neuen PächterInnen die Räumlichkeiten nach langer Zeit wieder öffentlich zugänglich. Die ehemalige Weinbar Limarutti, heutige Sushibar Yamamoto, ging einst aus einem italienischen Lebensmittelhandels hervor und wurde danach zu einem Stehcafé nach italienischem Vorbild. Das Projekt wurde 1990 mit dem Architekturpreis der GerambRose ausgezeichnet und entwickelte sich nicht nur, aber vor allem wegen eines Betontresen, den man über eine Zahnstangenmechanik in den öffentlichen Raum kurbeln kann, zu einem Szenetreff in Graz. In Zusammenarbeit mit der Schlosserei Golser konnte man die verlorene Kurbel rekonstruieren und in Anwesenheit von ehemaligen Stammgästen der Weinbar (darunter Hans Gangoly (IGL, TU Graz) oder Andreas Lichtblau (i_w, TU Graz) nach über 20 Jahren wieder in die Öffentlichkeit kurbeln. Begleitet wurde der Ortsbesuch von Architekt Norbert Müller und dem von ihm zur Verfügung gestellten Planmaterial in Form einer mobilen Ausstellung. Im Zuge der Veranstaltung ist es gelungen, die beiden Projekte als Vorlass in das Architekturarchiv Steiermark einzugliedern.

Michael Hafner

EnBeDe On-Site Event: Bar Limarutti and Gallery Konzett

On June 7, 2023, the Institute of Design in Existing Structures and Architectural Heritage Protection (EnBeDe, TU Graz), represented by Matthias Castorph (chair) and Michael Hafner, hosted a site visit in Graz's city center, prompted by two contributions by the Graz School that had faded into oblivion: Norbert Müller's Konzett Gallery situated in the Enge Gasse and the erstwhile Limarutti wine bar in the Prokopigasse. This on-site visit sought to reactivate Müller's architectural contributions from 1990 for one afternoon. The former Konzett Art Gallery, an architectural hybrid of the Graz School and Carlo Scarpa, was realized in collaboration with Wolfgang Wimmer. Following the gallery's closure, the premises were used solely as a storage space in recent years. For the on-site visit, the new tenants made the premises publicly accessible again after a long time. The previously named Limarutti wine bar, now Sushibar Yamamoto, emerged from an Italian grocery store and subsequently became an Italian-style stand-up café. In 1990, the project was awarded the GerambRose architecutral prize, evolving into an in-vogue venue in Graz, not only (but by and large) due to its concrete counter featuring a rack-and-pinion mechanism. Working together with the locksmiths Golser, the lost crank could be reconstructed and, in the presence of former regulars of the wine bar including the institute chairs Hans Gangoly (IGL) and Andreas Lichtblau (i_w), was cranked back into the public space after more than twenty years. Accompanying the site visit was the architect Norbert Müller, who also provided planning material in the form of a mobile exhibition. Following the event, both projects were successfully integrated into the Architectural Archive of Styria collection.

© TU Graz Archive

Grazer Architektinnen

Architektinnen werden bis auf wenige Ausnahmen in den bis heute maßgeblichen Standardwerken zur Grazer Architektur nach 1945 nicht genannt. Auch in aktuellen Publikationen gibt es kaum Spuren von ihnen. Wie ist das möglich? Wo sind die vielen Frauen geblieben, die ihr Studium in Graz absolviert und hier und anderswo gearbeitet haben? Ab dem Studienjahr 2023/24 werden am Institut für Architekturtheorie, Kunst- und Kulturwissenschaften erstmals die Absolventinnen der Architekturfakultät der TU Graz (vormals: Technische Hochschule Graz) seit der Ersten Republik systematisch erfasst. Der hegemonialen Erzählung der sogenannten „Grazer Schule" der Architektur als nahezu reiner Männerbund soll – im Sinne einer längst fälligen Kanonkorrektur – eine andere Geschichte entgegengesetzt werden: nämlich die der Architektinnen, die oft als Büropartnerinnen oder -mitarbeiterinnen einen wesentlichen Beitrag zum internationalen Erfolg dieser Architekturentwicklung geleistet haben. Ein Schwerpunkt liegt dabei auf den beiden Generationen der „Grazer Schule", die in den 1950er- bis 1970er-Jahren hier studiert haben. Die Ergebnisse der Recherchen sollen abschließend in eine Wikipedia-Rubrik „Absolventinnen der Architekturfakultät der TU Graz" mit ausgewählten Kurzbiographien einfließen. Gefördert wird das von Waltraud P. Indrist und Antje Senarclens de Grancy geleitete und von Clara Neuhold bearbeitete Projekt im Rahmen der Gender Taskforce durch das Dekanat der Fakultät für Architektur. Das Archiv der TU Graz ist Kooperationspartner.

Antje Senarclens de Grancy

Women Architects in Graz

With few exceptions, women architects are still not mentioned in the standard works on architecture in Graz after 1945. There are hardly any traces of them in current publications. How is that possible? Where are the many women who completed their studies in Graz and worked here and elsewhere? Starting with the academic year 2023/24, the Institute of Architectural Theory, Art History, and Cultural Studies (akk) is systematically documenting the female graduates of the Faculty of Architecture of TU Graz (formerly: Technical College Graz) for the first time since the First Austrian Republic. The hegemonic narrative of the so-called Graz School of architecture as a group composed almost exclusively of men will be countered with a different story — in a long-overdue correction: namely, that of the women architects, who made an essential contribution to the international success of this architectural movement, often as partners or employees of the firm. One focus is on the two generations of the Graz School that studied here from the 1950s to the 1970s. The results of this research will then be used to create a Wikipedia category "Women Graduates of the Faculty of Architecture of TU Graz," with selected brief biographies. This project, headed by Waltraud P. Indrist and Antje Senarclens de Grancy and compiled by Clara Neuhold, is funded by the Office of the Dean of the Faculty of Architecture. The TU Graz Archive is a cooperation partner.

© IAM, TU Graz

StudentsART

Die vom Institut für Architektur und Medien, Institut für Raumgestaltung und F+T Haus ins Leben gerufene Plattform StudentsART ermöglicht es Studierenden der TU Graz ihre im Rahmen des Studiums angefertigten Designobjekte in öffentlich zugänglichen Ausstellungen zu präsentieren und zu verkaufen. Im Dezember 2022 wurden beispielsweise Möbelstücke aus der Lehrveranstaltung „Handwerk" (Institut für Raumgestaltung, TU Graz), 3D-Drucke aus Keramik oder Akustikpaneele (Institut für Architektur und Medien, TU Graz) u.a. im Rahmen des Grazer Designmonats und der Weinverkostung „Kunst & Wein" in der Kiwis Mietbar (in Kooperation mit „Krenn.49") in Graz ausgestellt. Als Ergebnis der Zusammenarbeit mit Printkultur, dem Servicebetrieb der Österreichischen Hochschülerschaft der TU Graz, ging auch ein Webshop online, über den Studierende ihre Objekte nun auch auf einem Online-Marktplatz anbieten und verkaufen können. Mehr Infos unter: https://StudentsART.tugraz.at

Albert Wiltsche

• Launched by the Institute of Architecture and Media, the Institute of Spatial Design, and F+T House, the StudentsART platform enables students at TU Graz to showcase and sell the design objects they have created as part of their studies in publicly accessible exhibitions. In December 2022, for instance, pieces of furniture from the course "Handwerk" (Craftsmanship) at the Institute of Spatial Design and 3D prints made of ceramics or acoustic panels (Institute of Architecture and Media), among others, were exhibited during the Graz Design Month and at the wine tasting "Art & Wine" at Kiwis Mietbar (in cooperation with Krenn.49) in Graz. Following the collaboration with Printkultur, the Austrian National Students' Union service company at TU Graz, students can now list and sell their objects through an online marketplace. For more information, see: https:// StudentsART.tugraz.at

Institut Vierzehn: Unter der Stiege

Mit der Veranstaltungsserie „Unter der Stiege" wird seit März 2023 der unbeachtete Schwellenraum zwischen den Architekturzeichensälen 1-4 als Ort für niederschwelligen architektonischen Austausch genutzt. Fernab der Hörsäle und Seminarräume soll zum Nachdenken und zur kritischen Auseinandersetzung mit Architektur angeregt werden. Input lieferten bisher einerseits Filme mit Architekturbezug und andererseits plakativ aufbereitete Fragestellungen zu relevanten Themen im zeitgenössischen Architekturdiskurs. Mit der Absicht einen möglichst diversen Ausschnitt des Studierendenkörpers anzusprechen, wechseln Veranstaltungsart und Themen regelmäßig. Zukünftig soll der (Schwellen-) Raum weiterhin ein Ort für offenen Diskurs und lebendigen Architekturaustausch sein.

Institut Vierzehn

Institut Vierzehn: Beneath the Stairs

Since March of 2023, the event series "Unter der Stiege" (Beneath the Stairs) has been using the largely disregarded liminal space between the architectural drawing studios 1–4 as a place for low-threshold architectural exchange. Situated at a distance from the lecture halls and seminar rooms, the aim is to encourage reflection and a critical examination of architecture. So far, input has consisted

© GAM.Lab, TU Graz

of films relating to architecture, on the one hand, and strikingly worded questions pertaining to relevant issues in contemporary architectural discourse, on the other. In order to address as diverse a cross-section of the student body as possible, the type of events and topics regularly change. The (threshold) space should continue to be a place for open discussion and lively architectural exchange in the future.

© Simon Oberhofer

Restoring a Boat

Der deutsche Pavillon, der im Rahmen der Architekturbiennale in Venedig 2023 unter dem Motto „Open for Maintenance – Wegen Umbau geöffnet" stand, verwandelte sich unter der kuratorischen Leitung von ARCH+, SUMMACUMFEMMER und Büro Juliane Greb für die Dauer der diesjährigen Ausstellung in eine Werkstatt. Mit gebrauchten Materialien der Länderpavillons der Kunstbiennale aus dem Vorjahr wurde gemeinsam mit Studierenden und Auszubildenden des Handwerks und in Kooperation mit venezianischen Initiativen repariert, gepflegt und instandgesetzt. In einem einwöchigen Workshop des Instituts für Raumgestaltung haben 26 Studierende des Master Entwerfen „Anbauen" gemeinsam mit Studierenden der Iuav Venedig ein altes Boot aus Holz – ein repräsentatives Element des venezianischen Lebens – restauriert. Mit der Unterstützung des lokalen Bootsbauers FAP Cantiere Nautico wurde der Bootsrumpf abgedichtet und anschließend ein Boden, eine Sitzbank und eine verschließbare Klappe für den Stauraum des Bootes gebaut. Die Rampe vor dem Portikus des Pavillons wurde für die Dauer des Workshops zur Bootswerft. In einem gemeinsamen Entwurfs- und Bauprozess und im Arbeiten mit dem, was schon da ist, gingen Vorhandenes und Neues ineinander über. Der Workshop fand unter der Leitung von Carlotta Bonura, Eva Herunter, Büşra Köroğlu und Rainer Eberl und der Mitarbeit von Dominic Janisch statt.

Eva Herunter

• The German Pavilion for the Venice Biennale of Architecture in 2023, whose motto was "Open for Maintenance," was transformed for the duration of the exhibition into a workshop under the curatorial direction of ARCH+, SUMMACUMFEMMER, and the office of Juliane Greb. Using materials from the national pavilions of the Biennale of Art of the previous year, working with students and apprentices in the trades, and in cooperation with initiatives in Venice, repairs, maintenance, and restoration were performed there. In a one-week workshop of the Institute of Spatial Design, twenty-six students from the Design Studio "Anbauen," together with students from Iuav in Venice, restored an old wooden boat — a typical element of life in Venice. With support from the local boat builders FAP Cantiere Nautico, the hull of the boat was sealed, and then a floor, a bench, and a closable hatch for the stowage area were built. The ramp in front of the portico of the pavilion served as a shipyard for the duration of the workshop. In a joint process of designing and building, working with what was already there, the existing and the new blended. The workshop was headed by Carlotta Bonura, Eva Herunter, Büşra Köroğlu, and Rainer Eberl, with assistance from Dominic Janisch.

Architekturtheorietage 2023. Gründung der Gesellschaft für Architekturtheorie

Die Theorie lebt von einer vitalen Diskussionskultur. Dementsprechend ist ein ständiger Austausch wichtig, nicht nur innerhalb der einzelnen Architekturtheorie-Institute, sondern auch zwischen ihnen. Aus diesem Grund finden seit 2016 die Architekturtheorietage als informelles Fixum statt. Diesmal wurden sie zudem auch für den Mittelbau in der Architekturtheorie geöffnet, um die Debatte zu erweitern. Die teilnehmenden Universitäten wechseln sich dabei in der GastgeberInnenrolle ab. Die Architekturtheorietage 2023 fanden unter der Organisationsleitung von Tatjana Schneider (Leiterin des Instituts für Geschichte und Theorie der Architektur und Stadt) an der TU Braunschweig statt. Vom Institut für Architekturtheorie, Kunst- und Kulturwissenschaften der TU Graz nahmen Institutsvorstand Anselm Wagner sowie Daniel Gethmann, Waltraud P. Indrist und Ramona Kraxner teil. Beim diesjährigen Treffen der aus Deutschland und Österreich stammenden Teilnehmenden stand das Thema „Publizieren als kritische Praxis" im Mittelpunkt. Reflexionen über die Architekturtheorie als essenzielles Fragment einer ganzheitlichen universitären Architekturbildung rahmten die inhaltlichen Diskussionen über die Publikationstätigkeiten.

Missstände und hochschulpolitisches Taktieren, wie etwa fehlende Nachbesetzungen von Professuren, drängten einmal mehr zu einer autonomen Handlungsfähigkeit der Architekturtheorie als akademische Disziplin. Ebenfalls streben die einzelnen Institute eine intensivere Vernetzung an. Dies nahm man zum Anlass und rief die Gesellschaft für Architekturtheorie ins Leben. Sie dient als Grundlage für inhaltliche und organisatorische Vernetzungsmöglichkeit, den fachlichen sowie informellen Austausch und eine zentrale Sammelstelle für Publikationen, Debatten und Reaktionen. Dazu initiierten die teilnehmenden Hochschulen eine Task Force für die Umsetzung eines geplanten gemeinsamen Online-Auftritts. Ziel ist es, in den kommenden Monaten eine Webpage als erste Anlaufstelle über die Aktivitäten im Bereich der internationalen deutschsprachigen Architekturtheorie aufzubauen.

Ramona Kraxner

Architecture Theory Days 2023: Founding of the Society for Architectural Theory

Theory thrives on a vital culture of discussion. Accordingly, constant exchange is necessary, not only inside of individual institutions of architectural theory but also between them. For that reason, Architecture Theory Days 2023 have been an informal fixed quantity since 2016. This time, it was also open to nonprofessorial teaching staff in architectural theory to broaden the debate. The organization of Architecture Theory Days 2023 was led by Tatjana Schneider (head of the Institute of the History and Theory of Architecture and the City) at TU Braunschweig. From the Institute of Architectural Theory, Art History, and Cultural Studies of TU Graz, the institute chair, Anselm Wagner, took part, as did Daniel Gethmann, Waltraud P. Indrist, and Ramona Kraxner. This year's meeting of participants from Germany and Austria focused on the theme "Publication as Critical Practice." Reflections on architectural theory as an essential fragment of a complete university education in architecture framed the discussions of publication activities.

Shortcomings and university politics such as the failure to reappoint chairs have once again made it necessary for architectural theory to operate autonomously as an academic discipline. Individual institutions are also networking more intensively. This has been seen as an occasion to found the Gesellschaft für Architekturtheorie (Society for Architectural Theory). It provides a basis for networking on content and organization, for professional and informal exchange, and for a central gathering point for publications, debates, and reactions. To that end, the participating universities initiated a taskforce to implement a planned joint online presence. Its goal is to develop a webpage in the coming months as the first place to go to increase activities in the field of international architectural theory in German.

© IAM, TU Graz

Clay Column

Im Zuge einer Kollaboration der Universität Innsbruck und der Technischen Universität Graz wurde im Sommersemester 2022 im Rahmen der Lehrveranstaltung „Methoden der Materialisierung" eine knapp drei Meter hohe Säule aus 3D-gedruckten keramischen Bauelementen hergestellt. Eine Gruppe von 50 Studierenden der Universität Innsbruck war sowohl am Design als auch an der Produktion und dem Aufbau von 97 Einzelmodulen beteiligt. Die individuellen Designs nutzten Punktwolken, um strukturell informierte Druckpfade für den Herstellungsprozess via 3D-Druck zu erzeugen. Für die erfolgreiche Produktion kam die am Institut für Architektur und Medien der TU Graz, speziell für den 3D-Druck von Ton entwickelte Software Termite zum Einsatz. Das Projekt stellt eine Erkundung von Möglichkeiten und Herausforderungen des 3D-Druckes von Ton im Bereich der Architektur dar. Die Lehrveranstaltung wurde von Julian Jauk, Viktoria Sandor und Mathias Bank Stigsen am Institut für Gestaltung, Arbeitsgruppe Konstruktion und Gestaltung (Universität Innsbruck) geleitet.

Julian Jauk

• As part of a collaboration with the University of Innsbruck and Graz University of Technology, a column of 3D printed ceramic construction elements just over three meters tall was produced as part of the class "Methods of Materialization." A group of fifty students from the University of Innsbruck were involved in both designing and building ninety-seven modules. They were designed individually using point clouds to create structurally informed printing paths for manufacturing them using 3D printing. They were successfully produced using the software Termite, which was developed by the Institute for Architecture and Media of TU Graz especially for 3D printing in ceramics. The project explores the possibilities and challenges of 3D printing in ceramics in the field of architecture. The course was headed by Julian Jauk, Viktoria Sandor, and Mathias Bank Stigsen at the Institute of Design, in the Structure and Design working group (University of Innsbruck).

EinWERK Vortrag 2022: Kjetil Thorsen (Snøhetta)

Am 9. November 2022 hatte der Architekturzeichensaal 3 (AZ3) die Ehre, den Architekten Kjetil Thorsen nach 40 Jahren wieder im Zeichensaal zu begrüßen. Der Mitbegründer des renommierten Architekturbüros Snøhetta studierte in den 1980er-Jahren Architektur an der TU Graz. Im Rahmen des EinWERK-Vortrags sprach er über das zeitgenössische Design der neuen Bibliothek in Alexandria und die unzähligen Herausforderungen, die die Wiederbelebung der antiken Bibliothek mit sich brachte. Der Vortrag wurde in Zusammenarbeit mit KOJE1 (Universität Innsbruck) organisiert. Seit 2008 bereichern die „EinWERK"-Vorträge des AZ3 das Architekturstudium an der TU Graz. ArchitektInnen, darunter auch ehemalige AZ-Mitglieder, werden eingeladen, ein aktuelles oder ihnen am Herzen liegendes Projekt vorzustellen. Dabei können Konzept, Details und Prozesse geteilt und im Anschluss besprochen werden. Örtlich an der TU Graz sowie der Universität Innsbruck verankert, soll die Reihe Studierende aus den beiden Städten einen Einblick in die Architekturpraxis geben und einen Meinungsaustausch über das aktuelle Architekturgeschehen ermöglichen.

Dorotea Josić

© Paul Pacher

EinWERK Lecture 2022: Kjetil Thorsen (Snøhetta)

On November 9, 2022, the Architectural Drawing Studio (AZ3) had the honor of welcoming the architect Kjetil Thorsen back to the drawing studio after forty years. The co-founder of the renowned architecture firm Snøhetta had studied architecture at Graz University of Technology in the 1980s. As part of the "EinWERK" lecture, he spoke about the contemporary design behind the new library in Alexandria and the innumerable challenges associated with the restoration of the ancient library. The lecture was organized in conjunction with KOJE1 (University of Innsbruck). Since 2008, the "EinWERK" lectures, organized by AZ3, have been enriching architecture studies at TU Graz. Architects, including former AZ members, are invited to present a current project or one they are particularly passionate about. In doing so, the concept, details, and procedures are shared and later discussed. Embedded locally at TU Graz and the University of Innsbruck, the series is intended to give students in both cities insight into architectural practice(s) as well as to facilitate an exchange of ideas regarding current architectural developments.

© Institut Vierzehn/Anđela Marinković, TU Graz

Workshop „Claiming Graz“

Wer baut eigentlich für wen? Fast der gesamte Städtebau ist patriarchal geprägt. Dass Straßen vor Geh- und Fahrradwegen von Schnee befreit werden, dass Ampelschaltungen eine Behinderung von FußgängerInnen erzeugen, dass nicht alle Transportmittel des ÖPNV barrierefrei zugänglich sind oder dass Fahrradwege ‚unterwegs' enden, zeugt von einer Ignoranz und Benachteiligung vieler Menschen in der städtebaulichen Planung. Gemeinsam mit dem studentischen Kollektiv raum*f reagierte das Institut Vierzehn im Rahmen des CIS-Designmonats in Form eines zweitägigen Workshops auf diese Situation. Zum Einstieg in die Thematik wurde ein Spaziergang mit Kinderwagen, Rollstuhl und geschärftem Blick durch Graz unternommen, um Grenzen der Barrierefreiheit zu identifizieren. Um das Gesehene auch für andere sichtbar zu machen, wurden im Rahmen des Workshops Collagen erstellt, die im Haus der Architektur Graz und auf der Sommerausstellung der Technischen Universität Graz präsentiert wurden. Inhaltlich unterstützt wurde der Workshop von der Architektin und Stadtplanerin Gabu Heindl, der TU Graz-Absolventin Theresa Schleinitz und der stellvertretenden Leiterin des Instituts für Städtebau der TU Graz Eva Schwab. Am Workshop wirkten Naomi Baumann, Dorotea Josić, Martin Kern, Budour Khalil, Anđela Marinković, Lea Schuiki und Hannah Wohofsky mit.

Institut Vierzehn

• Who is actually building for whom? Almost all urban development is structured around patriarchy. The fact that streets are cleared of snow in front of paths for pedestrians and bicyclists, that traffic lights impede pedestrians, that not all means of public transport offer barrier-free access, or that cycling paths are terminated en route is evidence of ignorance and discrimination of numerous people in urban planning. Together with the student collective raum*f, Institut Vierzehn responded to this situation as part of the CIS Design Month in the form of a two-day workshop. In order to become better acquainted with the subject, a tour of Graz was conducted using baby strollers and wheelchairs, as well as with a discerning eye, to identify the limits of (barrier-free) accessibility. To make these observations visible to others, participants produced collages as part of the workshop, which were presented at the House of Architecture Graz and the summer exhibition of TU Graz. The workshop was further assisted by the architect and urban planner Gabu Heindl, TU Graz graduate Theresa Schleinitz, and Eva Schwab, deputy head of the Institute of Urbanism at TU Graz. Participants included Naomi Baumann, Dorotea Josić, Martin Kern, Budour Khalil, Anđela Marinković, Lea Schuiki, and Hannah Wohofsky.

Exhibitions

Graz Open Architecture 2023

Am 29. und 30. Juni wurde der Campus der Alten Technik wieder zum Austragungsort der öffentlichen Sommerausstellung „Graz Open Architecture“ und präsentierte in den Räumlichkeiten des Hauptgebäudes der Alten Technik, sowie jenen der Institute in der Lessingstraße einen Querschnitt durch das Ausbildungsangebot und die vielgestaltigen Lehrveranstaltungsergebnisse aus dem letzten Studienjahr.

Die Ausstellungen der 13 Institute richteten den inhaltlichen Fokus auf unterschiedliche Themenfelder der Disziplin. So sah man in diesem Jahr beeindruckende Modelle von Tragstrukturen für Hochbauten und große Spannweiten aus Holz (ITE), Entwürfe für gemeinschaftlich-öffentliche Räume in der Wüstenlandschaft des Emirats Sharjah (i a&l), Beispiele klimapositiver (Um-)Baukultur in der Münchner Goethestraße (Integral Architecture), atmosphärische Architekturvisualisierungen sowie Entwürfe eines „Handwerkappartements“ an der Schnittstelle von Architektur und Bildhauerei (IGL), strukturelle Figuren und Schlaglichter auf architektonische Nebensächlichkeiten (IRG), Erweiterungen der Traumstadt Tomaso Buzzis „La Scarzuola“ und eine ausführliche Dokumentation bereits zerstörter oder nachweislich gefährdeter Bauten der Grazer Schule (akk), sozial-ökologischeKonzepte zur Grazer Wohnraumproduktion und Vorschläge für ein Supergrätzl-Beteiligungskonzept in Ottakring (stdb), Holz(ge)schichten für ein bestehendes Grazer Siedlungsquartier (IAT/Holzbau), State of the Art-Ergebnisse der parametrischen Planung sowie digital gefertigtes Geschirr (IAM), Einblicke in den sorgsamen Umgang mit baulichem Bestand am Beispiel des Einfamilienhauses, Günther Domenigs Steinhaus oder der Erlebniswelt Schwarzl (EnDeBe), ästhetisch anspruchsvolle Designkonzepte für die Nutzung von Sonnenenergie (ige), zeitgenössische funktionsoffene Wohnprogrammatiken (i_w) oder aber die künstlerisch-wissenschaftliche Aufarbeitung des globalen Lithiumhandels und seinem Spannungsfeld zwischen Wirtschaftswachstum und Ausbeutung (IZK).

Beeindruckend war auch die Vielzahl an unterschiedlichen Architekturmodellen, die im Rahmen der „270 Days of Architecture“ am KOEN entstanden waren und auf raumhohen Regalen in einem der Korridore des Hauptgebäudes dicht aneinander zur Schau gestellt wurden. Teil der KOEN-Ausstellung waren auch die Modellbauprojekte des Wettbewerbs „Erinnerung bauen: Pionierinnen der TU Graz,“ in dem Studierende in Kooperation mit dem Alumni Frauennetzwerk der TU Graz Denkmäler entwarfen, die den ersten Absolventinnen der TU Graz gewidmet waren. Feierlich verliehen wurden die Preise durch Dekanin Petra Petersson und Vizerektor Horst Bischof. Der Campuspark war auch 2023 wieder der Schauplatz der alljährlichen Verleihung des Skizzenbuchpreises,

© GAM.Lab, TU Graz

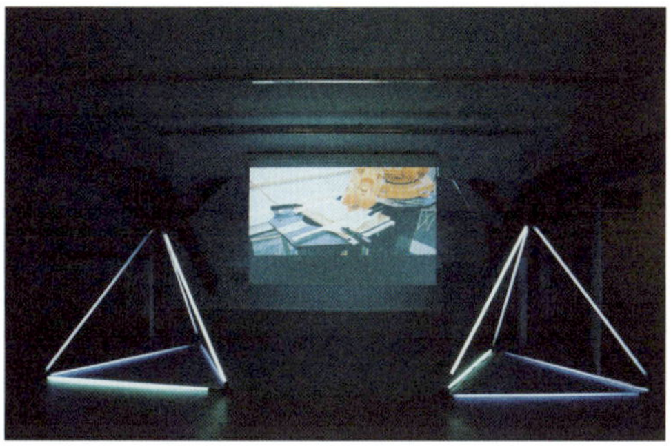

der von Dekanin und KOEN-Leiterin Petra Petersson persönlich überreicht wurde. Ausführliche Informationen zu den Preisverleihungen sind auf den Seiten 218–219 nachzulesen.

Das Rahmenprogramm von „Graz Open Architecture" wurde am Freitagvormittag mit einem Modellbauworkshop für SchülerInnen fortgesetzt. Das vom Institut Vierzehn betreute Kooperationsformat versammelte SchülerInnen der HTL-Zeltweg sowie der Ortweinschule Graz, und bot den SchülerInnen die Möglichkeit, Keramikmodelle zu entwerfen und eigenhändig zu gießen.

Zu den interessierten BesucherInnen der Sommerausstellung zählten auch Rektor Harald Kainz, Vizerektor Horst Bischof sowie die Universitätsrat-Mitglieder Barbara Steiner und Ulrike Farnik.

Petra Eckhard

• On June 29 and 30, the Alte Technik campus was once again host to the public summer exhibition "Graz Open Architecture". It showcased a cross-section of the program and multifaceted course results from the past academic year in the spaces of the main building of Alte Technik as well as those of the institutes in Lessingstraße.

The exhibitions staged by the thirteen institutes focused on different thematic aspects of the field. Thus, this year visitors were able to view impressive models of load-bearing structures for high-rise buildings and large span widths made of timber (ITE), designs for communal public spaces situated in the desert landscape of the Emirate of Sharjah (i a&l), examples of climate-positive (re)building practice in Munich's Goethestraße (Integral Architecture), atmospheric architectural visualizations and designs for a "tradespeople's flat" at the interface of architecture and sculpture (IGL), structural figures and spotlights on architectural trivialities (IRG), extensions of Tomaso Buzzi's dream city "La Scarzuola" and a detailed documentation of previously destroyed or verifiably endangered buildings of the Graz School (akk), socio-ecological concepts for housing production in Graz and proposals for a supergrätzl participatory concept in Ottakring (stdb), "Holz(ge)schichten" (wood hi/stories) for an existing settlement quarter in Graz (IAT/Timber Engineering), state-of-the-art results of parametric planning and digitally manufactured tableware (IAM), insights into the gentle treatment of existing buildings using the example of the single-family house typology, Günther Domenig's Steinhaus or the Erlebniswelt Schwarzl (EnDeBe), aesthetically demanding design concepts for the use of solar energy (ige), contemporary, functionally open residential living programs (i_w), and the artistically and scientifically based examination of the global lithium trade and its field of tension between economic growth and exploitation (IZK).

The many different architectural models created at KOEN as part of the "270 Days of Architecture" were equally impressive and were displayed close together on floor-to-ceiling shelves in one of the corridors of the main building. Another part of the KOEN display featured the model building projects from the competition "Building Remembrance: Female Pioneers of TU Graz," in which students, in cooperation with the alumni women's network of TU Graz, designed monuments dedicated to the first female graduates of TU Graz. The prizes were ceremonially awarded by Dean Petra Petersson and Vice-Rector Horst Bischof. As in previous years, the campus park served as the venue for the annual award ceremony of the Sketchbook Prize, which was personally presented by Dean and KOEN Director Petra Petersson. For more detailed information regarding the award ceremonies, please refer to pages 218–219.

The accompanying program of „Graz Open Architecture" continued on Friday morning with a model-building workshop for students. This cooperative format, supervised by Institut Vierzehn, brought together pupils from the HTL-Zeltweg and the Ortweinschule Graz, providing them with the opportunity to design ceramic models and cast them using their own hands.

Among the interested visitors to the summer exhibition were Rector Harald Kainz, Vice-Rector Horst Bischof, and University Council members Barbara Steiner and Ulrike Farnik.

Graz Open Architecture © GAM.Lab, TU Graz

Annenstrasse 53, Studierendenausstellungen

Der unabhängige Ausstellungsraum Annenstrasse 53, beherbergte 2023 verschiedene Ausstellungen, die am Institut für Zeitgenössische Kunst (IZK) entwickelt wurden. In der Ausstellung „Time Crystals, Rock, Stone and Mud", die im Januar 2023 stattfand, erforschten die Studierenden die Begriffe „site" und „non-site" und inwiefern Land Art die Vorstellung von Landschaft radikal verändert und die Grenzen bildhauerischer Praxis gesprengt hat. In ihren Arbeiten untersuchten sie diese Konzepte im Zusammenhang mit Robert Smithsons Auffassung von Zeit („Time Crystals") und reflektierten die Prozesse, durch die Kunst Akkumulation und Reduktion veranschaulicht und vermittelt. Dabei gingen sie der Frage nach, wie ein „Nichtort" (*non-site*) durch Architektur als Konkretisierung, als räumliche Praxis, zu einem „Ort" (*site*) werden kann. (Teilnehmende Studierende: Ada Basanović, Erna Costović, Inas Dizdarević, Alexia Eberl, Ariana Imsirović, Anastasiia Andriivna Kutsova, Joana Inês Saldanha Loureiro, Pedro Paes Morais, Julia Oberdieck, Guillermo José Ramirez Regolf, Stefan Schenkel, Ksenija Todorović, Sara Travar, Johanna Vogel)

Die Ausstellung „How Does One Get to Own a Mountain" fand ebenfalls im Januar 2023 statt. Im Rahmen des gleichnamigen Kurses, der von Rose-Anne Gush, Anousheh Kehar und Philipp Sattler geleitet wurde, war sie das Ergebnis eines kollaborativen Entwicklungsprozesses kollektiver Rechercheformate und künstlerischer Ausdrucksformen. Im Rahmen des Kurses fand auch eine Exkursion auf die Koralpe statt, bei der ein Bergwerkstollen erkundet wurde. Studierende analysierten dabei die gesellschaftlichen und territorialen Umwälzungen, die der Bergbau und insbesondere der Lithiumabbau für diesen Ort und die umliegenden Städte mit sich gebracht hat. Die Studierenden setzten sich mit der Definition von „primitiver Akkumulation" auseinander, welches sich von der Bergbaugeschichte des Mittelalters bis in die heutige Zeit erstreckt. Berücksichtigt wurde dabei auch die Politik des Green New Deals mit seinen Vorschlägen für eine kohlenstofffreie bzw. -arme Zukunft und den damit einhergehenden Veränderungen in Stadt und Land. Durch die Auseinandersetzung mit dem Gelände und künstlerischen Praktiken entwickelten die Studierenden einen investigativen Ansatz, um Spuren der Bergbaugeschichte in der Region und ihre Darstellungen zu erfassen. Im Mittelpunkt der Ausstellung standen die Auswirkungen des Lithium-Bergbau auf Körper und auf urbane und natürliche Landschaften. (Ein Gemeinschaftsprojekt von Žiljka Fajfar, Lena Marie Pucher, Nadica Stanojevic, Natalia Vasadze, Marie Line Furland, Luz Meliza Garcia Vittini, Nicole Sarafijanovic, Catherina Stacher, Tapio Pietari Tuomi, Ana-Mary Vadlja, Lisa-Marie Wagenthaler, Bettina Zengerer).

Die Ausstellung „When the Dust Unsettles", die im Juni 2023 stattfand, knüpfte an die Arbeit im Lithiumstollen im Koralmgebirge an und präsentierte Positionen und Arbeiten von Studierenden, die den Fragen nachgingen, wie Lithium in Beziehungen von Wirtschaftswachstum und wachsender Ungerechtigkeit verwickelt ist sowie welche Vorstellungen dem Umgang mit der Natur als Rohstoff entgegenstehen. Die Ausstellung umfasste Arbeiten von Momo Francesca Canzian Ferrari Trecate, Julia Castela Fernandez, Ahmad Darkhabani, Željka Fajfar, Fabian Fazio, Ana Garcia Marchena, Katharina Klug, Marry-Ann Lackner, Anna Schoissengeyer, Catherina Stacher, Alina Tamegger und Loriana Tomescu.

„Time Crystals, Rock, Stone and Mud" © IZK, TU Graz

Annenstrasse 53, Student Exhibitions

In 2023, the independent exhibition space Annenstrasse 53, housed various shows developed at the Institute of Contemporary Art (IZK). In "Time Crystals, Rock, Stone and Mud", held in January 2023, students explored the ideas of "site" and "non-site," considering how Land Art had radically changed the idea of landscape, having disrupted the limits of sculptural practice. The students' works investigated these concepts together with Robert Smithson's understanding of time ("Time Crystals") and reflected on the processes through which art visualizes and narrates accumulation and extraction. They asked how a "non-site" becomes a "site" through architecture as concretization, as a spatial practice. Participating students: Ada Basanović, Erna Costović, Inas Dizdarević, Alexia Eberl, Ariana Imsirović, Anastasiia Andriivna Kutsova, Joana Inês Saldanha Loureiro, Pedro Paes Morais, Julia Oberdieck, Guillermo José Ramirez Regolf, Stefan Schenkel, Ksenija Todorović, Sara Travar, Johanna Vogel.

The exhibition "How Does One Get to Own a Mountain" also took place in January 2023. Produced within a course of the same title, convened by Rose-Anne Gush, Anousheh Kehar, and Philipp Sattler, the exhibition was the result of a collaborative process of developing collective research formats and forms of artistic expression, including an excursion to the Koralpe mountain range to explore the site of a lithium tunnel. Students looked at the societal and spatial transformations that mining has brought to this site and the surrounding towns and cities. In their work, they investigated the meaning of "primitive accumulation" from the mining history of the Middle Ages to the present day, in light of the politics of the Green New Deal with its proposals for non- or low-carbon futures and the resulting urban and rural transformations. Through immersion in the site and artistic practices, students formulated an investigative approach to the traces of mining history in the region and the related representations. The topic of lithium mining and its impact on bodies and urban and natural landscapes was at the core of this exhibition. A collective project by Žiljka Fajfar, Lena Marie Pucher, Nadica Stanojevic, Natalia Vasadze, Marie Line Furland, Luz Meliza Garcia Vittini, Nicole Sarafijanovic, Catherina Stacher, Tapio Pietari Tuomi, Ana-Mary Vadlja, Lisa-Marie Wagenthaler, Bettina Zengerer.

The exhibition "When the Dust Unsettles," which took place during June 2023, continued the work on the lithium tunnel in the Koralm mountain range and presented positions and works by students who had investigated how lithium is entangled in relations that foster economic growth and growing inequality, as well as notions that counter the treatment of nature as a raw material. The exhibition included works by Momo Francesca Canzian Ferrari Trecate, Julia Castela Fernandez, Ahmad Darkhabani, Željka Fajfar, Fabian Fazio, Ana Garcia Marchena, Katharina Klug, Marry-Ann Lackner, Anna Schoissengeyer, Catherina Stacher, Alina Tamegger, and Loriana Tomescu.

Milica Tomić, Rose-Anne Gush, Anousheh Kehar, Philipp Sattler

„When the Dust Unsettles" © IZK, TU Graz

Haus des Werkzeugs

Zwölf Figuren
über — auf keinen Fall für — zwölf Werkzeuge.
Jedes Werkzeug hat Struktur und Fügung, und damit Gestalt, Charakter und einen Ausdruck.
Wir können sie beschreiben,
auch ohne ihre Nützlichkeiten.
Aus Strukturen werden Figuren.
Als Strukturelle Figuren
entwickeln sie ihre eigene Realität.
Ein Innen oder Außen gibt es nicht.
Es sind Häuser ohne Hülle.

Im Rahmen des steirischen herbst 2023 wurden in der alten Rösselmühle in Graz zwölf Figuren ausgestellt. Für ein halbes Jahr haben sich die Studierenden des Instituts für Raumgestaltung (IRG) in die Werkstatt eingeschlossen und heraus kam das Haus des Werkzeugs. Zu sehen waren die versetzte Reibung der Raspel (Patrizia Posch und Julia Schalk), der schlagbaumartige Tischlerhammer (Benedikt Probstmeier und Jakob Rescher), die Keile des Doppelhobels (Laura Huber und Lea Hudetz), die gestoppte Bewegung der Gestellsäge (Marchet Jangulbaewa und Lukas Livesu), die gegenseitige Sperrung des Streichmaß (Naomi Baumann und Jakob Übeleis), die Passivität der Zwinge (Lorenz Kerschensteiner und Matej Rozman), die Verjüngung vom Quadrat ins Runde des Schabhobels (Tamara Faber und Lukas Thurner), die Arbeit gegen den Tempel im Schnitzeisen (Daniela Tubin und Milena Ždrnja), das spitze Gewicht des Grundhobels (Florian Berger und Hannah Gilly), die Zentralität im Exzentrischen der Bohrwinde (Florentina Bachmann und Karla Matweber), das schattenhafte Zeichnen der Feinsäge (Umut Can) und das heimliche Zwingen des Körpers durch die Gratsäge (Alexander Postl und Kushtrim Vishi). Die Ausstellung fand in Kooperation mit dem steirischen herbst und APORON 21, Igor Petković statt.

Alex Lehnerer

© IRG, TU Graz

House of the Tool

Twelve figures
about—by no means for—twelve tools.
Each tool has structure and construction,
and hence form, character, and expression.
We can describe them,
even without their utility.
Structures become figures.
As Structural Figures,
they develop their own reality.
They have no inside or outside.
They are buildings without a covering.

As part of steirischer herbst 2023, twelve sculptures were exhibited in the Rösselmühle in Graz. Students from the Institute of Spatial Design (IRG) locked themselves in the workshop, and the result was the House of the Tool. The displaced attrition of the rasp (Patrizia Posch and Julia Schalk), the boom-barrier-like carpenter's hammer (Benedikt Probstmeier and Jakob Rescher), the wedges of the smoothing plane (Laura Huber and Lea Hudetz), the reciprocal locking of the marking gauge (Naomi Baumann and Jakob Übeleis), the passivity of the clamp (Lorenz Kerschensteiner and Matej Rozman), the tapering of square into round of the spokeshave (Tamara Faber and Lukas Thurner), working "against the temple with the chisel" (Daniela Tubin and Milena Ždrnja), the pointed weight of the router plane (Florian Berger and Hannah Gilly), the centrality in the eccentric of the drill brace (Florentina Bachmann and Karla Matweber), the shadowy drawing of the razor saw (Umut Can), and the uncanny forcing of the volume by the stair saw (Alexander Postl and Kushtrim Vishi). The exhibition was held in cooperation with steirischer herbst and APORON 21, Igor Petkovic.

Grazer Schule. Stil & Wert des Phänomens

Eindrucksvolle Kubaturen, facettenreiche Fassaden oder raffinierte Details – die Werke der „Grazer Schule" prägen bis heute das Bild der steirischen Landeshauptstadt. Dennoch sind viele dieser Bauten vom Abriss bedroht. In der im HDA Graz (23.03.–28.05.2023) und der ZT-Kammer Salzburg (10.11.–15.12.2023) gezeigten Ausstellung „Grazer Schule. Stil und Wert des Phänomens" widmeten sich Studierende des Instituts für Architekturtheorie, Kunst- und Kulturwissenschaften (akk) dem bedeutenden architektonischen Erbe. Gezeigt wurden neun ausgewählte Projekte. Zu diesen zählten neben dem bereits zerstörten Haus Fuchs (Heinz Wondra) oder dem kurz vor dem Abbruch befindlichen WIFI Werkstättenbau (Christine & Walther Kordon) auch das Studentenwohnheim Wienerstraße (Klaus Kada), das Institut für Biochemie & Biotechnologie (Michael Szyszkowitz & Karla Kowalski), die Wohnanlage Rettenbach (Bernhard Hafner), das Haus Rosegger (Konrad Frey), die Erweiterung Mathematik & Geodäsie (Günther Domenig & Hermann Eisenköck), die Wohnanlage Carl-Spitzweg-Gasse (Volker Giencke) sowie die Raiffeisenkasse Andritz (Team A). Veranschaulicht wurden diese Gebäude in Form von Originalplänen, Fotos und von den Studierenden angefertigten Modellen, um die raffinierten Details, den mehrschichtigen Fassadenaufbau und die plastischen Kubaturen herauszuarbeiten und den oft wenig bekannten Gebäuden neue Wertschätzung zukommen zu lassen.

Die Ausstellung wurde im Rahmen des Vertiefungsmoduls „Architekturkommunikation" im WS 2022/23 (Leitung: Anselm Wagner, Margareth Otti-Wagner) erarbeitet. Beteiligte Studierende: Lara Aichholzer, Angelika Alberer, Annalena Arminger, Marius Birnbreier, Gabriel Deinhammer, Esther Dullnigg, Julian Lança Gil, Kim Melissa Luu, Salim M'Barki, Clara Neuhold, Kerstin Neuhold, Katharina Platzer, Natalie Resch, Florentine Rom, Anna Söllinger, Sandra Sulzer, Katharina Weigl

Anselm Wagner

© The Schubidu Quartet, HDA

Graz School: Style & Value of a Phenomenon

Impressive cubatures, multifaceted façades, and refined details—the works of the Graz School define the image of the Styrian state capital even today. Nevertheless, many of these buildings are at risk of demolition. In the exhibition "Graz School: Style & Value of a Phenomenon," shown at the HDA Graz (March 23–May 28, 2023) and ZT-Kammer Salzburg (November 10–December 15, 2023), students of the Institute of Architectural Theory, Art History and Cultural Studies (akk) dedicated themselves to this important architectural legacy. Nine selected projects were shown. These included the Fuchs House (Heinz Wondra), which has already been destroyed; the WIFI workshop building (Christine & Walther Kordon) and the student dormitory on Wienerstrasse (Klaus Kada), which are about to be demolished; the Institute for Biochemistry & Biotechnology (Michael Szyszkowitz & Karla Kowalski); the Rettenbach apartment building (Bernhard Hafner); the Rosegger House (Konrad Frey); mathematics & geodesy extension (Günther Domenig & Hermann Eisenköck); the Carl-Spitzweg-Gasse residential complex (Volker Giencke); and the Andritz branch of the Raiffeisenbank (Team A). These buildings were presented in the form of original plans, photographs, and models made by the students in order to work out their refined details; they multilayered façades and their sculptural cubatures and gain a new appreciation of these frequently little-known buildings.

The exhibition was worked out as part of the specialization module "Architectural Communication" in the winter semester 2022/23 (leaders: Anselm Wagner, Margareth Otti-Wagner). Participating students: Lara Aichholzer, Angelika Alberer, Annalena Arminger, Marius Birnbreier, Gabriel Deinhammer, Esther Dullnigg, Julian Lança Gil, Kim Melissa Luu, Salim M'Barki, Clara Neuhold, Kerstin Neuhold, Katharina Platzer, Natalie Resch, Florentine Rom, Anna Söllinger, Sandra Sulzer, Katharina Weigl

© Design Forum

Architektur aus Licht und Schatten

Im Rahmen der Ausstellung „Licht Punkt Strich“, die von 26. Januar 2023 bis 24. Februar 2023 im Designforum Steiermark stattfand, präsentierten Studierende des Instituts für Architektur und Medien (IAM) die entstandenen Arbeiten des Vertiefungsfaches zum Thema „Architektur aus Licht und Schatten“.

Als Mittel zur Transformation von Raum dienten analoge Lichtquellen, digitale Projektionen und gezielt eingesetzte Materialien. Ein Ziel war die Kombination analoger Lichtquellen und digitaler Medien mit unterschiedlichen Materialien im Raumkontext des Designforums Graz.

Durch den Einsatz von State-of-the-Art Video Projektionen und Computational Design Tools wurden die transformierten Räume selbst zu Ausstellungsobjekten. Die Lehrveranstaltung unter der Leitung von Adam Sebestyen (IAM) wurde unterstützt und betreut von dem Grazer Film- und Projektions-KünstlerInnenkollektiv OchoReSotto sowie von Birgit Schulz und Alex Krug vom LightLab am Institut für Raumgestaltung (IRG, TU Graz).

Studierende: Annes Begovic, Ajla Bukvarević, Marie Lutgarde Goossens, Daniel Gradwohl, Christina Hain, Amina Huskic, Gregor Kaiser, Matea Kelava, Nikolas Keuschnig, Barbara Maria Langmann, Jasmin Monschein, Britta Nader, Valentina Ofner, Lena Ruisz, Sarah Schirz, Esra Sedik

Birgit Schulz, Adam Sebestyen

Architecture from Light and Shadow

In the exhibition “Licht Punkt Strich,” held from January 26 to February 24, 2023, at the Designforum Steiermark, students of the Institute of Architecture and Media (IAM) presented their works from the specialization module on the theme “Architecture from Light and Shadow.” Space was transformed by means of analog light sources, digital projections, and deliberately employed materials. One goal was combining analog light sources and digital media with different materials in the spatial context of the Designforum Graz. Through the use of state-of-the-art video projections and computational design tools, the transformed spaces became exhibition objects in their own right. The course headed by Adam Sebestyen (IAM, TU Graz) was supported and supervised by the Graz collective of film and projection artists OchoReSotto and by Birgit Schulz and Alex Krug from the LightLab at the Institute of Spatial Design (IRG, TU Graz).

Students: Annes Begovic, Ajla Bukvarević, Marie Lutgarde Goossens, Daniel Gradwohl, Christina Hain, Amina Huskic, Gregor Kaiser, Matea Kelava, Nikolas Keuschnig, Barbara Maria Langmann, Jasmin Monschein, Britta Nader, Valentina Ofner, Lena Ruisz, Sarah Schirz, Esra Sedik

MyCera – MaterialDistrict

Die dem Institut für Architektur und Medien (IAM) zugehörige Forschungsgruppe ShapeLab wurde eingeladen, ihre Arbeit auf der MaterialDistrict Utrecht im Februar 2023 zu präsentieren. Auf der alljährlich in den Niederlanden stattfindenden Messe finden zahlreiche Ausstellungen sowie eine angesehene Vortragsreihe statt, bei der ArchitektInnen, WissenschaftlerInnen, DesignerInnen, HerstellerInnen und Start-ups ihre innovativen Entwicklungen der Öffentlichkeit vorstellen. Die Ausstellung zeigte eine Reihe von Designobjekten sowie ziegelsteinähnliche Elemente aus MyCera, wobei zwei verschiedene Impfmethoden (Flüssigimpfung und kornbasierte Impfung) vorgestellt wurden. Der Verbundwerkstoff besteht aus Ton, Holzsägemehl und Myzel, die als gezielt angeordnete Faserarmierung fungieren. Dieser innovative Ansatz verbessert die statischen Fähigkeiten der im 3D-Druckverfahren hergestellten ungebrannten Tonelemente und ermöglicht das Bioverschweißen bereits gebrannter Tonelemente nach dem Zusammenbau. Diese interdisziplinäre Forschung vereint digitale Fertigungstechniken mit dem Wachstum von Myzelien und schafft so leistungsfähige und vielseitige Bauelemente. Die Objekte veranschaulichten eine Reihe von Möglichkeiten, von gänzlich organischen Strukturen bis hin zu hybriden Kreationen aus Ton und Myzel. Ziel dieser Ausstellung war es, das Potenzial natürlicher, auf Wachstum basierender Verbindungen zu verdeutlichen. Ein Vortrag der IAM-Mitglieder Hana Vašatko, Lukas Gosch und Julian Jauk vermittelte zusätzlich einen tieferen Einblick in die Entwicklung und die Anwendungsmöglichkeiten dieser neuartigen Materialien. ShapeLab-Team: Hana Vašatko, Lukas Gosch, Julian Jauk und Milena Stavrić.

© IAM, TU Graz

• The research group ShapeLab, affiliated with the Institute of Architecture and Media (IAM), was invited to showcase their work at the MaterialDistrict Utrecht in February 2023. The annual event organized in the Netherlands hosts numerous exhibitions and an esteemed lecture series featuring architects, scientists, designers, manufacturers, and start-ups who present their innovative advancements to the public. The exhibition presented a series of design objects as well as brick-like elements created using MyCera, highlighting two distinct inoculation methods (liquid inoculation and grain-based inoculation). The composite material consists of clay, wood sawdust, and mycelium, leveraged as strategically positioned fiber reinforcement. This innovative approach enhances the structural capabilities of unfired clay elements produced using 3D printing and enables the bio-welding of fired clay elements after assembly. This interdisciplinary research merges digital fabrication techniques with mycelial growth, resulting in the creation of high-performance and versatile building components. The objects showcased a range of possibilities, from fully organic structures to hybrid creations combining clay and mycelium. The exhibition aimed to emphasize the potential of natural growth-based connections. Additionally, a lecture by IAM members Hana Vašatko, Lukas Gosch, and Julian Jauk provided a more in-depth understanding of the research, offering further insights into the development and potential applications of these novel materials. ShapeLab team: Hana Vašatko, Lukas Gosch, Julian Jauk, and Milena Stavrić.

Hana Vašatko

Installation view: "meta.space/OÖLKG/Location: Francisco Carolinum" © Grasser-Parger.

Raumskulptur „Open Architectures"

Die von Alexander Grasser und Alexandra Parger am Institut für Architektur und Medien (IAM) konzipierte Raumskulptur „Open Architectures" wurde als Auftragsarbeit für die OÖLKG im Rahmen der von Markus Reindl und Fabian Müller-Nittel kuratierten Gruppenausstellung „Meta.Space – Raumvisionen" im Museum Francisco Carolinum in Linz realisiert. Die Ausstellung präsentierte im Zeitraum zwischen 01. September 2022 und 08. Januar 2023 diverse Arbeiten von mehr als 60 internationalen KünstlerInnen, die sich mit dem Thema Raum im Allgemeinen und im Kontext des Metaverse auseinandersetzten. Für den Ausstellungsbeitrag entwickelten Alexander und Alexandra eine Software, die es der Öffentlichkeit ermöglichte, aktiv am Entwurfsprozess der Raumskulptur teilzunehmen. Die benutzerfreundliche Anwendung war in eine Webseite integriert und ermöglichte in Echtzeit, in einer virtuellen Umgebung, die dem tatsächlichen Ausstellungsraum nachempfunden war, an der Gestaltung der Raumskulptur mitzuwirken. Über 500 Teilnehmende engagierten sich auf dieser kollaborativen Entwurfsplattform, auf der mehr als 50 „Community Structures" entstanden, die automatisch erfasst und dokumentiert wurden. Aus dieser vielfältigen Auswahl an Entwürfen wählten wir eine Community Structure aus, die wir als physische Raumskulptur im Francisco Carolinum Museum realisierten. Zusätzlich wurden die digitalen Entwürfe der nicht realisierten Strukturen in Form eines Videos neben der physischen greifbaren Community Structure ausgestellt.

Alexander Grasser-Parger

Spatial Sculpture "Open Architectures"

The spatial sculpture "Open Architectures" by Alexander Grasser and Alexandra Parger from the Institute of Architecture and Media (IAM, TU Graz) was commissioned for the OÖLKG as part of the group exhibition "Meta.Space — Visions of Space", curated by Markus Reindl and Fabian Müller-Nittel at the museum Francisco Carolinum in Linz. The exhibition was on display from September 1, 2022, to January 8, 2023, and showcased diverse works from more than sixty international artists who engaged with the concept of space in general and space within the context of the metaverse. Alexander Grasser and Alexandra Parger's contribution to this exhibition addressed the creation of space as a collective project and proposed a spatial sculpture that was co-created publicly in the metaverse and realized as a physical prototype on a 1:1 scale in the museum. Software was specifically developed for this project that allowed the public to actively participate in the joint design process. The user-friendly application was integrated into a website and offered the opportunity to participate in the design of the spatial sculpture. This took place in real-time within a virtual environment that was modeled after the actual exhibition space. More than 500 participants engaged with this collaborative design platform, on which over fifty community structures were co-created, automatically recorded, and documented. Grasser and Parger selected one Community Structure that was realized as a physical spatial sculpture at the Francisco Carolinum. In addition, the digital designs of the structures that were not realized were displayed as a video alongside the tangible physical Community Structure.

© Simon Oberhofer

Colors

Seit jeher ist Farbe ein wichtiges Ausdrucksmittel der Architektur. Durch das Konzept der universellen weißen Box hat sie allerdings an Bedeutung verloren. Sowohl in der architektonischen Praxis als auch in der Lehre ist uns die Sensibilität für Farbe als auch das Wissen um deren Einsatz abhandengekommen. Daher ist es ein Anliegen von Diskursiv, einem Verein zur Architekturforschung, die Farbe ins Zentrum ihres Diskurses zu stellen. Die Ausstellung, die von 12. bis 28. Januar 2023 im Forum Stadtpark gezeigt wurde, versammelte verschiedene Positionen, Ansätze und Arbeitsweisen von Architekturschaffenden zur Thematik „Farben".

Nuno Melo Sousas Zeichnungen wurden auf einem sieben Meter langem Tisch präsentiert. Im Kontrast zu seiner monochromen Architektur arbeitet er mit Buntstiften an Details und Konzepten. Die Skulptur von Michael Reindel hinterfragte Materialen und deren Farben im Modellbau. Luca Tommassis „Lobmys" thematisierte die Frage, wie Architektur von den Merkmalen von Farben lernen kann. Nikola Hergovich beschäftigte sich mit dem Fotografieren von anonymen Architekturen und zeigte acht Häuser an einem Strand mit acht verschiedenfarbigen Dächern. Das studentische Kollektiv Institut Vierzehn dokumentierte ihre Arbeit „Wir malen uns einen Raum", in der einem Leerstand durch experimentellen Umgang mit Farbe neues Leben eingehaucht wurde. An dem Konzept der Ausstellung wirkten Katharina Hohenwarter, Michael Hafner, Julian Brües, und Philipp Sternath mit.

Julian Brües

• Color has always been an important means of expression in architecture. It has, however, lost significance as a result of the concept of the universal white box. Both the practice and teaching of architecture have lost sensitivity to color and knowledge about its use. Diskursiv, an association for architectural research, is therefore making color the center of its discourse. The exhibition, which was shown at the Forum Stadtpark from January 12 to 28, 2023, brought together architects' varied positions, approaches and working methods on the theme "Colors."

Nuno Melo Sousa's drawings were presented on a table seven meters long. In contrast to his monochrome architecture, he works with colored pencils for details and concepts. The sculpture of Michael Reindel asked questions about materials and their colors in model building. Luca Tommassi's *Lobmys* addressed the issue of how architecture can learn from the qualities of colors. Nikola Hergovich photographed anonymous architecture and presented eight buildings on a beach with roofs in eight different colors. The student collective Institut Vierzehn documented their work "We are painting ourselves a room," which used color to breathe new life into an experimental approach to vacant buildings. Katharina Hohenwarter, Michael Hafner, Julian Brües, and Philipp Sternath helped conceive the exhibition.

HOW ON EARTH?!

Ausstellung anlässlich des
59. Oktobersalons, Belgrad Biennale
20. Oktober – 4. Dezember 2022

„Wer verdient an der Kunst und wer profitiert wirklich von ihr?“, fragte Raša Todosijević 1975 in seinem „Edinburgh Statement“, das von Milica Tomić in einer Dialog-Performance zur Eröffnung des 59. Oktobersalons 2022 in Belgrad neu interpretiert wurde. Ihre Einzelausstellung (ko-kuratiert von Jelena Vesić) erforscht die materiellen Auswirkungen einer Ideologie der Normalität im Kontext der Diskussion über zeitgenössische Kunst. Dabei geht es um die Institutionen und den Markt, die Abschaffung des Gemeineigentums und die Etablierung eines Kunstmarktes. Die Raum- und Videoinstallationen verwenden Fragmente reflektierender Erinnerung, die in einer Montage von Bildern und Worten, Haltungen und Positionen verankert und wieder freigesetzt werden, um die lokale zeitgenössische Kunstszene im ersten Jahrzehnt des Jahres 2000 darzustellen. Tomić konzentriert sich auf die Ruhe vor dem Sturm, die den Auftakt eines erbitterten, fortwährenden Konflikts zwischen der zeitgenössischen Kunst und der Kulturbranche einläutete, der die zeitgenössischen Kunstinstitutionen bis heute systematisch in Beschlag nimmt. Dabei untersucht sie die kulturpolitischen Kämpfe und Fantasien einer zukünftigen Gesellschaft in einer Zeit, in der die anti-jugoslawischen Kriege formell beendet, und von der globalen Politik- und Finanzkrise 2008 abgelöst wurden.

„HOW ON EARTH!?“ zeigt Arbeiten von Abdelrahman Elbashir, Amel Bešlagić, Olga Jevrić, Anousheh Kehar, Stevan Labudović, Milica Lopičić, Philipp Sattler und Branimir Stojanović; Zusammenarbeit mit Rosa El-Hassan und Branko Dimitrijevic. Grafikdesign: Žiga Testen. Ausstellungsarchitektur: Kuehn Malvezzi Architects.

• Exhibition within the 59th October Salon, Belgrade Biennale
October 20 – December 4, 2022

“Who makes a profit from art, and who gains from it honestly?” asked Raša Todosijević in his 1975 Edinburgh Statement, which was reinvented by Milica Tomić through a dialogue-performance at the opening of the 59th October Salon in 2022 in Belgrade. Her solo exhibition (co-curated with Jelena Vesić) investigates the material effects of the ideology of normality in the context of the discussion on contemporary art. It deals with the institutions and the market, the abolition of public property and the establishment of an art market. The spatial and video installations use fragments of reflective memory—fastened and unfastened in the montage of images and words, attitudes, and positions—to portray the local contemporary art scene in the first decade after 2000. Tomić focuses on the lull before the storm that heralded the beginning of a fierce ongoing struggle between contemporary art and cultural industries that was and still is an ongoing systemic occupation of contemporary art institutions. It investigates cultural-political struggles and fantasies of a society yet to come, during a period in which anti-Yugoslav wars had formally ended, succeeded by the global financial and political crisis of 2008.

“HOW ON EARTH!?” includes works by Abdelrahman Elbashir, Amel Bešlagić, Olga Jevrić, Anousheh Kehar, Stevan Labudović, Milica Lopičić, Philipp Sattler, and Branimir Stojanović; in collaboration with Rosa El-Hassan and Branko Dimitrijevic. Graphic design: Žiga Testen. Exhibition architecture: Kuehn Malvezzi Architects.

Milica Tomić, Jelena Vesić

© IZK, TU Graz

Four Faces of Omarska

Ausstellung im Rahmen des 6. Berliner Herbstsalons 2023 LOST – YOU GO SLAVIA
Berlin 28. September – 10. Dezember
(zurückgezogen am 18. Oktober 2023)

„Four Faces of Omarska" ist eine investigative Gedenkpraxis und Plattform, die sich mit den Strategien der Gedenkstättenproduktion auf der Grundlage von Erfahrungen und Kenntnissen beschäftigt, die unterjocht, abgewiesen und aus dem öffentlichen Gedächtnis sowie der öffentlichen Geschichte ausgeschlossen wurden. Das von Milica Tomić, Anousheh Kehar, Philipp Sattler, Dubravka Sekulić, Amel Beslagić und Abdelrahman Elbashir erarbeitete Konzept untersucht, wie ein Ort der Gräueltaten zu einem Ort des Lernens auf der Grundlage von Solidarität und Gleichberechtigung wird. Der Titel leitet sich aus den vier konstitutiven Ebenen der Geschichte des Bergbaukomplexes Omarska im Nordwesten Bosniens und Herzegowinas ab. Er bezieht sich auf Bereiche wie aktivistische Interventionen, Geisteswissenschaften, Kunst, Architektur und die Kritik an einer Politik der Wissenschaft und Traumabewältigung in Bosnien und Herzegowina. Mithilfe einer öffentlichen Montage wird die Komplexität der ineinander greifenden Schichten traumatischer Geschichten, Ausbeutung und anhaltender Gewalt untersucht und einander gegenübergestellt.

Die neueste Ausgabe von „Four Faces of Omarska", die im 6. Berliner Herbstsalon im Gorki Theater ihre Premiere feierte, rückt die ethnisch-gesellschaftliche Spaltung nach dem Genozid in den Mittelpunkt und zeigt, wie das politische Erbe eines Krieges durch globale wirtschaftliche Investitionen aufrechterhalten wird. Untersucht wurden die Architektur und die noch unerforschten neuartigen Formen von Konzentrations- und Kriegsgefangenenlagern, die mit Beginn des Krieges in Jugoslawien entstanden und durch neue Formen der Verstädterung, Wirtschaft und Sozialisierung in der Nachkriegszeit fortbestehen. In dieser neuen Ausgabe wurde die Anerkennung von Vergewaltigungen während des Krieges als Kriegsverbrechen gemäß dem Völkerrecht besonders hervorgehoben.

Die Ausstellung und alle Begleitprogramme wurden am 18. Oktober 2023 aus dem Berliner Herbstsalon zurückgezogen, als Reaktion auf eine Erklärung des Maxim Gorki Theaters, die „uns in die Realität drängt, die durch die Aufforderung, die Welt ohne Palästinenser zu akzeptieren, dominiert wird". Dieser Rückzug wird als „Protest angesehen, um einen Raum für die Produktion einer Möglichkeit zu bewahren, über den Völkermord und die Logistik des Konzentrationslagers zu sprechen [...] und festzustellen, dass nicht über Omarska gesprochen werden kann, ohne dass über Gaza gesprochen wird."

• Exhibition at the 6th Berlin Herbstsalon 2023 LOST – YOU GO SLAVIA
September 28 – December 10, 2023
(withdrawn October 18, 2023)

"Four Faces of Omarska" is an investigative memorialization practice and a platform engaged in exploring the strategies of memorial production from experiences and knowledges that have been subjugated, rejected, and excluded from public memory and public history. Conceptualized by Milica Tomić, Anousheh Kehar, Philipp Sattler, Dubravka Sekulić, Amel Beslagić, and Abdelrahman Elbashir, it asks how a site of atrocity becomes a site of learning based on solidarity and equality. The title comes from four constitutive layers in the history of the Omarska mining complex in northwest Bosnia and Herzegovina. It draws from fields such as activist interventions, humanities, art, architecture, and the critique of a politics of science and trauma management in Bosnia and Herzegovina. The exhibition employs the method of public montage to juxtapose and investigate the complexity of the intertwining layers of traumatic histories, exploitation, and continuing violence.

This newest edition of "Four Faces of Omarska," which premiered at the 6th Berlin Herbstsalon at Gorki, brought into focus post-genocide ethno-societal division and revealed how the political legacy of war is perpetuated through global economic investments. It investigated the architecture and still unexplored new forms of concentration and prisoner-of-war camps that emerged at the onset of the war in Yugoslavia and that persist through new forms of urbanity, economy, and socialization during the postwar transition. This new edition highlighted the recognition of wartime rape as a war crime under international law.

The exhibition and all accompanying programs were withdrawn from the Berlin Herbstsalon on October 18, 2023, in response to a statement issued by the Maxim Gorki Theater that "pushed us into the reality ruled by an injunction to accept the world without Palestinians." This withdrawal is considered "a protest to maintain a space for the production of a possibility to speak about genocide and the logic of the concentration camp ... [stating] that we cannot speak about Omarska without speaking about Gaza."

Milica Tomić, Philipp Sattler, Anousheh Kehar

© IZK, TU Graz

On Violence

Ausstellung in der Budapest Gallery
Milica Tomić
12. Mai – 30. Juli 2023

Milica Tomić stellte ihre Arbeit „Open Video Sequence. The Four Faces of Omarska | Safety on the Road" im Rahmen der internationalen Gruppenausstellung „On Violence" aus, die in der Budapest Gallery stattfand. Diese Gruppenausstellung präsentierte Gewalterfahrungen, Skripte sozialen Verhaltens und visuelle sowie politische Themen der Gewalt aus der Sicht von Frauen und Queers. Werke mit einer abstrakteren Herangehensweise an die komplexen Paradigmen der Zustände und Fallstricke des Missbrauchs, des Angstmachens und der Furcht wurden tagebuchähnlichen Arbeiten gegenübergestellt, in denen viszerale Reaktionen in Bezug auf die Lage in der Ukraine und auf allgegenwärtige Gewalt festgehalten wurden. Mehrere Künstlerinnen und Künstler in der Ausstellung setzten sich mit den anhaltenden Traumata der jüngsten Vergangenheit der Region auseinander, darunter die Jugoslawienkriege. Die politisch-ideologische Einflussnahme auf das gemeinsame Gedächtnis, ethnisch begründete Gewalt und kollektive Verantwortung wurden in dieser teils archivbasierten, investigativen Recherche untersucht.

In diesem Zusammenhang rückt Milica Tomićs Film Open Video Sequence. The Four Faces of Omarska | Safety on the Road die bosnische Richterin Nusreta Sivac in den Mittelpunkt, die als eine der weiblichen Insassinnen des Lagers Omarska regelmäßig vergewaltigt und gefoltert wurde. Nach der Schließung des Lagers im August 1992 wurde Sivac zusammen mit ihrer Kollegin Jadranka Cigelj zu einer Aktivistin für Vergewaltigungsopfer. Es wird ihnen zugeschrieben, dass sie maßgeblich dazu beitrugen, Vergewaltigungen während des Krieges als Kriegsverbrechen nach internationalem Recht anzuerkennen.

Milica Tomić: „Open Video Sequence. The Four Faces of Omarska | Safety on the Road," 40'47", 2006–2023, englische und serbische Sprache, mit Untertiteln
Schnitt: Ema Teokarević

• Exhibition in the Budapest Gallery
Milica Tomić
May 12 – July 30, 2023

Milica Tomić exhibited her work *Open Video Sequence: The Four Faces of Omarska | Safety on the Road* within the international group exhibition "On Violence" that took place at the Budapest Gallery. This group exhibition presented experiences of violence, scripts of social behavior, and visual and political themes of violence from women's and queer perspectives. Works with a more abstract approach to the complex patterns of states and trap situations of abuse, fear-mongering, and anxiety were juxtaposed with diary-like works recording visceral reactions to the situation in Ukraine and pervasive violence. Several artists in the exhibition dealt with the enduring traumas of the region's recent past, including the Yugoslav wars. This partly archive-based, investigative research examined the political-ideological manipulation of collective memory.

Within this context, Milica Tomić's film Open Video Sequence: The Four Faces of Omarska | Safety on the Road brings into focus Nusreta Sivac, the Bosnian judge who was one of the female inmates at Omarska camp, where women were regularly raped and tortured. After the camp's closure in August 1992, Sivac, together with her colleague Jadranka Cigelj, became an activist for victims of rape. They are credited with being instrumental in the recognition of wartime rape as a war crime under international law.

Milica Tomić, *Open Video Sequence: The Four Faces of Omarska | Safety on the Road*, 2006–2023, 40'47", in English and Serbian with subtitles
Editing: Ema Teokarević

Milica Tomić

International Cooperations

Andreas Lechner zu Gast am Mailänder Politecnico

Andreas Lechner (Institut für Gebäudelehre, TU Graz) war im WS 2022/23 Gastprofessor am renommierten Politecnico di Milano, wo er gemeinsam mit Gennaro Postiglione (Vize-Direktor des Department of Architecture and Urban Studies) ein neues Forschungsprojekt erarbeitete, in der Doctoral School des Departments unterrichtete, Joint-Degree Masterarbeiten betreute und Vorträge zu seinem Lehr- und Forschungsschwerpunkt „Counterintuitive Typologies“ hielt. Das am Mailänder Politecnico erarbeitete Projekt „Affordances of Architectural Typologies“ erweitert Lechners entwurfs- und forschungsgeleitete Arbeiten zum Um- und Weiterbau von kommerziellen Gewerbetypologien um historische und moderne Gebäudetypologien und versammelt Beiträge von PraktikerInnen und WissenschaftlerInnen in einem Planatlas. Diese Beiträge wurden nach einem „Call for Papers (through drawing)“ von einem neunköpfigen internationalen Beirat aus zahlreichen Einsendungen ausgewählt und werden die Resilienz und Dauerhaftigkeit von Gebäuden als über Zeichnungen und Pläne erzählte Umbaugeschichten sicht- bzw. als entsprechende Entwurfsaspekte für die Lehre und Forschung nachvollziehbar gemacht.

Das Projekt „Affordances of Architectural Typologies“ wird 2024 sowohl im Rahmen der internationalen ARCC-EAAE-Konferenz an der Aarhus School of Architecture in Dänemark vorgestellt als auch im Rahmen von Lehrveranstaltungen an der TU Berlin, am Mailänder Politecnico und an der TU Graz bearbeitet.

Andreas Lechner

Andreas Lechner at Politcenico di Milano

Andreas Lechner (Institute of Design and Building Typology, TU Graz) was a visiting professor at the renowned Politecnico di Milano in the winter semester of 2022/23. Together with Gennaro Postiglione (Vice-Director of the Department of Architecture and Urban Studies), he developed a new research project, taught in the department’s Doctoral School, supervised joint-degree master’s theses, and held lectures on his teaching and research focus “Counterintuitive Typologies.” Developed at Politecnico di Milano, the research project “Affordances of Architectural Typologies” expands Lechner’s design- and research-led work involving the conversion and extension of commercial building typologies by including historical and modern building typologies as well as bringing together contributions from practitioners and

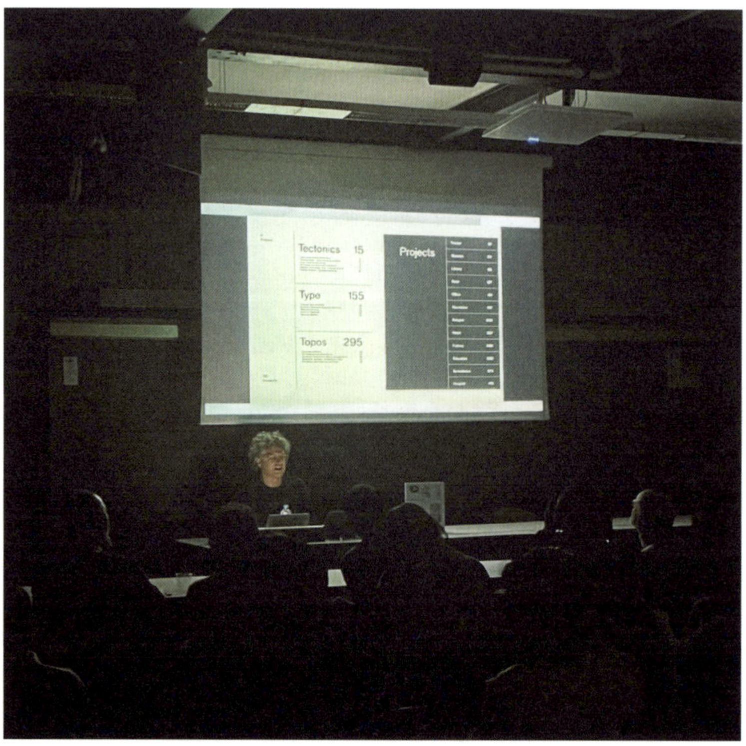

Andreas Lechner © IGL, TU Graz

academics within a plan atlas. Following a "Call for Papers (through Drawing)," these contributions were selected among numerous submissions by a nine-member international advisory board and will make the resilience and longevity of buildings visible in the form of conversion stories narrated through drawings and plans, or make them comprehensible as corresponding design aspects for teaching and research. The "Affordances of Architectural Typologies" project will be presented in 2024 as part of the international ARCC-EAAE conference at the Aarhus School of Architecture in Denmark and as part of courses at TU Berlin, Politecnico di Milano, and TU Graz.

© Università degli Studi di Napoli Federico II

„Learning from Pompeii". Kollaboration mit der Universität Neapel

Im Rahmen des Erasmus+ Blended Intensive Program (BIP) und in Kooperation mit der Università degli Studi di Napoli Federico II, der RWTH Aachen, der TU Eindhoven, der TU Dortmund und der FH Potsdam besuchte eine Gruppe von Architekturstudierenden der TU Graz im Juli 2023 den Sommerkurs „Learning from Pompeii (view from the North). The Ancient Urban Form for the Future City." Das von Prof. Federica Visconti (Neapel) geleitete didaktisch hybride Programm „Learning from Pompeii", ermöglichte den Studierenden, sich mit einer antiken Stadt vor Ort zu beschäftigen und Ideen mit anderen Lehrenden und Studierenden aus Italien, Deutschland und den Niederlanden auszutauschen. In einem zweimonatigen Online-Seminar untersuchten die Studierenden die architektonischen und städtebaulichen Ideen Pompejis, rekonstruierten die Ruinen und entwarfen analoge Häuser. Abgeschlossen wurde das Projekt in einer intensiven Workshop-Woche in Neapel und sowie einer Exkursion nach Pompeji, in der die Neugestaltung des Südeingangs der antiken Stadt bearbeitet wurde. Die typomorphologische Analyse und das analoge Entwerfen dienten als Grundlage, um zu erforschen, was wir von antiken Städten sowohl in kleinerem Maßstab (Haus) als auch in einem komplexeren städtebaulichen Maßstab in einer zeitgenössischen Situation lernen können: Konkret behandelt wurden unter anderem: Dichte, Funktionsmischung, Blockrandbebauung, Fußläufigkeit, belebte Erdgeschosszonen sowie eine klare Trennung von öffentlichem und privatem Raum.

Beteiligte Studierende der TU Graz: Christian Brügel, Daniel Lučić, Anđela Marinković, Anna Schoisssengeyer, Lisa-Marie Wagenthaler. Koordination: Anselm Wagner (akk)

Anđela Marinković

"Learning from Pompeii": Collaboration with the University of Naples Federico II

As part of the Erasmus+ Blended Intensive Program (BIP)—in cooperation with the University of Naples Federico II, RWTH Aachen University, TU Eindhoven, TU Dortmund, and the University of Applied Sciences Potsdam—a group of architecture students from TU Graz attended the summer course "Learning from Pompeii (View from the North): The Ancient Urban Form for the Future City." The didactically hybrid program "Learning from Pompeii," led by Prof. Federica Visconti (Naples), allowed students to engage with an ancient city on site and to exchange ideas with other teachers and students from Italy, Germany, and the Netherlands. During a two-month online seminar, students examined Pompeii's architectural and urban planning principles, reconstructed its ruins, and designed analog houses. The project was concluded through an intensive workshop week in Naples and an excursion to Pompeii, during which students worked on redesigning the ancient city's south entrance. The typo-morphological analysis and the analog design provided the framework to explore what we might learn from ancient cities on both a smaller scale (house) and a more complex urbanistic scale within a contemporary situation. Concretely, topics included density, mixed functions, perimeter block development, walking distance, lively ground floor areas, and a clear delineation of public and private spaces.

TU Graz students involved: Christian Brügel, Daniel Lučić, Anđela Marinković, Anna Schoisssengeyer, Lisa-Marie Wagenthaler. Coordination: Anselm Wagner (akk)

© stdb, TU Graz

Kooperation mit der Ain Shams University in Kairo

Rowaida Rashed forschte im Rahmen ihres Gastaufenthalts zum Thema sub- und periurbane Räume am Institut für Städtebau und initiierte gemeinsam mit Aglaée Degros, Eva Schwab und Patricia Lucena Ventura im WS 2023/24 eine Kooperation mit der Ain Shams University in Kairo. Daraus ging das Vertiefungsmodul „Territorial Habitat: P[re]ipheral Mosaic of Cairo" hervor, zu dem auch ein Besuch der Winterschool in Kairo im November 2023 gehörte. Während der Exkursion wurden verschiedene Teil- und Entwicklungsgebiete der Stadt Kairo analysiert, um in weiterer Folge eine gesamtheitliche Strategie für den Großraum Kairo zu entwickeln. Die Zusammenarbeit wird durch die gemeinsame Herausgeberschaft einer wissenschaftlichen Publikation fortgesetzt. Darin werden die Möglichkeiten zur Integration aktiver Mobilitätsformen in die Stadtentwicklung der neuen Verwaltungshauptstadt Ägyptens untersucht.

Sabine Bauer

Cooperation with Ain Shams University in Cairo

As part of her guest residency, Rowaida Rashed researched sub- and peri-urban spaces at the Institute of Urbanism and, together with Aglaée Degros, Eva Schwab, and Patricia Lucena Ventura, initiated a cooperation with Ain Shams University in Cairo during the winter semester of 2023/24. Culminating in the Specialization Module "P[re]ipheral Mosaic of Cairo," this included visiting the Winter School in Cairo in November 2023. During the excursion, various subareas and development areas within the city of Cairo were analyzed in order to subsequently devise a holistic strategy for Greater Cairo. This collaboration is being continued through the joint editing of a scientific publication, which will examine the potential for integrating active forms of mobility into the urban development of Egypt's new administrative capital.

KOEN-Sommerschule in Venedig

Mit seinem Beitrag „Open for Maintenance. Wegen Umbau geöffnet“ wurde der deutsche Pavillon im Rahmen der 18. Architekturbiennale in Venedig für sechs Monate zu einem experimentellen Arbeitsort für Architektur- und Handwerksschulen aus ganz Europa. Das KuratorInnenteam ARCH+, SUMMACUMFEMMER und Büro Juliane Greb verwandelten den deutschen Pavillon in eine temporäre Werkstatt, in der Materialien aus über 40 verschiedenen Länderpavillons der Kunstbiennale 2022 archiviert und katalogisiert wurden. Im Mittelpunkt des Programms stand das zirkuläre Bauen und die Pflege und Instandhaltung verschiedener Einrichtungen aus Venedig. Die Materialien für die Reparaturen oder gebauten Interventionen entnahm man aus dem Depot des deutschen Pavillons.

Das Institut für Grundlagen der Konstruktion und des Entwerfens (KOEN) wurde eingeladen, gemeinsam mit dem Lehrstuhl für nachhaltiges Bauen des KIT in Karlsruhe und dem gemeinnützigen Verein Baukreisel, einen Workshop zu organisieren. Mit 22 Studierenden von drei verschiedenen Hochschulen, davon 10 Studierende aus Graz, 10 aus Karlsruhe und 2 von der IUAV Venedig, wurden in der letzten Septemberwoche verschiedene Interventionen geplant und realisiert. Als Kooperationspartner vor Ort konnte der alternative Kunstverein „Spazio Punch“ auf der Insel Giudecca gewonnen werden. Die BetreiberInnen des „Spazio Punch“ wünschten sich verschiedene Interventionen für ihren überdachten Innenhof, darunter eine neue Bar, eine wetterfeste Einhausung für die Wintermonate, ein Lichtkonzept und ein neues Ordnungssystem für ihr

© Baukreisel

Materiallager. In den ersten Tagen wurden auf Grundlage der eingelagerten Materialien grobe Entwurfskonzepte und Mockups entwickelt. Eine große Herausforderung war es, die Objekte für venezianische Verhältnisse transportfähig zu planen, um sie mit einem Boot von den Giardini nach Giudecca überführen zu können. Die Gruppe war einerseits als Teil der Ausstellung im deutschen Pavillon mit dem Bau der Interventionen beschäftigt, andererseits mit dem Aufbau der Infrastrukturen im Spazio Punch. Die funktionalen Interventionen sind zu einem integrativen Bestandteil des „Spazio Punch“ geworden.

Studierende TU Graz: Florian Berger, Hanna Gilly, Julian Lança Gil, Budour Khalil, Sabeth Moschitz, Kerstin Neuhold, Nicole Pühringer, Christina Radl, Natalia Vasadze, Ludwig Albert Zibold

Petra Petersson, Barbara Gruber, Sebastian Pletzer

© Baukreisel

KOEN Summerschool in Venice

With its contribution “Open for Maintenance,” the German Pavilion at the eighteenth Venice Biennale of Architecture was turned into an experimental workplace for architectural and trade schools from all over Europe. The curatorial team of ARCH+, SUMMACUMFEMMER, and the office of Juliane Greb transformed the German Pavilion into a temporary workshop in which materials from forty different national pavilions from the Biennale of Art in 2022 were archived and cataloged. The program centered on circular building and the maintenance and upkeep of various facilities in Venice. The materials for repairs or built interventions were taken from the storeroom of the German Pavilion.

The Institute of Construction and Design Principles (KOEN) was invited to organize a workshop together with the Chair for Sustainable Building of the KIT in Karlsruhe and the nonprofit Baukreisel. With twenty-two students from three universities, ten from Graz, ten from Karlsruhe, and two from the IUAV in Venice, various interventions were planned and realized during the last week of September. The alternative arts society Spazio Punch on the island of Giudecca was won over as a local cooperation partner. The organizers of Spazio Punch wanted various interventions for their covered interior courtyard, including a new bar, an all-season shelter for the winter months, a lighting concept, and a new system to organize the storage of their materials. On the first days, rough design concepts and mockups were worked out on the basis of the stored materials. One big challenge was planning objects that could be transported in Venetian conditions so they could be brought by boat from the Giardini to Giudecca. The group was involved, on the one hand, in building the interventions as part of the exhibition in the German Pavilion and, on the other, in developing the infrastructure for Spazio Punch. The functional interventions have become an integral component of Spazio Punch.

Students from TU Graz: Florian Berger, Hanna Gilly, Julian Lança Gil, Budour Khalil, Sabeth Moschitz, Kerstin Neuhold, Nicole Pühringer, Christina Radl, Natalia Vasadze, Ludwig Albert Zibold

Call for Contributions

GAM 21
Confronting the Environmental Crisis: New Approaches in Architecture

Guest Editors: Alexander Passer, Marcella Ruschi Mendes Saade

Die globale Umweltkrise, mit der die Menschheit konfrontiert ist, zwingt uns zu einem Paradigmenwechsel, der die Art und Weise stark beeinflusst, wie wir bauen, gestalten und mit unseren natürlichen Umgebungen interagieren. Wie es der brasilianische Schriftsteller und Umweltschützer Ailton Krenak so treffend auf den Punkt gebracht hat, muss der grundlegende Wandel ein Ende des „extraktiven Modells" mit sich bringen, das vor allem in der westlichen Welt tief verwurzelt ist: „Es widerspricht völlig der Natur des Menschen, die Landschaften, in denen wir leben, nur als Werkzeuge oder Ressourcen wahrzunehmen."[1] Übertragen auf die Architektur bedeutet dies, dass im Zusammenspiel von Entwurf, Konstruktion und Baubranche die Zeit gekommen ist, um tiefgreifende Konsequenzen aus diesem Paradigmenwechsel zu ziehen.

Auch wenn es keine eindeutigen Lösungen für komplexe Herausforderungen, sogenannte *wicked problems*, wie den Klimawandel gibt, müssen unsere Planungsansätze berücksichtigen, dass gebaute Räume einen wesentlichen Bestandteil des gesamten Ökosystems ausmachen, für die sinnvollerweise die gleichen Grundsätze gelten: durchlässig, funktional und ausgewogen zu sein. Als Gegenpol zu künstlichen Strukturen, die an einem beliebigen Ort errichtet werden und lediglich auf eine minimal geringere Umweltbelastung als beim Status quo abzielen, haben die gebauten Räume der Zukunft zur Voraussetzung, die konventionellen Planungspraktiken zu überwinden, die den Bausektor zum größten Verursacher der vom Menschen verursachten CO_2-Emissionen weltweit gemacht haben. Das Erreichen von Netto-Null-Emissionen beim Bau und Betrieb künftiger Gebäude erfordert die aktive Mitwirkung von Entwurfs-, Konstruktions- und Baufachleuten und die rasche Umsetzung von Dekarbonisierungslösungen in den Produktionsprozessen seitens der Bauindustrie.

1 Krenak, Ailton zitiert in Baratto, Romullo: „Ailton Krenak: ‚Instead of Operating in the Landscape, We Should Blend in With It'", Interview übersetzt von Diogo Simões, *Archdaily*, 16. Oktober2023,www.archdaily.com/1007953/ailton-krenak-instead-of-operating-in-the-landscape-we-should-blend-in-with-it

The global environmental crisis facing humanity compels us to push toward a paradigm shift that also highly affects the way we build, design, and interact with our natural environments. As the Brazilian writer and environmentalist Ailton Krenak has aptly brought to the point, the essential shift needs to entail the end of the "extractive model" that is particularly ingrained in the mindset of the Western world: "It is fundamentally unnatural for humans to perceive the landscapes in which we dwell merely as tools or resources."[1] When applied to architecture, this means that the time has come to face the far-reaching consequences of this paradigm shift in the interaction between design, construction, and the building industry.

While there are no clear-cut solutions to wicked problems such as climate change, our design approaches must take into account that built spaces are an essential part of the overall ecosystem, to which, for logical reasons, the same principles should apply: permeability, functionality, and balance. As an antithesis to artificial structures transplanted into a given space, aiming solely at a marginally lower environmental impact than the status quo, the built spaces of the future need to disrupt conventional design practices that have "elevated" the building sector to the largest contributor of man-made CO_2 emissions globally. Achieving net-zero embodied and operational emissions in future construction calls for active participation from design, construction, and building professionals, and for the prompt implementation of decarbonization solutions in production processes by pertinent construction industries.

An analytical look at how the built environment has changed over the last few centuries, both in terms of architecture and engineering and in terms of construction technology and materials, can help us to see more clearly how we can accelerate the process and restructure or reinterpret how

1 Ailton Krenak, in Romullo Baratto, "Ailton Krenak: 'Instead of Operating in the Landscape, We Should Blend in With It,'" interview translated by Diogo Simões, *Archdaily*, October 16, 2023, www.archdaily.com/1007953/ailton-krenak-instead-of-operating-in-the-landscape-we-should-blend-in-with-it

Ein analytischer Blick darauf, wie sich die gebaute Umwelt in den letzten Jahrhunderten sowohl in Bezug auf Architektur und Ingenieurswesen wie auch hinsichtlich der Bautechnik und Materialien verändert hat, kann uns dabei helfen, klarer zu sehen, wie wir den Prozess beschleunigen und die Interaktion zwischen Menschen und ihren Ökosystemen neu strukturieren oder neu interpretieren können. Daher betrachtet GAM 21 die architektonischen Konsequenzen des Paradigmenwechsels aus zwei Perspektiven: erstens aus historischer Sicht, einschließlich einer gründlichen Bewertung der historischen Entwicklung der gebauten Umwelt unter Berücksichtigung ihrer Ressourcen und Umweltauswirkungen, und zweitens aus zukunftsorientierter Sicht, mit konkreten Vorschlägen, wie Veränderungen auf allen Ebenen von Entwurf und Konstruktion die Dekarbonisierung und die Regeneration der Natur fördern können. Letzteres bedeutet eine Neubewertung und Neuinterpretation der Rolle der Architektur als Triebkraft der Transformation. Das, was für die Architektur bei der Betrachtung von Aspekten der Nachhaltigkeit auf dem Spiel steht, ist ihre Rolle bei der Ausformulierung von notwendigen, radikalen Konsequenzen für die Gestaltung von Gebäuden.

Die nächste Ausgabe von GAM lädt zu Vorschlägen aus den Disziplinen Architektur, Bauingenieur-, Umweltwissenschaften, Städtebau oder Material- und Kulturwissenschaften ein, um die architektonische Gestaltung zu diskutieren, die ein Perspektivwechsel hin zur umweltökologischen Performance annehmen könnte. In diesem Zusammenhang sind auch Vorschläge willkommen, die sich mit pädagogischen Veränderungen befassen, deren es für eine Neubewertung der Disziplin bedarf. Abstracts zum Thema „Confronting the Environmental Crisis" können zusammen mit einer Kurzbiographie bis zum 31. Mai 2024 eingereicht werden. Die Einreichungsfrist für den Beitrag ist der 16. September 2024.

Übersetzung: Nikolaus G. Schneider

humans interact with their ecosystems. Therefore, GAM 21 looks at the architectural consequences of the paradigm shift from two perspectives: first, from a historical point of view, including a thorough assessment of the evolution of the built environment over time, in consideration of its resources and environmental impacts; and second, from a future-oriented point of view, with specific proposals for how changes at all levels of design and construction can promote decarbonization and the regeneration of nature. The latter entails a reevaluation and reinterpretation of the role of architecture and the discipline as such and, more specifically, of its role as a transformative agent. At stake for architecture, when considering aspects of sustainability, is its role in formulating the necessary radical consequences for the design of buildings.

The next issue of GAM invites proposals from the disciplines of architecture, civil engineering, environmental studies, urban planning, or material and cultural studies, to discuss the architectural design that a shift in perspective might take when it comes to environmental performance. In this context, we also welcome proposals discussing pedagogical shifts that are required for a reevaluation of the discipline. Abstracts on the topic "Confronting the Environmental Crisis" can be submitted together with a short biography until May 31, 2024. The submission deadline for the contribution is September 16, 2024.